Discover
India

Experience the best
of India

This edition written a

Abigail B....,
Paul Clammer, Mark Elliott, Paul Harding, Trent Holden, John
Noble, Iain Stewart, Michael Benanav, Anirban Mahapatra,
Daniel McCrohan, Isabella Noble, Kevin Raub, Sarina Singh

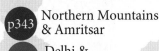

Northern Mountains
& Amritsar p343

Delhi &
the Taj Mahal p51

Rajasthan p139

Darjeeling, Varanasi
& the Northeast p293

Mumbai (Bombay)
& Around p109

Goa & Around p191

Kerala &
South India p227

● Delhi &
the Taj Mahal

Highlights....................................54

o Taj Mahal
o Red Fort
o Old Delhi's Bazaars
o Humayun's Tomb
o Qutb Minar

● Mumbai
(Bombay) &
Around

Highlights....................................112

o Mumbai's Colonial-Era
Architecture
o Eating in Mumbai
o Cave Temples at
Ellora & Ajanta
o Marine Drive &
Girgaum Chowpatty
o Elephanta Island

● Rajasthan

Highlights....................................142

o Jaisalmer Fort
o Udaipur
o Pushkar
o Jodhpur
o Tiger-Spotting,
Ranthambhore
National Park

● Kerala &
South India

Highlights....................................230

o Kerala Backwaters
o Meenakshi Amman Temple
o Munnar
o Fort Cochin
o Mysore Palace

● Darjeeling,
Varanasi &
the Northeast

Highlights....................................296

o Darjeeling
o Boat Ride in Varanasi
o Experiencing Kolkata
Culture
o Khajuraho
o Sunderbans Tiger
Reserve

● Northern
Mountains &
Amritsar

Highlights....................................346

o Golden Temple
o Adrenaline-Seeking in
Manali
o Corbett Tiger Reserve
o Tibetan Buddhism in
McLeod Ganj
o Rishikesh

Contents

Plan Your Trip

This is India	6
India Map	8
India's Top 25 Highlights	10
India's Top Itineraries	32
India Month by Month	42
Get Inspired	47
Need to Know	48

Discover

Delhi & the Taj Mahal   51

Highlights	54
Best...	56
Walking Tour	58
Delhi	60
Uttar Pradesh & the Taj Mahal	97
Agra	97
Fatehpur Sikri	104

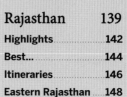

Mumbai (Bombay) & Around   109

Highlights	112
Best...	114
Walking Tour	116
Mumbai (Bombay)	118
Maharashtra	133
Aurangabad	133
Ellora	135
Ajanta	136

Rajasthan   139

Highlights	142
Best...	144
Itineraries	146
Eastern Rajasthan	148

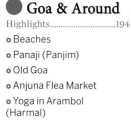

Goa & Around

Highlights	194

- Beaches
- Panaji (Panjim)
- Old Goa
- Anjuna Flea Market
- Yoga in Arambol (Harmal)

Contents

Discover India

Jaipur 148
Pushkar 159
Ranthambhore
National Park 163

**Southern
Rajasthan** **165**
Udaipur 165

Western Rajasthan **175**
Jodhpur 175
Jaisalmer 182

Goa &
Around 191

Highlights **194**
Best... .... **196**
Itineraries **198**
Central Goa **200**
Panaji (Panjim) 200
Old Goa 207
North Goa **208**
Calangute & Baga 208
Anjuna 209
Mandrem & Asvem 212
Arambol (Harmal) 212
South Goa **214**
Margao (Madgaon) 214
Colva & Benaulim 216
Benaulim to
Agonda 219
Palolem & Around 219
Karnataka **223**
Hampi 223

Kerala &
South India 227

Highlights **230**
Best... .... **232**
Itineraries **234**
Kerala **236**
Thiruvananthapuram
(Trivandrum) 236
Kovalam 240
Varkala 243
Alappuzha
(Alleppey) 245
Periyar Wildlife
Sanctuary 250
Munnar 253
Kochi (Cochin) 256
**Southern
Karnataka** **265**
Mysuru (Mysore) 265
Tamil Nadu **269**
Chennai (Madras) 269
Mamallapuram
(Mahabalipuram) 278
Puducherry
(Pondicherry) 282
Madurai 287

Darjeeling,
Varanasi &
the Northeast ... 293

Highlights **296**
Best... .... **298**
Itineraries **300**
Kolkata (Calcutta) **302**
Darjeeling **317**
Varanasi **325**
Madhya Pradesh **336**
Khajuraho 336

Northern
Mountains &
Amritsar 343

Highlights **346**
Best... .... **348**
Itineraries **350**
Uttarakhand **352**
Mussoorie 352
Rishikesh 354
Corbett Tiger
Reserve 359
Himachal Pradesh **361**
Shimla 361
Manali 366
McLeod Ganj 371
Punjab **377**
Amritsar 377

In Focus

India Today 384

History 386

Family Travel 397

The Way of Life 399

Hinduism 402

Delicious India 404

Architecture &
the Arts 407

Landscape &
Wildlife 410

Survival Guide

Directory 414

Accommodation 414

Customs
Regulations 416

Electricity 416

Gay & Lesbian
Travellers 416

Health 417

Insurance 420

Internet Access 421

Legal Matters 421

Money 422

Public Holidays 424

Safe Travel 425

Telephone 425

Time 427

Tourist Information 427

Travellers with
Disabilities 427

Visas 428

Transport 429

Getting There
& Away 429

Getting Around 429

Language 435

Behind the
Scenes 437

Index 438

How to Use
This Book 445

Our Writers 448

This Is India

India fires the imagination and stirs the soul like no other place on earth, bristling with a mind-stirring mix of landscapes and cultural traditions. Your journey through India, no matter how fleeting, will blaze in your memory long after you've left its shores.

Famously chaotic, India doesn't have to be intimidating.
True, the big cities can be bedlam, and the markets border on feverish, but there's a bounty of laid-back charms to explore too, from idyllic palm-fringed beaches and tranquil backwaters to sweeping deserts, snow-brushed mountains and lush green tea plantations.

Natural beauty abounds, but man-made gems also the dot the land.
India's history is one of the world's most epic tales, and it has carved its incredible, indelible mark throughout the subcontinent. Temples hide in forests, fortresses rise from the desert, and palaces, mausoleums and more line the banks of the holy rivers that feed India's deeply sacred essence.

Spirituality is the common thread that weaves its way through India.
Religion is alive, and thriving. It's woven into almost every aspect of daily life and it enriches your experiences at every turn. Follow pilgrims on a temple trail, place an offering on a roadside shrine, smell wafts of incense and feel the well-worn stone of the temple floor beneath your bare feet.

Nourishment of a different nature awaits you at restaurant tables everywhere.
You're about to jump on board one of the wildest culinary trips of your travelling life. Frying, simmering, sizzling, kneading, roasting and flipping a deliciously diverse repertoire of dishes, feasting your way through the subcontinent is a tongue-teasing ride to remember.

India is indeed a feast of opportunities.
And even on a short trip you can go surprisingly in-depth and experience a remarkable range of wonders. Just try not to fit too much onto your plate. It's more rewarding to experience a small amount more fully; so slow down, relax and above all enjoy the phenomenon that is India.

Priest at a Jain temple in Ranakpur (p165), Rajasthan

> 66
> Fiery India will blaze in your memory long after you've left its shores. 99

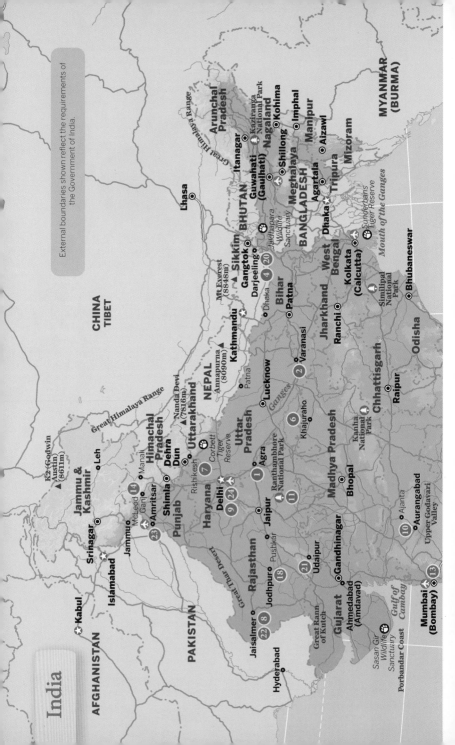

India

External boundaries shown reflect the requirements of the Government of India.

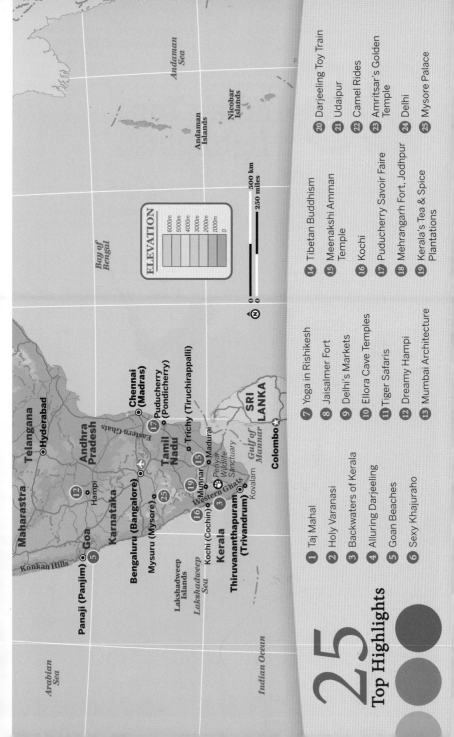

25
Top Highlights

1 Taj Mahal
2 Holy Varanasi
3 Backwaters of Kerala
4 Alluring Darjeeling
5 Goan Beaches
6 Sexy Khajuraho
7 Yoga in Rishikesh
8 Jaisalmer Fort
9 Delhi's Markets
10 Ellora Cave Temples
11 Tiger Safaris
12 Dreamy Hampi
13 Mumbai Architecture
14 Tibetan Buddhism
15 Meenakshi Amman Temple
16 Kochi
17 Puducherry Savoir Faire
18 Mehrangarh Fort, Jodhpur
19 Kerala's Tea & Spice Plantations
20 Darjeeling Toy Train
21 Udaipur
22 Camel Rides
23 Amritsar's Golden Temple
24 Delhi
25 Mysore Palace

ELEVATION

6000m
5000m
4000m
3000m
2000m
1000m
0

500 km
250 miles

N

25 India's Top Highlights

Taj Mahal

The Taj Mahal (p98) rises from the beaten earth of Uttar Pradesh as it does in dreams, but even the wildest imaginings leave travellers underprepared for that breath-stealing moment when its gates are traversed and this magnificent world wonder comes into focus. It is the embodiment of architectural perfection; the ultimate monument to love. Don't let fears of tour buses or hordes of visitors make you think you can skip the Taj – you can't.

CHRISTER FREDRIKSSON/GETTY IMAGES ©

2

Holy Varanasi

Everyone in Varanasi (p325) seems to be dying or praying or hustling or cremating someone, or swimming or laundering or washing buffaloes in the sewage-saturated Ganges. The goddess river will clean away your sins and help you escape from that tedious life-and-death cycle – and Varanasi is *the* place to take a sacred dip. So take a deep breath, put on a big smile for the ever-present touts, go to the holy water and get your karma in order.

Backwaters of Kerala

It's unusual in India to find a place as vast and tranquil as the backwaters (p248): 900km of interconnected rivers, lakes and lagoons lined with tropical flora. Even if you do, there won't be a way to experience it that's as peaceful and intimate as a few days on a teak-and-palm-thatch houseboat. Float along the water – as the sun sets behind the palms, or while eating to-die-for Keralan seafood, or as you sleep under a twinkling sky – and forget about life on land for a while.

The Best...
Quiet Retreats

BACKWATERS, KERALA
There are few things more relaxing than travelling through the 900km network of waterways fringing Kerala's coast. (p248)

SHIMLA, HIMACHAL PRADESH
An engaging blend of hilltop holiday town and Indian city, surrounded by rolling landscapes of green, reached via the 'toy train'. (p361)

MUNNAR, KERALA
Relax in a homestay at a remote tea plantation near this Kerala hill station. (p253)

SUNDERBANS TIGER RESERVE
Escape the city chaos of nearby Kolkata with a boat trip through part of the world's largest mangrove forest. (p314)

LINDSAY BROWN/GETTY IMAGES ©

13

The Best...
Beaches

PALOLEM
Nodding palms, beach huts on stilts and white sands – this is one of Goa's loveliest spots. (p219)

VARKALA
Dramatic russet sea cliffs drop down to a broad sandy beach that hosts a mix of Hindu priests, backpackers and local volleyball enthusiasts. (p243)

GIRGAUM CHOWPATTY
Mumbai's jostling, colourful city beach is a favoured spot for an evening stroll and a serve of *bhelpuri* (fried dough with rice, lentils and spices). (p121)

CHERAI BEACH
Kochin's best-kept secret, this long stretch of undeveloped white sand on nearby Vypeen Island also comes with miles of lazy backwaters just a few hundred metres from the seafront. (p260)

Alluring Darjeeling

4

Up in a tippy-top nook of India's far northeast is storied Darjeeling (p317). It's no longer a romantic mountain hideaway, but the allure remains. Undulating hills of bulbous tea shrubs are pruned by women in colourful dresses; the majestic Himalaya peek through puffy clouds as the sun climbs out from behind the mountains; and little alleys wend their way through mountain mist, past clotheslines and monasteries. Ride the 'toy train' and drink it all in – the tea and the town's legendary enchantment.

Goan Beaches

5

There's no better place in India to be lazy than on one of Goa's spectacular beaches (p201). With palm groves on one side of the white sands and gently lapping waves on the other, the best beaches live up to your image of a tropical paradise. But it's not an undiscovered one: the sands are peppered with fellow travellers and beach-shack restaurants. Goa's treasures are for fans of creature comforts who like their seafood fresh and their holidays easy. Palolem beach (p219)

Sexy Khajuraho

Are the sensuous statues on the temples of Khajuraho (p336) the Kamasutra, Tantric examples for initiates or allegories for the faithful? They're definitely naughty fun, with hot nymphs, a nine-person orgy and even men getting it on with horses. Once the titillation passes, you'll be pleasantly absorbed by the exquisite carving of these thousand-year-old temples and the magical feeling of 11th-century India.

Yoga in Rishikesh

Where better to do the downward dog than in the self-styled 'Yoga Capital of the World'? Rishikesh (p354) has a beautiful setting, surrounded by forested hills and cut through by the fast-flowing Ganges. There are masses of ashrams and all kinds of yoga, meditation classes and alternative therapies, from laughing yoga to crystal healing.

Jaisalmer Fort

Rising up from the deserts of Rajasthan, Jaisalmer's 12th-century citadel (p182) looks like something from a dream. The enormous golden sandstone fort, with its crenellated ramparts and undulating towers, is a fantastical structure, even while camouflaged against the desert sand. Inside, an ornate royal palace, fairy-tale mansions, intricately carved temples and narrow lanes conspire to create one of the world's best places to get lost.

BRENT WINEBRENNER/GETTY IMAGES ©

The Best...
Forts

JAISALMER FORT
A grand sandcastle of a fort, rearing out of the desert; once a stop on the ancient camel trade routes. (p182)

MEHRANGARH
Formidable fortress protruding out of a great rocky escarpment, which towers over the old city of Jodhpur. (p176)

AGRA FORT
With the Taj Mahal overshadowing it, it's easy to overlook one of the finest Mughal forts in India. (p97)

AMBER FORT
Mighty fortress of pale yellow and pink sandstone and white marble, just outside Jaipur. (p149)

KUMBHALGARH
A vast, isolated fortress in the forested hills near Udaipur. The journey here is almost as amazing as the sight itself. (p165)

Delhi's Markets

Shopaholics: be careful not to lose control. No interest in shopping? Get in touch with your consumerist side. Delhi (p91) is one of the world's finest places to shop, and its markets – Old Delhi, Khan Market or the specialty bazaars – have something you want, guaranteed (though you may not have known this beforehand). The range of technicolour saris, glittering gold and silver bling, mounds of rainbow vermilion, aromatic fresh spices, stainless-steel head massagers, bangles and bobby pins, heaping piles of fruit and marigold and coconut offerings is simply astounding. Paharganj bazaar

The Best...
Places for Food

DELHI
Dine on almost any international flavour in India's capital, with remarkably good food ranging from streetside stalls to creative-cuisine restaurants. (p83)

KERALA
With a long coastline, endless spice plantations and coconut groves, the fragrant cuisine of Kerala is refreshingly delicious. (p236)

GOA
Famous for fresh fish curries, often served on a banana leaf, Goan cuisine is perfumed with many influences brought by traders from overseas. (p191)

MUMBAI
One of India's great food centres, where a cornucopia of flavours from all over the country collides with international trends and tastebuds. (p125)

18

KEREN SU/GETTY IMAGES ©

10 Ellora Cave Temples

The pinnacle of ancient Indian rock-cut architecture, these astounding cave temples (p135) were chipped out laboriously through five centuries by generations of Buddhist, Hindu and Jain monks. The caves here are younger than those at nearby Ajanta, but are embellished with a profusion of remarkably detailed sculptures, and the location, strung along a 2km-long escarpment, allowed for more monumental designs, with elaborate courtyards carved in front of the shrines themselves.

Tiger Safaris

You have to be lucky to spot a tiger in India, but it can be done. Try Ranthambhore National Park (p163), in Rajasthan. It's one of India's most exciting experiences to steal through the undergrowth, surrounded by birds and butterflies, in search of a tiger. And even if you don't catch sight of one, the other wildlife, and the deep-forest setting of most tiger reserves, will prove a breathtaking distraction.

JOHN HAY/GETTY IMAGES ©

11

12

Dreamy Hampi

The surreal rockscape of Hampi (p223) was once the cosmopolitan capital of a powerful Hindu empire. The glorious ruins of its temples and royal structures join sublimely with the terrain: giant rocks balance on pedestals near an ancient elephant stable; temples tuck into crevices between boulders; boats float by rice paddies near a giant bathtub fit for a queen. Watching the sunset's rosy glow over the dreamy landscape, you might just forget what planet you're on.

13

Mumbai Architecture

Mumbai (Bombay; p118) has always absorbed everything in its midst and made it its own. The result is a heady mix of buildings with countless influences. The art deco and modern towers are flashy, but it's the Victorian-era structures, the neo-Gothic, Indo-Saracenic and Venetian Gothic, that have come to define Mumbai. All the spires, gables, arches and onion domes make for a pleasant walk through the city's past.
Chhatrapati Shivaji Terminus (p119)

Tibetan Buddhism

Up north, in places such as McLeod Ganj (p371), where the air is cooler and crisper, hill settlements give way to snow-topped peaks. Here, the cultural influences came not by coast but via mountain passes. Tibetan Buddhism thrives, and monasteries emerge from the forest or steep cliffs as vividly and poetically as the sun rises over mountain peaks. Weathered prayer flags on forest paths blow in the wind, the sound of monks chanting reverberates in meditation halls, and locals bring offerings and make merit, all in the shadow of the mighty Himalaya.

JEREMY WOODHOUSE/GETTY IMAGES ©

The Best...
Unesco World Heritage Sites

TAJ MAHAL
Just one of a trio of sites in Agra; see Agra Fort and Fatehpur Sikri too. (p98)

ELLORA CAVES
The epitome of ancient Indian rock-cut architecture, chipped out laboriously over five centuries. (p135)

AJANTA CAVES
Ancient caverns guarding a hoard of unparalleled artistic treasures. (p137)

KHAJURAHO
Famed temples carved with exquisite skill and erotic detail. (p336)

QUTB MINAR
Architecture reflecting different building styles over hundreds of years. (p68)

HAMPI
An incredible collection of 15th- and 16th-century temples just a short trip from Goa. (p223)

The Best...
Temples

MEENAKSHI AMMAN TEMPLE, MADURAI
Abode of a triple-breasted, fish-eyed goddess, a pinnacle of South Indian temple architecture. (p288)

KHAJURAHO
The erotic carvings of these temples are among the finest sacred art in the world. (p336)

SHORE TEMPLE, MAMALLAPURAM
A magnificent masterpiece of rock-cut elegance overlooking the sea. (p278)

VITTALA TEMPLE, HAMPI
Never finished, this 16th-century structure in boulder-strewn Hampi remains the pinnacle of Vijayanagar art. (p224)

GOLDEN TEMPLE, AMRITSAR
Gorgeous to look at and atmospheric to visit, this is Sikhism's holiest shrine. (p378)

KAILASA TEMPLE, ELLORA
The centrepiece of the Ellora caves took 150 years to carve from a rock face. (p135)

15

Meenakshi Amman Temple

A six-hectare complex (p288) enclosed by 12 tall *gopurams* (gateway towers), covered in a multicoloured stucco frenzy of thousands of deities, mythical creatures and monsters, Meenakshi Amman is the pinnacle of South Indian temple architecture. It's an inspirational dedication to Shiva, a work of utmost splendour that's an onslaught on the senses. Within is a hive of activity, with tranquil tanks and dramatic halls; it's one of India's key places to experience the vibrant wonder of religious life.

ABOVE: SUYOG GAIDHANI/GETTY IMAGES © LEFT: NEIL MCALLISTER/GETTY IMAGES ©

Kochi

It's easy to be beguiled in the ancient Keralan port of Kochi (p256). Its most charming district, Fort Cochin, displays a tantalising cocktail of influences, from the rambling Dutch, British and Portuguese villas to the cantilevered Chinese fishing nets still in use off the promenade, from the overgrown foreign cemeteries to the ancient synagogue, decorated with hand-painted Cantonese tiles. It's a laid-back place to wander and breathe in the living history of this wonderfully atmospheric spice port.

FELIX HUG/GETTY IMAGES ©

PAUL HARDING/GETTY IMAGES ©

Puducherry Savoir Faire

In this former French colony (p282), yellow houses line cobblestone streets, grand cathedrals are adorned with architectural frou-frou and the croissants are the real deal. But Puducherry (Pondicherry) is also a Tamil town – with all the history, temples and bustle that go along with that – and a classic retreat town, too, with the Sri Aurobindo Ashram at its heart. Turns out that yoga, *pain au chocolat*, Hindu gods and colonial-era architecture make for an atmospheric melange. Notre Dame des Anges (p286)

Mehrangarh Fort, Jodhpur

India is full of incredible, fantastical forts, but one of the most memorable you will see is Mehrangarh (p176), which towers over the blue city of Jodhpur like an illustration from the Brothers Grimm. It seems to grow out of the rock face, with imposing walls shooting skywards from the cliff on which it stands. The architecture is half solid fortress, half delicate palace. The blue-city views are enchanting.

18

LINDSAY BROWN/GETTY IMAGES ©

The Best...
Views

TIGER HILL, DARJEELING
A stunning 250km panorama of Himalayan horizon, including Everest (8848m), Lhotse (8501m), and Makalu (8475m). (p317)

TOP STATION, MUNNAR
On the Kerala–Tamil Nadu border, Top Station has spectacular views over the Western Ghats. (p253)

GUN HILL, MUSSOORIE
Take a cable car up to Gun Hill (2530m) on a clear day for views of several peaks. (p352)

TAJ MAHAL, AGRA
From the north bank of the Yamuna River, from a rooftop cafe in Taj Ganj, or from one of the towers in Agra Fort. (p98)

JAISALMER FORT
Your first glimpse of this sandcastle-like fortress is unforgettable. But don't miss climbing it for sweeping views of the Thar Desert. (p182)

Kerala's Tea & Spice Plantations

The southern state of Kerala is famous for its beaches and backwaters, but one of the region's highlights is its lush plantations in the hills, such as those around Munnar (p253). Travel inland and you'll discover more shades of green than you thought could possibly exist, with endless rolling clumps of tea, brilliantly bright rice paddies, spiky ginger plantations, and field after field of coffee, cardamom and pepper.

BARTOSZ HADYNIAK/GETTY IMAGES ©

The Best...
Places for Walks & Hikes

MANALI
Take a stroll along the Beas River, or hire a guide and hike into the mountains. (p366)

RISHIKESH
Walk to a waterfall or a riverside beach, or follow pilgrims on a temple trail. (p354)

DARJEELING
Trek into the hills, or just saunter around the tea plantations. (p317)

MUSSOORIE
Easy walks with great views, as well as longer guided treks. (p352)

MCLEOD GANJ
Short walks with fine mountain views. (p371)

UDAIPUR
Take a city walking tour, explore the surrounding countryside or walk the fort walls at nearby Khumbhalgarh. (p165)

20 Darjeeling Toy Train

India's quintessential journey is still the train ride, and one of the prettiest and quaintest journeys is the narrow-gauge train trip on the Darjeeling Himalayan Railway, aka the toy train (p320). This hilltop treasure made its first journey in 1881 and is one of the few hill railways still operating in India (there's another good one serving Shimla). Parts of the line are still served by steam locomotives, the views are often stunning, and such is the romantically slow speed of the train that you'll find locals hopping on and off as your chug your way up the mountain.

TOM COCKREM/GETTY IMAGES ©

Udaipur

On your honeymoon? No? Well, make as if you are and indulge in the storybook romance of Udaipur (p165), a town seemingly sculpted from faded lace and built around several beautiful lakes, framed by pale blue hills. It's a great place to laze on sun-bleached rooftops, kick back and read some good books, browse the city's stalls and shops and explore its labyrinthine lakeside palace. Jagdish Temple (p167)

OREN HARVEY/GETTY IMAGES ©

CHRISTER FREDRIKSSON/GETTY IMAGES ©

Camel Rides

Live out a maharaja fantasy and take a desert 'safari' around Jaisalmer (p186). You'll lollop through the rocky terrain atop the tall, goofy creatures, camp out among sand dunes under star-packed skies and visit remote villages where desert dwellers' clothes flicker like flames against the landscape, gaggles of children run out to see you and musicians sing about local life.

Amritsar's Golden Temple

The Sikhs' holiest shrine (p378) is a magical place for people of all religions to worship. Seeming to float atop a pool named for the 'nectar of immortality', the temple is a gorgeous structure, made even more so by its extreme goldness (the lotus-shaped dome is gilded with the real thing). Even when crowded with happy pilgrims, the temple is peaceful, with birds singing outside and the lake gently lapping against the godly abode.

(23)

The Best...
Places for Outdoor Activities

MANALI
Himalayan foothills form a backdrop for hiking, mountain biking, paragliding, rafting and more. (p366)

RISHIKESH
If yoga isn't your thing, try hiking, rafting, kayaking or just lazing around on a riverside beach. (p354)

PALOLEM, GOA
Kayak out to sea on dolphin-spotting trips, or take a guided hike into the surrounding jungle. (p219)

AROUND JAIPUR
Take a spectacular balloon ride above Amber Fort, or spend a day with the elephants at stables nearby. (p153)

JANE SWEENEY/GETTY IMAGES ©

Delhi

India's capital (p60) has had several incarnations over the past few thousand years, which partly explains why there's so much going on here. Dust, noise and chaos aside, Delhi is full of stunning architecture, culture (its residents come from all over the country), good food and even better shopping. The Mughal legacy is one of its biggest attractions: Old Delhi is all crumbling splendour, with the majestic Jama Masjid, the massive Red Fort and other monuments of the historic Mughal capital adorning the old city like royal jewels. Jama Masjid (p61)

The Best...
Places for Wildlife

RANTHAMBHORE NATIONAL PARK
With 1334 sq km of wild jungle hemmed in by rocky ridges, and the amazing 10th-century Ranthambhore Fort, this is a fantastic place for spotting tigers. (p163)

CORBETT TIGER RESERVE
This legendary park has around 200 tigers, and 200 to 300 wild elephants. (p359)

SUNDERBANS TIGER RESERVE
This 2585-sq-km reserve forms part of the world's largest mangrove forest, home to the largest single population of tigers on earth. (p314)

PERIYAR WILDLIFE SANCTUARY
Kerala's most popular wildlife reserve is home to around 1000 wild elephants and 35 to 40 tigers. (p250)

MERTEN SNIJDERS/GETTY IMAGES ©

25

Mysore Palace

Undoubtedly over the top, this 100-year-old Indo-Sarcenic marvel (p265) is a kaleidoscope of stained glass, mirrors and gaudy colours, and is among the grandest of India's royal buildings. Illuminated majestically on weekends, the palace's magnificent exterior houses sculptures, paintings, carved doorways, mosaic floors and numerous collections of artefacts, including an intriguing armoury containing more than 700 weapons.

India's
Top Itineraries

Delhi to Jaipur
The Golden Triangle

5 DAYS

This is the classic, awe-inspiring route: you can discover the many different sides of Delhi before visiting India's most famous monument, the Taj Mahal, taking a side trip to the deserted former capital of Fatehpur Sikri, then heading to the pink city of Jaipur, before returning to Delhi.

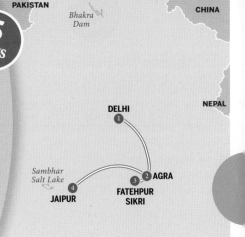

PAKISTAN
CHINA
Bhakra Dam
NEPAL
DELHI ①
Sambhar Salt Lake
AGRA ②
③ FATEHPUR SIKRI
④ JAIPUR

① Delhi (p60)

Explore the capital's highlights, from buzzing restaurants and astounding shops to the medieval old city with its imposing **Red Fort** and huge **Jama Masjid**. Try to include trips to **Qutb Minar** and **Humayun's tomb**.

DELHI ⟶ AGRA

🚆 **1½ to three hours** The 6am Bhopal Shatabdi Express from New Delhi station takes two hours; a new high-speed train should take 90 minutes from Nizamuddin; other trains (there are many) take three hours.
🚗 **Three hours** If taking the new expressway; otherwise, four to five hours.

② Taj Mahal, Agra (p98)

Rudyard Kipling called it 'the embodiment of all things pure', and somehow this epic monument to love really does live up to all the hype. Try to visit in the early morning and leave room for a side trip to **Agra Fort**. But don't forget, the Taj is closed on Friday!

AGRA ⟶ FATEHPUR SIKRI

🚌 **One hour** From Agra's Idgah bus stand, every 30 minutes. 🚗 **One hour** 40km southwest by road.

③ Fatehpur Sikri (p104)

The short-lived capital of the Mughal empire in the 16th century, the magnificent fortified ancient city of **Fatehpur Sikri**, 40km southwest of Agra, is a well-preserved and atmospheric Unesco World Heritage Site. The city was an Indo-Islamic masterpiece, but was erected in an area that suffered from water shortages and so was abandoned shortly after Emperor Akbar's death.

AGRA ⟶ JAIPUR

🚆 **3½ hours** The Shatabdi Express leaves every afternoon (except Thursdays) from Agra Fort train station. 🚗 **Six hours** It's around 230km from Agra to Jaipur.

④ Jaipur (p148)

The dusky, grubby pink city glitters with bazaars and centres around its sprawling **City Palace** as well as the **Hawa Mahal** – a honeycomb-like palace. Outside the city is the majestic **Amber Fort**, which you can reach on the back of a painted elephant.

Quwwat-ul-Islam Masjid (p69), Qutb Minar
DAMIEN SIMONIS/GETTY IMAGES ©

5 DAYS

Mumbai to Palolem
A Taste of Goa

This trip will immerse you in the mixed-up rhythms of Mumbai before you head south to relax on the white-sand beaches of Goa, eat delicious seafood and explore this fascinating region's culture.

ARABIAN SEA

1 MUMBAI (BOMBAY)

2 PANAJI (PANJIM)

3 PALOLEM

① Mumbai (Bombay) (p118)

Enjoy eating in some of India's best restaurants, browsing in some of its most atmospheric bazaars, admiring the grandiose frilliness of Mumbai's colonial-era architecture, strolling on **Girgaum Chowpatty** eating *kulfi* (ice cream) and taking the boat out to **Elephanta Island**.

MUMBAI ➡ PANAJI

✈ **One hour** Fly to Goa's Dabolim Airport, 29km south of Panaji, then take a taxi. **10½ hours** Take the 11.05pm Konkan Kanya Express from Mumbai's CST station, and get off the following morning at Karmali (Old Goa), a short taxi ride from Panaji.

② Panaji (Panjim) (p200)

Discover the Portuguese-flavoured old quarters of the Goan capital, **Panaji**, lingering over lunch at one of its ravishing restaurants and enjoying a tranquil boat trip on the Mandovi River. Take a day trip to **Old Goa** for elegantly crumbling grand cathedrals; vestiges of its former splendour.

PANAJI ➡ PALOLEM

🚗 **Two hours** It's a short drive south to Palolem. **One hour** The daily train from Karmali (Old Goa) to Cancona leaves you with a short taxi ride to Palolem, but it departs Old Goa at an awkwardly late 10.20pm.

③ Palolem (p219)

Formerly Goa's best-kept secret, Palolem is the perfect place to end your trip and relax for a couple of days, with a stunning crescent **beach**. There's not much nightlife, but it's ideal for chilling out, basking in the sunshine and swimming in limpid seas. There's also yoga, **massage therapies** and even **kayaking** on offer.

Girgaum Chowpatty (Chowpatty Beach; p121), Mumbai
CHRISTER FREDRIKSSON/GETTY IMAGES ©

10 DAYS

Delhi to Jaisalmer
The Land of the Kings

This royal journey includes Delhi and the Taj Mahal before it ventures across Rajasthan, the 'Land of the Kings'. Search for tigers in the jungles of Ranthambhore, then explore the forts and palaces of the 'Lake City' (Udaipur), the 'Blue City' (Jodhpur) and the 'Golden City' (Jaisalmer).

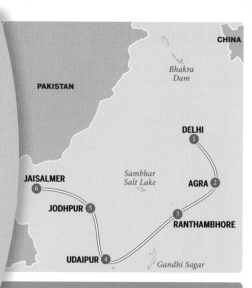

CHINA

PAKISTAN

Bhakra Dam

DELHI ①

Sambhar Salt Lake

JAISALMER ⑥

AGRA ②

JODHPUR ⑤

③ RANTHAMBHORE

UDAIPUR ④

Gandhi Sagar

Delhi (p60)

Starting your trip in Delhi, be sure to visit some of its major sights, including the **Qutb Minar**, **Humayun's tomb** and the **Red Fort**. Also, don't miss out on eating at some of best restaurants in India.

DELHI ⟳ AGRA

🚆 **Two to three hours** The 6am Bhopal Shatabdi Express from New Delhi station takes just two hours. Other trains (there are many) take three. 🚗 **Three hours** If taking the new expressway; otherwise, four to five hours.

 ## Agra (p97)

Make an early start to see the **Taj Mahal**, one of the wonders of the world, followed by a lazy lunch in Agra before visiting the magnificent Mughal **Agra Fort**.

AGRA ⟳ RANTHAMBHORE

🚗 **Five to six hours** It's around 250km drive from Agra to Ranthambhore. 🚆 **Five hours** There's only one daily train to Sawai Madhopur (for Ranthambhore); the 6.15am PNBE Kota Express from Agra Cant station, although others run on selected days from Agra Fort station.

❸ Ranthambhore (p163)

Visit **Ranthambhore National Park** to see wild jungle scrub, hemmed in by rocky ridges and dotted by ruined *chhatris* (domed kiosks), temples and a spectacularly overgrown **10th-century fort**, all the while keeping your eyes peeled for tigers.

RANTHAMBHORE ⟳ UDAIPUR

🚆 **7½ hours** The overnight Mewar Express leaves Sawai Madhopur for Udaipur at 11.50pm, arriving at 7.20am. 🚗 **Six to seven hours** It's 380km by road.

Mehrangarh (p176), overlooking Jodhpur
MARJI LANG/GETTY IMAGES ©

 ## Udaipur (p165)

Relax in what is perhaps India's most romantic city, framed by ancient Aravalli hills and ranged around the glassy waters of **Lake Pichola**. Visit the impressive **City Palace**, go **boating** on the lake then watch the sun set from a rooftop restaurant.

UDAIPUR ⟳ JODHPUR

🚗 **Six to seven hours** There are no trains to Jodhpur, so hire a car and driver. 🚆 **Eight hours** There are hourly buses until 10pm, but it's a long slog.

❺ Jodhpur (p175)

Towered over by the mighty fortress of **Mehrangarh**, the 'Blue City' of Jodhpur stretches out, a jumble of pale-painted houses – from the bird's-eye viewpoint of the fort, it looks like a fantastical, cubist painting.

JODHPUR ⟳ JAISALMER

🚆 **Six hours** There's a 5.10am train, but the better option is the overnight Jodhpur-Jaisalmer Express, which leaves Jodhpur at 11.45pm. 🚗 **Five hours** Your hotel can help arrange a car and driver, or else negotiate with drivers at the taxi stand outside the train station.

❻ Jaisalmer (p182)

Romantically remote, this desert citadel is home to India's most remarkable **fort**; a still-inhabited, 12th-century bastion that seems to rise, mirage-like from the surrounding desert. Wander the narrow streets of the old city and take a **camel safari** if you have time, before you board the 5.15pm Jaisalmer-Delhi Express back to Delhi, arriving at 11.10am the following day.

10 DAYS

Chennai to Mumbai
Sun, Sea & Temples

Laid-back Kerala is the highlight of this southern tour, which begins in Tamil Nadu and ends in Mumbai. From Chennai, head south to the incredible Meenakshi Amman Temple before crossing into Kerala where you'll enjoy the beach, the backwaters and a charming ancient spice port before ending your trip in massive Mumbai.

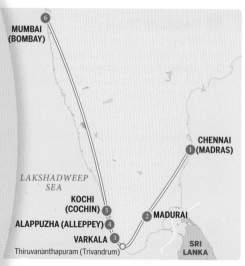

MUMBAI (BOMBAY) 6

CHENNAI (MADRAS) 1

LAKSHADWEEP SEA

KOCHI (COCHIN) 5

ALAPPUZHA (ALLEPPEY) 4

MADURAI 2

VARKALA 3

Thiruvananthapuram (Trivandrum)

SRI LANKA

① Chennai (Madras) (p267)

Take it easy in Chennai on your first day; visit a museum or two; perhaps hook up with one of the city's walking tours; certainly take a sunset stroll along **Marina Beach**.

CHENNAI ⟳ MADURAI

🚆 **Nine hours** The most convenient of the daily trains to Madurai Junction is the overnight Pandian Express, which leaves Chennai Central at 9.20pm. ✈ **One hour** Spice Jet flies daily to Madurai.

② Madurai (p287)

The heart and soul of Tamil Nadu, Madurai is one of India's oldest cities and home to the remarkable **Meenakshi Amman Temple**. Covering six hectares and including 12 tall *gopurams* (gateway towers), each encrusted with a staggering array of gods, goddesses, demons and heroes, this is one of India's greatest temple complexes.

MADURAI ⟳ VARKALA

🚆 **Nine hours** The 11.05pm Quilon Passenger is the best of three daily trains to Thiruvananthapuram. It arrives at 6.40am, giving you plenty of time to reach the beach at Varkala, by train (40 minutes), bus (1½ hours) or taxi (one hour)

③ Varkala (p243)

Hindu place of pilgrimage and laid-back **beach resort**, Varkala stretches out along the coast on the edge of some stunningly dramatic, russet-streaked sea cliffs. It's a great place to kick back for a day or two, resting up at its small-scale resorts and guesthouses and indulging in some **ayurvedic treatments**.

Kathakali dancer (p262), Kochi
KIMBERLEY COOLE/GETTY IMAGES ©

VARKALA ⟳ ALAPPUZHA

🚌 **Two hours** There are six daily trains to Alappuzha (Alleppey), although only the 10.25am, 6pm and 8pm are at convenient times. 🚗 **Three hours** Your hotel should be able to help arrange a taxi.

④ Alappuzha (Alleppey) (p245)

Alappuzha is the gateway to Kerala's fabled **backwaters**, a network of lakes and canals, lined by lush vegetation and waterside villages. It's one of India's most magical experiences to take an overnight **houseboat** and sleep on the water under the stars. Inquire about the possibility of taking a houseboat all the way to Kochi.

ALAPPUZHA ⟳ KOCHI

🚆 **1½ hours** Regular trains run from Alappuzha (Alleppey) to Ernakulam (Kochi). 🚗 **1½ hours** Ask your hotel to help arrange a taxi.

⑤ Kochi (Cochin) (p256)

Soak in 500 years of colonial history and stay in one of Fort Cochin's beautiful heritage hotels. See **giant fishing nets** from China, a 400-year-old **synagogue**, ancient mosques and charming Portuguese-era mansions.

KOCHI ⟳ MUMBAI

✈ **Two hours** The train takes 40 hours, but there are daily flights.

⑥ Mumbai (Bombay) (p118)

End your trip in cosmopolitan Mumbai, with its **colonial architecture**, great **shopping**, classy **cafes** and some of the best **restaurants** in India. Consider a side trip to the rock-cut temples on **Elephanta Island** and don't miss a sunset stroll along **Girgaum Chowpatty**.

2 WEEKS

Mumbai to Varanasi
The Best of India

Taking two weeks, you can see a surprising amount via a few canny domestic flights. This tour mixes the nation's best cities and most breathtaking sights with some of India's more laid-back natural charms.

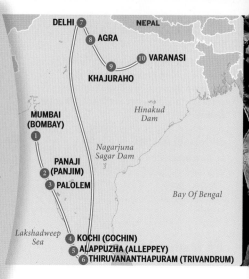

① Mumbai (Bombay) (p118)

Book yourself onto one of the excellent **heritage walking tours**; a hassle-free way of getting your bearings on your first day in India.

MUMBAI ⟶ PANAJI

✈ **One hour** Fly into Dabolim Airport and take a taxi to Panaji or Palolem. 🚆 **10½ hours** The 11.05pm Konkan Kanya Express from Mumbai arrives the following morning at Karmali, a short ride from Panaji.

② Panaji (Panjim) (p200)

Spend a day soaking up the Portuguese-flavoured charm of the Goan capital, including a trip to the crumbling remains of **Old Goa**.

PANAJI ⟶ PALOLEM

🚌 **Two hours**. 🚆 **One hour** The daily train from Karmali (Old Goa) to Cancona leaves you with a short autorickshaw or taxi ride to Palolem, but it departs Old Goa at an awkwardly late 10.20pm.

③ Palolem (p219)

Arguably India's best **beach**, Palolem is a wonderfully easygoing place in which to relax while you're still getting used to the

whole India thing. Chill out, enjoy a massage and go **dolphin spotting** in a kayak.

PALOLEM ⟶ KOCHI

✈ **5½ hours** Take a taxi (two hours) to Dabolin Airport, from where there are daily flights to Kochi. 🚆 **18 hours** Take a taxi (two hours) to Karmali (Old Goa) train station, then take the 10.20pm Netravati Express; it arrives at Ernakulam 2.10pm the next day.

④ Kochi (Cochin) (p256)

Head for **Fort Cochin**, where you can stay in a heritage property, visit the ancient **Pardesi Synagogue** and eat some splendid **seafood**.

KOCHI ⟶ ALAPPUZHA

🚆 **1½ hours** There are regular trains from Kochi to Alappuzha. 🚌 **1½ hours** Around 50km by road.

⑤ Alappuzha (Alleppey) (p245)

The gateway to the famed Keralan **backwaters**. Book yourself onto a houseboat and explore this network of waterways.

ALAPPUZHA ⟶ THIRUVANANTHAPURAM

🚆 **Three hours** To connect with the afternoon flight to Delhi, catch the 7am Trivandrum Express. There are

Keralan backwaters (p248) near Thiruvananthapuram
MARK DAFFEY/GETTY IMAGES ©

DELHI ➡ AGRA

🚆 **Two to three hours** The 6am Bhopal Shatabdi Express from New Delhi station takes just two hours. Other trains (there are many) take three.

🚗 **Three hours** If taking the new expressway; otherwise, four to five hours.

8 Agra (p97)

Visit the **Taj Mahal**, India's most iconic sight. It will not disappoint. Leave time to also see nearby **Agra Fort** and, if possible, the equally impressive **Fatephur Sikri**.

AGRA ➡ KHAJURAHO

🚆 **Seven to eight hours** The 11.20pm UP SMPRK KRNTI takes seven hours and leaves every evening except Wednesday. The 11.05am UDZ KURJ Express runs daily and takes 8½ hours. Both leave from Agra Cantonment station.

9 Khajuraho (p336)

With exquisitely fine carvings, the **Word Heritage temples** of Khajuraho are one of India's most extraordinary sights, swathed as they are in ancient erotica.

KHAJURAHO ➡ VARANASI

✈ **50 minutes** Air India has a 3.05pm flight on Monday, Wednesday and Saturday. 🚆 **11 hours** The 11.40pm Khajuraho-Varanasi Link Express leaves for Varanasi Junction every Tuesday, Friday and Sunday.

10 Varanasi (p325)

Varanasi makes a unique final stop on your tour of India. One of Hinduism's holiest cities, this is where pilgrims come to wash away a lifetime of sins in the sacred waters of the **Ganges**. It's a remarkable place to experience, particularly on an early-morning **boat trip** along the river. From here you can fly daily to Delhi, Mumbai or Kolkata to connect with your flight home.

---

also daily trains at 3.30pm, 5.43pm and 6.15pm.
🚆 **3½ hours** Buses for Thiruvananthapuram depart every 20 minutes. 🚗 **3½ hours** Your guesthouse can help arrange a taxi.

6 Thiruvananthapuram (Trivandrum) (p236)

If you can't leave Alappuzha early enough to connect with a flight to Delhi, lay up in Thiruvananthapuram for a day. The **zoological gardens** and **museums** are worth a visit, and it's only 15km to the beach at **Kovalam**.

THIRUVANANTHAPURAM ➡ DELHI

✈ **Four to five hours** Most flights include a short stop in either Mumbai or Bengaluru (Bangalore).

7 Delhi (p60)

Naturally, the nation's capital has tons for you see: magnificent **historical sights**, fabulous **restaurants** and super **shopping**. For best use of your short time, consider one of the many guided tours.

India Month by Month

Top Events

⭐ **Carnival**, February or March

⭐ **Holi**, February or March

⭐ **Ganesh Chaturthi**, August or September

⭐ **Navratri**, September or October

⭐ **Diwali (Festival of Lights)**, October or November

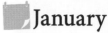 January

⭐ **Republic Day (Free India)**
Commemorates the founding of the Republic of India on 26 January 1950; the biggest celebrations are in Delhi, which holds a military parade along Rajpath and the Beating of the Retreat ceremony three days later.

⭐ **Kite Festival (Sankranti)**
This Hindu festival, marking the sun's passage into Capricorn, is celebrated in many ways – from banana-giving to cockfights. But it's the mass kite-flying in Uttar Pradesh and Maharashtra that steals the show.

⭐ **Pongal (Southern Harvest)**
The Tamil festival of Pongal marks the end of the harvest season. Southern families prepare pots of *pongal* (rice, sugar, dhal and milk), symbolic of prosperity and abundance, then feed it to decorated cows.

⭐ **Vasant Panchami**
Hindus dress in yellow and place books, musical instruments and other educational objects in front of idols of Saraswati, the goddess of learning, to receive her blessing. It can also fall in February.

February

⭐ **Losar (Tibetan New Year)**
Tantric Buddhists all over India – particularly in Himachal Pradesh and Ladakh – celebrate for 15 days, with the most important festivities during the first three. Losar is usually in February or March, though dates can vary between regions.

⭐ **Carnival in Goa**
The four-day party kicking off Lent is particularly big in Goa.

(left) September Ganesh Chaturthi, Mumbai
WIN INITIATIVE/GETTY IMAGES ©

Sabado Gordo (Fat Saturday) starts it off with parades of elaborate floats and costumed dancers, and the revelry continues with street parties, concerts and general merrymaking.

 # March

 ## Holi

One of North India's most ecstatic festivals; Hindus celebrate the beginning of spring according to the lunar calendar (either February or March) by throwing coloured water and *gulal* (powder) at anyone within range. Bonfires held the night before symbolise the death of the demoness Holika.

 ## Wildlife-Watching

When the weather warms up, water sources dry out and animals have to venture into the open to find refreshment – your chance to spot elephants, deer and, if you're lucky, tigers and leopards. Visit www.sanctuaryasia.com for detailed info.

 ## Rama's Birthday

During Ramanavami, which lasts from one to nine days, Hindus celebrate with processions, music, fasting and feasting, enactments of scenes from the Ramayana and, at some temples, ceremonial weddings of Rama and Sita idols.

 # April

 ## Mahavir's Birthday

Mahavir Jayanti commemorates the birth of Jainism's 24th and most important *tirthankar* (teacher and enlightened being). Temples are decorated and visited, Mahavir statues are given ritual baths, processions are held and offerings are given to the poor. It can also fall in March.

 # May

 ## Buddha's Birthday

Commemorating Buddha's birth, nirvana (enlightenment) and parinirvana (total liberation from the cycle of existence, or passing away), Buddha Jayanti is quiet but moving: devotees dress simply, eat vegetarian food, listen to dharma talks and visit monasteries or temples.

 ## Trekking

May and June, the months preceding the rains in the northern mountains, are surprisingly good times for trekking, with sunshine and temperate weather. Try trekking tour operators in Himachal Pradesh, Jammu & Kashmir and Uttarakhand.

 ## Ramadan (Ramazan)

Thirty days of dawn-to-dusk fasting mark the ninth month of the Islamic calendar. Muslims turn their attention to Allah, with a focus on prayer and purification.

 # July

 ## Eid al-Fitr

Muslims celebrate the end of Ramadan with three days of festivities, beginning 30 days after the start of the fast. Prayers, shopping, gift-giving and, for women and girls, *mehndi* (henna designs) may all be part of the celebrations.

 ## Snake Festival

The Hindu festival Naag Panchami is dedicated to Ananta, the coiled serpent Vishnu rested upon between universes. Women return to their family homes to fast, while snakes are venerated as totems against flooding and other evils. Falls in July or August.

and *rangoli* (chalk pictures), families dress up and eat special fish dishes and sweets, and offerings are made at the Fire Temple.

September

✷ Eid al-Adha

Muslims commemorate Ibrahim's readiness to sacrifice his son by slaughtering a goat or sheep and sharing it with family, the community and the poor.

✷ Ganesh Chaturthi

Hindus celebrate the birthday of Ganesh, the elephant-headed god, with verve, particularly in Mumbai. Clay idols of Ganesh are paraded through the streets before being ceremonially immersed in rivers, tanks (reservoirs) or the sea. Ganesh Chaturthi may also be in August.

October

✷ Gandhi's Birthday (2 October)

A solemn national celebration of Mohandas Gandhi's birth, with prayer meetings at his cremation site in Delhi. Schools and businesses close for the day.

✷ Durga Puja

The conquest of good over evil, exemplified by the goddess Durga's victory over the buffalo-headed demon Mahishasura, is celebrated, particularly in Kolkata (Calcutta), where images of Durga are displayed then ritually immersed in rivers and water tanks.

✷ Navratri

The Hindu 'Festival of Nine Nights' leading up to Dussehra, the following day, celebrates the goddess Durga in all her incarnations. Festivities, in September or October, are particularly vibrant in West Bengal, Gujarat

✷ Brothers & Sisters

On Raksha Bandhan (Narial Purnima) girls fix amulets known as *rakhis* to the wrists of brothers and close male friends to protect them in the coming year. Brothers reciprocate with gifts and promises to take care of their sisters.

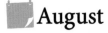 August

✷ Independence Day (15 August)

This public holiday marks the anniversary of India's independence from Britain in 1947. Celebrations are a countrywide expression of patriotism, with flag-hoisting ceremonies (the biggest one is in Delhi), parades and patriotic cultural programs.

✷ Pateti (Parsi New Year)

Parsis celebrate Pateti, the Zoroastrian new year, especially in Mumbai. Houses are cleaned and decorated with flowers and Maharashtra; in Kolkata, Durga images are ritually immersed in rivers and tanks.

 Dussehra

The nine-day festival of Navratri culminates in colourful Dussehra, which celebrates the victory of the Hindu god Rama over the demon-king Ravana. Dussehra is big in Kullu, where effigies of Ravana are ritually burned, and Mysuru (Mysore), which hosts one of India's grandest parades.

 Diwali (Festival of Lights)

In October or November, Hindus celebrate Diwali for five days, giving gifts, lighting fireworks, and burning oil lamps or hanging lanterns to lead Lord Rama home from exile. One of India's prettiest festivals.

 Muharram

A month of remembrance when Shiite Muslims commemorate the martyrdom of the Prophet Mohammed's grandson Imam with beautiful processions.

November

 Pushkar Camel Fair

This famous event attracts up to 200,000 people, who bring with them 50,000 camels, horses and cattle. The town becomes an extraordinary swirl of colour, thronged with musicians, mystics, tourists, traders, animals, devotees and camera crews.

December

 The Prophet Mohammed's Birthday

The Islamic festival of Eid-Milad-un-Nabi celebrates the birth of the Prophet Mohammed with prayers and processions, especially in Jammu & Kashmir.

 **Christmas Day (25 December)**

Festivities are especially big in Goa and Kerala, with musical events, elaborate decorations and special Masses.

Far left: October Diwali **Left: March** Holi

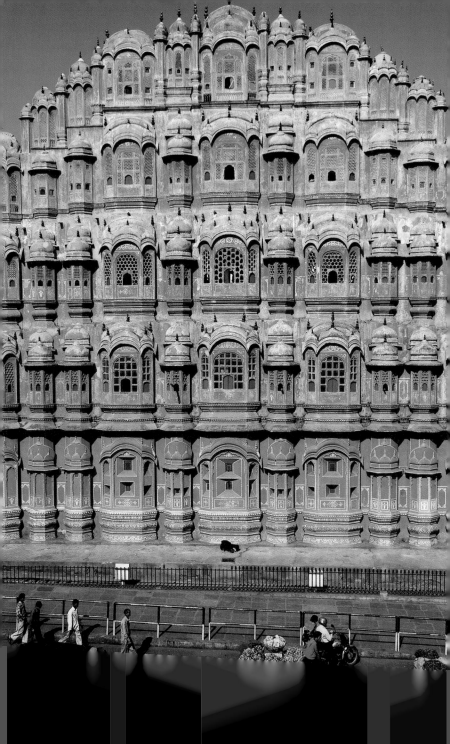

Get Inspired

 ## Books

○ **Ramayana** (1973) RK Narayan's condensed, novelistic retelling of the ancient classic.

○ **India's Struggle for Independence** (1989) Bipan Chandra expertly chronicles the history of India from 1857 to 1947.

○ **A Fine Balance** (1995) A moving and tragic Mumbai story by Rohinton Mistry.

○ **The God of Small Things** (1997) Vibrant, beautiful novel by Arundhati Roy, set in Kerala.

○ **Nine Lives** (2011) William Dalrymple's fascinating insight into the enduring nature of traditional culture in contemporary India.

 ## Films

○ **Gandhi** (1982) Hugely popular biographical film about the Great Soul.

○ **Fire** (1996) **Earth** (1998) **Water** (2005) Deepa Mehta's acclaimed trilogy.

○ **Lagaan** (2001) Critically acclaimed historical drama (with songs).

○ **Devdas** (2002) Lush Bollywood treat starring Aishwarya Rai.

○ **Slumdog Millionaire** (2008) Oscar-winning drama about a young man from the slums of Mumbai who is accused of cheating on *Who Wants to be a Millionaire?*.

Music

○ **Hare Rama Hare Krishna** (1971) Film soundtrack with fantastic 'Dum Maro Dum'.

○ **The Sounds of India** (1968) Legendary sitar player Ravi Shankar's finest.

○ **A Morning Raga/An Evening Raga** (1968) Beautiful raga played by virtuoso Ravi Shankar and tabla player Alla Rakha.

○ **Chaudhvin Ka Chand** (1960) Film music by Shankar with vocals by Asha Bhosle.

○ **Pakeezah** (1972) Sumptuous film soundtrack by Ghulam Mohammed and Naushad Ali.

 ## Websites

○ **Lonely Planet** (www.lonelyplanet.com) Country profile, accommodation information and traveller forums.

○ **Times of India** (www.timesofindia.com) India's largest English-language newspaper.

○ **Incredible India** (www.incredibleindia.org) Official India Tourism site.

○ **Saavn** (www.saavn.com) Free, legal streaming of Indian music, including Bollywood soundtracks and traditional classics.

Short on time?

This list will give you an instant insight into the country.

Read RK Narayan's novel *Ramayana* gives the low-down on the great epic.

Watch *Gandhi*, directed by Richard Attenborough, about the nation's favourite son.

Listen Ravi Shankar's *The Sounds of India* is a seminal sitar album.

Log on Incredible India (www.incredibleindia.org) is the tourist board's useful site.

Left: Hawa Mahal (p151), Jaipur

Need to Know

Currency
Indian rupees (₹)

Language
Hindi and English
(plus local languages)

ATMs
Most urban centres have
foreign-friendly ATMs;
carry cash as back-up.

Credit Cards
MasterCard and Visa
widely accepted.

Visas
Six-month tourist visa
valid from date of issue
(not date of arrival). Some
nationals granted 30-day
visas on arrival (VOA).

Mobile Phones
Use local networks to avoid
expensive roaming costs.

Wi-Fi
In many hotels and hostels
nationwide, in some cafes
and restaurants in cities.

Internet Access
Internet cafes in cities and
towns; few in rural areas.

Driving
Affordable car-with-driver hire
lets you avoid dealing with
hair-raising road conditions.

Tipping
Restaurants usually add
service charges (tipping more
is optional). Tip drivers for long
trips, plus hotel porters and
cycle-rickshaw riders.

When to Go

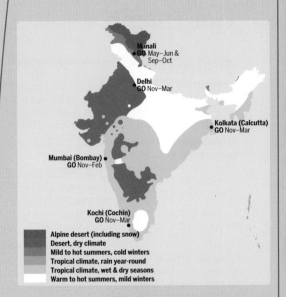

Manali
GO May–Jun &
Sep–Oct

Delhi
GO Nov–Mar

Kolkata (Calcutta)
GO Nov–Mar

Mumbai (Bombay)
GO Nov–Feb

Kochi (Cochin)
GO Nov–Mar

- Alpine desert (including snow)
- Desert, dry climate
- Mild to hot summers, cold winters
- Tropical climate, rain year-round
- Tropical climate, wet & dry seasons
- Warm to hot summers, mild winters

High Season
(Dec–Mar)
○ Pleasant
weather, mostly.
Peak crowds
and prices. Pre-
book flights and
accommodation.

○ In December and
January northern
cities can get cold,
bitterly so in the far
north.

Shoulder Season
(Jul–Nov)
○ July to early
September is the
prime time to visit
Ladakh.

○ Southeast coast
(and southern
Kerala) experiences
heavy rain any time
from October to
early December.

Low Season
(Apr–Jun)
○ April to June
can be unbearably
hot. Hotels prices
competitive.

○ June's southern
monsoons sweep
up north (except
Ladakh) by July.
Fatiguing humidity.

○ Beat the heat by
fleeing to the hills.

Advance Planning

○ **One to two months before** Check your passport is valid for at
least six months, and apply for a visa, unless you want/are eligible to
obtain a visa on arrival.

○ **Six weeks before** Seek advice regarding the necessary
vaccinations, and obtain malaria tablets if necessary.

○ **One week before** Get travel insurance and ensure it will cover
you for any activities you want to do.

Daily Costs

Budget less than ₹1000

○ Stay at cheap guesthouses with shared bathrooms, or in hostels.

○ Eat at roadside stalls or basic restaurants.

○ Travel by train and bus, and occasionally autorickshaw.

Midrange ₹1000 to ₹5000

○ Good accommodation (with private bathrooms) and restaurants.

○ Travel by train, autorickshaw and taxi.

Top End more than ₹5000

○ Sleep and dine like royalty in a restored palace.

○ Hire a car and driver, but take the train for romance and an autorickshaw for adventure!

Exchange Rates

Australia	A$1	₹47
Canada	C$1	₹50
Euro zone	€1	₹71
Japan	¥100	₹53
New Zealand	NZ$1	₹43
UK	UK£1	₹97
US	US$1	₹63

For current exchange rates see www.xe.com

What to Bring

○ **Non-revealing clothes** Covering up will win locals' respect; essential when visiting holy sites.

○ **Money belt** A well-concealed belt for valuables.

○ **Sunscreen & sunglasses** To be sure of good UV protection, bring them from home.

○ **Tampons** Usually found only in big (or touristy) towns, though sanitary pads are widely available.

○ **Mosquito repellent** Especially for malarial areas.

○ **Water bottle** Use water-purification tablets or filters.

○ **Sleeping sheet** If you're unsure about hotel linen or taking overnight train journeys.

Arriving in India

Ask if your hotel can arrange an airport pickup.

○ **Delhi**

Taxi Prepaid taxi booths at the airport

Metro Airport Express Metro Train (5.15am to 11.30pm) links up with metro system

○ **Mumbai**

Taxi Prepaid taxi booths at the airport

○ **Chennai**

Train MRTS train is cheapest way to the centre

Taxi & Autorickshaw Catch from prepaid booths

○ **Kolkata**

Taxi Prepaid fixed-price taxis available from the airport; very few after 10pm (when it costs more)

Bus Half-hourly AC buses from the airport

Getting Around

○ **Rail** Reliable; especially recommended for overnight journeys.

○ **Car** Easiest and safest to hire a car and driver. Advisable not to travel on the roads at night.

○ **Air** Quick and efficient for long distances; numerous airlines have competitive prices.

○ **Bus** From sleek AC coaches to decrepit vehicles. Take only if most convenient.

○ **Rickshaws** The easiest way to zip around towns; mostly motorised.

Sleeping

○ **Government-owned & tourist bungalows** Usually mid-priced, some heritage properties.

○ **Homestays/B&Bs** Family-run, small-scale places, from basic village huts to comfortable middle-class city homes.

○ **Top-end & heritage hotels** From modern five-star chains to glorious palaces and forts.

Be Forewarned

○ **Touts** Use recommended guides – ask other travellers or the official local tourist office.

○ **Taxi & rickshaw drivers** Disregard 'it's no good/closed/burnt down': they'll try to take you to places that pay them a commission.

○ **Gem scams** If a gem deal seems too good to be true, *it is*.

○ **Clean water** Drink bottled or purify your own.

Delhi & the Taj Mahal

Mystery, magic, mayhem.

Welcome to Delhi, City of Djinns, home to 25 million people, where the ruins of Mughal forts and medieval bazaars are scattered between the office blocks, shopping malls and tangled expressways. Like an eastern Rome, India's capital is littered with the relics of lost empires. A succession of armies stormed across the Indo-Gangetic plain and imprinted their identity onto the vanquished city, before vanishing into rubble and ruin like the conquerors who preceded them.

Modern Delhi, with its stellar restaurants and eclectic emporiums, is a chaotic tapestry of medieval fortifications, dusty bazaars and colonial-era town planning. And it's all just a short hop from the city of Agra, another former Mughal capital and home to India's most celebrated landmark of all: the Taj Mahal.

Humayun's Tomb (p67)
HUW JONES/PREMIUM ©

Delhi & the Taj Mahal

Welcome

Seelampur

SEELAMPUR

Marginal Bandh Rd

Yamuna River

Shastri Park

Boulevard Rd

Shastri Rd

Indraprastha Marg

Yamuna Bank

Hapur Bypass

Akshardham

Akshardham Temple

Ring Rd (MG Rd)

SUNDER NAGAR

Delhi Zoo (National Zoological Gardens)

GANDHI DARSHAN

Tilak Bridge Train Station

Pragati Maidan

PRAGATI MAIDAN

Pragati Maidan Train Station

Indraprastha

KAKA NAGAR

PANDARA PARK

Khan Market

Akbar Rd

MEENA BAGH

India Gate

Rajpath

Mandi House

See Old Delhi Map (p62)

Kashmere Gate

Delhi Train Station (Old Delhi)

Netaji Subhash Park

PARDA BAGH

Hindi Park

2

3

Chandni Chowk

OLD DELHI

Chawri Bazaar

Ramlila Grounds

New Delhi

Shivaji Bridge Train Station

Minto Bridge Train Station

Dr KB Hedgewar Marg

Vidhan Sabha

CIVIL LINES

Civil Lines

Tis Hazari

Delhi University

Sadar Bazaar Train Station

New Delhi Train Station

Qutb Rd

CONNAUGHT PLACE

Patel Chowk

Central Secretariat

Udyog Bhawan

KAMLA NAGAR

Sabzi Mandi Train Station

Pulbangash

Kishan Ganj Train Station

SADAR BAZAAR

RAM NAGAR

Karol Bagh

PAHARGANJ

Jhandewalan

RK Ashram Marg

See Connaught Place Map (p78)

Talkatora Gardens

Mughal Gardens

Willingdon Cres

DIPLOMATIC ENCLAVE

Grand Trunk Rd

Pratap Nagar

Desh Bandhu Gupta Rd

Pusa Rd

RAJENDRA NAGAR

Southern Ridge Forest

Delhi Polo Club

SABZI MANDI

Shastri Nagar

Sarai Rohilla Train Station

KAROL BAGH

Rajendra Place

Rajendra Nagar

See New Delhi & Around Map (p80)

Pusa Hill Forest

Upper Ridge Rd

Mahavir Jayanti Park

Inderlok

Daya Basti

PATEL NAGAR

Shadipur

Patel Nagar

NEW RAJENDRA NAGAR

Buddha Jayanti Smarak Park

Keshav

New Rohtak Rd

Patel Nagar Train Station

Kirti Nagar

Kirti Train Station

Naraina Train Station

Brar Square Train Station

Shakurbasti

Ring Rd

Ramesh Nagar

Ring Rd (MG Rd)

Station Rd

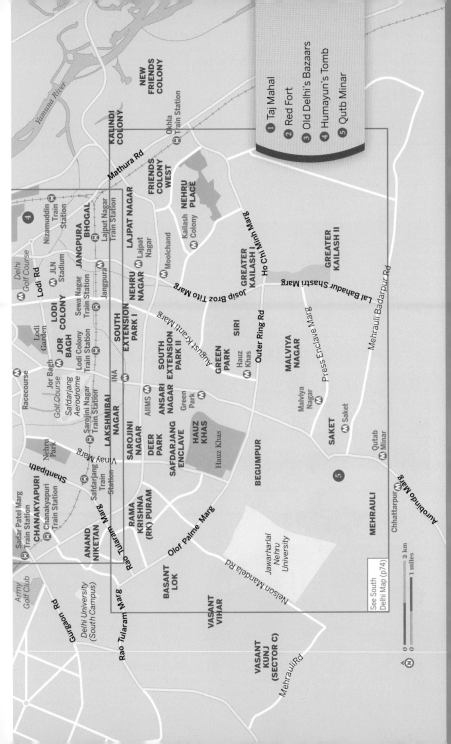

Delhi & the Taj Mahal's Highlights

Taj Mahal

A building that gleams, its perfection like something from a dream, the Taj Mahal (p98) will exceed all your expectations, however high they are. This was the pinnacle of Mughal architecture, and the building has not been diminished by age or any of the surrounding commercialism. If you don't make time to come here, you'll regret it.

1

DYLAN GOLDBY AT WELKINLIGHT PHOTOGRAPHY/GETTY IMAGES ©

2 ## Red Fort

The Red Fort (p60) is awash with splendour, a sandstone queen bee overlooking the Old Delhi hive. Surrounded by magnificent red walls, the remaining buildings might be a shadow of their former selves, but it's still possible to imagine the glories of the imperial court; the battered structures and grounds dotted with British-built barracks resonate with Delhi's tumultuous history.

DAMIEN SIMONIS/GETTY IMAGES ©

Old Delhi's Bazaars

Losing yourself in the madness of Old Delhi's bazaars (p91) is more than just a manic shopping experience – it's a head-spinning assault on the senses. Aromatic incense and pungent spices mix with car fumes, body odour and worse, while the soundtrack is a constant barrage of shouts, barks, music and car horns. It's not so much retail therapy as heightened reality; intense, but unforgettable.

3

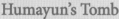

4

Humayun's Tomb

Desperate for a little piece of tranquillity amid the hubbub and traffic of Delhi? This great Mughal tomb (p67), built for the second Mughal emperor, was the inspiration for and forerunner of the Taj Mahal. Surrounded by manicured gardens, it is also one of the most serene places in the capital.

5

Qutb Minar

One of Delhi's most spectacular sights, the ruins of Qutb Minar (p68) date from the onset of Islamic rule in India. Not only is the site a beautiful place to wander, but it's fascinating to see the political and religious historical developments of the time through the adaptations of its architecture.

Delhi & the Taj Mahal's Best…

Wining & Dining

○ **Bukhara** Small menu, big reputation: regarded as Delhi's finest. (p87)

○ **Indian Accent** Creative new Indian cuisine at its best. (p89)

○ **Coast** Delightful South Indian flavours with views in hip Hauz Khas. (p88)

○ **Karim's** Sumptuous kebabs and other meaty treats, in the heart of the Old City. (p83)

○ **Hotel Saravana Bhavan** Down-to-earth atmosphere serving the best South Indian thali in town. (p86)

○ **Esphahan** Agra's finest restaurant and a stone's throw from the Taj Mahal. (p103)

Shopping

○ **Old Delhi's Bazaars** Sights, sounds and smells like no other shopping experience – an assault on the senses. (p91)

○ **Central Cottage Industries Emporium** Aladdin's cave of handicrafts. (p91)

○ **State Emporiums** Handicraft centres from regions across the country – a retail tour of India. (p91)

○ **Khan Market** Exclusive enclave for clothes, homewares and books. An expat favourite. (p92)

○ **Kamala** Crafts and curios with a touch of class. (p91)

Rooms with Panache

○ **Imperial** Raj-era class through and through; don't miss high tea! (p77)

○ **Devna** Charming hosts run Delhi's most charismatic guesthouse. (p79)

○ **Lodhi** Exquisite, cotemporary, spacious yet intimate five star, with views and pools. (p77)

○ **Hotel Palace Heights** The capital's coolest place to rest your head. (p77)

○ **Oberoi Amarvilas** View the Taj Mahal from your bathtub in Agra's finest hotel. (p102)

Need to Know

Places to Chill

○ **Sunset at India Gate**
Everyone gathers to wander
and eat ice cream. (p70)

○ **Humayun's Tomb**
Graceful Mughal tomb set in
serene symmetrical gardens.
(p67)

○ **Lodi Garden** Delhi's
loveliest escape, dotted by
crumbling tombs. (p66)

○ **Bahai House of Worship**
Designed for quiet
meditation, the petal-shaped
'Lotus Temple' welcomes
people of all religions. (p66)

○ **Lodhi Spa** Lush and laid-
back five-star relaxation.
(p72)

ADVANCE PLANNING

○ **Two months before**
Get your visa or check
regarding a Visa on Arrival
(VOA).

○ **Six weeks before** Have
any vaccinations.

○ **One month before** Book
hotel rooms and long train
journeys online.

○ **A few days before** Put
your name down for city
tours you wish to take.

RESOURCES

○ **Delhi Tourism** Free-
advertising city maps are
widely available; for street-
by-street detail, seek out the
excellent 245-page Eicher
City Map (₹340).

○ **Delhi Tourism** (www.
delhitourism.nic.in) Official
government tourism site.

○ **The Delhi Walla** (www.
thedelhiwalla.com) An
offbeat view of Delhi by
local journalist Mayank
Austen Soofi.

○ **Little Black Book Delhi**
(www.littleblackbookdelhi.
com) Curated listings on all
that's hot, from restaurants
to language schools.

○ **Lonely Planet** (www.
lonelyplanet.com/india/
delhi) For planning advice,
author recommendations,
traveller reviews and
insider tips.

GETTING AROUND

○ **Airport Pick-up** Save
yourself heaps of hassle

by getting your hotel to pick
you up when you arrive.

○ **Delhi Metro** The quickest
way to get around the city.

○ **Taxis & Autorickshaws**
They have meters, but they
rarely use them, so agree on
your fare beforehand.

○ **Taxi Tours** Arrange them
at prepaid taxi booths or
through your hotel. Prices
start at ₹1000 per day
without a guide.

○ **To Agra** The fastest trains
from Delhi take only 90 minutes. Expect at least three
hours and ₹3500 by car.

BE FOREWARNED

○ **Commission** Ensure
your taxi or autorickshaw
driver takes you where you
want to go, rather than a
hotel, souvenir shop or
unscrupulous travel agent
masquerading as a tourist
office.

○ **'English Students'** Be
dubious of chatty young
men claiming to be students
wanting to improve their
English – the conversation
is usually the preamble to
a scam.

○ **Tourist Office** Don't
believe anyone who tries
to direct you to a 'tourist
office' around Connaught
Place. There is only one
Government of India tourist
office, at 88 Janpath.

○ **Small Change** Carry
small denomination bills
(below ₹50), as rickshaw
drivers rarely have change.

Left: India Gate (p70)
Above: Spice market, Old Delhi
(LEFT) PHOTOSINDIA/GETTY IMAGES ©;
(ABOVE) CORMAC MCCREESH/GETTY IMAGES ©

Old Delhi Walking Tour

This loop visits Old Delhi's major bazaars and monuments. It's hectic walking through the crowds: if it gets too much, hail a cycle-rickshaw to glide through the mayhem.

WALK FACTS
- **Start** Red Fort
- **Finish** Fatehpur Mosque
- **Distance** 2.5km
- **Duration** Three hours

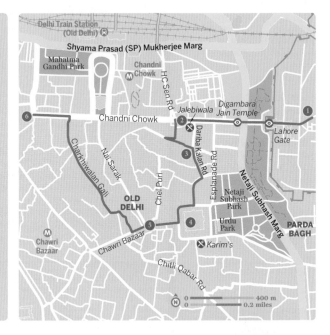

① Red Fort

Start your walk outside the Red Fort, looking up at Lahore Gate, with the walls of the Red Fort stretching out on either side of you. Then, turn your back on the fort and start down Chandni Chowk. Crossing the frantic road, the first thing you will see on your left is Digambara Jain Temple. It contains a bird hospital, reflecting the Jain philosophy of the preservation of all life.

② Sisganj Gurdwara

Continuing to walk down Chandni Chowk, you'll next pass the Jalebiwala on your left, where there's always a crowd of people waiting for the next freshly fried batch of sweet squiggles. Also on your left you'll see the Sisganj Gurdwara, a permanently thronged Sikh temple. It commemorates the martyrdom of Sikh Guru Tegh Bahadur, who was beheaded by the Mughals on this spot in 1675.

③ Kinari Bazaar

Just after the temple, dive left into one of the narrow lanes that snake off the main drag (the one just before the famous sweet shop of Ghantewala). First you'll find a delicious cluster of hole-in-the-wall restaurants, where you can eat a freshly fried *paratha* (bread) stuffed with vegetables and cheese, the perfect snack. Soon the lane meets busy Kinari Bazaar – turn left onto the bazaar. This market stocks everything you might need for a wedding: garlands, grooms' turbans, bridal jewellery and decorations.

4 Jama Masjid

Follow Kinari Bazaar until the junction with Dariba Kalan Rd, then turn right, following it until you meet another junction. Turn right again and follow the lane round a short distance until it opens out to look onto Jama Masjid. It's a surprise to see the imposing building, reached via tall flights of steps. For a bird's-eye view over where you've been walking, enter and climb the minaret.

5 Chawri Bazaar

If you haven't eaten lunch yet, you might want to stop at Karim's on the south side of the Jama Masjid, famous for its delicious Mughlai cuisine. Otherwise, take the street leading west from the great mosque to Chawri Bazaar. The stalls here are piled high with paper products, from greeting cards to wallpaper, and also specialise in brass and copper items. After about 200m take the lane on the right, Charkhiwalan Gali, and follow the bazaar lane straight until you hit the junction with Chandni Chowk.

6 Fatehpur Mosque

The western end of Chandni Chowk is marked by the mid-17th-century Fatehpuri Masjid, named after one of Shah Jahan's wives. It offers a striking tranquillity after the craziness of the streets. After the 1857 First War of Independence (Indian Uprising) the mosque was sold to a Hindu merchant, who used it as a warehouse, but it was later returned to local Muslims.

Delhi in...

TWO DAYS

On day one, acclimatise gently at tranquil sites such as the **National Museum** (p71), **Gandhi Smriti** (p72) and **Humayun's tomb** (p67). In the evening head to **Hazrat Nizam-ud-din Dargah** (p71) to hear the Sufis sing *qawwalis* (Islamic devotional singing).

On day two, follow our Old Delhi Walking Tour, launching into the Old City's action-packed **bazaars** (p91).

FOUR DAYS

The first day, wander around **Qutb Minar** (p68) and **Mehrauli** (p70) before some meditation at the **Bahai House of Worship** (p66). In the evening, check out a show or concert then kick back at a bar.

On day two visit Old Delhi's **Red Fort** (p60), then launch into the Old City's **bazaars** (p91) and visit the **Jama Masjid** (p61). Day three, visit some sights of New and South Delhi, including **Humayun's Tomb** (p76), then take an autorickshaw to **Connaught Place** (p66) to eat.

Day four, visit the laid-back **Crafts Museum** (p72) and finish off around **Connaught Place** (p66) to explore the government **emporiums** (p91).

Painting inside Gandhi Smriti
ANDERS BLOMQVIST /GETTY IMAGES ©

Discover Delhi & the Taj Mahal

At a Glance

○ **Delhi** India's multilayered capital is like numerous cities in one, and a feast for the senses.

○ **Agra** (p97) Visit Mughal emperor Shah Jahan's monument to love and wonder of the world.

○ **Fatehpur Sikri** (p104) This short-lived Mughal capital is now an evocative, beautifully preserved ghost town.

DELHI

011 / POP 25 MILLION

⊙ Sights

Most sights in Delhi are easily accessible via metro. Note that many places are closed on Monday.

OLD DELHI

Sprawling around the Red Fort, medieval-era Old Delhi is a constant barrage of noise, colour and smells that bombard the senses.

Red Fort Fort

(Map p62; Indian/foreigner/child ₹10/250/free, video ₹25, combined museum ticket ₹5, audio guide in Hindi/English & Korean ₹68/113; ⊙dawn-dusk Tue-Sun, museums 9am-5pm; MChandni Chowk) Converted into a barracks by the British, this massive fort is a carcass of its former self, but still conjures a picture of the splendour of Mughal Delhi. Protected by a dramatic 18m-high wall, the marble and sandstone monuments here were constructed at the peak of the dynasty's power, when the empire was flush with gold and precious stones. Shah Jahan founded the fortress between 1638 and 1648 to protect his new capital city of Shahjahanabad, but never took up full residence, as his disloyal son, Aurangzeb, imprisoned him in Agra Fort.

Lahore Gate   Historic Building

(Map p62) The main gate to the fort looks towards Lahore in Pakistan, the second most important city in the Mughal empire. During the struggle for Independence, nationalists promised to raise the Indian flag over the gate, an ambition that became a reality on 15 August 1947.

Lahore Gate

RAMESH LALWANI / GETTY IMAGES ©

JAMIE MITCHELL / GETTY IMAGES ©

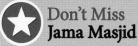 **Don't Miss**
Jama Masjid

A calm respite from the surrounding mayhem, India's largest mosque can hold a mind-blowing 25,000 people. Towering over Old Delhi, the 'Friday Mosque' was Shah Jahan's final architectural opus, built between 1644 and 1658. It has three gateways, four angle towers and two minarets standing 40m high, and is constructed of alternating vertical strips of red sandstone and white marble. You can enter from gate 1 or 3. The only prayer session where non-Muslims may be present is at 7.45am.

NEED TO KNOW
Map p62; camera & video each ₹300, tower ₹100; ⊙non-Muslims 8am-dusk, minaret 9am-5.30pm; MChawri Bazaar

Immediately beyond the gate is the regal **Chatta Chowk (Covered Bazaar; Map p62)**, which once sold silk and jewels, but now mainly sells souvenirs. At the eastern end of the bazaar, the arched **Naubat Khana (Drum House; Map p62)** once accommodated royal musicians and served as a parking lot for royal horses and elephants. Upstairs is the **Indian War Memorial Museum (Map p62; ⊙8am-5pm Tue-Sun)**, with a fearsome-looking collection of historic weaponry.

A short stroll north, housed in a colonial-era block, the **Museum on India's Struggle for Freedom (Map p62; ⊙9am-5pm Tue-Sun)** tells the story of the Independence struggle. If you walk on through the dilapidated barracks, you'll reach a deserted *baoli* (step-well), which the British used as a prison, and a causeway leading to the **Salimgarh (Map p62; ⊙10am-5pm Tue-Sun)**, a fortress built by Salim Shah Suri in 1546. It was likewise used as a prison, first by Aurangzeb, and later by the British; it's

61

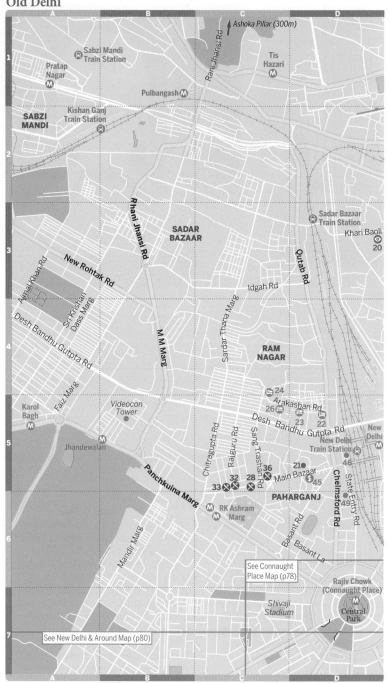

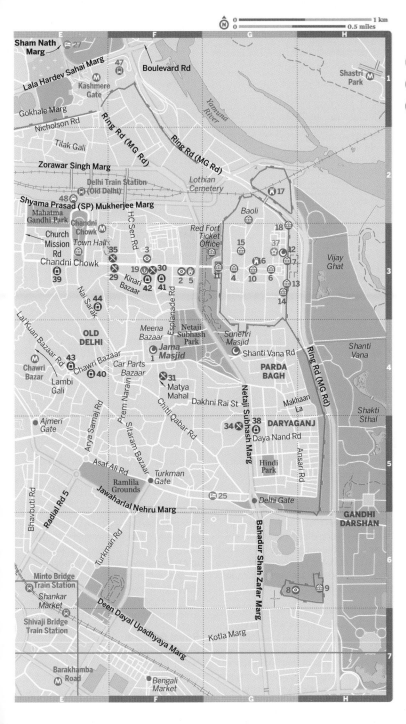

Old Delhi

◎ **Don't Miss Sights**
1 Jama Masjid.............................F4

◎ **Sights**
2 Bird Hospital............................F3
3 Chandni Chowk.......................F3
4 Chatta Chowk..........................G3
5 Digambara Jain Temple...........F3
6 Diwan-i-Am..............................G3
7 Diwan-i-Khas...........................G3
8 Feroz Shah Kotla.....................G6
9 Hawa Mahal.............................H6
10 Indian War Memorial
   Museum G3
11 Lahore Gate.............................G3
12 Moti Masjid...............................G3
13 Mumtaz Mahal.........................G3
14 Museum of Archaeology..........G3
15 Museum on India's Struggle
   for Freedom............................G3
   Naubat Khana ....(see 10)
16 Red Fort...................................G3
   Royal Baths ....(see 12)
17 Salimgarh................................G2
18 Shahi Burj................................G3
19 Sisganj Gurdwara F3
20 Spice Market D3

◎ **Activities, Courses & Tours**
21 Salaam Baalak Trust...............D5

◎ **Sleeping**
22 Bloom Rooms...........................D5
23 Hotel Ajanta.............................D5
24 Hotel Amax Inn........................C4
25 Hotel Broadway G5
26 Hotel Grand Godwin.................C5

27 Maidens Hotel..........................E1

◎ **Eating**
28 Brown Bread Bakery...............C5
   Chor Bizarre.......................(see 25)
29 Gali Paratha Wali F3
   Ghantewala ....(see 29)
30 Jalebiwala................................F3
31 Karim's.....................................F4
32 Malhotra..................................C5
33 Metropolis Restaurant & Bar...C5
34 Moti Mahal...............................G5
35 Natraj Dahi Balle Wala F3
36 Shimtur....................................C5

◎ **Entertainment**
37 Sound & Light Show.................G3

◎ **Shopping**
38 Aap Ki Pasand (San Cha).........G5
39 Ballimaran...............................E3
40 Chawri Bazaar..........................E4
41 Dariba Kalan.............................F3
42 Kinari Bazaar............................F3
43 Lal Kuan Main Bazaar..............E4
44 Nai Sarak.................................E3

◎ **Information**
45 Baluja Forex.............................D5

◎ **Transport**
46 International Tourist Bureau.....D5
47 Kashmere Gate Inter State
   Bus Terminal...........................F1
48 Prepaid Autorickshaws E2
49 Train Reservation Office..........D6

still occupied by the Indian army, but you can visit the ruined mosque and a small museum.

Diwan-i-Am   Historic Building

(Map p62) Beyond the Naubat Khana, a monumental arcade of sandstone columns marks the entrance to the Diwan-i-Am (Hall of Public Audience), where the emperor greeted guests and dignitaries from a pietra-dura covered balcony.

Diwan-i-Khas   Historic Building

(Map p62) Those in favour with the emperor, or conquered rivals begging for peace, were admitted to the white marble Diwan-i-Khas (Hall of Private Audience). This delicate, wedding cake–like pavilion features some outstanding carving and

inlay work. The legendary gold and jewel-studded Peacock Throne was looted from the pavilion by Nadir Shah in 1739.

Mumtaz Mahal   Historic Building

(Map p62) This pavilion once contained the quarters for other women of the royal household. Today it houses the **Museum of Archaeology** (Map p62; ◎9am-5pm Tue-Sun), with royal vestments, miniature paintings, astrolabes, Mughal scrolls and a shirt inscribed with verses from the Quran to protect the emperor from assassins.

Royal Baths & Moti Masjid   Historic Building

North of the Diwan-i-Khas are the **royal baths** (Map p62), which once contained a sauna and hot baths for the royal family, and the **Moti Masjid** (Pearl Mosque; Map p62), an elegant private place of worship for the emperor. The outer walls align with the fort walls, while the inner walls are slightly askew to correctly align with Mecca. Both are closed to visitors, but you can peer through the screen windows.

Shahi Burj   Historic Building
(Map p62) North of the Royal Baths is the Shahi Burj, a three-storey octagonal tower, where Shah Jahan planned the running of his empire. In front of the tower is what remains of an elegant formal garden, centred on the Zafar Mahal, a sandstone pavilion surrounded by a deep, empty water tank.

Sound & Light
Show   Cultural program
(Map p62; Tue-Fri ₹60, Sat & Sun ₹80; ⊘in English 8.30pm, 9pm May-Aug, 7.30pm Nov-Jan) Every evening, except Monday, the Red Fort is the setting for a bombastic sound-and-light show, with coloured spotlights and a portentous voiceover, highlighting key events in the history of the Red Fort.

Chandni Chowk   Area
(Map p62; MChandni Chowk) Old Delhi's main thoroughfare is a chaotic shopping street, mobbed by hawkers, motorcycles, stray dogs and porters and with narrow lanes running off it offering the full medieval bazaar experience. In the time of Shah Jahan, a tree-lined canal ran down its centre, reflecting the moon, hence the name Chandni Chowk, or 'Moonlight Place'.

Digambara Jain
Temple   Jain Temple
(Map p62; Chandni Chowk; ⊘6am-noon & 6-9pm; MChandni Chowk) In the cluster of temples at the Red Fort end of Chandni

Volunteering

There plenty of ways to assist Delhi's less fortunate residents. The Salaam Balaak Trust (p73) in Paharganj and the Hope Project (p73) in Nizamuddin often have openings for volunteers – contact them directly for opportunities. Mother Theresa's Missionaries of Charity runs projects in Delhi which may accept volunteers – contact its Kolkata office (p303) for information.

Chowk, the scarlet Digambara Jain Temple houses a fascinating **bird hospital** (Map p62; Chandni Chowk; donations appreciated; ⊘10am-5pm) established to further the Jain principle of preserving all life, with a capacity of 10,000. Only vegetarian birds are admitted (up to 60 per day), though predators are treated as outpatients.

Autorickshaw, Chandni Chowk
DAN HERRICK / GETTY IMAGES ©

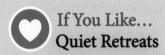

If You Like...
Quiet Retreats

If you're attracted to tranquil places such as Humayun's Tomb, try these calm oases.

1 LODI GARDENS
(Map p80; Lodi Rd; ⊙6am-8pm Oct-Mar, 5am-8pm Apr-Sep; MKhan Market or Jor Bagh) At this peaceful park the gardens are dotted with the crumbling tombs of Sayyid and Lodi rulers, including the impressive 15th-century **Bara Gumbad tomb** (Map p80) and mosque, and the strikingly different tombs of **Mohammed Shah** (Map p80) and **Sikander Lodi** (Map p80). There's a lake crossed by the Athpula (eight-piered) bridge, which dates from Emperor Akbar's reign.

2 BAHAI HOUSE OF WORSHIP
(Lotus Temple; Map p74; ☑26444029; www.bahaihouseofworship.in; Kalkaji; ⊙9am-7pm Tue-Sun, to 5.30pm winter; ☎; MKalkaji Mandir) Designed by Iranian-Canadian architect Fariburz Sahba in 1986, this Bahai temple, styled after a lotus flower with 27 white-marble petals, was created to bring faiths together; visitors are invited to pray or meditate silently according to their beliefs. The visitor centre tells the story of the Bahai faith. Photography is prohibited inside.

3 HAUZ KHAS
(Map p74; MGreen Park) The lake at Hauz Khas, meaning 'Royal Tank', was built by Sultan Allauddin Khilji in the 13th century to provide water for Siri Fort. Thronged by birds and fringed by parkland, it is fronted by the ruins of Firoz Shah's 14th-century madrasa (religious school) and **tomb** (Map p74).

4 PURANA QILA
(Old Fort; Map p80; ☑24353178; Mathura Rd; Indian/foreigner ₹5/100, video ₹25, sound & light show ₹80; ⊙dawn-dusk; MPragati Maidan) Purana Qila was constructed by Afghan ruler Sher Shah (1538–45), who briefly seized control of Delhi from the emperor Humayun. The monumental gatehouse opens onto a peaceful garden studded with ancient monuments. The graceful octagonal, red-sandstone **Sher Mandal** was used by Humayun as a library; it was a fall down its stairs that ended his reign, and life, in 1556. Beyond is the intricately patterned **Qila-i-Kuhran Mosque** (Mosque of Sher Shah).

Remove shoes and leather items before entering the temple.

Nearby, the 18th-century **Sisganj Gurdwara** (Map p62; Chandni Chowk) marks the the martrydom site of the ninth Sikh guru, Tegh Bahadur, executed by Aurangzeb in 1675 for resisting conversion to Islam.

Feroz Shah Kotla — Historic Site
(Map p62; Bahadur Shah Zafar Marg; Indian/foreigner ₹5/100, video ₹25; ⊙dawn-dusk; MPragati Maidan) Ferozabad, the fifth city of Delhi, was built by Feroz Shah in 1354 as a replacement for Tughlaqabad. Ringed by crumbling fortifications are a huge mosque, a *baoli* (step-well), and the pyramid-like **Hawa Mahal** (Map p62), topped by a 13m-high sandstone **Ashoka Pillar** inscribed with Ashoka's edicts. There's an otherworldly atmosphere to the ruins, which are still a place of worship – on Thursday afternoon, crowds gather to light candles and incense and leave bowls of milk to appease Delhi's djinns (invisible spirits). Shoes should be removed when entering the mosque and Hawa Mahal.

CONNAUGHT PLACE AREA

Connaught Place — Area
(Map p78; MRajiv Chowk) New Delhi's colonial-era heart is Connaught Place, named after George V's paternal uncle, and fashioned after the colonnades of Cheltenham and Bath to assuage British homesickness. Its whitewashed, grey-tinged streets radiate out from the central circle of Rajiv Chowk, lined with shops and restaurants. The outer circle (divided into blocks G to N) is technically called Connaught Circus, and the inner circle (divided into blocks A to F) is Connaught Place, but locals call the whole area 'CP'.

Jantar Mantar — Historic Site
(Map p78; Sansad Marg; Indian/foreigner ₹5/100, video ₹25; ⊙9am-dusk; MPatel Chowk) The most eccentric-seeming of Delhi's historic sites, Jantar Mantar

MUKUL BANERJEE PHOTOGRAPHY / GETTY IMAGES ©

⭐ Don't Miss
Humayun's Tomb

The most perfectly proportioned and captivating of Delhi's mausoleums, Humayun's Tomb seems to float above the gardens that surround it. Built in the mid-16th century by Haji Begum, the Persian-born senior wife of the Mughal emperor Humayun, the tomb brings together Persian and Mughal elements, creating a template that strongly influenced the Taj Mahal.

NEED TO KNOW
Map p80; Mathura Rd; Indian/foreigner ₹10/250, video ₹25; ⏲dawn-dusk; Ⓜ JLN Stadium

(derived from the Sanskrit word for 'instrument') is an odd collection of curving geometric buildings that are carefully calibrated to monitor the movement of the stars and planets. Maharaja Jai Singh II constructed the observatory in 1725.

Agrasen ki Baoli   Monument
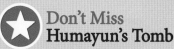
(Map p78; Hailey Lane; ⏲dawn-dusk; Ⓜ Barakhamba Rd) A remarkable thing to discover among the office towers southeast of Connaught Place, this atmospheric 14th-century step-well was once set in rural land, until the city grew up around it; 103

steps descend to the bottom, flanked by arched niches.

NEW DELHI & AROUND
Rajpath   Area
(Ⓜ Khan Market) The focal point of Edwin Lutyens' plan for New Delhi was Rajpath (Kingsway), a grand parade linking India Gate to the offices of the Indian government. Constructed between 1914 and 1931, these grand civic buildings, reminiscent of Imperial Rome, were intended to spell out in stone the might of the British empire – yet just 16 years

Don't Miss
Qutb Minar

In a city awash with ancient ruins, the Qutb Minar complex is something special. The first monuments here were erected by the sultans of Mehrauli, and subsequent rulers expanded on their work, hiring the finest craftspeople and artisans to create an exclamation mark in stone to record the triumph of Muslim rule.

Map p74

☏ 26643856

Indian/foreigner ₹10/250, video ₹25, decorative light show Indian/foreigner ₹20/250, audio guide ₹100

🕑 dawn-dusk

Ⓜ Qutab Minar

The complex, studded with ruined tombs and monuments, is dominated by the spectaclular Qutb Minar, a soaring Afghan-style victory tower and minaret, erected by sultan Qutb-ud-din in 1193 to proclaim his supremacy over the vanquished Hindu rulers of Qila Rai Pithora. The tower has five distinct storeys with projecting balconies, but Qutb-ud-din only completed the first level before being unfortunately impaled on his saddle while playing polo. His successors completed the job.

Quwwat-ul-Islam Masjid

At the foot of the Qutb Minar stands the Quwwat-ul-Islam Masjid, the first mosque built in India. Its design shows a fusion of Islamic and pre-Islamic styles. Altamish, Qutb-ud-din's son-in-law, expanded the original mosque with a cloistered court between 1210 and 1220, and Ala-ud-din added the exquisite marble and sandstone Alai Darwaza gatehouse in 1310.

Iron Pillar

Standing in the courtyard of the Quwwat-ul-Islam mosque is a 7m-high iron pillar that vastly predates the surrounding monuments. A six-line Sanskrit inscription indicates it was initially erected outside a Vishnu temple, possibly in Bihar, in memory of Chandragupta II, who ruled from AD 375 to 413. What the inscription does not tell is how it was made – scientists have never discovered how the iron, which has not rusted after 1600 years, could be cast using the technology of the time.

Alai Minar

When the Sultan Ala-ud-din made additions to the complex in the 14th century, he also conceived an ambitious plan to erect a second tower of victory, exactly like the Qutb Minar, but twice as high! Construction of the Alai Minar got as far as the first level before the sultan died; none of his successors saw fit to bankroll this extravagant piece of showboating. The 27m-high plinth can be seen just north of the Qutb Minar.

Local Knowledge

Qutb Minar Don't Miss List

DILLIWALA SUREKHA NARAIN PROVIDES WALKING TOURS AROUND DELHI SIGHTS, INCLUDING QUTB MINAR, WITH DELHI METRO WALKS

1 QUWWAT-UL-ISLAM MOSQUE
In AD 1192, Muhammad Ghori from Afghanistan defeated Prithviraj Chauhan, a Hindu and Rajput ruler, and left his slave, Qutbuddin Aibak, to establish the Qutb complex. Aibak demolished around 27 Hindu temples and built a mosque (known as Quwwat-ul-Islam or Might of Islam). The result is a blend of Hindu and Islamic elements. Hindu elements include conical domes with supporting pillars and beams. Islamic ideas are seen in the form of corbelled arches.

2 QUTB MINAR
This victory tower was established in 1193, and is the tallest stone tower in India: 72.5m high with 379 steps leading to five storeys. On each floor you can see details of stalactite corbelling and arabesque Islamic decoration with floral and geometrical patterns and calligraphy of Quranic verses.

3 ALAI DARWAZA
Alauddin Khilji, the invader who founded the second city of Delhi, added the Alai Darwaza – a stunning gateway in arabesque decoration – in 1311 by beautifully blending red sandstone and marble to create a southern entrance to the Qutb Minar.

4 TOMB OF IMAM ZAMIM
Next to the Alai Darwaza, this Lodhi-style square tomb has 12 pillars with red sandstone lattice work. Inside you see how a circle has been converted to a dome (circular structure) with the help of squinches. The marble sculpture of a small pen box on the lid of the tomb shows that this is the tomb of a man.

5 TOMB OF ILTUTMISH
At the far end of the complex is the stunning square tomb of Iltutmish, which has no Hindu features, and combines arabesque floral and geometrical patterns in sandstone and marble with a large pen sculpture on a male tomb, decorative prayer niche, and calligraphy from the Quran.

69

Mehrauli Archaeological Park

Bordering the Qutb Minar complex, but overlooked by most of the tourist hordes, the **Mehrauli Archaeological Park** (Map p74; ⊙dawn-dusk; Ⓜ Qutab Minar) preserves some of the most atmospheric relics of the second city of Delhi. Scattered around a forest park that spills into a chaotic basti (slum) are the ruins of dozens of tombs and palace buildings and several colonial-era follies. The most impressive structure is the Jamali Khamali mosque, attached to the tomb of the Sufi poet Jamali. Ask the caretaker to open the doors so you can see the intricate incised plaster ceiling. Nearby are the Rajon ki Baoli, a majestic 16th-century step-well with a monumental flight of steps, and the time-ravaged tombs of Balban and Quli Khan.

later, the British were out on their ear and Indian politicians were pacing the corridors of power.

Shielded by a wrought-iron fence at the western end of Rajpath, the official residence of the president of India, Rashtrapati Bhavan, is flanked by the mirror-image, dome-crowned **North Secretariat** (Map p80) and **South Secretariat** (Map p80), housing government ministries. The Indian parliament meets nearby at the **Sansad Bhavan** (Parliament House; Map p80), a circular, colonnaded edifice at the end of Sansad Marg.

At Rajpath's eastern end, and constantly thronged by tourists, is **India Gate** (Map p80). This 42m-high stone memorial arch, designed by Lutyens, pays tribute to around 90,000 Indian army soldiers who died in WWI, the Northwest Frontier operations, and the 1919 Anglo-Afghan War.

Rashtrapati Bhavan
Historic Building

(President's House; Map p80; ☏23012960; www.presidentofindia.nic.in/rashtrapati -bhavan.htm; 1hr tour ₹50; ⊙9am-4pm Fri-Sun;

Qutb Minar (p68)

BPPERRY / GETTY IMAGES ©

 Don't Miss
Hazrat Nizam-ud-din Dargah

Hidden away in a tangle of bazaars selling rose petals, attars (perfumes) and offerings, the marble shrine of the Muslim Sufi saint, Nizam-ud-din Auliya, offers a window through the centuries, full of music and crowded with devotees. The ascetic Nizam-ud-din died in 1325 at the ripe old age of 92, and his mausoleum became a point of pilgrimage for Muslims from across the empire. Later kings and nobles wanted to be buried as close to Nizam-ud-din as possible, hence the number of nearby Mughal tombs.

NEED TO KNOW

Map p80; off Lodi Rd; ⊘24hr; Ⓜ JLN Stadium

Ⓜ Central Secretariat) You have to book ahead online, but it's worth it to peek inside the grandiose President's House. Formerly home to the British Viceroy, it has 340 rooms, with 2.5km of corridors. However, visits are limited to the domed Durbar Hall, the presidential library, and the gilded Ashoka Hall.

You'll have to leave cameras and phones at the entrance, but there's a chance to take pictures close up of the outside before/after your visit.

National Museum Museum
(Map p80; ☎23019272; www.nationalmuseum india.gov.in; Janpath; Indian/foreigner ₹10/300, audio guide English, French or German ₹400, Hindi ₹150, camera Indian/foreigner ₹20/300; ⊘10am-5pm Tue-Sun; Ⓜ Central Secretariat) Offering a compelling if not always coherent snapshot of India's last 5000 years, this museum is not overwhelmingly large, but full of splendours. Exhibits include rare relics from the Harappan Civilisation, Buddha's 4th- to 5th-century BC effects,

If You Like...
Museums

If you like the National Museum (p71), Delhi has many other facinating museums.

1 GANDHI SMRITI
(Map p80; ☏ 23012843; 5 Tees Jan Marg; ⊙10am-5pm Tue-Sun, closed every 2nd Sat of month; Ⓜ Racecourse) This poignant memorial is where Mahatma Gandhi was shot dead by a Hindu zealot on 30 January 1948, after campaigning against intercommunal violence. Concrete footsteps lead to the spot where Gandhi died, marked by a small pavilion. Video prohibited.

2 NATIONAL GALLERY OF MODERN ART
(Map p80; ☏ 23382835; www.ngmaindia. gov.in; Jaipur House, Dr Zakir Hussain Marg; Indian/foreigner ₹10/150; ⊙10am-5pm Tue-Sun; Ⓜ Khan Market) Delhi's flagship art gallery displays a remarkable collection of paintings, including primitive-inspired artworks of Nobel Prize–winner Rabindranath Tagore. Photography prohibited.

3 CRAFTS MUSEUM
(Map p80; ☏ 23371641; Bhairon Marg; ⊙10am-5pm Tue-Sun; Ⓜ Pragati Maidan) Set up like a traditional village, this captivating, rambling museum aims to preserve the traditional crafts of India, from hand-loom weaving to Mithila wall painting.

4 NATIONAL RAIL MUSEUM
(Map p80; ☏ 26881816; Service Rd, Chanakyapuri; adult/child ₹20/10, video ₹100; ⊙9.30am-5.30pm Tue-Sun) Trainspotters and kids will adore this recently renovated museum, with its collection of steam locos and carriages and a toy train (adult/child ₹20/10) that chuffs around the grounds.

5 SULABH INTERNATIONAL MUSEUM OF TOILETS
(☏ 25031518; www.sulabhtoiletmuseum.org; Sulabh Complex, Mahavir Enclave, Palam Dabri Rd; ⊙10am-5pm summer, 10.30am-5pm winter) Run by a pioneering charity that has done extraordinary work bringing sanitation to the poor of India, this quirky museum displays toilet-related paraphernalia dating from 2500 BC to modern times.

antiquities from the Silk Route, exquisite miniature paintings (look out for the hand-painted playing cards), woodcarvings, textiles, statues, musical instruments, and an armoury with gruesomely practical weapons and a suit of armour for an elephant.

Allow at least two hours, preferably half a day. Bring identification to obtain an audio guide (worthwhile as labelling is minimal).

Activities

Lodhi Spa
Spa

(Map p80; ☏ 43633333; www.thelodhi.com; Lodhi Hotel, Lodi Rd, New Delhi; 1hr massage from ₹3800; Ⓜ JLN Stadium) The fragrant, rarified world of the Lodhi spa is open to nonguests who book treatments, such as massages, facials, and traditional ayurvedic treatments.

Aura
Spa

(Map p80; ☏ 8800621206; www.aurathai spa.com; Middle Lane, Khan Market; 1hr oil massage ₹2400; ⊙10am-9pm; Ⓜ Khan Market) Glitzy spa offering Thai-inspired massages and treatments. There are also branches at Karol Bagh, GK1, GK2 and Green Park.

Courses

Hush Cooking
Cooking

(Vasant Vihar; 3hr lesson ₹3200) The lovely Prabeen Singh, a former development worker, offers 1½-hour cookery lessons in her home, in a suburb close to the airport. After the lesson, you eat your creations.

Nita Mehta
Cooking

(☏ 26141185; www.nitamehta.com; Block TU, Uttari Pitampura, North Delhi; 3hr lesson ₹2000) Cookery writer, teacher and TV chef Nita Mehta offers Indian cookery courses.

Sivananda Yoga
Yoga

(Map p74; www.sivananda.org.in; A41 Kailash Colony; class ₹400; Ⓜ Kailash Colony) Excellent yoga ashram, with beginners and advanced courses, plus drop-in classes.

Tours

Tours are a good way to see Delhi without being overwhelmed, but avoid Monday when many sites are shut. Admission fees and camera/video charges aren't included in tour prices below, and rates are per person. Book several days in advance. For a bespoke tour, India Tourism Delhi can arrange multilingual, government-approved guides.

DelhiByCycle   Bicycle Tour
(9811723720; www.delhibycycle.com; per person ₹1850; 6.30-10am) Run by a Dutch journalist, this is a fantastic way to explore Delhi. Tours focus on specific neighbourhoods – Old Delhi, New Delhi, Nizamuddin, and the banks of the Yamuna – and start early to miss the worst of the traffic. The price includes chai and a Mughal breakfast. Child seats are available.

Salaam Baalak Trust   Walking Tour
(SBT; Map p62; 23584164; www.salaambaalak trust.com; Gali Chandiwali, Paharganj; suggested donation ₹200; Ramakrishna Ashram Marg) This charitable organisation offers

two-hour 'street walks' guided by former street children, who will show you first-hand what life is like for Delhi's homeless youngsters. The fees help the Trust assist children on the streets.

Hope Project   Walking Tour
(Map p80; 24353006; www.hopeprojectindia. org; 127 Hazrat Nizamuddin; 1½hr walk suggested donation ₹200) This charity runs fascinating walks around the Muslim *basti* (slum) of Nizamuddin. Take the walk in midafternoon to end at the *qawwali* (Islamic devotional singing) at the Hazrat Nizam-ud-din Dargah, or at the more intimate session at the shrine of Hazrat Inayat Khan on Friday. Wear modest clothing.

Street Connections   Walking Tour
(www.walk.streetconnections.co.uk; 3hr walk ₹500) This fascinating walk through Old Delhi is guided by former street children who have been helped by the Salaam Baalak Trust. It explores the hidden corners of Old Delhi, starting at Jama Masjid and concluding at one of the SBT shelters.

National Rail Museum

South Delhi

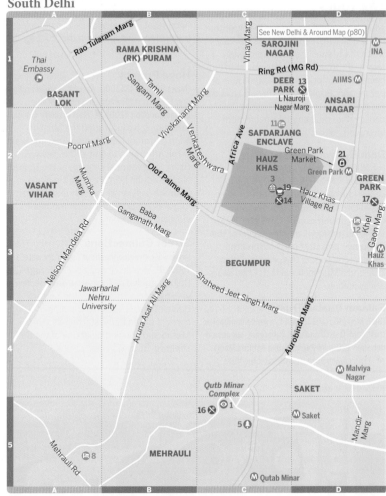

Indomania Cultural Tours   Tour
(☎ 8860223456; www.indomaniatours.com;
half-day tour per person ₹2000) 🖋 Excellent
tours by the knowledgeable Priyush,
exploring the parts of Delhi others don't
reach. Visit a Rajasthani pottery village
on Delhi's outskirts, cultural groups along
the Yamuna River, or Delhi's Tibetan enclave, in tours that operate in association
with local NGOs.

**Delhi Tourism &
Transport Development
Corporation**   Bus Tour
(DTTDC; Map p78; www.delhitourism.nic.in;
Baba Kharak Singh Marg; AC tour half/full day
₹200/350; ☯7am-9pm; Ⓜ Rajiv Chowk) Offers
bus tours of New Delhi (9am to 1.30pm)
and Old Delhi (2.15pm to 5.45pm)
visiting all the big sights (avoid Monday,
when most are shut). It also runs the
air-conditioned Ho Ho (Hop-on, Hop-off)

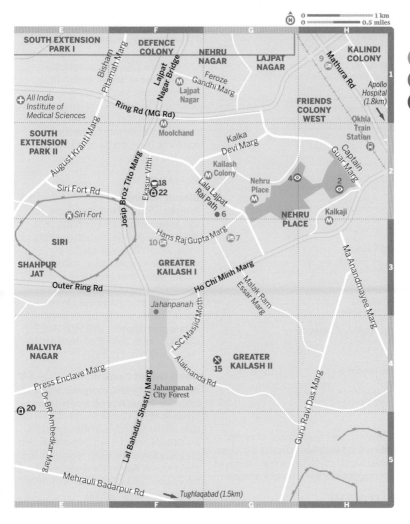

Dilli Dekho bus service, which circuits the major sights every 45 minutes or so from 8.30am to 6.30pm (Indian/foreigner ₹350/700, two-day ticket ₹600/1200) – buy tickets from the **booth (Map p78)** near the office.

🛏 Sleeping

It's wise to book in advance, as popular places can fill up in a flash, leaving new arrivals easy prey for commission sharks. Call or email ahead to confirm your

booking 24 hours before you arrive. Most hotels offer pick-up from the airport with advance notice. Homestays are becoming an attractive alternative to hotels. For details of government-approved places contact India Tourism Delhi, or check www.incredibleindianhomes.com and www.mahindrahomestays.com.

Hotels with a minimum tariff of ₹1000 charge luxury tax (10% at the time of research) and service tax (7.42% at the time of research), and some also add a service charge (up to 10%). Room rates

South Delhi

◎ **Don't Miss Sights**
1 Qutb Minar Complex C5

◎ **Sights**
2 Bahai House of Worship H2
3 Firoz Shah's Tomb..............................C2
   Hauz Khas.................................(see 3)
4 Iskcon Temple......................................G2
5 Mehrauli Archaeological Park............C5

◎ **Activities, Courses & Tours**
6 Sivananda Yoga G2

◎ **Sleeping**
7 Bed & Chai...G3
8 Chhoti Haveli.......................................A5
9 Manor...H1
10 Moustache Hostel...............................F3
11 Scarlette...C2
12 Treetops...D3

◎ **Eating**
13 Alkauser D1
14 Coast..C2
   Indian Accent ....(see 9)
15 Not Just Parathas...............................G4
16 Olive...C5
17 Potbelly D2

◎ **Drinking & Nightlife**
18 Café Turtle F2
19 Kunzum Travel Cafe............................C2

◎ **Shopping**
20 Fabindia...E4
21 Fabindia...D2
22 Fabindia..F2

in this chapter include taxes; all rooms have private bathrooms unless otherwise stated. Most hotels have a noon checkout and luggage storage is usually possible.

OLD DELHI

Hotel Broadway   Hotel $$
(Map p62; ☎43663600; www.hotelbroadway delhi.com; 4/15 Asaf Ali Rd; s/d incl breakfast ₹2295/3995; ❄@; ⓂNew Delhi) A surprising find in the Old City, Broadway was Delhi's first high rise when it opened in 1956. Today it combines comfort with charm and eccentricity and has a great restaurant and bar. Some rooms have old-fashioned wood panelling, while others have been quirkily kitted out by French designer Catherine Lévy. Ask for one with views over Old Delhi.

Maidens Hotel   Hotel $$$
(Map p62; ☎23975464; www.maidenshotel.com; 7 Sham Nath Marg; r from ₹12,000; ❄@🛜🛁; ⓂCivil Lines) Set in immaculate gardens, Oberoi-owned Maidens is a graceful wedding cake of a hotel, built in 1903. Lutyens stayed here while supervising the building of New Delhi, and the enormous high-ceilinged rooms have a colonial-era charm combined with contemporary comforts. There are two restaurants, a pool and a bar.

PAHARGANJ

Bloom Rooms   Hotel $$
(Map p62; ☎011-40174017; bloomrooms.com; 8591 Arakashan Road; s/d from ₹2200/2800; 🛜) Sunny lemon-yellow and gleaming white, Bloom Rooms is sparklingly designer-feeling and clean, with soft pillows, white linen, great wi-fi, and nice outdoor seating areas. This New Delhi branch is in a busy area but a haven inside. There's another balmy branch in **Jangpura** (Map p80; ☎011-41261400; 7 Link Rd) in South Delhi. Both have Amici restaurants (good pizza).

Hotel Grand Godwin   Hotel $$
(Map p62; ☎23546891; www.godwinhotels.com; 8502/41 Arakashan Rd; d incl breakfast from ₹2500; ❄@🛜) Located north of Main Bazaar, on the hotel strip of Arakashan Rd, the Grand Godwin is firmly midrange, and the glitzy feel of the lobby extends to the smart rooms. Run by the same owners, the nearby Godwin Deluxe offers similar facilities for similar prices.

Hotel Ajanta   Hotel $$
(Map p62; ☎42350000; www.ajantahotel.com; 8647 Arakashan Rd; d/ste ₹2642/4697; ❄@🛜) Some rooms are better than others at Ajanta; pay the higher rates and you'll be in for a more spacious room with a grand, polished-wood look. Some have private balconies. The downstairs **Vagabond** restaurant serves quality Mughlai food.

Hotel Amax Inn   Hotel $
(Map p62; ☎23543813; www.hotelamax.com; 8145/6 Arakashan Rd; s/d from ₹750/850;

✳@🛜) Set back from chaotic Arakashan Rd, the Amax offers fairly standard, good-value budget rooms, with bullet-hard pillows, but the friendly staff run the place with the globe-trotting traveller in mind. The rooftop terrace is a great spot to swap travel stories and there's wi-fi in reception.

CONNAUGHT PLACE & AROUND

The following places are close to Rajiv Chowk metro station.

Imperial   Hotel $$$
(Map p78; 📞23341234; www.theimperialindia.com; Janpath; r from ₹17,000; ✳@🛜🏊) The inimitable, Raj-era Imperial marries colonial-period classicism with gilded art deco. Rooms have high ceilings, flowing curtains, French linen and marble baths, and the hallways and atriums are lined with 18th- and 19th-century paintings and prints. The 1911 bar (p90) is highly recommended, and the **Atrium cafe** serves the perfect high tea.

Hotel Palace Heights   Hotel $$$
(Map p78; 📞43582610; www.hotelpalaceheights.com; 26-28 D-Block; s/d ₹7150/8250; ✳@🛜) This boutique hotel is cool enough to wear shades, offering Connaught Place's nicest rooms with gleaming white linen, black lampshades and caramel and amber tones. There's an excellent restaurant, Zäffrän (p86).

Prem Sagar Guest House
Guesthouse $$
(Map p78; 📞23345263; www.premsagarguesthouse.com; 1st fl, 11 P-Block, Connaught Place; s/d from ₹3523/4110; ✳@; MRajiv Chowk) A reliable, long-standing choice, with 12 snug rooms that aren't flash but are clean and

relatively cheap for the location. There's a pot-plant-filled rear terrace, and internet in reception.

NEW DELHI

Lodhi   Hotel $$$
(Map p80; 📞43633333; www.thelodhi.com; Lodi Rd; r from ₹27,000; ✳🛜🏊) Formerly the Aman, the Lodhi is one of Delhi's finest luxury hotels, with only 40 huge, lovely rooms and suites, and acres of space. Each room has a balcony with private plunge pool, and those on the upper floors have great views, some over to Humuyan's Tomb. Attention to detail is superb and the general managers greet everyone personally. There's also a top-notch spa.

Lutyens Bungalow   Guesthouse $$$
(Map p80; 📞24611341; www.lutyensbungalow.co.in; 39 Prithviraj Rd; s/d incl breakfast from ₹5500/7000; ✳@🛜🏊; MRace-course) This great rambling house is an atmospheric green oasis, ideal if you're travelling with kids and perfectly located for exploring New Delhi. The garden is

Jantar Mantar (p66)
ROSA RENDTORFF / EYEEM / GETTY IMAGES ©

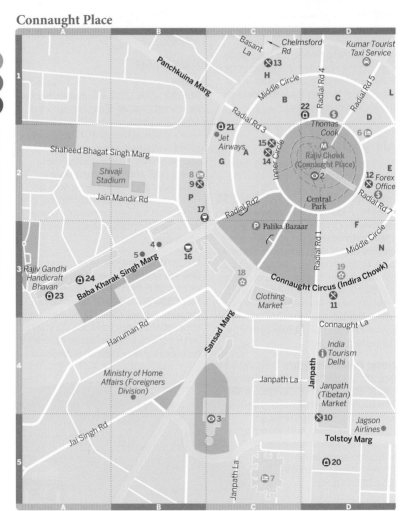

great – lawns, flowers and fluttering parrots – but rooms are a little stuffy and overpriced, though looking much better since recent renovations.

SOUTH DELHI

Bed & Chai   Hostel **$$**
(Map p74; www.bedandchai.com; R55 Hans Raj Gupta Marg; dm ₹850, d without/with bathroom from ₹2200/3000) This French-owned guesthouse has simple, stylish rooms, decorated with flashes of colour and lamps made out of teapots. There's

a sparkling clean dorm as well, a roof terrace and, of course, excellent chai. The owners also run Bed & Chai Masala, which has cheaper dorm beds.

Treetops   Guesthouse **$$**
(Map p74; ☑ 9899555704; baig.murad@gmail. com; R-8b Hauz Khas Enclave; s/d incl breakfast ₹3500/4000; ❄ @ 🛜; Ⓜ Hauz Khas) Cookery writer Tannie and journalist Murad have a gracious home and to stay here feels rather like visiting distant, upper-crust relatives. Treetops offers two large

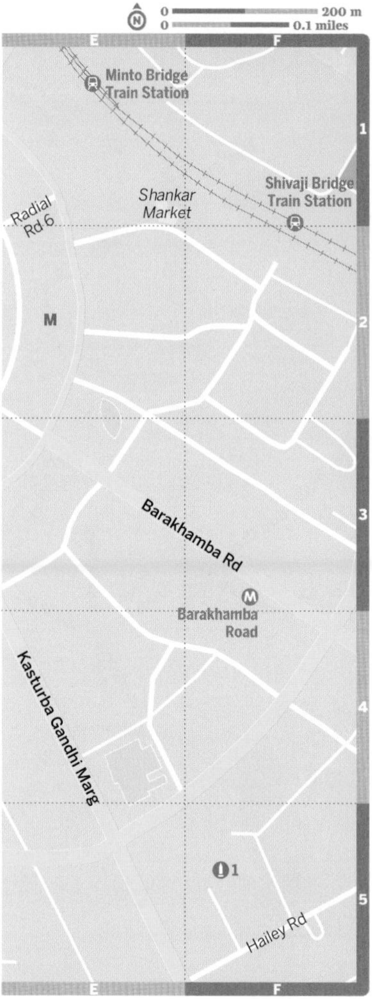

Connaught Place

Sights
1 Agrasen ki Baoli F5
2 Connaught Place D2
3 Jantar Mantar C5

Activities, Courses & Tours
4 Delhi Tourism & Transport Development Corporation B3
5 Delhi Tourism & Transport Development Corporation Booth B3

Sleeping
6 Hotel Palace Heights D2
7 Imperial C5
8 Prem Sagar Guest House B2

Eating
9 Hotel Saravana Bhavan B2
10 Hotel Saravana Bhavan D5
11 Rajdhani D3
12 United Coffee House D2
13 Véda C1
14 Wenger's C2
15 Wenger's Deli C2
Zāffrān .... (see 6)

Drinking & Nightlife
1911 .... (see 7)
16 Indian Coffee House B3
17 Monkey Bar B2

Entertainment
18 Attic C3
19 Blues D3

Shopping
20 Central Cottage Industries Emporium D5
21 Chandni Chowk C2
22 Fabindia D1
23 Kamala A3
24 State Emporiums A3

rooms opening onto a leafy rooftop terrace overlooking the park. Evening meals are available.

Devna Guesthouse **$$$**
(Map p80; ☎41507176; www.tensundernagar.com; 10 Sunder Nagar; s/d ₹5700/6000; ❄@☜) Fronted by a pretty courtyard garden, and run with panache by the charming Atul and Devna, this is one of Delhi's prettiest guesthouses. The walls are lined with photos of maharajas and works of art (yes, those are original Jamini Roys) and the rooms are decked out with quirky antiques. The upstairs rooms front onto tiny terraces.

Manor Boutique Hotel **$$$**
(Map p74; ☎26925151; www.themanordelhi.com; 77 Friends Colony West; d incl breakfast from ₹12,000; ❄@) A more intimate alternative to Delhi's five-star chains, this 16-room boutique hotel oozes privacy and elegance. Set amid lush lawns off Mathura Rd, the Manor offers the kind of designer touches normally found in the homes of Bollywood stars. There's a colonial air to the opulent rooms and the

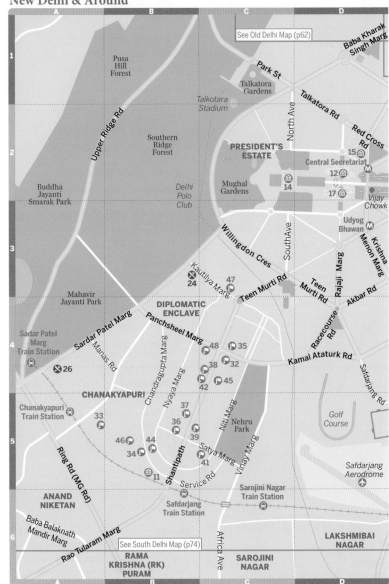

restaurant, Indian Accent (p89), is one of Delhi's finest.

Bnineteen Guesthouse $$$
(Map p80; ☎ 41825500; www.bnineteen.com;
B-19 Nizamuddin East; s/d incl breakfast from

₹7500/9000; ❄ @) Located in posh and peaceful Nizamuddin East, with views over Humayun's Tomb from the rooftop, this gorgeous place is owned by architects, and it shows. Rooms are modern

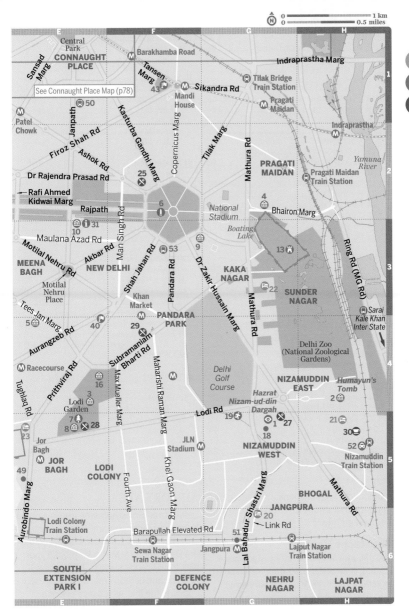

and refined, and there is a state-of-the-art shared kitchen on each floor.

Scarlette   Guesthouse **$$$**
(Map p74; ✆8826010278; www.scarlettenew delhi.com; B2/139 Safdarjung Enclave; d ₹8000;

❄ 🛜) In a serene residential area, close to the Deer Park and Hauz Khas, Scarlette is a lovely boutique *maison d'hotes* (guesthouse) with just four rooms and a large sitting room filled with books and interesting objects. It's French-owned and

New Delhi & Around

◉ Don't Miss Sights
1 Hazrat Nizam-ud-din Dargah...............G5
2 Humayun's Tomb H4

◎ Sights
3 Bara Gumbad Tomb............................E4
4 Crafts Museum G2
5 Gandhi Smriti......................................E4
6 India Gate...F2
7 Lodi Gardens E5
8 Mohammed Shah's Tomb E5
9 National Gallery of Modern Art...........F3
10 National Museum...............................E3
11 National Rail Museum B5
12 North Secretariat...............................D2
13 Purana Qila G3
14 Rashtrapati Bhavan............................C2
15 Sansad Bhavan D2
16 Sikander Lodi's Tomb E4
17 South Secretariat D2

◉ Activities, Courses & Tours
Aura ....(see 29)
18 Hope Project......................................G5
19 Lodhi Spa G5

⊜ Sleeping
20 Bloom Rooms @Link Rd G6
21 Bnineteen...H5
22 Devna...G3
Lodhi..(see 19)
23 Lutyens Bungalow E5

✕ Eating
24 Alkauser B3
25 Andhra Pradesh Bhawan
    Canteen...F2
26 Bukhara..A4
27 Karim's G5
28 Lodi Garden Restaurant......................E5
29 Sodabottleopenerwala........................F4

◗ Drinking & Nightlife
30 Café Turtle..H5
Café Turtle......................................(see 29)

⌂ Shopping
Anand Stationers ....(see 29)
Bahrisons ....(see 29)
Fabindia...(see 29)
Kama ....(see 29)
Khan Market....................................(see 29)
Mehra Bros.....................................(see 29)

ⓘ Information
31 Archaeological Survey of India.............E3
32 Australian High Commission.................C4
33 Bangladeshi High Commission A5
34 Bhutanese Embassy............................B5
35 British High Commission C4
36 Canadian High Commission B5
37 Dutch Embassy...................................B5
38 French Embassy..................................C4
39 German Embassy.................................B5
40 Israeli Embassy...................................E4
41 Malaysian High Commission C5
42 Myanmar Embassy...............................C4
43 Nepali Embassy...................................F1
44 New Zealand High Commission B5
45 Pakistani Embassy...............................C4
46 Singaporean High Commission............B5
47 Sri Lankan High Commission C3
48 US Embassy...C4

ⓘ Transport
49 Air India..E5
50 Himachal Pradesh Tourism
    Development Corporation E1
51 Metropole Tourist Service G6
52 Prepaid Autorickshaws H5
53 Rajasthan Tourism..............................F3

popular with French speakers. A set menu dinner (rather pricey at ₹900 to ₹1200) is served nightly.

Moustache Hostel
Hostel $

(Map p74; www.facebook.com/moustachehostel; S25, GK1, M-Block Market Main Rd; incl breakfast dm ₹600, d ₹2500; ❄ 🛜; Ⓜ Kailash Colony) This cheerful hostel has appealing, nicely kept small dorms, a few doubles decorated with bright prints, and a funky, welcoming vibe. It's about a 15- to 20-minute walk from the metro. There's a book-lined common room and lots of local info. It's a great place to chat to other 20-something travellers.

AIRPORT AREA

Delhi's brand-new Aerocity area is a bland but convenient conglomeration of hotels, only 4km from the airport. It's served by the Delhi Aerocity Metro stop. Take your pick from brands such as JW Marriott, Red Fox and Lemon Tree; the cheapest option is the Ibis, which also offers a free 24-hour shuttle pick-up from either terminal. There are also a few choices in nearby Vasant Kunj.

Chhoti Haveli
Homestay $$

(Map p74; ☏ 26124880; www.chhotihaveli.com; A1006, Pocket A, Vasant Kunj; s/d ₹3500/4000; ❄ @ 🛜) Set in a block of low-rise apartments, in a quiet, leafy area near the airport, this well-kept place offers tastefully decorated rooms. Potted plants and scattered petals on the doorstep show a personal touch.

Eating

Delhi is a foodie paradise, and locals graze throughout the day, whether munching the city's famous *Dilli-ka-Chaat* (Delhi street food) at stalls in the Old City, or sitting down to indulgent feasts at Delhi's fine-dining restaurants.

Midrange and upmarket restaurants charge a service tax of around 10%; drinks taxes can suck a further 20% (alcoholic) or 12.5% (nonalcoholic) from your wallet. Taxes haven't been included unless indicated. Many restaurants also levy a 10% service charge, in lieu of a tip.

Telephone numbers have been provided for restaurants where reservations are recommended.

OLD DELHI

Karim's
Mughlai $

(Map p62; Gali Kababyan; mains ₹45-460; ⊙9am-12.30am; M Chawri Bazaar) Just off the lane leading south from Jama Masjid, Karim's has been delighting carnivores since 1913. Expect meaty Mughlai treats such as mutton *burrah* (marinated chops), delicious mutton Mughlai, and the breakfast mutton and bread combo *nahari* (₹125 half portion). There's a second branch in **Nizamuddin West** (Map p80; 168/2 Jha House Basti).

Jalebiwala
Sweets $

(Map p62; Dariba Corner, Chandni Chowk; jalebis per 100g ₹30; ⊙8.30am-9.45pm; M Chandni Chowk) Century-old Jalebiwala does Delhi's, if not India's, finest

High Tea at the Imperial

Raise your pinkie finger! High tea at the Imperial (p77) is perhaps the most refined way to while away an afternoon in Delhi. Sip tea from bone-china cups and pluck dainty sandwiches and cakes from tiered stands, while discussing the latest goings-on in Shimla and Dalhousie. High tea is served in the **Atrium** (⊙3-6pm daily; weekday/weekend ₹750/1050). For ₹2500, you can add a 1½-hour tour of the Imperial's fantastic collection of Indian and colonial-era art.

jalebis (deep-fried, syrupy fried dough), so pig out and worry about the calories tomorrow.

Atrium, Imperial Hotel
JEREMY SUTTON-HIBBERT / ALAMY ©

Gali Paratha Wali   Street Food $

(Map p62; Gali Paratha Wali; parathas ₹15-35;
⊙7am-11pm; Ⓜ Chandni Chowk) Head to this
food-stall-lined lane off Chandni Chowk
for delectable *parathas* (traditional flat
bread) fresh off the *tawa* (hotplate).
Choose from a spectacular array of
stuffings, from green chilli and paneer to
lemon and banana.

Natraj Dahi
Balle Wala   Street Food $

(Map p62; 1396 Chandni Chowk; plate ₹50;
⊙10.30am-11pm; Ⓜ Chandni Chowk) This
hole-in-the-wall with the big red sign
and the big crowds is famous for its
dahi bhalle (fried lentil balls served with
yoghurt and garnished with chutney) and
deliciously crispy *aloo tikki* (spiced potato
patties).

Ghantewala   Sweets $

(Map p62; 1862A Chandni Chowk; mithai per 100g
from ₹25; ⊙8am-10pm; Ⓜ Chandni Chowk)
Delhi's most famous sweetery, the 'Bell
Ringer' has been churning out *mithai* (Indian sweets) since 1790. Try some *sohan
halwa* (ghee-dipped gram flour biscuits).

Moti Mahal   Mughlai $$

(Map p62; ☏23273661; 3704 Netaji Subhash
Marg; mains ₹170-540; ⊙11am-midnight) The
original, much-copied Moti Mahal has
been open for six generations – the food
is much more impressive than the faded
surroundings. Delhi-ites rate the place
for its superior butter chicken and dhal
makhani. There's live *qawwali* (Islamic devotional singing) Wednesday to Monday
(8pm to 11.30pm).

Chor Bizarre   Kashmiri $$$

(Map p62; ☏23273821; Hotel Broadway, 4/15
Asaf Ali Rd; mains ₹305-675; ⊙7.30-10.30am,
noon-3.30pm & 7.30-11.30pm; Ⓜ New Delhi) A
dimly lit cavern, filled with bric-a-brac, including a vintage car, Chor Bizarre (meaning 'thieves market') offers delicious and
authentic Kashmiri cuisine, including
wazawan, the traditional Kashmiri feast. It
offers an Old City walking tour combined
with lunch for ₹2500.

Left: Bara Gumbad tomb, Lodi Gardens (p66); **Below:** Yoga, Lodi Gardens
(LEFT) INTI ST CLAIR / GETTY IMAGES ©; (BELOW) MATTHEW WAKEM / GETTY IMAGES ©

PAHARGANJ

Brown Bread Bakery
Organic $

(Map p62; Ajay Guesthouse, 5084-A, Main Bazaar; snacks ₹65-150; ⏰7am-11pm; 📶; Ⓜ Ramakrishna Ashram Marg) With a rustic, wicker-heavy interior and a long menu of largely organic breads, cheeses, jams, soups, teas and more, the Brown Bread is a nice relaxing place to hang out among other travellers from all over the place. You can also buy ayurvedic products here.

Shimtur
Korean $$

(Map p62; 3rd fl, Navrang Guest House, Tooti Galli; meals ₹240-500; ⏰10am-11pm; Ⓜ Ramakrishna Ashram Marg) It's a mini-adventure to find this place, off the main drag and on top of the Navrang Guesthouse. Follow the stairs up several floors and you'll find a neat little bamboo-lined rooftop. The Korean food is fresh, authentic and delicious. Try the *bibimbap* (rice bowl with a mix of vegetables, egg and pickles; ₹240).

Malhotra
Multicuisine $$

(Map p62; 1833 Laxmi Narayan St; mains ₹100-600; ⏰7am-11pm) One street back from the Main Bazaar chaos, Malhotra is smarter than most, with a good menu of set breakfasts, burgers, Indian standards and spirited attempts at continental dishes.

Metropolis Restaurant & Bar
Multicuisine $$

(Map p62; Metropolis Tourist Home, Main Bazaar; mains ₹300-1000; ⏰11am-11pm) On the rooftop at Metropolis Tourist Home, this energetic travellers' haunt is a cut above the competition, with prices to match, proffering cold beer and tasty tandoori chicken.

CONNAUGHT PLACE

The following eateries are all close to the Rajiv Chowk metro stop.

Hotel Saravana Bhavan
South Indian $

(Map p78; 15 P-Block, Connaught Place; mains ₹65-165; ⏱8am-11pm; Ⓜ Rajiv Chowk) Delhi's best thali is served up in unassuming surroundings – a simple Tamil canteen on the edge of Connaught Place. There are queues every meal time to sample the splendid array of richly spiced veg curries, dips, breads and condiments that make it onto every thali plate. There's a second branch on **Janpath** (Map p78; 46 Janpath; Ⓜ Rajiv Chowk).

Wenger's
Bakery $

(Map p78; 16 A-Block, Inner Circle, Connaught Place; snacks from ₹30-90; ⏱10.45am-7.45pm; Ⓜ Rajiv Chowk) Legendary Wenger's has a wonderfully stuck-in-time feel having been baking since 1926. Come for cakes, sandwiches, biscuits, and savoury patties. Around the corner you can eat in at **Wenger's Deli** (Map p78), which has the most delicious milkshakes, including mango (₹90).

Rajdhani
Indian $$$

(Map p78; ☎43501200; 1/90 P-Block, Connaught Place; thalis ₹395, dinner & weekends ₹445; ⏱noon-4pm & 7-11pm; Ⓜ Rajiv Chowk) This pristine, nicely decorated two-level place serves up excellent-value, food-of-the-gods vegetarian thalis with a fantastic array of Gujarati and Rajasthani dishes. It's the same, sumptuous thali daily.

Véda
Indian $$$

(Map p78; ☎41513535; 27 H-Block, Connaught Place; mains ₹400-1300; ⏱12.30-11.30pm; Ⓜ Rajiv Chowk) Fashion designer Rohit Baal created Véda's sumptuous interior, making for Connaught Place's most dimly lit eatery, a dark boudoir with swirling neo-Murano chandeliers and shimmering mirror mosaics. The menu proffers tasty classic Mughlai dishes (butter chicken, dhal makhani and the like) and staff mix a mean Martini.

Zāffrān
Mughlai $$$

(Map p78; ☎43582610; Hotel Palace Heights, 26-28 D-Block; mains ₹435-800; ⏱noon-3.30pm & 7pm-midnight) An excellent restaurant serving Mughlai cuisine, with a lovely, calm bamboo-shuttered, glass-covered terrace and plenty of light.

Akshardham Temple

UNIQUELY INDIA / GETTY IMAGES ©

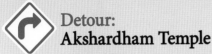

Detour:
Akshardham Temple

Rising dramatically over the eastern suburbs, the Hindu Swaminarayan Group's controversially ostentatious **Akshardham Temple** (22016688; www.akshardham. com; National Hwy 24, Noida turning; temple admission free, exhibitions ₹170, fountains ₹30; ☺9.30am-6.30pm Tue-Sun; [M]Akshardham) is a wedding-cake confection of salmon-coloured sandstone and white marble, drawing elements from traditional Orissan, Gujarati, Mughal and Rajasthani architecture. The interior offers an almost psychedelic journey through Hindu mythology, with 20,000 carved deities, saints and mythical beings.

Surrounding this spiritual showpiece is a series of Disneyesque exhibitions, including a boat ride through 10,000 years of Indian history, animatronics telling stories from the life of Swaminarayan, and musical fountains. Allow at least half a day to do it justice (weekdays are less crowded).

United Coffee House
Multicuisine $$$

(Map p78; ☏23416075; 15 E-Block, Connaught Place; mains ₹345-1000; ☺noon-midnight; [M]Rajiv Chowk) Not a coffee shop, but an upscale, high-ceilinged, chandeliered restaurant, with an old-world dining room full of characters who look as elderly as the fixtures and fittings. The menu covers everything from butter chicken to English high tea. Serves alcohol (a pint of Kingfisher costs ₹225).

NEW DELHI & AROUND

Andhra Pradesh Bhawan Canteen
South Indian $

(Map p80; 1 Ashoka Rd; breakfast ₹60, thalis ₹110; ☺7.30-10.30am, noon-3pm & 7.30-10pm; [M]Patel Chowk) A hallowed bargain, the canteen at the Andhra Pradesh state house serves cheap and delicious unlimited South Indian thalis to a seemingly unlimited stream of patrons. Come on Sunday for the Hyderabadi biryani (₹180).

Alkauser
Street Food $$

(Map p80; www.alkausermughlaifood.com; Kautilya Marg; kebabs from ₹130, biryani from ₹250; ☺6-10.30pm) The family behind this hole-in-the-wall takeaway earned their stripes cooking kebabs for the Nawabs of Lucknow in the 1890s. The house speciality is the kakori kebab, a pâté-smooth combination of lamb and spices, but other treats include biryani (cooked *dum puhkt* style in a *handi* pot sealed with pastry) and perfectly prepared lamb *burrah* (marinated chops) and *murg malai tikka* (chicken marinated with spices and paneer). There are several branches, including one in the **Safdarjand Enclave market** (Map p74; ☺6-10.30pm).

Sodabottleopenerwala
Parsi $$

(Map p80; Khan Market; ₹125-500; ☺11am-11.15pm; [M]Khan Market) Suggesting a typical Parsi surname (taken from a trade), this place emulates the Iranian cafes of Mumbai and the food is authentic Persian. The upstairs terrace has a good deal more charm. The menu includes Iranian cakes and 'Bombay specials' including delicious *kanda bhaji* (Mumbai-style crispy onion fritters).

Bukhara
Indian $$$

(Map p80; ☏26112233; ITC Maurya, Sadar Patel Marg; mains ₹750-2400; ☺12.30-2.45pm & 7-11.45pm) Widely considered Delhi's best restaurant, this glam hotel eatery serves Northwest Frontier–style cuisine at low tables, with delectable melt-in-the-mouth kebabs and its famous Bukhara dhal. Reservations are essential.

Lodi Garden Restaurant
Mediterranean $$$

(Map p80; ☎24652808; Lodi Rd; mains ₹400-1700; ⏰12.30pm-12.45am; Ⓜ Jor Bagh) Set in a funky garden with lanterns dangling from the trees and tables in curtained pavilions and wooden carts, this is the most romantic dinner spot in New Delhi. Although not quite as impressive as the surroundings, the menu traverses Europe and the Middle East, and there's a popular Sunday brunch.

SOUTH DELHI

Coast
South Indian $$

(Map p74; above Ogaan, Hauz Khas; set meals ₹340-440; ⏰noon-midnight; Ⓜ Green Park) A beautifully light, bright restaurant on several levels, with wonderful views over the parklands of Hauz Khas, Coast serves delicious, elegant cuisine, with light southern Indian dishes, such as *avial* (South Indian vegetable curry) with pumpkin *erisheri* (with black lentils) or European cuisine, such as salad with orange and walnuts.

Not Just Parathas
Indian $$

(Map p74; 84 M-Block, Great Kailash II; dishes ₹90-625; ⏰noon-midnight) They don't just serve *parathas* (stuffed flat bread), they serve 120 types of *parathas!* Try them stuffed with kebabs, veg curries, shredded chicken and untold other fillings.

Potbelly
Bihari $$

(Map p74; 116C Shahpur Jat Village; mains ₹190-350; ⏰12.30-11pm; Ⓜ Hauz Khas) In the hip, boutique-filled urban village of Shahpur Jat: climb several flights of higgeldy piggeldy stairs to reach Potbelly, a rooftop cafe with views out across the rooftops and a lovely artsy mix of painted watering cans and cane furniture. The food is delicious – try the Bihari burger or *keema goli* (mutton meatballs).

Olive
Mediterranean $$$

(Map p74; ☎29574443; One Style Mile, Mehrauli; dishes ₹450-1350; ⏰noon-midnight; Ⓜ Qutab Minar) Uberchic Olive with its uberchic clientele creates a little piece of the Mediterranean in the suburbs. The *haveli* (tra-

ditional, ornately-decorated residence) setting, combined with beach-house colours, is unlike anywhere else in Delhi. Come for inventive Mediterranean dishes, such as scallops with mascarpone, quinoa, amaranth, pumpkin seeds, and apricot-orange puree, and astoundingly good pizza.

Indian Accent Indian $$$

(Map p74; ☎26925151; Manor, 77 Friends Colony; tasting menu veg/nonveg ₹2595/2695) Overlooking lush lawns at the Manor hotel (p79), this exclusive restaurant serves inspired modern Indian cuisine. Familiar and unfamiliar ingredients are thrown together in surprising and beautifully creative combinations. The tasting menu is recommended, though its portions are remarkably small. But the food is delicious: sample delights such as *cheeni ki roti* (a hard bread stuffed with jaggary), and bacon-stuffed *kulcha* (soft-leavened Indian-style bread).

Drinking

Chain coffeeshops abound – Café Coffee Day is the most prolific (you'll rarely have to walk more than a hundred yards to find a branch), but there are also abundant branches of Costa and Barista, particularly around Connaught Place.

Café Turtle Cafe

(Map p80; Full Circle Bookstore, Khan Market; ⊙9.30am-9.30pm; Ⓜ Khan Market) Allied to the Full Circle Bookstore, this boho cafe ticks all the boxes when you're in the mood for coffee, cake and a calm reading space. There are branches in GK1's **N-Block Market** (Map p74; N-Block, Greater Kailash Part I) and in **Nizamuddin East** (Map p80).

Kunzum Travel Cafe
Cafe

(Map p74; www.kunzum.com; T49 Hauz Khas Village; ⏰11am-7.30pm Tue-Sun; 🛜; Ⓜ Green Park) 🏷 Run by the team of travel writers behind the informative *Delhi 101* guidebook, Kunzum has a pay-what-you-like policy for the self-service French-press coffee and tea. There's free wi-fi and travel books and magazines to browse. It also runs heritage walks.

Indian Coffee House
Cafe

(Map p78; 2nd fl, Mohan Singh Place, Baba Kharak Singh Marg; ⏰9am-9pm; Ⓜ Rajiv Chowk) Stuck-in-time Indian Coffee House has lots of faded (to the point of dilapidation) charm. The roof terrace is a popular hang-out thanks to the staggeringly cheap menu of snacks (₹20 to ₹50) and serves up South Indian coffee; there's a 'ladies and families' section.

Monkey Bar
Bar

(Map p78; P3 Connaught Circus; ⏰noon-12.30am; Ⓜ Rajiv Chowk) With exposed brick walls and piping, Monkey Bar is CP's coolest choice, with a friendly, buzzy vibe, and a '90s neo-industrial look. It's the kind of place the cast of *Friends* might have hung out, if they lived in Delhi. Try the excellent buffalo burgers with gruyère, gouda, whiskey glaze, bloody mary tomatoes and umami ketchup and sample out-there cocktails (goat cheese as an ingredient?).

1911
Bar

(Map p78; Imperial Hotel, Janpath; cocktails ₹750-1200, beer from ₹400; ⏰noon-12.45am; Ⓜ Rajiv Chowk) The elegant bar at the Imperial is the ultimate neocolonial extravagance. Sip perfectly prepared cocktails in front of murals of cavorting maharajas.

☆ Entertainment

To access Delhi's dynamic arts scene, check local listings. October and March is the 'season', with shows and concerts (often free) happening nightly.

Blues
Live Music

(Map p78; 18 N-Block, Connaught Place; ⏰noon-1am; Ⓜ Rajiv Chowk) A dark den with reasonably priced beers and random photos of rock stars on its brick walls. It's a lively, snob-free zone with a live band daily from 6.30pm.

Attic
Cultural Program

(Map p78; 📞23746050; www.theattic delhi.org; 36 Regal Bdg, Sansad Marg; Ⓜ Rajiv Chowk) Small arts organisation set up to promote textiles and arts and crafts, with regular free or inexpensive exhibitions, music and dance lectures and workshops.

🔒 Shopping

Away from the government-run emporiums and other fixed-price shops, haggle like you mean it. Many taxi and autorickshaw drivers earn commissions (via

Chandni Chowk
EMAD ALJUMAH / GETTY IMAGES ©

Old Delhi's Bazaars

Old Delhi's bazaars are a head-spinning assault on the senses: an aromatic barrage of incense, spices, car fumes, body odour and worse, with a constant soundtrack of shouts, barks, music and car horns. This is less retail therapy, more heightened reality. The best time to come is midmorning, when you actually move through the streets.

Whole districts here are devoted to individual items. **Chandni Chowk** (Map p78; Old Delhi; ☉10am-7pm Mon-Sat; Ⓜ Chandni Chowk) is all clothing, electronics and break-as-soon-as-you-buy-them novelties. For silver jewellery, head for **Dariba Kalan** (Map p62), the alley near the Sisganj Gurdwara. Off this lane, the **Kinari Bazaar** (Trimmings Market; Map p62) is famous for *zardozi* (gold embroidery), temple trim and wedding turbans. Running south from the old Town Hall, **Nai Sarak** (Map p62) is lined with stalls selling saris, shawls, chiffon and *lehanga* (long skirts with a waist cord), while nearby **Ballimaran** (Map p62) has sequinned slippers and fancy, curly-toed jootis.

Beside the Fatehpuri Masjid, on Khari Baoli, is the nose-numbing **Spice Market** (Gadodia Market; Map p62), ablaze with piles of scarlet-red chillis, knobbly ginger and turmeric roots, peppercorns, cumin, coriander seed, cardamoms, dried fruit and nuts. For gorgeous wrapping paper and wedding cards, head to **Chawri Bazaar** (Map p62), leading west from the Jama Masjid. For steel cookpots and cheap-as-chapattis paper kites, continue northwest to **Lal Kuan Main Bazaar** (Map p62).

your inflated purchase price) by taking travellers to dubious, overpriced emporiums – don't fall for it.

OLD DELHI

Aap Ki Pasand (San Cha)   Drink
(Map p62; 15 Netaji Subhash Marg; ☉9.30am-7pm Mon-Sat) An elegant tea shop selling a full range of Indian teas, from Darjeeling and Assam to Nilgiri and Kangra. You can try before you buy, and teas come lovingly packaged in drawstring bags. There's another branch at **Santushti Shopping Complex** (☎264530374; www.sanchatea.com; Santushti Shopping Complex, Chanakyapuri, Racecourse Rd; ☉10am-6.30pm Mon-Sat).

CONNAUGHT PLACE

State Emporiums   Handicrafts, Clothing
(Map p78; Baba Kharak Singh Marg; ☉11am-7pm Mon-Sat; Ⓜ Rajiv Chowk) Nestling side by side are the treasure-filled official emporiums of the different Indian states.

Shopping here is like taking a tour around India – top stops include Kashmir, for papier mâché and carpets; Rajasthan, for miniature paintings and puppets; Uttar Pradesh, for marble inlaywork; Karnataka, for sandalwood sculptures; Tamil Nadu, for metal statues; and Odisha, for stone carvings.

Kamala   Handicrafts
(Map p78; Baba Kharak Singh Marg; ☉10am-6.45pm Mon-Sat; Ⓜ Rajiv Chowk) Upscale crafts and curios, designed with real panache, from the Crafts Council of India.

Central Cottage Industries Emporium   Handicrafts
(Map p78; ☎23326790; Janpath; ☉10am-7pm; Ⓜ Rajiv Chowk) This government-run, fixed-price multilevel Aladdin's cave of India-wide handicrafts is a great place to browse. Prices are higher than in the state emporiums, but the selection of wood-carvings, jewellery, pottery, papier mâché,

jootis, brassware, textiles, beauty products and miniature paintings is superb.

Fabindia
Clothing, Homewares

(Map p78; www.fabindia.com; 28 B-Block, Inner Circle, Connaught Place; ⏰11am-8pm; Ⓜ️Rajiv Chowk) Reasonably priced ready-made clothes in funky Indian fabrics, from elegant kurtas and dupattas to Western-style shirts, plus stylish homewares. There are branches at **Green Park** (Map p74), **Khan Market** (Map p80), **N-Block Market** (Map p74; Greater Kailash I) and **Select Citywalk** (Map p74; Saket).

NEW DELHI

Khan Market
Market

(Map p80; ⏰around 10.30am-8pm Mon-Sat; Ⓜ️Khan Market) 🍴 Favoured by expats and Delhi's elite, Khan Market's boutiques focus on fashion, books and homewares. For handmade paper, check out **Anand Stationers**, or try **Mehra Bros** for cool papier mâché ornaments and Christmas decorations. Literature lovers should head to **Full Circle Bookstore** and **Bahrisons** (www.booksatbahri.com). For ethnic-inspired fashions and homeware, hit **Fabindia**, **Anokhi** and **Good Earth**, and for elegantly packaged ayurvedic remedies, browse **Kama**.

ℹ️ Information

Dangers & Annoyances

Shop & Hotel Touts

Taxi-wallahs at the international airport and around tourist areas frequently act as touts for hotels, claiming that your chosen hotel is full, poor value, overbooked, dangerous, burned down or closed, or that there are riots in Delhi, as part of a ruse to steer you to a hotel where they'll get a commission. Insist on being taken to where you want to go – making a show of writing down the registration plate number may help. Drivers at Connaught Place run a similar scam for private souvenir emporiums.

Travel Agent Touts

Many travel agencies in Delhi claim to be tourist offices, even branding themselves with official tourist agency logos. There is only one

tourist office – at 88 Janpath – and any other 'tourist office' is just a travel agency. Should you legitimately need the services of a travel agent, ask for a list of recommended agents from the bona-fide tourist office. Be wary of booking a multistop trip out of Delhi, particularly to Kashmir. Travellers are often hit for extra charges, or find out the class of travel and accommodation is less than they paid for.

Train Station Touts

Touts at New Delhi train station endeavour to steer travellers away from the legitimate International Tourist Bureau (on level 1 in the main building on the Paharganj side) and into private travel agencies where they earn a commission. Don't believe any claims about the station booking office until you have seen it with your own eyes.

Internet Access

Most hotels offer internet access (often with wi-fi), but internet cafes can be found everywhere, including in Khan Market, Paharganj and Connaught Place. Rates start at ₹35 per hour.

Medical Services

Pharmacies are found on most shopping streets and in most suburban markets. Reputable hospitals include the following:

All India Institute of Medical Sciences (IIMS; Map p74; ☎40401010; www.aiims.edu; Ansari Nagar; Ⓜ️AIIMS)

Apollo Hospital (☎29871090; www.apollohospdelhi.com; Mathura Rd, Sarita Vihar)

Money

There are banks with ATMs everywhere you look in Delhi. Foreign exchange offices are concentrated around Connaught Place, particularly along Radial Rd 7. Travel agents and moneychangers offer international money transfers.

Baluja Forex (Map p62; 4596 Main Bazaar, Paharganj; ⏰9am-7.30pm; Ⓜ️New Delhi)

Thomas Cook (Map p78; ☎66271900/23; C33, 335 Inner Circle, Connaught Circus; ⏰9.30am-6.30pm Mon-Sat; Ⓜ️Rajiv Chowk)

Tourist Information

The only official tourist information centre is India Tourism Delhi. Ignore touts who (falsely) claim to be associated with this office. Most states around India have their own regional tourist offices in

Delhi – ask at India Tourism Delhi for contact details.

India Tourism Delhi (Government of India; Map p78; ☎23320008, 23320005; www.incredibleindia.org; 88 Janpath; ⊙9am-6pm Mon-Fri, to 2pm Sat; MRajiv Chowk) This is the only official tourist information centre outside of the airport. Ignore touts who (falsely) claim to be associated with this office. Anyone who 'helpfully' approaches you is certainly not going to take you to the real office. It's a useful source of advice on Delhi, getting out of Delhi, and visiting surrounding states. Has a free Delhi map and brochures, and publishes a list of recommended agencies and B&Bs. Come here to report tourism-related complaints.

ⓘ Getting There & Away

Delhi's airport can be prone to thick fog in December and January (often disrupting airline schedules) – it's wise to allow a day between connecting flights during this period.

Air

Indira Gandhi International Airport (☎0124-3376000; www.newdelhiairport.in) is about 14km southwest of the centre. International and domestic flights use the gleaming new Terminal 3. Ageing Terminal 1 is reserved for low-cost carriers.

Free shuttle buses run between the two terminals every 20 minutes.

The arrivals hall at Terminal 3 has 24-hour foreign exchange, ATMs, prepaid taxi and car-hire counters, tourist information, bookshops, cafes and a **Premium Lounge** (☎61233922; 3hr s/d ₹2350/3520) with short-stay rooms.

For comprehensive details of domestic routes, pick up *Excel's Timetable of Air Services Within India* (₹55) from news-stands. Note that prices fluctuate and seats can be much cheaper if you book online with low-cost carriers.

Air India (Indian Airlines; Map p80; ☎24622220; www.airindia.in; Aurobindo Marg; ⊙8.30am-7pm; MJor Bagh)

Jagson Airlines (Map p78; ☎23721593; Vandana Bldg, 11 Tolstoy Marg; ⊙10am-6pm Mon-Sat)

Jet Airways (Map p78; ☎39893333; www.jetairways.com; 11/12 G-Block, Connaught Place; ⊙10am-9pm)

SpiceJet (☎1800-1803333; www.spicejet.com)

Bus

Most travellers enter and leave Delhi by train, but buses are a useful option if the trains are booked up.

Services to destinations north and west of Delhi leave from the **Kashmere Gate Inter State Bus Terminal** (ISBT; Map p62; ☎23860290)

Chandni Chowk (p91)

DAN HERRICK / GETTY IMAGES ©

PETER ADAMS / GETTY IMAGES ©

in Old Delhi, accessible by metro. For buses to destinations east of Delhi, including Dehra Dun, Haridwar and Rishikesh, head to the Anand Vihar ISBT in the eastern suburbs, accessible on the blue Metro line. Services to destinations south of Delhi leave from the Sarai Kale Khan ISBT on the ring road near Nizamuddin train station.

All the bus stands are chaotic so arrive at least 30 minutes ahead of your departure time. You can avoid the hassle by paying a little more for private deluxe buses that leave from locations in central Delhi – enquire at travel agencies or your hotel for details.

Considering the traffic situation at either end, the train is your best bet for Agra. Himachal Pradesh Tourism Development Corporation (HPTDC; Map p80) runs a bus for Dharamsala (₹1100, 12 hours) from Chanderlok House on Janpath. For Rishikesh, the luxury Royal Cruiser leaves from the Anand Vihar ISBT at 10am, 9pm and 11pm daily (₹643, six hours).

Rajasthan Tourism runs deluxe buses from Bikaner House (Map p80; ☏ 23381884; www. rtdc.com; Bikaner House, Pandara Rd), near India Gate, to the following destinations:

Ajmer (Volvo; ₹923, nine hours, one daily)

Jaipur (super deluxe/Volvo ₹500/780, six hours, hourly)

Jodhpur (super deluxe/Volvo ₹965/1256, 11 hours, two daily)

Udaipur (Volvo; ₹1375, 15 hours, one daily)

Train

There are three main stations in Delhi – (Old) Delhi train station (aka Delhi Junction) in Old Delhi, New Delhi train station near Paharganj, and Nizamuddin train station, south of Sunder Nagar. Make sure you know which station your train is leaving from.

There are two options for foreign travellers – you can brave the queues at the main reservation office (Map p62; Chelmsford Rd; ☉ 8am-8pm, to 2pm Sun), or visit the helpful International Tourist Bureau (ITB; Map p62; ☏ 23405156; 1st fl, New Delhi Train Station; ☉ 8am-8pm Mon-Sat, to 2pm Sun) on the 1st floor in the main building at New Delhi railway station. Do not believe anyone who tells you it has shifted, closed or burnt down!

When making reservations here, you can pay in foreign currency, in travellers cheques (Thomas Cook cheques in US dollars, euros or pounds sterling, Amex cheques in US dollars and euros, or Barclays cheques in US dollars) or in rupees, backed up by money-exchange certificates (or ATM receipts). Bring your passport.

When you arrive, complete a reservation form, then queue to check availability, before paying for your booking at the relevant counter. This is the best place to get last-minute bookings for quota seats to popular destinations, but the queues can be outrageous.

If you prefer to brave the standard reservation office, check the details for your journey (including the train number) in advance on the Indian Railways (www.indianrail.gov.in) website or Erail (http:\\erail.in), or in the invaluable publication *Trains at a Glance* (₹45), available at news-stands. You'll need to fill out a reservation form and queue – after 7pm is the quietest time to book.

ⓘ Getting Around

The metro system has transformed getting around the city, making it incredibly easy to whiz out to the remotest suburbs. Keep small change handy for rickshaw fares.

To/From the Airport

International flights often arrive at ghastly hours, so it pays to book a hotel in advance and notify staff of your arrival time. Organised city transport runs to/from Terminal 3; a free shuttle bus runs every 20 minutes between Terminal 3 and Terminal 1.

Prearranged Pick-ups Hotels offer pre-arranged airport pick-up, but you'll pay extra to cover the airport parking fee (up to ₹140) and a ₹80 charge to enter the arrivals hall. To avoid the entry fee, drivers may wait outside Gates 4 to 6.

Metro The Airport Express (www.delhiairportexpress.com) line runs every 13 minutes from 5.15am to 11.30pm, completing the journey from Terminal 3 to New Delhi train station in around 40 minutes (₹150).

Bus Air-conditioned buses run from outside Terminal 3 to Kashmere Gate ISBT every 20 minutes, via the Red Fort, LNJP Hospital, New Delhi Station Gate 2, Connaught Place, Parliament St and Ashoka Rd (₹50).

Taxi In front of the arrivals buildings at Terminal 3 and Terminal 1 are Delhi Traffic Police Prepaid Taxi counters (📞 23010101; www.delhitrafficpolice.nic.in) offering fixed-price taxi services. You'll pay about ₹350 to New or Old Delhi, and ₹450 to the southern suburbs, plus a 25% surcharge between 11pm and 5am. Insist that the driver takes you to your chosen destination and only surrender your voucher when you arrive.

You can also book a prepaid taxi at the Megacabs (p97) counter outside the arrivals building at both the international and domestic terminals. It costs ₹600 to ₹700 to the centre, but you get a cleaner car with air-con.

Autorickshaw & Taxi

Local taxis (recognisable by their black and yellow livery) and autorickshaws have meters but these are effectively ornamental as most drivers refuse to use them. Delhi Traffic Police runs a network of prepaid autorickshaw booths (www.delhitrafficpolice.nic.in/prepaid-booths.htm) where you can pay a fixed fare, including 24-hour stands at the New Delhi, Old Delhi and Nizamuddin train stations; elsewhere, you'll need to negotiate a fare before you set off.

Subway station, New Delhi
URBANCOW / GETTY IMAGES ©

Fares are invariably elevated for foreigners so haggle hard, and if the fare sounds too outrageous, find another cab. For an autorickshaw ride from Connaught Place, expect to pay around ₹30 to Paharganj, ₹40 to India Gate, ₹60 to the Red Fort, ₹70 to Humayan's Tomb and ₹100 to Hauz Khas. The website www.taxiautofare.com can provide suggested fares for other journeys.

Taxis typically charge twice the autorickshaw fare. Note that fares may vary as fuel prices go up and down. From 11pm to 5am there's a 25% surcharge for autorickshaws and taxis.

Car

Numerous operators will rent out a car with a driver, or you can negotiate directly with taxi drivers at taxi stands around the city. Note that some taxis can only operate inside the city limits, or in certain surrounding states. For a day of local sightseeing, there is normally an eight-hour, 80km limit – anything over this costs extra. The following companies get positive reports from travellers.

Kumar Tourist Taxi Service (Map p78; ☏23415930; www.kumarindiatours.com; 14/1 K-Block, Connaught Place; ⊙9am-9pm) Rates are among Delhi's lowest – a day of Delhi sightseeing costs from ₹1200 (the eight hours and 80km limit applies).

Metropole Tourist Service (Map p80; ☏24310313; www.metrovista.co.in; 224 Defence Colony Flyover Market; ⊙7am-7pm) Under the Defence Flyover Bridge (on the Jangpura side).

Cycle-Rickshaw

Cycle-rickshaws are useful for navigating Old Delhi and the suburbs, but are banned from many parts of New Delhi, including Connaught Place, and from the clogged main artery of Chandni Chowk. Negotiate a fare before you set off – expect to pay about ₹30 for the trip from Paharganj to Connaught Place.

Metro

Delhi's magnificent **metro** (☏23417910; www.delhimetrorail.com) is fast and efficient, with signs and arrival/departure announcements in Hindi and English. Trains run from around 6am to 11pm and the first carriage in the direction of travel is reserved for women only. Note that trains can get insanely busy at peak commuting times (around 9am to 10am and 5pm to 6pm) – avoid travelling with luggage during rush hour if at all possible.

Radiocab

You'll need a local mobile number to order a radiocab, or ask a shop or hotel to assist. These air-conditioned cars are clean, efficient, and use

Marble detail, Taj Mahal (p98)

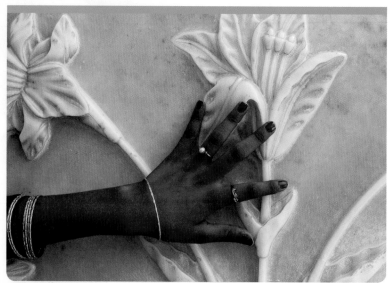

Taj Mahal History

The Taj was built by Shah Jahan as a memorial for his third wife, Mumtaz Mahal, who died giving birth to their 14th child in 1631. The death of Mumtaz left the emperor so heartbroken that his hair is said to have turned grey virtually overnight. Construction of the Taj began the following year and, although the main building is thought to have been built in eight years, the whole complex was not completed until 1653. Not long after it was finished Shah Jahan was overthrown by his son Aurangzeb and imprisoned in Agra Fort where, for the rest of his days, he could only gaze out at his creation through a window. Following his death in 1666, Shah Jahan was buried here alongside Mumtaz.

In total, some 20,000 people from India and Central Asia worked on the building. Specialists were brought in from as far away as Europe to produce the exquisite marble screens and pietra dura (marble inlay work) made with thousands of semiprecious stones.

The Taj was designated a World Heritage Site in 1983 and looks as immaculate today as when it was first constructed – though it underwent a huge restoration project in the early 20th century.

reliable meters, charging ₹20 at flagfall then ₹20 per kilmetre.

Some reliable companies:

Easycabs (43434343; www.easycabs.com)

Megacabs (41414141; www.megacabs.com) You can book a prepaid taxi at the Megacabs counter outside the arrivals building at both the international and domestic terminals. It costs ₹600 to ₹700 to the centre, but you get a cleaner car with air-con.

Quickcabs (45333333; www.quickcabs.in)

UTTAR PRADESH & THE TAJ MAHAL

Agra
0562 / POP 1.7 MILLION

Sights

Agra Fort
Fort

(Indian/foreigner ₹20/300, video ₹25; ⊙dawn-dusk) With the Taj Mahal overshadowing it, one can easily forget that Agra has one of the finest Mughal forts in India. Construction of the massive red-sandstone fort, on the bank of the Yamuna River, was begun by Emperor Akbar in 1565.

Taj Museum
Museum

(⊙9am-5pm, closed Fri) **FREE** Within the Taj complex, on the western side of the gardens, is the small but excellent Taj Museum, housing a number of original Mughal miniature paintings, including a pair of 17th-century ivory portraits of Emperor Shah Jahan and his beloved wife Mumtaz Mahal.

Tours

Amin Tours
Cultural Tours

(9837411144; www.daytourtajmahal.com) If you can't be bothered handling the logistics, look no further than this recommended agency for all-inclusive private Agra day trips from Delhi by car (₹6000) or train (₹6500). Caveat: if they try to take you shopping and you're not interested, politely decline.

Don't Miss
Taj Mahal

Indian/foreigner ₹20/750, video ₹25

⏲ dawn-dusk Sat-Thu, closed Fri

Rabindranath Tagore described it as 'a teardrop on the cheek of eternity', while its creator, Emperor Shah Jahan, said it made 'the sun and the moon shed tears from their eyes'. Every year, tourists numbering more than twice the population of Agra pass through its gates to catch a glimpse of what is widely considered the most beautiful building in the world. Few leave disappointed.

The Taj can be accessed through the west, south and east gates. Independent travellers tend to use the south gate, which is nearest to Taj Ganj, the main area for budget accommodation. There are separate queues for men and women at all three gates. Cameras and videos are permitted but you cannot take photographs inside the mausoleum itself. A 500mL bottle of water and shoe covers are included with your ticket. If you keep your ticket you get small entry-fee reductions when visiting Agra Fort, Fatehpur Sikri, Akbar's Tomb or the Itimad-ud-Daulah on the same day. You can store your luggage for free beside the ticket offices. The Taj is arguably at its most atmospheric at sunrise, which is also the most comfortable time to visit, with far fewer crowds. Sunset is another magical viewing time. You can also view the Taj for five nights around full moon. Entry numbers are limited, though, and tickets must be bought a day in advance from the **Archaeological Survey of India office** (Map p80; 011-23010822; www.asi.nic.in; Janpath, New Delhi; 9.30am-1pm & 2-6pm Mon-Fri).

Inside the Grounds

The Taj itself stands on a raised marble platform at the northern end of the classical Mughal *charbagh* (ornamental gardens), with its back to the Yamuna River. Its raised position means that the backdrop is only sky. Purely decorative 40m-high white minarets grace each corner. The red sandstone **mosque** to the west is an important gathering place for Agra's Muslims. The identical building to the east, the **jawab**, was built for symmetry. The central structure is made of semitranslucent white marble, carved with flowers and inlaid with semiprecious stones in beautiful patterns. Inside, directly below the main dome is the **Cenotaph of Mumtaz Mahal**, an elaborate false tomb surrounded by a perforated marble screen inlaid with semiprecious stones. Beside it, offsetting the symmetry of the Taj, is the **Cenotaph of Shah Jahan**, who was interred here with little ceremony by his usurping son Aurangzeb in 1666. The real tombs are in a locked basement room below.

HISTORIAN AND WRITER DR NEVILLE SMITH'S FAMILY HAS LIVED IN AGRA FOR OVER FOUR GENERATIONS

Local Knowledge

Taj Mahal Don't Miss List

1 PERFECT SYMMETRY
There is a perfect balance of structures to the left and right of an imaginary middle line cut through the building's centre. You see the same number of turrets, cupolas and pavilions on the left and right of the central dome, as well as on the main structure.

2 MATHEMATICAL ACCURACY
If you stand in front of the main tomb in the Cenotaph Chamber and look straight towards the main gateway due south, you will find that the tomb aligns with the middle of the gateway. That such accuracy was achieved, without the technical instruments of today, says much about the architectural and engineering skills of the builders.

3 OPTICAL ILLUSION
The Quranic verses on the mausoleum do not appear to decrease in size as they go up to the base of the main dome, which would be the case if they were chiselled in equal size and placed in their grooves. The letters were increased in size along with the grooves in which they were to be inserted, so that a person looking at them from the ground would see them as equal in size and the optical effect of their tapering to the top would be avoided.

4 ARCHITECTURAL SYMBOLISM
The Taj can be seen as conceptualising the feminine grace of Mumtaz Mahal. The dome has been likened to the head of a woman and its base as her neck, around which the marble inlay gives the appearance of Mumtaz Mahal arrayed in all her finery.

5 LANDSCAPING INNOVATION
Unlike other Mughal and, indeed, Muslim garden tombs, which all have a tomb set in the centre of a garden with waterways radiating from it, the Taj has been placed at the northen end of a garden. Shah Jahan broke away from the typical Muslim garden tomb for better effect, so the edifice dominates the garden, instead of being dominated by it.

99

Taj Mahal

TIMELINE

1631 Emperor Shah Jahan's beloved third wife, Mumtaz Mahal, dies in Buhanpur while giving birth to their 14th child. Her body is initially interred in Buhanpur itself, where Shah Jahan is fighting a military campaign, but is later moved, in a golden casket, to a small building on the banks of the Yamuna River in Agra.

1632 Construction of a permanent mausoleum for Mumtaz Mahal begins.

1633 Mumtaz Mahal is interred in her final resting place, an underground tomb beneath a marble plinth, on top of which the Taj Mahal will be built.

1640 The white-marble mausoleum is completed.

1653 The rest of the Taj Mahal complex is completed.

1658 Emperor Shah Jahan is overthrown by his son Aurangzeb and imprisoned in Agra Fort.

1666 Shah Jahan dies. His body is transported along the Yamuna River and buried underneath the Taj, alongside the tomb of his wife.

1908 Repeatedly damaged and looted after the fall of the Mughal empire, the Taj receives some long-overdue attention as part of a major restoration project ordered by British viceroy Lord Curzon.

1983 The Taj is awarded Unesco World Heritage Site status.

2002 Having been discoloured by pollution in more recent years, the Taj is spruced up with an ancient recipe known as multani mitti – a blend of soil, cereal, milk and lime once used by Indian women to beautify their skin.

Today More than three million tourists visit the Taj Mahal each year. That's more than twice the current population of Agra.

GO BAREFOOT

Help the environment by entering the mausoleum barefoot instead of using the free disposable shoe covers.

Pishtaqs
These huge arched recesses are set into each side of the Taj. They provide depth to the building while their central, latticed marble screens allow patterned light to illuminate the inside of the mausoleum.

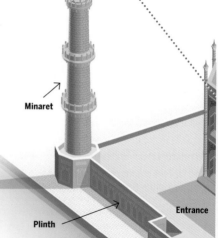

Minaret

Entrance

Plinth

Marble Relief Work
Flowering plants, thought to be representations of paradise, are a common theme among the beautifully decorative panels carved onto the white marble.

BE ENLIGHTENED

Bring a small torch into the mausoleum to fully appreciate the translucency of the white marble and semiprecious stones.

Filigree Screen
This stunning screen was carved out of a single piece of marble. It surrounds both cenotaphs, allowing patterned light to fall onto them through its intricately carved *jali* (latticework).

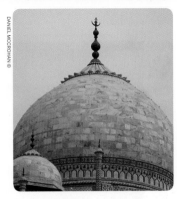

Central Dome
The Taj's famous central dome, topped by a brass finial, represents the vault of heaven, a stark contrast to the material world, which is represented by the square shape of the main structure.

Yamuna River

NORTH →

Pietra Dura
It's believed that 35 different precious and semi-precious stones were used to create the exquisite pietra dura (marble inlay work) found on the inside and outside of the mausoleum walls. Again, floral designs are common.

Calligraphy
The strips of calligraphy surrounding each of the four pishtaqs get larger as they get higher, giving the impression of uniform size when viewed from the ground. There's also calligraphy inside the mausoleum, including on Mumtaz Mahal's cenotaph.

Cenotaphs
The cenotaphs of Mumtaz Mahal and Shah Jahan, decorated with pietra dura inlay work, are actually fake tombs. The real ones are located in an underground vault closed to the public.

CULTURA RM EXCLUSIVE/BEN PIPE PHOTOGRAPHY / GETTY IMAGES ©

UP Tourism   Coach Tours

(www.up-tourism.com; incl entry fees Indian/foreigner ₹500/2000) Agra Cantonment train station (☎2421204; ⏱6.30am-9.30pm) Taj Rd (☎0562-2226431; www.up-tourism.com; 64 Taj Rd; ⏱10am-5pm Mon-Sat) UP Tourism runs coach tours that leave Agra Cantonment train station at 10.30am Saturday to Thursday, after picking up passengers arriving from Delhi on the Taj Express. The tour includes the Taj Mahal, Agra Fort and Fatehpur Sikri with a 1¼-hour stop in each place.

 ## Sleeping

It's possible to see Agra on a day trip from Delhi, but it's a rush. If you want to see more than just the Taj, or just fancy a change of scene, consider booking a night or two at one of the following places.

Hotel Sheela   Hotel $

(☎0562-2333074; www.hotelsheelaagra.com; Taj East Gate Rd; s/d with fan ₹500/600, with AC ₹800/900; ❄🛜) It draws its fair share of complaints from travellers (cold in winter, indifferent management, questionable hygiene), but if you're not fussed about looking at the Taj Mahal 24 hours a day, and don't mind doing a little legwork for an autorickshaw, Sheela teeters on being an acceptable budget option.

N Homestay   Homestay $$

(☎9690107860; www.nhomestay.com; 15 Ajanta Colony, Vibhav Nagar; s/d incl breakfast ₹1600/1800; ❄@🛜) Matriarch Naghma and her helpful sons are a riot at this wonderful homestay. Their beautiful home, tucked away in a residential neighbourhood 15 minutes' walk from the Taj's western gate, is nothing short of a fabulous place to stay.

Oberoi Amarvilas   Hotel $$$

(☎0562-2231515; www.oberoihotels.com; Taj East Gate Rd; d with/without balcony ₹62,955/53,961; ❄@🛜🏊) Following Oberoi's iron-clad MO of Maharaja-level service, exquisite dining and properties that pack some serious wow, Agra's best hotel by far oozes style and luxury. Elegant interior design is suffused with Mughal themes, a composition carried over into the exterior fountain courtyard and swimming pool, both of which are set in a delightful water garden.

Eating

Saniya Palace Hotel
Multicuisine $$

(South Gate; mains ₹50-200; ⏱6am-11pm; 🛜) With cute tablecloths, dozens of potted plants and a bamboo pergola for shade, this is the most pleasant rooftop restaurant in Taj Ganj. It also has the best rooftop view of the Taj bar none. The kitchen isn't the cleanest in town, but its usual mix of Western dishes and Western-friendly Indian dishes usually go down without complaints.

Dasaprakash
South Indian $$

(www.dasaprakashgroup.com; Meher Theater Complex, Gwailor Rd; meals ₹100-300; ⏱noon-10.45pm) Fabulously tasty and religiously clean, Dasaprakash whips up consistently great South Indian vegetarian food, including spectacular thalis (₹190 to ₹270), dosa and a few token Continental dishes. The ice-cream desserts (₹80 to ₹210) are another speciality. Comfortable booth seating and wood-lattice screens make for intimate dining.

Pinch of Spice
North Indian $$$

(www.pinchofspice.in; Opp ITC Mughal Hotel, Fatahabad Rd; mains ₹280-410; ⏱noon-11.30pm) This modern North Indian superstar at the beginning of Fatahabad Rd is the best spot outside five-star hotels to indulge yourself in rich curries and succulent tandoori kebabs. The *murg boti masala* (chicken tikka swimming in a rich and spicy country gravy) and the paneer *lababdar* (fresh cheese cubes in a spicy red gravy with sauteed onions) are outstanding.

Esphahan
North Indian $$$

(📞2231515; Oberoi Amarvilas Hotel, Taj East Gate Rd; mains ₹1125-2250; ⏱dinner 6.30pm & 9pm) There are only two sittings each evening at Agra's finest restaurant so booking a table is essential. The exquisite menu is chock-full of unique delicacies and rarely seen regional heritage dishes.

ℹ Information

Agra is more wired than most, even in restaurants. Taj Ganj is riddled with internet cafes, most charging between ₹30 and ₹40 per hour. ATMs are all over the city. There are three close to the Taj, one near each gate.

Medical Services

Amit Jaggi Memorial Hospital
(📞9690107860; www.ajmh.in; Vibhav Nagar, off Minto Rd) If you're sick, Dr Jaggi, who runs this private clinic, is the man to see. He accepts most health-insurance plans from abroad; otherwise a visit runs ₹1000 (day) or ₹2000 (night). He'll even do house calls.

ℹ Getting There & Away

Air

Commercial flights to Agra's Kheria Airport began again in late 2012 after a long absence. Air India (p93) now flies Mondays, Wednesdays and Saturdays to Varanasi (1.50pm) via Khajuraho. A new international airport, something Delhi lobbyists have fought against for years, was also greenlighted at the time of research, but don't expect to see it in this edition's lifespan.

To access the airport, part of Indian Air Force territory, your name must be on the list of those with booked flights that day. Tickets must be purchased online or by phone. See p104 for sample destinations and fares.

Train

Most trains leave from Agra Cantonment (Cantt) train station, although some go from Agra Fort station. A few trains, such as the Marudhar Exp, run as slightly different numbers on different days than those listed, but timings remain the same.

Express trains are well set up for day trippers to/from Delhi but trains run to Delhi all day. If you can't reserve a seat, just buy a 'general ticket' for the next train (about ₹62), find a seat in Sleeper class then upgrade when the ticket collector comes along. Most of the time, he won't even make you pay any more.

ℹ Getting Around

Autorickshaw

Agra's green-and-yellow autorickshaws run on CNG (compressed natural gas) and are less environmentally destructive. Just outside Agra Cantt station is the prepaid autorickshaw booth, which gives you a good guide for haggling elsewhere. Note, autos aren't allowed to go to Fatehpur Sikri.

Agra Train Services

DELHI–AGRA TRAINS FOR DAY TRIPPERS

TRIP	TRAIN NO & NAME	FARE (₹)	DURATION (HR)	DEPARTURES
New Delhi-Agra	12002 Shatabdi Exp	384/805 (A)	2	6am (except Fri)
Agra-New Delhi	12001 Shatabdi Exp	415/850 (A)	2	8.35pm (except Fri)
Hazrat Nizamuddin-Agra	12280 Taj Exp	75/273 (B)	3	7.10am
Agra-Hazrat Nizamuddin	12279 Taj Exp	75/273 (B)	3	6.55pm

Fares: (A) AC chair/1AC, (B) 2nd-class/AC chair

OTHER TRAINS FROM AGRA

DESTINATION	TRAIN NO & NAME	FARE (₹)	DURATION (HR)	DEPARTURES
Jaipur*	12036 Shatabdi Exp	415/890 (C)	3½	4.20pm (except Thu)
Khajuraho	12448 UP SMPRK KRNTI	207/546/805 (A)	8	11.20pm (except Wed)
Mumbai (CST)	12138/12137 Punjab Mail	410/1139/1770 (A)	23	8.55am
Varanasi	93238/13237 Kota PNBE Exp	262/733/1110 (A)	12	11.30pm

Fares: (A) sleeper/3AC/2AC, (B) sleeper/3AC only, (C) AC chair/1AC only
* leaves from Agra Fort station

Sample prices from Agra Cantt station: Fatahabad Rd ₹100; Sadar Bazaar ₹60; Taj Mahal ₹100, Shilpgrarm (Taj East Gate) ₹120; half-day (four-hour) tour ₹400; full-day (10-hour) tour ₹500. Prices do not include a ₹5 booking fee.

Cycle-Rickshaw

Agree fares beforehand. Price estimates from the Taj Mahal include: Agra Cantt train station ₹40; Agra Fort ₹30; Fatahabad Rd ₹20; Sadar Bazaar ₹30; half-day tour ₹200.

Taxi

Outside Agra Cantt the prepaid taxi booth gives a good idea of what taxis should cost. Non-AC prices include: Delhi ₹3000; Fatahabad Rd ₹150; Sadar Bazaar ₹100; Taj Mahal ₹150; half-day (four-hour) tour ₹650; full-day (eight-hour) tour ₹850. Prices do not include a ₹10 booking fee.

Fatehpur Sikri

✆05613 / POP 29,000

This magnificent fortified ancient city, 40km west of Agra, was the short-lived capital of the Mughal empire between 1571 and 1585, during the reign of Emperor Akbar. Akbar visited the village of Sikri to consult the Sufi saint Shaikh Salim Chishti, who predicted the birth of an heir to the Mughal throne. When the prophecy came true, Akbar built his new capital here, including a stunning mosque – still in use today – and three palaces for each of his favourite wives, one a Hindu, one a Muslim and one a Christian (though Hindu villagers in Sikri dispute a few of these claims). The city was an Indo-Islamic masterpiece, but erected in an area that supposedly suffered from water shortages and so was abandoned shortly after Akbar's death.

◉ Sights

Jama Masjid   Mosque
This beautiful, immense mosque was completed in 1571 and contains elements of Persian and Indian design. The main entrance, at the top of a flight of stone steps, is through the spectacular 54m-high **Buland Darwaza** (Victory Gate), built to commemorate Akbar's military victory in Gujarat.

Palaces & Pavilions   Palaces
(Indian/foreigner ₹20/260, video ₹25; ⊙dawn-dusk) The main sight at Fatehpur Sikri is the stunning imperial complex of pavilions and palaces spread among a large abandoned 'city' peppered with Mughal masterpieces: courtyards, intricate carvings, servants quarters, vast gateways and ornamental pools.

☞ Tours

Official Archaeological Society of India guides can be hired from the ticket office for ₹300 (English), but they aren't always the most knowledgeable (some have been birthrighted in). Official Uttar Pradesh Tourism guides have gone through more rigorous training and can be hired for ₹750. Our favorite is **Pankaj Bhatnagar** (☏8126995552; www.tajinvitation.com).

✂ Eating

Fatehpur Sikri's culinary speciality is *khataie*, the biscuits you can see piled high in the bazaar below Jama Masjid.

If you want to stop for lunch, try the basic but friendly guesthouse

Hotel Ajay Palace (☏9548801213; Agra Rd; mains ₹40-120), where you can sit on the rooftop at the large, elongated marble table and enjoy a view of the village streets with the Jama Masjid towering above you. Note it is not 'Ajay Restaurant By Near Palace' at the bus stand – it's 50m down the road, back towards Agra.

ⓘ Getting There & Away

Tours and taxis all arrive at the Gulistan Tourist Complex parking lot, from which shuttle buses (₹5) depart for Fatehpur Sikri's Diwan-i-Am entrance (right side of the street) and Jodh Bai entrance (left side of the street). Note that if you have hired an unauthorised guide, you will not be allowed to enter at Diwan-i-Am.

Buses run to Agra's Idgah Bus Stand from the bazaar every half-hour (₹34), from 6am to 7pm.

Diwan-i-Khas (p106)
PETER ZELEI IMAGES / GETTY IMAGES ©

Fatehpur Sikri

A WALKING TOUR OF FATEHPUR SIKRI

You can enter this fortified ancient city from two entrances, but the northeast entrance at Diwan-i-Am (Hall of Public Audiences) offers the most logical approach to this remarkable Unesco World Heritage site. This large courtyard (now a garden) is where Emperor Akbar presided over the trials of accused criminals. Once through the ticket gate, you are in the northern end of the **Pachisi Courtyard ❶**. The first building you see is **Diwan-i-Khas ❷** (Hall of Private Audiences), the interior of which is dominated by a magnificently carved central stone column. Pitch south and enter **Rumi Sultana ❸**, a small but elegant palace built for Akbar's Turkish Muslim wife. It's hard to miss the **Ornamental Pool ❹** nearby – its southwest corner provides Fatehpur Sikri's most photogenic angle, perfectly framing its most striking building, the five-storey Panch Mahal, one of the gateways to the Imperial Harem Complex, where the **Lower Haramsara ❺** once housed more than 200 female servants. Wander around the Palace of Jodh Bai and take notice of the towering ode to an elephant, the 21m-high **Hiran Minar ❻**, in the distance to the northwest. Leave the palaces and pavilions area via Shahi Darwaza (King's Gate), which spills into India's second-largest mosque courtyard at **Jama Masjid ❼**. Inside this immense and gorgeous mosque is the sacred **Tomb of Shaikh Salim Chishti ❽**. Exit through the spectacular **Buland Darwaza ❾** (Victory Gate), one of the world's most magnificent gateways.

Buland Darwaza
Most tours end with an exit through Jama Masjid's Victory Gate. Walk out and take a look behind you: Behold! The magnificent 15-storey sandstone gate, 54m high, is a menacing monolith to Akbar's reign.

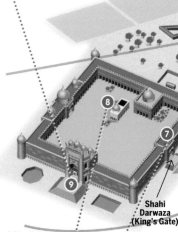

Shahi Darwaza (King's Gate)

Tomb of Shaikh Salim Chishti
Each knot in the strings tied to the 56 carved white marble designs of the interior walls of Shaikh Salim Chishti's tomb represents one wish of a maximum three.

Jama Masjid
The elaborate marble inlay work at the Badshahi Gate and throughout the Jama Masjid complex is said to have inspired similar work 82 years later at the Taj Mahal in Agra.

Hiran Minar
This bizarre, seldom-visited tower off the north-west corner of Fatehpur Sikri is decorated with hundreds of stone representations of elephant tusks. It is said to be the place where Minar, Akbar's favourite execution elephant, died.

Pachisi Courtyard
Under your feet just past Rumi Sultana is the Pachisi Courtyard where Akbar is said to have played the game *pachisi* (an ancient version of ludo) using slave girls in colourful dress as pieces.

Diwan-i-Khas
Emperor Akbar modified the central stone column inside Diwan-i-Khas to call attention to a new religion he called Din-i-Ilahi (God is One). The intricately carved column features a fusion of Hindu, Muslim, Christian and Buddhist imagery.

Panch Mahal

Diwan-i-Am (Hall of Public Audiences)

Lower Haramsara
Akbar reportedly kept more than 5000 concubines, but the 200 or so female servants housed in the Lower Haramsara were strictly business. Knots were tied to these sandstone rings to support partitions between their individual quarters.

Ornamental Pool
Tansen, said to be the most gifted Indian vocalist of all time and one of Akbar's treasured nine *Navaratnas* (Gems), would be showered with coins during performances from the central platform of the Ornamental Pool.

Rumi Sultana
Don't miss the headless creatures carved into Rumi Sultana's palace interiors: a lion, deer, an eagle and a few peacocks were beheaded by jewel thieves who swiped the precious jewels that originally formed their heads.

Mumbai (Bombay) & Around

Mumbai is big. It's full of dreamers and hard-labourers, starlets and gangsters, stray dogs and exotic birds, artists and servants, fisherfolk and *crorepatis* (millionaires) and lots and lots of other people. It has a prolific film industry, some of Asia's biggest slums, the world's most expensive home, and the largest tropical forest in an urban zone. It's India's financial powerhouse and fashion epicentre, and a pulse point of religious tension. The city's furious energy, limited public transport and punishing pollution makes it challenging for visitors. That said, its incredibly grand colonial-era architecture, unique bazaars, hidden temples, hipster enclaves and premier-league restaurants beg to be investigated. And while you're here, seize the chance to visit the nearby Unesco sites of Ellora and Ajanta, epic cave temples containing some astounding religious art.

Girgaum Chowpatty (p121)
CHRISTER FREDRIKSSON/GETTY IMAGES ©

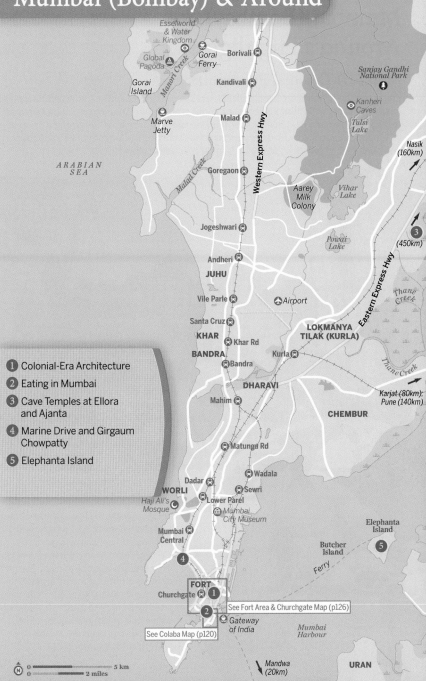

Mumbai (Bombay) & Around

Esselworld & Water Kingdom

Global Pagoda

Gorai Ferry

Borivali

Gorai Island

Kandivali

Marve Jetty

Malad

ARABIAN SEA

Goregaon

Western Express Hwy

Jogeshwari

Andheri

JUHU

Vile Parle

Santa Cruz

KHAR

Khar Rd

BANDRA

Bandra

DHARAVI

Mahim

Matunga Rd

Dadar

WORLI

Lower Parel

Haji Ali's Mosque

Mumbai Central

Churchgate

FORT

Sanjay Gandhi National Park

Kanheri Caves

Tulsi Lake

Vihar Lake

Aarey Milk Colony

Powai Lake

Airport

LOKMANYA TILAK (KURLA)

Kurla

Eastern Express Hwy

Thane Creek

Nasik (160km)

(450km)

Karjat (80km); Pune (140km)

CHEMBUR

Wadala

Sewri

Mumbai City Museum

Elephanta Island

Butcher Island

Ferry

Mumbai Harbour

Gateway of India

Mandwa (20km)

URAN

1 Colonial-Era Architecture

2 Eating in Mumbai

3 Cave Temples at Ellora and Ajanta

4 Marine Drive and Girgaum Chowpatty

5 Elephanta Island

See Fort Area & Churchgate Map (p126)

See Colaba Map (p120)

0 ____ 5 km
0 ____ 2 miles

Mumbai (Bombay) & Around's Highlights

Mumbai's Colonial-Era Architecture

The grandiose frilliness of Mumbai's fabulous 19th-century colonial-era architecture is epitomised by the crazy Gothic facade of the famous train station, Chhatrapati Shivaji Terminus (p119), and marries well with the larger-than-life feel of the city itself. Some of the architectural detail is incredible, with dog-faced gargoyles adorning the magnificent central tower and peacock-filled windows above the central courtyard. Chhatrapati Shivaji Terminus

DAVE ABRAM/GETTY IMAGES ©

2 Eating in Mumbai

Mumbai is shaped by flavours from all over India and the world. You can dine like a maharaja at high-end restaurants (try Peshwari for starters), but the street food here also shouldn't be missed. The most famous is *bhelpuri,* readily available at Girgaum Chowpatty (p121). These crisp-fried thin rounds of dough are mixed with puffed rice, lentils, lemon juice, onions, herbs, chilli and tamarind chutney and piled high onto takeaway paper plates.

ORIEN HARVEY/GETTY IMAGES ©

Cave Temples at Ellora & Ajanta 3

These ancient sites, 350km to 400km from Mumbai, represent some of the finest rock carvings in India. Ajanta (p136), the older, dates back around 2000 years and includes exquisite Buddhist wall paintings. Ellora (p135) contains the standout Kailasa Temple, one of the world's largest rock-cut sculptures, hewn against a rocky slope by 7000 labourers over a 150-year period. Ellora cave temple

4 Marine Drive & Girgaum Chowpatty

Mumbai is at its most visually dramatic along this spectacular crescent-shaped shoreline, lined with art deco apartment blocks and high-rises, and known as the 'Queen's Necklace'. It's a great spot for an evening amble, finishing at Chowpatty Beach with a snack of *bhelpuri*. During the Ganesh Chaturthi festival (in August/September) you'll see glorious colour and mayhem as huge effigies of the elephant god are dunked in the sea.

5 Elephanta Island

If you don't have time to make it all the way out to Ellora or Ajanta then Elephanta Island (p123), just a short boat ride from the city centre, makes a great half-day trip. This tranquil island and Unesco World Heritage Site is home to a labyrinth of cave temples carved into the basalt rock, and the artwork here also represents some of the most impressive temple carving in all of India. There's a classical music festival in February.

Mumbai (Bombay) & Around's Best...

Wining & Dining

○ **Peshwari** A gastro-temple of tandoori cusine where you eat with your hands. (p128)

○ **Indigo** A gourmet haven serving inventive European cuisine. (p125)

○ **Koh** Mumbai's outstanding Thai restaurant. (p128)

○ **Dakshinayan** Traditional, village-fresh South Indian goodness. (p128)

○ **Revival** Belt-bursting all-you-can-eat thali stronghold. (p125)

Places for a Drink

○ **Aer** Sky lounge where the city views are out of this world. (p129)

○ **Bluefrog** Best place in Mumbai to check out local bands and DJ talent. (p130)

○ **Harbour Bar** Affordable drinks, fabulous views. (p128)

○ **Colaba Social** Mix with South Mumbai's hip young things over a mojito. (p129)

○ **Leopold's Cafe** Wobbly fans and a lively atmosphere: a Mumbai travellers' institution. (p129)

Shopping

○ **Crawford Market** Bas-reliefs by Rudyard Kipling's father adorn the Norman Gothic exterior to this British Bombay fruit-and-veg market. (p130)

○ **Mangaldas Market** Like a mini town, complete with its own lanes, this is one of the city's prime clothing and fabrics markets. (p130)

○ **Contemporary Arts & Crafts** Inventive takes on traditional crafts. (p130)

○ **Phillips** 150-year-old antiques shop containing a multitude of things you never knew you wanted. (p130)

Need to Know

Pockets of Tranquillity

o **Global Pagoda** A haven for *vipassana* meditation, built to promote peace. (p121)

o **Jijamata Udyan** Home of the Dr Bhau Daji Lad Mumbai City Museum and lush 19th-century gardens. (p121)

o **Elephanta Island** A peaceful place with ancient rock-cut temples. (p123)

ADVANCE PLANNING

o **One month before** Book your accommodation; start even earlier if you're travelling over Christmas and New Year. Book any domestic flights and long-distance train tickets.

o **One week before** Book city tours and restaurant tables.

o **On arrival** Arrange any long-distance taxi rides via a recommended local agency or your hotel.

RESOURCES

o **Mumbai Magic** (www. mumbai-magic.blogspot. com) An excellent blog on the city's hidden corners.

o **Mumbai Boss** (www. mumbaiboss.com) Seriously the boss of what's on in Mumbai.

o **Maharashtra Tourism Development Corporation** (www. maharashtratourism.gov. in) Official tourism site.

o **Lonely Planet** (www. lonelyplanet.com/ india/mumbai) For planning advice, author recommendations, traveller reviews and insider tips.

GETTING AROUND

o **Premier taxi** The black-and-yellow cabs are the easiest way to get around the city, and in South Mumbai drivers usually use the meter without prompting.

o **Autorickshaw** Confined to the suburbs from Bandra north.

o **Car hire** Cars with driver are generally hired for an eight-hour day and an 80km maximum, with additional charges if you go over. For an air-conditioned car the going rate is about ₹1600. For a day trip from Aurangabad to Ajanta/Ellora rates are around ₹2400/2100.

BE FOREWARNED

o **Bring directions** Print a map or detailed landmark directions for your hotel – many airport taxi drivers don't speak English.

o **Touts** Keep your wits about you around the Gateway of India – touts tend to hang around here.

Left: Fruit at Crawford Market (p130) **Above:** Sunset at Girgaum Chowpatty (Chowpatty Beach; p121)

EFT) KEREN SU/GETTY IMAGES ©: (ABOVE) HUW JONES/GETTY IMAGES ©

Mumbai's Colonial-Era Architecture Walking Tour

The grandiose colonial-era architecture of Mumbai is a remarkable feature of the cityscape. Take this stroll to see its most spectacular 19th-century hits. Be warned: heavy traffic and exhaust fumes taint the route in places; take cover in the cafes of Kala Ghoda.

WALK FACTS

- **Start** Gateway of India
- **Finish** Eros Cinema
- **Distance** 2.5km
- **Duration** Two hours

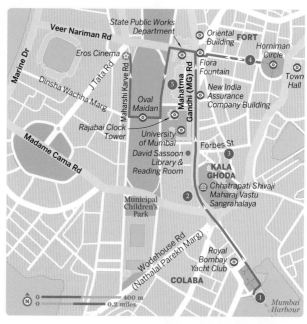

➊ Gateway of India

Starting from the Gateway of India walk up Chhatrapati Shivaji Marg, past the members-only colonial relic Royal Bombay Yacht Club on one side and the art deco complex Dhunraj Mahal on the other, towards Regal Circle. The car park in the middle of the circle has the best view of the surrounding buildings, including the old Sailors Home which dates from 1876 and is now the Maharashtra Police Headquarters, as well as the art deco cinema Regal and the old Majestic Hotel, now the Sahakari Bhandar cooperative store.

➋ National Gallery of Modern Art

Continue up Mahatma Gandhi (MG) Rd, past the restored facade of the National Gallery of Modern Art. Opposite is the Chhatrapati Shivaji Maharaj Vastu Sangrahalaya; step into the front gardens to admire this grand building. Back across the road is the 'Romanesque Transitional' Elphinstone College and the David Sassoon Library & Reading Room, where members escape the afternoon heat lazing on planters' chairs on the upper balcony.

3 Keneseth Eliyahoo Synagogue

Cross back over to Forbes St to visit the synagogue before returning to MG Rd and continuing north along the left-hand side of the road, to admire the art deco stylings of the New India Assurance Company Building. In a traffic island ahead lies the pretty Flora Fountain, erected in 1869 in honour of Sir Bartle Frere, the Bombay governor responsible for dismantling the fort. From here, there's a nice view of the 1885 Oriental Building to the north.

4 St Thomas' Cathedral

Turn east down Veer Nariman Rd, walking towards St Thomas' Cathedral. Ahead lies the stately Horniman Circle, an arcaded ring of buildings laid out in the 1860s around a botanical garden. The circle is overlooked from the east by the neoclassical town hall, which contains the regally decorated members-only Asiatic Society of Bombay Library and Mumbai's State Central Library.

5 High Court

As you retrace your steps back to Flora Fountain, glance to the north at the striking red Bombay Samachar building, home to the oldest continuously published newspaper in India, before continuing west past the Venetian Gothic-style State Public Works Department, now the entrance to the High Court. Turn south on to Bhaurao Patil Marg to see the High Court in full glory and the equally venerable and ornately decorated University of Mumbai. The university's 80m-high Rajabai Clock Tower and the facade of the High Court are best observed from within the Oval Maidan. Turn around to compare the colonial-era edifices with the row of art deco beauties lining Maharshi Karve (MK) Rd, culminating in the wedding-cake tower of the Eros Cinema.

Mumbai in...

TWO DAYS

In the morning, follow part or all of our walking tour, before having lunch in the Fort area. Dive into the maze of bazaars just to the north; colourful **Crawford Market** (p130) is a good place to start.

The next day, visit the ornate **Dr Bhau Daji Lad Mumbai City Museum** (p121), then take in a beach sunset at **Girgaum Chowpatty** (p121) before heading for dinner at one of Mumbai's stand-out restaurants.

FOUR DAYS

Follow the two-day itinerary above, then on day three hop on a ferry to nearby **Elephanta Island** (p123). Finish the day with a meal in Colaba before swapping tales with fellow travellers at **Leopold's Cafe** (p129).

Head out to **Global Pagoda** (p121) on your final day, returning in the afternoon to visit the museums and galleries of **Kala Ghoda** (p119). Dine in style in the evening, but leave enough time to take in a show; either a concert at the **National Centre for the Performing Arts** (p130) or a gig at **Bluefrog** (p130).

St Thomas' Cathedral (p122)

Discover Mumbai (Bombay) & Around

At a Glance

○ **Mumbai** (Bombay) Crazy, charismatic yet businesslike metropolis.

○ **Ellora** (p135) Unesco-listed cave temples.

○ **Ajanta** (p136) Unesco-listed Buddhist rock caves.

○ **Elephanta Island** (p123) Tranquil island temples.

○ **Aurangabad** (p133) Former Mughal capital, gateway to Ellora and Ajanta.

MUMBAI (BOMBAY)
 022 / POP 21 MILLION

◎ Sights

Mumbai is an island connected by bridges to the mainland. The southernmost peninsula is Colaba, traditionally the travellers' nerve centre, with many of the major attractions, and directly north of Colaba is the busy commercial area known as Fort, where the British fort once stood.

COLABA

Taj Mahal Palace, Mumbai
Landmark

(Map p120; Apollo Bunder) Mumbai's most famous landmark, this stunning hotel is a fairy-tale blend of Islamic and Renaissance styles, and India's second-most photographed monument. It was built in 1903 by the Parsi industrialist JN Tata, supposedly after he was refused entry to one of the European hotels on account of being 'a native'. Dozens were killed inside the hotel when it was targeted during the 2008 terrorist attacks, and images of its burning facade were beamed across the world. The fully restored hotel reopened on Independence Day 2010.

Gateway of India
Monument

(Map p120) This bold basalt arch of colonial triumph faces out to Mumbai Harbour from the tip of Apollo Bunder. Incorporating Islamic styles of 16th-century Gujarat, it was built to commemorate the 1911 royal visit of King George V, but wasn't completed until 1924. Ironically, the British builders of the gateway used it just 24 years later to parade the last British regiment as India marched towards independence.

Gateway of India
LONELY PLANET / GETTY IMAGES ©

Detour:
Great Wall of Mumbai

Started as an initiative by artists to add colour to a suburban street in Bandra, the **Wall Project** (www.thewallproject.com) has introduced public art, murals and graffiti across the city. There's no official membership, and art has been created by amateurs and professionals. No advertising, political statements, religious content or obscene messaging should be used. Social messaging that's too preachy is not encouraged either.

Hundreds of individuals have joined the project, with most murals dealing with personal stories: dreams, desire for change, criticisms and frustrations.

Perhaps the most spectacular stretch is a 2km canvas along **Senapati Bapat Marg** (Tulsi Pipe Rd), between Mahim Junction and Dadar railway stations on the Western Line, where the art parallels the tracks. It's a very thought-provoking and enriching experience take in; allow an hour and a half to explore. Around four hundred people contributed.

Many murals on Senapati Bapat Marg have a theme that's relevant to India and Mumbai such as the environment, pollution and the pressures of metropolitan life. One mural of a Mumbai cityscape simply says 'Chaos is our Paradise'.

Bandra is another area rich in street art, where many walls and bridges have been customised: Chapel Lane is a good place to start investigating.

FORT & CHURCHGATE

Lined up in a row and vying for your attention with aristocratic pomp, many of Mumbai's majestic Victorian buildings pose on the edge of **Oval Maidan**. This land, and the **Cross** and **Azad Maidans** immediately to the north, was on the oceanfront in those days, and this series of grandiose structures faced west directly out to the Arabian Sea.

Kala Ghoda, or 'Black Horse', is a sub-neighbourhood of Fort just north of Colaba and contains many of Mumbai's museums and galleries alongside a wealth of colonial-era buildings.

Chhatrapati Shivaji Terminus
Historic Building

(Victoria Terminus; Map p126) Imposing, exuberant and overflowing with people, this monumental train station is the city's most extravagant Gothic building and an aphorism for colonial-era India. It's a meringue of Victorian, Hindu and Islamic styles whipped into an imposing Dalíesque structure of buttresses, domes, turrets, spires and stained glass. As historian Christopher London put it, 'the Victoria Terminus is to the British Raj what the Taj Mahal is to the Mughal empire'.

Chhatrapati Shivaji Maharaj Vastu Sangrahalaya
Museum

(Prince of Wales Museum; Map p126; http://csmvs.in; K Dubash Marg, Kala Ghoda; Indian/foreigner ₹50/300, camera/video ₹200/1000; ☉10.15am-6pm) Mumbai's biggest and best museum displays a mix of exhibits from across India. The domed behemoth, an intriguing hodgepodge of Islamic, Hindu and British architecture, is a flamboyant Indo-Saracenic design by George Wittet (who also designed the Gateway of India).

Its vast collection includes impressive Hindu and Buddhist sculpture, terracotta figurines from the Indus Valley, Indian miniature paintings, porcelain and some particularly vicious-looking weaponry. Good information is provided in English, and audio guides are available in seven languages.

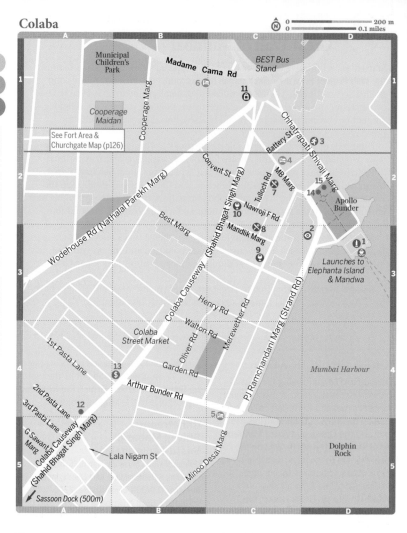

Municipal Children's Park

Madame Cama Rd

BEST Bus Stand

Cooperage Maidan

See Fort Area & Churchgate Map (p126)

Chhatrapati Shivaji Marg

Convent St

Apollo Bunder

Nawroji F Rd

Mandlik Marg

Launches to Elephanta Island & Mandwa

Best Marg

Wodehouse Rd (Nathalal Parekh Marg)

Colaba Causeway (Shahid Bhagat Singh Marg)

Henry Rd

Merewether Rd

PJ Ramchandani Marg (Strand Rd)

Mumbai Harbour

Colaba Street Market

Walton Rd

Oliver Rd

1st Pasta Lane

13

Garden Rd

Arthur Bunder Rd

2nd Pasta Lane

12

3rd Pasta Lane

G Sawant Marg

Colaba Causeway (Shahid Bhagat Singh Marg)

Lala Nigam St

Dolphin Rock

Minoo Desai Marg

Sassoon Dock (500m)

Keneseth Eliyahoo Synagogue
Synagogue

(Map p126; www.jacobsassoon.org; Dr VB Gandhi Marg, Kala Ghoda; camera/video ₹100/500; ⊙11am-6pm Mon-Sat, 1-6pm Sun) Built in 1884, this unmistakable sky-blue synagogue still functions and is tenderly maintained by the city's dwindling Jewish community. It's protected by very heavy security, but the caretaker is welcoming (and will point out a photo of Madonna, who dropped by in 2008).

KALBADEVI TO MAHALAXMI

Marine Drive
Promenade

(Map p126; Netaji Subhashchandra Bose Rd) Built on reclaimed land in 1920, Marine Dr arcs along the shore of the Arabian Sea from Nariman Point past Girgaum Chowpatty and continues to the foot of Malabar Hill. Lined with flaking art deco apartments, it's one of Mumbai's most popular promenades and sunset-watching spots. Its twinkling night-time lights earned it the nickname 'the Queen's Necklace'.

Colaba

◎ Sights
1 Gateway of India D3
2 Taj Mahal Palace, Mumbai..........D3

✛ Activities, Courses & Tours
3 Palm Spa D2

⬢ Sleeping
4 Abode Bombay C2
5 Sea Shore Hotel C4
Taj Mahal Palace, Mumbai..........(see 2)
6 YWCA B1

✕ Eating
7 Bademiya C2
8 Indigo C3

◉ Drinking & Nightlife
9 Colaba Social.............................C3
Harbour Bar ....(see 2)
10 Leopold Cafe C2

◈ Shopping
11 Phillips C1

ⓘ Information
12 Akbar Travels A4
13 Thomas Cook B4

ⓘ Transport
14 MTDC Booth D2
15 PNP Ticket Office........................D2

Hundreds gather on the promenade around Nariman Point in the early evening to snack and chat, when it's a good place to meet Mumbaikers.

Dr Bhau Daji Lad Mumbai City Museum
Museum

(www.bdlmuseum.org; Dr Babasaheb Ambedkar Rd; Indian/foreigner ₹10/100; ⊘10am-6pm Thu-Tue) This gorgeous museum, built in Renaissance revival style in 1872 as the Victoria & Albert Museum, contains 3500-plus objects centering on Mumbai's history – photography and maps, textiles, books and manuscripts, bidriware (metal handicrafts), laquerware, weaponry and exquisite pottery. It's set in the lush mid-19th-century **Jijimata Udyan** gardens.

The landmark building was renovated in 2008, with its Minton tile floors, gilded ceiling mouldings, ornate columns, chandeliers and staircases all restored to their former glory. Contemporary music, dance and drama feature in the new Plaza area, where there's a cafe and shop.

Girgaum Chowpatty
Beach

This city beach is a favourite evening spot for courting couples, families, political rallies and anyone out to enjoy what passes for fresh air. Evening *bhelpuri* at the throng of stalls at the beach's southern end is an essential part of the Mumbai experience. Forget about taking a dip: the water's toxic.

JUHU

Iskcon Temple
Hindu Temple

(www.iskconmumbai.com; Juhu Church Rd; ⊘4.30am-1pm & 4-9pm) A focus for intense, celebratory worship in the sedate suburbs, this temple is a compelling place to visit. Iskcon Juhu has a key part in the Hare Krishna story, as founder AC Bhaktivedanta Swami Prabhupada spent extended periods here (you can visit his modest living quarters in the adjacent building). The temple compound comes alive during prayer time as the faithful whip themselves into a devotional frenzy of joy, with *kirtan* dancing accompanied by crashing hand symbols and drum beats.

GORAI ISLAND

Global Pagoda
Buddhist Temple

(www.globalpagoda.org; Gorai; ⊘9am-7pm, meditation classes 10am-6pm) Rising up like a mirage from polluted Gorai Creek is this breathtaking, golden 96m-high stupa modelled on Myanmar's Shwedagon Pagoda. Its dome, which houses relics of Buddha, was built entirely without supports using an ancient technique of interlocking stones, and the meditation hall beneath it seats 8000.

There's a museum dedicated to the life of the Buddha and his teaching. Twenty-minute meditation classes are offered daily; an on-site meditation centre also offers 10-day courses.

✦ Activities

Yoga House
Yoga

(☏65545001; www.yogahouse.in; 53 Chimbai Rd, Bandra; class ₹700; ⊘8am-10pm) A variety of yoga traditions are taught at this homey, Western-style yoga centre,

If You Like...
Colonial-Era Architecture

If you love Mumbai's sumptuous colonial-era buildings such as Chhatrapati Shivaji, seek out the following fantastic examples in the Fort area:

1 HIGH COURT
(Map p126; Eldon Rd; ⏱10.45am-2pm & 2.45-5pm Mon-Fri) A hive of daily activity, packed with judges, barristers and other cogs in the Indian justice system, the High Court is an elegant 1848 neo-Gothic building. The design was inspired by a German castle and was obviously intended to dispel any doubts about the authority of the justice dispensed inside.

2 ST THOMAS' CATHEDRAL
(Map p126; Veer Nariman Rd; ⏱7am-6pm) This charming cathedral, begun in 1672 and finished in 1718, is the oldest British-era building standing in Mumbai: it was once the eastern gateway of the East India Company's fort (the 'Churchgate'). The cathedral is a marriage of Byzantine and colonial-era architecture, and its airy interior is full of grandiose colonial memorials.

housed in a Portuguese-style bungalow by the sea. There's also a charming cafe.

Yoga Cara
Yoga, Massage
(☎022-26511464; www.yogacara.in; 1st fl, SBI Bldg, 18A New Kant Wadi Rd, Bandra; ⏱yoga per class/week ₹600/1500) Classic hatha and iyengar yoga institute. Massages (from ₹1850 per hour) and treatments are excellent here; the SoHum rejuvenating massage is recommended. Ayurvedic cooking classes are also offered.

Palm Spa
Spa
(Map p120; ☎022-66349898; www.thepalms spaindia.com; Chhatrapati Shivaji Marg, Colaba; 1hr massage from ₹3200; ⏱9.30am-10.30pm) Indulge in a rub, scrub or tub at this renowned Colaba spa. The exfoliating lemongrass and green-tea scrub is ₹2500.

Tours

Fiona Fernandez' *Ten Heritage Walks of Mumbai* (₹395) contains walking tours in the city, with fascinating historical background.

The Government of India tourist office (p131) can provide a list of approved multilingual guides; most charge ₹750/1000 per half/full day.

Reality Tours & Travel
Slum Tour
(Map p126; ☎9820822253; www.reality toursandtravel.com; 1/26, Unique Business Service Centre, Akber House, Nowroji Fardonji Rd; most tours ₹750-1500) Compelling tours of the Dharavi slum, with 80% of post-tax profits going to the agency's own NGO, **Reality Gives** (www.realitygives.org). Street food, market, bicycle and Night Mumbai tours are also excellent.

Mumbai Magic Tours
City Tour
(☎9867707414; www.mumbaimagic.com; 2hr tour per person from ₹1750) Designed by the authors of the fabulous **Mumbai Magic blog** (www.mumbai-magic.blogspot.com), these city tours focus on food markets, traditional dance and music, and Jewish heritage, among others.

Bombay Heritage Walks
Walking Tour
(☎23690992, 9821887321; www.bombayher itagewalks.com; per 2hr tour for up to 5 people from ₹2500) Run by two enthusiastic architects, BHW has terrific tours of heritage neighbourhoods.

Nilambari Bus Tours
Bus Tour
(MTDC; ☎020-22845678; www.maharash tratourism.gov.in; 1hr tour lower/upper deck ₹60/180; ⏱7pm & 8.15pm Sat & Sun) Maharashtra Tourism runs open-deck bus tours of illuminated heritage buildings on weekends. Buses depart from and can be booked at both the **MTDC booth** (Map p120) and the **MTDC office** (☎22841877; Madame Cama Rd, Nariman Point; ⏱9.45am-5.30pm Mon-Sat).

Detour:
Elephanta Island

Northeast of the Gateway of India in Mumbai Harbour, the rock-cut temples on Gharapuri, better known as **Elephanta Island** (Gharapuri; Indian/foreigner ₹10/250; ⏱caves 9am-5pm Tue-Sun), are a Unesco World Heritage Site. Created between AD 450 and 750, the labyrinth of cave temples represent some of India's most impressive temple carving. The main Shiva-dedicated temple is an intriguing latticework of courtyards, halls, pillars and shrines; its magnum opus is a 6m-tall statue of Sadhashiva, depicting a three-faced Shiva as the destroyer, creator and preserver of the universe, his eyes closed in eternal contemplation.

The Portuguese dubbed the island Elephanta because of a large stone elephant near the shore (this collapsed in 1814 and was moved by the British to Mumbai's Jijamata Udyan). There's a small **museum** on-site, with informative pictorial panels on the origin of the caves.

Pushy, expensive guides are available – but Pramod Chandra's *A Guide to the Elephanta Caves*, widely for sale, is more than sufficient.

Launches (economy/deluxe ₹130/160) head to Gharapuri from the Gateway of India every half-hour from 9am to 3.30pm. Buy tickets at the booths lining Apollo Bunder. The voyage takes about an hour.

The ferries dock at the end of a concrete pier, from where you can walk or take the **miniature train** (₹10) to the **stairway** (admission ₹10) leading up to the caves. It's lined with souvenir stalls and patrolled by pesky monkeys. Wear good shoes.

 Sleeping

Mumbai has the most expensive accommodation in India. Colaba and Fort are convenient for the main sites and train stations. Top-end places are dotted along Marine Dr and out in the suburbs.

No matter where you stay, always book ahead.

COLABA

Sea Shore Hotel Guesthouse $
(Map p120; ☎22874237; 4th fl, 1-49 Kamal Mansion, Arthur Bunder Rd; s/d without bathroom ₹700/1100; 🛜) This place is really making an effort, with small but immaculately clean and inviting rooms, all with flat-screen TVs, set off a railway carriage-style corridor. Half the rooms even have harbour views (the others don't have a window). The modish communal bathrooms are well-scrubbed and have a little gleam and sparkle. Wi-fi in the reception area only.

YWCA Guesthouse $$
(Map p120; ☎22025053; www.ywcaic.info; 18 Madame Cama Rd; s/d/tr with AC incl breakfast & dinner ₹2400/3640/5450; ❄@🛜) Efficiently managed, and within walking distance of all the sights in Coloba and Fort, the YMCA is a good deal and justifiably popular. The spacious, well-maintained rooms boast desks and wardrobes and multi-chanelled TVs (though wi-fi is restricted to the lobby). Tariffs include a buffet breakfast, dinner and a daily newspaper.

Taj Mahal Palace, Mumbai Heritage Hotel $$$
(Map p120; ☎66653366; www.tajhotels.com; Apollo Bunder; s/d tower from ₹15,800/17,620, palace from ₹23,530/25,990; ❄@🛜≋) The grand dame of Mumbai is one of the world's most iconic hotels and has hosted a roster of presidents and royalty. Sweeping arches, staircases and domes and a glorious garden and pool ensure an

Mumbai for Children

Kidzania (www.kidzania.in; 3rd flr, R City, LBS Marg, Ghatkopar West; ⊘child/adult Tue-Fri ₹950/500, Sat & Sun ₹950/700) is an educational activity centre where children can learn about piloting a plane, fighting fires, policing and get stuck into lots of art- and craft-making.

Little tykes with energy to burn will love the Gorai Island amusement parks, **Esselworld** (www.esselworld.in; adult/child ₹790/490; ⊘11am-7pm, from 10am weekends) and **Water Kingdom** (www.waterkingdom.in; adult/child ₹690/490; ⊘11am-7pm, from 10am weekends). Both have lots of rides, slides and shade. Combined tickets are ₹1190/990 per adult/child.

unforgettable stay. Rooms in the adjacent tower lack the period details of the palace itself, but many have spectacular, full-frontal views of the Gateway to India.

Abode Bombay Boutique Hotel $$$
(Map p120; ☏8080234066; www.abodebou tiquehotels.com; 1st fl, Lansdowne House, MB Marg; r with AC incl breakfast ₹5850-14,400; ❄🔊) Terrific new hip hotel, stylishly designed using colonial-era and art deco furniture, reclaimed teak flooring and original artwork; the luxury rooms have glorious free-standing bath tubs. Staff are very switched on to travellers' needs, and breakfast is excellent with fresh juice and delicious local and international choices. A little tricky to find, it's located behind the Regal Cinema.

FORT & CHURCHGATE

Traveller's Inn Hotel $
(Map p126; ☏22644685; 26 Adi Marzban Path; dm/d ₹630/1880, d with AC incl breakfast ₹2550; ❄@🔊) On a quiet, tree-lined street, this small hotel is a very sound choice

with clean, if tiny, rooms with cable TV that represent good value. The three (fan-cooled) dorms can get Hades-hot in summer but are a steal for Mumbai – bring your own ice pack (and exorcist). The location's excellent, staff are helpful and there's free wi-fi in the lobby.

Residency Hotel Hotel $$
(Map p126; ☏22625525; www.residencyhotel.com; 26 Rustom Sidhwa Marg, Fort; s/d with AC incl breakfast from ₹4430/4670; ❄@🔊) The best-run midranger in Mumbai, the Residency is the kind of dependable place where you can breathe a sigh of relief after a long journey and be certain you'll be looked after well. It's fine value too, with contemporary rooms that boast mood lighting, fridges, flat-screen TVs and hip en suite bathrooms.

WESTERN SUBURBS

Juhu Residency Boutique Hotel $$
(☏67834949; www.juhuresidency.com; 148B Juhu Tara Rd, Juhu; s/d with AC incl breakfast & wi-fi from ₹5850; ❄@🔊) Essential oil aromas greet you in the lobby at this excellent boutique hotel with an inviting, relaxing atmosphere (and a fine location, five minutes' walk from Juhu beach). The chocolate-and-coffee colour scheme in the modish rooms works well, each boasting marble floors, dark woods, artful bedspreads and flat-screen TVs. There are three restaurants – good ones – for just 18 rooms.

To top it all, free airport pick-ups are included.

Anand Hotel Hotel $$
(☏26203372; anandhote@yahoo.co.in; Gandhigram Rd, Juhu; s/d with AC from ₹2580/4230; ❄🔊) Yes, the decor's in 50 shades of beige but the Anand's rooms are comfortable, spacious and represent decent value, considering the prime location on a quiet street next to Juhu beach. The excellent in-house Dakshinayan restaurant (p128) scores highly for authentic, inexpensive meals too. It's a particularly good deal for solo travellers.

Eating

COLABA

Bademiya
Mughlai, Fast Food $

(Map p120; Tulloch Rd; light meals ₹60-150; ⏲8pm-1.30am) Formerly a tiny, outrageously popular late-night street stall, Bademiya now encompasses a (dingy) seating area too. Yes, prices have risen, but it remains a key Colaba hang-out for its trademark buzz and bustle, plus its delicious meat-heavy menu. Expect spicy, fresh-grilled kebabs, mutton and chicken curries, and tikka rolls.

Indigo
Fusion, Continental $$$

(Map p120; ☎66368980; www.foodindigo.com; 4 Mandlik Marg; mains ₹780-1250; ⏲noon-3pm & 6.30pm-midnight; 🛜) This incredibly classy Colaba institution is a colonial-era property converted into a temple of fine dining. Serves inventive, expensive European and Asian cuisine and offers a long wine list, sleek ambience and a gorgeous rooftop deck. Favourites include the pulled duck tortellini, Kochi oysters, and pork belly with maple-glazed apple. Reserve ahead.

FORT & CHURCHGATE

Pradeep Gomantak Bhojanalaya
Maharashtrian $

(Map p126; Sheri House, Rustom Sidhwa Marg; mains ₹60-150; ⏲11am-4pm & 7.30-10pm) A simple but satisfying place that serves Malvani cuisine and gets very busy at lunchtime. Its *bombil* rice plate (₹70) and crab masala (₹65) are very flavoursome and prepared with real care and attention. Wash your meal down with *sol kadhi* (a soothing, spicy drink of coconut milk and kokum).

Revival
Indian $$

(www.revivalindianthali.com; 361 Sheikh Memon St, Kalbadevi, opp Mangaldas market; mains ₹200-360, thali from ₹350; ⏲noon-4pm & 7.30-10.30pm, lunch only Sun) Thali mecca near Crawford Market where waiters in silken dhoti come one after another to fill your plates with dozens of delectable (veg-only) curries, sides, chutneys, rotis and rice dishes in an all-you-can-eat gastro onslaught. The thali menu changes daily and the premises are air-conditioned.

La Folie
Cafe $$

(Map p126; Ropewalk Lane, Kala Ghoda; croissants/cakes from ₹110/220; ⏲noon-11pm) Chocoholics and cake fetishistas look no further, this miniscule Kala Ghoda place will satisfy your cravings, and then some. Owner Sanjana Patel spent seven years in France studying the art (addiction?) of pastry- and chocolate-making, which was obviously time well spent. Try the delectable Madagascar cake (chocolate with raspberry mousse) with a latte (₹130) or the 70% cocoa Venezuelan-sourced chocolates.

Miniature train,
Elephanta Island (p123)
MARK WILLIAMSON / GETTY IMAGES ©

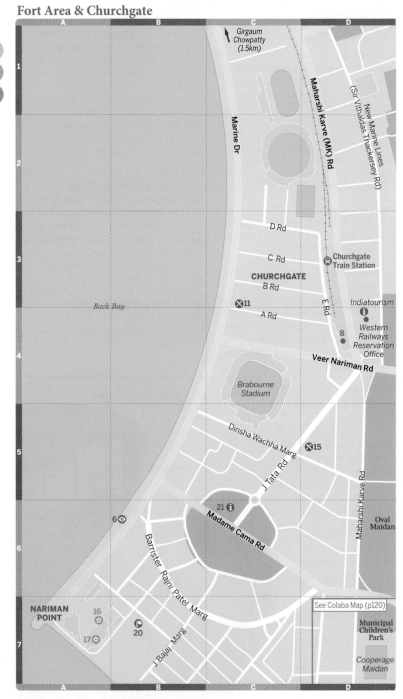

MUMBAI (BOMBAY) & AROUND

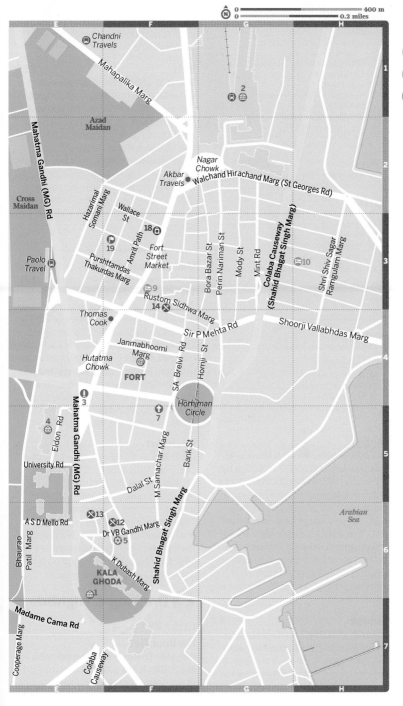

Chandni
Travels

Mahapalika Marg

Azad
Maidan

2

Nagar
Chowk
Akbar   Walchand Hirachand Marg (St Georges Rd)
Travels

Cross
Maidan

Mahatma Gandhi (MG) Rd

Hazarimal
Somani Marg

Wallace
St

18

19

Amrit Path

Fort
Street
Market

Bora Bazar St

Perin Nariman St

Mody St

Mint Rd

Colaba Causeway
(Shahid Bhagat Singh Marg)

10

Shri Shiv Sagar
Ramgulam Marg

Paolo
Travel

Purshttamdas
Thakurdas Marg

9

Rustom Sidhwa Marg
14

Thomas
Cook

Sir P Mehta Rd

Shoorji Vallabhdas Marg

Janmabhoomi
Marg
@

Hutatma
Chowk

FORT

SA Brelvi Rd

Homji St

Horniman
Circle

Mahatma Gandhi (MG) Rd

3

4

Eldon Rd

University Rd

M Samachar Marg

Bank St

Dalal St.

Shahid Bhagat Singh Marg

A S D Mello Rd

13

12

Dr VB Gandhi Marg

5

Arabian
Sea

Bhaurao Patil Marg

K Dubash Marg

KALA
GHODA

1

Madame Cama Rd

Cooperage Marg

Colaba Causeway

Fort Area & Churchgate

◎ **Sights**
1 Chhatrapati Shivaji Maharaj
   Vastu Sangrahalaya E6
2 Chhatrapati Shivaji Terminus G1
3 Flora Fountain E4
4 High Court..E5
5 Keneseth Eliyahoo Synagogue F6
6 Marine Drive B6
7 St Thomas' Cathedral F5

◐ **Activities, Courses & Tours**
8 Reality Tours & Travel.........................D4

◎ **Sleeping**
9 Residency Hotel.....................................F3
10 Traveller's Inn..H3

✖ **Eating**
11 Koh...C3
12 La Folie F6
13 Pantry...E6
14 Pradeep Gomantak
    Bhojanalaya...F3
15 Samrat..D5

◉ **Entertainment**
16 National Centre for the
    Performing Arts A7
17 NCPA Box Office...................................A7

◎ **Shopping**
18 Contemporary Arts & Crafts..............F3

ℹ **Information**
19 Dutch Consulate...................................F3
20 German Consulate................................B7
21 Maharashtra Tourism
    Development Corporation..............C6

Pantry · Cafe $$

(Map p126; www.thepantry.in; B Bharucha Rd; snacks/meals from ₹200/270; ⊙8.30am-11pm; 🛜) Pantry is a bakery-cafe that offers a choice of fine pies and pastries, soups and sandwiches plus delicious mains (such as curry leaf chicken with burgal pilaf). Breakfasts are legendary: try the tomato scrambled eggs with parmesan and rosti, or some organic-flour waffles with fruit. The elegantly restored historic premises are also perfect for a coffee and slab of cake.

Samrat · Gujarati $$

(Map p126; 📞42135401; www.prashantcater ers.com; Prem Ct, J Tata Rd; thali ₹400, mains ₹160-290; ⊙noon-11pm) Samrat has an à la carte menu but most rightly opt for the famous Gujarati thali – a cavalcade of taste and texture, sweetness and spice that includes four curries, three chutneys, curd, rotis and other bits and pieces. It's air-conditioned and beer is available.

Koh · Thai $$$

(Map p126; 📞39879999; InterContinental, Marine Dr; mains ₹850-1850; ⊙12.30-3pm & 7.30-midnight) Destination Thai restaurant with a real wow factor, where celeb chef Ian Kittichai works his native cuisine into an international frenzy of flavour. The massamun curry (Thai Muslim-style spiced lamb shank with cucumber relish) is his signature (and most expensive) dish, but there are lots of sublime seafood and vegetarian choices too. Well worth a splurge.

WESTERN SUBURBS

Dakshinayan · South Indian $$

(Anand Hotel, Gandhigram Rd; Juhu; light meals ₹90-170; ⊙11am-3pm & 6-11pm, from 8am Sun) With *rangoli* on the walls, servers in lungis and sari-clad women lunching (*chappals* off under the table), Dakshinayan channels Tamil Nadu. There are delicately textured dosas (₹110 to ₹165), *idli* and *uttapam,* village-fresh chutneys and perhaps the best *rasam* (tomato soup with spices and tamarind) in Mumbai. Finish off with a South Indian filter coffee – served in a stainless-steel set.

Peshawri · North Indian $$$

(📞28303030; ITC Maratha, Sahar Rd, Andheri East; meals ₹1100-2700; ⊙12.45-2.45pm & 7-11.45pm) Make this Northwest Frontier restaurant, outside the international airport, your first or last stop in Mumbai. The buttery *dhal bukhara* (a thick black dhal cooked for a day; ₹700) is perhaps the signature dish, but its kebabs are sublime: try the *peshawri* (chargrilled lamb marinated in yoghurt and spices).

Drinking & Nightlife

COLABA

Harbour Bar · Bar

(Map p120; Taj Mahal Palace, Mumbai, Apollo Bunder; ⊙11am-11.45pm) With unmatched views of the Gateway of India and harbour, this timeless bar inside the Taj is an essential visit. Drinks aren't uber-expensive (₹395/800 for a beer/cocktail) given the surrounds and the fact they come with very generous portions of nibbles (including jumbo cashews).

Colaba Social   Bar
(Map p120; www.socialoffline.in; ground fl, Glen Rose Bldg, BK Boman Behram Marg, Apollo Bunder; ⏰9am-1.30am; 📶) The Social opened with a bang in late 2014, thanks to its stellar cocktail list (most are just ₹300 or so; try the Longest Island Ice Tea) and fab Colaba location. During the day it's a social-cum-workspace for laptop-toting brunching creative types, but by 6pm the place is rammed with a raucous young crowd. Snacks (₹120 to ₹380) and espresso coffee are available.

Also hosts DJ and live-music events, art and photography exhibits and stand-up comedy acts.

Leopold Cafe   Bar
(Map p120; www.leopoldcafe.com; cnr Colaba Causeway & Nawroji F Rd, Colaba; ⏰7.30am-12.30am) Love it or hate it, most tourists end up at this Mumbai travellers'

institution-cum-cliché at one time or another. Around since 1871, Leopold's has wobbly ceiling fans, crap service and a rambunctious atmosphere conducive to swapping tales with strangers. There's also food and a cheesy DJ upstairs on weekend nights.

WESTERN SUBURBS

Aer   Lounge
(Four Seasons Hotel, 34th fl, 114 Dr E Moses Rd, Worli; cover Fri & Sat after 8pm ₹2500; ⏰5.30pm-midnight; 📶) Boasting astounding sea, sunset and city views, Aer is Mumbai's premier sky bar. Drink prices are steep, but that's kind of the point: cocktails cost around ₹900, beers start at ₹350 and happy hour is 5.30pm to 8pm. A DJ spins house and lounge tunes nightly from 9pm.

Bonobo   Bar
(www.facebook.com/BonoboBandra; Kenilworth Mall, 33rd Rd, Bandra West, off Linking Rd; ⏰6pm-1am; 📶) The scenesters' first choice in Bandra, this bar champions underground and alternative music. DJs spin drum 'n' bass and electronica, big beats and funk tech-house, and musicians

Leopold Cafe

RICHARD I'ANSON / GETTY IMAGES ©

play folk and blues. There's a great rooftop terrace.

 Entertainment

Consult **Mumbai Boss** (www.mumbaiboss. com), **Time Out Mumbai** (www.timeout.com/ mumbai) and www.nh7.in for live-music listings.

Bluefrog Live Music, Nightclub
(☎61586158; www.bluefrog.co.in; D/2 Mathuradas Mills Compound, Senapati Bapat Marg, Lower Parel; admission ₹300-1200; ☺6.30pm-1.30am Tue-Sat, from 11.30am Sun) Mumbai cultural mecca, a world-class venue for concerts (everything from indie to Mexican), stand-up comedy and lots of DJ-driven clubby nights (hip hop, house and techno). There's also a restaurant with space-age pod seating (book ahead for dinner) in the intimate main room. Happy hour is 6.30pm to 9pm. It's 1km north of Mahalaxmi train station.

National Centre for the Performing Arts Theatre, Live Music
(NCPA; Map p126; ☎66223737, box office 22824567; www.ncpamumbai.com; Marine Dr & Sri V Saha Rd, Nariman Point; tickets ₹200-800; ☺box office 9am-7pm) This vast cultural centre is the hub of Mumbai's high-brow music, theatre and dance scene. In any given week, it might host experimental plays, poetry readings, photography exhibitions, a jazz band from Chicago or Indian classical music. Many performances are free. The **box office** (Map p126) is at the end of NCPA Marg.

 Shopping

COLABA

Phillips Antiques
(Map p120; www.phillipsantiques.com; Wodehouse Rd, Colaba; ☺10am-7pm Mon-Sat) Art deco and colonial-era furniture, wooden ceremonial masks, silver, Victorian glass and also high-quality reproductions of old photos, maps and paintings.

FORT & CHURCHGATE

Contemporary Arts & Crafts Homewares
(Map p126; www.cac.co.in; 210 Dr Dadabhai Naoroji Rd, Fort; ☺10.30am-7.30pm) Modish, high-quality takes on traditional crafts: these are not your usual handmade souvenirs.

KALBADEVI TO MAHALAXMI

Crawford Market Market
(Mahatma Phule Market; cnr DN & Lokmanya Tilak Rds) Crawford Market is the largest in Mumbai, and contains the last whiff of British Bombay before the tumult of the central bazaars begins. Bas-reliefs by Rudyard Kipling's father, Lockwood Kipling, adorn the Norman Gothic exterior. Fruit and vegetables, meat and fish are mainly traded, but it's also an excellent place to stock up on spices.

Mangaldas Market Market
Mangaldas Market, traditionally home to traders from Gujarat, is a mini town, complete with lanes of fabrics. Even if you're not the type to have your clothes tailored, drop by **DD Dupattawala** (Shop No 217, 4th Lane, Mangaldas Market; ☺9.30am-6.30pm) for pretty scarves and dupattas at fixed prices. **Zaveri Bazaar** for jewellery and **Bhuleshwar Market** (cnr Sheikh Menon St & M Devi Marg) for fruit and veg are just north of here. Just a few metres further along Sheikh Menon Rd from Bhuleshwar is a Jain pigeon-feeding station, flower market and a religious market.

Chor Bazaar Antiques
Chor Bazaar is known for its antiques, though nowadays much of it is reproductions; the main area of activity is Mutton St, where shops specialise in 'antiques' and miscellaneous junk. Dhabu St, to the east, is lined with fine leather goods.

 Information

Internet Access

Anita CyberCafé (Map p126; Cowasji Patel Rd, Fort; per hr ₹30; ☺9am-10pm Mon-Sat, 2-10pm

Sun) Opposite one of Mumbai's best chai stalls (open evenings).

Medical Services

Breach Candy Hospital (☎23672888, emergency 23667809; www.breachcandyhospital.org; 60 Bhulabhai Desai Marg, Breach Candy) The best in Mumbai, if not India. It's 2km northwest of Chowpatty Beach.

Money

ATMs are everywhere, and foreign-exchange offices changing cash and travellers cheques – including Akbar Travels and Thomas Cook's Fort and **Colaba** (Map p120; ☎66092608; Colaba Causeway; ◷9.30am-6pm) branches – are also plentiful.

Tourist Information

Indiatourism (Government of India Tourist Office; Map p126; ☎22074333; www.incredibleindia.com; Western Railways Reservation Complex, 123 Maharshi Karve Rd; ◷8.30am-6pm Mon-Fri, to 2pm Sat) Provides information for the entire country, as well as contacts for Mumbai guides and homestays.

Maharashtra Tourism Development Corporation (MTDC; Map p126; ☎22044040; www.maharashtratourism.gov.in; Madame Cama Rd, Nariman Point; ◷10am-5pm Mon-Sat, closed 2nd & 4th Sat) The MTDC's head office has helpful staff and lots of pamphlets to give away.

Travel Agencies

Akbar Travels (www.akbartravelsonline.com; ◷10am-7pm Mon-Fri, to 6pm Sat) Colaba (Map p120; ☎22823434; 30 Alipur Trust Bldg, Shahid Bhagat Singh Marg); Fort (Map p126; ☎22633434; 167/169 Dr Dadabhai Naoroji Rd) Extremely helpful and can book cars/drivers and buses. Also has good exchange rates.

Thomas Cook (Map p126; ☎61603333; www.thomascook.in; 324 Dr Dadabhai Naoroji Rd, Fort; ◷9.30am-6pm Mon-Sat) Flight and hotel bookings, plus foreign exchange.

ℹ Getting There & Away

Air

Mumbai's **Chhatrapati Shivaji International Airport** (BOM; ☎66851010; www.csia.in), about 30km from the city centre, was nearing the end of a US$2 billion modernisation program at the time of research. The impresssive international terminal is complete, while its new domestic terminal should be fully operational some time in 2015, creating a fully integrated airport.

Crawford Market

However at the time of writing there were still two airports: one international terminal and a separate domestic terminal (also known locally as Santa Cruz airport), 5km away. A free shuttle bus runs between the two every 30 minutes (journey time 15 minutes) for ticket-holders. Both terminals have ATMs, foreign-exchange counters and tourist-information booths.

Bus

Long-distance government-run buses depart from the well-organised **Mumbai Central bus terminal** (✆enquiries 23024075; Jehangir Boman Behram Rd) right by Mumbai Central train station. They're cheaper and more frequent than private services, but the quality and crowd levels vary.

Private buses depart from Dr Anadrao Nair Rd near Mumbai Central train station, or from Paltan Rd, near Crawford Market. To check on departure times and current prices, visit **Citizen Travels** (✆23459695; www.citizenbus.com; D Block, Sitaram Bldg, Paltan Rd) or **National CTC** (✆23015652; Dr Anadrao Nair Rd). More convenient for Goa and southern destinations are the private buses run by **Chandni Travels** (Map p126; ✆22713901, 22676840), running six daily from in front of Azad Maidan, and **Paolo Travel** (Map p126; ✆0832-6637777; www.paulotravels.com), which has an 8pm daily departure from Fashion St.

Train

Three train systems operate out of Mumbai, but the most important services for travellers are Central Railways and Western Railways.

Central Railways (✆139), handling services to the east, south, plus a few trains to the north, operates from CST. Foreign tourist–quota tickets can be bought at Counter 52.

Some Central Railways' trains depart from Dadar (D), a few stations north of CST, or Lokmanya Tilak (LTT), 16km north of CST.

Western Railways (✆139) has services to the north from Mumbai Central train station (BCT). The **reservation centre** (Map p126; ⏰8am-8pm Mon-Sat, to 2pm Sun), opposite Churchgate station, has foreign tourist–quota tickets.

🛈 Getting Around

To/From the Airports

International

The international airport has a prepaid-taxi booth, with set fares. Taxis are ₹700/800 (non-AC/AC) to Colaba and Fort. The journey to Colaba takes about an hour at night (via the Sealink) and 1½ to two hours during the day.

Autorickshaws are available but they only go as far south as Bandra (daytime/night around ₹180/240).

A taxi from South Mumbai to the international airport should be around ₹500. Allow two hours for the trip if you travel between 4pm and 8pm.

Domestic

There's a prepaid taxi counter in the arrivals hall. A non-AC/AC taxi costs ₹600/700 to Colaba or Fort.

Car

Cars with driver are generally hired for an eight-hour day and an 80km maximum; air-conditioned vehicles cost around ₹1600.

Taxis, Mumbai
CULTURA TRAVEL / PLANET PICTURES / GETTY IMAGES ©

Metro

The first section of Line 1, Mumbai's new **metro** (www.mumbaimetroone.com) opened in 2014. Initially it only connected seven stations in the far northern suburbs. However Line 1 is scheduled to be extended to Jacob Circle (5km north of Chhatrapati Shivaji Terminus) sometime in 2015, bringing it past nightlife hub Lower Parel. Single fares cost between ₹10 and ₹20.

Taxi & Autorickshaw

Mumbai's black-and-yellow taxis are very inexpensive and the most convenient way to get around southern Mumbai; drivers *almost* always use the meter without prompting. The minimum fare is ₹21 (for up to 1.6km), a 5km trip costs about ₹50.

Autorickshaws are the name of the game north of Bandra. The minimum fare is ₹17, up to 1.6km, a 3km trip is about ₹30.

Both taxis and autorickshaws tack 25% onto the fare between midnight and 5am.

MAHARASHTRA

Aurangabad

📞 0240 / POP 1.28 MILLION / ELEV 515M

Aurangabad lay low through most of the tumultuous history of medieval India and only hit the spotlight when the last Mughal emperor, Aurangzeb, made the city his capital from 1653 to 1707. This brief period of glory saw the building of some fascinating monuments, including a Taj Mahal replica (Bibi-qa-Maqbara). But for most visitors the city is simply a convenient base for exploring the magnificent World Heritage Sites of Ellora and Ajanta.

Selected Trains from Mumbai

DESTINATION	TRAIN NO & NAME	SAMPLE FARE (₹)	DURATION (HR)	DEPARTURE
Agra	12137 Punjab Mail	580/1515/2195/3760 (A)	22	7.40pm CST
Ahmedabad	12901 Gujarat Mail	315/805/1135/1915 (A)	9	10pm BCT
	12009 Shatabdi Exp	960/1870 (C)	7	6.25am BCT
Aurangabad	11401 Nandigram Exp	235/620/885 (B)	7	4.35pm CST
	17617 Tapovan Exp	140/500 (C)	7	6.15am CST
Delhi	12951 Rajdhani Exp	2030/2810/4680 (D)	16	4.35pm BCT
Jaipur	12955 Jaipur Exp	535/1405/2025/3455 (A)	18	6.50pm BCT
Madgaon (Goa)	10103 Mandovi Exp	390/1055/1520/2575 (A)	12	7.10am CST
	12133 Mangalore Exp	420/1100/1570 (B)	9	10pm CST

Station abbreviations: CST (Chhatrapati Shivaji Terminus), BCT (Mumbai Central)
Fares: (A) sleeper/3AC/2AC/1AC, (B) sleeper/3AC/2AC, (C) sleeper/CC, (D) 3AC/2AC/1AC

 Sights

Bibi-qa-Maqbara _Monument_
(Indian/foreigner ₹5/100; ⏲dawn-10pm) Built by Aurangzeb's son Azam Khan in 1679 as a mausoleum for his mother Rabia-ud-Daurani, Bibi-qa-Maqbara is widely known as the poor man's Taj. With its four minarets flanking a central onion-domed mausoleum, the white structure certainly does bear a striking resemblance to Agra's Taj Mahal. It is much less grand, however, and apart from having a few marble adornments, namely the plinth and dome, much of the structure is finished in lime mortar.

Tours

Classic Tours (☎2337788; www.classictours.info; MTDC Holiday Resort, Station Rd East) and the **Indian Tourism Development Corporation** (ITDC; ☎2331143; MTDC Holiday Resort, Station Rd East) both run daily bus tours to the Ajanta and Ellora caves. The trip to Ajanta caves costs ₹450 and the tour to Ellora caves ₹325; prices include a guide but don't cover admission fees.

For private tours in an air-conditioned car, **Ashoka Tours & Travels** (☎2359102, 9890340816; www.touristaurangabad.com; Hotel Panchavati, Station Rd West; ⏲8am-8pm) has good rates to Ajanta (₹2400 for up to four people) and Ellora (₹1400).

Sleeping

Hotel Panchavati _Hotel $_
(☎2328755; www.hotelpanchavati.com; Station Rd West; s/d ₹1000/1130, with AC ₹1150/1250; ❄@🛜) The best budget hotel in town, Panchavati is run by ever-helpful, switched-on management who understand travellers' needs. Rooms are compact but thoughtfully appointed, with comfortable beds that have paisley style bedspreads and 24-hour hot water (and room service). There are two restaurants, a bar and it's a great place to hook up with other travellers.

Lemon Tree _Hotel $$$_
(☎6603030; www.lemontreehotels.com; R7/2 Chikalthana, Airport Rd; r incl breakfast from ₹5590; ❄@🛜🏊) The Lemon Tree offers elegance and class, looking more like a billionaire's luxury whitewashed Mediterranean villa than an Indian hotel. It's well designed too: all rooms face inwards, overlooking perhaps the best pool in the Decca plateau, all 50m of it. The standard rooms, though not large, are brightened by vivid tropical tones offset against snow-white walls. Located near the airport, 6km from the centre.

Eating

Bhoj _Indian $$_
(Station Rd West; thali ₹180; ⏲11am-3pm & 7-11pm) Rightly famous for its delicious unlimited Rajasthani and Gujarati thalis, Bhoj is a wonderful place to refuel and relax after a hard day on the road (or rail). It's on the 1st floor of a somewhat scruffy little shopping arcade, but the decor, ambience, service and presentation are all first rate.

ⓘ Getting There & Away

Air
The airport is 10km east of town. There are direct daily flights to Delhi (around ₹8500) and Mumbai (around ₹4500).

Bus
Ordinary buses head to Ellora from the MSRTC bus stand (Station Rd West) every half-hour (₹30, one hour), and hourly to Jalgaon (₹155, four hours) via Fardapur (₹95, 2½ hours), the drop-off point for Ajanta.

Private bus agents are mainly located around the corner from the MSRTC bus stand, where Dr Rajendra Prasad Marg becomes Court Rd. Deluxe overnight bus destinations include Mumbai (with/without AC from ₹550/350, sleeper ₹900 to ₹1500; 7½ to 9½ hours).

Train
Aurangabad's train station (Station Rd East) is not on a main line, but has four daily direct trains to/from Mumbai. The Tapovan Express (2nd class/chair ₹140/500, 7½ hours) departs Aurangabad at

2.35pm. The Janshatabdi Express (2nd class/chair ₹172/575, 6½ hours) departs Aurangabad at 6am.

ⓘ Getting Around

Autorickshaws are very common. The taxi stand is next to the MSRTC bus stand.

Ellora

☏ 02437

Give a man a hammer and chisel, and he'll create art for posterity. Come to the World Heritage Site **Ellora cave temples** (Indian/foreigner ₹10/250; ⊘ dawn-dusk Wed-Mon), located 30km from Aurangabad, and you'll know exactly what we mean. The epitome of ancient Indian rock-cut architecture, these caves were chipped out laboriously over five centuries by generations of Buddhist, Hindu and Jain monks. Monasteries, chapels, temples – the caves served every purpose, and they were stylishly embellished with a profusion of remarkably detailed sculptures.

The caves line a 2km-long escarpment, the gentle slope of which allowed the architects to build elaborate courtyards in front of the shrines, and render them with sculptures of a surreal quality.

Ellora has 34 caves in all: 12 Buddhist (AD 600–800), 17 Hindu (AD 600–900) and five Jain (AD 800–1000). The grandest, however, is the awesome Kailasa Temple (Cave 16), the world's largest monolithic sculpture, hewn top to bottom against a rocky slope by 7000 labourers over a 150-year period. Dedicated to Lord Shiva, it is clearly among the best that ancient Indian architecture has to offer.

Official guides can be hired at the ticket office in front of the Kailasa Temple for ₹1072 (up to five people).

◎ Sights

Kailasa Temple   Hindu Temple

One of Incredible India's greatest monuments, this astonishing temple, carved from solid rock, was built by King Krishna I in AD 760 to represent Mt Kailasa (Kailash), Shiva's Himalayan abode. To say that the assignment was daring would be an understatement. Three huge trenches were bored into the sheer cliff

Ellora cave temples

face, a process that entailed removing 200,000 tonnes of rock by hammer and chisel, before the temple could begin to take shape, and its remarkable sculptural decoration added.

Buddhist Caves
Caves

Calm and contemplation infuse the 12 Buddhist caves, which stretch to the south of Kailasa. All are Buddhist *viharas* (monasteries) used for study and worship, but these multistoreyed structures also included cooking, living and sleeping areas.

The one exception is Cave 10, which is a *chaitya* (assembly hall). While the earliest caves are simple, Caves 11 and 12 are more ambitious; both comprise of three stories and are on par with the more impressive Hindu temples.

Hindu Caves
Caves

Drama and excitement characterise the Hindu group (Caves 13 to 29). In terms of scale, creative vision and skill of execution, these caves are in a league of their own.

All these temples were cut from the top down, so it was never necessary to use scaffolding – the builders began with the roof and moved down to the floor. Highlights include caves 14, 15, 16, 21 and 29.

Jain Caves
Caves

The five Jain caves, the last created at Ellora, may lack the ambitious size of the best Hindu temples, but they are exceptionally detailed, with some remarkable paintings and carvings.

The caves are 1km north of the last Hindu temple (Cave 29) at the end of the bitumen road; autorickshaws run here from the main car park.

Ellora Visitor Centre
Tourist Information

(⏱9am-5.30pm Wed-Mon) Ellora's impressive new visitor centre, 750m west of the site, is worth dropping by to put the caves in historical context. It features modern displays and information panels, a 15-minute video presentation, and two galleries: one on the Kailasa Temple (with a diorama of the temple) and other dedicated to the site itself. A cafe, craft centre and restaurant are planned.

ℹ Getting There & Away

The temples are closed on Tuesday. Buses (₹30) and packed share jeeps (₹70) regularly ply the road between Aurangabad and Ellora; the last depart from Ellora at 8pm. A full-day autorickshaw tour to Ellora costs ₹700; taxis charge around ₹1400.

....

Ajanta
✆02438

Set superbly in a remote river valley 105km northeast of Aurangabad, the remarkable cave temples of Ajanta are this region's second

Ajanta caves
JOHN BORTHWICK / GETTY IMAGES ©

Ellora cave temple

CALEB KENNA / GETTY IMAGES ©

World Heritage Site. Much older than Ellora, these secluded caves date from around the 2nd century BC to the 6th century AD and were among the earliest monastic institutions to be constructed in the country.

One of primary reasons to visit Ajanta is to admire its renowned 'frescoes', actually temperas, which adorn many of the caves' interiors.

Authorised guides are available here for ₹750.

Sights

Ajanta Caves
Cave

(Indian/foreigner ₹10/250, video ₹25, authorised guide ₹750; ⏰9am-5.30pm Tue-Sun) Ajanta's caves line a steep face of a horseshoe-shaped gorge bordering the Waghore River. Five of the caves are *chaityas* (prayer halls) while others are *viharas* (monasteries). Caves 8, 9, 10, 12, 13 and part of 15 are early Buddhist caves, while the others date from around the 5th century AD (Mahayana period). In the austere early Buddhist school, the Buddha was never represented directly but always alluded to by a symbol such as the footprint or wheel of law.

Ajanta Visitor Centre
Tourist Information

(⏰9am-5.30pm Tue-Sun) This state-of-the-art new facility is one of India's very best, with highly impressive replicas of four caves (No 1, 2, 16 and 17) in real scale, audio guides available in many languages, excellent painting and sculpture galleries, and the story of Buddhism in India, an audio-visual arena and large cafe.

❶ Getting There & Away

The caves are closed on Monday. Buses from Aurangabad or Jalgaon will drop you off at a T-junction, 4km from the site. From here buses (with/without AC ₹20/15) take you to the caves; the last returning to the T-junction at 5pm.

137

Rajasthan

It is said that there is more history in Rajasthan than the rest of India put together.
Welcome to the Land of the Kings; a fabled realm of maharajas, majestic forts and lavish palaces.

India is littered with splendid ruined bastions but nowhere will you find fortresses quite as magnificent as those in Rajasthan, which rise imperiously from the desert landscape like fairy-tale mirages of a bygone era. As enchanting as they are, though, there is more to this most royal of regions than its seemingly timeless architectural wonders.

This is also a land of sand dunes and jungle, of camel trains and wild tigers, of glittering jewels, vivid colours and vibrant culture. There are festivals galore, and the shopping and cuisine are nothing short of spectacular. In truth, Rajasthan just about has it all. It is the must-see state of this must-see country; brimming with startling, thought-provoking and, ultimately, unforgettable attractions.

Elephant and keeper in Jaipur (p148)
HUW JONES/GETTY IMAGES ©

Rajasthan

PAKISTAN

THAR DESERT

Anupgarh

Gajner Wildlife Sanctuary

Kolayat

GREAT

Indira Gandhi Canal

15

Ramgarh

Lodhruva

Phalodi

Sam **Jaisalmer** ①

Pokaran

Mandore

Jodhpur ④

Khuri

Desert National Park

Rohet

Pali

Barmer ○

Balotra

① Jaisalmer Fort

② Udaipur

③ Pushkar

④ Jodhpur

⑤ Tiger-Spotting, Ranthambhore National Park

15

Luni River

Mt Abu Wildlife Sanctuary

Guru Shikar (1721m) ▲

Mt Abu

Abu Rd

Palanpur

GUJARAT

Radhanpur

15

8A

Gandhidham

Gandhinagar ◉

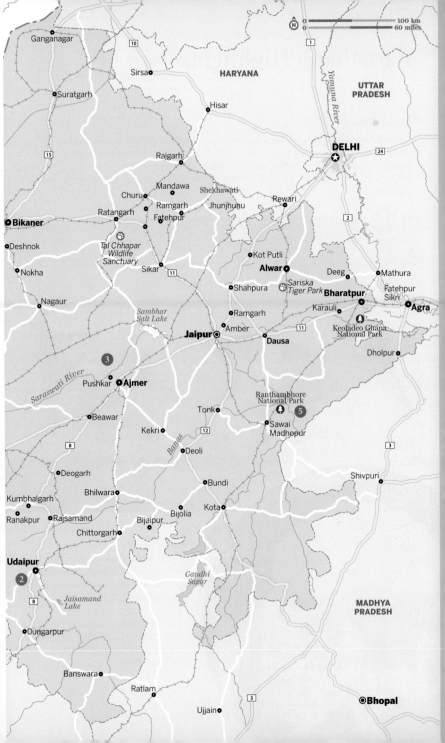

Rajasthan's Highlights

Jaisalmer Fort

Rising from the desert scrub like a beautiful, oversized sandcastle, surrounded by 99 bastions, the city of Jaisalmer resonates with its history. Despite today's commercialism, it retains a sense of epic romance. Visiting the ancient citadel (p182) and exploring the desert on camelback are mirage-like, otherworldly experiences that will stay with you long after you leave.

Udaipur

Surrounded by the wooded ridges of the Aravalli Hills and centred on two glimmering, mirror-calm lakes, Udaipur (p165) is Rajasthan's most romantic city, home to serene views on sunny rooftops; fantastical, lace-like, cupola-topped palaces, temples and *havelis* (noble houses); and narrow, crooked, colourful streets.

Pushkar

3

The pastel-hued pilgrimage destination of Pushkar (p159) is a mystical small town set around a holy lake. Although it's a popular travellers' stop, the town feels essentially spiritual, and there's always something going on at one of the temples around the lake. The diminutive town also hosts one of India's most famous fairs, the Pushkar Camel Fair.

4

Jodhpur

The Blue City (p175) really is blue, as you'll see when you climb up to its majestic fortress, Mehrangarh, which rears out of its rocky escarpment like a vision from a fairy tale. Listen to the city's secrets from its soaring ramparts, and get lost in its glittering bazaars, where you can buy polished tubas and trumpets, heaped spices, jewellery and shimmering temple decorations.

5

Tiger-Spotting, Ranthambhore National Park

Ranthambhore (p163) is one of India's most spectacular national parks, an area of lush, tangled jungle dotted by ruined *chhatris* (cenotaphs) and temples, topped by a magical clifftop fortress, and inhabited by exotic birds and wild animals, including, of course, tigers. The big cats are used to visitors and you have a good chance of spotting one here.

Rajasthan's Best...

Heritage Hotels

○ **Taj Lake Palace** The icon of Udaipur. (p170)

○ **Rohet Garh** Countryside manor with literary connections. (p178)

○ **Narain Niwas Palace Hotel** Ramshackle splendour set among tree-shaded gardens in Jaipur. (p154)

○ **Pal Haveli** Jodhpur's most charming *haveli*. (p178)

○ **Hotel Nachana Haveli** 280-year-old Jaisalmer *haveli*, set around three courtyards. (p187)

○ **Alsisar Haveli** Beautifully renovated *haveli* in the heart of Jaipur. (p153)

Wining & Dining

○ **Indique** Jodhpur's candle-lit rooftop restaurant, with old-city views. (p180)

○ **Ambrai** Udaipur's loveliest waterfront restaurant.(p172)

○ **Millets of Mewar** Healthy, friendly, delicious: another Udaipur gem. (p172)

○ **Saffron** Sublime Indian cuisine in an open-air Jaisalmer setting. (p188)

○ **Honey & Spice** Wholefood heaven, and Pushkar's best homemade cakes to boot. (p162)

○ **Handi Restaurant** Top-notch but down-to-earth vegetarian restaurant in Jaipur. (p155)

Forts

○ **Jaisalmer** Mirage-like sandstone fortress rising up from the Thar Desert. (p182)

○ **Mehrangarh** Mighty rock fort overlooking Jodhpur's 'Blue City'. (p176)

○ **Amber** Magnificent fort in a village outside Jaipur. (p149)

○ **Ranthambhore** Jungle fort secreted away inside a tiger-inhabited national park. (p163)

○ **Kumbhalgarh** Vast yet remote; in the Aravali Hills beyond Udaipur. (p165)

Need to Know

Adventures

○ **Ranthambhore National Park** The best place to spot tigers in the wild. (p163)

○ **Jaisalmer** Camel safaris in the desert. (p186)

○ **Amber Fort** Take a balloon ride over Jaipur's famous citadel. (p153)

○ **Udaipur** Head to Krishna Ranch for countryside horse treks. (p165)

○ **Jodhpur** Enjoy high-adrenaline views on Mehrangarh fort's flying fox zip-line. (p175)

ADVANCE PLANNING

○ **Two months before** Book any particularly special palace hotels, especially if you're travelling in the high season (October to March).

○ **One week before** Book train tickets for longer journeys.

○ **One day before** Call your hotel to confirm your booking.

RESOURCES

○ **Festivals of India** (www.festivalsofindia.in) All about Indian festivals.

○ **Incredible India** (www.incredibleindia.org) Official India tourism site.

○ **Rajasthan Tourism** (www.rajasthantourism.gov.in) Rajasthan government tourism site.

○ **Lonely Planet** (www.lonelyplanet.com/india/rajasthan) Destination information, accommodation reviews and travellers' forum.

GETTING AROUND

○ **Car & driver** Between ₹8 and ₹12 per kilometre, with a minimum of 250km per day and ₹150 extra for overnight stays. Note, you'll have to pay for the driver's return trip even if you only travel one way.

○ **Train** Jaipur, Sawai Madohpur (for Ranthambhore), Jaipur, Udaipur, Jodhpur and Jaisalmer are all served by rail. Pushkar's nearest rail hub is Ajmer, 30 minutes' drive away.

○ **Bus** All destinations are served by bus; AC Volvo buses tend to be the most comfortable.

BE FOREWARNED

○ **Gem scams** Don't get smooth-talked into buying gems with an eye to making a profit.

○ **Camel safaris** Ask other travellers for recommendations of the best operators.

○ **Hotel touts** Prepare to be besieged in Jaipur and Jodhpur. Prearrange hotel pick-up if possible.

ft: Traditional dancers inside Mehrangarh (p176)
Above: Amber Fort (p149)
(LEFT) AMAR GROVER/GETTY IMAGES ©;
(ABOVE) TIM MAKINS/GETTY IMAGES ©

Rajasthan Itineraries

The first of these itineraries covers the eastern highlights of Rajasthan, while the second takes in several of the most spectacular desert cities of the western part of the region. For a longer stay you could combine the two journeys.

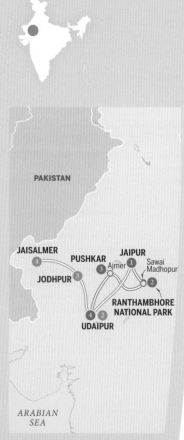

5 DAYS

JAIPUR TO UDAIPUR
EASTERN PROMISE

Start your trip in the pink city of **① Jaipur**, visiting its colourful bazaars, City Palace, Amber Fort and Hawa Mahal. Next, take a train from here to Sawai Madhopur, the nearest station to **② Ranthambhore National Park** (p163), to explore the lush jungle landscape of the park with its myriad wildlife, see its ancient, overgrown fort, and go tiger spotting.

Returning from Sawai Madhopur, take the train to Ajmer, from where it's a short hop by taxi or bus to the magical small town of **③ Pushkar** (p159). Spend a day chilling out in this beguilingly pretty pilgrim and traveller centre, lazing in rooftop cafes and seeing the sun set behind its holy lake.

You can either hire a taxi for the next leg of the journey, or return to Ajmer to travel to **④ Udaipur** (p165) by train. The milk-white city, built across several lakes, is the ideal place to end your journey on a high, exploring its impressive City Palace and spending your last day boating on beautiful Lake Pichola, before taking the train back to Jaipur or flying to Delhi or Mumbai (Bombay).

Above: City Palace (p149), Jaipur
Top Right: Backstreet, Jodhpur (p175)
(TOP LEFT) GETTY IMAGES ©; (TOP RIGHT) INDIA PHOTOGRAPHY/GETTY IMAGES ©

1 WEEK

JAIPUR TO JAISALMER
WESTERN DESERT

Again start your trip in the Rajasthani capital, **❶ Jaipur** (p148), visiting the sights of the Pink City, including the City Palace and Amber Fort, and seeing a blockbuster Bollywood film at the sumptuous, meringue-like Rajmandir Cinema. Next, make your way via train or taxi to the laid-back town of **❷ Udaipur** (p165) to visit its City Palace, indulge in some lakeside lazing, and take boats across Lake Pichola against a backdrop of misty blue hills.

The easiest and quickest way to reach **❸ Jodhpur** (p175) from Udaipur is to hire a taxi. Known as the Blue City, Jodhpur features an amazing impressionistic cityscape overlooked by the magnificent fortifications of Mehrangarh. Spend your time here visiting the fort itself, for wonderful views over the city, and don't miss the old city's glittering bazaars. Make sure you book ahead for the overnight train to (and back from) the desert city of **❹ Jaisalmer** (p182), where you can explore the golden sandstone fort, see its beautifully carved *havelis* and Jain temples, and take an overnight trip into the desert on camelback, spending the night under a firmament of stars.

Discover Rajasthan

At a Glance

○ **Jaipur** The dusty 'Pink City' capital of Rajasthan.

○ **Pushkar** (p159) Temple town, a magnet for pilgrims and travellers.

○ **Ranthambhore National Park** (p163) Rajasthan's No 1 tiger park.

○ **Udaipur** (p165) Romantic, pale, palace-dotted lake city.

○ **Jodhpur** (p175) The 'Blue City' dominated by its magnificent fort.

○ **Jaisalmer** (p182) Golden sandstone desert fortress.

EASTERN RAJASTHAN

Jaipur

☑0141 / POP 3 MILLION

Jaipur, Rajasthan's capital, is an enthralling historical city and the gateway to India's most flamboyant state.

The city's colourful, chaotic streets ebb and flow with a heady brew of old and new. Careering buses dodge dawdling camels, leisurely cycle-rickshaws frustrate swarms of motorbikes, and everywhere buzzing autorickshaws watch for easy prey. In the midst of this mayhem, the splendours of Jaipur's majestic past are islands of relative calm evoking a different pace and another world. At the city's heart, the City Palace continues to house the former royal family, while the Jantar Mantar (the royal observatory) maintains a heavenly aspect, and the honeycomb Hawa Mahal gazes on the bazaar below. And just out of sight, in the arid hill country surrounding the city, is the fairy-tale grandeur of Amber Fort, Jaipur's star attraction.

 Sights

Consider buying a composite ticket (Indian/foreigner/foreign student ₹50/300/150), which gives you entry to Amber Fort, Central Museum, Jantar Mantar, Hawa Mahal and Narhargarh, and is valid for two days from the time of purchase.

OLD CITY (PINK CITY)

The 18th-century Old City (known as the Pink City by some) is partially encircled by a crenellated wall punctuated at intervals

Amber Fort garden
ERICK TSENG (VISIGLOW.COM) / GETTY IMAGES ©

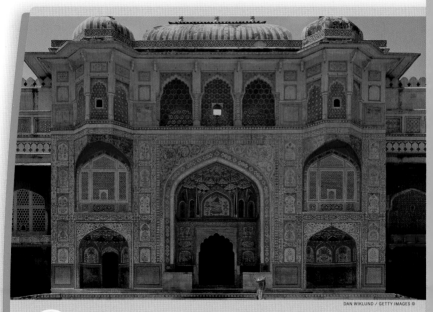

DAN WIKLUND / GETTY IMAGES ©

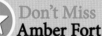

Don't Miss
Amber Fort

The magnificent, honey-hued 17th-century **Amber Fort** (Indian/foreigner ₹25/200, guide ₹200, audio guide Hindi/other ₹100/150; ⊙8am-6pm, last entry 5.30pm), an ethereal example of Rajput architecture, rises from a rocky mountainside about 11km northeast of Jaipur, and is the city's must-see sight.

It is made up largely of a royal palace, built from pale-yellow and pink sandstone and white marble, and divided into four main sections, each with its own courtyard.

You can trudge up to the fort from the road in about 10 minutes. Cold drinks are available at the top. The ticket office is also here. You can ride up to the entrance on an elephant (₹900 one way for two people), but animal rights groups have recently started to criticise the allegedly poor treatment of the elephants in their stables.

Hiring a guide (₹200) at the ticket office, or grabbing an audio guide (₹150) is highly recommended as there are very few signs and many blind alleys.

There are frequent buses (non-AC/AC ₹10/20, 15 minutes) to Amber from near the Hawa Mahal in Jaipur city centre. They drop you opposite where you start your climb up to the entrance of Amber Fort. The elephant rides start 100m further down the hill from the bus drop-off. An autorickshaw/taxi will cost at least ₹200/600 for the return trip from Jaipur city centre. RTDC city tours (p151) include Amber Fort.

by grand gateways. The major gates are Chandpol (*pol* means 'gate'), Ajmeri Gate and Sanganeri Gate.

City Palace   Palace
(Indian/foreigner incl camera ₹100/400, video ₹200, audio guide free, human guide from ₹300,

Royal Grandeur tour ₹2500; ⊙9.30am-5pm)
A complex of courtyards, gardens and buildings, the impressive City Palace is right in the centre of the Old City. The outer wall was built by Jai Singh, but within it the palace has been enlarged and adapted over the centuries. There

149

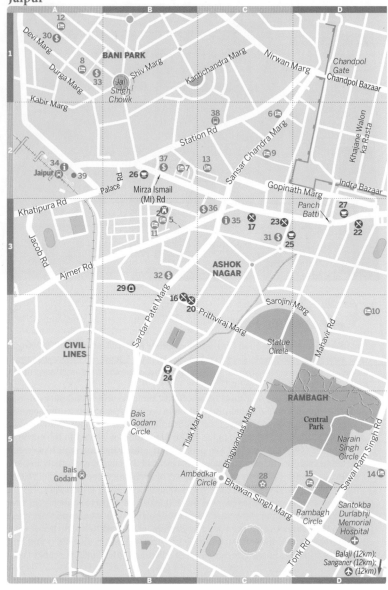

are palace buildings from different eras, some dating from the early 20th century. Despite the gradual development, the whole is a striking blend of Rajasthani and Mughal architecture.

Jantar Mantar Historic Site
(Indian/foreigner ₹40/200, audio guide ₹150, human guide ₹200; ⏰9am-4.30pm) Adjacent to the City Palace is Jantar Mantar, an observatory begun by Jai Singh in 1728

that resembles a collection of giant bizarre sculptures. Built for measuring the heavens, the name is derived from the Sanskrit *yanta mantr,* meaning 'instrument of calculation', and in 2010 it was added to India's list of Unesco World Heritage Sites. Paying for a local guide is highly recommended if you wish to learn how each fascinating instrument works.

Hawa Mahal Historic Building

(Johari Bazaar; Indian/foreigner incl camera ₹10/50, audio guide Hindi/English ₹80/110, human guide ₹200; ⏰9am-5pm) Jaipur's most distinctive landmark, the Hawa Mahal is an extraordinary, fairy-tale, pink sandstone, delicately honeycombed hive that rises a dizzying five storeys. It was constructed in 1799 by Maharaja Sawai Pratap Singh to enable ladies of the royal household to watch the life and processions of the city. The top offers stunning views over Jantar Mantar and the City Palace one way, and over Siredeori Bazaar the other.

Tours

RTDC Sightseeing Tour

(📞2200778; tours@rtdc.in; RTDC Tourist Office, Platform 1, Jaipur Train Station; half-/full-day tour ₹300/350; ⏰8am-6.30pm Mon-Sat) Full-day tours (9am to 6pm) take in all the major sights of Jaipur (including Amber Fort), with a lunch break at Nahargarh. The lunch break can be as late as 3pm, so have a big breakfast. Rushed half-day tours still squeeze in Amber (8am to 1pm, 11.30am to 4.30pm and 1.30pm to 6.30pm) – some travellers recommend these, as you avoid the long lunch break. The tour price doesn't include admission charges.

Cyclin' Jaipur Cycling Tour

(📞28060965; www.cyclinjaipur.com; 4hr tour ₹1800; ⏰tour 6.30am) Get up early to beat the traffic for a tour of the Pink City by bike, exploring the hidden lanes, temples, markets and food stalls of Jaipur. It's a unique and fun way to learn about the workings and culture of the city. Breakfast and refreshments during the tour are included, and helmets are provided on demand. Tours start at Karnot Mahal, on Ramganj Chaupar in the Old City.

Jaipur

◎ Sights
1 City Palace.................................F1
2 Hathroi Fort..............................B3
3 Hawa Mahal.............................F2
4 Jantar Mantar..........................F1

◎ Activities, Courses & Tours
RTDC .... (see 34)

◎ Sleeping
5 All Seasons Homestay B3
6 Alsisar Haveli............................C2
7 Atithi Guest House.....................B2
8 Hotel Anuraag Villa....................A1
9 Hotel Arya Niwas C2
10 Hotel Diggi Palace.....................D4
11 Hotel Pearl Palace B3
12 Jas Vilas A1
13 Karni Niwas..............................C2
14 Narain Niwas Palace Hotel D5
15 Rambagh Palace........................D5

◎ Eating
16 Anokhi Café B4
17 Copper Chimney........................C3
18 Ganesh Restaurant.....................E3
Handi Restaurant........................(see 17)
19 Indian Coffee House....................F3
20 Little Italy B4
21 LMB..F2
22 Niro's D3

23 Old Takeaway The Kebab Shop C3
Peacock Rooftop Restaurant .... (see 11)

◎ Drinking & Nightlife
24 100% Rock...............................B4
25 Brewberry's..............................C3
26 Café Coffee Day.........................B2
27 Lassiwala.................................D3

◎ Entertainment
28 Polo Ground.............................C5

◎ Shopping
29 Mojari B3

◎ Information
30 HDFC ATM.................................A1
31 HDFC Bank................................C3
32 HSBC ATM.................................B3
33 IDBI ATM..................................A1
RTDC Tourist Office....................(see 38)
34 RTDC Tourist Office....................A2
35 RTDC Tourist Office Main branch........C3
36 State Bank of India ATM.............C3
37 Thomas Cook............................B2

◎ Transport
38 Main Bus Stand..........................C2
Reservation Office.....................(see 38)
39 Reservation Office......................A2

Sleeping

AROUND MIRZA ISMAIL (MI) ROAD

Hotel Pearl Palace   Hotel $
(☎2373700, 9414066311; www.hotelpearlpalace.
com; Hathroi Fort, Hari Kishan Somani Marg; dm
₹200, r ₹400-1400; ❄@ 🛜) The delightful
Pearl Palace continues to raise the bar for
budget digs. There's a range of rooms to
choose from – small, large, shared bathroom, private bathroom, some with balconies, some with AC or fan cooling, and all
are spotless. Services include free pick-up,
moneychanging and travel arrangements,
and the hotel boasts the excellent Peacock
Rooftop Restaurant (p155). Advance booking is highly recommended.

Karni Niwas   Guesthouse $$
(☎2365433; www.hotelkarniniwas.com; C5, Mo-
tilal Atal Marg; r ₹1000, with AC ₹1500; ❄@ 🛜)
This friendly hotel has clean, cool and
comfortable rooms, often with balconies.
There's no restaurant, but there are
relaxing plant-decked terraces to enjoy
room service on. And being so central,
restaurants aren't far away. The owner
shuns commissions for rickshaw drivers;
free pick-up from the train or bus station
is available.

Atithi Guest House   Guesthouse $$
(☎2378679; www.atithijaipur.com; 1 Park House
Scheme Rd; s/d ₹1000/1400; ❄@ 🛜) This
nicely presented modern guesthouse,
well situated between MI and Station Rds,
offers strikingly clean, simple rooms dotted around a quiet courtyard. It's central
but peaceful, and the service is friendly
and helpful. Meals are available (the thali
is particularly recommended) and you
can have a drink on the very pleasant
rooftop terrace.

Hotel Arya Niwas   Hotel $$
(☎4073456; www.aryaniwas.com; Sansar
Chandra Marg; r from ₹1200, s/d with AC from
₹1500/1650; ❄@ 🛜) Just off Sansar

Chandra Marg, behind a high-rise tower, this very popular travellers' haunt has a travel desk, bookshop and yoga lessons. For a hotel of 92 rooms it is very well run, though its size means it's not as personal as smaller guesthouses. The spotless rooms vary in layout and size so check out a few.

All Seasons Homestay
Homestay $$

(9460387055; www.allseasonshomestay jaipur.com; 63 Hathroi Fort; s ₹1300-1900, d ₹1400-2000;) Ranjana and her husband Dinesh run this welcoming homestay in their lovely bungalow on a quiet back street behind deserted Hathroi Fort. There are only four guestrooms but each is lovingly cared for and two have small kitchens. There's a pleasant lawn and home-cooked meals. Advance booking is recommended.

Alsisar Haveli
Heritage Hotel $$$

(2368290; www.alsisar.com; Sansar Chandra Marg; r from ₹7700;) A genuine heritage hotel that has emerged from a gracious 19th-century mansion. Alsisar Haveli is set in beautiful green gardens, and boasts a lovely swimming pool and grand dining room. Its bedrooms don't disappoint either, with elegant Rajput arches and antique furnishings. This is a winning choice, though a little impersonal, perhaps because it hosts many tour groups.

BANI PARK

Upmarket Bani Park is a relatively peaceful area (away from the main roads, at least), about 2km west of the Old City (₹50 in a cycle-rickshaw).

Hotel Anuraag Villa
Hotel $$

(2201679; www.anuraagvilla.com; D249 Devi Marg; r ₹790-990, with AC ₹1650-2050;) This quiet and comfortable option has no-fuss, spacious rooms and an extensive lawn where you can find some quiet respite from the hassles of sightseeing. It has a recommended restaurant with its kitchen on view, and efficient, helpful staff.

Jas Vilas
Guesthouse $$$

(2204638; www.jasvilas.com; C9 Sawai Jai Singh Hwy; s/d ₹4440/5080;) This small but impressive hotel was built in 1950 and is still run by the same charming family. It offers 11 spacious rooms, most of which face the large sparkling pool set in a romantic courtyard. Three garden-facing rooms are wheelchair accessible. In addition to the relaxing courtyard and lawn, there is a cosy dining room and helpful management.

RAMBAGH ENVIRONS

Hotel Diggi Palace
Heritage Hotel $$

(2373091; www.hoteldiggipalace.com; off Sawai Ram Singh Rd; s/d incl breakfast from ₹4000/5000;) About 1km south of Ajmer Gate, this former splendid residence of the *thakur* (nobleman) of Diggi is surrounded by vast shaded lawns. Once a budget hotel, the more expensive rooms

Hot-Air Ballooning

For something a little bit special, consider treating yourself to a sunrise balloon ride above Amber Fort with India's leading hot-air balloon company, **Sky Waltz** (9717295801; www.skywaltz.com; adult/ child US$250/150). Run by Aussie expat Paul Macpherson, and with a team of highly experienced foreign pilots, Sky Waltz offers spectacular early-morning balloon flights over the fort and surrounding countryside.

The package includes pick-up from your hotel in Jaipur (at around 6am), tea, coffee and cookies, watching the balloon inflation, the flight itself and drop-off at your hotel afterwards. The whole thing lasts around three hours, including the one-hour flight.

Balloon-flight season is from September to March.

are substantially better than the cheaper options. There's free pick-up from the bus and train stations.

Management prides itself on using organic produce from the hotel's own gardens and farms in the restaurant.

Narain Niwas Palace Hotel
Heritage Hotel **$$$**

(☏2561291; www.hotelnarainniwas.com; Narain Singh Rd; s/d incl breakfast from ₹5610/7670; ❄@ 🛜 ☲) In Kanota Bagh, just south of the city, this genuine heritage hotel has wonderful ramshackle splendour. There's a lavish dining room with liveried staff, an old-fashioned verandah on which to drink tea, and antiques galore. The high-ceilinged rooms vary in atmosphere and the bathrooms also vary greatly – inspect before committing.

Rambagh Palace
Heritage Hotel **$$$**

(☏2211919; www.tajhotels.com; Bhawan Singh Marg; r from ₹38,500; ❄@ 🛜 ☲) This splen-

did palace was once the Jaipur pad of Maharaja Man Singh II and, until recently, his glamorous wife Gayatri Devi. Veiled in 19 hectares of gardens, the hotel – now run by the luxury Taj Group brand – has fantastic views across the immaculate lawns. More expensive rooms are naturally the most sumptuous.

AMBER FORT AREA

Mosaics Guesthouse
Guesthouse **$$**

(☏8875430000, 2530031; www.mosaicsguest house.com; Siyaram Ki Doongri, Amber; s/d incl breakfast ₹3200/3500; ❄@ 🛜) Get away from it all at this gorgeous arty place (the French owner is a mosaic artist and will show off his workshop) with four lovely rooms and a rooftop terrace with beautiful fort views. Set-price Franco-Indian meals cost ₹500. It's about 1km past the fort near Kunda Village – head for Siyaram Ki Doongri, where you'll find signs.

Left: Amber Fort (p149); **Below:** Rambagh Palace
(LEFT) PIERRE TURTAUT / GETTY IMAGES ©; (BELOW) ALTRENDO TRAVEL / GETTY IMAGES ©

Eating

AROUND MIRZA ISMAIL (MI) ROAD

Indian Coffee House Cafe **$**
(MI Rd; coffee ₹11-15, snacks from ₹40; ⏰8am-9.30pm) Set back from the street, down an easily missed alley, this traditional coffee house (a venerable co-op–owned institution) offers a very pleasant cup of filtered coffee in very relaxed surroundings. Aficionados of Indian Coffee Houses will not be disappointed by the fan-cooled ambience. Inexpensive samosas, *pakoras* (deep-fried battered vegetables) and dosas grace the snack menu.

**Old Takeaway
The Kebab Shop** Kebabs **$**
(151 MI Rd; kebabs ₹90-180; ⏰6-11pm) One of a few similarly named roadside kebab shops on this stretch of MI Road, this one (next to the mosque) is the original (so we're told) and the best (we agree). It knocks up outstanding tandoori kebabs, including *paneer* shish, mutton shish and tandoori chicken. Like the sign says: 'a house of delicious nonveg corner'.

**Peacock Rooftop
Restaurant** Multicuisine **$$**
(☎2373700; Hotel Pearl Palace, Hari Kishan Somani Marg; mains ₹80-260; ⏰7am-11pm) This multilevel rooftop restaurant at the Hotel Pearl Palace gets rave reviews for its excellent, inexpensive cuisine (Indian, Chinese and Continental) and relaxed ambience. The mouth-watering food, attentive service, whimsical furnishings and romantic view towards Hathroi Fort make it a first-rate restaurant. There are great-value thalis, and alcohol is served.

Handi Restaurant North Indian **$$**
(MI Rd; mains ₹140-300; ⏰noon-3.30pm & 6-11pm) Handi has been satisfying customers for years, with scrumptious tandoori and barbecued dishes and rich Mughlai curries. In the evenings it sets up a smoky

155

kebab stall at the entrance to the restaurant. Good vegetarian items are also available. No beer.

It's opposite the main post office, tucked at the back of the Maya Mansions.

Copper Chimney
Indian $$

(2372275; Maya Mansions, MI Rd; mains ₹150-400; noon-3.30pm & 6.30-11pm) Copper Chimney is casual, almost elegant and definitely welcoming, with the requisite waiter army and a fridge of cold beer. It offers excellent veg and nonveg Indian cuisine, including aromatic Rajasthani specials. Continental and Chinese food is also on offer, as is a small selection of Indian wine, but the curry-and-beer combos are hard to beat.

Anokhi Café
Organic $$

(2nd fl, KK Square, C-11, Prithviraj Marg; mains from ₹230; 10am-7.30pm;) A relaxing cafe with a quietly fashionable coffee-shop vibe about it, Anokhi is the perfect place to come if you're craving a crunchy, well-dressed salad, quiche or thickly filled sandwich – or just a respite from the hustle with a latte or an iced tea. The delicious organic loaves are made to order and can be purchased separately.

Niro's
Indian $$$

(2374493; MI Rd; mains ₹200-500; 10am-11pm) Established in 1949, Niro's is a long-standing favourite on MI Rd that continues to shine. Escape the chaos of the street by ducking into its cool, clean, mirror-ceiling sanctum to savour veg and nonveg Indian cuisine. Classic Chinese and Continental food are available but the Indian menu is definitely the pick. Alcohol served.

Little Italy
Italian $$$

(4022444; 3rd fl, KK Sq, Prithviraj Marg; mains ₹300-500; noon-11pm) Easily the best Italian restaurant in town, Little Italy is part of a small national chain that offers excellent vegetarian pasta, risotto and wood-fired pizzas in cool, contemporary surroundings. The menu is extensive and includes some Mexican items and first-rate Italian desserts. There's a lounge bar attached so you can accompany your vegetarian dining with wine or beer.

OLD CITY (PINK CITY)

Ganesh Restaurant
Vegetarian $

(Nehru Bazaar; mains ₹60-120; 9am-11.30pm) This pocket-sized outdoor restaurant is in a fantastic location on the top of the Old City wall near New Gate. The cook is in a pit on one side of the wall, so you can check out your pure vegetarian food being cooked. If you're looking for a local eatery with fresh tasty food such as paneer butter masala, you'll love it.

There's an easy-to-miss signpost, but no doubt a stallholder will show you the narrow stairway.

LMB
Vegetarian $$

(2560845; Johari Bazaar; mains ₹180-340; 8am-11pm) Laxmi Misthan Bhandar, LMB to you and me, is a sattvik (pure vegetarian) restaurant in the Old City that's been going strong since 1954. A welcoming AC refuge from frenzied Johari Bazaar, LMB is also an institution with its singular decor, attentive waiters and extensive sweet counter.

Drinking & Entertainment

Lassiwala
Cafe

(MI Rd; lassi small/jumbo ₹18/36; 7.30am till sold out) This famous, much-imitated institution is a simple place that whips up fabulous, creamy lassis in clay cups. Get here early to avoid disappointment! Will the real Lassiwala please stand up? It's the one that says 'Shop 312' and 'Since 1944', directly next to the alleyway. Imitators spread to the right as you face it.

100% Rock
Bar

(Hotel Shikha, Yudhishthir Marg, C-Scheme; beer from ₹160; 10am-11.30pm) Attached to, but separate from Hotel Shikha, this is the closest thing there is to a beer garden in Jaipur, with plenty of outdoor seating as well as AC-cooled side rooms and a clubby main room with a small dance floor. Two-for-one beer offers are common, making this popular with local youngsters.

Brewberry's
Cafe

(G-2, Fortune Heights; coffee from ₹40; 🕐8am-midnight; 📶) Modern wi-fi-enabled cafe with fresh coffee and a good mix of Indian and Continental food and snacks. Has some patio seating. It's located opposite HDFC Bank.

Café Coffee Day
Cafe

(Country Inn Hotel, MI Rd; coffee ₹60-90; 🕐10am-10pm) The franchise that successfully delivers espresso to coffee addicts, as well as the occasional iced concoction and muffin, has several branches in Jaipur. In addition to this one, sniff out the brews at Paris Point on Sawai Jai Singh Hwy (aka Collectorate Rd), and near the exit point at Amber Fort.

Polo Ground
Sports

(🖉ticket info 2385380; Ambedkar Circle, Bhawan Singh Marg) Maharaja Man Singh II indulged his passion for polo by building an enormous polo ground next to Rambagh Palace, which is still a polo-match hub today. A ticket to a match also gets you into the lounge, which is adorned with historic photos and memorabilia. The polo season extends over winter, with the most important matches played during January and March. Contact the Rajasthan Polo Club (rajasthanpoloclub.co.in) for info about tickets.

🔒 Shopping

Jaipur is a shopper's paradise. Commercial buyers come here from all over the world to stock up on the amazing range of jewellery, gems, artefacts and crafts that come from all over Rajasthan. You'll have to bargain hard though, as shops have seen too many cash-rich, time-poor tourists.

The Old City is still loosely divided into traditional artisans quarters:

Bapu Bazaar is lined with saris and fabrics, and is a good place to buy trinkets. **Johari Bazaar** is where many jewellery shops are concentrated, selling gold, silver and highly glazed enamelwork known as *meenakari*, a Jaipur speciality.

Kishanpol Bazaar is famous for textiles, particularly *bandhani* (tie-dye). **Nehru Bazaar** also sells fabric, as well as jootis, trinkets and perfume. MI Rd is another good place to buy jootis. The best place for bangles is the Old City alleyway called **Maniharon ka Rasta**.

Mojari
Clothing

(Shiv Heera Marg; 🕐10am-6.30pm Mon-Sat) Named after the traditional decorated shoes of Rajasthan, Mojari is a UN-supported project that helps rural leatherworkers, traditionally among the poorest members of society. A wide variety of footwear is available (₹500 to ₹750), including embroidered, appliquéd and open-toed shoes, mules and sandals.

Bangle shop, Jaipur Old City
RICHARD I'ANSON / GETTY IMAGES ©

There's a particularly good choice for women, plus a small selection of hand-made leather bags and purses.

ℹ Information

Medical Services

Most hotels can arrange a doctor on-site.

Santokba Durlabhji Memorial Hospital (SDMH; ☎2566251; www.sdmh.in; Bhawan Singh Marg) Private hospital, with 24-hour emergency department, helpful staff and clear bilingual signage. Consultancy fee ₹400.

Money

There are plenty of places to change money, including numerous hotels and masses of ATMs (especially around MI Rd), most of which accept foreign cards; we've marked a selection on our map.

Thomas Cook (☎2360940; Jaipur Towers, MI Rd; ⊙9.30am-6pm) Changes cash and travellers cheques.

Tourist Information

RTDC Tourist Office (www.rajasthantourism. gov.in) Main branch (☎5155137; Room 21, former RTDC Tourist Hotel, MI Rd; ⊙9.30am-6pm Mon-Fri); Airport (☎2722647); Amber Fort (☎253026); Jaipur train station (☎2200778; Platform 1; ⊙24hr); main bus station (☎5064102; Platform 3; ⊙10am-5pm Mon-Fri) Has maps and brochures on Jaipur and Rajasthan.

ℹ Getting There & Away

Air

Air India, IndiGo and Jet Airways all fly daily between Jaipur and various other Indian cities.

Bus

Rajasthan State Road Transport Corporation (RSRTC) buses all leave from the **main bus stand (Station Rd)**, where there's a left-luggage 'cloakroom' (₹10 per bag for 24 hours), as well as a prepaid autorickshaw stand.

Deluxe buses leave from platform 3, tucked away in the right-hand corner of the bus station, and can be booked in advance from the **reservation office (**☎5116032) here.

Car

Most hotels can arrange car and driver hire. Or else go to the RTDC Tourist Office at the train station.

Pushkar

Train

The efficient **railway reservation office** (☎135; ⏰**8am-9pm Mon-Sat, to 2pm Sun**) is to your left as you enter Jaipur train station. It's open for advance reservations only (more than five hours before departure).

For same-day travel, buy your ticket at the northern end of the train station on platform 1, window 10.

Nine daily trains go to Delhi, three to Agra, four to Jodhpur and three to Udaipur. Eleven daily trains go to Ajmer (for Pushkar), while six go to Sawai Madhopur (for Ranthambore National Park). Only one daily train (11.45pm) goes to Jaisalmer.

ⓘ Getting Around

To/From the Airport

An autorickshaw/taxi costs at least ₹250/450. There's a prepaid taxi booth inside the airport.

Autorickshaw

There are prepaid autorickshaw stands at the bus and train stations. Rates are fixed by the government, which means you don't have to haggle. Keep hold of your docket, though, until you reach your destination. Your driver won't get paid without it.

In other cases you should be prepared to bargain hard. Expect to pay at least ₹80 from the train or bus station to the Old City.

Cycle-Rickshaw

Slightly cheaper than autorickshaws, but not much. Tips are appreciated – these guys work *hard*.

Taxi

There are unmetered taxis available which will require negotiating a fare, or you can try **Mericar** (☎4188888; www.mericar.in; flagfall incl 2km ₹50, afterwards per km ₹13, 25% night surcharge 10pm-5am; ⏰24hr). It's a 24-hour service and taxis can also be hired for sightseeing for four-/ six-/eight-hour blocks, costing ₹600/1000/1500.

Pushkar

☎0145 / POP 15,000

Pushkar has a magnetism all of its own, and is quite unlike anywhere else in Rajasthan. It's a prominent Hindu pilgrimage town and devout Hindus should visit at least once in their lifetime. The town curls around a holy lake, said to have appeared when Brahma dropped a lotus flower. It also has one of the world's few Brahma temples. With 52 bathing ghats and 400 milky-blue temples, the town often hums with *puja*s (prayers) generating an episodic soundtrack of chanting, drums and gongs, and devotional songs.

Major Trains from Jaipur

DESTINATION	TRAIN	DEPARTURE TIME	ARRIVAL TIME	FARE (₹)
Agra (Cantonment)	19666 Udaipur-Kurj Exp	6.15am	11am	175/485 (A)
Ahmedabad	12958 Adi Sj Rajdhani	12.25am	9.40am	1190/1635 (B)
Ajmer	Ajmer-Agra Fort Intercity	9.40am	11.50am	90/305 (C)
Delhi (New Delhi)	12016 Ajmer Shatabdi	5.50pm	10.40pm	720/1365 (D)
Delhi (S Rohilla)	12985 Dee Double Decker	6am	10.30am	480/1175 (D)
Jaisalmer	14659	11.45pm	11.15am	340/910 (A)
Jodhpur	22478 Jaipur-Jodhpur SF Exp	6am	10.30am	495/600 (E)
Sawai Madhopur	12466 Intercity Exp	11.05am	1.15pm	170/305/535 (F)
Udaipur	12965 Jaipur–Udaipur Exp	11pm	6.45am	260/690 (A)

Fares: (A) sleeper/3AC, (B) 3AC/2AC, (C) 2nd-class seat/AC chair, (D) AC chair/1AC, (E) AC chair/3AC, (F) sleeper/AC chair/3AC

JONATHAN KINGSTON / GETTY IMAGES ©

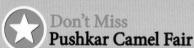

Don't Miss
Pushkar Camel Fair

Come the month of Kartika (November), the eighth lunar month of the Hindu calendar and one of the holiest, Thar camel drivers spruce up their ships of the desert and start the long walk to Pushkar in time for Kartik Purnima (Full Moon). Each year around 200,000 people converge here, bringing with them some 50,000 camels, horses and cattle. The place becomes an extraordinary swirl of colour, sound and movement, thronging with musicians, mystics, tourists, traders, animals, devotees and camera crews.

It's hard to believe, but this seething mass is all just a sideshow. Kartik Purnima is when Hindu pilgrims come to bathe in Pushkar's sacred waters. The religious event builds in tandem with the camel fair in a wild, magical crescendo of incense, chanting and processions to dousing day, the last night of the fair, when thousands of devotees wash away their sins and set candles afloat on the holy lake.

The result is a muddle of religious and tourist scenes. The main street is one long bazaar, selling anything to tickle a traveller's fancy, from hippie-chic tie-dye to didgeridoos. Despite the commercialism and banana pancakes, the town remains enchantingly small and authentically mystic.

Sights

Fifty-two bathing ghats surround the lake, where pilgrims bathe in the sacred waters. If you wish to join them, do so with respect. Remember, this is a holy place: remove your shoes and don't smoke, kid around or take photographs.

Some ghats have particular importance: Vishnu appeared at **Varah**

Ghat in the form of a boar, Brahma bathed at **Brahma Ghat**, and Gandhi's ashes were sprinkled at **Gandhi Ghat**, formerly Gau Ghat.

Pushkar boasts hundreds of temples, though few are particularly ancient, as they were mostly desecrated by Aurangzeb and subsequently rebuilt.

Shiva Temples
Hindu Temple

About 8km southwest of the town (past the turn-off to Saraswati Temple) is a collection of Shiva temples near Ajaypal, which make a great trip by motorbike (or bike if you're fit and start early in the day), through barren hills and quiet villages. Be warned: the track is hilly and rocky.

Another Shiva temple is about 8km north of Pushkar, tucked down inside a cave, which would make for a good excursion.

Activities

Nonguests can use the pool at **Hotel Navaratan Palace** (2772145; www.pushkarnavaratanpalace.co.in) for ₹100.

Camel Rides

Plenty of people in Pushkar offer short **camel rides** (per hr around ₹200), which are a good way to explore the starkly beautiful landscape – a mixture of desert and the rocky hills – around town. Sunset rides are most popular. It's best to ask at your hotel. Inn Seventh Heaven is reliable.

Shannu's Riding School
Horse Riding

(2772043; www.shannus.weebly.com; Panch Kund Marg; ride/lesson per hr ₹400) French-Canadian and long-time Pushkar resident Marc Dansereau can organise riding lessons and horse safaris on his graceful Marwari steeds. You can stay here too (single/double/suite ₹1000/1500/2000). The ranch is on the southeastern fringes of Pushkar, off the Ajmer Road.

Young Rajasthani women in festival attire

RICHARD I'ANSON / GETTY IMAGES ©

🛏 Sleeping

Shyam Krishna Guesthouse
Guesthouse $

(☎2772461; skguesthouse@yahoo.com; Sadar Bazaar; s/d ₹500/600, without bathroom ₹300/500; 🛜) Housed in a lovely old blue-washed building with lawns and gardens, this guesthouse has ashram austerity and genuinely friendly management. Some of the cheaper rooms are cell-like, though all share the simple, authentic ambience. The outdoor kitchen and garden seating are a good setting for a relaxing meal of hearty vegetarian fare, but watch out for passing troops of monkeys.

Hotel White House
Guesthouse $

(☎2772147; www.pushkarwhitehouse.com; off Heloj Rd; r ₹250-850, with AC ₹1000-1300; ❄@) This place is indeed white, with spotless rooms. Some are decidedly on the small side, but the nicest are generous and have balconies to boot. There is good traveller fare and green views from the plant-filled rooftop restaurant. It's efficiently run by a tenacious businesslike mother-and-son team. Yoga is offered.

Inn Seventh Heaven
Heritage Hotel $$

(☎5105455; www.inn-seventh-heaven.com; Chotti Basti; r ₹1100-3000; ❄@🛜) You enter this lovingly converted *haveli* through heavy wooden doors into an incense-perfumed courtyard, centred with a marble fountain and surrounded by tumbling vines. There are just a dozen individually decorated rooms situated on three levels, all with traditionally crafted furniture and comfortable beds. Rooms vary in size, from the downstairs budget rooms to the spacious Asana suite.

Hotel Pushkar Palace
Heritage Hotel $$$

(☎2772001; www.hotelpushkarpalace.com; r incl breakfast ₹7000; ❄@) Once belonging to the maharaja of Kishangarh, the top-end Hotel Pushkar Palace boasts a romantic lakeside setting. The rooms have carved wooden furniture and beds, and the suites look directly out onto the lake: no hotel in Pushkar has better views. A pleasant outdoor dining area overlooks the lake.

🍴 Eating

Honey & Spice
Multicuisine $$

(Laxmi Market, off Sadar Bazaar; mains ₹90-340; ⏰7.30am-6.45pm) 🍽 Run by a friendly family, this tiny wholefood breakfast and lunch place has delicious South Indian coffee and home-made cakes. Even better are the salads and hearty vegetable stews served with brown rice; delicious, wholesome and a welcome change from frequently oil-rich Indian food.

Festival dancers, Rajasthan
RICHARD I'ANSON / GETTY IMAGES ©

Sunset Café Multicuisine $$
(mains ₹75-200; ⏱7.30am-midnight; 📶)
Right on the eastern ghats, this cafe has sublime lake views. It offers the usual traveller menu, including curries, pizza and pasta, plus there's a German bakery serving reasonable cakes. The lakeside setting is perfect at sunset and gathers a crowd.

Out of the Blue Multicuisine $$
(Sadar Bazaar; mains ₹100-200; ⏱8am-11pm; 📶) Distinctly a deeper shade of blue in this sky-blue town, Out of the Blue is a reliable restaurant. The menu ranges from noodles and *momos* (Tibetan dumplings) to pizza, pasta (those *momos* occasionally masquerade as ravioli) and pancakes. A nice touch is the street-level espresso coffee bar and German bakery.

Sixth Sense Multicuisine $$
(Inn Seventh Heaven, Chotti Basti; mains ₹80-200; ⏱8.30am-4pm & 6-10pm; 📶) This chilled rooftop restaurant is a great place to head to even if you didn't score a room in its popular hotel. The pizza and Indian seasonal vegetables and rice are all serviceable, as are the filter coffee and fresh juice. Its ambience is immediately relaxing and the pulley apparatus that delivers food from the ground-floor kitchen is very cunning.

🛍 Shopping

Pushkar's Sadar Bazaar is lined with enchanting little shops and is a good place for picking up gifts. Many of the vibrant textiles come from the Barmer district south of Jaisalmer. There's plenty of silver and beaded jewellery catering to foreign tastes, and some old tribal pieces, too.

Lala International Clothing
(Sadar Bazaar; ⏱9.30am-8pm) Brilliantly colourful women's clothing, with modern designs but Indian in theme. Dresses and skirts start from around ₹500. Prices are clearly labelled and fixed.

ℹ Getting There & Away

The nearest major train station is Ajmer, 11km away. Frequent buses link Pushkar with Ajmer (₹14, 30 minutes, every 10 minutes).

A taxi to/from Ajmer train station costs ₹300 to ₹400, plus a ₹20 toll fee, which bus passengers do not have to pay.

Ranthambhore National Park
☑ 07462

This famous national park, open from 1 October to 30 June, is the best place to spot wild tigers in Rajasthan. Comprising 1334 sq km of wild jungle scrub hemmed in by rocky ridges, at its centre is the amazing 10th-century Ranthambhore Fort. Scattered around the fort are ancient temples and mosques, hunting pavilions, crocodile-filled lakes and vine-covered *chhatris* (cenotaphs).

Seeing a tiger (there were 28 at last count) is partly a matter of luck; leave time for two or three safaris to improve your chances.

It's 10km from Sawai Madhopur (the gateway town for Ranthambore) to the first gate of the park, and another 3km to the main gate and Ranthambhore Fort. There's a bunch of cheap (and rather grotty) hotels near Sawai Madhopur train station, but the nicest accommodation is stretched out along Ranthambhore Rd, which eventually leads to the park.

It's ₹50 to ₹100 for an auto from the train station to Ranthambhore Rd, depending on where you get off. Many hotels, though, will pick you up from the train station for free if you call ahead.

◎ Sights & Activities

Safaris take place in the early morning and late afternoon, starting between 6am and 7am, and between 2pm and 3pm, depending on the time of year. Each safari lasts for around three hours. The mornings can be exceptionally chilly in the open vehicles, so bring warm clothes.

The best option is to travel by **gypsy** (per safari per person ₹1500), a five-person open-topped 4WD. You still have a good chance of seeing a tiger from a **canter** (₹1200), a 20-seater open-topped truck; though sometimes other passengers can be rowdy.

Be aware that the rules for booking safaris (and prices) are prone to change. You can also book online through the park's official website (www.rajasthan wildlife.com), which we highly recommend you do, or go in person on the day of your safari to the Safari Booking Office, which is inconveniently located 3km from Ranthambhore Rd, in the opposite direction to the park. Booking with hotels is much simpler, although be aware that they add commission to the rates.

🛏 Sleeping

Hotel Tiger Safari Resort   Hotel $$

(☎221137; www.tigersafariresort.com; Ranthambhore Rd; r ₹1600-2200; ❄@🛜🏊) A reasonable budget option, with spacious doubles and so-called cottages (larger rooms with bigger bathrooms) facing a garden and small pool. The management is adept at organising safaris, wake-up calls and early breakfasts before the morning safari, although like the other hotels it throws in a chunky commission. There's an expensive restaurant attached.

Vatika Resort   Hotel $$

(☎222457; www.ranthambhorevatikaresort. com; Ranthambhore Rd; r ₹1800, incl breakfast/ all meals ₹2250/3000; ❄@🛜) A lovely little guesthouse with simple but immaculate rooms, each with terrace seating overlooking a beautifully tended, flower-filled garden. It's about 1km beyond the main strip of accommodation on Ranthambhore Rd (although still 5km before the park's main gate) so much quieter than elsewhere. It's 3km from Hammir Circle.

Hotel Ankur Resort   Hotel $$

(☎220792; www.hotelankurresort.com; r incl breakfast ₹2000, cottage ₹2500; ❄@🛜) Ankur Resort is good at organising safaris, wake-up calls and early breakfasts for

Bengal tigers, Ranthambhore National Park (p163)

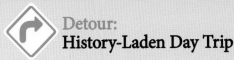

Detour:
History-Laden Day Trip

If you like fantastic forts or exquisite temples, then consider hiring a taxi for the day from Udaipur to visit the huge, remote fort of Kumbhalgarh and the sublime Jain temples at Ranakpur. It will cost you around ₹1800 per vehicle for the return trip. The drive through the forested Aravalli Hills is a highlight in itself.

An incredible stone fort, **Kumbhalgarh** (Indian/foreigner ₹5/100, Light & Sound Show ₹200; ⏲9am-6pm, Light & Sound Show 6.30pm) is situated 84km north of Udaipur. Built by Maharana Kumba in the 15th century, the colossal structure fulfills romantic expectations of Rajput grandeur. The fort's thick walls stretch for around 12km and it's possible to walk along them to complete a circuit of the fort (allow four to five hours). The walls enclose hundreds of temples (some intact, others in ruins), some of which date back to the 2nd-century BC, plus palaces, gardens, step-wells and cannon bunkers.

Ninety kilometres north of Udaipur, the Jain Temples at **Ranakpur** (camera/video ₹100/300; ⏲Jains 6am-7pm, non-Jains noon-5pm) are an incredible feat of religious devotion. Carved from milk-white marble, the main temple contains a complicated series of 29 halls, supported by a forest of 1444 pillars (no two alike). It is the finest of its type in Rajasthan, and one the most important in India.

---

tiger spotters. Standard rooms are fairly unadorned but clean and comfortable with TVs. The cottages boast better beds, fridge and settee overlooking the surrounding gardens and pool.

❶ Getting There & Away

There are six daily trains to Jaipur (2.05am, 9.10am, 9.40am, 10.40am, 2.35pm and 7.15pm), although plenty of others run on selected days so you rarely have to wait more than an hour. The journey takes two hours. Unreserved 2nd-class seats cost ₹90; sleepers cost ₹170.

Ten trains run daily around the clock to Delhi. Journey times vary from 5½ to eight hours. Sleeper/3AC tickets cost around ₹250/635.

A daily train goes to Agra (Agra Fort station) at 11.15pm (six hours). The service is sleeper only (₹200).

Two daily trains go to Udaipur, at 3.10pm and midnight. The latter takes seven hours (four hours fewer than the afternoon service). Sleeper/3AC tickets cost around ₹350/910.

SOUTHERN RAJASTHAN

Udaipur

📞0294 / POP 451,000

Beside shimmering Lake Pichola, with the ochre and purple ridges of the wooded Aravalli Hills stretching away in every direction, Udaipur has a romantic setting unmatched in Rajasthan and arguably in all India. Fantastical palaces, temples, *havelis* and countless narrow, crooked, colourful streets add the human counterpoint to the city's natural charms. Its tag of 'the most romantic spot on the continent of India' was first applied in 1829 by Colonel James Tod, the East India Company's first Political Agent in the region. Today the romance is wearing ever so slightly thin as Udaipur strains to exploit this reputation for tourist rupees.

Take a step back from the hustle, however, and Udaipur still has its

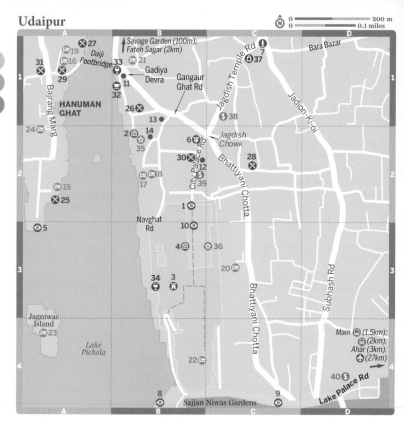

magic, not just in its marvellous palaces and monuments but in its matchless setting, the tranquillity of boat rides on the lake, the bustle of its ancient bazaars, the quaint old-world feel of its better hotels, its tempting shops and lovely surrounding countryside, which can be explored on foot, by bike or on horseback.

◉ Sights

Lake Pichola   Lake

Limpid and large, Lake Pichola reflects the cool grey-blue mountains on its rippling mirrorlike surface. It was enlarged by Maharana Udai Singh II, following his foundation of the city, by flooding Picholi village, which gave the lake its name. The lake is now 4km long and 3km wide, but remains shallow and dries up completely during severe droughts. The City Palace complex, including the gardens at its southern end, extends nearly 1km along the lake's eastern shore.

City Palace   Palace

(www.eternalmewar.in; adult/child ₹30/15, not charged if visiting City Palace Museum; ⊙7am-11pm) Surmounted by balconies, towers and cupolas towering over the lake, the imposing City Palace is Rajasthan's largest palace, with a facade 244m long and 30.4m high. Construction was begun in 1599 by Maharana Udai Singh II, the city's founder, and it later became a conglomeration of structures (including 11 separate smaller palaces) built and extended by various maharanas, though it still manages to retain a surprising uniformity of design.

Udaipur

◉ Sights
1 Badi Pol	B2
2 Bagore-ki-Haveli	B2
3 City Palace	B3
4 City Palace Museum	B3
5 Dhobi (Washing) Ghats	A3
6 Jagdish Temple	B2
7 Old Clock Tower	C1
8 Rameshwar Ghat	B4
9 Sheetla Mata Gate	C4
10 Tripolia Gate	B3

⊕ Activities, Courses & Tours
11 Art of Bicycle	B1
12 Heritage Walks	B2
Krishna Ranch	(see 20)
13 Shashi Cooking Classes	B1
14 Sushma's Cooking Classes	B2

🛏 Sleeping
15 Amet Haveli	A2
16 Dream Heaven	A1
17 Jagat Niwas Palace Hotel	B2
18 Kankarwa Haveli	B2
19 Karohi Haveli	A1
20 Kumbha Palace	C3
21 Nukkad Guest House	B1
22 Shiv Niwas Palace Hotel	B4
23 Taj Lake Palace	A4
24 Udai Kothi	A2

⊗ Eating
25 Ambrai	A2
26 Cafe Edelweiss	B1
Jagat Niwas Palace Hotel	(see 17)
27 Jasmin	A1
28 Lotus Cafe	C2
29 Millets of Mewar	A1
30 O'Zen Restaurant	B2
Paantya Restaurant	(see 22)
31 Queen Cafe	A1

☕ Drinking & Nightlife
32 Jheel's Ginger Coffee Bar	B1
Panera Bar	(see 22)
33 Paps Juice	B1
34 Sunset Terrace	B3

⊛ Entertainment
35 Dharohar	B2
36 Mewar Sound & Light Show	C3

⊟ Shopping
37 Sadhna	C1

⊙ Information
38 Axis Bank ATM	C1
39 State Bank of India ATM	B2
40 Thomas Cook	D4

City Palace Museum
Museum

(adult/child ₹115/55, camera or video ₹225, ticket plus audio guide ₹225, human guide ₹200; ⊙9.30am-5.30pm, last entry 4.30pm) The main part of the palace is open as the City Palace Museum, with rooms extravagantly decorated with mirrors, tiles and paintings, and housing a large, varied collection of artefacts. It's entered from Ganesh Chowk, which you reach from Manek Chowk.

Jagdish Temple
Hindu Temple

(⊙5.30am-2pm & 4-10pm) Reached by a steep, elephant-flanked flight of steps, 150m north of the City Palace's Badi Pol entrance, this busy Indo-Aryan temple was built by Maharana Jagat Singh in 1651. The wonderfully carved main structure enshrines a black stone image of Vishnu as Jagannath, Lord of the Universe. There's also a brass image of the Garuda (Vishnu's man-bird vehicle) in a shrine facing the main structure.

Bagore-ki-Haveli
Historic Building

(admission ₹30; ⊙10am-5pm) This gracious 18th-century *haveli*, set on the water's edge in the Gangaur Ghat area, was built by a Mewar prime minister and has since been carefully restored. There are 138 rooms set around courtyards, some arranged to evoke the period during which the house was inhabited, while others house cultural displays, including – intriguingly enough – the world's biggest turban.

🏃 Activities & Courses

Several hotels allow nonguests to use their swimming pools, including **Udai Kothi** (☎2432810; www.udaikothi.com; Hanuman Ghat; r ₹300), with the only rooftop pool in town.

Krishna Ranch
Horse Riding

(☎9828059505; www.krishnaranch.com; full-day incl lunch ₹1200) Situated in beautiful countryside near Badi village, 7km northwest of Udaipur, and run by the owners of **Kumbha Palace guesthouse** (☎9828059506, 2422702; www.hotelkumbha palace.com; 104 Bhattiyani Chotta; r ₹550-600, with AC ₹1000; ❋@🛜). Experienced owner-guide Dinesh Jain leads most trips himself, riding local Marwari horses through the surrounding hills. There are also attractive cottages (p167) at the ranch.

Art of Bicycle Trips — Cycling
(☎08769822745; www.artofbicycletrips.com; 27 Gadiya Devra, inside Chandpol; half day per person ₹1950) This well-run outfit offers a great way to get out of the city. The Lake-city Loop is a 30km half-day tour that quickly leaves Udaipur behind to have you wheeling through villages, farmland and along the shores of Fateh Sagar and Badi Lakes. Other options include a vehicle-supported trip further afield to Kumbalgarh and Ranakpur. Bikes are well maintained and all come with helmets.

Heritage Walks — Walking
(☎9414164680; www.heritageroyalrajasthan. com; City Palace Rd; per person ₹200; ⌚tours 8am & 5pm) If you want to really drill into Udaipur's history, architecture and religious sites, you could do a lot worse than joining one of the twice-daily expert-led tours from Heritage Walks, which will show you the Lal Ghat area that exists beyond the souvenir shops. Tours last two hours.

Shashi Cooking Classes — Cooking
(☎9929303511; www.shashicookingclasses. blogspot.com; Sunrise Restaurant, 18 Gangaur Ghat Rd; 4hr class ₹1500, max 4 students) Readers rave about Shashi's high-spirited classes, teaching many fundamental Indian dishes.

Sushma's Cooking Classes — Cooking
(☎7665852163; www.cookingclassesinudaipur. com; Hotel Krishna Niwas, 35 Lal Ghat; 2hr class ₹1000) A highly recommended cooking class run by the enthusiastic Sushma. Classes offer up anything from traditional Rajasthani dishes and learning how to make spice mixes, through bread-making to the all-important method of making the perfect cup of chai.

🛏 Sleeping

LAL GHAT AREA

Nukkad Guest House — Guesthouse $
(☎2411403; nukkad_raju@yahoo.com; 56 Ganesh Ghati; s/d without bathroom ₹100/200, r ₹300-500; @🛜) Nukkad has simple, fan-cooled, very clean, good-value rooms, plus a sociable, breezy, upstairs restaurant with very good Indian and international dishes. You can join afternoon cooking classes and morning yoga sessions (by

Kumbhalgarh (p165)
RBB / GETTY IMAGES ©

donation) without stepping outside the door – just don't stay out past curfew or get caught washing your clothes in your bathroom.

Jagat Niwas Palace Hotel   Heritage Hotel $$$

(2420133; www.jagatniwaspalace.com; 23-25 Lal Ghat; r ₹3250-4250, without lake view ₹1850-2950; ❄ @ 🛜) This leading top-end hotel set in two converted lakeside *havelis* takes the location cake. The lake-view rooms are charming, with carved wooden furniture, cushioned window seats and pretty prints. Rooms without a lake view are almost as comfortable and attractive, and considerably cheaper.

Kankarwa Haveli   Heritage Hotel $$$

(2411457; www.kankarwahaveli.com; 26 Lal Ghat; s/d incl breakfast ₹3200/4200, ste ₹5800; ❄ @ 🛜) This is one of Udaipur's few hotels that are genuine old *havelis* (as opposed to new buildings made to look like old *havelis,* or places that simply stick 'Haveli' on the end of their name). It's right by the lake, and the whitewashed rooms, set around a courtyard, have a lovely simplicity with splashes of colour.

HANUMAN GHAT AREA

Dream Heaven   Guesthouse $

(2431038; www.dreamheaven.co.in; Hanuman Ghat; r ₹300-1000; ❄ @ 🛜) This popular place is in a higgledy-piggledy building with clean rooms with wall hangings and paintings. Bathrooms are small-ish, though some rooms have a decent balcony and/or views. The food at the rooftop **restaurant** (dishes ₹40-110), which overlooks the lake and shows Udaipur at its best, is fresh and tasty – the perfect place to chill out on a pile of cushions.

Karohi Haveli   Heritage Hotel $$$

(2430026; www.karohihaveli.com; r ₹3500, with lake view ₹4400; ❄ @ 🛜 🏊) A beautifully renovated three-storey *haveli* with tastefully decorated rooms off a cool central marble courtyard. Quiet but welcoming, it has a rooftop restaurant, bar, garden lawn with lake views, lovely pool and wi-fi throughout. Rooms with lake views attract a premium.

Amet Haveli   Heritage Hotel $$$

(2431085; www.amethaveliudaipur.com; Hanuman Ghat; s/d ₹5400/6600; ❄ @ 🛜) A 350-year-old heritage building on the

City Palace (p166)

TOM LAU / GETTY IMAGES ©

Below: Detail of inlay work, City Palace (p166); **Right:** City Palace

(BELOW) AYAN82 / GETTY IMAGES ©; (RIGHT) ALEX TREADWAY / GETTY IMAGES ©

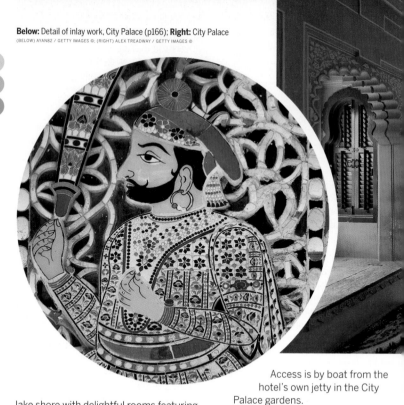

lake shore with delightful rooms featuring cushioned window seats and coloured glass with little shutters. They're set around a pretty little courtyard and pond. Splurge on one with a balcony or giant bathtub. One of Udaipur's most romantic restaurants, Ambrai (p172), is part of the hotel.

CITY PALACE AREA

Taj Lake Palace
Heritage Hotel **$$$**

(✆2428800; www.tajhotels.com; r from ₹48,000; ❄@🛜🏊) The icon of Udaipur, this romantic white-marble palace seemingly floating on the lake is extraordinary, with open-air courtyards, lotus ponds and a small, mango-tree-shaded pool. Rooms are hung with breezy silks and filled with carved furniture. Some of the cheapest overlook the lily pond rather than the lake; the mural-decked suites will make you truly feel like a maharaja.

Access is by boat from the hotel's own jetty in the City Palace gardens.

Shiv Niwas Palace Hotel
Heritage Hotel **$$$**

(✆2528016; www.eternalmewar.in; City Palace Complex; r ₹15,000-42,000; ❄@🛜🏊) This hotel, in the former palace guest quarters, has opulent common areas such as its pool courtyard, bar and lawn garden. Some of the suites are truly palatial, filled with fountains and silver, but the standard rooms are poorer value. Go for a suite, or just for a drink (p173), **meal** (mains ₹500-1000; ⏱noon-3pm & 7-10.30pm), massage or swim in the gorgeous marble pool (nonguests ₹300).

FURTHER AFIELD

Krishna Ranch
Cottages **$$**

(✆9602192902, 3291478; www.krishnaranch.com; s/d incl meals ₹2000/2500) 🌿 This delightful countryside retreat has five cottages set around the grounds of a small farm. Each comes with attached

bathroom (with solar-heated shower), tasteful decor and farm views. All meals are included and are prepared using organic produce grown on the farm. The ranch is 7km from town, near Badi village, but there's free pick-up from Udaipur.

 Eating

LAL GHAT AREA

Cafe Edelweiss   Cafe **$**

(73 Gangaur Ghat Rd; coffee from ₹50, sandwiches from ₹180; 8.30am-8pm; 🛜) The Savage Garden restaurant folks run this itsy piece of Europe that appeals to homesick and discerning travellers with superb baked goods and good coffee. Offerings included sticky cinnamon rolls, squidgy blueberry chocolate cake, spinach-and-mushroom quiche or apple strudel, good muesli or eggs for breakfast, and great sandwiches (the unexpected appearance of ham and bacon feels deliciously transgressive).

Jagat Niwas Palace Hotel   Indian **$$**

(☑2420133; 23-25 Lal Ghat; mains ₹150-375; 7am-10am, noon-3pm & 6-10pm) A wonderful, classy, rooftop restaurant with superb lake views, delicious Indian cuisine and good service. Choose from an extensive selection of rich curries (tempered for Western tastes) — mutton, chicken, fish, veg — as well as the tandoori classics. There's a tempting cocktail menu and the beer is icy. Book ahead for dinner.

Lotus Cafe   Multicuisine **$**

(15 Bhattiyani Chotta; dishes ₹50-210; 9am-10.30pm) This funky little restaurant serves up fabulous chicken dishes (predominantly Indian), plus salads, baked potatoes and plenty of vegetarian fare. It's ideal for meeting and greeting other travellers, with a mezzanine to loll about on and cool background sounds.

O'Zen Restaurant   Multicuisine **$$**

(City Palace Rd; coffee ₹50-70, mains ₹100-300; 8.30am-11pm; 🛜) A swish location

171

on City Palace Rd, this stylish 1st-floor restaurant-cafe does a range of Indian curries plus Italian pizza and pasta. It's bright and modern, does good coffee and beer (₹180), and has views of the street below.

Savage Garden
Mediterranean **$$$**

(🖉2425440; 22 inside Chandpol; mains ₹220-520; ⊙11am-11pm) Tucked away in the backstreets near Chandpol, Savage Garden does a winning line in soups, chicken and homemade pasta dishes. We loved the ravioli with lamb ragu, and the sweet-savoury stuffed chicken breast with nuts, cheese and carrot rice. The setting is a 250-year-old *haveli* with indigo walls and bowls of flowers, and tables in alcoves or a pleasant courtyard.

The bar is slick, with red, white and sparkling Indian wines from Nasik, Maharashtra.

HANUMAN GHAT AREA

Millets of Mewar
Indian **$**

(www.milletsofmewar.com; Hanuman Ghat; mains ₹80-140; ⊙8.30am-10.30pm; 🕾) 🥢 This place does the healthiest food in town. Local millets are used where possible instead of less environmentally sound wheat and rice. There are vegan options, gluten-free dishes, fresh salads and juices and herbal teas. Also on the menu are multigrain sandwiches and millet pizzas, plus regular curries, Indian street food snacks, pasta and even pancakes.

Jasmin
Multicuisine **$**

(mains ₹60-90; ⊙8.30am-11pm) Very tasty vegetarian dishes are cooked up in a lovely, quiet, open-air spot looking out on the quaint Daiji Footbridge. There are plenty of Indian options, and some original variations on the usual multicuisine theme including Korean and Israeli dishes. The ambience is super-relaxed and service friendly.

Queen Cafe
Indian **$**

(14 Bajrang Marg; mains ₹60-75; ⊙8am-10pm) This tiny restaurant-cum-family-front-room serves up good home-style Indian

vegetarian dishes. Try the pumpkin curry with mint and coconut, and the Kashmir pilao with fruit, vegies and coconut. Host Meenu also offers cooking classes and slightly overpriced walking tours, but some diners may find that the hard sell she serves up with the food leaves a slightly bitter taste.

Ambrai
North Indian **$$$**

(🖉2431085; www.amethaveliudaipur.com; Amet Haveli; mains ₹250-400; ⊙12.30-3pm & 7.30-10.30pm) The cuisine at this scenic restaurant – set at lake-shore level, looking across to Lal Ghat and the City Palace – does justice to its fabulous position. Highly atmospheric at night, Ambrai feels like a French park, with its wrought-iron furniture, dusty ground and large shady trees, and there's a terrific bar to complement the dining, which is strong on Rajashani dishes and nonveg options.

OTHER AREAS

1559 AD
Multicuisine **$$$**

(🖉2433559; PP Singhal Marg; mains ₹200-650; ⊙11am-11pm) Waiters in embroidered-silk waistcoats serve up lovely Indian, Thai and Continental dishes in elegant surroundings at this secluded restaurant near the northwestern side of Fateh Sagar. There are garden tables as well as several different rooms with just a few candlelit tables in each, and Indian classical music in the evenings. Includes a coffee shop with the best coffee we tasted in Udaipur.

Drinking

Most guesthouses have a roof terrace serving up cold Kingfishers with views over the lazy waters of Lake Pichola. Particularly worth considering are Jagat Niwas Palace and Dream Heaven. For a (nonalcoholic) drink beside the water's edge, try Jasmin restaurant or its equally shanty neighbour The Little Prince. For something more upmarket, head to Ambrai restaurant.

Jheel's Ginger Coffee Bar Cafe
(Jheel Palace Guest House, 56 Gangaur Ghat; coffee ₹50-100; ⊘8am-8pm; 📶) This small but slick air-con-cooled cafe by the edge of the water is on the ground floor of Jheel Palace Guest House. Large windows afford good lake views, and the coffee is excellent. Also does a range of cakes and snacks. Note, you can take your coffee up to the open-air rooftop restaurant if you like, but there's no alcohol served here.

Paps Juice Juice Bar
(inside Chandpol; juices ₹40-100; ⊘9am-8pm) This bright-red spot is tiny but very welcoming, and it's a great place to refuel during the day with a shot of vitamin C from a wide range of delicious juice mixes. If you want something more substantial, the muesli mix is pretty good too.

Panera Bar Bar
(Shiv Niwas Palace Hotel; beer from ₹475, shots from ₹250; ⊘11.30am-10pm) Sink into plush sofas surrounded by huge mirrors, royal portraits and beautiful paintwork, or sit out by the pool and be served like a maharaja.

Sunset Terrace Bar
(Fateh Prakash Palace Hotel; ⊘7am-10.30pm) On a terrace overlooking Lake Pichola, this is perfect for a sunset gin and tonic. It's also a restaurant, with live music performed every night.

⭐ Entertainment

Dharohar Dance, Puppetry
(📱2523858; Bagore-ki-Haveli; Indian/foreigner ₹60/100, camera ₹100; ⊘7-8pm) The beautiful Bagore-ki-Haveli (p167) hosts the best (and most convenient) opportunity to see Rajasthani folk dancing, with nightly shows of colourful, energetic Marwari, Bhil and western Rajasthani dances, as well as traditional Rajasthani puppetry.

Mewar Sound & Light Show Cultural Program
(Manek Chowk, City Palace; adult/child ₹100/200; ⊘7pm Sep-Feb, 7.30pm Mar-Apr, 8pm May-Aug) Fifteen centuries of intriguing Mewar history are squeezed into one atmospheric hour of commentary and light switching – in English from September to April, in Hindi other months.

🔒 Shopping

Tourist-oriented shops – selling miniature paintings, wood carvings, silver, bangles and other jewellery, traditional

Traditional puppet, Udaipur
ATREECALLEDLIFE / GETTY IMAGES ©

Below: Goats, Jodhpur; **Right:** Street scene, Jodhpur

(BELOW) FRANCESCO PAVANETTO / GETTY IMAGES ©; (RIGHT) JEREMY WOODHOUSE / GETTY IMAGES ©

shoes, spices, leather-bound hand-made-paper notebooks, ornate knives, camel-bone boxes and a large variety of textiles – line the streets radiating from Jagdish Chowk. Bargain hard. Udaipur is known for its local crafts, particularly its miniature paintings in the Rajput-Mughal style.

Sadhna   Clothing
(🖉 2454655; www.sadhna.org; Jagdish Temple Rd; 🕙 10am-7pm) 🖉 This is the crafts outlet for Seva Mandir, a long-established NGO working with rural and tribal people. The small shop sells attractive fixed-price textiles; profits go to the artisans and towards community development work.

🅸 Information

Medical Services

GBH American Hospital (🖉 24hr enquiries 2426000, emergency 9352304050; www.gbhamericanhospital.com; Meera Girls College Rd, 101 Kothi Bagh, Bhatt Ji Ki Bari) Modern, reader-recommended private hospital with 24-hour emergency service, about 2km northeast of the Old City.

Money

There are a couple of ATMs near the Jagdish Temple.

Thomas Cook (Lake Palace Rd; 🕙 9.30am-6.30pm Mon-Sat) Changes cash and travellers cheques.

🅸 Getting There & Away

Air

Air India (🖉 2410999, airport office 2655453; www.airindia.com; 222/16 Mumal Towers, Saheli Rd) Flies daily to Mumbai (Bombay) and Delhi (via Jodhpur).

Jet Airways (🖉 5134000; www.jetairways.com; Airport) Flies direct to Delhi twice daily, and Mumbai daily.

Train

An autorickshaw between the train station and Jagdish Chowk should cost around ₹50. There's a prepaid autorickshaw stand at the station, though, so use that when you arrive.

There are no direct trains to Jodhpur or Jaisalmer.

For Pushkar, four daily trains make the five-hour journey to Ajmer (6.15am, 2.15pm, 5.20pm and 10.20pm). A sleeper ticket costs ₹480.

Three trains run daily to Jaipur (6.15am, 2.15pm and 10.20pm), taking around seven hours. A sleeper ticket costs ₹590.

Two daily trains (5.20pm and 6.15pm) make the 12-hour trip to Delhi. Sleeper tickets are ₹390.

Only one daily train runs to Agra (10.20pm). Sleeper tickets cost ₹360.

🛈 Getting Around

To/From the Airport

A prepaid taxi to the Lal Ghat area costs ₹400.

WESTERN RAJASTHAN

Jodhpur

🕿 0291 / POP 1 MILLION

Mighty Mehrangarh, the muscular fort that towers over the Blue City of Jodhpur, is a magnificent spectacle and an architectural masterpiece. Around Mehrangarh's base, the old city, a jumble of Brahmin-blue cubes, stretches out to the 10km-long , 16th-century city wall.

The 'Blue City' really is blue! Inside is a tangle of winding, glittering, medieval streets, which never seem to lead where you expect them to, scented by incense, roses and sewers, with shops and bazaars selling everything from trumpets and temple decorations to snuff and saris.

Jodhpur

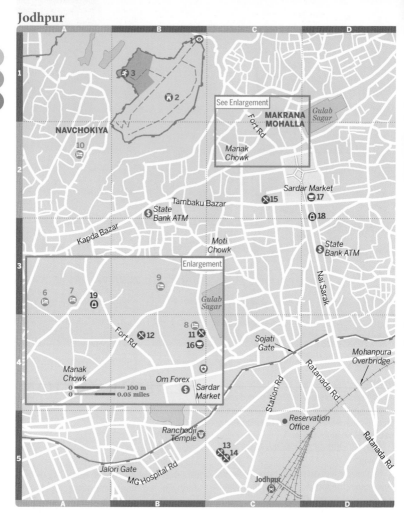

◉ Sights & Activities

Mehrangarh
Fort

(www.mehrangarh.org; Indian/foreigner incl audio guide ₹60/400, camera/video ₹100/250, human guide ₹225; ⏰9am-5pm) Rising perpendicular and impregnable from a rocky hill that itself stands 120m above Jodhpur's skyline, Mehrangarh is one of the most magnificent forts in India. The battlements are 6m to 36m high, and as the building materials were chiselled from the rock on which the fort stands, the structure merges with its base. Still run by the Jodhpur royal family, Mehrangarh is packed with history and legend. Mehrangarh's main entrance is at the northeast gate, **Jai Pol**. You don't need a ticket to enter the fort itself, only the museum section.

Rao Jodha Desert Rock Park
Park

(☎9571271000; www.raojodhapark.com; Mehrangarh; admission ₹50, guide ₹100; ⏰8am-6pm Oct-Mar, 7am-7pm Apr-Sep) This 72-hectare

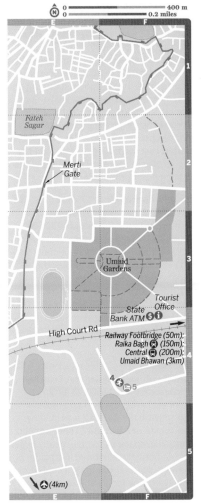

Jodhpur

⊙ Sights
1 Jai Pol B1
2 Mehrangarh B1

✪ Activities, Courses & Tours
3 Flying Fox B1
4 Sambhali Trust F4

🛏 Sleeping
5 Durag Niwas Guest House F4
6 Kesar Heritage Hotel A3
7 Krishna Prakash Heritage
   Haveli A3
8 Pal Haveli B4
9 Raas B3
10 Singhvi's Haveli A2

✖ Eating
11 Indique B4
12 Jhankar Choti Haveli B4
13 Kalinga Restaurant C5
14 Mid Town C5
15 Nirvana C2

☕ Drinking & Nightlife
16 Cafe Sheesh Mahal B4
17 Shri Mishrilal Hotel D2

🛍 Shopping
18 MV Spices D2
19 Sambhali Boutique A3

Flying Fox   Outdoor Adventure

(www.flyingfox.asia; tour ₹1800; ⊙9am-5pm)
This circuit of six zip-lines flies back and
forth over walls, bastions and lakes on
the northern side of Mehrangarh. A brief
training session is given before you start
and safety standards are good: awesome
is the verdict of most who dare. Flying Fox
has a desk near the main ticket office and
its starting point is in the Chokelao Bagh.
Tours last up to 1½ hours, depending on
the group size. Book online for a discount
on the walk-up price.

🛏 Sleeping

The Old City has something like 100
guesthouses, most of which scramble for
your custom as soon as you get within
breathing distance of Sardar Market
(many autorickshaw drivers also operate
on commission).

park – and model of intelligent ecotourism – sits in the lee of Mehrangarh. It has
been lovingly restored and planted with
native species to show the natural diversi-
ty of the region. The park is criss-crossed
with walking trails that take you up to the
city walls, around Devkund Lake, spotting
local birds, butterflies and reptiles. For an
extra insight into the area's native flora
and fauna, take along one of the excellent
local guides.

To avoid the madness, arrange a hotel pick-up from the train or bus station if you can.

OLD CITY & NAVCHOKIYA

Kesar Heritage Hotel
Guesthouse **$**

(☏09983216625; www.kesarheritage.com; Makrana Mohalla; r ₹700-1200) A popular recent addition to Jodhpur's budget accommodation scene, Kesar plays a good hand with large airy rooms (a few of which have balconies) and friendly, helpful management, plus a side-street location that puts noisily sputtering rickshaws out of earshot of light sleepers. The rooftop restaurant looks up to Mehrangarh.

Krishna Prakash Heritage Haveli
Heritage Hotel **$$**

(☏2633448; www.kpheritage.net; Nayabas; r incl breakfast ₹1500-4000; ❄@🔊❄) This multilevel heritage hotel right under the fort walls is a good-value and peaceful choice. It has prettily painted furniture and murals, and rooms are well proportioned; the deluxe ones are a bit more spruced up, generally bigger, and set on the upper floors, so airier. There's an undercover swimming pool and a relaxing terrace restaurant. Free bus and train station pick-ups are offered.

Singhvi's Haveli
Guesthouse **$$**

(☏2624293; www.singhvihaveli.com; Ramdevji-ka-Chowk, Navchokiya; r ₹900-2600; ❄@🔊) This red-sandstone, family-run, 500-odd-year-old *haveli* is an understated gem. Run by two friendly brothers, Singhvi's has 13 individual rooms, ranging from the simple to the magnificent Maharani Suite with 10 windows and a fort view. The relaxing vegetarian restaurant is decorated with sari curtains and floor cushions.

Pal Haveli
Heritage Hotel **$$$**

(☏3293328; www.palhaveli.com; Gulab Sagar; r incl breakfast ₹5500-8500; ❄@🔊) This stunning *haveli,* the best and most attractive in the Old City, was built by the Thakur of Pal in 1847. There are 21 charming, spacious rooms, mostly large and elaborately decorated in traditional heritage style, surrounding a cool central courtyard. The family still live here and can show you their small museum. Three restaurants serve excellent food and the rooftop Indique (p180) boasts unbeatable views.

Raas
Boutique Hotel **$$$**

(☏2636455; www.raasjodhpur.com; Tunvarji-ka-Jhalra; r incl breakfast ₹21,000-40,000; ❄@🔊❄) Developed from a 19th-century city mansion, Jodhpur's first contemporary-style boutique hotel is a splendid retreat of clean, uncluttered style, hidden behind a big castlelike gateway. The red-sandstone-and-terrazzo rooms come with plenty of luxury touches. Most have balconies with great Mehrangarh views – also to be enjoyed from the lovely pool in the neat garden-courtyard. There are two restaurants and a highly indulgent spa.

SOUTH OF THE OLD CITY

Durag Niwas Guest House
Guesthouse $$

(☎2512385; www.durag-niwas.com; 1st Old Public Park Lane; r ₹1200-1600; ❄) ✦ A friendly place set away from the hustle of the Old City. Good home-cooked veg and nonveg dishes are available, and there's a cushion-floored, sari-curtained area on the roof for relaxing. There are deals for long-termers: a double room with full board is ₹9000 per month. Management offers cultural tours and the opportunity to volunteer with the **Sambhali Trust** (www.sambhali-trust.org).

 Eating

As well as the places reviewed here, remember that most guesthouses have restaurants (usually on the roof, with a fort view).

Jhankar Choti Haveli
Multicuisine $

(Makrana Mohalla; mains ₹90-150; ⏱8am-10pm; 📶) Stone walls and big cane chairs in a leafy courtyard, prettily painted woodwork and whirring fans set the scene at this semi-open-air travellers' favourite. It serves up good Indian vegetarian dishes plus pizzas, burgers and baked cheese dishes.

Nirvana
Indian $$

(1st fl, Tija Mata ka Mandir, Tambaku Bazar; mains ₹120-160, regular/special thali ₹160/250; ⏱10.30am-10pm) Sharing premises with a Rama temple, Nirvana has both an indoor cafe, covered in 150-year-old Ramayana wall paintings, and a rooftop eating area with panoramic views. The Indian vegetarian food is among the most delicious you'll find in Rajasthan. The special thali is enormous and easily enough for two. Continental and Indian breakfasts are served in the cafe.

Kalinga Restaurant
Indian $$

(off Station Rd; mains ₹130-300; ⏱8am-11pm) This restaurant near Jodhpur train station is smart and popular. It's in a dimly lit setting and has AC, a well-stocked bar, and tasty veg and nonveg North Indian tandooris and curries. Try the *lal maans*, a mouthwatering Rajasthani mutton curry.

Mid Town
Indian $$

(off Station Rd; mains ₹100-150; ⏱7am-10.30pm) This clean, air-con restaurant does great veg food, including some

Feeding a sacred cow, Jodhpur
GUYLAIN DOYLE / GETTY IMAGES ©

Rajasthani specialities, and some particular to Jodhpur, such as *chakki-ka-sagh* (wheat dumpling cooked in rich gravy), *bajara-ki-roti pachkuta* (pearl millet roti with local dry vegetables) and kabuli (vegetables with rice, milk, bread and fruit).

Indique
Indian $$$
(☏3293328; Pal Haveli Hotel; mains ₹250-350; ⊙11am-11pm) This candlelit rooftop restaurant at the Pal Haveli hotel is the perfect place for a romantic dinner, with superb views to the fort, clock tower and Umaid Bhawan. The food covers traditional tandoori, biryanis and North Indian curries, but the Rajasthani *laal maas* (mutton curry) is a delight. Ask the barman to knock you up a gin and tonic before dinner.

🍷 Drinking

Coffee drinkers will enjoy the precious beans and espresso machines at the deliciously air-conditioned **Cafe Sheesh Mahal** (Pal Haveli Hotel; coffee from ₹80; ⊙9am-9pm), which also has free wi-fi.

Plenty of rooftop restaurants do real coffee too, with varying results. For a dose of double-shot espresso, you'll find chain coffee shops in the mall on High Court Rd.

Shri Mishrilal Hotel
Cafe
(Sardar Market; lassi ₹30; ⊙8.30am-10pm) Just inside the southern gate of Sardar Market, this place is nothing fancy but whips up the most superb creamy *makhania* (saffron-flavoured) lassis. These are the best in town, probably in all of Rajasthan, possibly in all of India.

Shopping

MV Spices
Food & Drink
(www.mvspices.com; Nai Sarak; ⊙9am-9pm) The most famous spice shop in Jodhpur (and believe us, there are lots of pretenders!), MV Spices has several small branches around town that are run by the seven daughters of the founder of the original stall. It will cost around ₹80 to ₹100 for 100g bags of spices, and the owners will email you recipes so you

Rohet Garh (p178)

KEREN SU / GETTY IMAGES ©

can use your spices correctly when you get home.

Sambhali Boutique
Clothing, Accessories

(Makrana Mohalla; ⏰10am-8pm Mon-Sat, noon-8pm Sun) 🍃 This small but interesting shop sells goods made by women who have learned craft skills with the Sambhali Trust (p179), which works to empower disadvantaged women and girls. Items include attractive *salwar* trousers, cute stuffed silk or cloth elephants and horses, bracelets made from pottery beads, silk bags, and block-printed muslin curtains and scarves.

ℹ Information

There are foreign-friendly **ATMs** dotted around the city. We've marked some on our map. There are very few in the Old City, though, one exception being near Shahi Guest House. Internet cafes charge around ₹30 to ₹40 per hour. Again, they're dotted around town, especially in the Old City.

Om Forex (Sardar Market; internet per hr ₹30; ⏰9am-10pm) Also exchanges currency and travellers cheques.

Police (Sardar Market; ⏰24hr) Small police post inside the market's northern gate.

Tourist Office (☎2545083; High Court Rd; ⏰9am-6pm Mon-Fri) Offers a free map and willingly answers questions.

ℹ Getting There & Away

Air

Jet Airways (☎5102222; www.jetairways.com; Residency Rd) and Air India both fly daily to Delhi and Mumbai.

Taxi

You can organise taxis for intercity trips (or longer) through most accommodation places, or deal direct with drivers. There's a taxi stand outside Jodhpur train station.

Train

The computerised **booking office** (Station Rd; ⏰8am-8pm Mon-Sat, to 1.45pm Sun) is 300m northeast of Jodhpur train station.

Four daily trains make the six-hour trip to Jaisalmer (5.30am, 7.35am, 5.45pm and 11.45pm). Eleven go to Jaipur throughout the day in five to six hours. Four daily trains go to Delhi (6.25am, 7pm, 8pm and 11pm), taking 11 to 14 hours: the early-evening departures are fastest. There are six a day to Mumbai, with a journey time of 16 to 19 hours.

For Pushkar, there are two daily trains to Ajmer (6.25am, 7am), taking 5½ hours. There are no direct trains to Udaipur.

ℹ Getting Around

To & From the Airport

The airport is 5km south of the city centre; at least ₹150/300 by autorickshaw/taxi.

Autorickshaw

Autorickshaws between the clock tower area and the train stations or central bus stand should be about ₹20 to ₹30.

Major Trains from Jodhpur

DESTINATION	TRAIN	DEPARTURE TIME	ARRIVAL TIME	FARE (₹; SLEEPER/3AC)
Ajmer	54801 Jodhpur-Ajmer Fast Passenger	7am	12.35pm	175/485
Bikaner	14708 Ranakpur Exp	10am	3.35pm	190/485
Delhi	12462 Mandor Exp	8pm	6.45am	370/955
Jaipur	14854 Marudhar Exp	9.45am	3.30pm	210/555
Jaisalmer	14810 Jodhpur-Jaisalmer Exp	11.45pm	5.25am	205/540
Mumbai	14707 Ranakpur Exp	2.45pm	9.40am	445/1195

Jaisalmer

02992 / POP 78,000

The fort of Jaisalmer is a breathtaking sight: a massive sandcastle rising from the sandy plains like a mirage from a bygone era. No place better evokes exotic camel-train trade routes and desert mystery. Ninety-nine bastions encircle the fort's still-inhabited twisting lanes. Inside are shops swaddled in bright embroideries, a royal palace and numerous businesses looking for your tourist rupee. Despite the commercialism it's hard not to be enchanted by this desert citadel. Beneath the ramparts, particularly to the north, the narrow streets of the Old City conceal magnificent *havelis*, all carved from the same golden-honey sandstone as the fort – hence Jaisalmer's designation as the Golden City.

◉ Sights

JAISALMER FORT

Founded in 1156 by the Rajput ruler Jaisal and reinforced by subsequent rulers, Jaisalmer Fort was the focus of a number of battles between the Bhatis, the Mughals of Delhi and the Rathores of Jodhpur. You enter the fort from its east side, near Gopa Chowk, and pass through four massive gates on the zigzagging route to the upper part. The fourth gate opens into a square, Dashera Chowk, where Jaisalmer Fort's uniqueness becomes apparent: this is a living fort, with about 3000 people residing within its walls.

Fort Palace   Palace

(Indian/foreigner incl compulsory audio guide ₹50/300, camera/video ₹100/200; ⊙8am-6pm Apr-Oct, 9am-6pm Nov-Mar) Towering over the fort's main square, and partly built on top of the Hawa Pol (the fourth fort gate), is the former rulers' elegant seven-storey palace.

Much of the palace is open to the public – floor upon floor of small rooms provide a fascinating sense of how such buildings were designed for spying on the outside world. The doorways connecting the rooms of the palace are quite low. This isn't a reflection on the stature of the Rajputs, but was a means of forcing people to adopt a humble, stooped

Jaisalmer Fort

DINESH MANEER / GETTY IMAGES ©

position in case the room they were entering contained the maharawal.

The 1½-hour audio-guide tour, available in six languages, is worthwhile but you must deposit ₹2000 or your passport, driving licence or credit card.

Jain Temples
Jain Temple

(Indian/foreigner ₹30/200, camera ₹50; ⊙Chandraprabhu 7am-1pm, other temples 11am-1pm) Within the fort walls is a mazelike, interconnecting treasure trove of seven beautiful yellow sandstone Jain temples, dating from the 15th and 16th centuries. Opening times have a habit of changing, so check with the caretakers. The intricate carving rivals that of the marble Jain temples in Ranakpur and Mt Abu, and has an extraordinary quality because of the soft, warm stone. Shoes and all leather items must be removed before entering the temples.

OTHER SIGHTS

Desert Cultural Centre & Museum
Museum

(Gadi Sagar Rd; Indian/foreigner ₹20/50, puppet show ₹30/50, camera/video ₹20/50, combined museum & show ticket ₹70; ⊙9am-8pm, puppet shows 6.30pm & 7.30pm) This interesting little museum tells the history of Rajasthan's princely states and has exhibits on traditional Rajasthani culture. Features include Rajasthani music (with video), textiles, a *kaavad* mobile temple, and a *phad* scroll painting depicting the story of the Rajasthani folk hero Pabuji, used by travelling singers as they recite Pabuji's epic exploits. It also hosts nightly half-hour **puppet shows** with English commentary. The ticket includes admission to the Jaisalmer Folklore Museum.

Tours

The tourist office runs a handful of tours, including sunset tours to the Sam sand dunes (₹200 per person, minimum four people). Add ₹100 if you'd like a short camel ride too.

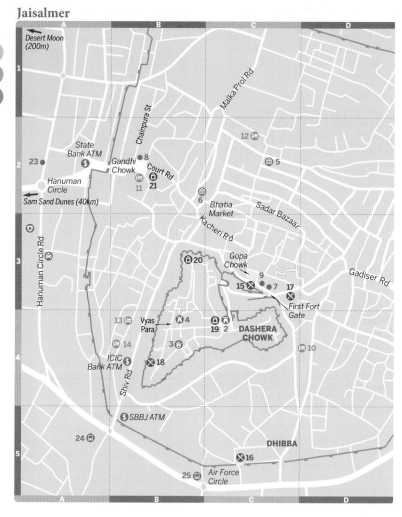

🛏 Sleeping

Staying in the fort is the most atmospheric and romantic choice, but be aware of the pressure tourism is exerting on the fort's infrastructure.

Residency Centre Point
Guesthouse $

(☏252883, 9414760421; residency_guest
house@yahoo.com; Kumbhara Para; r ₹600-1500;
@) Near Patwa-ki-Haveli, this friendly,

family-run guesthouse has five clean, spacious doubles in a lovely 250-year-old building. Rooms vary in size – they are budget by price but mostly midrange in quality (those in the bottom of the house are rather dark). The rooftop restaurant has superb fort views and offers home-cooked food.

Roop Mahal
Hotel $

(☏251700; www.hotelroopmahal.com; off Shiv
Rd; r ₹600-1500; 🛜) A solid budget choice

Jaisalmer

◎ Sights
1 Desert Cultural Centre &
   Museum E4
2 Fort Palace...C4
3 Jain Temples B4
4 Jaisalmer Fort B4
5 Kothari's Patwa-ki-Haveli
   Museum C2
6 Nathmal-ki-Haveli...........................B2
   Patwa-ki-Haveli ....(see 5)

◆ Activities, Courses & Tours
7 Sahara Travels C3
8 Thar Desert Tours B2
9 Trotters C3

◉ Sleeping
10 1st Gate D4
11 Hotel Nachana Haveli.....................B2
12 Residency Centre Point C2
13 Roop Mahal.......................................B4
14 Shahi Palace B4

✕ Eating
   1st Gate ....(see 10)
15 Bhang Shop C3
16 Desert Boy's Dhani..........................C5
17 Monica Restaurant C3
   Saffron...(see 11)
18 Sun Set Palace B4

⊕ Shopping
19 Bellissima...C4
20 Hari Om Jewellers............................B3
21 Jaisalmer Handloom B2

ⓘ Transport
22 Buses to Khuri...................................F4
23 Hanuman Travels..............................A2
24 Main Bus Stand.................................A5
25 Private Bus Stand.............................B5
   Swagat Travels..............................(see 23)

with clean spacious rooms, trustworthy management, fort views from the rooftop cafe, and free wi-fi throughout. Cheaper rooms have fan only and windows facing inside; some fancier rooms have AC and views.

Desert Moon　　　Guesthouse **$$**
(☑250116, 9414149350; www.desertmoonguest house.com; Achalvansi Colony; s ₹600-1000, d ₹1000-1600; ❄@🛜) On the northwestern edge of town, 1km from Gandhi Chowk,

Desert Moon is in a remote-feeling location beneath the Vyas Chhatari sunset point. The guesthouse is run by a friendly Indian-Kiwi couple who offer free pick-ups from the train and bus stations. The 11 rooms are cool, clean and comfortable, with polished stone floors, tasteful decorations and sparkling bathrooms.

Shahi Palace　　　Hotel **$$**
(☑255920; www.shahipalacehotel.com; off Shiv Rd; r ₹600-2500; ❄@🛜) Shahi Palace is a deservedly popular option. It's a modern building in the traditional style with

Jaisalmer Camel Safaris

Trekking by camel is the most evocative and fun way to sample Thar Desert life. Don't expect dune seas – it's mostly arid scrubland sprinkled with villages and wind turbines, with occasional dune areas popping out here and there.

Most trips now include jeep rides to get you to less frequented areas. The camel riding is then done in two-hour batches, one before lunch, one after. It's hardly camel *trekking*, but it's a lot of fun nevertheless.

Competition between safari organisers is cut-throat and standards vary. Most hotels are very happy to organise a camel safari. While many provide a good service, some may cut corners and take you for the kind of ride you didn't have in mind. A few low-budget hotels in particular exert considerable pressure on guests to take 'their' safari. Others specifically claim 'no safari hassle'.

You can also organise a safari directly with one of the several reputable specialist agencies in Jaisalmer. Since these agencies depend exclusively on safari business it's particularly in their interest to satisfy their clients. It's a good idea to talk to other travellers and ask two or three operators what they're offering.

The best known dunes, at Sam (40km west of Jaisalmer), are always crowded in the evening and are more of a carnival than a back-to-nature experience. The dunes near Khuri are quite busy at sunset, but quiet the rest of the time. Operators all sell trips now to 'nontouristy' and 'off the beaten track' areas. Ironically, this has made Khuri quieter again, although Sam still hums with day-dripper activity.

With jeep transfers included, typical rates are between ₹1100 and ₹1700 per person for a one-day-one-night trip (leaving one morning, returning the next). This should include meals, mineral water and blankets, and sometimes a thin mattress. Check there will be one camel for each rider. You can pay for greater levels of comfort (eg tents, better food), but *always* get it all down in writing.

Women should consider wearing a sports bra, as a trotting camel is a bumpy ride. A wide-brimmed hat, long trousers, long-sleeved shirt, insect repellent, toilet paper, torch, sunscreen, water bottle (with a strap), and cash (for a tip to the camel men) are also recommended. It can get cold at night, so if you have a sleeping bag bring it along, even if you're told blankets will be supplied.

You should get a cheaper rate (₹900 to ₹1500 per person) if you leave Jaisalmer in the afternoon and return the following morning. A quick sunset ride in the dunes at Sam costs around ₹550 per person, including jeep transfer.

WHICH SAFARI?

Sahara Travels (📞252609; www.saharatravelsjaisalmer.com; Gopa Chowk; 🕐6am-8pm) Now run by the son of the late LN Bissa (aka Mr Desert), a real Jaisalmer character, this place is still very professional and transparent. Trips are to 'nontouristy' areas only. An overnight trip costs ₹1400 per person, all inclusive.

Trotters (📞9828929974; www.trottersjaisalmer.net; Gopa Chowk; 🕐5.30am-7.30pm) Run by 'Del Boy', this company is also run transparently, with a clear price list showing everything on offer. Does trips to 'nontouristy' areas as well as cheaper jaunts to Sam or Khuri. An overnight trip costs ₹1100 to 1200 per person, all inclusive.

Thar Desert Tours (📞255656; www.tharcamelsafarijaisalmer.com; Gandhi Chowk; 🕐8.30am-7.30pm) Located at Gandhi Chowk, this well-run operator charges ₹950 per person per day, adjusted depending on trip times. They are slightly pricier than Sahara or Trotters, but we receive good feedback about them.

carved sandstone. It has attractive rooms with raw sandstone walls, colourful embroidery, and carved stone or wooden beds. The cheaper rooms are mostly in two annexes along the street, **Star Haveli** and **Oasis Haveli**. The rooftop **restaurant** (mains ₹80-200) is excellent.

Indian veg and nonveg dishes are available plus some European fare, cold beer and a superb evening fort view.

Hotel Nachana Haveli
Heritage Hotel $$$

(📞252110; www.nachanahaveli.com; Gandhi Chowk; r ₹3750; ✳@) This 280-year-old royal *haveli*, set around three courtyards – one with a tinkling fountain – is a fascinating hotel. The raw sandstone rooms have arched stone ceilings and the ambience of a medieval castle. They are sumptuously and romantically decorated, though some lack much natural light. The common areas come with all the Rajput trimmings, including swing chairs and bearskin rugs.

1st Gate
Hotel $$$

(📞9462554462; www.1stgate.in; First Fort Gate; r incl breakfast ₹8500; ✳@🛜) Italian-designed and super slick, this is Jaisalmer's most sophisticated modern hotel and it is beautiful throughout with a desert-meets-contemporary boutique vibe. The location lends it one of the finest fort views in town, especially from its split-level open-air restaurant-cafe (p188) area. Rooms are immaculate and the food (Italian and Indian) and coffee are both top-notch.

Eating

Sun Set Palace
Multicuisine $

(Vyas Para, Fort; mains ₹90-200; ⏰8am-10pm) This restaurant has cushions and low tables on an airy terrace on (as the name implies) the fort's western side. Pretty good vegetarian Indian dishes are prepared, as well as Chinese and Italian options.

Bhang Shop
Cafe $

(Gopa Chowk; lassi from ₹100) Jaisalmer's infamous lassi shop is a simple, pocket-sized place. The added ingredient is bhang: cannabis buds and leaves mixed into a paste with milk, ghee and spices. It also does a range of bhang-laced cookies. Bhang is legal here, but it doesn't agree with everyone so if you're not used to this sort of thing, go easy or avoid altogether.

Monica Restaurant
Multicuisine $$

(Amar Sagar Pol; mains ₹100-280) The airy open-air dining room at Monica just about squeezes in a fort view, but if you end up at a non-view table, console yourself with the excellent veg and nonveg options. Meat from the tandoor is particularly well-flavoured and succulent, the thalis well-varied, and the salads fresh and clean.

Desert Boy's Dhani   Indian $$
(Dhibba; mains ₹100-135; ⊙11am-4pm & 7-11pm) A walled-garden restaurant where tables are spread around a large, stone-paved courtyard with a big tree. There's also traditional cushion seating under cover. Rajasthani music and dance is performed from 8pm to 10pm nightly, and it's a very pleasant place to eat excellent, good-value Rajasthani and other Indian veg dishes.

Saffron   Multicuisine $$$
(Hotel Nachana Haveli, Gandhi Chowk; mains ₹250-370) On the spacious roof terrace of Hotel Nachana Haveli, the veg and nonveg food here is excellent. The Indian food is hard to beat, though the Italian isn't too bad either. It's a particularly atmospheric place in the evening. Alcohol is served.

1st Gate   Italian $$$
(📞9462554462; First Fort Gate; mains ₹300-650; ⊙7am-11pm; 📶) A small but good menu of authentic vegetarian Italian dishes as well as some delicious Indian food served on a split-level, open-air terrace with dramatic fort views. Also does good strong Italian coffee (₹100 to ₹150). A wood-fired oven was being built when we visited, so look out for a pizza menu.

🔒 Shopping

Hari Om Jewellers   Handicrafts
(Chougan Para, Fort; ⊙10am-8.30pm) This family of silversmiths makes beautiful, delicate silver rings and bracelets featuring world landmarks and Hindu gods. Asking prices for rings start at ₹1800 (at a rate of ₹300 per day's work).

Jaisalmer Handloom   Handicrafts
(www.jaisalmerhandloom.com; Court Rd; ⊙9am-10pm) This place has a big array of bedspreads, tapestries, clothing (ready-made and custom-made, including silk) and other textiles, made by its own workers

Jewellery seller, Jaisalmer

Major Trains from Jaisalmer

DESTINATION	TRAIN	DEPARTURE TIME	ARRIVAL TIME	FARE (₹; SLEEPER/3AC)
Delhi (Old Delhi)	14660 Jaisalmer-Delhi Exp	5pm	11.10am	440/1185
Jaipur	14660 Jaisalmer-Delhi Exp	5pm	4.50am	340/910
Jodhpur	14809 Jaisalmer-Jodhpur Exp	6.15am	12.15pm	205/540

and others. Staff don't belabour you with too much of a hard sell.

Bellissima   Handicrafts
(Dashera Chowk, Fort; ☺8am-9pm) This small shop near the fort's main square sells beautiful patchworks, embroidery, paintings, bags, rugs, cushion covers and all types of Rajasthani art. Proceeds assist underprivileged women from surrounding villages, including those who have divorced or been widowed.

ℹ Information
There are several internet cafes scattered around town; typical cost is ₹40 per hour. ATMs include State Bank and SBBJ near Hanuman Circle, SBBJ and ICIC Bank on Shiv Rd, and State Bank outside the train station. There are licensed money changers in and around Gandhi Chowk.

Hanuman Travels (☏9413362367)

Swagat Travels (☏252557)

Tourist Office (☏252406; Gadi Sagar Rd; ☺9.30am-6pm) Friendly office; free town map.

ℹ Getting There & Away

Taxi
One-way taxis should cost about ₹1800 to Jodhpur or ₹6500 to Udaipur. There's a taxi stand on Hanuman Circle Rd.

Train
Three daily trains go to Jodhpur (1.20am, 6.15am and 5pm). They take five to six hours.
   One daily train goes to Delhi (5pm, 18 hours) via Jaipur (12 hours).

ℹ Getting Around

Autorickshaw
Around ₹40 from the train station to Gandhi Chowk.

Car
It's possible to hire taxis or jeeps from the stand near Hanuman Circle Rd. To Khuri or the Sam sand dunes expect to pay ₹800 to ₹1000 one way.

Goa & Around

It's green, it's glistening and it's gorgeous: just three of the reasons Goa has lured travellers for decades. They come for the silken sand, crystalline shores, coconut culture and *susegad* – a Portuguese-derived term that translates loosely to 'laid-backness'.

But Goa is far more than its old-school reputation as a hippie haven or its relatively new status as a package-holiday beach getaway. Goa is as beautiful and culturally rich as it is tiny and hassle-free, so you can go birdwatching in a butterfly-filled forest, marvel at centuries-old cathedrals, venture out to waterfalls or meander the capital's charming alleyways. Add a dash of Portuguese-influenced food and architecture, infuse with a colourful blend of religious traditions, pepper with parties and you've got a heady mix that makes Goa easy to enjoy and extremely hard to leave – although the pull of nearby Hampi, a stunning World Heritage Site just across the state border in Karnataka, might well be strong enough to finally lure you away.

Palolem beach (p219)
KIMBERLEY COOLE/GETTY IMAGES ©

Church of St Francis of Assisi (p207)
YADID LEVY / GETTY IMAGES ©

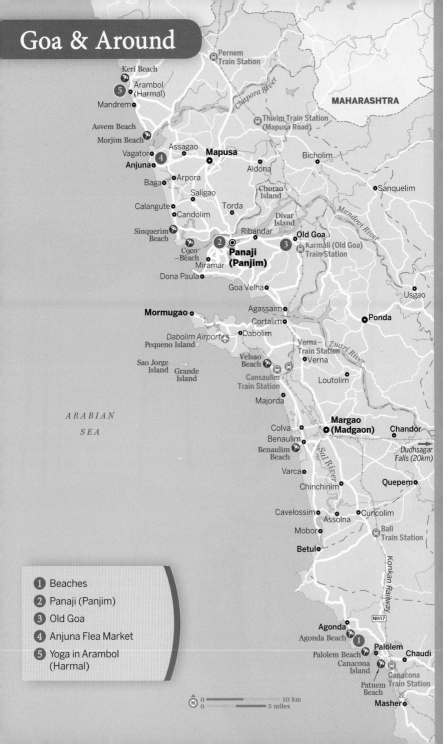

Goa & Around

Keri Beach
Arambol (Harmal)
Mandrem

Pernem Train Station

Chapora River

MAHARASHTRA

Thivim Train Station (Mapusa Road)

Asvem Beach
Morjim Beach
Vagator
Anjuna
Baga
Arpora
Saligao
Calangute
Candolim
Sinquerim Beach
Coco Beach
Miramar
Dona Paula

Assagao
Mapusa
Aldona
Bicholim

Chorao Island
Torda
Divar Island
Ribandar

Panaji (Panjim)

Goa Velha

Sanquelim

Mandovi River

Old Goa
Karmali (Old Goa) Train Station

Usgao

Agassaim
Cortalim
Mormugao
Pequeno Island
Dabolim Airport
Dabolim
Sao Jorge Island
Grande Island

Velsao Beach
Cansaulim Train Station

Verna Train Station
Verna
Loutolim

Ponda

Zuari River

A R A B I A N

S E A

Majorda

Colva
Benaulim
Benaulim Beach
Varca

Chinchinim

Cavelossim
Mobor
Betul

Margao (Madgaon)

Sal River

Assolna
Curcolim
Bali Train Station

Chandor

→ *Dudhsagar Falls (20km)*

Quepem

Konkan Railway

Agonda
Agonda Beach
Palolem Beach
Canacona Island
Patnem Beach

NH17

Palolem
Chaudi
Canacona Train Station

Masher

1 Beaches
2 Panaji (Panjim)
3 Old Goa
4 Anjuna Flea Market
5 Yoga in Arambol (Harmal)

N
0 ———————— 10 km
0 ———————— 5 miles

Goa & Around's Highlights

Beaches

Goa is one of India's best places to kick back on powder-white beaches. In some places the coast has become built up, but there's still plenty of paradise-style, palm-shaded coastline where it's easy to escape, relax and tuck into fresh-from-the-boat seafood. Arguably, Palolem (p219) is the best beach in the south, while Mandrem (p212) gets our vote for prettiest in the north, but there are dozens to choose from along the length of the Goan coastline. Mandrem beach

Panaji (Panjim)

Is Panaji (p200) India's cutest capital? It's a friendly, manageable, walkable city and its Portuguese-era charms make it a perfect place to spend a day or two. Stroll the peaceful streets, take a kitschy river cruise, eat delicious vindaloos and end the evening in a cosy local bar. Viva Panjim (p204)

YADID LEVY / GETTY IMAGES ©

Old Goa

Gaze at the cathedral-filled remains of Old Goa (p207), which from the 16th to the 18th centuries was the 'Rome of the East'. Only shadows of this history remain, but it's a picturesque place that's full of faded vestiges of Catholic splendour, adapted to the local environment. It's home to the largest church in Asia, as well as some beautiful 16th- and 17th-century chapels. Basilica of Bom Jesus (p206)

GREG ELMS/GETTY IMAGES ©

Anjuna Flea Market

Once an infamous hang-out for hippies smoking jumbo joints, the weekly Wednesday flea market in Anjuna (p211) is more mainstream these days. Peruse the multitude of open-air stalls for clothes, souvenirs and knick-knacks before retreating to a beach bar for sunset.

Yoga in Arambol (Harmal)

Goa is a great place to practise some alternative therapies and yoga. From ashtanga through to Zen, every kind of spiritually oriented health regime is to be found here. There are plenty of places all over the state to take courses or have treatments such as ayurvedic massage. Try the lovely beach of Arambol (p212) to track down some local practitioners.

195

Goa & Around's Best...

Wining & Dining

- **Black Sheep Bistro** Impressive boutique restaurant serves tapas and world food done well. (p204)

- **Viva Panjim** Streetside eatery in an old Portuguese-style house. (p204)

- **Longhuino's** Old wooden chairs, whirring fans and very good Goan food. (p215)

- **Café Inn** Great nighttime barbecue in Palolem. (p221)

- **Home** Hip Mediterranean-style restaurant on Patnem beach. (p222)

- **Seasonal beach shacks** Fresh fish on the menu, toes in the sand; found all over.

Rooms with Character

- **Hotel Bougainvillea** Ridiculously pretty hotel in a 200-year-old mansion. (p211)

- **Nilaya Hermitage** Ultimate in Goan boutique and spa luxury. (p209)

- **Panjim Inn** A 19th-century hotel with four-poster beds, colonial-era furniture and local artworks. (p203)

- **Yab Yum** Stylish huts in secluded beachfront jungle gardens. (p212)

- **Ciaran's** Rustic yet sophisticated Palolem beach huts. (p221)

Local Culture

- **Panaji** Chilled-out Goan capital. (p200)

- **Old Goa** Centre of Indian Catholicism, full of colonial-era churches. (p207)

- **Braganza House** Glorious, faded 17th-century mansion. (p216)

- **Goa Chitra** Ethnographic museum preserving Goa's domestic past. (p217)

Adventures & Activities

○ **Paragliding** Popular on the cliffs above Arambol beach, but also possible in Anjuna on flea-market day. (p212)

○ **Yoga** You can find yoga classes and courses all over, including Arambol, Mandrem, Anjuna and Palolem.

○ **Kayaking** Rent kayaks at Palolem beach. (p220)

○ **Trekking** French-run Goa Jungle Adventure, based in Palolem, gets great reviews. (p220)

○ **Dudhsagar Falls** India's second-highest waterfall makes a fun day trip from Panaji or Margao. (p215).

ADVANCE PLANNING

○ **One month before** Book any particularly special accommodation or any accommodation for the Christmas and New Year peak.

○ **Two weeks before** Reserve long train trips.

○ **One or two days before** Arrange any local tours that take your fancy.

RESOURCES

○ **Goa Tourism** (www. goa-tourism.com) Good background and tour info.

○ **What's Up Goa** (www. whatsupgoa.com) Goa's version of *Time Out* with lots of listings and events.

○ **Goa's English dailies** (www.navhindtimes.in, www.oheraldo.in) For the news.

GETTING AROUND

○ **Taxi** Cars and drivers are available for hire in most towns; try your hotel or the local taxi stand. Full-day tours cost ₹1000 to ₹1500. Women and families can take advantage of the **Womens Taxi Service** (📞0832-2437437).

○ **Pilots** Motorcycles, known as 'pilots', are also a licensed form of taxi in Goa. They're cheap, easy to find and can be identified by a yellow front mudguard.

○ **Motorcycles & mopeds** Many tourists rent these (₹200 to ₹500 per day), but take care on the potholed, haphazard Goan roads and insist on using a helmet.

○ **Bus** There's an extensive network of buses serving even the smallest towns.

○ **Arriving at the airport** There are two prepaid taxi counters at Dabolim airport. Use them.

BE FOREWARNED

○ **Illegal substances** Being caught, even with small quantities of illegal drugs, can mean a hefty sentence in jail.

○ **Strong currents** Check where it's safe to swim before launching into the Arabian Sea.

○ **Christmas & New Year** If you're looking for peace and quiet, be aware that this is the most crowded and expensive period.

Left: Panaji (Panjim; p200)
Above: Braganza House (p216), Chandor
(LEFT & ABOVE) LONELY PLANET/GETTY IMAGES ©;

Goa & Around Itineraries

Central Goa is the state's most cultural region – with its gracious capital Panaji – while the north is the liveliest, harbouring the last remnants of the region's fabled party scene. For utter peace and relaxation, head to the quieter beaches in the south.

5 DAYS

PANAJI TO ARAMBOL
NORTH GOA EXPLORER

Start your trip in the charming Goan capital, **❶ Panaji** (Panjim; p200), where you can wander the old town, see its historic buildings, take cruises along the Mandovi River and dine at delicious, laid-back restaurants. Factor in a side-trip to **❷ Old Goa** (p207), the former state capital that was abandoned in the 17th century but which still houses some architectural gems, including the largest cathedral in Asia.

Return to Panaji before hitting the northern beaches. First up: **❸ Anjuna** (p209), the much-loved former hippie hangout. Try to time your visit to coincide with the weekly Wednesday flea market, or else drop in on a yoga class and then just chill with a drink at a beach bar. From here you could head still further north to the appealing beach town of **❹ Arambol** (Harmal; p212), a corner of Goa that's a well-known traveller magnet with something of a mainstream festival vibe – the main drag leading to the beach is known as 'Glastonbury St'. This is also the best place in Goa for yoga, there are beach huts aplenty and you can even try your hand at paragliding.

ARAMBOL (HARMAL) ❹

ANJUNA ❸

OLD GOA ❷

❶❶ PANAJI (PANJIM)

MARGAO (MADGAON)

BENAULIM ❸ ❺ CHANDOR ❹

ARABIAN SEA

PALOLEM ❺

Above: Sé Cathedral (p207)
Top Right: Palolem beach (p219)
(TOP LEFT) STEVEN MIRIC/GETTY IMAGES ©; (TOP RIGHT) NICHOLAS PITT/GETTY IMAGES ©

1
WEEK

PANAJI TO PALOLEM

SOUTH GOA RELAXER

This itinerary explores the tranquil coastal stretches in the south of Goa, with its white-sand beaches and unspoiled coves, but you can kick off in the relaxed regional capital of **1 Panaji** (Panjim; p200), as with the first itinerary.

Next travel south, either taking a bus or taxi to the transport hub of **2 Margao** (Madgaon; p214) and then taking a taxi, or by hiring a taxi all the way to the coastal resort of **3 Benaulim** (p216), to relax on its long white-sand beach, and explore the surrounding empty and gorgeous coastline, dotted with Portuguese-era mansions and whitewashed churches. From here you can also take a trip to explore inland, heading to the town of **4 Chandor** (p216), which is home to several fantastical mansions, including the sumptuous, 17th-century Braganza House. Back on the coast, follow the picturesque road south via Varca and Cavelossim, crossing the Sal River to the far south. From here it's a beautiful winding coastal drive past Agonda Beach to **5 Palolem** (p219) and Patnem, two of Goa's most beautiful spots, with calm seas and plenty of opportunities for yoga and to indulge in alternative therapies while resting up in picturesque beach huts or lusher, low-key resorts set back from the beach.

Discover
Goa & Around

At a Glance

○ **Panaji** (Panjim) Goa's picturesque capital.

○ **Old Goa** (p207) Asia's most impressive churches and cathedrals

○ **Anjuna** (p209) Famous ex-hippie flea market.

○ **Arambol** (Harmal; p212) Backpacker beach, a traveller favourite.

○ **Margao** (Madgaon; p214) Market town and transport hub.

○ **Palolem** (p219) South Goa's most idylic beach.

○ **Hampi** (p223) Ancient ruins, unearthly landscape.

CENTRAL GOA

Panaji (Panjim)

POP 15,000

One of India's smallest and most relaxed state capitals, Panaji (formerly Panjim) crowds around the mouth of the broad Mandovi River and boasts a fabulous whitewashed church and a fascinating old quarter with a tangle of narrow streets. Nowhere is the Portuguese influence felt more strongly than here, where the late-afternoon sun lights up yellow houses with purple doors, and around each corner you'll find restored ochre-coloured mansions with terracotta-tiled roofs, wrought-iron balconies and arched oyster-shell windows. Panjim is a place for walking, enjoying the peace of the afternoon siesta, eating well and meeting real Goans.

Sights & Activities

One of the pleasures of Panaji is long, leisurely strolls through the Portuguese-era Sao Tomé, Fontainhas and Altinho districts.

Church of Our Lady of the Immaculate Conception   Church

(cnr Emilio Gracia & Jose Falcao Rds; ⊙10am-12.30pm & 3-5.30pm Mon-Sat, 11am-12.30pm & 3.30-5pm Sun, English Mass 8am) Panaji's spiritual, as well as geographical, centre is this elevated, pearly white church, built in 1619 over an older, smaller 1540 chapel and stacked like a fancy white wedding cake. When Panaji was little more than a sleepy fishing village, this church was the

Church of Our Lady of the Immaculate Conception
EXOTICA.IM / GETTY IMAGES ©

first port of call for sailors from Lisbon, who would give thanks for a safe crossing, before continuing to Ela (Old Goa) further east up the river. The church is beautifully illuminated at night.

Goa State Museum Museum

(📞0832-2438006; www.goamusem.gov.in; EDC Complex, Patto; 🕑9.30am-5.30pm Mon-Sat) **FREE** This spacious museum east of town houses an eclectic, if not extensive, collection of items tracing aspects of Goan history. As well as some beautiful Hindu and Jain sculptures and bronzes, there are nice examples of Portuguese-era furniture, coins, an intricately carved chariot and a pair of quirky antique rotary lottery machines.

The most interesting exhibit is in the furniture room: an elaborately carved table and high-backed chairs used by the notoriously brutal Portuguese Inquisition in Goa during its reign of terror. The table's legs feature carved lions and an eagle on one side and four human figures on the other.

 Tours

Mandovi River Cruises Cruise

(sunset cruise ₹200, dinner cruise ₹650, backwater cruise ₹900; 🕑sunset cruise 6pm, sundown cruise 7.15pm, dinner cruise 8.45pm Wed & Sat, backwater cruise 9.30am-4pm Tue & Fri) Goa Tourism operates a range of entertaining hour-long cruises along the Mandovi River aboard the *Santa Monica* or *Shantadurga*. All include a live band and usually performances of Goan folk songs and dances. There are also twice-weekly, two-hour dinner cruises and a twice-weekly, all-day backwater cruise, which takes you down the Mandovi to Old Goa, stopping for lunch at a spice plantation and then heading back past Divar and Chorao Islands. All cruises depart from the Santa Monica Jetty next to the Mandovi Bridge, where you can purchase tickets.

Panaji (Panjim)

0   0.2 miles
0   400 m

Mandovi Bridge

Mapusa (13km)

Santa Monica Jetty

Private Bus Stand (80m);
Old Goa (9km);
Karmali (12km);
Ponda (34km)

3

PATTO

Dabolim (29km);
Margao (34km)

14

15

13

Vasco da Gama (32km);
Margao (34km)

Mandovi River

New Patto Bridge

Old Patto Bridge

Goa Tourism
Development
Corporation

Ourem Creek

MG Rd

Dr Alvaro Costa Rd

P

2

Statue of Abbé Faria

Avenida Dom João Castro

12

Steps

X 9

SÃO TOMÉ

31st January Rd

GP Rd

5

Emilio Gracia Rd

CA Rd

Rua de Natal

X 10

4

Footbridge

Ourem Rd

St Sebastian Rd

7

Dabolim (29km);
Margao (34km)

Panaji Jetty

José Falcao Rd

Dr RS Rd

1

Municipal Gardens
(Church Square)

Jama Masjid

Avenida Pe Agnelo

FONTAINHAS

31st January Rd

Fountain

6

MG Rd

Cunha-Rivara Rd

Ormuz Rd

Menezes Braganza Rd

Dr Pisurlekar Rd

Dr P Shirgaonkar Rd

Mahalaxmi Temple

ALTINHO

Cafe Bodega (100m)

Ferry to Betim

Azad Maidan

Malaca Rd

11

Swami Vivekanand Rd

X 8

Dr Dada Vaidya Rd

Goa Marriott Resort (1.8km)

Dayanand Bandodkar Marg

Heliodoro Salgado Rd

Municipal Market

General Bernardo Guedes Rd

Gen Costa Alvares Rd

18th June Rd

Dr Atmaram Borkar Rd

Vintage Hospitals (1.5km)

Sleeping

Old Quarter Hostel
Hostel **$**

(☎0832-6517606; www.thehostelcrowd.com; 31st Jan Rd, Fontainhas; dm ₹450, d with AC from ₹2000; ❄ 🛜) Backpackers rejoice! This cool new hostel in an old Portuguese-style house in historic Fontainhas offers slick four-bed dorms with lockers and two comfortable doubles upstairs, along with a cafe, arty murals, good wi-fi and bikes for hire. Noon checkout.

Afonso Guesthouse
Guesthouse **$$**

(☎9764300165, 0832-2222359; www.afonso guesthouse.com; St Sebastian Rd; d ₹1800-3000; ❄ 🛜) Run by the friendly Jeanette, this pretty Portuguese-era townhouse offers spacious, well-kept rooms with timber ceilings. The little rooftop terrace makes for sunny breakfasting (extra) with Fontainhas views. Add ₹200 for air-con. It's a simple, serene stay in the heart of the most atmospheric part of town. Checkout

Panaji (Panjim)

◎ Sights
1 Church of Our Lady of the
    Immaculate Conception D2
2 Goa State Museum...............................F4

🟢 Activities, Courses & Tours
3 Mandovi River Cruises G2

🛏 Sleeping
4 Afonso Guesthouse.............................E3
5 Casa Nova...E2
6 Old Quarter Hostel.............................E4
7 Panjim Inn..E4

🍴 Eating
8 Black Sheep Bistro B3
9 Hotel Venite..E2
   Verandah.......................................(see 7)
10 Viva Panjim..E3

🍷 Drinking & Nightlife
11 Cafe Mojo...B2

▸ Entertainment
12 Deltin Royale......................................E1

ⓘ Transport
13 Kadamba Bus Stand............................ G3
   Konkan Railway
      Reservation Office .... (see 13)
14 Paulo Travels..G3
15 Private Bus Agents G3

is 9am and bookings are accepted online but not by phone.

Panjim Inn
Heritage Hotel **$$**

(☎0832-2226523, 9823025748; www.panjiminn. com; 31st Jan Rd; s ₹3400-6000, d ₹3900-6500, ste ₹5950; ❄ 🛜) One of the original heritage hotels in Fontainhas, the Panjim Inn has been a long-standing favourite for its character and charm, friendly owners and helpful staff. This beautiful 19th-century mansion has 12 charismatic rooms in the original house, along with 12 newer rooms with modern touches, but all have four-poster beds, colonial-era furniture and artworks. Buffet breakfast is included, and the **Verandah restaurant** mains ₹180-360; 🕙11am-11pm) serves excellent Goan food.

Casa Nova
Guesthouse **$$**

(☎9423889181; www.goaholidayaccommoda tion.com; Gomes Pereira Rd; ste ₹4300; ❄ 🛜) In a gorgeous Portuguese-style house (c 1831) in Fontainhas, Casa Nova comprises just one stylish, exceptionally comfy double-bed apartment, accessed via a little alley and complete with arched windows, wood-beam ceilings, and mod-cons such as a kitchenette and wi-fi.

Goa Marriott Resort
International **$$$**

(☎0832-2463333; www.marriott.com; Miramar Beach; d ₹7000-15,000; ❄ 🛜 🏊) Miramar's plush Goa Marriot Resort is the best in the Panaji area. Expertly choreographed, with the five-star treatment beginning in the lobby and extending right up to the rooms-with-a-view. The 24-hour **Waterfront Terrace & Bar** is a great place for a sundowner overlooking the pool, while its **Simply Grills** restaurant is a favourite with well-heeled Panjimites.

Eating

A stroll down 18th June or 31st January Rds will turn up a number of great, cheap canteen-style options, as will a quick circuit of the Municipal Gardens.

Viva Panjim
Goan $$

(☏0832-2422405; 31st Jan Rd; mains ₹100-170; ⏲11.30am-3.30pm & 7-11pm Mon-Sat, 7-11pm Sun) Well known to tourists, this little side-street eatery, in an old Portuguese house and with a few tables out on the laneway, still delivers tasty Goan classics at reasonable prices. There's a whole page devoted to pork dishes, along with tasty *xacuti* (spicy chicken or meat dish with coconut) and *cafreal*-style dishes, seafood such as kingfish vindaloo and crab *xec xec* (curry), and desserts such as *bebinca* (richly layered Goan dessert made from egg yolk and coconut).

Hotel Venite
Goan $$

(31st Jan Rd; mains ₹210-260; ⏲9am-10.30pm) With its cute rickety balcony tables overhanging the cobbled street, Venite has long been among the most atmospheric of Panaji's old-school Goan restaurants. The menu is traditional, with spicy sausages, fish curry rice, pepper steak and *bebinca* featuring, but Venite is popular with tour-ists and prices are consequently rather inflated. It's not to be missed though.

Cafe Bodega
Cafe $$

(☏0832-2421315; Altinho; mains ₹120-320; ⏲10am-7pm Mon-Sat, to 4pm Sun; 🛜) It's well worth a trip up to Altinho Hill for this se-rene cafe-gallery in a lavender-and-white Portuguese-era mansion in the grounds of Sunaparanta Centre for the Arts. Enjoy good coffee, juices and fresh-baked cakes around the inner courtyard or lunch on super pizzas and sandwiches.

Black Sheep Bistro
European, Tapas $$$

(☏0832-2222901; www.blacksheepbistro.in; Swami Vivekanand Rd; tapas ₹180-225, mains ₹320-450) One of the new breed of Panaji boutique restaurants, Black Sheep's impressive pale-yellow facade gives way to a sexy dark-wood bar and loungy din-ing room. The tapas dishes are light, fresh and expertly prepared in keeping with their farm-to-table philosophy. Salads,

Left & Below: Palolem beach (p219)
(LEFT) ANDERS BLOMQVIST / GETTY IMAGES ©; (BELOW) KIMBERLEY COOLE / GETTY IMAGES ©

pasta, local seafood and dishes such as lamb osso bucco also grace the menu, while an internationally trained sommelier matches food to wine.

🍷 Drinking & Nightlife

Cafe Mojo
Bar

(www.cafemojo.in; Menezes Braganza Rd; ⏰10am-4am Mon-Thu, to 6am Fri-Sun) The decor is cosy English pub, the clientele young and up for a party, and the hook is the e-beer system. Each table has its own beer tap and LCD screen: you buy a card (₹1000), swipe it at your table and start pouring – it automatically deducts what you drink (you can also use the card for spirits, cocktails or food). Wednesday night is ladies night, Thursday karaoke and the weekends go until late.

Deltin Royale
Casino

(📞8698599999; www.deltingroup.com/deltin-royale; Noah's Ark, RND Jetty, Dayanand Bandod-

kar Marg; weekday/weekend ₹2500/3000, premium weekend ₹4000-4500; ⏰24hr, entertainment 9pm-1am) Goa's biggest luxury floating casino, with 123 tables, the Vegas Restaurant, a Whisky Bar and a creche. Entry includes gaming chips worth ₹1500/2000 per weekday/weekend and to the full value of your ticket with the premium package. Unlimited food and drinks included.

ℹ️ Information

ATMs are plentiful, especially on 18th June Rd and around the Thomas Cook office.

Goa Tourism Development Corporation (Goa Tourism, GTDC; 📞0832-2437132; www.goa-tourism.com; Paryatan Bhavan, Dr Alvaro Costa Rd; ⏰9.30am-5.45pm Mon-Sat) The GTDC office is in the slick new Paryatan Bhavan building across the Ourem Creek and near the bus stand. However, it's more corporate office than tourist office and is of little use to casual visitors, unless you want to book one of the GTDC's host of tours.

RAMESH LALWANI / GETTY IMAGES ©

 ## Don't Miss
Basilica of Bom Jesus

Famous throughout the Roman Catholic world, the imposing Basilica of Bom Jesus
in Old Goa contains the tomb and mortal remains of St Francis Xavier, the so-called
Apostle of the Indies. St Francis Xavier's missionary voyages throughout the East
became legendary. His 'incorrupt' body is in the mausoleum to the right, in a glass-
sided coffin amid a shower of gilt stars.

Construction on the basilica began in 1594 and was completed in 1605, to create
an elaborate late-Renaissance structure, fronted by a facade combining elements of
Doric, Ionic and Corinthian design.

NEED TO KNOW
⊙7.30am-6.30pm

Vintage Hospitals (☎ 0832-6644401,
ambulance 9764442220; www.vintagehospitals.
com; Caculo Enclave, St Inez; ⊙24hr) Central
Panaji's best hospital in an emergency; it's just
west of the centre near Caculo Mall.

 ## Getting There & Away

A taxi from Panaji to Dabolim airport takes about
an hour and costs ₹800. A prepaid taxi from
Dabolim is ₹670.

Bus

All government buses depart from the huge
and busy Kadamba bus stand (☎ interstate
enquiries 0832-2438035, local enquiries
0832-2438034; www.goakadamba.com;
⊙reservations 8am-8pm), with local services
heading out every few minutes. To get to south
Goan beaches, take an express bus to Margao and
change there.

○ Margao (express shuttle; ₹30, 35 minutes)

○ Old Goa (₹10, 15 minutes)

State-run long-distance services also depart from the Kadamba bus stand. Private operators have booths outside Kadamba, but the buses depart from the interstate bus stand next to New Patto Bridge. One reliable company is **Paulo Travels** (☎0832-2438531; www.phmgoa.com; **G1, Kardozo Bldg**). Destinations include Hampi (private sleeper; ₹800 to ₹1000, 10 to 11 hours) and Mumbai (₹900, 12 to 14 hours).

Train

Panaji's closest train station is Karmali (Old Goa), 12km to the east, where some long-distance services stop (check timetables). A taxi there costs ₹350. Panaji's **Konkan Railway reservation office** (☎0832-2712940; www.konkanrailway.com; ⊙8am-8pm Mon-Sat) is on the 1st floor of the Kadamba bus stand.

❶ Getting Around

Panaji, particularly the Old Quarter, is generally a pleasure to explore on foot. An autorickshaw from Kadamba to the city centre will cost ₹80.

Scooters/motorbikes can easily be hired from around the post office from around ₹200/300 per day.

Old Goa

From the 16th to the 18th centuries, when Old Goa's population exceeded that of Lisbon or London, this former capital of Goa was considered the 'Rome of the East'. You can still sense that grandeur as you wander the site, with its towering churches, cavernous cathedrals and majestic convents. Its rise under the Portuguese, from 1510, was meteoric, but cholera and malaria outbreaks forced the abandonment of the city from the 1700s. In 1843 the capital was officially shifted to Panaji.

Some of the most imposing churches are still in use and are remarkably well-preserved, while other historical buildings have become museums or ruined sites. It's a fascinating day trip, but it can get crowded: consider visiting on a weekday morning, when you can take in Mass (in Konkani) at Sé Cathedral or

❤ If You Like…
Churches

If you enjoy Old Goa churches and architecture, seek out these two gems.

1 SÉ CATHEDRAL
(⊙9am-6pm, Mass 7am & 6pm Mon-Sat, 7.15am, 10am & 4pm Sun) At over 76m long and 55m wide, the cavenerous Sé Cathedral is the largest church in Asia. Building work commenced in 1562, on the orders of King Dom Sebastiao of Portugal, and the finishing touches where finally made some 90 years later. The exterior of the cathedral is notable for its plain style, in the Tuscan tradition. Also of note is its rather lopsided look resulting from the loss of one of its bell towers, which collapsed in 1776 after being struck by lightning. The remaining tower houses the famous **Sino de Ouro** (Golden Bell), the largest in Asia and renowned for its rich tone, which once tolled to accompany the Inquisition's notoriously cruel *autos-da-fé* (trials of faith), held out the front of the cathedral on what was then the market square.

2 CHURCH OF ST FRANCIS OF ASSISI
West of the Sé Cathedral, the Church of St Francis of Assisi is no longer in use for worship, and consequently exudes a more mournful air than its neighbours.

the Basilica of Bom Jesus (remember to cover your shoulders and legs in the churches and cathedral).

◉ Sights

Museum of Christian Art
Museum
(www.museumofchristianart.com; admission ₹50, camera ₹100; ⊙9am-6pm) This excellent museum, in a stunningly restored space within the 1627 Convent of St Monica, contains a collection of statues, paintings and sculptures, though the setting warrants a visit in its own right. Interestingly, many of the works of Goan Christian art made during the Portuguese era, including some of those on display here, were produced by local Hindu artists.

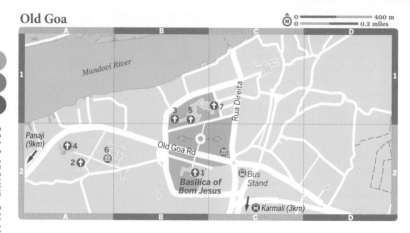

Old Goa

◉ Don't Miss Sights
1 Basilica of Bom Jesus B2

◉ Sights
2 Chapel of St Anthony A2
3 Chapel of St Catherine.......................B1
4 Church of Our Lady of the
   Rosary A2
5 Church of St Francis of Assisi.............B1
6 Museum of Christian Art.....................A2
7 Sé Cathedral..C1

❶ Getting There & Away

Frequent buses from Old Goa head to Panaji's Kadamba bus stand (₹10, 25 minutes) from Old Goa Rd, just beside the Tourist Inn and at the main roundabout to the east. A taxi costs around ₹350.

NORTH GOA

Calangute & Baga

Love it or loathe it, Calangute and Baga are Goa's most popular and crowded beaches with wall-to-wall beach shacks and plenty of watersports on offer. Baga, to the north, is notorious for drinking and dancing. Further south, Candolim and Sinquerim are two more long stretches of beach with lots of midrange and top-end accommodation, beach shacks, and restaurants and shops lining Fort Aguada Rd.

Tours

Day Tripper   Tour

(☎0832-2276726; www.daytrippergoa.com; Gaura Vaddo, Calangute; ⊙9am-5.30pm Mon-Sat Nov-Apr) Calangute-based Day Tripper is one of Goa's biggest and most reliable tour agencies. It runs a wide variety of minibus and boat trips around Goa, including two-hour dolphin trips (₹500 per person), trips to Dudhsagar Falls (₹1530), a houseboat stay (₹5300 per person) and also interstate tours to Hampi and the Kali River (for rafting and birdwatching trips) in Karnataka.

Sleeping & Eating

Ospy's Shelter   Guesthouse $

(☎7798100981, 0832-2279505; ospeys. shelter@gmail.com; d ₹800-900) Tucked away between the beach and St Anthony's Chapel, in a quiet, lush little area full of palms and sandy paths, Ospey's is a traveller favourite and only a two-minute walk from the beach. Spotless upstairs rooms have fridges and balconies and the whole place has a cosy family feel. Take the road directly west of the chapel – but it's tough to find, so call ahead.

Alidia Beach
Cottages   Guesthouse $$

(☎0832-2279014; Calungute-Baga Rd, Saunta Waddo; d ₹2000, with AC from ₹3300; ❄️🛜🏊)

Set back behind a whitewashed church off busy Baga Rd, this convivial but quiet place has beautifully kept Mediterranean-style rooms orbiting a gorgeous pool. The cheaper, non-AC rooms at the back are not as good, but all are in reasonably good condition, staff are eager to please, and there's a path leading directly to Baga Beach.

Nilaya Hermitage
Hotel $$$

(0832-2269793; www.nilaya.com; Arpora; ✳@🛜🐕🏊) The ultimate in Goan luxury, set 3km inland from the beach at Arpora, a stay here will see you signing the guestbook with Bollywood stars and the likes of Giorgio Armani, Sean Connery and Kate Moss. Eleven beautiful red-stone rooms undulate around a swimming pool. The food is as dreamy as the surroundings, and the spa will see you spoiled rotten.

Infantaria
Bakery, Italian $$

(Calangute-Baga Rd; pastries ₹50-200, mains ₹160-440; 🕖7.30am-midnight) Infanteria began life as Calangute's best bakery but has developed into an extremely popular Italian-cum-Indian restaurant. The bakery roots are still there, though, with homemade cakes, croissants, little flaky pastries and real coffee. Get in early for breakfast before the good stuff runs out. For lunch and dinner it's Goan and Italian specialities and a full bar. Regular live music in season.

Go With the Flow
International, Brazilian $$$

(7507771556; www. gowiththeflowgoa.com; Baga River Rd; dishes ₹200-650; 🕕from 6pm Mon-Sat) Stepping into the fantasy neon-lit garden of illuminated white-wicker furniture is wow factor enough, but the food is equally out of this world. With a global menu leaning towards European and South American flavours, Brazilian chef Guto brings a wealth of experience and culinary imagination to the table. Try some of the small bites (ask about a tasting plate) or go straight for the pork belly or duck ravioli.

Anjuna

Dear old Anjuna. The stalwart of India's hippie scene still drags out the sarongs and sandalwood each Wednesday for its famous flea market. With its long beach, rice paddies and cheap guesthouses huddled in relatively peaceful pockets, it continues to pull in droves of backpackers and long-term hippies, while midrange tourists are also increasingly making their way here. The village itself might be a bit ragged around the edges, but that's all part of its haphazard charm, and Anjuna remains a favourite of long-stayers and first-timers alike.

Fishing boat, Baga
LONELY PLANET / GETTY IMAGES ©

⊙ Sights & Activities

Anjuna's charismatic **beach** runs for almost 2km from the northern village area to the flea market. The northern end is mostly cliffs lined with cheap cafes and basic guesthouses, while the beach proper is a narrow but lovely stretch of sand with a bunch of beach bars at the southern end.

YOGA

There's lots of yoga, reiki and ayurvedic massage offered around Anjuna, and at the nearby village of Assagao; look for notices at Artjuna Cafe and the German Bakery.

Brahmani Yoga   Yoga
(☎ 9545620578; www.brahmaniyoga.com; Tito's White House, Aguada-Siolim Rd; classes ₹600, 10-class pass ₹4500) This friendly drop-in centre offers daily classes from from November to April in ashtanga, vinyasa, hatha and dynamic yoga, as well as pranayama meditation. No need to book: just turn up 15 minutes before the beginning of class, to secure space enough to spread your yoga mat.

🛏 Sleeping

Red Door Hostel   Hostel $
(☎ 0832-2274423; reddoorhostels@gmail.com; dm without/with AC ₹500/600, d without/with AC ₹1600/2000; ❄ 🛜) A recent addition to north Goa's hostel scene, Red Door is a welcoming place close to Anjuna's central crossroads. Clean four- and six-bed dorms plus a few private rooms. Facilities include lockers, free wi-fi, garden and good communal areas, including a well-equipped kitchen. Laid-back vibe and resident pet dogs.

Paradise   Guesthouse $
(☎ 9922541714; janet_965@hotmail.com; Anjuna-Mapusa Rd; d ₹800-1000, with AC ₹2000; ❄ @ 🛜) This friendly place is fronted by an old Portuguese-era home and offers neat, clean rooms with well-decorated options in the newer annexe. The better rooms have TV, fridge and hammocks on the balcony. Friendly owner Janet and family also run the pharmacy, general store, restaurant, internet cafe, Connexions travel agency and money exchange!

Anjuna Flea Market

KIMBERLEY COOLE / GETTY IMAGES ©

Banyan Soul
Boutique Hotel **$$**

(☏9820707283; www.thebanyansoul.com; d ₹2200; ❄️🛜) A slinky 12-room option, tucked down the lane off Market Rd, and lovingly conceived and run by Sumit, a young Mumbai escapee. Rooms are chic and well equipped with AC and TV, and there's a lovely library and shady seating area beneath a banyan tree.

Hotel Bougainvillea
Heritage Hotel **$$$**

(Granpa's Inn; ☏0832-273270; www.granpasinn. com; Anjuna-Mapusa Rd; d/ste incl breakfast from ₹4400/5000; ❄️🛜🏊) An old-fashioned hotel housed in a pretty, yellow 200-year-old ancestral mansion, 'Granpa's Inn' offers charm and a touch of luxury with a lovely pool and well-decorated cottages. The grounds are lush, shady and make a cool retreat, though some find it a little far from the beach for this price.

Eating & Drinking

The southern end of Anjuna beach boasts a string of supersized semipermanent beach shacks serving all-day food and drinks; good ones include Cafe Lilliput and Janet & John's. At the far end, **Curlie's** (www.curliesgoa.com; ⏰9am-3am) is a notorious spot for late-night parties.

Artjuna Cafe
Cafe **$**

(☏0832-2274794; www.artjuna.com; Market Rd; mains ₹80-290; ⏰8am-10.30pm) Right up there with our favourite cafes in Anjuna. Along with all-day breakfast, outstanding espresso coffee, salads, sandwiches and Middle Eastern surprises such as baba ganoush, tahini and felafel, this sweet garden cafe has an excellent craft and lifestyle shop, yoga classes and one of Anjuna's best noticeboards. Great meeting place.

German Bakery
Multicuisine **$$**

(www.german-bakery.in; bread & pastries ₹50-90, mains ₹100-450; ⏰8.30am-11pm; 🛜) Leafy and filled with prayer flags, occasional live music and garden lights, German Bakery is a long-standing favourite for hearty and healthy breakfasts, fresh-baked bread and organic food, but these days the menu runs to pasta, burgers and

Anjuna Flea Market

Wednesday's weekly **flea market** (⏰8am-late Wed, Nov-late Apr) at Anjuna is as much part of the Goan experience as a day on the beach. More than three decades ago it was the sole preserve of hippies smoking jumbo joints and convening to compare experiences on the heady Indian circuit. Nowadays things are far more mainstream and the merchandise comes from all over India: sculptures and jewellery courtesy of the Tibetan and Kashmiri traders; colourful Gujarati tribal women selling T-shirts; richly colourful saris, bags and bedspreads from Rajasthan; sacks of spices from Kerala; and the lamari tribal girls from Karnataka.

It's still a great day out, with live music, food and drink stalls and a few bargains to be had. The best time to visit is early morning (from 8am) or late afternoon (around 4pm until close just after sunset). The first market of the season is around mid-November, continuing until the end of April.

pricey seafood. Prices are up and service is down though. Healthy juices (think wheatgrass) and espresso coffee.

Heidi's Beer Garden
German **$$**

(☏9886376922; Market Rd; mains ₹100-400; ⏰11am-11pm) It may well be Goa's first German-style beer garden and restaurant, which is reason enough to call into Heidi's. Another is the range of some 40 international beers from Germany, Belgium, Mexico, Japan, Portugal and more. Imported beers are relatively expensive, but you can still order local beers, including a Goan draught. The food is mostly German and European, including bratwurst sausages and the acclaimed German thali (₹400).

Information

Anjuna has three ATMs, clustered together on the main road to the beach and one near the bus stand.

Getting There & Away

Buses to Mapusa (₹15), where you can get onward connections, depart every half-hour or so from the main bus stand near the beach; some from Mapusa continue on to Vagator and Chapora. Taxis and pilots (motorcycle taxis) gather at the bus stop, and you can hire scooters and motorcycles easily from the crossroads.

Mandrem & Asvem

Mellow Mandrem and neighbouring Asvem have developed in recent years from an in-the-know bolt-hole for those seeking respite from the relentless traveller scene of Arambol and Anjuna to a fairly mainstream but still incredibly lovely beach hang-out with lots of yoga, meditation and ayurveda on offer.

Activities

Vaayu Waterman's Village Surfing
(☏9850050403; www.vaayuvision.org; Aswem; surfboard hire per hr ₹500, lessons ₹2700) Goa's only surf shop is also an activity and art centre where you can arrange lessons and hire equipment for surfing, kiteboarding, stand-up paddleboarding, kayaking and wakeboarding. Enthusiastic young owners also run an art gallery, cafe and funky accommodation across the road from Asvem beach.

Sleeping & Eating

Dunes Holiday Village Beach Hut $
(☏0832-2247219; www.dunesgoa.com; r & hut ₹900-1100; @🛜) The pretty huts here are peppered around a palm-filled lane leading to the beach; at night, globe lamps light up the place like a palm-tree dreamland. Huts range from basic to more sturdy 'treehouses' (huts on stilts). It's a friendly, good-value place with a decent beach restaurant, massage, yoga classes and a marked absence of trance.

Yab Yum Hut $$$
(☏0832-6510392; www.yabyumresorts.com; hut from ₹5800; 🛜) 🌿 This top-notch choice has unusual, stylish, dome-shaped huts – some look like giant hairy coconuts – made of a combination of all-natural local materials, including mud, stone and mango wood. A whole host of yoga and massage options are available, and it's all set in one of the most secluded beachfront jungle gardens you'll find in Goa.

La Plage Mediterranean $$
(mains ₹210-400; ⊙9am-10pm Nov-Mar) Renowned in these parts, La Plage takes beach shack to the next level with its inspired gourmet French-Mediterranean food. Along with excellent salads, seafood and fabulous desserts (try the chocolate thali), La Plage stocks great wines. It's usually open from late November to April.

Arambol (Harmal)

Beautiful Arambol, with its craggy cliffs and sweeping beach, first emerged in the 1960s as a mellow paradise for long-haired long-stayers, and ever since, travellers attracted to the hippie atmosphere have been drifting up to this blissed-out corner of Goa. As a result, in the high season the beach and the road leading down to it (known as Glastonbury St) can get pretty crowded – with huts, people and nonstop stalls selling the usual tourist stuff.

Activities & Courses

The cliffs north of Arambol beach are a popular spot for **paragliding**. Tandem flights cost around ₹1500. Numerous places also offer **yoga** classes and courses – look for notices around town.

Follow the cliff path north of Arambol Beach to pretty **Kalacha Beach**, which meets the small 'sweetwater' lake, a great spot for swimming.

Himalayan Iyengar Yoga Centre
Yoga

(www.hiyogacentre.com; Madhlo Vaddo; 5-day yoga course ₹4000; ⏱9am-6pm Tue-Sun Nov-Mar) Arambol's reputable Himalayan Iyengar Yoga Centre, which runs five-day courses in hatha yoga from mid-November to mid-March, is the winter centre of the iyengar yoga school in Dharamkot, near Dharamsala in North India. First-time students must take the introductory five-day course, then can continue with more advanced five-day courses at a reduced rate.

🛏 Sleeping

Arambol is well known for its sea-facing, cliff-hugging budget huts – trawl the cliffside to the north of Arambol's main beach stretch for the best hut options. It's almost impossible to book in advance: simply turn up early in the day to check who's checking out.

Chilli's
Hotel $

(☎9921882424; d ₹600, apt with AC ₹1000; ⏱year-round; ❄) Near the beach entrance on Glastonbury St, this clean and friendly canary-yellow place is one of Arambol's better non-beachfront bargains. Chilli's offers 10 decent, no-frills rooms, all with attached bathroom, fan and a hot-water shower. The top-floor apartment with AC and TV is great value. Owner Derek hires out motorbikes and scooters and give free advice.

Shree Sai Cottages
Hut $

(☎0832-3262823, 9420767358; shreesai_cottages@yahoo.com; hut without bathroom ₹400-600) A good example of what's on offer along the cliffs, Shree Sai has simple, cute, sea-facing huts on the cliffs overlooking Kalacha Beach.

Arambol Plaza Beach Resort
Hotel $$

(☎9545550731, 0832-2242052; Arambol Beach Rd; r & cottage ₹1800-2500; ❄🛜🏊) On the road between the upper village and the beach, Arambol Plaza is a reasonable midrange choice with cute timber cottages around a decent pool. All rooms are AC but avoid the poorly maintained rooms in the building at the side.

Paragliding, Benaulim (p216)

AMIT BASU PHOTOGRAPHY / GETTY IMAGES ©

Eating & Drinking

Beach shacks with chairs and tables on the sand and parachute-silk canopies line the beach at Arambol.

Shimon Middle Eastern **$**
(meals ₹100-160; ⏱9am-11pm) Just back from the beach, and understandably popular with Israeli backpackers, Shimon is the place to fill up on exceptional felafel. For something more unusual go for *sabich,* crisp slices of eggplant stuffed into pita bread along with boiled egg, boiled potato and salad. The East-meets-Middle-East thali (₹360) comprises a little bit of almost everything on the menu.

Fellini Italian **$$**
(mains ₹180-350; ⏱from 6.30pm) On the left-hand side just before the beach, this unsignposted but long-standing Italian joint is perfect if you're craving a carbonara or calzone. More than 20 wood-fired, thin-crust pizza varieties are on the menu, but save space for a very decent rendition of tiramisu.

Double Dutch Multicuisine **$$**
(mains ₹110-390, steaks ₹420-470; ⏱7am-10pm) In a peaceful garden set back from the main road to the Glastonbury St beach entrance, Double Dutch has long been popular for its steaks, salads, Thai and Indonesian dishes, and famous apple pies. It's a very relaxed meeting place with secondhand books, newspapers and a useful noticeboard for current Arambolic affairs.

ℹ Information

Internet outfits, travel agents and money changers are plentiful on the road leading down to Arambol's beach. The nearest ATM is in Arambol village near the bus stop.

ℹ Getting There & Around

Buses to Mapusa (₹27, 1½ hours) depart from Arambol village every half-hour. It's only about 1.5km from the main beach area, but you're lucky if you get a cab, or even an autorickshaw, for ₹60. A prepaid taxi to Arambol from Dabolim airport costs ₹1200; from Mapusa it's ₹500.

Lots of places in Arambol rent scooters/motorbikes for ₹250/350 per day.

SOUTH GOA

Margao (Madgaon)

POP POP 94,400

Margao (also known by its train station name of Madgaon) is the main population centre of south Goa and for travellers is chiefly a transport hub, with the state's major train and bus stations.

◎ Sights

It's worth a walk around the lovely, small **Largo de Igreja** district, home to lots of atmospherically

Dudhsagar Falls
RAKESH AYILLIATH / GETTY IMAGES ©

crumbling and gorgeously restored old Portuguese homes, and the quaint and richly decorated 17th-century **Church of the Holy Spirit**.

 Sleeping

Hotel Tanish Hotel $

(0832-2735858; www.hoteltanishgoa. com; Reliance Trade Centre, Valaulikar Rd; s/d ₹900/1200, s/d/ste with AC ₹1100/1500/2000;) Oddly situated inside a modern mall, this top-floor hotel offers good views of the surrounding countryside, with stylish, well-equipped rooms. Suites come with a bathtub, a big TV and a view all the way to Colva; just make sure you get an outside-facing room, as some overlook the mall interior.

Nanutel Margao Hotel $$

(0832-6722222; Padre Miranda Rd; s/d incl breakfast ₹3780/4100, ste ₹4750-5300;) Margao's best business class hotel by some margin, Nanutel is modern and slick with a lovely pool, good restaurant, bar and coffee shop, and clean air-con rooms. The location, between the Municipal Gardens and Largo de Igreja district, is convenient for everything.

 Eating

Ruta's World Cafe American, International $$

(0832-2710757; www.caferuta.com; Fr Miranda Rd; mains ₹150-350; 10am-7pm Mon-Sat) Ruta's is a quality addition to Margao's otherwise average dining scene and an excellent reason to get off the beach. After years working as an award-winning cook, teacher and recipe book author on the San Francisco scene, chef Ruta Kahate has brought some of her culinary magic to Goa – there's another restaurant in **Mapusa** (0832-2250757; www.caferuta. com; St Xavier's College Rd, opp Ashirwad Bldg; mains ₹110-270; 10am-8pm Mon-Sat).

Simple things such as soups, salads and toasties sit alongside 'comfort food' such as pulled-pork burgers and New Orleans jambalaya.

Detour:
Dudhsagar Falls

On the eastern border with Karnataka, Dudhsagar Falls (603m) are Goa's most impressive waterfalls and the second highest in India, best seen as soon as possible after the rains. To get here, take a taxi, tour or train (8.13am from Margao) to Colem and from there catch a jeep for the bumpy 40-minute trip to the falls (₹400 per person for the six passengers). It's then a short but rocky clamber to the edge of the falls themselves. The GTDC offers a **tour** (₹1200; Wed & Sun) from Panaji or arrange an excursion with travel agencies at any of the beach resorts.

Longhuino's Goan, Multicuisine $$

(Luis Miranda Rd; mains ₹95-205; 8.30am-10pm) A local institution since 1950, quaint old Longhuino's has been serving up tasty Indian, Goan and Chinese dishes, popular with locals and tourists alike. Go for a Goan dish like *ambot tik,* and leave room for the retro desserts such as rum balls and tiramasu. Service is as languid as the slowly whirring ceiling fans but it's a great place to watch the world go by over a coffee or beer.

ℹ Information

Banks offering currency exchange and 24-hour ATMs are located around the Municipal Gardens.

ℹ Getting There & Around

Bus

Government and private long-distance buses both depart from Kadamba bus stand, about 2km north of the Municipal Gardens. Shuttle buses (₹30, 35 minutes) run to Panaji every few minutes. For north Goa destinations, head to Panaji and change

215

Detour:
Chandor

The lush village of Chandor, 15km east of Margao (Madgoan), makes a perfect day away from the beaches and it's here more than anywhere else in the state that the opulent lifestyles of Goa's former landowners, who found favour with the Portuguese aristocracy, are still visible in its quietly decaying colonial-era mansions.

Braganza House, built in the 17th century, is possibly the best example of what Goa's scores of once grand and glorious mansions have today become. Built on land granted by the King of Portugal, the house was divided from the outset into two wings, to house two sides of the same family. The **West Wing** (📞0832-2784201; donation ₹150; 🕙9am-5pm) belongs to one set of the family's descendants, the Menezes-Bragança, and is filled with gorgeous chandeliers, Italian marble floors, rosewood furniture and antique treasures from Macau, Portugal, China and Europe. Despite the passing of the elderly Mrs Aida Menezes-Bragança in 2012, the grand old home, which requires considerable upkeep, remains open to the public. Next door the **East Wing** (📞0832-2784227; donation ₹100; 🕙10am-6pm) is owned by the Braganza-Pereiras, descendants of the other half of the family. It's not as grand, but it's beautiful in its own lived-in way and has a small but striking family chapel that contains a carefully hidden fingernail of St Francis Xavier – a relic that's understandably a source of great pride. Both homes are open daily and there's almost always someone around to let you in.

The best way to get here is by taxi from Margao: ₹400 round trip, including waiting time.

there. Local buses to Benaulim (₹10, 20 minutes), Colva (₹10, 20 minutes) and Palolem (₹40, one hour) stop at the bus stop on the east side of the Municipal Gardens every 15 minutes or so.

Private and government buses, usually overnight, ply major interstate routes several times daily, and can be booked at offices or travel agents around town; try **Paulo Travel Masters** (📞0832-2702405; ww.phmgoa.com; Hotel Nanutel, Padre Miranda Rd) High-season fares include the following:

○ Hampi (private sleeper; ₹900 to ₹1100, 10 to 11 hours)

○ Mumbai (₹350 to ₹1100, 12 to 14 hours)

Taxi

Taxis are plentiful around the Municipal Gardens, train station and Kadamba bus stand, and they'll go anywhere in Goa, including Palolem (₹900), Panaji (₹900), Dabolim airport (₹600) and Anjuna (₹1200). Except for the train station, where there's a prepaid booth, you'll have to negotiate the fare with the driver.

Train

Margao's well-organised train station, about 2km south of town, serves the Konkan Railway and other routes. Its **reservation hall** (📞PNR enquiry 0832-2700730, information 0832-2712790; 🕙8am-2pm & 2.15-8pm Mon-Sat, 8am-2pm Sun) is on the 1st floor. Services to Mumbai, Mangalore, Ernakulum and Thiruvananthapuram are the most frequent. A 7.50am train runs to Hospet (for Hampi) on Tuesdays, Thursdays, Fridays and Sundays. It takes seven hours. Sleeper/3AC/2AC tickets cost ₹225/600/855.

A taxi or autorickshaw between the train station and the town centre is around ₹100.

Colva & Benaulim
POP 12,000

Colva and Benaulim boast broad, open beaches, but are no longer the first place backpackers head in south Goa. There's no party scene as in north Goa and they lack the beauty and traveller vibe of Palolem. Still, these are the closest beaches to the major transport hubs of Margao and Dabolim airport. And from here you can explore this part of the southern coast (the beach stretches unbroken as far as Velsao in the north and the mouth of the Sal River at Mobor in the south), which in many parts is empty and gorgeous. The inland road that runs this length is perfect for gentle cycling and scootering, with lots of picturesque Portuguese-era mansions and white-washed churches along the way.

 Sights & Activities

The beach entrances at Colva, and to a lesser extent Benaulim, throng with operators keen to sell you **parasailing** (per ride ₹7800), **jet-skiing** (s/d per 15min ₹300/500), and one-hour **dolphin-watching trips** (per person from ₹3400).

Goa Chitra   Museum
(☎0832-6570877; www.goachitra.com; St John the Baptist Rd, Mondo Vaddo, Benaulim; admission ₹200; ☉9am-6pm Tue-Sun) Artist and restorer Victor Hugo Gomes first noticed the slow extinction of traditional objects –

from farming tools to kitchen utensils to altarpieces – as a child in Benaulim. He created this ethnographic museum from the more than 4000 cast-off objects that he collected from across the state over 20 years (he often had to find elderly people to explain their uses). Admission to this fascinating museum is via a one-hour guided tour, held on the hour. Goa Chitra is 3km east of Maria Hall – ask locally for directions.

Sleeping

COLVA

Sam's Guesthouse   Hotel $
(☎0832-2788753; r ₹650; ☎) Away from the fray, north of Colva's main drag on the road running parallel to the beach, Sam's is a big, cheerful place with friendly owners and spacious rooms that are a steal at this price. Rooms are around a pleasant garden courtyard and there's a good restaurant and whacky bar.

Skylark Resort   Hotel $$
(☎0832-2788052; www.skylarkresortgoa.com; d with AC ₹2885-3639; f ₹4270; ❄☎☲) A serious step up from the budget places,

Braganza House, Chandor

Skylark's clean, fresh rooms are graced with bits and pieces of locally made teak furniture and block-print bedspreads, while the lovely pool makes a pleasant place to lounge. The best (and more expensive) rooms are those facing the pool.

BENAULIM

Rosario's Inn   Guesthouse $

(📞0832-2770636; r without/with AC ₹450/800; ❄️) Across a football field flitting with young players and dragonflies, family-run Rosario's is a large establishment with very clean, simple rooms and a restaurant. Excellent value.

Anthy's Guesthouse   Guesthouse $

(📞0832-2771680; anthysguesthouse@rediff mail.com; Sernabatim Beach; d ₹1300, with AC ₹1700; ❄️) One of a handful of places lining Sernabatim Beach itself, Anthy's is a firm favourite with travellers for its good restaurant, book exchange, and its well-kept chalet-style rooms, which stretch back from the beach surrounded by a garden. Ayurvedic massage is available here.

Palm Grove Cottages   Hotel $$

(📞0832-2770059; www.palmgrovegoa.com; Vaswado; d incl breakfast ₹2020-3700; ❄️📶) Old-fashioned, secluded charm and Benaulim's leafiest garden wecomes you at this great midrange choice. The quiet AC rooms, some with balcony, all have a nice feel but the best are the spacious deluxe rooms in a separate Portuguese-style building. The **Palm Garden Restaurant** here is exceptionally good.

🍴 Eating & Drinking

COLVA

Colva's beach has a string of shacks that offer the standard fare and fresh seafood.

Sagar Kinara   Indian $

(Colva Beach Rd; mains ₹60-180; ⏰7am-10.30pm) A pure-veg restaurant upstairs (nonveg is separate, downstairs) with tastes to please even committed carnivores, this place is clean, efficient and offers cheap and delicious North and South Indian cuisine all day.

Beach cottage, Agonda

Leda Lounge & Restaurant Bar

(7.30am-midnight) Part sports bar, part music venue, part cocktail bar, Leda is Colva's best nightspot by a long shot. There's live music from Thursday to Sunday, fancy drinks (Mojitos, Long Island iced teas) and good – but pricey – food (mains ₹270 to ₹600).

BENAULIM

Pedro's Bar & Restaurant Goan, Multicuisine $$

(Vasvaddo Beach Rd; mains ₹110-350; 7am-midnight) Set amid a large, shady garden on the beachfront and popular with local and international travellers, Pedro's offers standard Indian, Chinese and Italian dishes, as well as Goan choices and 'sizzlers'.

Club Zoya Nightclub

(9822661388; www.clubzoya.com; from 8pm) The party scene has hit sleepy little Benaulim in the form of barn-sized Club Zoya, with international DJs, big light shows and a cocktail bar featuring speciality flavoured and infused vodka drinks. Something's on most nights here in season but check the website for upcoming events and DJs.

❶ Information

Colva has plenty of banks and ATMs strung along the east–west Colva Beach Rd. Benaulim has a Bank of Baroda ATM at Maria Hall and an HDFC ATM on the back road to Colva. Most useful services (pharmacies, supermarkets, internet, travel agents) are clustered around Benaulim village, which runs along the east–west Vasvaddo Beach Rd.

❶ Getting There & Around

As with other beaches, scooters can be rented at Colva and Benaulim for around ₹250.

Colva

Buses run from Colva to Margao every few minutes (₹10, 20 minutes) until around 7pm. An autorickshaw/taxi to Margao costs ₹200/250.

Benaulim

Buses from Benaulim to Margao are also frequent (₹10, 20 minutes); they stop at the Maria Hall crossroads, 1.2km east of the beach. Some from Margao continue south to Varca and Cavelossim. Autorickshaws and pilots charge around ₹200 for Margao, and ₹60 for the five-minute ride to the beach.

Benaulim to Agonda

Immediately south of Benaulim are the beach resorts of **Varca** and **Cavelossim**, with wide, pristine sands and a line of flashy five-star hotels set amid landscaped private grounds fronting the beach. About 3km south of Cavelossim, at the end of the peninsula, **Mobor** and its beach is one of the prettiest spots along this stretch of coast, with simple beach shacks serving good food. From here you can cross the new bridge over the Sal River to Assolna and on to the small fishing village of Betul.

From Betul heading south to Agonda, the road winds over gorgeous, undulating hills thick with palm groves. About 2.5km before Agonda is a 2km dirt track leading to **Cola Beach**, one of south Goa's most gorgeous hidden beach gems complete with emerald-green lagoon.

Agonda is a small village with a wide, lovely stretch of white-sand beach lined (in season) with a string of upmarket beach huts and restaurants. Agonda is low-key compared with Palolem, partly due to strong currents that can make swimming dangerous, but it's a fine place to relax for a while.

Palolem & Around

Palolem is undoubtedly one of Goa's most postcard-perfect beaches and while it has long been 'discovered' it's still the tropical star of Goa's beaches. The stunning crescent of sand, calm waters and leaning coconut palms lend it a castaway vibe, but it does get crowded in season! It's a backpacker- and family-friendly, laid-back sort of place with lots of bamboo-hut budget accommodation along the sands, good places to eat, safe swimming and kayaking in calm seas, and all the yoga, massage and alternative therapies you could wish for.

If even Palolem's version of action is too much for you, head further south, along the small rocky cove named **Colomb Bay**, which hosts several basic places to stay, to **Patnem beach**, where a fine selection of beach huts, and a less pretty – but infinitely quieter – stretch of sand awaits.

Palolem, even more so than other beach towns, operates seasonally and many places aren't up and running until November. If you want to see what Palolem looked like 10 or 15 years ago, turn up in September or early October, before the beach huts start to go up.

 Activities

YOGA

Yoga courses and classes are plentiful in season, but locations and teachers tend to change seasonally. **Bhakti Kutir** (0832-2643469, 9823627258; www.bhakti kutir.com; Colomb Bay; cottage ₹2200-3300;

@) offers daily drop-in yoga classes, as well as longer residential courses, while Space Goa is a centre for spirituality. You'll find info on daily yoga classes (₹300) and cooking classes (₹1200) at **Butterfly Book Shop** (9341738801; 9am-10.30pm).

BEACH ACTIVITIES

Kayaks are available for rent on both Patnem and Palolem beaches; an hour's paddling will cost ₹150, including life jacket. Fishermen and other boat operators hanging around the beach offer dolphin-spotting trips or rides to beautiful Butterfly Beach, north of Palolem, for ₹1200 for two people, including one hour's waiting time.

TREKKING

Goa Jungle Adventure   Outdoors (9850485641; www.goajungle.com; trekking & canyoning trips ₹1890-3590) This adventure company, run by an experienced French guide, will take you out for thrilling trekking and canyoning trips in the Netravali area at the base of the Western Ghats, where you climb, jump and abseil into remote water-filled plunges. Trips run from a half-day to several days, and extended rafting trips into Karnataka are also sometimes offered.

 Sleeping

Most of Palolem's accommodation is of the simple seasonal beach-hut variety. Since the huts are dismantled and rebuilt each year, standards and ownership can vary – for this reason the places listed here are either permanent guesthouses or well-established hut operations.

Cotigao Wildlife Sanctuary
LONELY PLANET / GETTY IMAGES ©

My Soulmate
Guesthouse $

(9823785250; mysolmte@gmail.com; d ₹1000, with AC ₹1500; ❄) This friendly and spotless two-storey guesthouse in a good location just off the main Palolem beach road is a good nonbeach bet. Neat rooms come with TV and hot water and the newer ones have sexy circular beds. Good cafe, nice staff.

Art Resort
Hut $$

(9665982344; www.art-resort-goa.com; Ourem Rd; hut ₹1500-2500; 🕾) The nicely designed cottages behind an excellent beachfront restaurant have a Bedouin camp feel with screened sit-outs and modern artworks sprinkled around. The resort hosts art exhibitions and has regular live music.

Ciaran's
Hut $$

(0832-2643477; www.ciarans.com; hut incl breakfast ₹3000-4000, r with AC ₹4500; ❄🕾) Ciaran's has some of the most impressive huts on the beachfront. Affable owner John has worked hard over the years to maintain a high standard and his beautifully designed cottages around a plant-filled garden and pond are top-notch. The sea-view cottages are the more expensive and there are some air-con rooms – including a Jacuzzi room. There's a popular multicuisine restaurant, tapas restaurant and quality massage and spa centre.

Dreamcatcher
Hut $$

(0832-2644873; www.dreamcatcher.in; hut ₹1750-2500) Probably the largest resort in Palolem, Dreamcatcher's 60 sturdy huts are nevertheless secluded, set in a coconut grove just back from the far northern end of the beach. One of the highlights here is the riverside restaurant and cocktail bar, and the wide range of holistic treatments, massage and yoga on offer, with daily drop-in yoga and reiki courses available. Access it from the back road running parallel to the beach.

Village Guesthouse
Guesthouse $$

(9960487627, 0832-2645767; www.villageguesthousegoa.com; d incl breakfast

Detour:
Cotigao Wildlife Sanctuary

About 9km southeast of Palolem, and a good day trip, is the beautiful, remote-feeling **Cotigao Wildlife Sanctuary** (0832-2965601; adult/child ₹20/10, camera/video ₹30/150; ⏱7am-5.30pm), Goa's second-largest sanctuary and easily its most accessible, if you have your own transport. Don't expect to bump into its more exotic residents (including gaurs, sambars, leopards and spotted deer), but frogs, snakes, monkeys, insects and blazingly plumed birds are in no short supply.

₹3400-4300; ❄🕾) The Village is a lovely expat-run boutique hotel with eight spotless and spacious air-con rooms that are a cut above most Palolem hotels. Nicely furnished with sparkling bathrooms, four-poster beds, TV and homely touches, it makes a good base if you value peace more than being on the beach. Breakfast is served in the rear garden.

Eating

Café Inn
Cafe $$

(Palolem Beach Rd; meals ₹150-550; ⏱10am-11pm; 🕾) If you're craving a cappuccino, semi-open-air Café Inn, which grinds its own blend of beans to perfection, is one of Palolem's favourite hang-outs – and it's not even on the beach. Its breakfasts are immense, and comfort-food burgers and panini sandwiches hit the spot. From 6pm there's an excellent barbecue. Free wi-fi.

Space Goa
Cafe $$

(80063283333; www.thespacegoa.com; mains ₹90-250; ⏱8.30am-5pm) On the Agonda road, Space Goa combines an excellent

organic wholefood cafe with a gourmet deli, craft shop and a wellness centre offering reiki and reflexology. The food is fresh and delicious, with fabulous salads, panini and meze, and the desserts – such as chocolate beetroot cake – are divine. Drop-in morning yoga classes are ₹500.

Fern's By Kate's
Goan **$$**

(☎9822165261; mains ₹200-450; ⏱8.30am-10.30pm; 🛜) Back from the beach, this solid timber place with a vague nautical feel serves up excellent authentic Goan food such as local sausages, fish curry rice and shark *ambot tik*.

Home
Continental **$$**

(☎0832-2643916; www.homeispatnem.com; Patnem Beach; mains ₹180-290; ⏱8.30am-9.30pm; 🛜) Standing out from the beach shacks like a beacon, this bright white, relaxed vegetarian restaurant is run by a British couple and serves up Patnem's best breakfasts, pastas, risotto and salads, continental-style. A highlight here is the dessert menu – awesome chocolate brownies, apple tart and cheesecake. Home also rents out eight nicely decorated, light rooms (from ₹1500). Email to book or ask at the restaurant.

Ourem 88
Fusion **$$$**

(☎8698827679; mains ₹440-650; ⏱6-10pm Tue-Sat) Big things come in small packages at British-run Ourem 88, a gastro sensation with just a handful of tables and a small but masterful menu. Try tender calamari stuffed with Goan sausage, slow-roasted pork belly, fluffy souffle or fillet steak with Béarnaise sauce. Worth a splurge.

ⓘ Information

Palolem's main road is lined with travel agencies, internet places and money changers. The nearest ATM is about 1.5km away, where the main highway meets Palolem Beach Rd, or head to nearby Chaudi.

ⓘ Getting There & Around

Scooters and motorbikes can easily be hired along the main road leading to the beach from ₹200.

Bus

Services to Margao (₹40, one hour, every 30 minutes) and Chaudi (₹7, every 15 minutes), the nearest town, depart from the bus stand down by the beach and stop at the Patnem turn-off. Chaudi has good bus connections, but for Panaji and north Goa, you'll need to change buses at Margao.

Taxi & Autorickshaw

An autorickshaw from Palolem to Patnem costs ₹80, or ₹120 to Chaudi. To Agonda it's ₹200. A prepaid taxi from Dabolim airport to Palolem costs ₹1200.

Train

Many trains that run north or south out of Margao stop at the train station in Canacona, 2km from Palolem's beach entrance.

KARNATAKA

Hampi
📞08394

Unreal and bewitching, the forlorn ruins of Hampi dot an unearthly landscape that will leave you spellbound the moment you cast your eyes on it. Heaps of giant boulders perch precariously over miles of undulating terrain, their rusty hues offset by jade-green palm groves, banana plantations and paddy fields. A World Heritage Site, Hampi is a place where you can lose yourself among wistful ruins, or simply be mesmerised by the vagaries of nature.

◎ Sights

Set over 36 sq km, there are some 3700 monuments to explore here, and it would take months if you were to do it justice. The ruins are divided into two main areas: the Sacred Centre, around Hampi

JOHN GOLLINGS / GETTY IMAGES ©

Don't Miss
Vittala Temple

The undisputed highlight of the Hampi ruins, the 16th-century Vittala Temple stands amid the boulders 2km from Hampi Bazaar. Work possibly started on the temple during the reign of Krishnadevaraya (r 1509–29). It was never finished or consecrated, yet the temple's incredible sculptural work remains the pinnacle of Vijayanagar art.

The ornate **stone chariot** that stands in the courtyard is the temple's showpiece and represents Vishnu's vehicle with an image of Garuda within. Its wheels were once capable of turning.

NEED TO KNOW
Indian/foreigner ₹10/250, child under 15yr free; ⊙8.30am-5.30pm

Bazaar; and the Royal Centre, towards Kamalapuram.

Be aware that the ₹250 ticket for Vittala Temple entitles you to same-day admission into most of the paid sites across the ruins, so don't lose your ticket.

Virupaksha Temple   Hindu Temple
(admission ₹2, camera ₹50; ⊙dawn-dusk) The focal point of Hampi Bazaar is the Virupaksha Temple, one of the city's oldest structures, and Hampi's only remaining working temple. The main *gopuram*

(gateway tower), almost 50m high, was built in 1442, with a smaller one added in 1510. The main shrine is dedicated to Virupaksha, an incarnation of Shiva.

If Lakshmi, the **temple elephant**, and her attendant are around, she'll smooch (bless) you for a coin; she gets her morning bath at 8am down by the river ghats.

Royal Centre   Historic Site
While it can be accessed by a 2km foot trail from the Achyutaraya Temple, the

Royal Centre is best reached via the Hampi–Kamalapuram road. A number of Hampi's major sites stand here.

The **Mahanavami-diiba** is a 12m-high three-tired platform with intricate carvings and panoramic vistas of the walled complex of ruined temples, stepped tanks and the King's audience hall. The platform was used as a royal viewing area for the Dasara festivities, religious ceremonies and processions.

There's also the **Hazarama Temple**, with exquisitve carvings that depict scenes from the Ramayana, and polished black granite pillars.

Northeast from here within the walled ladies' quarters is the **Zenana Enclosure**. Its peaceful grounds and lush lawns feel like an oasis amid the arid surrounds. Here is the **Lotus Mahal**, a delicately designed pavilion which was supposedly the queen's recreational mansion. It overlooks the 11 grand **Elephant Stables** with arched entrances and domed chambers. There's also a small museum and army barracks within the high-walled enclosure. Further south, you'll find various temples and elaborate waterworks, including the **Queen's Bath**, deceptively plain on the outside but amazing within, with its Indo-Islamic architecture.

Another interesting stop-off along the road to the Virupaksha Temple is the 6.7m monolithic statue of the bulging-eyed **Lakshimi Narasmiha** in a cross-legged yoga position and topped by a hood of seven snakes. Nearby is the **Krishna Temple** built in 1513, which is fronted by a D-cupped apsara and 10 incarnations of Vishnu.

🛏 Sleeping & Eating

Due to Hampi's religious significance, meat is strictly off the menu in all restaurants, and alcohol is banned (though some restaurants can order it for you).

Padma Guest House   Guesthouse $

(☎ 08394-241331; padmaguesthouse@gmail.com; d from ₹800; ❄ 🛜) In a quiet corner of Hampi Bazaar, this amiable guesthouse feels more like a homestay, with basic, squeaky-clean rooms, many of which have views of Virupaksha Temple.

Laughing Buddha   Multicuisine $

(mains from ₹80; ⊙8am-10pm; 🛜) Now that Hampi's famous riverside restaurants have closed on the other side, Laughing Buddha has taken over as the most atmospheric place to eat, with serene river views that span beyond to the temples and ruins. Its menu is curries, burgers, pizzas – you know the drill…

ℹ Information

There's no ATM in Hampi; the closest is 3km away in Kamalapuram – a ₹100 autorickshaw return trip.

Internet (per hour ₹40) is ubiquitous; some guesthouses have paid wi-fi. A good tourist resource for Hampi is www.hampi.in.

ℹ Getting There & Away

The first bus from Hospet (₹22, 30 minutes, half-hourly) is at 5.45am; the last one back leaves Hampi Bazaar at 7.30pm. An autorickshaw costs ₹150 to ₹200.

The Amaravathi Express and Kcg Ypr Express head to Magdaon, Goa (sleeper/2AC ₹225/855, 7½ hours) at 6.30am on Monday, Wednesday Thursday and Saturday.

Numerous travel agents in Hampi Bazaar book onward tickets or arrange taxis.

ℹ Getting Around

Bicycles cost about ₹30 per day in Hampi Bazaar, while mopeds cost ₹100 to ₹150.

Walking around the ruins is recommended too, but expect to cover at least 7km just to see the major sites. Hiring an autorickshaw for the day costs ₹750.

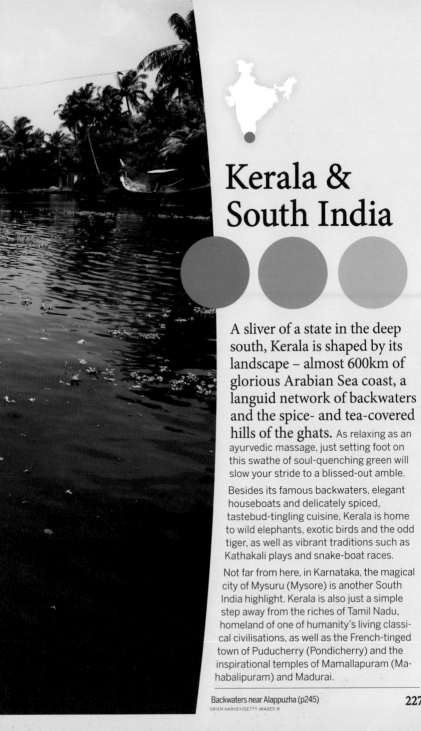

Kerala & South India

A sliver of a state in the deep south, Kerala is shaped by its landscape – almost 600km of glorious Arabian Sea coast, a languid network of backwaters and the spice- and tea-covered hills of the ghats. As relaxing as an ayurvedic massage, just setting foot on this swathe of soul-quenching green will slow your stride to a blissed-out amble.

Besides its famous backwaters, elegant houseboats and delicately spiced, tastebud-tingling cuisine, Kerala is home to wild elephants, exotic birds and the odd tiger, as well as vibrant traditions such as Kathakali plays and snake-boat races.

Not far from here, in Karnataka, the magical city of Mysuru (Mysore) is another South India highlight. Kerala is also just a simple step away from the riches of Tamil Nadu, homeland of one of humanity's living classical civilisations, as well as the French-tinged town of Puducherry (Pondicherry) and the inspirational temples of Mamallapuram (Mahabalipuram) and Madurai.

Backwaters near Alappuzha (p245)

Meenakshi Amman Temple (p288)
ANTONIA TOZER/GETTY IMAGES ©

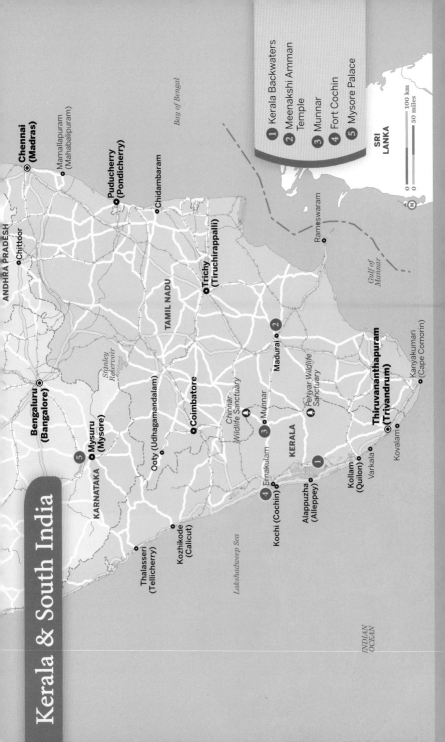

Kerala & South India

ANDHRA PRADESH

Chittoor

Chennai (Madras)

Mamallapuram (Mahabalipuram)

Puducherry (Pondicherry)

Chidambaram

Bay of Bengal

TAMIL NADU

Trichy (Tiruchirappalli)

Rameswaram

Gulf of Mannar

Madurai ❷

Periyar Wildlife Sanctuary

Chinnar Wildlife Sanctuary

Munnar ❸

❹

KERALA

Ernakulam

Kochi (Cochin) ❹

Alappuzha (Alleppey)

❶

Kollam (Quilon)

Varkala

Thiruvananthapuram (Trivandrum)

Kovalam

Kanyakumari (Cape Comorin)

Coimbatore

Ooty (Udhagamandalam)

Stanley Reservoir

KARNATAKA

Bengaluru (Bangalore)

Mysuru (Mysore)

❺

Kozhikode (Calicut)

Thalasseri (Tellicherry)

Lakshadweep Sea

INDIAN OCEAN

❶ Kerala Backwaters
❷ Meenakshi Amman Temple
❸ Munnar
❹ Fort Cochin
❺ Mysore Palace

SRI LANKA

100 km
50 miles

0
0

Kerala & South India's Highlights

Kerala Backwaters

Exploring Kerala's 900km network of waterways that fringe the coast and trickle inland is an experience not to be missed. The main jumping-off point to explore Kerala's southern backwaters is Alappuzha (Alleppey; p245) – from here you can hire an overnight houseboat or travel around through the narrower canals by canoe.

1

Meenakshi Amman Temple

2

The labyrinthine Meenakshi Amman Temple (p288) is one of India's most breathtaking religious sites, a 6-hectare complex enclosed by 12 *gopurams* (gateway towers). It's the pinnacle of South Indian temple architecture and an amazing place to observe the busy rituals and constant activity that centre on the shrine.

MAHESH/GETTY IMAGES ©

Munnar

The countryside around Munnar (p253) consists of rolling tea plantations, hued in a thousand shades of green. The hills are covered by a sculptural carpet of tea trees and the mountain scenery is magnificent. Stay in a remote guesthouse and take a trek – you'll often find yourself up above the clouds, watching veils of mist cling below the mountaintops.

3

4

Fort Cochin

The historic port area of Kochi (Cochin; p256) is full of old colonial-era mansions, many turned into some of South India's loveliest heritage hotels. It's the ideal place to splash out on some atmospheric, stately accommodation and India's best homestays to use as a base for your explorations of Kochi's islands, synagogue, museums and excellent restaurants.

5

Mysore Palace

For many travellers, a trip to Mysuru (Mysore; p265), this most royal of ancient cities, is a highlight of South India. Most are enticed by the magnificent maharaja's palace, but it's the bustling markets, cosmopolitan culture and famously friendly locals that persuade visitors to linger longer than they first planned.

Kerala & South India's Best...

Wining & Dining

○ **Villa Maya** Sumptuous dining in a magnificent 18th-century Dutch mansion in Trivandrum. (p238)

○ **Dal Roti** Fort Cochin's finest, with the freshest, tastiest Indian cuisine. (p261)

○ **Malabar Junction** Another Fort Cochin culinary gem; come here for European cuisine, seafood and healthy indulgence. (p261)

○ **Sapphire** Food fit for a king, served in the grand ballroom of Mysuru's Lalitha Mahal Palace hotel. (p268)

Heritage Accommodation

○ **Raheem Residency** Lovely 1860s beachside home in the backwater hub of Alleppey. (p247)

○ **Malabar House** Old world meets uber-hip at this Fort Cochin gem. (p259)

○ **Brunton Boatyard** Faithful 16th- and 17th-century Dutch and Portuguese architecture in Fort Cochin. (p260)

○ **Les Hibiscus** Arguably the pick of Puducherry's impressive collection of heritage hotels. (p285)

○ **Lalitha Mahal Palace** Majestic heritage accommodation in a former maharaja's guesthouse in Mysuru. (p267)

Architecture

○ **Meenakshi Amman Temple, Madurai** A labyrinthine structure that ranks among the greatest temples of India. (p288)

○ **Mysore Palace, Mysuru** Fantastic 20th-century palace – among the grandest of India's royal buildings. (p265)

○ **French Quarter, Puducherry** Romantic white and mustard colonial-era buildings on the cobbled streets of old Pondi. (p283)

○ **Pardesi Synagogue, Kochi** Exquisite synagogue in the spice port of Mattancherry. (p257)

○ **Shore Temple, Mamallapuram** Rock-cut elegance by the sea. (p278)

Need to Know

Chill-Out Spots

○ **Kerala Backwaters** Kick back on a houseboat and watch the coconut groves float by. (p248)

○ **Varkala** Stunning red-streaked coastal cliffs and white-sand beaches at Kerala's beachside traveller hot spot. (p243)

○ **Munnar** Trek, chill and sip chai in the tea plantations around Munnar. (p253)

○ **Periyar** Explore wildlife and trek the jungle in this popular national park. (p250)

○ **Mamallapuram** Tamil Nadu's beach hang-out is also the site of World Heritage–listed temples and carvings. (p278)

ADVANCE PLANNING

○ **One month before** Book ahead at heritage hotels.

○ **Two weeks before** Reserve train tickets, or arrange a car and driver through an agency.

○ **One day before** Call to reconfirm hotel bookings and reserve a place on your favoured tours.

RESOURCES

○ **Kerala Tourism** (www.keralatourism.org) Kerala's official tourism site.

○ **Manorama Online** (www.manoramaonline.com) Keralan newspaper with an online English edition.

○ **Kerala.com** (www.kerala.com) News, tourism and loads of links.

○ **Tamilnadu** (www.tamilnadu.com) News and directory.

○ **Tamil Nadu Tourism** (www.tamilnadutourism.org)

GETTING AROUND

○ **Train** Usually the quickest and most comfortable transport between towns along the coast and between major cities.

○ **Car & driver** A taxi – for one or several days – is the most convenient way to travel, but can be slower than the train on some routes, especially after the monsoon.

○ **Boat** Ferries serve towns around Kerala's backwaters or for longer trips if the trains are booked out.

○ **Bus** Good for getting to smaller towns.

BE FOREWARNED

○ **High season** Kerala's backwaters and beach resorts have a high season around November to March; around mid-December to mid-January, prices creep up further.

○ **Great deals** To be had during the monsoon (June to September).

○ **Festivals** Colourful temple festivals happen almost daily in Kerala between November and February; ask around locally for times and locations.

Left: Fish seller near Kovalam (p240)
Above: Paths connect Kerala's waterside villages

Kerala & South India Itineraries

The first of these itineraries concentrates on the temple-rich state of Tamil Nadu, while the second allows time to explore the gloriously laid-back region of Kerala.

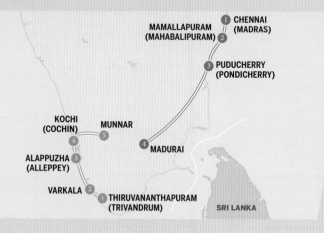

5 DAYS

CHENNAI TO MADURAI
TAMIL NADU TEMPLE HOP

This tour starts in ❶ **Chennai** (Madras; p269), the underrated state capital that's thin on top-draw sights but great for top-notch food. Build up an appetite by poking around the Government Museum complex and taking an early-evening stroll along Marina Beach before tucking into the city's culinary delights.

The following day, head south to nearby ❷ **Mamallapuram** (Mahabalipuram; p278), where you can pick your way through the dramatic ruined temples and impressive ancient rock carvings, before gorging on fresh seafood as the sun goes down. If time

allows, sign up for a bicycle tour around the neighbouring villages, before making your way to French-tinged ❸ **Puducherry** (Pondicherry; p282). With its colonial-era buildings and bohemian vibe, you'll want to base yourself here for a couple of days – eat steak, browse boutiques and practise some yoga – before heading further south to ❹ **Madurai** (p287). The highlight here is the extraordinary Meenakshi Amman Temple, a riot of Dravidian sculpture that's regarded as South India's finest temple complex and ensures a dramatic to end your tour.

THIRUVANANTHAPURAM TO MUNNAR
A TASTE OF KERALA

Launch off from Kerala's gentle state capital, ❶ **Thiruvananthapuram** (Trivandrum; p236), seeing its appealing museums and zoo park before heading straight for the beach. The laid-back, traveller-oriented resort of ❷ **Varkala** (p243) straggles along the top of stunning coastal cliffs and is formed of a cluster of small hotels and guesthouses. It's a Hindu place of pilgrimage as well as a holiday destination and you'll see priests doing *puja* (worship) on the beach. From here, head to ❸ **Alappuzha** (Alleppey; p245) for a boat trip along Kerala's magical backwaters. Continue north (by boat, bus or a combination of the two) to the fascinating historic spice port of ❹ **Kochi** (Cochin; p256). Stay in lovely Fort Cochin, with its colonial-era mansions, excellent restaurants and age-old cantilevered Chinese fishing nets. The marvellous synagogue is within walking distance, in nearby Mattancherry. If you still have some time, it's an easy trip from Kochi into the foothills of the Western Ghats to the scrappy-looking town of ❺ **Munnar** (p253), which is sublimely set, surrounded by rolling tea plantations. It's the perfect place to stay in a remote mansion, relax and go trekking into the hills.

Five Rathas (p278), Mamallapuram
IMAGES OF INDIA/GETTY IMAGES ©

Discover Kerala & South India

At a Glance

- **Varkala** (p243) Cliff-lined beach; laid-back vibe.

- **Alappuzha** (Alleppey; p245) Gateway to the backwaters.

- **Munnar** (p253) South India's tea-growing capital.

- **Kochi** (Cochin; p256) Delightful ancient port town.

- **Mysuru** (Mysore; p265) Flamboyant city; fantastical palace.

- **Mamallapuram** (Mahabalipuram; p278) Unesco-listed temples.

- **Puducherry** (Pondicherry; p282) French-flavoured coastal town.

- **Madurai** (p287) Home to one of India's greatest temples.

Krishna's Butter Ball, Mamallapuram (p278)
SACHIN SAXENA / GETTY IMAGES ©

KERALA

Thiruvananthapuram (Trivandrum)

☎0471 / POP 752,490

Kerala's capital – often still referred to by its colonial name, Trivandrum – is an energetic place and an easygoing introduction to city life down south. Most travellers merely springboard from here to the nearby beachside resorts of Kovalam and Varkala, but Trivandrum has enough sights – including its zoo and cluster of Victorian museums in glorious neo-Keralan buildings – to justify a stay.

◉ Sights

Zoological Gardens   Zoo
(☎0471-2115122; adult/child ₹20/5, camera/video ₹50/100; ⊙9am-5.15pm Tue-Sun) Yann Martel famously based the animals in his *Life of Pi* on those he observed in Trivandrum's zoological gardens. Shaded paths meander through woodland, lakes and native forest, where tigers, macaques and hippos gather in reasonably large open enclosures.

Napier Museum   Museum
(adult/child ₹10/5; ⊙10am-5pm Tue & Thu-Sun, 1-5pm Wed) Housed in an 1880 wooden building designed by Robert Chisholm, a British architect whose Fair Isle–style version of the Keralan vernacular shows his enthusiasm for local craft, this museum has an eclectic display of bronzes, Buddhist sculptures, temple carts and ivory carvings. The carnivalesque interior is stunning and worth a look in its own right.

Museum of History & Heritage
Museum

(☏9567019037; www.museumkeralam.org; Park View; adult/child Indian ₹20/10, foreigner ₹200/50, camera ₹25; ☉10am-5.30pm Tue-Sun) In a lovely heritage building within the Kerala Tourism complex, this beautifully presented museum traces Keralan history and culture through superb static displays and interactive audiovisual presentations. Exhibits range from Iron Age implements to bronze and terracotta sculptures, murals, *dhulichitra* (floor paintings) and recreations of traditional Keralan homes.

Shri Padmanabhaswamy Temple
Hindu Temple

(☉inner sanctum 3.30am-7.30pm, Hindus only) Trivandrum's spiritual heart is this 260-year-old temple in the Fort area. The main entrance is the 30m-tall, seven-tier eastern *gopuram* (gateway tower). In the inner sanctum (Hindus only), the deity Padmanabha reclines on the sacred serpent and is made from over 10,000 *salagramam* (sacred stones) that were purportedly transported from Nepal by elephant. The path around to the right of the gate offers good views of the *gopuram*.

Tours

KTDC (Kerala Tourist Development Corporation) runs several tours, all leaving from the Tourist Reception Centre (p239) at the KTDC Hotel Chaithram on Central Station Rd. They include a City Tour (₹300), Kanyakumari Day Tour (₹700) and Neyyar Dam (₹400).

Sleeping

Princess Inn
Hotel $

(☏0471-2339150; princess_inn@yahoo.com; Manjalikulam Rd; s/d from ₹450/550, with AC from ₹950/1125; ❄☎) In a glass-fronted building, the Princess Inn promises a relatively quiet sleep in a central sidestreet location. It's comfortable, with satellite TV and immaculate bathrooms; it's worth paying a little more for the spacious 'deluxe' rooms.

Graceful Homestay
Homestay $$

(☏9847249556, 0417-2444358; www.graceful homestay.com; Pothujanam Rd, Philip's Hill; s/d incl breakfast downstairsd ₹1450/1650, upstairs & ste ₹2200/2750; @☎) In Trivandrum's leafy western suburbs, this lovely, serene house set in a couple of hectares of garden is owned by Sylvia and run by her brother Giles. The four rooms are all neatly furnished with individual character and access to kitchen, living areas and balconies. The pick of the rooms has an amazing covered terrace with views overlooking a sea of palms. It's around 6km from the train station and 5km from the airport; call ahead for directions.

Varikatt Heritage
Homestay $$

(☏9895239055, 0417-2336057; www.varikatt heritage.com; Punnen Rd; r/ste incl breakfast ₹4000/5000; ☎) Trivandrum's most charismatic place to stay is the 250-year-old home of Colonel Roy Kuncheria. It's a wonderful Indo-Saracenic bungalow with four rooms flanked by verandahs facing a pretty garden. Every antique – and the home itself – has a family story attached. Lunch and dinner available (₹500).

Eating

Indian Coffee House
Indian $

(Maveli Cafe; Central Station Rd; snacks ₹10-60; ☉7am-10.30pm) This branch of Indian Coffee House serves its strong coffee and snacks in a crazy red-brick tower that looks like a cross between a lighthouse and a pigeon coop, and has a spiralling interior lined with concrete benches and tables. You have to admire the hard-working waiters.

Cherries & Berries
Cafe $$

(☏0471-2735433; www.cherriesandberries. in; Carmel Towers, Cotton Hill; dishes ₹100-195; ☉10am-10pm; ☎) For serious comfort food, icy air-con and free wi-fi that really works, take a trip east of the centre to Cherries & Berries. The menu includes waffles, mini-pizzas, hot dogs, toasties, good coffee and indulgent chocolate-bar milkshakes – try the Kit Kat shake (₹150).

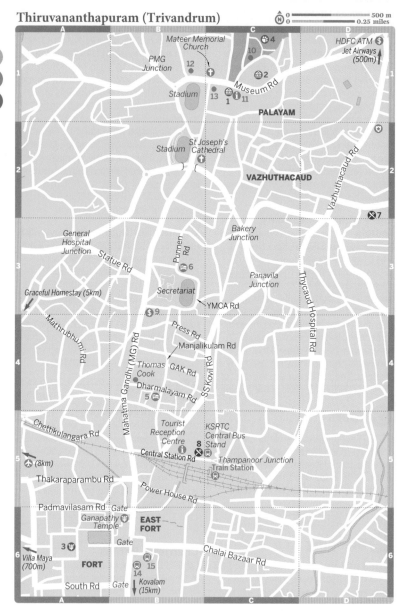

Villa Maya Keralan **$$$**

(☏0471-2578901; www.villamaya.in; 120 Airport Rd, Injakkal; starters ₹350-600, mains ₹450-1050; ☺11am-11pm) Villa Maya is more an experience than a restaurant. Dining is either in the magnificent 18th-century Dutch mansion or in private curtained niches in the tranquil courtyard garden, where you'll be lulled by lily ponds and trickling fountains. The Keralan cuisine itself is expertly crafted, delicately spiced and beautifully

Thiruvananthapuram (Trivandrum)

◉ Sights
1 Museum of History & Heritage C1
2 Napier Museum.....................................C1
3 Shri Padmanabhaswamy Temple A6
4 Zoological Gardens................................C1

🛏 Sleeping
5 Princess Inn...B4
6 Varikatt Heritage..................................B3

✴ Eating
7 Cherries & Berries D2
8 Indian Coffee House.............................B5

❶ Information
9 State Bank of India ATM........................B3
10 Ticket Counter (for Zoo &
    Museums) C1
11 Tourist Facilitation Centre C1

❶ Transport
12 Air India...B1
13 Airtravel Enterprises............................C1
14 East Fort Bus Stand (buses &
    taxis to Kovalam).............................B6
15 Municipal Bus Stand............................B6

presented. Seafood is a speciality, with dishes like stuffed crab with lobster butter, but there are some tantalising veg dishes too. Between lunch and dinner (3pm to 7pm) you can order snacks like sandwiches, pizzas and calzones. Ask the friendly staff for a free tour of the historic manor.

❶ Information

KIMS (Kerala Institute of Medical Sciences; ☏0471-3041000, emergency 0471-3041144; www.kimskerala.com; Kumarapuram; ☻24hr) Best choice for medical problems; about 7km northwest of Trivandrum train station.

Tourist Facilitation Centre (☏0471-2321132; Museum Rd; ☻24hr) Near the zoo; supplies maps and brochures.

Tourist Reception Centre (KTDC Hotel Chaithram; ☏0471-2330031; Central Station Rd; ☻7am-9pm daily) Arranges KTDC-run tours.

❶ Getting There & Away

Air

Between them, **Air India** (☏0471-2317341; www.airindia.in; Mascot Sq), **Jet Airways** (☏0471-2728864; www.jetairways.com; Sasthamangalam Junction) and **SpiceJet** (☏09871803333; www.spicejet.com; Trivandrum airport) fly from Trivandrum airport to Mumbai (Bombay), Kochi,

Transport from Trivandrum

BUSES FROM TRIVANDRUM (KSRTC BUS STAND)

DESTINATION	FARE (₹)	DURATION (HR)	FREQUENCY
Alleppey	120, AC 211	3½	every 15min
Ernakulam (Kochi)	167, AC 281	5½	every 20min
Kollam	60	1½	every 15min
Kumily (for Periyar)	231	8	2 daily
Munnar	35	7	2 daily
Varkala	60	1¼	hourly

MAJOR TRAINS FROM TRIVANDRUM

DESTINATION	TRAIN NO & NAME	FARE (₹; SLEEPER/3AC/2AC)	DURATION (HR)	DEPARTURES (DAILY)
Chennai	12696 Chennai Exp	470/1230/1760	16½	5.20pm
Mumbai	16346 Netravathi Exp	670/1785/2625	31	9.50am

Bengaluru (Bangalore), Chennai (Madras) and Delhi.

There are also direct flights from Trivandrum to Colombo in Sri Lanka, Male in the Maldives and major Gulf regions such as Dubai, Kuwait, Sharjah and Bahrain.

All airline bookings can be made at the efficient **Airtravel Enterprises** (☏0471-3011300; www.ate.travel; MG Rd, New Corporation Bldg).

Bus

State-run and private buses use Trivandrum's giant new concave **KSRTC Central Bus Stand** (☏0471-2462290; www.keralatc.com; Central Station Rd, Thampanoor), opposite the train station.

Buses leave for Kovalam beach (₹15, 30 minutes, every 20 minutes) between 6am and 9pm from the southern end of the East Fort bus stand on MG Rd.

Train

Within Kerala there are frequent express trains to Varkala (2nd/sleeper/3AC ₹45/140/485, one hour), Kollam (₹55/170/535, 1¼ hour) and Ernakulam (₹95/195/535, 4½ hours), with trains passing through either Alleppey (₹80/170/535, three hours) or Kottayam (₹80/140/485, 3½ hours). There are also numerous daily services to Kanyakumari (₹80/140/485, three hours).

❶ Getting Around

The **airport** (☏0471-2501424) is 10km from the city and 15km from Kovalam; take local bus 14 from the East Fort and City Bus stand (₹9). Prepaid taxi vouchers from the airport cost ₹350 to the city and ₹500 to Kovalam.

Autorickshaws are the easiest way to get around, with short hops costing ₹30 to ₹50.

....

Kovalam
☏0471

Once a calm fishing village clustered around its crescent beaches, these days Kovalam is Kerala's most developed resort. The main stretch, **Lighthouse Beach**, is touristy with hotels and restaurants built up along the shore, while **Hawa Beach** to the north is usually crowded with day-trippers.

About 2km further north, **Samudra Beach** has several upmarket resorts, restaurants and a peaceful but steep beach.

There are strong rips at both ends of Lighthouse Beach that carry away several swimmers every year. Swim only between the flags in the area patrolled by

Lighthouse Beach, Kovalam

DETHAN PUNALUR / GETTY IMAGES ©

lifeguards and avoid swimming during the monsoon.

Sights & Activities

Vizhinjam Lighthouse Lighthouse
(Indian/foreigner ₹10/25, camera/video ₹20/25; ◷10am-5pm) Kovalam's most distinguishing feature is the working candy-striped lighthouse at the southern end of the beach. Climb the spiral staircase for vertigo-inducing views up and down the coast.

Kovalam Surf Club Surfing
(☏9847347367; www.kovalamsurfclub.com; behind Lighthouse Beach; 1½ hr lessons ₹1000, board rental half-/full day ₹500/1000) This surf shop and club on Lighthouse Beach offers lessons (from introductory to performance), board rental and a community focus.

Santhigiri Ayurveda
(☏0471-2482800; www.santhigiriashram.org; Lighthouse Beach Rd; from ₹1100; ◷9am-8pm) Recommended massages and ayurvedic treatments.

Sleeping

Paradesh Inn Guesthouse $$
(☏9995362952; inn.paradesh@yahoo.com; Avaduthura; d incl breakfast from ₹1800; @) Back from the beach high above the palms, tranquil Italian-run Paradesh Inn resembles a whitewashed Greek island hideaway. Each of the six fan-cooled rooms has a hanging chair outside; there are views from the rooftop, nice breakfasts and satya cooking ('yoga food') for guests.

Beach Hotel II Hotel $$$
(☏9400031243, 0471-2481937; www.thebeachhotel-kovalam.com; d ₹4500, with AC ₹5600; ❄🛜) Tucked into the southern end of Lighthouse Beach, this stylish pad has 10 sea-facing rooms all with balcony and large sliding French windows. Decor is simple chic. It's also home to the excellent Fusion terrace restaurant (p242).

Jeevan Ayurvedic Beach Resort Resort $$
(☏9846898498, 0471-2480662; www.jeevanresort.net; d ₹1800-4200, with AC ₹2400-12,000; ❄🛒) Beachfront Jeevan is an inviting sort of place with one of the only seafront pools on this strip. Expect inoffensively decorated, decent-sized rooms with bathtubs. All but the cheapest ground-floor rooms have sea views and balconies.

Leela Hotel $$$
(☏0471-2480101; www.theleela.com; d/ste from ₹16,200/40,000; ❄@🛜🛒) The sumptuous Leela is set in extensive grounds on the headland north of Hawah beach. You'll find three swimming pools, an ayurvedic centre, a gym, two 'private beaches', several restaurants and more. Spacious rooms have period touches, colourful textiles and Keralan artwork.

Eating & Drinking

Lighthouse Beach is the main restaurant hub and each evening numerous places lining the beach promenade display the catch of the day – just pick a fish or lobster, settle on a price and decide how you want it prepared. Market price varies enormously depending on the day's catch, but at the time of research it was around ₹350 per fish fillet, ₹900 per half kilo of tiger prawns, and ₹3500 per kilo of lobster. Unlicensed places might serve alcohol in mugs, or with the bottles hidden discreetly out of sight (or not depending on current government rules).

Samudra Beach, to the north, is quieter but also has some restaurants worth seeking out. For a romantic dining splurge, the restaurants at Leela and Vivanta by Taj are pricey but top class.

Varsha Restaurant South Indian $
(mains ₹100-175; ◷8am-10pm) This little restaurant just back from Lighthouse Beach serves some of Kovalam's best vegetarian food at budget prices. Dishes are fresh and carefully prepared. A great spot for breakfast and lunch in particular.

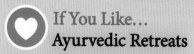

If You Like…
Ayurvedic Retreats

Around 8km south of Kovalam, amid seemingly endless swaying palms, colourful village life and some empty golden-sand beaches, are some ayurvedic resorts that make tantalising high-end alternatives to Kovalam's crowded centre.

1 DR FRANKLIN'S PANCHAKARMA INSTITUTE

(☎0471-2480870; www.dr-franklin.com; Chowara; s/d hut €23/30, r from €28/37, with AC €41/60; @🛜🏊) For those serious about ayurvedic treatment, this is a reputable and less expensive alternative to the flashier resorts. Daily treatment with full meal plan costs €70. Accommodation is tidy and comfortable but not resort style.

2 NIRAAMAYA SURYA SAMUDRA

(☎0471-2480413; www.niraamaya.in; Pulinkudi; r incl breakfast ₹18,000-32,000; ❄🛜🏊) The latest incarnation of Surya Samudra offers A-list-style seclusion. The 22 transplanted traditional Keralan homes come with four-poster beds and open-air bathrooms, set in a palm grove above sparkling seas. There's an infinity pool carved out of a single block of granite, the renowned Niraamaya Spa, ayurvedic treatments, gym and spectacular outdoor yoga platforms.

3 BETHSAIDA HERMITAGE

(☎0471-2267554; www.bethsaidahermitage. com; Pulinkudi; s €90-150, d €150-165; ❄🛜🏊) This charitable organisation helps support two nearby orphanages and several other worthy causes. As a bonus, it's also a luxurious and remote beachside escape, with sculpted gardens, seductively slung hammocks, putting-green-perfect lawns, palms galore and professional ayurvedic treatments and yoga classes.

Waves Restaurant & German Bakery
Multicuisine $$

(Beach Hotel; breakfast ₹80-450, mains ₹250-450; ⊙7.30am-11pm; 🛜) With its broad, burnt-orange balcony, ambient soundtrack and wide-roaming menu, Waves is usually busy with foreigners. It morphs into the German Bakery, a great spot for breakfast with fresh bread, croissants, pastries and decent coffee, while dinner turns up Thai curries, German sausages, pizza and seafood. There's a small bookshop attached. Wi-fi is ₹40.

Fusion
Multicuisine $$

(mains ₹150-450; ⊙7.30am-10.30pm; 🛜) The terrace restaurant at Beach Hotel II is one of the best dining experiences on Lighthouse Beach with an inventive East-meets-West menu, a range of Continental dishes, Asian fusion, and interesting seafood numbers like lobster steamed in vodka. Also serves French press coffee and herbal teas.

Curry Leaf
Multicuisine $$

(mains ₹100-350; ⊙8am-8.30pm) On a small hilltop overlooking Samudra Beach, this new two-storey restaurant boasts enviable ocean and sunset views, eager staff and good food ranging from fresh seafood and tandoori to Continental dishes. It requires a bit of a walk along paths or uphill from the beach, but the uncrowded location is part of the charm.

ⓘ Information

About 500m uphill from the beach are HDFC and Axis ATMs. There are several small internet cafes charging around ₹30 per hour.

Tourist Facilitation Centre (☎0471-2480085; Kovalam Beach Rd; ⊙9.30am-5pm) Helpful; in the entrance to Government Guesthouse near the bus stand.

Upasana Hospital (☎0471-2480632) Has English-speaking doctors who can take care of minor injuries.

ⓘ Getting There & Around

Bus

Buses start and finish at an unofficial stand on the main road outside the entrance to Leela resort and all buses pass through Kovalam Junction, about 1.5km north of Lighthouse Beach. Buses connect Kovalam and Trivandrum every 20 minutes between 5.30am and 10pm (₹15, 30 minutes).

For northbound onward travel it's easiest to take any bus to Trivandrum and change there, but there are two buses daily to Ernakulam (₹210, 5½ hours), stopping at Kallambalam (for Varkala, ₹750, 1½ hours), Kollam (₹85, 2½ hours) and Alleppey (₹125, four hours).

For Kanyakumari there are a couple of buses (₹80, two hours).

Taxi

A taxi between Trivandrum and Kovalam beach is around ₹400; an autorickshaw should cost ₹300. From the bus stand to the north end of Lighthouse Beach costs around ₹50.

Varkala

✆0470 / POP 42,270

Perched almost perilously along the edge of 15m-high red laterite cliffs, the resort of Varkala has a naturally beautiful setting and the cliff-top stretch has steadily grown into Kerala's most popular backpacker hang-out. It's not hard to escape the crowds further north or south where the beaches are cleaner and quieter.

Despite its backpacker vibe, Varkala is essentially a temple town, and the main Papanasham beach is a holy place where Hindus come to make offerings for passed loved ones, assisted by priests who set up shop beneath the Hindustan Hotel.

 Activities

Laksmi's　　　　　Beauty & Massage
(✆9895948080; Clafouti Beach Resort; manicure & pedicure ₹600-1000, henna designs ₹500, massages ₹1200; ⏰9am-7pm) This tiny place at Clafouti offers quality ladies-only treatments such as threading and waxing, manicures and massage.

Haridas Yoga　　　　　　　　　Yoga
(www.pranayogavidya.com; Hotel Green Palace; classes ₹300; ⏰8am & 4.30pm Aug-May) Recommended drop-in 1½-hour hatha yoga classes with experienced teachers.

Eden Garden　　　　　　　Massage
(✆0470-2603910; www.edengarden.in; massages from ₹1000) Offers a more upmarket ayurvedic experience, including single treatments and packages.

Sleeping

Jicky's　　　　　Guesthouse $
(✆9846179325, 0470-2606994; www.jickys.com; s ₹500, d ₹800-1200, AC cottage ₹3000; ❄🛜) In the palm groves just back from the cliffs and taxi stand, family-run Jicky's remains as friendly as they come and has blossomed into several buildings offering plenty of choice for travellers. The rooms in the main whitewashed building are fresh, and nearby are two charming octagonal double cottages, and some larger air-con rooms. Offers good off-season discounts.

Kaiya House　　　　Guesthouse $$
(✆9746126909, 9995187913; www.kaiyahouse.com; d incl breakfast ₹2750, with AC ₹3300; ❄🛜) What Kaiya House lacks in sea views it makes up for with charm, welcoming owners and sheer relaxation. Each of the five rooms is thoughtfully furnished and themed (African, Indian, Chinese, Japanese and English) with four-poster beds and artworks on the walls. There's a lovely rooftop terrace and rear courtyard with calming vibe. Expat owner Debra will welcome you with tea, advice and free walking tours. The clifftop is 10 minutes' walk away.

Kerala Bamboo House　　Resort $$
(✆9895270993; www.keralabamboohouse.com; huts d ₹2500-3500, r with AC ₹5000; ❄🛜) For that simple bamboo-hut experience, this popular place squishes together dozens of pretty Balinese-style huts and a neatly maintained garden about half-way along the North Cliff walk. Ayurvedic treatments, yoga and cooking classes (₹600 per person, minimum two people) are on offer.

Omsam Guest Home　　Guesthouse $$
(✆0470-2604455; www.omsamguesthome.com; South Cliff; d ₹2500-3500, with AC ₹4500; ❄🛜) The seven rooms in this beautiful Keralan-style guesthouse are a delight, with heavy timber stylings and furniture. Good location south of the main beach.

Environmental Issues

Pollution from houseboat motors is becoming a major problem as boat numbers swell every season. The Keralan authorities have introduced an ecofriendly accreditation system for houseboat operators. Among the criteria an operator must meet before being issued with the 'Green Palm Certificate' are the installation of solar panels and sanitary tanks for the disposal of waste – ask operators whether they have the requisite certification. Consider choosing one of the few remaining punting, rather than motorised, boats if possible, though these can only operate in shallow water.

Gateway Hotel Janardhanapuram   Hotel $$$

(📞0470-6673300; www.thegatewayhotels.com; d incl breakfast from ₹9000, ste ₹12,500; ❄@🛜🏊) Varkala's flashiest hotel, the rebadged Gateway, is looking hot with gleaming linen and mocha cushions in rooms overlooking the garden, while the more expensive rooms have sea views and private balconies. There's a fantastic pool with bar (nonguests ₹500), tennis court and well-regarded GAD restaurant.

Eating & Drinking

Most restaurants in Varkala offer the same traveller menu of Indian, Asian and Western fare to a soundtrack of easy-listening trance and Bob Marley, but the quality of the cliffside 'shacks' has improved out of sight over the years and most offer free wi-fi. Join in the nightly Varkala saunter till you find a place that suits.

Sreepadman   South Indian $

(thalis ₹75; ⏱5am-10pm) For cheap and authentic Keralan fare – think dosas and thalis – where you can rub shoulders with rickshaw drivers and pilgrims rather than tourists, pull up a seat at hole-in-the-wall Sreepadman, opposite the Janardhana temple and overlooking the large bathing tank.

Coffee Temple   Cafe $

(coffee ₹70-100, mains ₹80-250; ⏱6am-7pm; 🛜) For your early-morning coffee fix it's hard to beat this English-run place, where the beans are freshly ground, and there's fresh bread and a daily paper. The menu has also expanded into crepes and Mexican burritos, fajitas and tacos – and it's no worse for that.

Cafe Italiano   Italian $$

(mains ₹200-400; ⏱7am-11pm; 🛜) As well as good pizza, pasta and crepes, two-storey Italiano is worth a visit for its library and book exchange and for the tree growing through the upper deck.

ℹ️ Information

A 24-hour ATM at Temple Junction takes Visa cards, and there are several more ATMs in Varkala town. Many of the travel agents lining the cliff do cash advances on credit cards and change travellers cheques. Most restaurants and cafes offer free wi-fi.

Dangers & Annoyances

The beaches at Varkala have strong currents; even experienced swimmers have been swept away. This is one of the most dangerous beaches in Kerala. Take care walking on the cliff path, especially at night – much of it is unfenced and can be slippery in parts.

If women wear bikinis or even swimsuits on the beach at Varkala, they are likely to feel uncomfortably exposed to stares.

ℹ️ Getting There & Away

There are frequent local and express trains to Trivandrum (2nd/sleeper/3AC ₹45/140/485, one hour) and Kollam (₹45/140/485, 40 minutes), as well as seven daily services to Alleppey (2nd/sleeper/3AC ₹95/140/485, two hours). From Temple Junction, three daily buses pass by on their way to Trivandrum (₹60, 1½ to two hours), with one heading to Kollam (₹40, one hour).

ⓘ Getting Around

It's about 2.5km from the train station to Varkala beach, with autorickshaws going to Temple Junction for ₹80 and North Cliff for ₹100. Local buses also travel regularly between the train station and Temple Junction (₹5).

Alappuzha (Alleppey)

🎵 0477 / POP 174,200

Alappuzha – still better known as Alleppey – is the hub of Kerala's backwaters, home to a vast network of waterways and more than 1000 houseboats.

Wandering around the small but chaotic city centre, with its modest grid of canals, you'd be hard-pressed to agree with the 'Venice of the East' tag. But step out of this mini-mayhem – west to the beach or in practically any other direction towards the backwaters – and Alleppey is graceful and greenery-fringed, disappearing into a watery world of villages, punted canoes, toddy shops and, of course, houseboats. Float along and gaze over paddy fields of succulent green, curvaceous rice barges and village life along the banks. This is one of Kerala's most mesmerisingly beautiful and relaxing experiences.

◉ Sights & Activities

RKK Memorial Museum   Museum

(🎵 0477-2242923; www.rkkmuseum.com; NH47, near Powerhouse Bridge; Indian/foreigner ₹150/350; ⊙ 9am-5pm Tue-Sun) The Revi Karuna Karan (RKK) Memorial Museum, in a grand building fronted by Greco-Roman columns, contains a lavish collection of crystal, porcelain, ivory, Keralan antiques, furniture and artworks from the personal collection of wealthy businessman Revi Karuna Karan. The museum was created as a memorial after he passed away in 2003.

Kerala Kayaking   Kayaking

(🎵 0477-2245001, 9846585674; www.keralakayaking.com; 4/7/10hr per person ₹1500/3000/4500) The original kayaking outfit in Alleppey, with a young crew offering excellent guided kayaking trips through narrow backwater canals. Paddles in single or double kayaks include a support boat and motorboat transport to your starting point. There are four-hour morning and afternoon trips, seven- or 10-hour day trips, and multiday village tours can also be arranged.

Passenger boat, Alappuzha
LINDSAY BROWN / GETTY IMAGES ©

Tours

Any of the dozens of travel agencies in town, guesthouses, hotels, or the KTDC can arrange canoe or houseboat tours of the backwaters. See p248.

Sleeping

Even if you're not planning on boarding a houseboat, Alleppey has some of the most charming and best-value accommodation in Kerala.

Mandala Beach House
Guesthouse $

(☏8589868589; www.mandalabeachhouse. com; Alleppey Beach; d ₹600-900, cottage ₹750, ste ₹2000; 🛜) Beachfront accommodation on a budget doesn't get much better than this in Alleppey. Super-laid-back Mandala sits on the edge of the sand and has a range of simple rooms – the best being the glass-fronted 'penthouse' with unbeatable sunset views. Impromptu parties are known to crank up here in season, and there's a quieter nearby annexe.

Johnson's
Guesthouse $

(☏9846466399, 0477-2245825; www. johnsonskerala.com; d ₹500-850; @ 🛜) This backpacker favourite in a tumbledown mansion is as quirky as its owner, the gregarious Johnson Gilbert. It's a rambling residence with themed rooms filled with funky furniture, loads of plants outside and a canoe-shaped fish tank for a table. Johnson also hires out his **'eco-house-boat'** (www.ecohouseboat.com; ₹7000-13,000) and has a secluded riverside guesthouse in the backwaters.

Cherukara Nest
Homestay $$

(☏9947059628, 0477-2251509; www.cherukara nest.com; d/tr incl breakfast ₹900/1100, with AC ₹1500, AC cottage ₹1500; ❄@🛜) Set in well-tended gardens, with a pigeon coop at the back, this lovely heritage home has the sort of welcoming family atmosphere that makes you want to stay. In the main house there are four large characterful rooms, with high ceilings, lots of polished wood touches and antediluvian doors with ornate locks – check out the spacious split-level air-con room. Owner Tony also has a good-value **houseboat** (2/4

Backwaters, Alappuzha

people ₹6000/8000) – one of the few that still uses punting power.

Malayalam
Resort **$$**

(📞9496829424, 0477-2234591; malayalam resorts@yahoo.com; Punnamada; r ₹1600-2500; 🛜) This little family-run pad has four cute bamboo cottages and a pair of spacious two-storey four-room houses facing the lake. Views from the upstairs rooms with balcony are sweet. It's a bit hard to find: walk past the Keraleeyam resort reception and along the canal bank.

Raheem Residency
Hotel **$$$**

(📞0477-2239767; www.raheemresidency.com; Beach Rd; d €120-150; ❄🛜🏊) This thoughtfully renovated 1860s heritage home is a joy to visit, let alone stay in. The 10 rooms have been restored to their former glory and have bathtubs, antique furniture and period fixtures. The common areas are airy and comfortable, and there are pretty indoor courtyards, a well-stocked library, a great little pool and an excellent restaurant. Creative types should enquire about Raheem's writers' retreats.

Eating & Drinking

Mushroom
Arabian, Indian **$**

(near South Police Station; mains ₹70-140; 🕐noon-midnight) Breezy open-air restaurant with wrought-iron chairs specialising in cheap, tasty and spicy halal meals like *murg kali mirch* (black pepper chicken), fish tandoori and chilli mushrooms. Lots of locals and travellers give it a good vibe.

Kream Korner Art Cafe
Multicuisine **$**

(📞0477-2252781; www.kreamkornerartcafe.com; Mullackal Rd; dishes ₹40-250; 🕐9am-10pm) The most colourful dining space in town, this food-meets-art restaurant greets you with brightly painted tables and contemporary local art on the walls. It's a relaxed, airy place popular with Indian and foreign families for its inexpensive and tasty menu of Indian and Chinese dishes.

Detour:
Green Palm Homes

Just 12km from Alleppey on a backwater island, **Green Palm Homes** (📞9495557675, 0477-2724497; www.greenpalmhomes.com; Chennamkary; r without bathroom incl full board ₹2250, with bathroom ₹3250-4000; ❄) is a series of homestays that seem a universe away, set in a picturesque village, where you sleep in simple rooms in villagers' homes among rice paddies (though 'premium' rooms with attached bathroom and air-con are available). It's splendidly quiet, and there are no roads in sight; you can take a guided walk, hire bicycles (₹50 per hour) and canoes (₹100 per hour), or take cooking classes with your hosts (₹150). To get here, call ahead and catch one of the hourly ferries from Alleppey to Chennamkary (₹10, 1¼ hours).

Dreamers
Multicuisine **$$**

(📞8086752586; www.dreamersrestaurant.com; Alleppey Beach; mains ₹130-450; 🕐11am-10.30pm) Designed to vaguely resemble a *kettuvallam* (rice barge), Dreamers, across from Alleppey Beach, is a rustic but cool little restaurant with an upper deck, serving a wide variety of dishes from Tibetan momos and Thai curries to seafood and pizzas.

Chakara Restaurant
Multicuisine **$$$**

(📞0477-2230767; Beach Rd; mini Kerala meal ₹500, mains from ₹450; 🕐12.30-3pm & 7-10pm) The restaurant at Raheem Residency is Alleppey's finest, with seating on a bijou open rooftop with views over the beach. The menu creatively combines traditional Keralan and European cuisine, specialising in locally caught fish.

Don't Miss
Kerala's Backwaters

The highlight of a trip to Kerala is travelling through the 900km network of waterways that fringe the coast and trickle inland. Trips traverse palm-fringed lakes studded with cantilevered Chinese fishing nets, and wind their way along narrow, shady canals where coir (coconut fibre), copra (dried coconut kernels) and cashews are loaded onto boats.

tourist cruise per person ₹400; budget houseboat per 24hr 2 people ₹6000-8000, 4 people ₹10,000-12,000, larger/AC houseboat ₹15,000-30,000; village tours per person ₹400-800

⊘ tourist cruise daily Aug-Mar, every second day Apr-Jul; departs Kollam or Alleppey at 10.30am, arrives at 6.30pm

Tourist Cruises

The popular tourist cruise between Kollam and Alleppey is a scenic way to get between the two towns, but the boat travels along only the major canals. Many travellers get off halfway for the **Matha Amrithanandamayi Mission** (☏0476-2897578; www.amritapuri.org; Amritapuri), the ashram of the 'Hugging Mother'.

Houseboats

Houseboats cater for couples and groups. Food (and a chef to cook it) is generally included in the quoted cost, as is a driver/captain. They can be chartered through private operators in Alleppey, Kollam and Kottayam. The quality of boats varies widely – try to inspect the boat before agreeing on a price. Travel-agency reps will be pushing you to book a boat as soon as you set foot in Kerala, but it's better to wait till you reach a backwater hub: choice is greater in Alleppey (an extraordinary 1000-plus boats). Most guesthouses and home-stays can also book you on a houseboat. In the busy high season, when prices peak, you're likely to get caught in backwater-gridlock – some travellers are disappointed by the number of boats on the water. It's possible to travel by houseboat between Alleppey and Kollam and part way to Kochi – though these trips spend more time on open lakes and large canals than true backwaters and take longer than most travellers expect. Shop around to negotiate a bargain; this will be harder in the peak season. Prices triple from around 20 December to 5 January.

Village Tours

Village tours usually involve small groups of five to six people, a knowledgeable guide and an open canoe or covered *kettuvallam* (rice barge). The tours (from Kochi, Kollam or Alleppey) last from 2½ to six hours. They include visits to villages to watch coir-making, boat building, toddy (palm beer) tapping and fish farming.

Local Knowledge

Kerala Backwaters Don't Miss List

BROUGHT UP ALONGSIDE THE BACKWATERS, DINESH KUMAR RUNS LOCAL TOURS AND HOUSEBOAT TRIPS

1 CANOE & CHAVARA
A motorised canoe ride through Alleppey's inland waters allows a glimpse of the local social life, the nature and its landscape. I recommend seeing a church, the 250-year-old birth house and Chavara Bhavan (Kuttamangalam) of the Reverend Kuriakose Elias. The journey will take you through the zigzagging canals, past rice fields – really you are in the lap of nature.

2 COIR MAKING
In 1902, Londoner William Goodacre started a coir handloom in Muhamma, a village 16km north of Alleppey. When the British left India, Goodacre gave his workers ownership – Kerala's first co-operative society. There are 150 workers here. Take a bus from Alleppey and alight at Muhamma junction (40 minutes). Entry is free and it's open Monday to Saturday.

3 RICE PADDIES & A CHURCH
There are three famous rice fields below the water level, called Q, S and T Kayals. Kayal, in Malayalam, refers to the rice fields artificially created from Vembanad Lake. The project was led by local man Paul Murikkan, and it was his dream that he and his wife should be buried near the rice fields, so he built a church and burial grounds here. Sadly, his dream was never fulfilled, and he died alone in Trivandrum, but the church still exists on the deserted lakeshore.

4 HOUSEBOAT ROUTE
There are many routes, but I suggest leaving Alleppey at noon, docking overnight in Vattakayal Lake, south of C-block rice fields. It's surrounded by paddy fields and the landscape is lush and green.

5 PUBLIC FERRY
I recommend the public ferries: Alleppey to Nedumudy (via Venattukadu) and Alleppey to Kavalam (via Venattukadu). These are some of the loveliest routes.

❶ Information

DTPC Tourist Reception Centre (☎0477-2253308; www.dtpcalappuzha.com; Boat Jetty Rd; ⏰9am-5pm) Close to the bus stand and boat jetty. Staff are helpful and can advise on homestays and houseboats.

❶ Getting There & Away

Boat

Public ferries operate between Alleppey and Kottayam (₹19, 2½ hours) five times daily from the jetty on VCSB (Boat Jetty) Rd. The trip crosses Vembanad Lake and has a more varied landscape than the Kollam–Alleppey cruise.

Bus

From the KSRTC bus stand, frequent buses head to Trivandrum (₹122, 3½ hours, every 20 minutes), Kollam (₹70, 2½ hours) and Ernakulam (Kochi, ₹52, 1½ hours). Buses to Kottayam (₹43, 1¼ hours, every 30 minutes) are much faster than the ferry. One bus daily leaves for Kumily at 6.40am (₹120, 5½ hours). The Varkala bus (₹89, 3½ hours) leaves at 9am and 10.40am daily.

Train

There are several trains to Ernakulam (2nd-class/sleeper/3AC ₹39/120/218, 1½ hours) and Trivandrum (₹59/120/267, three hours) via Kollam (₹66/140/250, 1½ hours). Four trains a day stop at Varkala (2nd-class/AC chair ₹71/218, two hours). The train station is 4km west of town.

❶ Getting Around

An autorickshaw from the train station to the boat jetty and KSRTC bus stand is around ₹60.

Periyar Wildlife Sanctuary
☎04869

South India's most popular wildlife sanctuary, **Periyar** (☎04869-224571; www.periyartigerreserve.org; Indian/foreigner ₹25/450; ⏰6am-6pm, last entry 5pm) encompasses 777 sq km and a 26-sq-km artificial lake created by the British in 1895. The vast region is home to bison, sambar, wild boar, langur, 900 to 1000 elephants and 35 to 40 hard-to-spot tigers. Firmly established on both the Indian and foreigner tourist trails, the place can sometimes feel a bit like Disneyland-in-the-Ghats, but its mountain scenery and jungle walks make for an enjoyable visit. Bring warm and waterproof clothing.

Kumily, 4km from the sanctuary, is the closest town and home to a growing strip of hotels, spice shops, chocolate shops and Kashmiri emporiums. **Thekkady** is the sanctuary centre with the KTDC hotels and boat jetty. Confusingly, when people refer to the sanctuary they tend to use Kumily, Thekkady and Periyar interchangeably.

◎ Sights & Activities

Various tours and trips access Periyar Wildlife Sanctuary, all arranged

Monkeys, Periyar Wildlife Sanctuary
RACHEL DUNSDON PHOTOGRAPHY / GETTY IMAGES ©

through the Ecotourism Centre. Most hotels and agencies around town can arrange all-day jeep **jungle safaris (per person ₹1600-2000;** ☉**5am-6.30pm),** which cover over 40km of trails in jungle bordering the park, though many travellers complain that at least 30km of the trip is on sealed roads.

Cooking classes (₹300-450) are offered by many local homestays. There are recommended four-hour classes (₹500) at **Bar-B-Que (** 🖉**04869-320705; KK Rd),** about 1km from the bazaar on the road to Kottayam.

Several **spice plantations** are open to visitors and most hotels can arrange tours (₹450/750 by autorickshaw/taxi for two to three hours).

Periyar Lake Cruise   Boating
(adult/child ₹150/50; ☉departures 7.30am, 9.30am, 11.15am, 1.45pm & 3.30pm) These 1½-hour boat trips around the lake are the main way to tour the sanctuary without taking a guided walk. You might see deer, boar and birdlife but it's generally more of a cruise – often a rowdy one – than a wildlife-spotting experience. Boats are operated by the forest department and by KTDC – the ticket counters are together in the main building above the boat jetty, and you must buy a ticket before boarding the boat. In high season get to the ticket office 1½ hours before each trip to buy tickets. The first and last departures offer the best prospects for wildlife spotting, and October to March are generally the best time to see animals.

Ecotourism
Centre   Outdoor Adventure
(🖉8547603066, 04869-224571; www.periyar tigerreserve.org; Thekkady Rd; ☉9am-1pm & 2-5pm) The main operator of explorations into the park is the Ecotourism Centre, run by the Forest Department. These include border hikes (₹1500), 2½-hour nature walks (₹300), half-/full-day bamboo rafting (₹1500/200) and 'jungle patrols' (₹1000), which cover 4km to 5km and are the best way to experience the park close up, accompanied by a trained tribal guide. Rates are per person and

trips usually require a minimum of four. There are also overnight 'tiger trail' treks (per person ₹5000), which are run by former poachers retrained as guides, and cover 20km to 30km.

Elephant Junction   Elephant Rides
(programs ₹400-5000; ☉8.30am-6pm) In a lovely 16-hectare patch of forest about 2km from Kumily, you can wash, feed and ride elephants. Programs start from a half-hour ride (₹400) up to a full day that includes elephant bathing, plantation tours, breakfast and lunch. This is a better option for interacting with elephants than the touristy operation in Kumily village.

Sleeping

INSIDE THE SANCTUARY

The KTDC runs three steeply priced hotels in the park, including Periyar House, Aranya Nivas and the grand **Lake Palace** (🖉04869-223887; www.lakepalacethekkady. com; r incl all meals ₹24,000-30,000). Make reservations (at any KTDC office), particularly for weekends. Note that there's effectively a curfew at these places – guests are not permitted to roam the sanctuary after 6pm.

The Ecotourism Centre can arrange tented accommodation inside the park at the **Jungle Camp (per person inc meals ₹2000).** Rates include trekking and meals but not the park entry fee. Also ask about **Bamboo Grove (d incl breakfast ₹1500),** a group of basic cottages and tree houses not far from Kumily town.

KUMILY

Mickey Homestay   Guesthouse $
(🖉9447284160, 04869-223196; www.mickey homestay.com; Bypass Rd; r & cottages ₹700-1000; 🛜) Mickey is a genuine homestay with just a handful of intimate rooms in a family house and a rear cottage, all with homely touches that make them some of the cosiest in town. Balconies have rattan furniture and hanging bamboo seats and the whole place is surrounded by greenery.

Green View Homestay
Homestay $$

(☎9447432008, 04869-224617; www.
sureshgreenview.com; Bypass Rd; r incl break-
fast ₹500-1750; 🛜) It has grown from its
humble homestay origins but Greenview
is a lovely place that manages to retain
its personal and friendly family welcome
from owners Suresh and Sulekha. The
two buildings house several classes
of well-maintained rooms with private
balconies – the best are the upper-floor
rooms overlooking a lovely rear spice
garden. Excellent vegetarian meals and
cooking lessons (veg/nonveg ₹350/450)
are available.

Spice Village
Hotel $$$

(☎0484-3011711; www.cghearth.com; Thekkady Rd; villas ₹18,700-24,000; 🛜🏊) 🌿 This
CGH Earth place takes its green creden-
tials very seriously and has captivating,
spacious cottages that are smart yet
cosily rustic, in pristinely kept grounds.
Its restaurant does lavish lunch
and dinner buffets (₹1400 to ₹1800),
there's a colonial-style bar and you can
find the **Wildlife Interpretation Centre**

(☎04869-222028; ⏱6am-6pm) here, which
has a resident naturalist showing slides
and answering questions about the park.
Good value out of high season when
rates halve.

Eating

There are plenty of good cheap veg
restaurants in the bazaar area.

French Restaurant & Bakery
Cafe, Bakery $$

(meals ₹90-200; ⏱8am-9.30pm) This family-
run shack set back from the main road is
a good spot for breakfast or lunch, mainly
for the fluffy tuna or cheese baguettes
baked on-site, but also pasta and noodle
dishes.

Chrissie's Cafe
Multicuisine $$

(www.chrissies.in; Bypass Rd; meals ₹150-
350; ⏱8am-10pm) A perennially popular
traveller haunt, this clean, airy 1st-floor
and rooftop cafe satisfies with cakes and
snacks, excellent coffee, well-prepared
Western faves like pizza and pasta and
even a Middle Eastern platter (₹275).

Lake cruise (p251), Periyar Wildlife Sanctuary

ANDERS BLOMQVIST / GETTY IMAGES ©

Detour:
Chinnar Wildlife Sanctuary

About 10km past Marayoor and 60km northeast of Munnar, this **wildlife sanctuary** (www.chinnar.org; Indian/foreigner ₹100/150, camera/video ₹25/150; ⏰7am-6pm) hosts deer, leopards, elephants and the endangered grizzled giant squirrel. Trekking and tree-house or hut accommodation within the sanctuary are available, as well as ecotour programs like river-trekking, cultural visits (two tribal groups inhabit the sanctuary) and waterfall treks (around ₹600 per person). For details contact the Forest Information Centre in Munnar. Buses from Munnar can drop you off at Chinnar (₹40, 1½ hours), or taxi hire for the day will cost around ₹1500. The best time for wildlife spotting is early morning or evening.

❶ Information

There's a Federal Bank ATM accepting international cards at the junction with the road to Kottayam, and several internet cafes in the bazaar area.

Ecotourism Centre (📞8547603066, 04869-224571; www.periyartigerreserve.org; Thekkady Rd; ⏰9am-1pm & 2-5pm) For park tours, information and guided walks.

❶ Getting There & Away

Eleven buses daily operate between Ernakulam (Kochi) and Kumily (₹145, five hours). Buses leave every 30 minutes for Kottayam (₹84, four hours), with two direct buses to Trivandrum at 8.45am and 11am (₹210, eight hours) and one daily bus to Alleppey at 1.10pm (₹120, 5½ hours). Private buses to Munnar (₹80, 4-5 hours) also leave from the bus stand at 6am, 9.45am and noon.

Tamil Nadu buses leave every 30 minutes to Madurai (₹90, four hours) from the Tamil Nadu bus stand just over the border.

❶ Getting Around

It's only about 1.5km from Kumily bus stand to the main park entrance, but another 3km from there to Periyar Lake; take an autorickshaw from the entry post (₹70) or set off on foot – there's no walking path so you'll have to dodge traffic on the road. Autorickshaws will take you on short hops around town for ₹30.

Kumily town is small enough to explore on foot but some guesthouses hire bicycles (₹200) and

most can arrange scooter hire (₹500) if you want to explore further afield.

Munnar

🎵04865 / POP 68,200 / ELEV 1524M

The rolling hills around Munnar, South India's largest tea-growing region, are carpeted in emerald-green tea plantations, contoured, clipped and sculpted like ornamental hedges. The low mountain scenery is magnificent – you're often up above the clouds watching veils of mist clinging to the mountaintops. Munnar town itself is a scruffy administration centre, not unlike a North Indian hill station, but wander just a few kilometres out of town and you'll be engulfed in a sea of a fifty shades of green.

◎ Sights & Activities

The best way to experience the hills is on a guided trek, which can range from a half-day 'soft trekking' around tea plantations (from ₹600 per person) to more arduous full-day mountain treks (from ₹800), which open up some stupendous views. Trekking guides can easily be organised through hotels and guesthouses or the DTPC (p256).

Bear in mind that the tea plantations are private property and trekking around without a licensed guide is trespassing.

Below: Local bus, Chinnar Wildlife Sanctuary (p253)
Right: Tea plantation, Munnar (p253)

(BELOW) ANDERS BLOMQVIST / GETTY IMAGES ©; (RIGHT) EMAD ALJUMAH / GETTY IMAGES ©

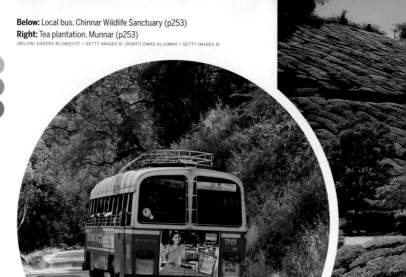

Nimi's Lip Smacking Classes
Cooking

(☎ 9745513373, 9447330773; www.nimisrecipes. com; classes ₹1500; ⏰ 5pm Mon-Fri, 2pm Sat & Sun) Nimi Sunilkumar has earned a solid reputation for Keralan cooking, publishing her own cookbook, website and blog, and now offers daily cooking classes in Munnar. You'll learn traditional Keralan recipes and the class includes a copy of her book *Lip Smacking Dishes of Kerala*. She's based in an unassuming building next to the DTPC.

Tours

The DTPC (p256) runs three fairly rushed full-day tours to points around Munnar. The **Sandal Valley Tour** (per person ₹400; ⏰ tour 9am-6pm) visits Chinnar Wildlife Sanctuary, several viewpoints, waterfalls, plantations, a sandalwood forest and villages. The **Tea Valley tour** (per person ₹400; ⏰ tour 10am-6pm) visits Echo Point, Top Station and Rajamalai (for Eravikulam National Park), among other places. The **Village Sightseeing Tour** (per person ₹400; ⏰ tour 9.30am-6pm) covers Devikulam, Anayirankal Dam, Ponmudy and a farm tour among others. You can hire a day's taxi to visit the main local sights for around ₹1300.

Sleeping

AROUND TOWN

JJ Cottage
Homestay $

(☎ 9447228599, 04865-230104; jjcottagemun nar@gmail.com; d ₹350-800; @ 🛜) The sweet family at this little purple place 2km south of town (but easy walking distance from the main bus stand) will go out of its way to make sure your stay is comfortable. The varied and uncomplicated rooms are ruthlessly clean, bright and great value, with TV and hot water. The one deluxe room on the top floor has a separate sitting room and sweeping views.

Green View   Guesthouse **$**
(☏ 9447825447, 04865-230940; www.green
viewmunnar.com; d ₹500-800; @ 🛜) This tidy
guesthouse has 10 fresh budget rooms,
a friendly welcome and reliable tours and
treks. The best rooms are on the upper
floor and there's a super rooftop garden
where you can sample 15 kinds of tea. The
young owner organises **trekking trips**
(www.munnartrekking.com) and also runs
Green Woods Anachal (☏ 04865-230189;
Anachal; d incl breakfast ₹750), a four-room
budget house out in the spice plantations,
10km outside of Munnar.

MUNNAR HILLS

Green Valley Vista   Guesthouse **$$**
(☏ 9447432008, 04865-263261; www.green
valleyvista.com; Chithirapuram; d incl breakfast
₹1500-2000; 🛜) The valley views are su-
perb, facilities top-notch and the welcome
warm at this new guesthouse. There are
three levels but all rooms face the valley
and have private balconies with dreamy
greenery views, as well as flat-screen TVs
and modern bathrooms with hot water.

Staff can organise trekking, jeep safaris
and village tours. It's about 11km south of
Munnar.

Rose Gardens   Homestay **$$**
(☏ 9447378524, 04864-278243; www.munnar
homestays.com; NH49 Rd, Karadipara; r incl
breakfast ₹4500; @ 🛜) Despite its handy
location on the main road to Kochi,
around 10km south of Munnar and with
good bus connections, this is a peaceful
spot overlooking the owner Tomy's idyllic
plant nursery and mini spice and fruit
plantation. The five rooms are large and
comfortable with balconies overlooking
the valley, and the family is charming.
Cooking lessons are free, including fresh
coconut pancakes for breakfast and delicately spiced Keralan dishes for dinner.

Windermere Estate   Resort **$$$**
(☏ 0484-2425237; www.windermeremunnar.com;
Pothamedu; s/d incl breakfast from ₹8300/9600,
villa ₹18,300/21,600; ❄ @ 🛜) Windermere
is a charming boutique-meets-country-
retreat 4km southeast of Munnar. There

255

are supremely spacious garden and valley view rooms, but the best are the suite-like 'Plantation Villas' with spectacular views, surrounded by 26 hectares of cardamom and coffee plantations. There's a cosy library above the country-style restaurant. Book ahead at its Kochi office.

Eating

Early-morning food stalls in the bazaar serve breakfast snacks and cheap meals, but some of the best food is served up at the homestays and resorts.

Rapsy Restaurant   Indian $

(Bazaar; dishes ₹50-140; ⏰8am-9pm) This spotless glass-fronted sanctuary from the bazaar is packed at lunchtime, with locals lining up for Rapsy's famous *paratha* or biryani. It also makes a decent stab at fancy international dishes like Spanish omelette, Israeli *shakshuka* (eggs with tomatoes and spices) and Mexican salsa.

Sree Mahaveer
Bhojanalaya   North Indian $$

(Mattupetty Rd; meals ₹100-250; ⏰8.30am-10.30pm) This pure veg restaurant attached to SN Annex Hotel has a nice deep-orange look with slatted blinds at the windows. It's madly popular with families for its great range of thalis: take your pick from Rajasthani, Gujarati, Punjabi and more, plus a dazzling array of veg dishes.

ℹ Information

There are ATMs near the bridge, south of the bazaar.

DTPC Tourist Information Office (☎04865-231516; keralatourismmunnardtpc@gmail.com; Alway-Munnar Rd; ⏰8.30am-6.30pm) Marginally helpful; operates a number of tours and can arrange trekking guides.

ℹ Getting There & Away

Roads around Munnar are in poor condition and can be affected by monsoon rains. The main **KSRTC bus station** (AM Rd) is south of town, but it's best to catch buses from stands in Munnar town (where more frequent private buses also depart). The main stand is in the bazaar.

There are around 13 daily buses to Ernakulam (Kochi, ₹114, 5½ hours), two direct buses to Alleppey (₹158, five hours) at 6.20am and 1.10pm, and four to Trivandrum (₹231, nine hours). Private buses go to Kumily (₹80, four hours) at 11.25am, 12.20pm and 2.25pm.

A taxi to Ernakulam costs around ₹3000, and to Kumily ₹2500.

ℹ Getting Around

Autorickshaws ply the hills around Munnar with bone-shuddering efficiency; they charge up to ₹800 for a full day's sightseeing.

Kochi (Cochin)

📞0484 / POP 601,600

Serene Kochi has been drawing traders and explorers to its shores for over 600 years. The result is an unlikely blend of medieval Portugal, Holland and an English village grafted onto the tropical Malabar Coast. It's a delightful place to spend some time and nap in some of India's finest homestays and heritage accommodation.

Mainland **Ernakulam** is the busy transport and cosmopolitan hub of Kochi, while the historical towns of **Fort Cochin** and **Mattancherry**, though well-touristed, remain wonderfully serene.

◎ Sights

FORT COCHIN

A popular promenade winds around to the unofficial emblems of Kerala's backwaters: cantilevered **Chinese fishing nets**. A legacy of traders from the AD 1400 court of Kublai Khan, these enormous, spiderlike contraptions require at least four people to operate their counterweights at high tide. Unfortunately, modern fishing techniques are making these labour-intensive methods less and less profitable.

Indo-Portuguese
Museum   Museum

(☎0484-2215400; Indian/foreigner ₹10/25; ⏰9am-1pm & 2-6pm Tue-Sun) This museum in the garden of the Bishop's House

MELVYN LONGHURST / GETTY IMAGES ©

 ## Don't Miss
Pardesi Synagogue

Originally built in 1568, this synagogue was partially destroyed by the Portuguese in 1662, and rebuilt two years later when the Dutch took Kochi. It features an ornate gold pulpit and elaborate hand-painted, willow-pattern floor tiles from Canton, China, which were added in 1762. It's magnificently illuminated by Belgian chandeliers and coloured-glass lamps. The graceful clock tower was built in 1760. There is an upstairs balcony for women, who worshipped separately according to Orthodox rites. Note that shorts, sleeveless tops, bags and cameras are not allowed inside.

NEED TO KNOW

admission ₹5; ☺10am-1pm & 3-5pm Sun-Thu, closed Jewish holidays

preserves the heritage of one of India's earliest Catholic communities, including vestments, silver processional crosses and altarpieces from the Cochin diocese. The basement contains remnants of the Portuguese Fort Immanuel.

MATTANCHERRY & JEW TOWN

About 3km southeast of Fort Cochin, Mattancherry is the old bazaar district and centre of the spice trade. These days it's packed with spice shops and over-priced Kashmiri-run emporiums. In the midst of this, Jew Town is a bustling port area with a fine synagogue.

Mattancherry Palace Museum
(Dutch Palace; ☎0484-2226085; Palace Rd; adult/child ₹5/free; ☺9am-5pm Sat-Thu) Mattancherry Palace was a generous gift presented to the Raja of Kochi, Veera Kerala Varma (1537–61), as a gesture of goodwill by the Portuguese in 1555. The Dutch renovated the palace in 1663, hence its alternative name, the Dutch Palace. The star attractions here are the astonishingly

257

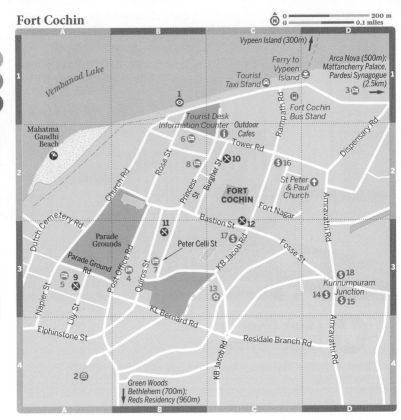

preserved Hindu murals, depicting scenes from the Ramayana, Mahabharata and Puranic legends in intricate detail.

Tours

Most hotels and tourist offices can arrange the popular day trip out to the **Elephant training camp** (Kodanuda; ⏱7am-6pm) at Kodanadu, 50km from Kochi. Here you can go for a ride (₹200) and even help out with washing the gentle beasts if you arrive at 8am. Entry is free, though the elephant trainers will expect a small tip. A return trip out here in a taxi should cost around ₹1200 to ₹1500.

Tourist Desk
Information Counter   Tours
(📞9847044688, 0484-2371761; www.tourist-desk.in; Ernakulam Boat Jetty & Tower Rd, Fort

Kochi) This excellent private tour agency runs the popular full-day **Water Valley Tour** (₹850; ⏱departs 8am) by houseboat through local backwater canals and lagoons. A canoe trip through smaller canals and villages is included, as is lunch and hotel pick-ups. It also offers a **sunset dinner cruise** (per person ₹750) by canoe from Narakkal Village on Vypeen Island, with the option of an overnight stay at a beach bungalow, and an overnight **Munnar Hillstation Tour** (per person ₹3000) with transport, accommodation and meals. Staff here are the best source of information on local temple festivals.

Kerala Bike Tours   Motorcycle Tour
(📞0484-2356652, 9388476817; www.keralabike tours.com; Kirushupaly Rd, Ravipuram) Organises motorcycle tours around Kerala and the Western Ghats and hires out touring

Fort Cochin

◉ Sights
1 Chinese Fishing Nets	B1
2 Indo-Portuguese Museum	A4

🛏 Sleeping
3 Brunton Boatyard	D1
4 Delight Home Stay	B3
5 Malabar House	A3
6 Old Harbour Hotel	B2
7 Raintree Lodge	B3
8 Spice Fort	B2

✖ Eating
9 Dal Roti	A3
10 Kashi Art Cafe	C2
Malabar Junction	(see 5)
11 Teapot	B3
12 Upstairs Italian	C3

⊕ Entertainment
13 Kerala Kathakali Centre	C3

ⓘ Information
14 Federal Bank ATM	D3
15 ICICI ATM	D3
16 SBI ATM	C2
17 South India Bank ATM	C3
18 UAE Exchange	D3

quality Enfield Bullets (from US$155 per week) with unlimited mileage, full insurance and free recovery/maintenance options.

🛏 Sleeping

Book ahead during December and January. At other times you can bargain for a discount.

FORT COCHIN

Green Woods Bethlehem
Homestay $

(🕿 9846014924, 0484-3247791; greenwoods bethlehem1@vsnl.net; opposite ESI Hospital; d incl breakfast ₹1000-1200, with AC ₹1500; ❄🛜) With a smile that brightens weary travellers, welcoming owner Sheeba looks ready to sign your adoption papers the minute you walk through her front door. Down a quiet laneway and with a walled garden thick with plants and palms, this is one of Kochi's most serene homestays. The rooms are humble but cosy; breakfast is served in the fantastic, leafy rooftop cafe, where cooking classes and demonstrations are often held.

Reds Residency
Homestay $$

(🕿 0484-3204060, 9388643747; www.redsresi dency.in; 11/372A, KJ Herschel Rd; d incl breakfast ₹900-1200, with AC from ₹1200, AC rooftop cottage ₹1500; ❄@🛜) Reds is a lovely homestay with hotel-quality rooms but a true family welcome from knowledgeable hosts Philip and Maryann. The seven rooms – including a triple and four-bed family room – are modern and immaculate, and there's a brilliant self-contained 'penthouse' cottage with kitchen on the rooftop. It's in a peaceful location south of the centre.

Delight Home Stay
Guesthouse $$

(🕿 98461121421, 0484-2217658; www.delightful homestay.com; Post Office Rd; r incl breakfast ₹1600-1800, with AC ₹2500; ❄🛜) And delightful it is. This grand house's exterior is adorned with frilly white woodwork, and the six rooms are spacious and polished. There's a charming little garden, an elegant breakfast room and an imposing sitting room covered in wall-to-wall teak. Good food is served and cooking classes are offered in the open kitchen.

Raintree Lodge
Guesthouse $$

(🕿 9847029000, 0484-3251489; www. fortcochin.com; Peter Celli St; r ₹2800; ❄🛜) The intimate and elegant rooms at this historic place flirt with boutique-hotel status. Each of the five rooms has a great blend of contemporary style and heritage carved-wood furniture and the front upstairs rooms have gorgeous vine-covered Juliet balconies. Good value.

Malabar House
Hotel $$$

(🕿 0484-2216666; www.malabarhouse.com; Parade Ground Rd; r €240, ste incl breakfast €330-380; ❄@🏊) What may just be one of the fanciest boutique hotels in Kerala, Malabar flaunts its uber-hip blend of modern colours and period fittings like it's not even trying. While the suites are huge and lavishly appointed, the standard rooms are more snug. The award-winning restaurant and wine bar (p261) are top notch.

Detour:
Cherai Beach

On Vypeen Island, 25km from Fort Cochin, Cherai Beach makes a nice day trip or getaway from Kochi, especially if you hire a scooter or motorbike in Fort Cochin. The main beach entrance can get busy at times but with miles of lazy backwaters just a few hundred metres from the seafront, it's a pleasant place to explore. To get here from Fort Cochin, catch the vehicle-ferry to Vypeen Island (₹3 per person) and either hire an autorickshaw from the jetty (around ₹400) or catch one of the frequent buses (₹15, one hour) and get off at Cherai village, 1km from the beach.

Hidden back from the beach but with the backwaters on your doorstep, **Les 3 Elephants** (✆0484-2480005, 9349174341; www.3elephants.in; Convent St; cottages ₹5000-10,000; ❄@🛜) is a superb French-run ecoresort.

Old Harbour Hotel — Hotel $$$
(✆0484-2218006; www.oldharbourhotel.com; 1/328 Tower Rd; r/ste ₹10,200/17,600; ❄@🛜) Set around an idyllic garden with lily ponds and a small pool, the dignified Old Harbour is housed in a 300-year-old Dutch/Portuguese heritage building. The elegant mix of period and modern styles lensd it a more intimate feel than some of the more grandiose competition. There are 13 rooms and suites, some facing directly onto the garden, and some with plant-filled, open-air bathrooms.

Spice Fort — Boutique Hotel $$$
(✆9364455440; www.duneecogroup.com; Princess St; r ₹8500-11,000; ❄🛜) Chic red-and-white spice-themed rooms here have TVs built into the bedheads, cool tones and immaculate bathrooms. They all orbit an inviting pool in a heritage courtyard shielded from busy Princess St. Great location, excellent restaurant, friendly staff.

Brunton Boatyard — Hotel $$$
(✆0484-2215461; bruntonboatyard@cgh earth.com; River Rd; r/ste ₹26,000/34,000; ❄@🛜) This imposing hotel faithfully reproduces 16th- and 17th-century Dutch and Portuguese architecture in its grand complex. All of the rooms look out over the harbour, and have bathtubs and balconies with a refreshing sea breeze that beats air-con any day. The hotel is also home to the excellent History Restaurant and Armoury Bar, along with a couple of open-air cafes.

MATTANCHERRY & JEW TOWN

Caza Maria — Homestay $$
(✆9846050901; cazamaria@rediffmail.com; Jew Town Rd, Mattancherry; r incl breakfast ₹4500; ❄) Right in the heart of Jew Town, this unique place has just two large heritage rooms overlooking the bazaar. Fit for a maharaja, the rooms feature an idiosyncratic style, with each high-ceilinged room painted in bright colours, and filled to the brim with antiques.

🍴 Eating & Drinking

FORT COCHIN

Behind the Chinese fishing nets are several fishmongers, from whom you can buy fish (or prawns, scampi, lobster), then take your selection to one of the row of simple but popular restaurants on nearby Tower Rd where the folks there will cook it and serve it to you for an additional charge. Market price varies.

Teapot — Cafe $
(Peter Celli St; mains ₹70-140; 🕐8.30am-8.30pm) This atmospheric cafe is the perfect venue for 'high tea', with 16 types of tea, sandwiches, cakes and a few meals served in chic, airy rooms. Witty tea-themed accents include loads of

antique teapots, tea chests for tables and a gnarled, tea-tree-based glass table.

Kashi Art Cafe   Cafe $$
(Burgher St; breakfast & snacks ₹90-250; ⏰8.30am-10pm) An institution in Fort Cochin, this natural-light-filled place has a zen-but-casual vibe and solid wood tables that spread out into a semi-court-yard space. The coffee is as strong as it should be and the daily Western breakfast and lunch specials are excellent. A small gallery shows off local artists.

Dal Roti   Indian $$
(📞9746459244; 1/293 Lily St; meals ₹100-230; ⏰noon-3.30pm & 6.30-10.30pm Wed-Mon) There's a lot to like about busy Dal Roti. Friendly and knowledgeable owner Ramesh will hold your hand through his expansive North Indian menu, which even sports its own glossary, and help you dive into his delicious range of vegetarian, eggetarian and nonvegetarian options. From kati rolls to seven types of thali, you won't go hungry. No alcohol.

Arca Nova   Seafood $$
(2/6A Calvathy Rd; mains ₹190-650; ⏰7.30am-10.30pm) The waterside restaurant at the Fort House Hotel is a prime choice for a leisurely lunch. It specialises in fish dishes and you can sit out at tables overlooking the water or in the serenely spacious covered garden area.

Malabar Junction
International $$$
(📞0484-2216666; Parade Ground Rd; mains ₹360-680, 5-course degustation ₹2000; ⏰lunch & dinner) Set in an open-sided pavilion, the restaurant at Malabar House is movie-star cool, with white-clothed tables in a courtyard close to the pool. There's a seafood-based, European-style menu – the signature

dish is the impressive seafood platter with grilled vegetables. Upstairs, the wine bar serves upmarket tapas-style snacks and fine wine by the glass.

Upstairs Italian   Italian $$$
(📞9745682608; Bastion St; mains ₹250-600; ⏰10am-11pm) For authentic Italian – imported gorgonzola, prosciutto, olive oil, Parmesan cheese – head upstairs to this cosy little place serving Kochi's best pizza, pasta and antipasto. Pricey but worth a splurge.

MATTANCHERRY & JEW TOWN

Ramathula Hotel   Indian $
(Kayikka's; Kayees Junction, Mattancherry; biryani ₹40-60; ⏰lunch & dinner) Legendary among locals for chicken and mutton biryanis – get here early or miss out. It's better known by the chef's name, Kayikka's.

Ginger House   Indian $$$
(Bazaar Rd; mains ₹190-700; ⏰8.30am-6pm) Hidden behind a massive antique-filled go-down (warehouse) is this fantastic water-front restaurant, where you can feast on

Cherai Beach
EYESWIDEOPENR / GETTY IMAGES ©

Indian dishes and snacks – ginger prawns, ginger ice cream, ginger lassi… you get the picture. To get to the restaurant, walk through the astonishing Heritage Arts showroom with amazing sculptures and antiques – check out the giant snake-boat canoe. If you ask, the owner might show you the rest of the collection upstairs.

Entertainment

There are several places in Kochi where you can view Kathakali. The performances are designed for tourists, but they're an excellent introduction to this intriguing art form. The standard program starts with the intricate make-up application and costume-fitting, followed by a demonstration and commentary on the dance and then the performance – usually two hours in all. The fast-paced traditional martial art of *kalarippayat* can also be easily seen in Fort Cochin.

FORT COCHIN

Kerala Kathakali Centre   Cultural Program
(☎0484-2217552; www.kathakalicentre.com; KB Jacob Rd; shows ₹250-300; ☺make-up

Kathakali performers

from 5pm, show 6-7.30pm) In an intimate, wood-lined theatre, this recommended place provides a useful introduction to Kathakali, complete with translations of the night's story. The centre also hosts performances of the martial art of *kalarippayat* from 4pm to 5pm daily, traditional music from 8pm to 9pm Sunday to Friday and classical dance from 8pm to 9pm Saturday.

ERNAKULAM

See India Foundation   Cultural Program
(☎0484-2376471; devankathakali@yahoo.com; Kalathiparambil Lane; shows ₹300; ☺make-up 6pm, show 7-8pm) One of the oldest Kathakali theatres in Kerala, it has small-scale shows with an emphasis on the religious and philosophical roots of Kathakali.

❶ Information

Internet Access

There are several internet cafes around Princess St in Fort Cochin charging ₹40 per hour, and most homestays and hotels offer free wi-fi.

Medical Services

Lakeshore Hospital (☎0484-2701032; www.lakeshorehospital.com; NH Bypass, Marudu) Modern hospital 8km southeast of central Ernakulam.

Money

UAE Exchange (◷9.30am-6pm Mon-Fri, to 2pm Sat) Ernakulam (☎0484-2383317; MG Rd, Perumpillil Bldg); Ernakulam (☎0484-3067008; Chettupuzha Towers, PT Usha Rd Junction); Fort Cochin (☎0484-2216231; Amravathi Rd) Foreign exchange and travellers cheques.

Tourist Information

KTDC Tourist Reception Centre (☎0484-2353234; Shanmugham Rd, Ernakulam; ◷8am-7pm) Also organises tours. There's another office at the jetty at Fort Cochin.

Tourist Desk Information Counter Ernakulam (☎9847044688, 0484-2371761; www.touristdesk.in; Boat Jetty; ◷8am-6pm); Fort Cochin (☎0484-2216129; ◷8am-7pm) At this private tour agency, with offices at Ernakulam's ferry terminal and in Fort Cochin, staff are extremely knowledgeable and helpful about Kochi and beyond. They run several popular and recommended tours, including a festival tour, and publish information on festivals and cultural events.

ℹ Getting There & Away

Air

Kochi International Airport is a popular hub, with international flights to/from the Gulf states, Sri Lanka, Maldives, Malaysia and Singapore.

On domestic routes, Jet Airways, Air India, Indigo and Spicejet fly direct daily to Chennai, Mumbai, Bengaluru, Hyderabad, Delhi and Trivandrum (but not Goa). Air India flies to Delhi

Ernakulam Bus & Train Services

MAJOR BUSES FROM ERNAKULAM

The following bus services operate from the KSRTC bus stand and Vyttila Mobility Hub.

DESTINATION	FARE (₹)	DURATION (HR)	FREQUENCY
Alleppey	52	1½	every 10min
Chennai	590	16	1 daily, 2pm
Kollam	114	3½	every 30min
Kottayam	57	2	every 30min
Kumily (for Periyar)	130	5	8 daily
Munnar	100	4½	every 30min
Trivandrum	170	5	every 30min

MAJOR TRAINS FROM ERNAKULAM

The following are major long-distance trains departing from Ernakulam Town.

DESTINATION	TRAIN NO & NAME	FARE (₹; SLEEPER/3AC/2AC)	DURATION (HR)	DEPARTURES (DAILY)
Bengaluru	16525 Bangalore Exp	345/930/1335	13	5.35pm
Chennai	12624 Chennai Mail	395/1035/1470	12	7.30pm
Delhi	12625 Kerala Exp (A)	885/2275/3375	46	3.45pm
Goa (Madgaon)	16346 Netravathi Exp (A)	415/1120/1620	15	2.10pm
Mumbai	16346 Netravathi Exp (A)	615/1635/2400	27	2.10pm

(A) Departs from Ernakulam Junction

daily and to Agatti in the Lakshadweep islands six times a week.

Bus

All long-distance services operate from Ernakulam. The **KSRTC bus stand** (☎0484-2372033; ⊗reservations 6am-10pm) still has a few services but most state-run and private buses pull into the massive new **Vyttila Mobility Hub** (☎0484-2306611; www.vyttilamobilityhub.com; ⊗24hr), a state-of-the-art transport terminal about 2km east of Ernakulam Junction train station. Numerous private bus companies have super-deluxe, air-con, video and Volvo buses to long-distance destinations such as Bengaluru, Chennai, Mangalore, Trivandrum and Coimbatore; prices vary depending on the standard but the best buses are about 50% higher than government buses. Agents in Ernakulam and Fort Cochin sell tickets. Private buses also use the Kaloor bus stand, 1km north of the city.

A prepaid autorickshaw from Vyttila costs ₹73 to the boat jetty, ₹190 to Fort Cochin and ₹370 to the airport.

Train

Ernakulam has two train stations, Ernakulam Town and Ernakulam Junction. Reservations for both are made at the Ernakulam Junction **reservations office** (☎132; ⊗8am-8pm Mon-Sat, 8am-2pm Sun).

There are local and express trains to Trivandrum (2nd-class/sleeper/3AC ₹95/195/535, 4½ hours), via either Alleppey (₹50/170/535, 1½ hours) or Kottayam (₹55/140/485, 1½ hours).

ⓘ Getting Around

An above-ground **metro** (www.kochmetro.org) is under construction in Ernakulam, which will connect the airport with the city when completed. The first phase is due in 2016.

To/From the Airport

Kochi International Airport (☎0484-2610125; www.cochinairport.com) is at Nedumbassery, 30km northeast of Ernakulam. C buses run between the airport and Fort Cochin (₹80, one hour, eight daily), some going via Ernakulam. Taxis to/from Ernakulam cost around ₹850, and to/from Fort Cochin around ₹1200, depending on the time of night.

Boat

Ferries are the fastest and most enjoyable form of transport between Fort Cochin and the mainland. The jetty on the eastern side of Willingdon Island is called Embarkation; the west one, opposite Mattancherry, is Terminus; and the main stop at Fort Cochin is Customs, with another stop at the Mattancherry Jetty near the synagogue. One-way fares are ₹4 (₹6 between Ernakulam and Mattancherry).

Ernakulam

There are services to both Fort Cochin jetties (Customs and Mattancherry) every 25 to 50 minutes from Ernakulam's main jetty between 4.40am and 9.10pm.

Ferries also run every 20 minutes or so to Willingdon and Vypeen Islands.

Fort Cochin

Ferries run from Customs Jetty to Ernakulam regularly between 5am and 9.50pm. Ferries also hop between

Mysore Palace
FAMELEAF PHOTOS / GETTY IMAGES ©

Customs Jetty and Willingdon Island 18 times a day.

Car and passenger ferries cross to Vypeen Island from Fort Cochin virtually nonstop.

Local Transport

There are no regular bus services between Fort Cochin and Mattancherry Palace, but it's an enjoyable 30-minute walk through the busy warehouse area along Bazaar Rd. Autorickshaws should cost around ₹70, much less if you promise to look in a shop. Most short autorickshaw trips around Ernakulam shouldn't cost more than ₹50.

To get to Fort Cochin after ferries (and buses) stop running you'll need to catch a taxi or autorickshaw – Ernakulam Town train station to Fort Cochin should cost around ₹400; prepaid autorickshaws during the day cost ₹250.

Scooters (per day ₹300) and Enfields (per day ₹400 to ₹600) can be hired from a number of agents in Fort Cochin.

SOUTHERN KARNATAKA

Mysuru (Mysore)

☎ 0821 / POP 895,000 / ELEV 707M

One of South India's most famous tourist destinations, Mysuru (which recently changed its name from Mysore) is known for its glittering royal heritage and magnificent monuments and buildings. Its World Heritage–listed palace may be what brings most travellers here, but it's also a thriving centre for the production of premium silk, sandalwood and incense. These days ashtanga yoga is another drawcard – Mysuru attracts visitors worldwide with its reputation as one of India's best places to practice yoga.

◎ Sights

Mysore Palace   Palace

(Maharaja's Palace; www.mysorepalace.gov.in; Indian/foreigner incl audio guide ₹40/200, child under 10 free; ⊙10am-5.30pm) Among the grandest of India's royal buildings, this fantastic palace was the former seat of the Wodeyar maharajas. The old palace was gutted by fire in 1897; the one you

see now was completed in 1912 by English architect Henry Irwin at a cost of ₹4.5 million. The interior of this Indo-Saracenic marvel – a kaleidoscope of stained glass, mirrors and gaudy colours – is lavish and undoubtedly over the top. The decor is further embellished by carved wooden doors, mosaic floors and a series of paintings depicting life in Mysuru during the Edwardian Raj era.

Devaraja Market   Market

(Sayyaji Rao Rd; ⊙6am-8.30pm) Dating from Tipu Sultan's reign, this lively bazaar has local traders selling traditional items such as flower garlands, spices and conical piles of *kumkum* (coloured powder used for bindi dots), all of which makes for some great photo-ops. Refresh your bargaining skills before shopping.

Chamundi Hill   Viewpoint

At a height of 1062m, on the summit of Chamundi Hill, stands the **Sri Chamundeswari Temple** (⊙7am-2pm, 3.30-6pm & 7.30-9pm), dominated by a 40m-high *gopuram* (tower gateway). It's a fine half-day excursion, offering spectacular views of the city below. Queues are long at weekends, so visit during the week. From the Central bus stand take bus 100 (₹17, 25 minutes) or 201 (₹28, AC) that rumbles up the narrow road to the summit. A return autorickshaw will cost about ₹400.

Jaganmohan Palace   Palace

(Jaganmohan Palace Rd; adult/child ₹120/60; ⊙8.30am-5pm) Built in 1861 as the royal auditorium, this stunning palace just west of the Mysore Palace, houses the **Jayachamarajendra Art Gallery**. Set over three floors it has a huge collection of Indian paintings, including works by noted artist Raja Ravi Varma and traditional Japanese art. There's also regal memorabilia from the Mysuru royal family, weapons and rare musical instruments.

St Philomena's Cathedral   Church

(St Philomena St; ⊙8am-5pm) The beauty of towering St Philomena's Cathedral, built between 1933 and 1941 in neo-Gothic style, is emphasised by beautiful

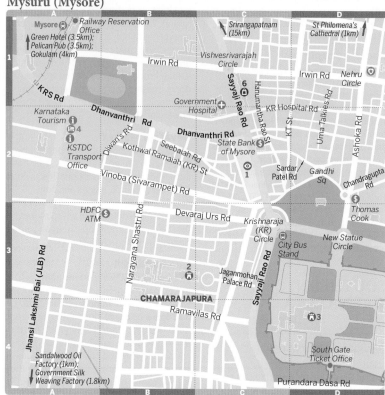

stained-glass windows. It's on the northern outskirts of town.

Tours

KSTDC (p268) runs a daily Mysuru city tour (₹210), taking in city sights (excluding the palace), Chamundi Hill, Srirangapatnam and Brindavan Gardens. It starts daily at 8.30am, ends at 8.30pm and is likely to leave you breathless!

Royal Mysore Walks　Walking Tour
(☑9632044188; www.royalmysorewalks.com; 2hr walk ₹600-1500) An excellent way to familiarise yourself with Mysuru's epic history and heritage, these weekend walks offer a range of themes from royal history to food walks.

Sleeping

Hotel Mayura Hoysala　Hotel **$$**
(☑0821-2426160; www.karnatakaholidays.net; 2 Jhansi Lakshmi Bai Rd; s/d incl breakfast with fan ₹1350/1500, with AC ₹2480/2750; ❈) The potential of this beautiful historic building remains unrealised as this government-owned hotel continues to offer its blend of mothballed heritage. It's still worthy of consideration, especially at these rates. The bar here is popular with Mysuru's tipplers.

Mystic School & Om Cafe　Hotel **$$**
(☑0821-4288490; www.mysoreyoga.in; 100 3rd Main Rd, Gokulam; r without/with kitchen per month ₹18,000/25,000; ❈🛜☒) This is the most stylish accommodation in Gokulam offering squeaky-clean studios with

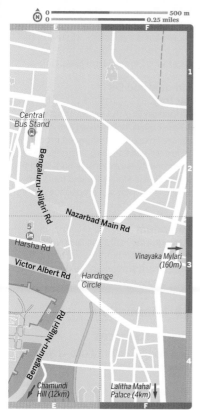

Map scale: 0 — 500 m / 0 — 0.25 miles

Central Bus Stand

Bengaluru-Nilgiri Rd

Nazarbad Main Rd

Harsha Rd

Victor Albert Rd

Hardinge Circle

Vinayaka Mylari (160m)

Bengaluru-Nilgiri Rd

Chamundi Hill (12km)

Lalitha Mahal Palace (4km)

Mysuru (Mysore)

◎ Sights
1 Devaraja Market..................................C2
2 Jaganmohan Palace B3
3 Mysore Palace...................................D4

⊜ Sleeping
4 Hotel Mayura Hoysala.........................A2
5 Parklane Hotel...................................E3

⊜ Shopping
6 Cauvery Arts & Crafts Emporium.......C1

filled hotel has undergone several fascinating reincarnations over the years. It was originally built as the Chittaranjan Palace in the 1920s by the maharajah for his three daughters, before becoming a major film studio from the 1950s to 1987. Today its 31-rooms, set among charming gardens, are all run on solar power and those in the Palace building include themes such as a writers room or kitschy Bollywood decor.

Lalitha Mahal Palace
Heritage Hotel $$$

(📞0821-2526100; www.lalithamahalpalace.in; r incl breakfast ₹4830-12,080; ❄ @ 🛜) A former maharaja's guesthouse built in 1921, this majestic heritage building has been operating as a hotel since 1974. Old-world charm comes in bucket loads from the 1920s birdcage elevator to mosaic tiled floors. The heritage classic rooms are where you'll feel the history. Spacious four-poster beds sit next to antique furniture, claw-foot baths sit on marble bathroom floors, and shuttered windows look out to stately landscaped gardens. It's around 5km from the centre of town.

🍴 Eating & Drinking

Malgudi Café
Cafe $

(Green Hotel; cakes from ₹40, sandwiches ₹60; 🕙10am-7pm; 🛜) 🖉 Set around an inner courtyard within the Green Hotel, this ambient cafe brews excellent coffees and Himalayan teas to be enjoyed with tasty cakes and sandwiches. Staff come from underprivileged backgrounds and are mostly women, and profits assist with disadvantaged communities, so you can do your bit by ordering a second cuppa.

kitchenettes, as well as an atmospheric rooftop cafe (8am to 8.30pm), Finnish sauna and plunge pool.

Parklane Hotel
Hotel $$

(📞0821-4003500; www.parklanemysore.com; 2720 Harsha Rd; r from ₹2000; ❄ @ 🛜 🏊) Travellers' central on Mysuru's tourist circuit, the Parklane is over-the-top kitsch but hard to dislike with its massive and immaculate rooms, ultra comfortable and thoughtfully outfitted with mobile-chargers and toiletry kits. Its lively open-air restaurant is always buzzing, and it has a small rooftop pool too.

Green Hotel
Heritage Guesthouse $$$

(📞0821-4255000; www.greenhotelindia.com; 2270 Vinoba Rd, Jayalakshmipuram; s/d incl breakfast from ₹3880/4480; 🛜) 🖉 This character-

Vinayaka Mylari
South Indian $

(769 Nazarbad Main Rd; mains ₹30-50; ⊙6.30am-1.30pm & 4-8pm) Local foodies say this is one of the best eateries in town to try the South Indian classics *masala dosa* (large savoury crepe stuffed with spiced potatoes) and *idlis* (spongy, round, fermented rice cakes). There's a similar branch up the road, Hotel Mylari, run by the owner's brother, and both are as good as each other.

Sapphire
Indian $$

(Lalitha Mahal Palace; mains ₹250-1000; ⊙12.30-7.45pm & 8-11pm) Dine in absolute royal Indian style in the grand ballroom of the Lalitha Mahal Palace hotel. And grand it is, with high stained-glass ceilings, lace tablecloths and polished teak floors. Order the royal Mysore silver thali (₹485) which gets you an assortment of vegetables, breads and sweets served on lavish brassware. Weekends are buffet menu only. Note that the nonguest ₹1000 entrance fee is refundable if you're here to eat.

Pelican Pub
Pub

(Hunsur Rd; mains ₹100-190; ⊙11am-11pm) A popular watering hole located on the fringes of upmarket Gokulam, this laid-back joint serves beer for ₹65 a mug in the indoor classic pub or alfresco style garden setting out back. There's live music Wednesday.

🔒 Shopping

Mysuru is a great place to shop for its famed sandalwood products, silk saris and wooden toys. It is also one of India's major incense-manufacturing centres.

Look for the butterfly-esque 'Silk Mark' on your purchase; it's an endorsement for quality silk.

Government Silk Weaving Factory
Clothing

(☎8025586550; www.ksicsilk.com; Mananthody Rd, Ashokapuram; ⊙8.30am-4pm Mon-Sat, outlet 10.30am-7pm daily) Given that Mysuru's prized silk is made under its very sheds, this government-run outlet, set up in 1912, is the best and cheapest place to shop for the exclusive textile. Behind the showroom is the factory, where you can drop by to see how the fabric is made. It's around 2km south of town.

Sandalwood Oil Factory
Souvenirs

(Mananthody Rd, Ashokapuram; ⊙outlet 9.30am-6.30pm, factory closed Sun) A quality-assured place for sandalwood products including incense, soap, cosmetics and the prohibitively expensive pure sandalwood oil (if in stock). Guided tours are available to show you around the factory.

Cauvery Arts & Crafts Emporium
Crafts, Souvenirs

(Sayyaji Rao Rd; ⊙10.30am-8pm) Not the cheapest place, but the selection at this government emporium is extensive and there's no pressure to buy.

ℹ️ Information

Medical Services

Government Hospital (☎0821-4269806; Dhanvanthri Rd) Has a 24-hour pharmacy.

Money

State Bank of Mysore (cnr Irwin & Ashoka Rds; ⊙10.30am-2.30pm & 3-4pm Mon-Fri, 10.30am-12.30pm Sat) Changes cash and ATM.

Thomas Cook (☎0821-2420090; Silver Tower, 9/2 Ashoka Rd; ⊙9.30am-6pm Mon-Sat) Foreign currency.

Tourist Information

Karnataka Tourism (☎0821-2422096; www.karnatakatourism.org; 1st fl, Hotel Mayura Hoysala, 2 Jhansi Lakshmi Bai Rd; ⊙10am-5.30pm Mon-Sat) Extremely helpful and has plenty of brochures.

KSTDC Transport Office (☎0821-2423652; www.karnatakaholidays.net; Yatri Navas Bldg, 2 Jhansi Lakshmi Bai Rd; ⊙8.30am-8.30pm) Offers general tourist information and provides a useful map. Has counters at the train station and Central bus stand, as well as this main office.

ℹ️ Getting There & Away

Bus

The **Central bus stand** (Bengaluru-Nilgiri Rd) handles all KSRTC long-distance buses. The **City bus stand** (Sayyaji Rao Rd) is for city, Srirangapatnam and Chamundi Hill buses.

Train

Train tickets can be bought from Mysuru's **railway booking office** (☏131; ⊙8am-8pm Mon-Sat, to 2pm Sun). To Bengaluru catch the 6.45am Chamundi Express (2nd class/AC ₹75/255, 2½ hours) or the 11.15am Tippu Express (2nd class/AC chair ₹90/305, 2½ hours). The 2.15pm Shatabdi Express also connects Bengaluru (AC chair/AC executive chair ₹370/765, two hours) and Chennai (AC chair/AC executive chair ₹935/1830, seven hours) daily except Wednesday. The 6.40pm Hampi Express (3AC/2AC sleeper ₹1000/1440, 11½ hours) heads to Hospet (for Hampi) daily, while the 10.30pm Mysore Dharwad Express goes to Hubli (sleeper/2AC ₹275/1055, 9½ hours).

ℹ️ Getting Around

Agencies at hotels and around town rent cabs from ₹8 per kilometre, with a minimum of 250km per day, plus a daily allowance of ₹200 for the driver.

Count on around ₹800 for a day's sightseeing in an autorickshaw.

TAMIL NADU

Chennai (Madras)

☏044 / POP 7.7 MILLION

The 'capital of the south' has always been the rather dowdy sibling among India's four biggest cities, with its withering southern heat, roaring traffic, and scarcity of outstanding sights. For many travellers, it is as much a gateway as a destination in itself. If you're just caught here between connections, it's certainly worth poking around one of the museums or taking a sunset stroll along Marina Beach. If you have more time to explore Chennai's varied neighbourhoods and appreciate its role as keeper of South Indian artistic and religious traditions, the odds are this 70-sq-km conglomerate of urban villages will grow on you. Recent years have added a new layer of cosmopolitan glamour in the shape of luxury hotels, shiny boutiques,

Temple festival, Chennai

PADDY PHOTOGRAPHY / GETTY IMAGES ©

classy contemporary restaurants and even a smattering of clubs and bars open into the wee hours.

ⓘ Dangers & Annoyances

Never get into an autorickshaw before agreeing the fare, and never pay the driver upfront. Tempting offers of ₹50 'city tours' by autorickshaw drivers precede a day being dragged from one shop or emporium to another.

◎ Sights

CENTRAL CHENNAI

Government Museum   Museum
(www.chennaimuseum.org; Pantheon Rd, Egmore; Indian/foreigner ₹15/250, camera/video ₹200/500; ⏰9.30am-5pm Sat-Thu) Housed across the British-built Pantheon Complex, this excellent museum is Chennai's best. The big highlight is building 3, the **Bronze Gallery**, with a superb collection of South Indian bronzes from the 7th-

century Pallava era through to modern times, and English-language explanatory material.

Marina Beach   Beach
Take an early-morning or evening stroll (you really don't want to roast here at any other time) along the 3km-long main stretch of Marina Beach and you'll pass cricket matches, flying kites, fortune-tellers, fish markets, corn-roasters and families enjoying the sea breeze. Don't swim: strong rips make it dangerous. At its southern end, the newly reopened, ridiculously popular **Madras Lighthouse** (Indian/foreigner ₹20/50, camera ₹25; ⏰10am-1pm & 3-5pm Tue-Sun) is India's only lighthouse with a lift; the panoramic city and beach views are fabulous.

Fort St George   Fort
(Rajaji Salai; ⏰9am-5pm) Finished in 1653 by the British East India Company, the fort has undergone many facelifts over the years. Inside the vast perimeter walls is now a precinct housing Tamil Nadu's

Legislative Assembly & Secretariat, and a smattering of older buildings. One of these, the **Fort Museum** (Indian/foreigner ₹5/100; ⊙9am-5pm Sat-Thu), has displays on Chennai's origins and the fort itself, and interesting military memorabilia and artwork from colonial times. The 1st-floor portrait gallery of colonial-era VIPs includes a very assured-looking Robert Clive (Clive of India).

Tours

The Tamil Nadu Tourism Development Corporation (p276) conducts half-day city tours (non-AC/AC ₹300/370) and day trips to Mamallapuram (₹450/550). Book ahead for weekends and holidays; be ready for cancellations on quiet weekdays. Every full moon there's an overnight pilgrimage trip to Tiruvanna-malai (₹600/780).

Detours   Walking Tour
(☏9000850505, 9840060393; www.detours india.com; RM Towers, 108 Chamiers Rd, Alwarpet)

A fantastic way to explore Chennai is with Detours' off-beat, in-depth history, faith and food tours, run by local experts. Four-hour early-morning food walks cost ₹5000 to ₹6000 per person.

Sleeping

EGMORE & AROUND

**YWCA International
Guest House**   Guesthouse $$
(☏044-25324234; igh@ywcamadras.org; 1086 Poonamallee High Rd; incl breakfast s ₹1500-1980, d ₹1800-2400, s/d without AC ₹900/1350; ✹@☎) The YWCA guesthouse, set in shady grounds, offers very good value along with a calm atmosphere. Efficiently run by helpful staff, it has good-sized, brilliantly clean rooms, spacious common areas and solid-value meals (₹175/275 for veg/nonveg lunch or dinner). Wi-fi (in the lobby) costs ₹100 per day. Renovations were underway at the time of research.

Chennai (Madras)

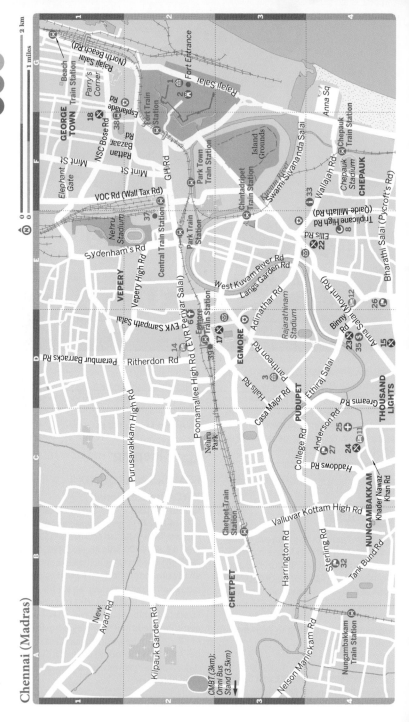

2 km

1 miles

GEORGE TOWN

Beach Train Station

Rajaji Salai (North Beach Rd)

Parry's Corner

Esplanade Rd

NSC Bose Rd

Rattan Bazaar Rd

Fort Train Station

Elephant Gate

Mint St

Mint St

GH Rd

VOC Rd (Wall Tax Rd)

Nehru Stadium

Central Train Station

Park Train Station

Park Train Station

Fort Entrance

Rajaji Salai

Island Grounds

Chintadripet Train Station

Swami Sivananda Salai

Cooum River

CHEPAUK

Chepauk Train Station

Chepauk Stadium

Anna Sq

Wallajah Rd

Triplicane High Rd (Qaide-Millath Rd)

Ellis Rd

Bharathi Salai (Pycroft's Rd)

VEPERY

Sydenham's Rd

Vepery High Rd

EVK Sampath Salai

West Kuvam River Rd

Langs Garden Rd

Adinathar Rd

Rajarathinam Stadium

Binny Rd

Anna Salai (Mount Rd)

Perambur Barracks Rd

Ritherdon Rd

Poonamallee High Rd (EVR Periyar Salai)

Egmore Train Station

EGMORE

Pantheon Rd

Halls Rd

Casa Major Rd

PUDUPET

Ethiraj Salai

Greams Rd

THOUSAND LIGHTS

Purusavakkam High Rd

Nehru Park

College Rd

Haddows Rd

Anderson Rd

NUNGAMBAKKAM

Khader Nawaz Khan Rd

CHETPET

Chetpet Train Station

Harrington Rd

Valluvar Kottam High Rd

Sterling Rd

Tank Bund Rd

New Avadi Rd

Kilpauk Garden Rd

CMBT (3km); Omni Bus Stand (3.5km)

Nelson Manickam Rd

Nungambakkam Train Station

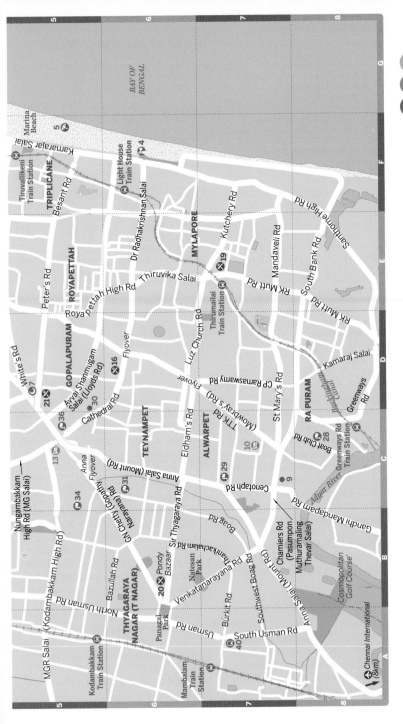

273

Chennai (Madras)

◎ Sights
1 Fort Museum G2
2 Fort St George G2
3 Government Museum D3
4 Madras Lighthouse F6
5 Marina Beach F5
6 St Andrew's Church D2
7 Thousand Lights Mosque D5
8 Wallajah Big Mosque E4

◎ Activities, Courses & Tours
9 Detours C7

🛌 Sleeping
10 Footprint B&B C7
11 Hanu Reddy Residences C4
12 La Woods E4
13 Park Hotel C5
14 YWCA International Guest House D2

✖ Eating
15 Amethyst D4
16 Copper Chimney D6
17 Hotel Saravana Bhavan D3
18 Hotel Saravana Bhavan (George
      Town) F1
19 Hotel Saravana Bhavan (Mylapore) E7
20 Hotel Saravana Bhavan (T Nagar) B6

21 Hotel Saravana Bhavan (Thousand
      Lights) D5
22 Hotel Saravana Bhavan (Triplicane) E4
23 Raintree D4
24 Tuscana Pizzeria C4

ℹ Information
25 Apollo Hospital C4
26 Australian Consulate E4
27 British Deputy High Commission C4
28 German Consulate C8
29 Malaysian Consulate C7
30 New Zealand Honorary Consul D5
31 Singaporean Consulate C6
32 Sri Lankan Deputy High
      Commission B4
33 Tamil Nadu Tourism Development
      Corporation F4
34 Thai Consulate C5
35 Thomas Cook D4
36 US Consulate C5

ℹ Transport
37 Advanced Computerised
      Reservation Office E2
38 Broadway Bus Terminus F1
39 Passenger Reservation Office D2
40 T Nagar Bus Terminus A7

Hanu Reddy Residences   B&B **$$**
(☎044-45038413; www.hanureddyresidences.
com; 6A/24 3rd St, Wallace Garden, Nungam-
bakkam; r incl breakfast ₹3600-4200; ❄🤖)
Spread across two residential buildings
engulfed by greenery in upmarket Wal-
lace Garden, Hanu Reddy is exactly the
kind of peaceful homey hideaway that
central Chennai needs. The eight cosy,
unpretentious rooms come with air-con,
free wi-fi, tea/coffee sets and splashes
of colourful artwork; the teensy terraces
have bamboo lounging chairs. Service
hits the perfect personal-yet-professional
balance.

TRIPLICANE & AROUND

La Woods   Hotel **$$**
(☎044-28608040; www.lawoodshotel.com;
1 Woods Rd; r incl breakfast ₹3500; ❄🤖)
Wonderfully erratic colour schemes
throw fresh whites against lime-greens
and turquoises at this friendly modern

hotel, new in 2013. The shiny, well-kept,
contemporary rooms are perfectly comfy,
with free wi-fi and mountains of pillows,
as well as kettles, hairdryers and 'global'
plug sockets.

SOUTHERN CHENNAI

Footprint B&B   B&B **$$**
(☎9840037483; www.chennaibedandbreak
fast.com; Gayatri Apts, 16 South St, Alwarpet;
r incl breakfast ₹4500; ❄@🤖) This is a
beautifully comfortable, relaxed base for
your Chennai explorations, spread over
four apartments on a quiet street in a
leafy neighbourhood. Bowls of wild roses
and old-Madras photos set the scene
for twelve cosy, spotless rooms, with
king-size or wide twin beds. Breakfasts
(Continental or Indian) are generous, wi-fi
is free and the welcoming owners are
full of Tamil Nadu tips. Book ahead. It's
behind the Sheraton Park Hotel.

Park Hotel
Boutique Hotel $$$

(044-42676000; www.theparkhotels.com; 601 Anna Salai; s ₹12,590-14,990, d ₹13,790-16,190, ste from ₹19,190; ❄@🛜🏊) We love this super-chic boutique hotel, which flaunts design everywhere you look, from the towering lobby's bamboo, steel and gold cushions to the posters from classic South Indian movies shot in Gemini Studios, the site's previous incarnation. Rooms have lovely lush bedding and stylish touches like feathered lamps and glass-walled bathrooms. There are three restaurants, a rooftop pool, a luxury spa and three packed-out nightspots too!

 Eating

Hotel Saravana Bhavan
Indian $

(www.saravanabhavan.com; 21 Kennet Lane; mains ₹75-140; 🕒6am-10pm) Dependably delish, South Indian thali 'meals' at this famous Chennai vegetarian chain run around ₹80 to ₹100. It's also excellent for South Indian breakfasts (idlis and vadas from ₹33), filter coffee and other Indian vegetarian fare. Branches include **George Town** (209 NSC Bose Rd; 🕒6am-10pm), **Triplicane** (Shanthi Theatre Complex, 44 Anna Salai;

🕒7am-11pm), **Thousand Lights** (293 Peter's Rd; 🕒7.30am-11pm), **Mylapore** (70 North Mada St; 🕒6am-10pm) and **T Nagar** (102 Sir Thyagaraya Rd; 🕒7am-10.30pm), along with London, Paris and New York!

Amethyst
Multicuisine, Cafe $$$

(044-45991633; www.amethystchennai. com; White's Rd, Royapettah; mains ₹240-450; 🕒10am-11pm; 🛜) Set in an exquisitely converted warehouse with a wraparound verandah from which tables spill out into lush gardens, Amethyst is a nostalgically posh haven that's outrageously popular with expats and well-off Chennaiites. Topnotch, European-flavoured treats range over quiches, pasta, crepes, creative salads (watermelon and feta), and even afternoon tea. Fight for your table, then check out the stunning Indian couture boutique.

Tuscana Pizzeria
Italian $$$

(044-45038008; http://tuscanakryptos.in; 19 3rd St, Wallace Garden; pizzas & pasta ₹480-780; 🕒noon-11pm) This, my pizza-loving friends, is the real deal, and Chennai has well and truly embraced it. Tuscana turns out authentic thin-crust pizzas with toppings

Temple entranceway, Chennai

like prosciutto and mozzarella, as well as creative takes such as spiced paneer masala pizza, and tasty pastas. It even has whole-wheat and gluten-free options. Best to book ahead.

Raintree Chettinadu $$$
(www.vivantabytaj.com; Vivanta by Taj – Connemara, Binny Rd; mains ₹500-1000; ⊙12.30-2.45pm & 7.30-11.45pm) This 25-year-old wood-ceilinged restaurant is probably the best place in Chennai to savour the delicious flavours of Tamil Nadu's Chettinadu region. Chettinadu cuisine is famously meat-heavy and superbly spicy without being chilli-laden, but veg dishes are good too. When the weather behaves, you can dine outside in the leafy garden with water lilies.

Copper Chimney North Indian $$$
(☎044-28115770; 74 Cathedral Rd, Gopalapuram; mains ₹290-700; ⊙noon-3pm & 7-11pm) Meat-eaters will drool over the yummy North Indian tandoori dishes served here in stylishly minimalist surroundings, but the veg food is fantastic too (even some Jain specialities). The *machchi* tikka – skewers of tandoori-baked fish – is superb, as is the spiced paneer kebab.

ℹ Information

Medical Services

Apollo Hospital (☎044-28296569, emergency 044-28293333; www.apollohospitals.com; 21 Greams Lane) State-of-the-art, expensive hospital, popular with 'medical tourists'.

Money

ATMs are everywhere, including at Central train station, the airport and the main bus station.

Thomas Cook (Phase I, Spencer Plaza, Anna Salai; ⊙9.30am-6.30pm) Changes foreign cash and American Express travellers cheques.

Tourist Information

Tamil Nadu Tourism Development Corporation (TTDC; ☎044-25383333; www.tamilnadutourism.org; Tamil Nadu Tourism Complex, 2 Wallajah Rd, Triplicane; ⊙10am-6pm) The state tourism body's main office takes bookings for its own bus tours, answers questions and hands out leaflets. In the same building are state tourist offices from all over India, mostly open 10am to 6pm. The TTDC has counters at Central and Egmore stations.

ℹ Getting There & Away

Air

Chennai Airport is at Tirusulam in the far southwest of the city. A brand-new domestic terminal was due to open soon at the time of research, with the international terminal expanding to occupy the whole of the old building. There are direct flights to over 20 Indian cities plus Colombo, Singapore, Kuala Lumpur and Bangkok, as well as the Gulf states.

Chennai Egmore train station
PANORAMIC IMAGES / GETTY IMAGES ©

Bus

Most government buses operate from the large but surprisingly orderly **CMBT (Chennai Mofussil Bus Terminus; Jawaharlal Nehru Rd, Koyambedu)**, 6km west of the centre. Routes include to Madurai (₹420, 10 hours, frequent), Mamallapuram (₹80, two hours, twice hourly) and Puducherry (₹100, four hours, twice hourly).

The **T Nagar Bus Terminus (South Usman Rd)** has a few daily departures to Bengaluru, Madurai, Mysuru, Thanjavur and Trichy, plus bus 599 to Mamallapuram (₹27, 1½ hours, every 30 minutes).

Car

Renting a car with a driver is the easiest way of getting anywhere and is easily arranged through most travel agents, midrange or top-end hotels, or the airport's prepaid taxi desks. Sample rates for non-AC/AC cars are ₹700/800 for up to five hours and 50km, and ₹1400/1600 for up to 10 hours and 100km.

Train

Interstate trains and those heading west generally depart from Central station, while trains heading south mostly leave from Egmore. The **advance reservations office (1st fl, Chennai Central local station; ⏰8am-8pm Mon-Sat, 8am-2pm Sun)**, with its extremely helpful Foreign Tourist Cell, is in a separate 11-storey building just west of the main Central station building. The **Passenger Reservation Office (Chennai Egmore station; ⏰8am-8pm Mon-Sat, 8am-2pm Sun)** at Egmore station keeps the same hours.

🛈 Getting Around

To/From the Airport

The Chennai Metro Rail system, expected to open in late 2015, will provide a cheap, easy link between the airport and city. Meanwhile, the cheapest option is a suburban train to/from Tirusulam station opposite the parking areas of the domestic terminal, accessed by a pedestrian subway under the highway. Trains run every 10 to 20 minutes from 4am to midnight to/from Chennai Beach station (₹5, 42 minutes) with stops including Kodambakkam, Egmore, Chennai Park and Chennai Fort.

Prepaid taxi kiosks outside the airport's international terminal charge ₹480/580 for a non-AC/AC cab to Egmore, and ₹400/500 to T Nagar. Rates are slightly lower at prepaid taxi kiosks outside the domestic terminal.

Autorickshaw

Drivers rarely use meters. Expect to pay at least ₹40 for a short trip down the road, around ₹80 for

Major Trains from Chennai

DESTINATION	TRAIN NO & NAME	FARE (₹)	DURATION (HR)	DEPARTURE
Bengaluru	12007 Shatabdi Exp*	529/1155 (A)	5	6am CC
	12609 Chennai-Bangalore Intercity Exp	110/386 (B)	6½	1.35pm CC
Delhi	12621 Tamil Nadu Exp	780/2020/2970 (C)	33	10pm CC
Goa	17311 Vasco Exp (Fri only)	475/1275/1850 (C)	22	2.10pm CC
Kochi (Cochin)	16041 Alleppey Exp	395/1035/1470 (C)	11½	8.45pm CC
Kolkata (Calcutta)	12842 Coromandel Exp	665/1730/2520 (C)	27	8.45am CC
Madurai	12635 Vaigai Exp	180/655 (B)	8	1.20pm CE
	12637 Pandyan Exp	315/805/1135 (C)	9	9.20pm CE
Mumbai (Bombay)	11042 Mumbai Exp	540/1440/2100 (C)	26	11.55am CC
Mysuru (Mysore)	12007 Shatabdi Exp*	915/1805 (A)	7	6am CC
	16222 Kaveri Exp	285/755/1085 (C)	10	9pm CC
Trivandrum	12695 Trivandrum Mail	470/1230/1760 (C)	16	3.25pm CC

Departure codes: CC – Chennai Central, CE – Chennai Egmore
*Daily except Wednesday
Fares:(A) chair/executive; (B) 2nd/chair; (C) sleeper/3AC/2AC

a 3km trip and ₹100 to ₹120 for 5km. Prices are at least 25% higher after 10pm. There are prepaid booths outside the CMBT (₹125 to Egmore) and Central station.

....

Mamallapuram (Mahabalipuram)

☎ 044 / POP 17,666

Mamallapuram was the major seaport of the ancient Pallava kingdom based at Kanchipuram, and today a wander round the town's great, World Heritage–listed temples and carvings inflames the imagination, especially at sunset.

◉ Sights

You can easily spend a full day exploring Mamallapuram's marvellous temples and rock carvings . Most of them were carved from the rock in the 7th century during the reign of Pallava king Narasimhavarman I, whose nickname Mamalla (Great Wrestler) gave the town its name. Apart from the Shore Temple and Five Rathas, admission is free. Official Archaeological Survey of India guides can be hired at the sites for around ₹100.

Shore Temple   Hindu Temple
(combined 1-day ticket with Five Rathas Indian/ foreigner ₹10/250, video ₹25; ⊙6am-6pm) Standing like a magnificent fist of rock-cut elegance overlooking the sea, the two-towered Shore Temple symbolises the heights of Pallava architecture and the maritime ambitions of the Pallava kings. Its small size belies its excellent proportion and the supreme quality of the carvings, many of which have been eroded into vaguely Impressionist embellishments. Built under Narasimhavarman II in the 8th century, it's the earliest significant free-standing stone temple in Tamil Nadu.

Five Rathas   Hindu Temple
(Pancha Ratha; Five Rathas Rd; combined 1-day ticket with Shore Temple Indian/foreigner ₹10/250, video ₹25; ⊙6am-6pm) Huddled together at the southern end of Mamallapuram, the Five Rathas look like buildings, but they were, astonishingly, all carved from single large rocks. Each of these 7th-century temples was dedicated to a Hindu god and is now named after one or more of the Pandavas, the five hero brothers of the epic Mahabharata, or

Five Rathas

JEBARAJ JOHN / GETTY IMAGES ©

 Don't Miss
Arjuna's Penance

The crowning masterpiece of Mamallapuram's stonework, this giant relief carving is one of India's greatest ancient art works. Inscribed on two huge, adjacent boulders, the Penance bursts with scenes of Hindu myth and everyday vignettes of South Indian life. In the centre *nagas* (snake-beings) descend a once water-filled cleft, representing the Ganges. To the left Arjuna (hero of the Mahabharata) performs self-mortification (fasting on one leg), so that the four-armed Shiva will grant him his most powerful weapon, the god-slaying Pasupata.

NEED TO KNOW
West Raja St

their common wife, Draupadi. The *rathas* were hidden in the sand until excavated by the British 200 years ago.

 Tours

Travel XS   Cycling, Birdwatching
(📞044-27443360; www.travel-xs.com; 123 East Raja St; bicycle tours ₹450-500; ⏰9.30am-6pm Mon-Fri, 9.30am-2pm Sat) Runs half-day bicycle tours to nearby villages, visiting local potters and observing activities like *kolam* drawing (the 'welcome' patterns outside doorways, also called *rangoli*),

and organises day trips to places including Kanchipuram and Vedanthangal Bird Sanctuary.

 Sleeping

Butterball Bed 'n Breakfast   B&B $$
(📞9094792525; www.butterball.in; 9/26 East Raja St; s/d incl breakfast ₹1700/2000; ❄️🛜) There's a great view of the eponymous giant rock (Krishna's Butter Ball) from the roof terrace, and a lovely lawn. The smallish but clean, pleasant rooms have

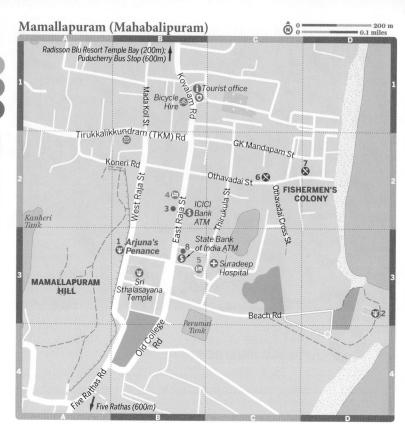

Mamallapuram (Mahabalipuram)

old English prints, writing desks and blue-tiled bathrooms, and breakfast is served in **Burger Shack** (mains ₹120-300; ⏱10am-10pm) restaurant out the front.

Hotel Mahabs
Hotel **$$**

(☏044-27442645; www.hotelmahabs.com; 68 East Raja St; r ₹2140-2930; ❄@🛜🏊) Friendly Mahabs is centred on a pretty mural-lined pool (₹300 for nonguests) surrounded by tropical greenery. Boring brown is the room theme, but they're very clean and comfy. There's a decent in-house restaurant.

Radisson Blu Resort
Temple Bay
Resort **$$$**

(☏044-27443636; www.radissonblu.com/hotel-mamallapuram; 57 Kovalam Rd; r incl breakfast from ₹9880; ❄@🛜🏊) The Radisson's 144 luxurious chalets, villas and bungalows are strewn across manicured gardens stretching 500m to the beach. Somewhere in the midst is India's longest swimming pool, all 220m of it. Rooms range from large to enormous; the most expensive have private pools. The Radisson also offers Mamallapuram's finest (and priciest) dining and a top-notch ayurvedic spa. Best rates online.

Eating

Eateries on Othavadai and Othavadai Cross Sts provide semi-open-air settings, decent Continental mains and bland Indian curries. Most of them can serve you a beer. For real Indian food, there are a few decent cheap veg and biryani places near the bus stand.

Mamallapuram (Mahabalipuram)

◎ Don't Miss Sights
1 Arjuna's Penance.................................... B3

◎ Sights
2 Shore Temple.. D3

◎ Activities, Courses & Tours
3 Travel XS... B2

◎ Sleeping
4 Butterball Bed 'n Breakfast................... B2

5 Hotel Mahabs... B3

◎ Eating
Burger Shack .... (see 4)
6 Gecko Restaurant C2
7 Le Yogi D2

◎ Transport
8 Southern Railway Reservation
Centre B3

Le Yogi   Multicuisine $$

(19 Othavadai St; mains ₹100-200; ⊙7.30am-11pm) This is some of the best Continental food in town; the pasta, pizza, sizzlers and crepes are genuine and tasty (if small), service is good, and the chilled-out setting, with bamboo posts and pretty lamps dangling from a thatched roof, has a touch of the romantic.

Gecko Restaurant   Multicuisine $$

(www.gecko-web.com; 37 Othavadai St; mains ₹150-270; ⊙9am-10pm; 🛜) Two friendly brothers run this cute blue-and-yellow-walled spot sprinkled with colourful artwork and wood carvings. The offerings

and prices aren't that different from other tourist-oriented spots, but there's more love put into the cooking here and it's tastier.

Water's Edge Cafe   Multicuisine $$$

(Radisson Blu Resort Temple Bay, 57 Kovalam Rd; mains ₹480-900; ⊙24hr) The Radisson's pool-side 'cafe' offers everything from American pancakes to grilled tofu, Indian veg dishes and a fantastic breakfast buffet (₹970). Also here is **The Wharf** (mains ₹550-1600; ⊙noon-3pm & 7-11pm), which looks like a beach shack but is actually a gourmet multicuisine seaside restaurant.

Shore Temple (p278)

KEVIN CLOGSTOUN / GETTY IMAGES ©

Below & Right: Street scenes, Puducherry

(BELOW) JOHN ELK III / GETTY IMAGES ©; (RIGHT) CLAUDE RENAULT / GETTY IMAGES ©

ℹ Information

Head to East Raja St for ATMs.

Suradeep Hospital (📞044-27442448; 15 Thirukula St; ⏱24hr) Recommended by travellers.

Tourist office (📞044-27442232; Kovalam Rd; ⏱10am-5.45pm Mon-Fri)

ℹ Getting There & Away

From the bus stand, bus 599 heads to Chennai's T Nagar Bus Terminus (₹27, 1½ hours) every 30 minutes from 7am to 8.30pm, and AC bus 568C (588C on Saturday and Sunday) runs to Chennai's CMBT (₹85, two hours) every two hours, 6am to 8pm. For Chennai Airport take bus 515 to Tambaram (₹40, 1½ hours, every 30 minutes), then a taxi, autorickshaw or suburban train. There are also nine daily buses to Kanchipuram (₹40, two hours).

Buses to Puducherry (₹60, two hours) stop about every 30 minutes at the junction of Kovalam Rd and the Mamallapuram bypass, 1km north of the town centre.

Taxis are available from the bus stand, travel agents and hotels.

You can make train reservations at the **Southern Railway Reservation Centre** (32 East Raja St, 1st fl; ⏱10am-1pm & 2.30-5pm Mon-Sat, 8am-1pm Sun)

ℹ Getting Around

The easiest way to get around is on foot, though on a hot day it's quite a hike to see all the monuments. Bicycles can be hired at some guesthouses and hotels, and at a few rental stalls, usually for ₹80 per day.

Puducherry (Pondicherry)

📞0413 / POP 241,773

Puducherry (formerly called Pondicherry and almost always referred to as 'Pondy') is certainly no Provençal village, but the older part of this former French colony (where you'll probably spend most of

your time) does have a lot of quiet, clean, shady, cobbled streets, lined with mustard-yellow colonial-era townhouses. In fact, if you've come from Chennai or some of the inland cities, old Pondy may well seem a sea of tranquillity.

◉ Sights

French Quarter   Area

Pocketed away just behind the seafront is a series of cobbled streets, white-and-mustard buildings in various states of romantic dishevelment, and a slight sense of Gallic glory gone by, otherwise known as the French Quarter. A do-it-yourself heritage walk could start at the **French Consulate** (☎ 0413-2231000; 2 Marine St) near the north end of seafront Goubert Ave, then gradually head south.

Sri Aurobindo Ashram   Ashram

(www.sriaurobindoashram.org; Marine St; ⊗ general visits 8am-noon & 2-6pm) Founded in 1926 by Sri Aurobindo and a French-born woman known as 'the Mother', this spiritual community now has about 1200 members working in its many departments. Aurobindo's teachings focus on an 'integral yoga' as the path towards a 'supramental consciousness which will divinise human nature'; devotees work in the world, rather than retreating from it. General visits to the main ashram building are cursory – you just see the flower-festooned samadhi of Aurobindo and the Mother, then the bookshop, then you leave.

Sri Manakula Vinayagar Temple   Hindu Temple

(Manakula Vinayagar Koil St; ⊗ 5.45am-12.30pm & 4-9pm) Pondy may have more churches than most towns, but this is still India, and the Hindu faith still reigns supreme. Don't miss the chance to watch tourists, pilgrims and the curious get a head pat from the temple elephant at this temple dedicated to Ganesh, which also contains over 40 skilfully painted friezes.

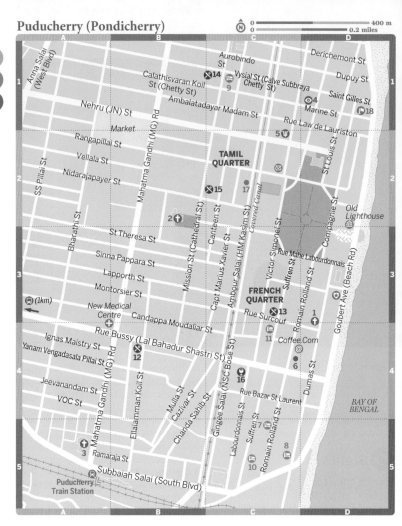

KERALA & SOUTH INDIA PUDUCHERRY (PONDICHERRY)

0   400 m
0   0.2 miles

Anna Salai (West Blvd)

Aurobindo St

Derichemont St

Dupuy St

Calathisvaran Koil St (Chetty St)

Vysial St (Calve Subbraya Chetty St)

14

9

Saint Gilles St

4

18

Nehru (JN) St

Ambalatadayar Madam St

Marine St

Rue Law de Lauriston

Market

Rangapillai St

5

Mahatma Gandhi (MG) Rd

TAMIL QUARTER

Vellala St

Nidarajapayer St

SS Pillai St

St Louis St

15

17

2

Covered Canal

Bharath St

St Theresa St

Mission St (Cathedral St)

Canteen St

Capt Marius Xavier St

Ambour Salai (HM Kasim St)

Sinna Pappara St

Old Lighthouse

Lapporth St

Montorsier St

Victor Simonel St

Suffren St

Compagnie St

FRENCH QUARTER

Rue Mahe Labourdonnais

Goubert Ave (Beach Rd)

(1km)

New Medical Centre

Candappa Moudaliar St

Rue Surcouf

13

Romain Rolland St

1

Ignas Maistry St

Rue Bussy (Lal Bahadur Shastri St)

11

Coffee.Com

Yanam Vengadasala Pillai St

Mahatma Gandhi (MG) Rd

12

6

Dumas St

Jeevanandam St

Ellaiamman Koil St

Mulla St

Cazivar St

Gingee Salai (NSC Bose St)

16

Rue Bazar St Laurent

VOC St

Chanda Sahib St

Labourdonnais St

Suffren St

BAY OF BENGAL

3

Ramaraja St

Romain Rolland St

7

8

Subbaiah Salai (South Blvd)

10

Puducherry Train Station

 ## Tours

Shanti Travel   Walking Tour

(☎ 0413-4210401; www.shantitravel.com; 13 Romain Rolland St; ⊙ 10am-1.30pm & 2.30-7pm) Shanti Travels offers recommended two-hour walking tours (per person ₹500) of Puducherry with English- or French-speaking guides.

 ## Sleeping

Sri Aurobindo Ashram (p283) has several simple but clean guesthouses. They're primarily intended for ashram visitors, but many accept other guests who are willing to abide by their rules: 10.30pm curfew and no smoking, alcohol or drugs. Only some accept advance bookings. The ashram's **Bureau Central** (☎ 0413-2233604; bureaucentral@sriaurobindoashram.

Puducherry (Pondicherry)

⊚ Sights
1 Notre Dame des Anges D3
2 Our Lady of the Immaculate
   Conception Cathedral.....................B2
3 Sacred Heart Basilica...........................A5
4 Sri Aurobindo Ashram D1
5 Sri Manakula Vinayagar Temple.........C2

⊙ Activities, Courses & Tours
6 Walking Tours C4

⊜ Sleeping
7 Coloniale Heritage Guest
   House C5
8 Hotel de Pondichéry............................C5
9 Kailash Guest House C1
10 Les Hibiscus C5
11 Villa Shanti..C4

⊗ Eating
12 Baker Street B4
13 Café des Arts......................................C3
14 La Pasta C1
Le Club ....(see 8)
15 Surguru C2
Villa Shanti.....................................(see 11)

⊙ Drinking & Nightlife
16 L'e-Space C4

⊙ Information
17 Bureau Central....................................C2
18 French Consulate................................D1
Shanti Travel ....(see 6)

org; Ambour Salai; ⊙6-7.30am, 9am-noon & 3-7pm) has a list.

Kailash Guest House
Guesthouse $

(☏0413-2224485; www.kailashguesthouse.in; 43 Vysial St; s/d ₹800/1000, d with AC ₹1250; ✳) The best value for money in this price range, Kailash has simple, super-clean rooms with well mosquito-proofed windows, friendly management and superb city views from the top floors. It's geared to traveller needs, with loungey communal areas, clothes-drying facilities and a bar on the way.

Les Hibiscus
Guesthouse $$

(☏9442066763, 0413-2227480; www.leshibiscus.in; 49 Suffren St; s/d incl breakfast ₹2400/2700; ✳@🖙) A strong contender for our favourite Tamil Nadu hotel, Hibiscus has just four pristine, high-ceilinged rooms with gorgeous antique beds, coffee-makers and a mix of quaint Indian art and old-Pondy photos, at incredibly reasonable prices. The whole place is immaculately tasteful, breakfast is fabulous, internet is free and management is genuinely friendly and helpful. Make sure you book ahead.

Coloniale Heritage Guest House
Guesthouse $$

(☏0413-2224720; www.colonialeheritage.com; 54 Romain Rolland St; r incl breakfast ₹2000-3300; ✳🖙) This colonial-era home with six comfy rooms (some up steep stairs) is chock-full of character thanks to the owner's amazing collection of gem-studded Tanjore paintings, Ravi Varma lithographs and other 19th- and 20th-century South Indian art. One room even has a swing. Breakfast is served in a sunken patio beside the leafy garden.

Hotel de Pondichéry
Heritage Hotel $$

(☏0413-2227409; www.hoteldepondichery.com; 38 Dumas St; incl breakfast s ₹2000, d ₹3000-5000; ✳🖙) A colourful heritage spot with 14 comfy, quiet, high-ceilinged, colonial-style rooms and a dash of original modern art. Its excellent restaurant, Le Club (p286), takes up the pretty front courtyard. Staff are lovely and there's free wi-fi in the lobby.

Villa Shanti
Heritage Hotel $$$

(☏0413-4200028; www.lavillashanti.com; 14 Suffren St; r incl breakfast ₹7870-10,117; ✳✳🖙) Set in a 100-year-old building revamped by two French architects, Villa Shanti puts an exquisitely contemporary twist on the traditional Pondy heritage hotel. Beautiful fresh rooms combine super-chic design with typically Tamil materials and colonial-style elegance: four-poster beds, Chettinadu tiles, Tamil murals. The courtyard houses a popular **restaurant** (mains ₹225-495; ⊙12.30-2.30pm & 7-10.30pm) and cocktail bar, so book upper-floor beds for early snoozing.

If You Like...
Colonial-Era Architecture

Puducherry has one of the best collections of over-the-top churches and cathedrals in India. If you enjoyed strolling around the French Quarter, go in search of these too.

1 OUR LADY OF THE IMMACULATE CONCEPTION CATHEDRAL
(Mission St; ⏰7-11am & 4-8.30pm) Our Lady of the Immaculate Conception Cathedral, completed in 1791, is a robin's-egg-blue-and-cloud-white typically Jesuit edifice in a Goa-like Portuguese style.

2 SACRED HEART BASILICA
(Subbayah Salai; ⏰7-11am & 4-8.30pm) The brown-and-white grandiosity of the Sacred Heart Basilica is set off by stained glass and a Gothic sense of proportion.

3 NOTRE DAME DES ANGES
(Dumas St; ⏰6-10am & 4-7pm) The twin towers and dome of the mellow pink-and-cream Notre Dame des Anges, built in the 1850s, look sublime in the late-afternoon light. The smooth limestone interior was made using eggshells in the plaster.

🍴 Eating & Drinking

Puducherry is a culinary highlight of Tamil Nadu; you get good South Indian cooking plus several restaurants specialising in well-prepped French and Italian cuisine.

Baker Street
Cafe $
(123 Rue Bussy; items ₹40-130; ⏰7am-9pm; 📶) A popular upmarket, French-style bakery with delectable cakes, croissants and biscuits. Baguettes, brownies and quiches aren't bad either. Eat in or take away.

Surguru
South Indian $
(235 (old 99) Mission St; mains ₹70-120; ⏰7am-10.30pm) Simple South Indian in a relatively posh setting. Surguru is the fix for thali (lunchtime only) and dosa addicts who like their veg with good strong aircon.

La Pasta
Italian $$
(📞9994670282; www.lapastapondy.blogspot.com; 55 Vysial St; mains ₹230-350; ⏰noon-2pm & 5-9pm Tue-Sat) Pasta lovers should make a pilgrimage to this little spot with just four check-cloth tables, where a real Italian whips up her own authentically yummy sauces and concocts her own perfect pasta in an open-plan kitchen as big as the dining area. No alcohol: it's all about the food.

Café des Arts
Cafe $$
(10 Suffren St; dishes ₹130-230; ⏰8.30am-7pm Wed-Mon; 📶) This bohemian, vintage-style cafe would look perfectly at home in Europe, but this is Pondy, so there's a cycle rickshaw in the garden. Refreshingly light dishes range from crisp salads, baguettes and toasties to crepes, and the coffees and fresh juices are great. The old-townhouse setting is lovely, with low tables and lounge chairs spilling out in front of a quirky boutique.

Le Club
Continental, Indian $$$
(📞0413-2339745; 38 Dumas St; mains ₹300-500; ⏰noon-3.30pm & 7-11pm Tue-Sun) The steaks (with sauces like blue cheese or Béarnaise), pizzas and crepes are all top-class at this super-popular romantically lit garden restaurant. Tempting local options include creole prawn curry, veg-paneer kebabs and Malabar-style fish, and there are plenty of wines, mojitos and margaritas to wash it all down.

L'e-Space
Bar, Cafe
(2 Labourdonnais St; cocktails ₹200; ⏰5-11pm) A quirky little semi-open-air upstairs bar/cafe lounge that's friendly and sociable, and does good cocktails (assuming the barman hasn't disappeared).

Information

ATMs are plentiful and there are numerous currency-exchange offices on Mission St near the corner of Nehru St.

Rue Bussy between Bharathi St and MG Rd is packed with clinics and pharmacies.

Coffee.Com (11A Romain Rolland St; per hr ₹80; ⏰10.30am-10pm) A genuine internet cafe, with good coffee and light food (₹60 to ₹300).

New Medical Centre (☎0413-2225287; www.nmcpondy.com; 470 MG Rd; ⏰24hr) Recommended private clinic and hospital.

ℹ️ Getting There & Away

Bus

The **bus stand** (Maraimalai Adigal Salai) is in the west of town, 2km from the French Quarter.

Train

Puducherry station has just a few services. Two daily trains go to Chennai Egmore, with unreserved seating only (₹45 to ₹75, four to five hours). You can connect at Villupuram for many more services north and south. Puducherry station has a computerised booking office for trains throughout India.

ℹ️ Getting Around

One of the best ways to get around Pondy's flat streets is by walking. Autorickshaws are plentiful. Official metered fares are ₹40 for up to 2km and then ₹15 per kilometre, but most drivers refuse to use their meters. A trip from the bus stand to the French Quarter costs around ₹60.

Madurai

☎0452 / POP 1.02 MILLION

Chennai may be the capital of Tamil Nadu, but Madurai claims its soul. Madurai is Tamil-born and Tamil-rooted, one of the oldest cities in India, a metropolis that traded with ancient Rome and was a great capital long before Chennai was even dreamt of.

Tourists, Indian and foreign, usually come here to see the Meenakshi Amman Temple (p288), a labyrinthine structure ranking among the greatest temples of India. Otherwise, Madurai, perhaps appropriately given her age, captures many of India's glaring dichotomies with a centre dominated by a medieval temple and an economy increasingly driven by IT, all overlaid with the energy and excitement of a large Indian city and slotted into a much more manageable package than Chennai's sprawl.

◎ Sights

Gandhi Memorial Museum

Museum

(Gandhi Museum Rd; camera ₹50; ⏰10am-1pm & 2-5.45pm Sat-Thu) **FREE** Housed in a 17th-century Nayak queen's palace, this excellent museum contains an impressively moving and comprehensive account of India's struggle for independence from 1757 to 1947, and the English-language text spares no detail about British rule. Included in the exhibition is the blood-stained dhoti (long loincloth) that Gandhi was wearing when he was assassinated in Delhi in 1948; it was here in Madurai, in 1921, that he first took up wearing the dhoti as a sign of native pride.

🛏️ Sleeping

Hotel West Tower

Hotel $

(☎0452-2349600; 42/60 West Tower St; s/d ₹500/800, with AC ₹1200/1800; ❄️) The West Tower's best asset is that it's very near the temple, but it's also acceptably clean and friendly.

Buses from Puducherry (Pondicherry) Bus Stand

DESTINATION	FARE (₹)	DURATION (HR)	FREQUENCY (DAILY)
Bengaluru	310	7	8pm & 10pm
Chennai	97 (Volvo AC 190)	4	every 30min (6 Volvo AC 6.30am-6pm)
Mamallapuram	80	2	36

Don't Miss

Meenakshi Amman Temple

Indian/foreigner ₹5/50, phone camera ₹50

🕐 4am-12.30pm & 4-9.30pm

The abode of the triple-breasted warrior goddess Meenakshi ('fish-eyed' – an epithet for perfect eyes in classical Tamil poetry) is considered by many to be the height of South Indian temple architecture, as vital to the aesthetic heritage of this region as the Taj Mahal to North India.

The Temple Complex

Not so much a temple as a 6-hectare complex with 12 tall *gopurams* (gateway towers), all encrusted with a staggering array of gods, goddesses, demons and heroes (1511 of them on the south *gopuram* alone).

The four streets surrounding the temple are pedestrian-only. The main entrance is by the eastern *gopuram*. First, have a look round the **Pudhu Mandapa (East Chitrai St)**, the 100m-long, 16th-century pillared hall facing the *gopuram*. It's filled with colourful textile and craft stalls and tailors at sewing machines, partly hiding some of the lovely pillar sculptures, but it's easy to find the triple-breasted Meenakshi near the southeast corner, and her marriage to Shiva, accompanied by Vishnu, just inside the western entrance. A particularly handsome light-blue Nandi bull (Shiva's vehicle) sits outside the *mandapa's* eastern entrance.

Inside

Once inside the eastern *gopuram*, you'll find the Nayak-period Thousand Pillar Hall on your right. This is now an **Art Museum** (Indian/foreigner ₹5/50, phone camera ₹50; ✆6.30am-1pm & 4-9pm) where you can admire at your leisure a Shiva shrine with a large bronze Nataraja at the end of a corridor of superbly carved pillars, plus many other fine bronzes and colourful painted panels. Moving on into the temple, you'll reach a Nandi shrine surrounded by more beautifully carved columns. Ahead is the main Shiva shrine, and further ahead to the left is the main Meenakshi shrine, both of which only Hindus can enter. Anyone can, however, wander round the temple tank, and leave the temple from there via a hall of flower sellers and the arch-ceilinged Ashta Shakti Mandapa. Note, dress codes are fairly strict for the temple itself: no women's shoulders, or legs of either gender, may be exposed.

1 THE SOUTH GOPURAM

This is the only *gopuram* (gateway tower) with parabolic design, and is one of the most beautiful *gopurams* structurally. The *gopuram* was constructed during the late 16th century, and has both Vijayanagar and Nayak architectural characteristics.

2 SCULPTURE ON THE SHIVA SHRINE

There is some marvellous marriage-ceremony sculpture on one of the pillars in front of the Sundareswar or Shiva shrine. In this scene, Lord Vishnu offers his sister Meenakshi or Parvati to Sundareswarar or Shiva. Vishnu is in a gentle mood, Parvati looks shy, and Shiva courageous – it's a visual feast. This sculpture, along with the Nandi *mandapa* (pillared pavilion), is housed under a high ceiling supported by ornamental pillars typical of the Nayak period.

3 THOUSAND PILLAR HALL

This is a wonder because of the remarkable angularity between all the pillars. The *mandapa* is a huge edifice located in the northeast corner of the temple that actually houses 985 pillars. The group of figures on two rows of pillars at the entrance is a masterpiece in itself.

4 THE GOLDEN VIMANAS

You may view the two golden *vimanas* (towers) from the eastern side of the golden lotus tank. The two *vimanas* and the tank are as old as the legends connected with the origin of the shrine.

5 PATH AROUND THE SHIVA SHRINE

I advise visitors to walk around the outside of the Shiva shrine: this circular route is particularly stunning. The monolithic pillars and granite roof are dazzling structures – you can see how the engineering of the era embraced artistry.

Madurai

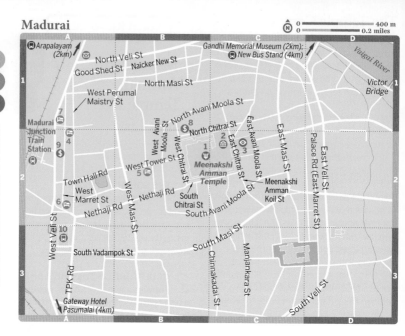

Madurai

⊙ Don't Miss Sights
1 Meenakshi Amman Temple B2

⊙ Sights
2 Art Museum..C2
3 Pudhu Mandapa.....................................C2

⊜ Sleeping
4 Hotel Supreme......................................A2
5 Hotel West Tower.................................B2
6 Madurai Residency..............................A2
7 Royal Court..A1

⊗ Eating
Surya ....(see 4)

ⓘ Information
8 ICICI Bank ATM....................................B1
9 State Bank of India A2
Supreme Web...................................(see 4)

ⓘ Transport
10 Shopping Complex Bus Stand............A3

Madurai Residency
Hotel **$$**

(📞0452-4380000; www.madurairesidency.com; 15 West Marret St; s ₹2380-2860, d ₹2760-3220, all incl breakfast; ❄ 🛜) The service is stellar and the rooms are comfy and fresh at this winner, which has one of the highest rooftop restaurants in town. It's very popular, so book at least a day ahead.

Hotel Supreme
Hotel **$$**

(📞0452-2343151; www.hotelsupreme.in; 110 West Perumal Maistry St; s ₹2390-3270, d ₹2710-3470, all incl breakfast; ❄🛜) The Supreme is a well-presented, slightly faded hotel with friendly service that's very popular with domestic tourists. There's good food at the rooftop Surya restaurant (p291) and free in-room wi-fi, and the spaceship-themed basement bar will make you wonder if someone laced your lassi last night.

Royal Court
Hotel **$$**

(📞0452-4356666; www.royalcourtindia.com; 4 West Veli St; s ₹3960-4910, d ₹4800-5640, all incl breakfast; ❄@🛜) The Royal Court blends a bit of white-sheeted, hardwood-floored colonial-era elegance with comfort, good eating options, free wi-fi and friendly yet professional service. Rooms come with tea/coffee sets. It's an excellent, central choice for someone in need of a treat.

Government Buses from Madurai

DESTINATION	FARE (₹)	DURATION (HR)	FREQUENCY
Chennai	325	9-10	every 30min 4am-11.30pm
Ernakulam (Kochi)	325	9-10	9am & 9pm
Mysuru (Mysore)	300-440	10	4 buses 4.30-9pm
Puducherry (Pondicherry)	250	8	9pm

Eating

For a great evening tasting Madurai specialities with a local food enthusiast, call or email **Foodies Day Out** (☏9840992340; www.foodiesdayout.com; 2nd fl, 393 Anna Nagar Main Rd; per person ₹2000).

Surya Multicuisine $$
(110 West Perumal Maistry St; mains ₹80-190; ⊙4-11.30pm) The Hotel Supreme's rooftop restaurant offers excellent service, good pure-veg food and superb city and temple views, but the winner here has got to be the iced coffee, which might have been brewed by God when you sip it on a hot, dusty day.

Garden All Day Multicusine $$$
(Gateway Hotel, 40 TPK Rd, Pasumalai; mains ₹300-525; ⊙7am-10.30pm) If you fancy splashing out, the panoramic all-day restaurant at the Gateway Hotel (5km southwest of central Madurai) does a fantastic multicuisine dinner buffet (₹800 to ₹1000). Dine outside in the gardens or inside in air-con comfort.

🛈 Information

State Bank of India (West Veli St) Foreign-exchange desks and ATM.

Supreme Web (110 West Perumal Maistry St; per hr ₹30; ⊙7.30am-9.30pm) Take your passport.

🛈 Getting There & Away

Air

SpiceJet (www.spicejet.com) flies at least once daily to Bengaluru, Chennai, Colombo, Delhi, Hyderabad and Mumbai. Further Chennai flights are operated by **Jet Airways** (www.jetairways.com) and **Air India** (☏0452-2690333; www.airindia.com).

Bus

Most government buses arrive and depart from the **New Bus Stand** (Melur Rd), 4km northeast of the Old City. Tickets for more expensive (and mostly more comfortable) private buses are sold by agencies on the south side of the **Shopping Complex Bus Stand** (btwn West Veli St & TPK Rd). Most travel overnight.

Train

From Madurai Junction station, 13 daily trains head north to Trichy (two to five hours) and 10 to Chennai, the fastest being the 7am Vaigai Express (Trichy 2nd/chair class ₹93/340, two hours; Chennai ₹180/655, 7¾ hours). A good overnight train for Chennai is the 8.35pm Pandyan Express (sleeper/3AC/2AC/1AC ₹315/805/1135/1915, nine hours). Trivandrum (three daily), Coimbatore (three daily), Bengaluru (two daily) and Mumbai (one daily) are other destinations.

🛈 Getting Around

The airport is 12km south of town and taxis cost ₹300 to the centre. Alternatively, bus 10A runs to/from the Shopping Complex Bus Stand. From the New Bus Stand, bus 75 (₹11) shuttles into the city; an autorickshaw is ₹100.

Darjeeling, Varanasi & the Northeast

Up in the cool northern hills the toy train of the Darjeeling Himalayan Railway chugs its way to the British-era hill station of Darjeeling. It's a quintessential remnant of the Raj, where views of massive Khangchendzonga towering over the surrounding tea estates rank as one of the region's most inspiring sights. The West Bengal capital Kolkata (Calcutta) is a cultural and gastronomic, somewhat mind-blowing feast, peppered with remnants of grandiose colonial-era architecture. It's a fascinating metropolis full of head-spinning contrasts, and forms a perfect springboard to exploring the region, including the tiger-sheltering swamps of the Sunderbans. An overnight train ride away, on the central plains, life and death rituals are played out on the banks of the Ganges in the extraordinary holy city of Varanasi, while tourists flock to Khajuraho to marvel at the breathtaking, virtuoso erotic carvings of its Unesco-protected temples.

Tea estate, Darjeeling hills
RICHARD I'ANSON/GETTY IMAGES ©

Ghats, Varanasi (p325)
SARA-JANE CLELAND/GETTY IMAGES ©

Darjeeling, Varanasi & the Northeast

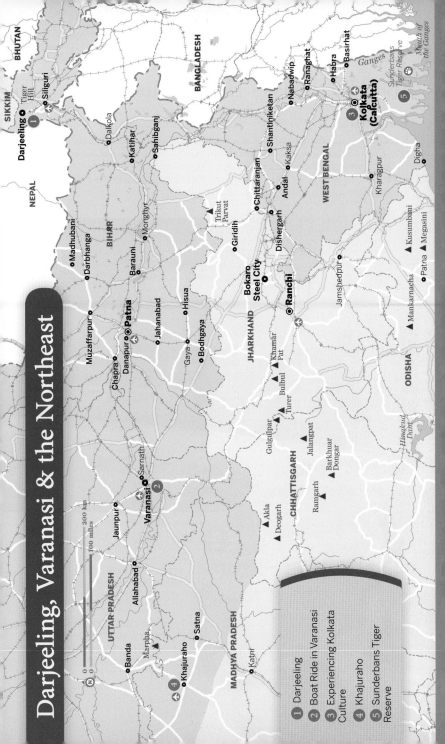

BHUTAN

SIKKIM

Tiger Hill

Darjeeling ● ⬤1

Siliguri ●

NEPAL

Dalkola ●

Katihar ●

Sahibganj ●

Madhubani ●

Darbhanga ●

BIHAR

Monghyr ●

Barauni ●

Muzaffarpur ●

Chapra ●

Danapur ⊙ Patna ⊙ ✈

Jahanabad ●

Hisua ●

Gaya ●

Bodhgaya ●

Giridih ●

Trikut Parvat ▲

BANGLADESH

Shantiniketan ●

Chittaranjan ●

Dishergarh ●

Bokaro Steel City ●

JHARKHAND

Ranchi ◉

Khamar Pat ▲

Bulbul ▲

Turer ▲

Gulgulpar ▲

Akla ▲

Deogarh ▲

CHHATTISGARH

Jalangpat ▲

Barkhuar Dongar ▲

Ramgarh ▲

Nabadwip ● Ranaghat ●

Habra ● Basirhat ●

Ganges

Kolkata (Calcutta) ⊙ ✈ ⬤3

Kaksa ●

Andal ●

WEST BENGAL

Kharagpur ●

Jamshedpur ●

Mankarnacha ▲

ODISHA

Patna ▲ Megasini ▲

Kusumbani ▲

Hinakrud Dam

Digha ●

Sunderbans Tiger Reserve

Mouth of the Ganges

⬤5

UTTAR PRADESH

Jaunpur ●

Sarnath ●

Varanasi ● ✈ ⬤2

Allahabad ●

Banda ●

Marpha ●

Khajuraho ● ✈ ⬤4

Satna ●

Katni ●

MADHYA PRADESH

200 km

100 miles

N

① Darjeeling
② Boat Ride in Varanasi
③ Experiencing Kolkata Culture
④ Khajuraho
⑤ Sunderbans Tiger Reserve

Darjeeling, Varanasi & the Northeast's Highlights

Darjeeling

A quintessential Indian hill station, Darjeeling (p317) is a place to escape the heat of the plains, relax and drink tea. It resonates with Raj-era history, its views of massive Khangchendzonga towering over the surrounding tea estates rank as one of the region's most inspiring sights, and the approach via toy train through the mountains is one of India's iconic journeys. Darjeeling Himalayan Railway (p320)

Boat Ride in Varanasi

The best way to see the tumultuousness of the holy city of Varanasi (p325) is to take a dawn boat trip along the Ganges. It's inspiring to see the colour and clamour of pilgrims bathing and performing *puja* (worship) in the mellow morning light. Early evening is another great time to be by the ghats, lighting a lotus candle and letting it float away on the water.

Experiencing Kolkata Culture ③

Kolkata (Calcutta; p302) is a frenetic, bamboozling mass of contradictions. India's intellectual and cultural capital, it's a place of astonishing festivals, chaotic merchant alleys and colonial-era architecture both grandiose and faded. Friendlier than other Indian mega-cities, it's a fantastic place to wander without being hassled, and feast on everything from street snacks to superb Bengali cuisine.

④

Khajuraho

The temples at Khajuraho (p336) are exquisite examples of Indo-Aryan architecture, but it's their liberally embellished carvings that have made them famous. Around the outsides of the temples are bands of virtuoso stonework showing a storyboard of life a millennium ago – gods, goddesses, warriors, musicians, real and mythological animals, and lots and lots of sex.

⑤

Sunderbans Tiger Reserve

The Sunderbans is a 10,000-sq-km delta of broad channels and semisubmerged mangroves, an area split roughly 40-60 between India and Bangladesh. In the swamps of its tiger reserve (p314) lurks the world's largest population of Royal Bengal tigers (around 300) and plenty more wildlife that's easier to glimpse, including spotted deer, 2m-long water monitors and darting kingfishers. Guided tours from Kolkata typically stay overnight on boats or in 'eco-villages'.

297

Darjeeling, Varanasi & the Northeast's Best…

Wining & Dining

Oh! Calcutta Don't let the shopping-mall location fool you; this is Bengali fusion with a touch of class. One of Kolkata's best. (p312)

Bhojohori Manna Top-notch Bengali food at bargain prices in this great-value Kolkata chain. (p313)

Glenary's Elegant dining above a famous Darjeeling teahouse. (p322)

Brown Bread Bakery Well worth hunting for in Varanasi's back alleys, Brown Bread is organic, international and terrifically tasty…and all for a good cause. (p332)

Raja's Café Khajuraho's classic; lovely setting and wide-ranging menu. (p340)

Heritage Hotels

Oberoi Grand Transporting you from the chaos of Kolkata's streets to an oasis of genteel calm. (p308)

Windamere Hotel Rambling relic of the Raj and one-time boarding house for Darjeeling's British tea planters. (p322)

Hotel Ganges View Beautifully renovated, colonial-style house overlooking the Ganges in the holy city of Varanasi. (p331)

Gateway Hotel Ganges The maharaja's former guesthouse is Varanasi's finest hotel. No river views, but luxury abounds. (p331)

Views

Bhutia Busty Gompa Darjeeling monastery with Khangchendzonga providing a spectacular backdrop. Picture perfect. (p321)

Tiger Hill Darjeeling's most famous sweeping view takes in half a dozen giant peaks (including Everest) and is best seen at dawn. (p317)

Victoria Memorial The magnificently photogenic view across reflecting ponds from the northeast. (p302)

Sunderbans Nature at every turn as you float your way through the mangrove forests. (p314)

Need to Know

Sacred Sites

o **Ganges River, Varanasi**
The river ghats here are
where some of the most
intimate rituals of life and
death are played out in
public. (p325)

o **Observatory Hill**
Sacred to both Buddhists
and Hindus, the site of
the original Dorje Ling
monastery that gave
Darjeeling its name. (p318)

o **Sarnath** Where the
Buddha came to preach after
he achieved enlightenment
at Bodhgaya. (p333)

o **Kalighat Temple** Pilgrims
queue to shower Kali with
hibiscus flowers at Kolkata's
holiest Hindu temples.
(p306)

ADVANCE PLANNING

o **One month before**
Book accommodation,
especially in high season
(usually November to
March). Book any long-
distance rail journeys and
internal flights.

o **One week before**
Book your tour of the
Sunderbans.

o **One or two days before**
Book your seat on the
Darjeeling Himayalan
Railway (toy train), and any
tours that take your fancy.

RESOURCES

o **West Bengal Tourist
Department** (www.wb
tourism.gov.in) Includes
Kolkata and Darjeeling.

o **Bengali Recipes** (www.
sutapa.com)

o **Calcutta Web** (www.
calcuttaweb.com) Kolkata
news and listings.

o **Uttar Pradesh Tourism**
(www.up-tourism.com)
Includes Varanasi.

o **Madhya Pradesh
Tourism** (www.mp
tourism.com) Includes
Khajuraho.

GETTING AROUND

o **Air** Kolkata has a well-
connected international
airport. There are small
airports at Varanasi,
Khajuraho and Bagdogra
(for Darjeeling). You can fly
Agra-Khajuraho direct but
NOT in reverse.

o **Train** Numerous long-
distance trains serve
Kolkata and Varanasi.
Service to Khajuraho is
limited. No through trains
reach Darjeeling but the
ultra-slow toy train from
Siliguri is a picturesque
attraction in itself.

BE FOREWARNED

o **Avoid the crowds**
During the month-long
'puja season', starting
from Durga Puja and
stretching to Diwali, hotels,
jeeps and trekking huts
are often booked out by
travelling Bengali tourists.
Pack a jumper and visit
in November to avoid the
crowds.

o **Touts** Touts are an
annoyance in Khajuraho
and especially Varanasi
where many tourists get
scammed. Most of Kolkata
is contrastingly low-hassle.

Darjeeling, Varanasi & the Northeast Itineraries

The first trip takes you from Kolkata to Varanasi before ending at Khajuraho. The second lets you sample the best of Bengal: its capital, Kolkata; its tiger domain, the Sunderbans; and its picturesque hill station, Darjeeling.

KOLKATA TO KHAJURAHO
THE SPIRITUAL & THE SACRED

5 DAYS

Start your trip in the frenetic, fascinating city of ❶ **Kolkata** (Calcutta; p302). Book into a heritage hotel, then take in the city's charming colonial-era architecture by signing up for one of Kolkata's excellent walking tours. Don't miss sampling a range of gustatory delights from street fare to fine Bengali cuisine.

From Kolkata, board an overnight train westwards to the mesmerising holy city of ❷ **Varanasi** (p325) a place that encompasses life and death in an extraordinary swirl of colour, ritual and mayhem. Take an early-morning boat ride along the Ganges to experience a sense of otherworldly spirituality. And don't miss a

half-day trip to nearby ❸ **Sarnath** (p333), one Buddhism's four most sacred places.

In India's steamy centre, ❹ **Khajuraho** (p336) is worth the trek for its Unesco-listed temples featuring a dazzling symphony of virtuoso carving, most famously the numerous fecund images of rampant sexuality. To get there from Varanasi you'll need to fly or plan carefully as only three trains a week connect those stations.

Overnight trains continue to Delhi, but to combine this route with the Taj Mahal, consider reversing direction and flying Agra-Khajuraho on Air India's inexpensive thrice-weekly hopper (eastbound only).

1 WEEK

KOLKATA TO DARJEELING
THE BEAUTY OF BENGAL

Again, start your trip in ❶**Kolkata** (Calcutta; p302), the capital of West Bengal and the home of Bengali cuisine. After a couple of days sightseeing, leave the city chaos behind and make your way to the wilds of the ❷**Sunderbans Tiger Reserve** (p314). This network of channels and mangrove swamps is part of the world's largest river delta and is home to the magnificent Royal Bengal tiger. Book yourself onto an all-inclusive tour and sleep on board a riverboat or in an 'eco-village' on the riverbank, before exploring the thickly forested reserve with a good pair of binoculars and an expert guide.

Return to Kolkata then start your journey towards India's lush green northeast with an overnight train or bus to Siliguri. From there, loco-lovers might have the chance to take the slow but romantic toy train to chug scenically into ❸**Darjeeling** (p317) in the lush northeastern corner of India. This graceful hill station is spread over a steep mountain ridge, surrounded by tea plantations, with a backdrop of jagged Himalayan peaks. Climb Tiger Hill, visit a tea estate and explore the local gompas and pagodas set in breathtaking scenery.

Buddhist devotees at Sarnath (p333)
TIM GRAHAM/GETTY IMAGES ©

Darjeeling, Varanasi & the Northeast

At a Glance

o **Kolkata** (Calcutta) India's intellectual capital and the heart of Bengali culture.

o **Sunderbans Tiger Reserve** (p314) Home to the elusive Royal Bengal tiger.

o **Darjeeling** (p317) North India's quintessential hill station.

o **Varanasi** (p325) Rituals of life and death by the Ganges.

o **Sarnath** (p333) Among Buddhism's holiest sites.

o **Khajuraho** (p336) Virtuoso temple carvings with an erotic twist.

KOLKATA (CALCUTTA)

033 / POP 14.1 MILLION

India's second-biggest city is a daily festival of human existence, simultaneously noble and squalid, cultured and desperate. By its old spelling, Calcutta conjures up images of human suffering to most foreigners. But locally, Kolkata is regarded as India's intellectual and cultural capital. While poverty is certainly in your face, the dapper Bengali gentry continues to frequent grand old gentlemen's clubs, back horses at the Calcutta Racetrack and tee off at some of India's finest golf courses.

As the former capital of British India, Kolkata retains a feast of colonial-era architecture, albeit some in a photogenic state of disrepair. Kolkata is also the ideal place to experience the mild, fruity tang of Bengali cuisine.

Sights

CENTRAL KOLKATA

Victoria Memorial Historic Building
(VM; Map p312; 033-22235142; www.victoriamemorial-cal.org; Indian/foreigner incl park ₹10/150; 10am-5pm Tue-Sun, last tickets 4.30pm) The incredible Victoria Memorial is a vast, beautifully proportioned festival of white marble: think US Capitol meets Taj Mahal. Had it been built for a beautiful Indian princess rather than a dead colonial queen, this would surely be considered one of India's greatest buildings. It was designed to commemorate Queen Victoria's 1901 diamond jubilee, but construction wasn't completed until nearly 20 years after her death.

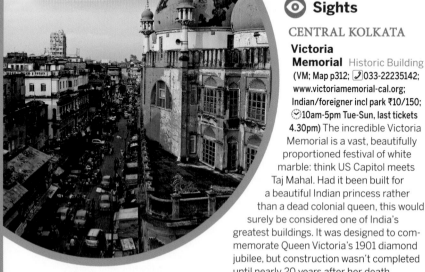

Kolkata streetscape
TUUL AND BRUNO MORANDI / GETTY IMAGES ©

St Paul's Cathedral   Church

(Map p312; Cathedral Rd; ⊙**9am-noon & 3-6pm)** With its central crenellated tower, St Paul's would look quite at home in Cambridgeshire. Built between 1839 and 1847, it has a remarkably wide nave and features a stained-glass west window by pre-Raphaelite maestro, Sir Edward Burne-Jones.

Indian Museum   Museum

(Map p308; ☎**033-22861702; www.indian museumkolkata.org; 27 Chowringhee Rd; Indian/ foreigner ₹10/150, camera ₹50;** ⊙**10am-4.30pm Tue-Sun, last entry 4pm)** India's biggest and oldest major museum celebrated its bicentenary in February 2014. It's mostly a loveably old-fashioned place that fills a large colonnaded palace ranged around a central lawn. Extensive exhibits include fabulous sculptures dating back two millennia, notably the lavishly carved 2nd-century-BC Barhut Gateway.

South Park Street Cemetery   Cemetery

(Map p312; donation ₹20, guide booklet ₹100; ⊙**8am-4.45pm)** Active from 1757 to 1840, this historic cemetery remains a wonderful oasis of calm featuring mossy Raj-era graves from rotundas to soaring pyramids, all jostling for space in a lightly manicured jungle.

Mother Teresa's Motherhouse   Historic Building

(Map p308; ☎**033-22497115, 033-22172277; www.motherteresa.org; 54A AJC Bose Rd;** ⊙**8am-noon & 3-6pm Fri-Wed)** A regular flow of mostly Christian pilgrims visit the Missionaries of Charity's 'Motherhouse' to pay homage at Mother Teresa's large,

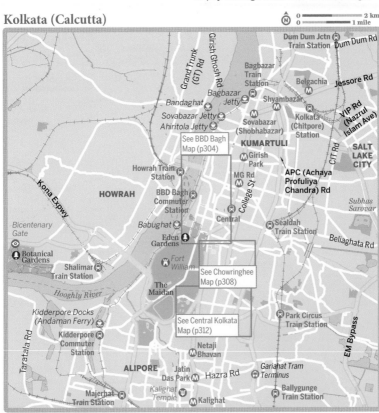

Kolkata (Calcutta)

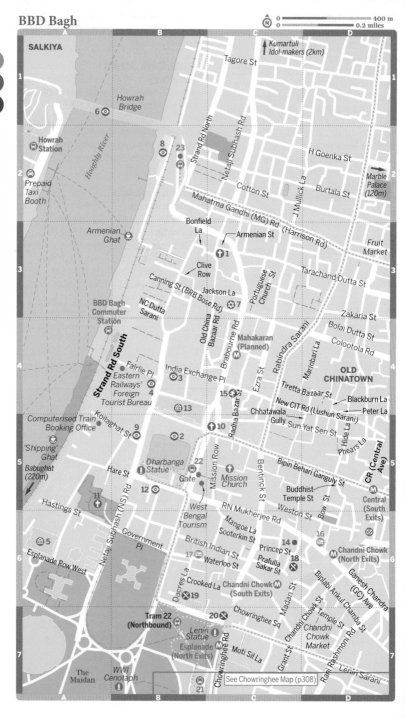

DARJEELING, VARANASI & THE NORTHEAST

sober tomb. A small adjacent museum room displays Teresa's worn sandals and battered enamel dinner bowl. Located upstairs is the room where she worked and slept from 1953 to 1997, preserved in all its simplicity.

From Sudder St, walk around 15 minutes along Alimuddin St, then two minutes' south. It's in the second alley to the right (after Hotel Heaven).

BBD BAGH & NORTH KOLKATA

Raj-era Calcutta is centred on **BBD Bagh** (Map p304; Dalhousie Sq), with its central palm-ringed reservoir-lake. Splendid colonial-era facades here include the 1780 **Writers' Building**, the vaguely Moorish **Chartered Bank Building** (India Exchange Pl), the 1860s **GPO** with its soaring rotunda and the cherub-festooned **Standard Life Building** (32 BBD Bagh). Find a moment's peace in **St John's**

BBD Bagh

⊙ **Sights**
1 Armenian Church of Nazareth............C3
2 BBD Bagh...B5
3 Chartered Bank Building B4
4 Eastern Railways Building B4
5 High Court...A6
6 Howrah Bridge A1
7 Maghen David Synagogue.................C3
8 Mullik Ghat Flower Market................B2
9 Old GPO Building B5
10 St Andrews Church C5
11 St John's Church....................................A5
12 Standard Life Building........................B5
13 Writers' Building....................................B4

⊙ **Activities, Courses & Tours**
14 Calcutta Walks C6
15 Sahaja Yoga Meditation..................... C4

⊙ **Sleeping**
16 Broadway Hotel D6
17 Lalit Great Eastern..............................B6

⊗ **Eating**
18 Anand C6
19 Dacres Lane...B6
20 KC Das...C7

⊙ **Drinking & Nightlife**
Broadway Bar............................(see 16)

⊙ **Transport**
21 Airport Bus VS1.....................................B7
22 Minibus Station B5
23 Tram 26 Terminus B2

(☎ 033-22436098; KS Roy Rd; admission on foot/with car ₹10/25; ⊙8am-5pm) an 1787 stone church set in an oasis of greenery. Or head north past Wren-like **St Andrew's Church** (14-15 BBD Bagh) into the frantic bustle of Old China Bazaar St where alleys teem with traders, rickshaw couriers and baggage wallahs balancing impossibly huge packages. Hidden away here is the spire-crowned **Maghen David Synagogue** (Canning St) and the **Armenian Church of Nazareth** (Armenian St; ⊙9am-4pm Mon-Sat), the city's oldest place of Christian worship. Northwest lies Kolkata's 1940s architectural icon, **Howrah Bridge** (Rabindra Setu). It's a 705m abstraction of steel cantilevers, sweat and traffic fumes that's best admired from the riverbank behind the colourfully chaotic **Mullik Ghat Flower Market**. Or from a river ferry. From Armenian ghat, you could ferry-hop via Howrah to 'Shipping' jetty to return to the BBD Bagh area. Or change at Howrah to a Bagbazar ferry for Kumartuli.

High Court   Historic Building

(Map p304; www.calcuttahighcourt.nic.in; Esplanade Row West; ⊙10am-5pm Mon-Fri) One of Kolkata's greatest architectural triumphs, the High Court building was built between 1864 and 1872, loosely modelled on the medieval Cloth Hall in Ypres (Flanders). The grand Gothic exterior is best viewed from the south. Sometimes foreigners can simply wander in but more likely you'll be asked to go around to the eastern entrance security desk and apply for an entry pass (free).

Marble Palace   Museum

(☎ 033-22393310; 46 Muktaram Babu St; ⊙10am-3pm, closed Mon & Thu) This resplendent 1835 raja's mansion is overstuffed with dusty statues of thinkers and dancing girls, much Victoriana, ample Belgian glassware and fine if bedraggled paintings, including supposedly original works by Murillo, Joshua Reynolds and Rubens.

Admission is free, but before arriving you need to get a permission note from one of the tourist offices. To find Marble

Palace from MG Rd metro, walk north and turn left at the first traffic light (171 Chittaranjan Ave). Coming from the east it's on the lane that leaves Rabindra Sarani between #198 and #200.

Kumartuli Idol-Makers   Area

Countless effigies of deities are immersed in the holy Hooghly during Kolkata's colourful *pujas* (offering or prayers). Most have been created in specialist *kumar* (sculptor) workshops in this enthralling district, notably along Banamali Sakar St, the lane running west from 499 Rabindra Sarani. Craftsmen are busiest from August to October, creating straw frames, adding clay coatings and painting the divine features for the Durga and Kali festivals. In November, old figures wash up on river banks and are refurbished.

SOUTH KOLKATA

Kalighat Temple   Hindu Temple

(5am-10pm, central shrine closed 2-4pm) This ancient Kali temple is Kolkata's holiest spot for Hindus and possibly the source of the city's name. Today's version is a 1809 rebuild with floral- and peacock-

motif tiles that look more Victorian than Indian. More interesting than the architecture are the jostling pilgrim queues that snake into the main hall to fling hibiscus flowers at a crowned, three-eyed Kali image. There's no need to join them to feel the atmosphere.

Activities

Royal Calcutta Golf Club   Golf

(033-24731288, 033-24731352; www.rcgc.in; 18 Golf Club Rd; non-member green-fees ₹7303, 9-/18-hole caddy fee ₹225/449) The magnificent Royal Calcutta Golf Club was established in 1829, making it the oldest golf club in the world outside Britain.

Tours

See p314 for info about excursions to the Sunderbans.

Kali Travel Home   Walking Tour

(033-25550581, 9432145532, 9748588366; www.traveleastindia.com) The 'original' Kolkata walking outfit offers tailored walks by day or night and a 3pm gallery exploration.

Mural near Kalighat Temple

Calcutta Walks   Walking Tour

(Map p304; ☏9830604197, 033-40052573, Ifte 9830184030; www.calcuttawalks.com; 9A Khairu Pl) Well organised with a wide range of walking, cycling and motorbike tours, plus homestays with local characters. It produces what is arguably the best printed map of Kolkata.

Backpackers   Motorcycle Tour

(Map p308; ☏9836177140; www.tourde sundarbans.com; Tottee Lane) Best known for their excellent Sunderban Mangrove trips (p314), the spirited 'brothers' at Backpackers also offer innovative six-hour city tours on the back of a motorbike (₹2200).

Sleeping

SUDDER STREET AREA

The nearest Kolkata gets to a traveller ghetto is the area around helpfully located Sudder St. There's a range of backpacker-oriented services, and if you haven't got an advance booking a big advantage of arriving here is that virtually every second building is a guesthouse or hotel. But be aware that many cheapies are utterly dismal.

Afridi International   Hotel $

(Map p308; ☏033-66077525; afridiinthotel@ goldenapplehotel.in; 3 Cowie Lane; r ₹995) Possibly the most professionally managed budget hotel in Sudder St; the furniture and fittings are top notch and the entrance is floored in crystalline Italian marble. Some rooms are small and suffer a little from damp but maintenance is regular and the 35-room 'old building' should be totally renovated by the time you read this.

Hotel Kempton   Hotel $$

(Map p308; ☏033-40177888; www.hotelkemp ton.in; 3 Marquis St; s/d from ₹3757/4461; ❄🛜) The Kempton welcomes guests with a light-suffused feast of white marble and artificial orchids. Landings have attractive watercolours and rooms are sturdily well built with Springwel mattresses and

Durga Puja

Much as Carnival transforms Rio or New Orleans, Durga Puja brings Kolkata to a fever pitch of colourfully chaotic mayhem as the city's biggest festival celebrates the maternal essence of the divine. For five days in the Bengali month of Aswin (usually October) people venerate gaudily painted idols of the 10-armed goddess Durga and her entourage displayed in fantastically elaborate *pandals* (temporary shrines) that dominate yards and block roads. At the festival's climax, myriad Durga idols are thrown into the sacred Hooghly River amid singing, water throwing, fireworks and indescribable traffic congestion.

walk-in showers. Prices include a buffet breakfast.

Golden Apple Hotel   Guesthouse $$

(Map p308; ☏033-66077500; www.golden applehotel.in; 9 Sudder St; cubicle ₹500, r ₹1800-2500) The Golden Apple has accommodation that's mostly fresh and stylishly appointed for the price. Even the cramped cheapest rooms somehow jam in a small desk. A handy backpacker feature is the set of 15 top-floor budget 'cubicles': like a dorm deluxe, each is a lockable bedspace partitioned off by smoked-glass walls and with a storage area beneath the mattress.

Fairlawn Hotel   Hotel $$

(Map p308; ☏033-22521510; www.fairlawn hotel.com; 13A Sudder St; s/d incl breakfast & afternoon tea ₹3550/4545; ❄🛜) Taking guests since 1936, the Fairlawn is a characterful 1783 Raj-era home fronted by tropical greenery. The stairs and sitting room are smothered with photos, family mementos and articles celebrating the hotel's long-term owner who passed away aged 94 in September 2014. Rooms are mostly spacious but

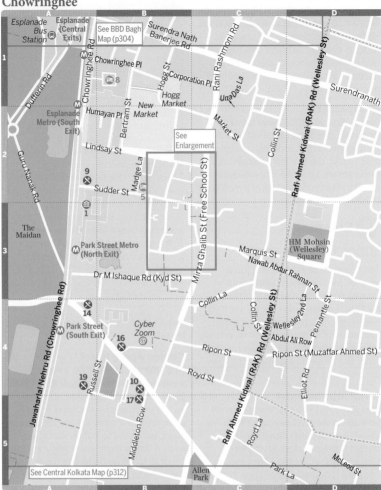

less polished than you might anticipate. Indeed some are downright plain with little charm and old bathtubs over-painted rather than re-enamelled.

Oberoi Grand   Heritage Hotel **$$$**
(Map p308; ☎033-22492323; www.oberoi hotels.com; 15 Chowringhee Rd; s/d/ste from ₹23,484/25,245/46,968; ❄@☎☀) Saluting guards usher you out of the chaos of Chowringhee Rd into a regal oasis of genteel calm that deserves every point on its five stars. Immaculate accommoda-tion exudes timeless class, the swimming pool is ringed with five-storey palms, and proactive staff anticipate your every need. Remarkably comfortable beds come with a five-choice pillow menu.

CENTRAL KOLKATA

Astor   Hotel **$$**
(Map p312; ☎033-22829950; www.astor kolkata.com; 15 Shakespeare Sarani; s/d/ste ₹5871/6458/8220) Artful evening flood-lighting brings out the best of the Astor's

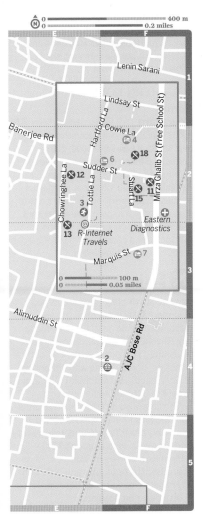

Chowringhee

Sights
1 Indian Museum A3
2 Mother Teresa's Motherhouse F4

Activities, Courses & Tours
3 Backpackers...E2

Sleeping
4 Afridi International................................F2
5 Fairlawn Hotel B2
6 Golden Apple Hotel.............................F2
7 Hotel Kempton F3
8 Oberoi Grand B1

Eating
9 1658 ....A2
10 Au Bon Pain B4
11 Bhoj Company.......................................F2
12 Blue Sky Cafe E2
13 Delish E3
14 Hot Kati Rolls.......................................A4
15 JoJo's Cafe F2
16 Kusum Rolls..B4
17 Peter Cat B5
18 Raj's Spanish Cafe F2
19 Teej A4

Drinking & Nightlife
Fairlawn Hotel Beer-Garden........(see 5)

whose exterior looks like a seven-storey computer punch-card and whose rooms have optical-illusion decor. Bedboards carry up across the ceiling and sweep down the wall to emerge as a dagger of desk. It's all done without compromising comfort, the foyer is spaciously inviting and the rooftop swimming pool nestles beside hip Henry's Lounge Bar.

BBD BAGH

Broadway Hotel   Hotel **$**
(Map p304; ☎033-22363930; www.broadway
hotel.in; 27A Ganesh Chandra Ave; s/d/tr/ste
₹825/925/1585/1940, s/d without bathroom
₹765/850) The Broadway is a simple colonial-era hotel that's kept all its character without going even slightly upmarket. An antiquated lift accesses plain but well-maintained rooms with high ceilings and re-upholstered 1950s-style furniture. Good value, with free newspaper under the door, but hot water's by bucket in the cheaper rooms.

solid 1905 architecture, while inside, walls are lavished with B&W photos of old Kolkata. A creative palate of chocolate, beige and iridescent butterfly blue brings to life beautifully furnished rooms, fully refurbished in 2012. Some suites include a four-poster bed. Sizes and shapes vary. There's no lift.

Park Prime   Hotel **$$$**
(Map p312; ☎033-30963096; www.chocolate
hotels.in; 226 AJC Bose Rd; s/d ₹11,742/12,330;
✻@🛜≋) Sleep in an artistic statement

Bengali Food

Fruity and mildly spiced, Bengali food favours the sweet, rich notes of *jaggery* (palm sugar), *daab* (young coconut), *malaikari* (coconut milk) and *posto* (poppy seed). Typical Bengali curry types include the light, coriander-scented *jhol,* drier spicier *jhal* and richer, ginger-based *kalia*. Strong mustard notes feature in *shorshe* curries and *paturi* dishes that come steamed in a banana leaf. Rather than meat opt for *chingri* (river prawns) or excellent fish, particularly *rohu* (white rui), fatty *chital* or cod-like *bhekti*. Excellent vegetarian choices include *mochar ghonto* (mashed banana-flower) and *doi begun* (eggplant in curd).

Distinctive on Kolkata's vibrant street-food scene is the kati roll: a *paratha* roti, fried with a coating of egg then filled with sliced onions, chilli and your choice of stuffing (curried chicken, grilled meat or paneer). Buy from hole-in-the-wall windows like **Kusum** (Map p308; 21 Park St; rolls from ₹25; ⏱noon-11.30pm) and **Hot Kati Rolls** (Map p308; 1/1 Park St; rolls from ₹23; ⏱11am-10.30pm).

Bengali desserts and sweets are legendary. Most characteristic are *mishti doi* (curd deliciously sweetened with *jaggery*), *cham-cham* (double-textured curd-based fingers) and *rasgulla* (syrupy sponge balls) reputedly invented at **KC Das** (Map p304; Lenin Sarani; mishti doi ₹18; ⏱7.30am-9.30pm) in 1868.

Lalit Great Eastern Hotel **$$$**
(Map p304; 📞033-44447777; www.thelalit. com/the-lalit-great-eastern-kolkata; Old Court House St; r from ₹11,000) The 1840 Great Eastern Hotel was once one of India's finest hotels. It lay derelict for years and the original west-facing facade remains a work in progress. Behind that, however, is an entirely new, sleek business hotel. Rooms are spacious and modernist with very comfortable super-king beds and stylish black-pebble surround showers (albeit leaky). Enter via Waterloo St.

SOUTHERN KOLKATA

Corner Courtyard Boutique Hotel **$$**
(📞033-40610145; www.thecornercourtyard. com; 92B Sarat Bose Rd; r ₹4000) Eight perfectly pitched rooms are named for colours but also take sub-themes – Bengali movies in 'Charcoal', Kumartuli goddesses in 'Vermilion'. They're on two storeys above a superb little restaurant in a recently restored 1904 townhouse that includes a charming little roof garden drooping with bougainvillea.

 Eating

Don't miss sampling Bengali cuisine, a wonderful discovery once you've mastered a whole new culinary vocabulary. Cheaper Bengali places often serve tapas-sized portions so order two or three dishes per person along with either rice or *luchi* (deep-fried flatbread) plus some sweet *khejur* (chutney).

A Kolkata-wide delight is making street-side tea stops for mini cuppas served in disposable *bhaar* (environmentally friendly earthenware thimbles; around ₹5).

Plentiful branches of Starbucks-style chains Barista, Aqua Java and Café Coffee Day make air-conditioned oases in which to sip a decent macchiato.

Most restaurants add 19.4% tax to food bills (included in prices quoted here). Posher places add service fees too. Tips are welcome at cheaper places and expected at most expensive restaurants. **Times Food Guide** (www.timescity.com/ kolkata; book ₹199) and **Zomato** (www.zomato. com/kolkata) offer hundreds of restaurant reviews.

CHOWRINGHEE

Around the Sudder St area, traveller cafes, like **Blue Sky** (Map p308; Chowringhee Lane; mains ₹70-270, curries ₹70-150, rice ₹35; ⏱8am-11pm), **Jojo's** (Map p308; www.facebook.

com/jojoskolkata; Stuart Lane; snacks ₹50-70, mains ₹80-120, rice ₹20; ☺8am-11pm; 📶), **Raj's Spanish Cafe** (Map p308; off Sudder St; mains ₹80-150; ☺8.30am-10pm; 📶) and somewhat snazzier **Delish** (Map p308; www.delishrestaurant.in; 9 Chowringhee Lane; mains ₹100-180), serve backpacker favourites including banana pancakes, muesli, fresh fruit juices plus good-value Indian dishes. Numerous Kolkata classic restaurants are ten minutes' walk south around Park St.

Bhoj Company   Bengali $

(Map p308; Sudder St; veg dishes ₹40-90, fish mains ₹100-330, small/large rice ₹20/30; ☺8.30am-11.30pm) Excellent, inexpensive Bengali food served in a bijou little restaurant, where colourful naive art sets off white walls inset with little terracotta-statuette niches. If you're not familiar with Bengali menu names, a deliciously safe bet is *ruhi kalia* (ginger-based curry) with *doi begun* (eggplant in curd; ₹190 with rice). Or giant prawn *malaikari* (coconut milk; ₹220 with rice plus *jhuri alu bhaja* – crispy potato whisps to add crunch).

1658   European, Fusion $$$

(Map p308; 📞033-40611658; 26 Chowringhee Rd; most mains ₹350-450, lobster ₹1500, beer/wine/cocktails from ₹175/320/700; ☺noon-3pm Wed-Mon & 7.30-11.30pm daily, kitchen closes 10.30pm; 📶) Although it offers inventive gourmet-standard cuisine, prices are sensible and the atmosphere relaxed yet very special. The name references the start of Italy's baroque period, but the decor prefers an early 20th-century sense of retro with low-wattage filament lamps and Charlie Chaplin–era movies playing on designer-stark walls beside the six-stooled cocktail bar that takes centre stage.

Teej   Rajasthani $$$

(Map p308; 📞033-22170730; www.teej.in; 1st fl, 2 Russell St; mains ₹230-350, rice ₹175, thalis ₹360, beer ₹180; ☺noon-3.30pm & 7-10.30pm) Superbly painted with Mughal-style murals, the interior feels like an ornate Rajasthani *haveli* (traditional residence) and the excellent, 100% vegetarian food is predominantly Rajasthani, too.

Peter Cat   Multicuisine $$

(Map p308; Middleton Row; mains ₹160-360, beer ₹183; ☺11am-11.15pm) This phenomenally popular Kolkata institution is best known for its Iranian style *chelo*-kebabs (barbecued fingers of spiced, ground-meat on buttered rice). Beer comes in pewter tankards and waiters wear Rajasthani costumes. No reservations – just join the queue!

Au Bon Pain   Bakery, Salads $

(Map p308; Park St; snacks ₹65-350, coffee from ₹70; ☺7.30am-10.30pm; 📶) This large, central bakery-cafe could have made more of its large, heritage building but there's lots of well-lit space to sit and read over

Street food, Chowringhee
GRAHAM CROUCH / GETTY IMAGES ©

egg and pesto croissants (₹70) and very acceptable espressos.

CENTRAL KOLKATA

Chocolate Room
Bakery Cafe **$**
(Map p312; www.thechocolateroomindia.com; Rawdon St; cake slices from ₹60; ⏰8am-10pm) Chocolate everything! Waffles, fondue, choco-pizza, varieties of hot chocolate and hot, moist cake slices that are rich yet light and eggless.

Oh! Calcutta
Bengali **$$$**
(Map p312; ☎033-22837161; 4th fl, Forum Mall, Elgin Rd; mains ₹390-1000, rice ₹196, cocktails from ₹350; ⏰12.30-3.15pm & 7.30-10.45pm) Although it's situated within a shopping mall, shutter-edged mirror 'windows', bookshelves, large paintings and B&W photography create a casually upmarket feel for enjoying what remains some of the city's best Bengali-fusion food. Mild, subtle and creamy *daab chingri* (prawns in coconut; ₹780) is served in a green coconut, the subtleties brought out particularly well by a side dish of fragrant lime salad (₹86).

Amigos
Mexican **$$$**
(Map p312; ☎033-40602507; www.facebook. com/Amigos.calcutta; 11/1A Ho Chi Minh Sarani; mains ₹350-700; ⏰12.30-3.30pm & 7.30-10.30pm) The excellent Tex-Mex spread is sometimes missing the guacamole (avocados are apparently awkward imports) but makes amends with exquisite mango salsa. The atmosphere has a warm buzz – partly stone-clad walls are picked out with a band of colourful patterned tiles, softly illuminated by swallows-nest lamps and tickled with low-volume salsa music.

Central Kolkata

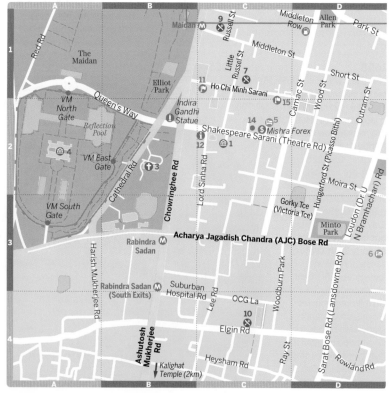

Fire and Ice
Italian $$$

(Map p312; ☏033-22884073; www.fireandicepiz
zeria.com; Kanak Bldg, Middleton St; mains ₹530-
730, water/beer/cocktails from ₹130/210/480;
⊙11.30am-11.30pm) Founded and directed
by an Italian from Naples, Fire and Ice has
waiters sporting black shirts, red aprons
and bandanas, who bring forth real Italian-
style pastas and Kolkata's best thin-crust
pizzas. Old film posters give character to
the spacious dining room set behind foli-
age in a huge heritage building. Few other
Kolkata restaurants keep serving as late.

BBD BAGH AREA

Dacres Lane
Street Food $

(James Hickey Sarani; Map p304; mains from
₹16; ⊙8am-9pm) A whole series of food
stalls that open comparatively late (for
street food) are interspersed by various
somewhat dodgy bar-restaurants whose
fairy lights add some warmth to the
grungy lane.

Anand
South Indian $

(Map p304; ☏033-22128344; 19 CR Ave; dosas
₹67-133, fresh juice ₹70; ⊙9am-9.30pm, closed
Wed) Prize-winning pure-veg dosas served
in a well-kept if stylistically dated family
restaurant with octagonal mirror-panels
and timber strips on the somewhat low
upper ceiling. Good air-con.

GARIAHAT AREA

Bhojohori Manna 6
Bengali $$

(☏033-24663941; www.bhojohorimanna.com;
18/1 Hindustan Rd; dishes ₹50-270, small/large
thali ₹220/265, rice ₹55; ⊙12.30-10.30pm)
Each Bhojohori Manna branch feels
very different, but all feature top-quality
Bengali food at sensible prices. Branch
6 on Hindustan Rd is comparatively spacious, decorated with tribal implements,
and offers live traditional music some
Saturdays. The menu allows you to pair a
wide selection of fish types with the sauce
of your choice.

🍷 Drinking & Nightlife

Most better bars are in hotels or restaurants. Cheaper places are usually dingy
and overwhelmingly male-dominated.

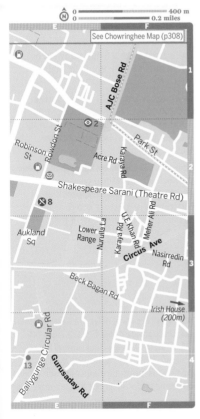

Central Kolkata
⊙ **Sights**
1 Aurobindo Bhawan C2
2 South Park Street Cemetery..............E2
3 St Paul's Cathedral............................B2
4 Victoria Memorial A2
🛏 **Sleeping**
5 Astor C2
6 Park Prime D3
🍴 **Eating**
7 Amigos C1
8 Chocolate Room E2
9 Fire and Ice C1
10 Oh! Calcutta.....................................C4
ℹ **Information**
11 British Deputy High Commission C1
12 India Tourism C2
13 Manipur State Office E4
14 Nagaland State Office.......................C2
15 USA Consulate C2

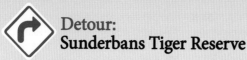

Detour:
Sunderbans Tiger Reserve

This Unesco World Heritage-listed **reserve** (admission/video ₹50/200; ☉dawn-dusk) forms the world's largest river delta and mangrove sanctuary. It is best known as home to one of the planet's largest concentrations of Royal Bengal tigers. Official estimates put the tiger population around 300 but they're shy and lurk within 2585 sq km of impenetrable mangrove forests and riverine channels. So don't be disappointed if you don't see one. Cruising the broad waterways is meditative and there's plenty of other wildlife to watch for, be it spotted deer, 2m-long water monitors or iridescent kingfishers.

The reserve is about three hours' drive south from Kolkata, its over-riding calm making a stark contrast to the chaotic bustle of the city. The best time to visit is between November and March, while entry is restricted during the monsoon months. Organised tours are the best way to navigate this confusing landscape, not least because all your permits, paperwork, guiding duties and logistical problems are taken care of. Travelling alone here is not recommended.

TOURS

Backpackers (☎9836177140; www.tourdesundarbans.com; 11 Tottee Lane, Kolkata; 1/2 nights per person all-inclusive ₹4000/4500; ☉10am-7pm) Reliable yet laid-back, fun yet spiritual, this very knowledgeable 'three brothers' outfit conducts highly recommended tours of the jungle, including birdwatching and local music. Accommodation is either in a cruise boat converted from a fishing trawler, or a traditional village-style guesthouse, with folk music in the evenings. Rates depend on group size and number of days.

Sunderban Tiger Camp (☎033-32935749; www.waxpolhotels.com; 71 Ganesh Chandra Ave, Kolkata; 1/2 nights per person all-inclusive from ₹4290/7290) This well-managed outfit provides expert guides and quality accommodation (on dry land) in tents, huts and lovely red-brick cottages with forest-themed wall murals. The tents are cheapest, but come with a sense of adventure.

Help Tourism (☎033-24550917; www.helptourism.com; 67A Kali Temple Rd, Kalighat, Kolkata; 2 nights per person all-inclusive ₹16,400) Actively associated with local communities, this tour operator takes you up close to rural life in the delta, and provides wonderful access into the forest. Accommodation is in a luxury eco-themed camp. Prices drop dramatically as group size increases; enquire with them directly.

Fairlawn Hotel
Beer-Garden   Bar
(Map p308; 13A Sudder St; beers ₹185; ☉10am-10pm) The small tropical garden of the historic Fairlawn Hotel is the most appealing place on Sudder St to down a cold brew.

Broadway Bar   Bar
(Map p304; Broadway Hotel, 27A Ganesh Chandra Ave; small/standard beer ₹75/135, shots ₹41-120; ☉11am-10.30pm) Back-street Paris? Chicago 1930s? Prague 1980s? This cavernous, unpretentious old-men's pub defies easy parallels but has a compulsive

left-bank fascination with cheap booze, 20 ceiling fans, bare walls, marble floors and, thankfully, no music.

Irish House   Pub
(www.facebook.com/IrishHouseKolkata; Quest Mall, Syed Amir Ali Ave; ⏰noon-11.30pm) While not really Irish at all, this is the nearest Kolkata gets to a fully fledged non-hotel pub/sports bar. Lots of weekend ambience and a showman at the bar.

🔒 Shopping

Dakshinapan
Shopping Centre   Shopping Centre
(Gariahat Rd; ⏰10.30am-7.30pm Mon-Sat) It's worth facing the soul-crushing 1970s architecture for Dakshinapan's wide range of government emporia. There's plenty of tack but many shops offer excellent-value souvenirs, crafts and fabrics. Several shops close by 7pm.

ℹ Information

Medical Services

Eastern Diagnostics (Map p308; 📞033-22178080; www.easterndiagnostics.com; 13C Mirza Ghalib St; ⏰9am-2pm Mon-Sat, longer some days) Polyclinic for doctors' consultations; handy for Sudder St.

Money
Many private moneychangers around Sudder St offer commission-free exchange rates significantly better than banks. In the city centre, **Mishra Forex** (Map p312; 11 Shakespeare Sarani; ⏰10am-8.30pm Mon-Sat, 10am-6pm Sun) is a good choice.

Tourist Information

India Tourism (Map p312; 📞033-22825813; www.incredibleindia.org; 4 Shakespeare Sarani; ⏰9am-6pm Mon-Fri, 9am-1pm Sat) Free maps of greater Kolkata.

West Bengal Tourism (Map p304; 📞033-22488271; www.wbtdc.gov.in; 3/2 BBD Bagh; ⏰10.30am-1.30pm & 2-5.30pm Mon-Fri, 10.30am-1pm Sat) Useful websites. The office primarily sells its own tours (last sales 4.30pm) but has good free city maps and an interesting line in philosophical conversation.

ℹ Getting There & Away

Air
Rebuilt in 2013, **Netaji Subhash Bose International Airport** (NSBIA; 📞033-25118787; www.aai.aero/kolkata/index.jsp) has an impressive departures area but screening bottlenecks persist so arrive in ample time.

Domestic flights link to numerous major Indian cities plus several international destinations including Bangkok, Chittagong, Dhaka, Hong Kong, Kathmandu, Kuala Lumpur, Kunming, Paro, Singapore and Yangon.

Major Trains from Kolkata

DESTINATION	TRAIN NO & NAME	DURATION (HR)	DEPARTURES (DAILY)	FARES(₹; SLEEPER/3AC/2AC)
Chennai	12841 Coromandal	26½	2.50pm (HWH)	665/1730/2520
	12839 Chennai Mail	28	11.45pm (HWH)	665/1730/2520
Delhi	12303/12381 Poorva	23½	8.05am/8.15am (HWH)	630/1650/2395
	12313 SDAH Rajdhani	19½	4.50pm (SDAH)	3AC/1AC 2080/4830
Mumbai CST	12810 Mumbai Mail	33	8.15pm (HWH)	740/1930/2820
New Jalpaiguri	12343 Darjeeling Mail	10	10.05pm (SDAH)	350/910/1285
Varanasi	13005 Amritsar Mail	14	7.10pm (HWH)	385/1045/1510

HWH=ex-Howrah, SDAH=ex-Sealdah

Bus

For Darjeeling, start by taking a bus to Siliguri (12 to 14 hours) departing **Esplanade bus station (Map p308)** between 5pm and 8pm (from ₹400/500 seat/sleeper, ₹1000/1200 AC).

Train

Stations

Long-distance trains depart from three major stations:

Howrah (Haora; HWH) Across the river, often best reached by ferry.

Sealdah (SDAH) At the eastern end of MG Road.

Kolkata (Chitpore; KOAA) Around 5km further north, nearest metro Belgachia.

Tickets

To buy 'tourist quota' long-distance train tickets, foreigners should use the **Eastern Railways' Foreign Tourist Bureau (Map p304; ☎033-22224206; 6 Fairlie Pl; ⊙10am-5pm Mon-Sat, 10am-2pm Sun).** Bring a book to read as waits can be very long but there are seats. On arrival take and fill in a booking form (forms are numbered and double as queuing chits).

For a certain commission, Sudder St travel agencies can save you the trek to the ticket office and can sometimes manage to find tickets on 'full' trains.

ⓘ Getting Around

Beware: Around 1pm the city's one-way road system reverses direction so bus routes invert and taxis can prove reluctant to make journeys at this time.

To/From the Airport

Bus

Airport bus **VS1 (Map p304; one-way ₹50; ⊙8am-7.30pm)** runs every half-hour to Esplanade bus station taking around one hour. Bus VS2 runs to Howrah.

Metro

A spur line of the metro should link the airport to Noapara station by 2017.

Taxi

Fixed-price taxis cost ₹345/455 to Sudder St/Howrah. Pre-pay at booth 12 in the new airport arrivals area (between exits 3B and 4).

Autos

Tuk-tuk-style autorickshaws ('autos') operate as fixed-route hop-on share-taxis with three passengers in the back and one beside the driver. Fares from ₹6.

Ferry

Ferries cross the Hoogly roughly every 15 minutes on various routes between Howrah train station and central Kolkata jetties.

Metro

Kolkata's busy **metro (www.mtp.indianrailways.gov.in; ⊙7am-9.45pm Mon-Sat, 2-9.45pm Sun)** has trains every five to 15 minutes. The new Line 2 (www.kmrc.in), under construction between Howrah, Sealdah and Salt Lake, will massively improve the city's navigability once it opens.

Makaibari Estate (p323)
INDIA PHOTOGRAPHY / GETTY IMAGES ©

Rickshaw

Human-powered 'tana rickshaws' work within limited areas, notably around New Market.

Taxi

Kolkata's trademark yellow Ambassador cabs have a minimum charge of ₹25 for up to 1.9km. Most have 'new' digital meters that simply show the fare due. However, a few have old mechanical meters which require a conversion chart to give the real rate (around 2.5 times more). Taxis are generally easy to flag down except during the 5pm to 6pm rush hour and after 10pm. After 9pm drivers might reasonably ask double fare if they can't expect to find a return ride.

DARJEELING

☑ 0354 / POP 120,400 / ELEV 2135M

India's quintessential hill station, Darjeeling spreads in ribbons over a steep mountain ridge, surrounded by emerald-green tea plantations and towered over by the majestic Khangchendzonga (8598m). When you stopped gazing open-mouthed at the white-topped horizon, explore colonial-era architecture, visit Buddhist monasteries and spot snow leopards and red pandas at the nearby zoo.

The town's narrow, winding streets bustle with an array of Himalayan faces from Sikkim, Bhutan, Nepal and Tibet and when energies start to flag a good, steaming Darjeeling cuppa is never far away. Most tourists visit Darjeeling in October, November or spring (mid-March to mid-May) when panoramas are clear and temperatures are pleasant. Winters can be cold while summer (June to September) can be extremely wet and is best avoided.

◉ Sights

Tiger Hill   Viewpoint

To watch the dawn light break over a spectacular 250km stretch of Himalayan horizon, including Everest (8848m), Lhotse (8501m) and Makalu (8475m) to the far west, rise early and jeep out to Tiger Hill (2590m), 11km south of Darjeeling, above Ghum. The skyline is dominated

---

Local Knowledge

Darjeeling Don't Miss List

TEA EXPERT RAJAH BANERJEE IS THE FOURTH GENERATION OF THE BANERJEE FAMILY TO OWN AND RUN THE MAKAIBARI TEA ESTATE, NEAR KURSEONG

1 **THE TOY TRAIN**
The heritage Darjeeling toy train, a unique steam-powered narrow gauge chugging up from Kurseong ('land of the white orchid') to Darjeeling ('land of the thunderbolt'), is a must for visitors. Passengers can almost touch the flora from the windows, and hop off, make a swift purchase from a shop and hop on, such is the romantic speed of the train. It meanders through the three main valleys of the region, Kurseong, Sonada and Darjeeling, with views of spectacular flora interspersed with well-groomed tea gardens.

2 **HISTORICAL REMNANTS**
The remnants of the British Raj resonate at the Windamere Hotel and in the memorabilia of its Tea Planters Club. The Himalayan Mountaineering Institute offers a rare insight into the famous mountaineers who have conquered Everest, while also grooming future conquerors.

3 **SUNRISE FROM TIGER HILL**
The early-morning sunrise from Tiger Hill is an event to be treasured forever. It's the only spot in the world – regally poised at nearly 3000m – to offer the broad sweep of the eternal Himalayan range from Everest and Khangchendzonga to Makalu. The miracle is not only to witness this majestic display, but also to experience the rapid emergence of the sun over the horizon.

4 **TEA PLANTATION VISIT**
To discover more about what makes Darjeeling tick, visit a tea plantation for a day trip to understand the process. It's also possible to participate as a long-term volunteer, working on a tea estate – some of the plantations offer programs where you can work as a volunteer while staying with a local village family.

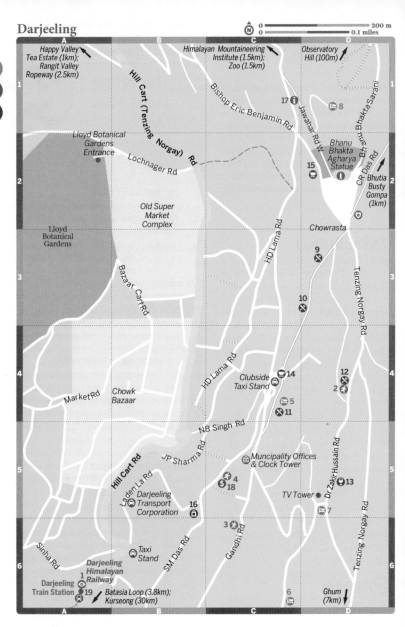

by Khangchendzonga ('great five-peaked snow fortress'), India's highest peak and the world's third-highest. On either side of the main massif are Kabru (7338m), Jannu (7710m) and Pandim (6691m), all serious peaks in their own right.

Observatory Hill   Sacred Site

Sacred to both Buddhists and Hindus, this hill was the site of the original Dorje Ling monastery that gave the town its name. Today, devotees come to a temple in a small cave to honour Mahakala, a

Darjeeling

◎ **Don't Miss Sights**
  1 Darjeeling Himalayan Railway.............A6

⊕ **Activities, Courses & Tours**
  2 Adventures Unlimited D4
  3 Himalayan Travels C6
  4 Samsara Tours, Travels & Treks C5

⊜ **Sleeping**
  5 Dekeling Hotel.................................... C4
  6 Hotel Aliment....................................... C6
  7 Hotel Tranquillity D5
  8 Windamere Hotel................................ D1

⊗ **Eating**
  9 Foodsteps..D3
  10 Glenary's..D3
  11 Kunga C4
     Lunar Restaurant.........................(see 5)
  12 Sonam's Kitchen................................ D4

⊖ **Drinking & Nightlife**
  13 Gatty's Cafe..D5
     Glenary's ....(see 10)
  14 House of Tea C4
  15 Sunset Lounge D2
     Windamere Hotel.........................(see 8)

⊕ **Shopping**
  16 Rink Mall..B5

ℹ **Information**
  17 GTA Tourist Reception Centre............C1
  18 Poddar's...C5

ℹ **Transport**
  19 Darjeeling Train Station A6

Buddhist protector deity also worshiped in Hinduism as a wrathful avatar of Shiva the destroyer. The summit is marked by several shrines, a flurry of colourful prayer flags and the ringing notes from numerous devotional bells.

Rangit Valley Ropeway
Cable Car

(return-ticket child/adult ₹75/150; ☺10am-2pm, closed 19th of every month) This scenic ropeway reopened in 2012, after a fatal accident halted operations in 2003. The 40-minute ride takes you from North Point down to the Takvar Valley tea estate, gliding over manicured tea bushes that look like giant broccoli growing on mountain slopes. Get here early if you want to explore the village and tea plantation.

Padmaja Naidu Himalayan Zoological Park
Zoo

(☎0354-2254250; www.pnhzp.gov.in; admission incl Himalayan Mountaineering Institute Indian/foreigner ₹40/100, camera/video ₹10/25; ☺8.30am-4.30pm Fri-Wed, ticket counter closes 4pm) This zoo, one of India's best, was established in 1958 to study, conserve and preserve Himalayan fauna. Housed within its rocky and forested environment are species such as Himalayan bears, clouded leopards, red pandas and Tibetan wolves. The zoo, and its attached snow-leopard-breeding centre (closed to the public), are home to the world's largest single captive population of snow leopards. The zoo is a pleasant 20-minute downhill walk from Chowrasta along Jawahar Rd West.

Himalayan Mountaineering Institute
Museum

(HMI; ☎0354-2254087; www.hmi-darjeeling. com; admission incl zoo Indian/foreigner ₹40/100, museum Indian/foreigner ₹20/50; ☺8.30am-4.30pm Fri-Wed) Tucked away within the grounds of the zoo, this prestigious mountaineering institute was founded in 1954 and has provided training for some of India's leading mountaineers. Within the complex is the fascinating **Mountaineering Museum**. It houses sundry details and memorabilia from the 1922 and 1924 Everest expeditions, which set off from Darjeeling, as well as more recent summit attempts. While browsing the displays, look for the Carl Zeiss telescope presented by Adolf Hitler to the head of the Nepalese Army.

Just beside the museum, near the spot where Tenzing Norgay was cremated, stands the **Tenzing Statue**. The intrepid Everest summiteer lived in Darjeeling for most of his life and was the director of the institute for many years.

The HMI runs 28-day basic and advanced **mountaineering courses** (Indian/foreigner ₹4000/US$650) from March to May and September to December. These courses are oriented to teach candidates a broad range of skills required for high-altitude climbing. Foreigners should apply at least three

GREG ELMS / GETTY IMAGES ©

★ Don't Miss
The Toy Train

On the Unesco World Heritage list since 1999, the charming, narrow-gauge **Darjeeling Himalayan Railway** is known affectionately as the 'toy train'. Locos first came panting along its precipice-topping, 2ft-wide (610mm) tracks in September 1881. Chugging up a series of loops and zigzag reverses, the tiny trains take seven tortuous hours to cover the 88km route between New Jalpaiguri station (Siliguri) and Darjeeling (2nd/1st class ₹50/280), gaining over 2km of vertical elevation en route. Landslides at Pagla Jhora and Tindharia meant that much of the line was out of action from 2010 to early 2015. But even then the line's most popular upper section – the 31km between Kurseong and Darjeeling via Ghum – remained active, with whistle-tooting trains weaving to and fro across the main road and in places passing within an arm's reach of local storefronts.

During the high season there are morning and afternoon steam-powered 'joy rides' from Darjeeling to Ghum (₹625, two hours return, www.irctctourism.com). Both of these services pause for 10 minutes at the scenic Batastia Loop and give you 20 minutes in Ghum, India's highest railway station, to visit the small **railway museum** (admission ₹20;  10am-1pm & 2-4pm). Alternatively, for a budget ride, take the twice-daily diesel Kurseong-bound passenger service.

The morning train from Darjeeling (52544) leaves at 10.15am, reaching Ghum (₹21) at 10.45am and Kurseong (₹30) at 1.10pm; the afternoon train (52488) leaves Darjeeling at 4pm, reaching Ghum at 4.30pm and Kurseong at 6.40pm. Going the other direction, the morning train (52587) leaves Kurseong at 7am, reaching Ghum at 8.55am and Darjeeling at 9.45am. The afternoon train (52545) from Kurseong leaves at 3pm, reaches Ghum at 5.03pm and arrives in Darjeeling at 5.50pm.

Book at least a day or two ahead. For more on the line and efforts to maintain it, see www.dhrs.org. Enthusiasts who don't have time for the journey can still see steam locomotives up close in the shed across the road from Darjeeling station.

months in advance. There are also a number of 15-day adventure courses for those aged between 14 and 40. These courses combine a range of adventure activities such as trekking, camping, rock climbing and water sports.

Tours

The GTA tourist information centre (p324), taxi stands and travel agencies offer a variety of tours around Darjeeling, usually including the zoo, Himalayan Mountaineering Institute, Tibetan Refugee Self-Help Centre and several viewpoints. Taxis can be hired for custom tours for ₹1000 per half-day.

Adventures Unlimited
Outdoor Adventure

(☏9933070013; www.adventuresunlimited. in; Dr Zakir Hussain Rd; ☉10am-8pm Mon-Sat) Offers treks (US$50 to US$60 per person per day), kayaking, motor paragliding, Enfield motorbike hire and mountain-bike trips.

Himalayan Travels
Trekking

(☏0354-2252254; 18 Gandhi Rd) Experienced company arranging treks (US$60 to US$70 per person per day) and mountaineering expeditions in Darjeeling and Sikkim.

Sleeping

Prices given are for the high season (October to early December and mid-March to mid-May), when it's wise to book ahead. Low season prices can drop by 50%. Foreigners are usually required to present a passport photo when checking in to a hotel.

Hotel Tranquillity
Hotel $

(☏0354-2257678; hoteltranquillity@yahoo. co.in; Dr Zakir Hussain Rd; d/tr ₹700/800; ☏) This good-value place is sparkling clean, with 24-hour hot water, nice lobby seating and small but neat baby-blue rooms. The helpful owner is a local schoolteacher,

❤ If You Like...
Temples with a View

If you enjoyed the panoramas from Tiger Hill, then consider tracking down these sacred sights which have great views of their own.

1 BHUTIA BUSTY GOMPA
This temple originally stood on Observatory Hill, but was rebuilt in its present location by the chogyals of Sikkim in the 19th century. It houses fine murals depicting the life of Buddha, with Khangchendzonga providing a spectacular backdrop. To get here, follow CR Das Rd downhill for five minutes from Chowrasta Sq, past a trinity of Buddhist rock carvings.

2 GHUM
The junction of Ghum, 7km southwest from Darjeeling, is home to a number of colourful Buddhist monasteries. **Yiga Choling Gompa**, the region's most famous monastery, has wonderful old murals and is home to some 30 monks of the Gelugpa school. Built in 1850, it enshrines a 5m-high statue of Jampa (Maitreya or 'Future Buddha') and 300 beautifully bound Tibetan texts. It's just west of Ghum, about a 10-minute walk off Hill Cart Rd. Ghum is 7km from Darjeeling, accessible by toy train or shared taxi.

and can provide all kinds of info about the area. Wi-fi costs ₹100 per day.

Dekeling Hotel
Guesthouse $$

(☏0354-2254159; www.dekeling.com; Gandhi Rd; d from ₹1650; @☏) Spotless Dekeling is full of charming touches such as coloured diamond-pane windows, a traditional *bukhari* (an enclosed cylindrical wood-fired oven) in the cosy and sociable lounge/library, wood panelling and sloping attic ceilings, plus superb views. Tibetan owners Sangay and Norbu play perfect hosts, and the whole place is a superb combination of clean and homey, right down to the adorable dog, Drolma.

Hotel Aliment
Hotel **$$**

(☎0354-2255068; alimentweb98@gmail.com; 40 Dr Zakir Hussain Rd; s/d from ₹800/1600; @) A budget travellers' favourite, with a good top-floor restaurant (and cold beer), lending library, helpful owners and wood-lined rooms. The upstairs rooms (₹1800) have a TV and valley views. All the double rooms have geysers, but they only operate between 6pm and 8pm. The overall hostel-like ambience is a throwback to the classic backpacker era.

Windamere Hotel
Heritage Hotel **$$$**

(☎0354-2254041; www.windamerehotel.com; Jawahar Rd West; s/d incl full board from ₹10,500/13,500; @) This quaint, rambling relic of the Raj on Observatory Hill offers one of Darjeeling's most atmospheric digs. The charming colonial-era Ada Villa was once a boarding house for British tea planters, and the well-tended grounds are spacious with lots of pleasant seating areas. The comfortable rooms, fireplaces and hot-water bottles offer just the right measures of comfort and charm.

Glenburn
Heritage Hotel **$$$**

(☎9830070213; www.glenburnteaestate.com; s/d incl full board ₹19,900/31,500) Located close to the Sikkim border about an hour's drive from Darjeeling, this stylish, uber-luxury tea estate is a true indulgence for those looking to splurge. This lovely estate sits pretty amid rolling tea plantations and makes for a perfect luxury hideaway, with five personalised butlers for every guest, and a number of elegant suites packed with colonial-era comforts.

Rates include all meals, transport and sundry activities offered within the estate premises.

✖ Eating & Drinking

Most restaurants close by 8pm or 9pm. Tax will add on 13.5% to most bills. The Windamere's classy bar is the most atmospheric place to kick back with an early-evening G&T (₹300). See 'Tea Tourism' for suggestions on where to sample Darjeeling's eponymous beverage.

Glenary's
Teahouse **$**

(Nehru Rd; small pot ₹65, pastries ₹20-50; ◷8am-8pm; 🛜) This teahouse and bakery has massive windows and good views. Order your tea, select a cake, grab your book and sink into a cosy wicker chair. It's a good place to grab breakfast.

Sonam's Kitchen
Continental **$**

(142 Dr Zakir Hussain Rd; mains ₹80-120; ◷8am-2.30pm & 5.30-8pm Mon-Sat, 8am-2pm Sun) Sonam's serves up real brewed coffee, authentic French toasts, fluffy pancakes, fresh soups (nettle in season) and yummy pasta, all within its tiny ration-store-like interior that seats barely a dozen people. The deliciously

Tea pickers, Darjeeling
HEMIS / ALAMY ©

Detour:
Tea Tourism

Darjeeling's most famous export is its aromatic muscatel black tea, known for its tannic astringence and musky, spicy flavour. Sample a pot at **Sunset Lounge** (Chowrastra Sq; cup of tea ₹50-150; ⊙9am-8pm; 🛜), the **House of Tea** (Nehru Rd; tea ₹50-80; ⊙10am-7pm) or at a pukka colonial-style afternoon tea in the **Windamere Hotel** (₹450; ⊙4-6pm).

To learn more about tea production visit one of the tea estates, notably **Happy Valley** (Pamphawati Gurungni Rd; ⊙8am-4pm Tue-Sun) 𝗙𝗥𝗘𝗘 or **Makaibari Estate** (📞9733004577; www.makaibari.com; Pankhabari Rd; ⊙Tue-Sat) 𝗙𝗥𝗘𝗘 in Kurseong. The latter allows you to **homestay** (📞033-22878560; per person incl full board US$25) overnight with a tea pickers family, joining your hosts for a morning's work in the tea bushes. Pick your own leaves, watch them being processed and then return home with a batch of your very own hand-plucked Darjeeling tea. Note that March to May is the busiest harvest time, but occasional plucking also occurs from June to November. There's no plucking on Sunday, which means most of the machinery isn't working on Monday.

For luxurious pampering, relax at exclusive **Glenburn** (p322). A stay at that working tea estate is rumoured to have given director Wes Anderson inspiration for his film *The Darjeeling Limited*.

chunky wholemeal sandwiches can be packed to go for picnics.

Kunga   Tibetan $
(51 Gandhi Rd; mains ₹100-140) A cosy wood-panelled place run by a friendly Tibetan family, which goes strong on noodles and *momos* (dumplings), with excellent juice, fruit muesli curd and *shabhaley* (Tibetan pies). The clientele includes locals, which is a mark of its culinary authenticity. It's next to Dekeling Hotel.

Lunar Restaurant   Indian $$
(51 Gandhi Rd; mains ₹120-160; ⊙11am-9pm) This bright and clean space just below Dekeling Hotelis perhaps the best veg-etarian Indian restaurant in town, with good service and great views from the large windows. The *masala dosas* come with yummy dried fruit and nuts. Access to this 1st-floor joint is via the same stair-case as Dekeling Hotel.

Foodsteps   Multicuisine $$
(19 Nehru Rd; mains ₹160-240; ⊙8.30am-9.30pm) There's a refreshing focus on

healthy options at this upstairs place, with gluten-free baked goods and brown breads on the menu. The best options are the all-day breakfasts, particularly the waffles and pancakes, but there are also good grilled sandwiches and dinner thalis. Cookies and muffins are served with a Darjeeling brew as afternoon set teas.

Glenary's   Multicuisine $$
(Nehru Rd; mains ₹150-250; ⊙noon-9pm) This elegant restaurant sits atop the famous bakery and cafe of the same name. It receives rave reviews and caters to diners round the clock. Of note are the yummy Continental sizzlers, Chinese dishes, tan-doori specials and veg gratin. The wooden floors and linen tablecloths add to the classy atmosphere. Oh, and there's booze to go with it all.

Gatty's Cafe   Bar
(Dr Zakir Hussain Rd; ⊙11am-11pm; 🛜) Back-packer-friendly Gatty's is the only place in town that has a pulse after 9pm, with live music on the weekend and open-mic and movie nights during the week. The food

Below & Right: *Ganga aarti* (river worship ceremony), Dashashwamedh Ghat (p327), Varanasi

(BELOW) AKASH BANERJEE PHOTOGRAPHY / GETTY IMAGES ©; (RIGHT) CHN-CHANGSHU-TRACELESS-LUXIN / GETTY IMAGES ©

includes housemade ravioli and decent breakfasts (mains ₹150 to ₹200), with Lavazza coffee and free wi-fi on the side.

ⓘ Information

Internet Access

There are dozens of internet cafes around town; all generally charge ₹30 per hour.

Money

Poddar's (☏ 0354-2252841; Laden La Rd; ⌚9.30am-8pm) Better rates, longer hours and shorter queues than the State Bank next door. Changes most currencies and travellers cheques at no commission. It accepts credit cards and is a Western Union agent. It's inside a clothing store.

Tourist Information

GTA Tourist Reception Centre (☏ 0354-2255351; Jawahar Rd West, Silver Fir Bldg; ⌚10am-5pm Mon-Sat, 9am-1pm every 2nd & 4th Sat, 9am-1pm Sun Mar-May & Oct-Nov) The staff are friendly, well organised and the best source of information on Darjeeling.

ⓘ Getting There & Away

For all long-distance transport you'll first need to get to Siliguri. Although that's barely 80km south of Darjeeling, budget three to four hours by taxi or shared jeep, or at least seven hours on the toy train.

Air

Bagdogra Airport (IXB) is 12km west of Siliguri, ₹250/400 by autorickshaw/taxi. Prepaid taxis from the airport direct to Darjeeling cost ₹2200.

Air India, GoAir, Indigo, Jet Airways and SpiceJet all operate flights from Bagdogra to Delhi and Kolkata. Several weekly Druk Air international flights stop at Bagdogra between Bangkok (Thailand) and Paro (Bhutan).

Bus

NBSTC and numerous private bus companies operate overnight buses to Kolkata (from ₹390/1000 seat/sleeper, from ₹430/1200 AC, 12 to 14 hours) starting from Siliguri's central **Tenzing Norgay Terminal** (Hill

Cart Rd). In Darjeeling Samsara Tours, Travels & Treks (☏0354-2252874; www.samsaratourstravelsandtreks.com; Laden La Rd) can pre-book certain ex-Siliguri services for you.

Jeep & Taxi

Between 7am and 3.30pm, numerous shared jeeps leave Darjeeling's crowded Chowk Bazaar bus/jeep stand for Siliguri (₹150, around three hours) and Kurseong (₹80, 1½ hours). Chartering your own jeep through Darjeeling Transport Corporation (Laden La Rd) to Kurseong/Siliguri/Bagdogra Airport costs ₹1400/2200/2400.

Train

The toy train from Darjeeling runs twice daily to Ghum (1st/2nd class ₹160/21, 30 minutes) and Kurseong (₹210/30, three hours). Landslides allowing, it runs daily to New Jalpaiguri (NJP) on the edge of Siliguri. From NJP, the Darjeeling Mail (train 12344) overnight to Kolkata (sleeper/3AC ₹350/910, 10 hours) departs at 8pm. For Delhi, the 1.15pm Rajdhani Express (train 12435) is your best bet (3AC /2AC ₹2155/2960, 21 hours).

Tickets for major services out of NJP can be purchased at Darjeeling train station (☏0354-2252555; www.irctc.co.in; Hill Cart Rd; ⊗8am-5pm Mon-Sat, to 2pm Sun).

ⓘ Getting Around

There are several taxi stands around town, but rates are absurdly high for short hops. Darjeeling's streets can be steep and hard to navigate. You can hire a porter to carry your bags up to Chowrasta from Chowk Bazaar for around ₹100.

Share jeeps to Ghum (₹20) depart along Hill Cart Rd.

VARANASI

☏0542 / POP 1.4 MILLION

Brace yourself. You're about to enter one of the most blindingly colourful, unrelentingly chaotic and unapologetically indiscreet places on earth. Varanasi takes no prisoners. But if you're ready for it, this may just turn out to be your favourite stop in all of India.

Also known at various times in history as Kashi (City of Life) and Benares, this is one of the world's oldest continually

Varanasi

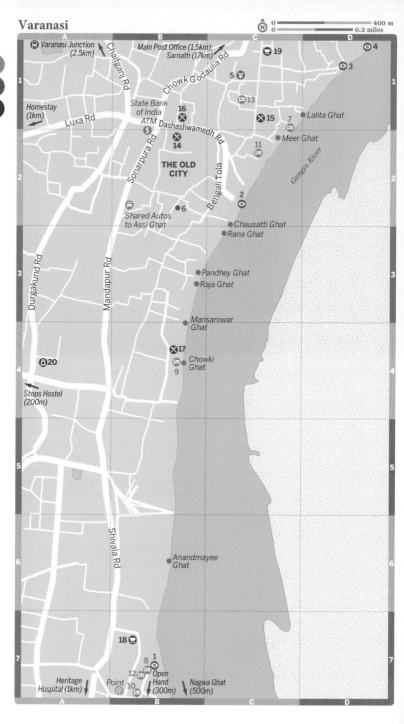

0   400 m
0   0.2 miles

Varanasi Junction (2.5km)

Chaitganj Rd

Main Post Office (1.5km);
Sarnath (17km)

Chowk Godaulia Rd

19

4

3

5

Homestay (1km)

Luxa Rd

State Bank of India
ATM   Dashashwamedh Rd

13

16

15   7   Lalita Ghat

Meer Ghat

Sonarpura Rd

14

11

THE OLD CITY

Bengali Tola

2

Ganges River

Shared Autos to Assi Ghat

6

Chausatti Ghat

Rana Ghat

Durgakund Rd

Mandapur Rd

Pandhey Ghat

Raja Ghat

Mansarowar Ghat

20

17

Chowki Ghat

9

Stops Hostel (200m)

Shivala Rd

Anandmayee Ghat

18

8   1

12   Open Hand (300m)

Point @   10

Heritage Hospital (1km)

Nagwa Ghat (500m)

Varanasi

◎ Sights
1 Assi Ghat..B7
2 Dashashwamedh Ghat......................C2
3 Manikarnika Ghat..............................D1
4 Scindhia Ghat.....................................D1
5 Vishwanath Temple...........................C1

◆ Activities, Courses & Tours
6 International Music Centre
   Ashram...B2

🛏 Sleeping
7 Hotel Alka..C1
8 Hotel Ganges View............................B7
9 Kedareswar...B4
10 Palace on Ganges B7
11 Rashmi Guest House.........................C2
12 Sahi River View Guesthouse B7
13 Teerth Guesthouse............................C1

✖ Eating
14 Ayyar's Cafe B2
15 Brown Bread Bakery C1
   Dolphin Restaurant......................(see 11)
16 Keshari Restaurant...........................B1
17 Lotus Lounge......................................B4

◎ Drinking & Nightlife
18 Aum Cafe B7
19 Blue Lassi...C1

◎ Shopping
20 Baba Blacksheep A4

inhabited population centres and is regarded as one of Hinduism's seven holy cities. Ghats lining the sacred Ganges River are where pilgrims come to wash away a lifetime's sins or to cremate their loved ones. Here the most intimate rituals of life and death take place in public. The sights, sounds and smells in and around the ghats – not to mention the almost constant attention from touts – can be overwhelming. Persevere. Varanasi is unique, and a walk along the ghats or a boat ride on the river will live long in the memory.

◎ Sights

Spiritually enlightening and fantastically photogenic, Varanasi is at its brilliant best by the ghats, the long stretch of steps leading down to the water on the western bank of the Ganges. Most are used for bathing but there are also several 'burning ghats' where bodies are cremated in public. The main one is Manikarnika: you'll often see funeral processions threading their way through the backstreets to this ghat.

Manikarnika Ghat   Sacred Site
Manikarnika Ghat, the main burning ghat, is the most auspicious place for a Hindu to be cremated. Dead bodies are handled by outcasts known as *doms*, and are carried through the alleyways of the Old City to the holy Ganges on a bamboo stretcher swathed in cloth. The corpse is doused in the Ganges prior to cremation.

Dashashwamedh Ghat   Sacred Site
Varanasi's liveliest and most colourful ghat is Dashashwamedh Ghat, easily reached at the end of the main road from **Godaulia Crossing**. The name indicates that Brahma sacrificed (*medh*) 10 (*das*) horses (*aswa*) here. In spite of the oppressive boat owners, flower sellers and touts trying to drag you off to a silk shop, it's a wonderful place to linger and people-watch while soaking up the atmosphere.

Every evening at 7pm an elaborate *ganga aarti* (river worship ceremony) with puja, fire and dance is staged here.

Assi Ghat   Sacred Site
Assi Ghat, the furthest south of the main ghats and one of the biggest, is particularly important as the River Assi meets the Ganges near here and pilgrims come to worship a Shiva lingam (phallic image of Shiva) beneath a peepul tree. Evenings are particularly lively, as the ghat's vast concreted area fills up with hawkers and entertainers. It's a popular starting point for boat trips.

Vishwanath Temple   Hindu Temple
(Golden Temple; ⏲3am-11am, 12.30-8pm & 9-11pm) There are temples at almost every turn in Varanasi, but this is the most famous of the lot. It is dedicated to Vishveswara – Shiva as lord of the universe. The current temple was built in 1776 by Ahalya Bai of Indore; the 800kg of gold plating on the tower and dome was

The Varanasi Shakedown

If you thought the touts and rickshaw-wallahs were annoying in Agra, wait till you get to Varanasi. The attention here is incredible, particularly around the ghats and the Old City. Expect persistent offers from touts and drivers claiming to offer 'cheapest and best' boat trips, guides, tour operators, travel agents, silk shops and moneychangers (to name but a few). Take it in good humour but politely refuse.

Words to live by in Varanasi:

○ Don't take photos at the 'burning' ghats and resist offers to 'follow me for a better view', where you'll be pressured for money and possibly be placed in an uncomfortable situation.

○ Do not go to any shop with a guide or autorickshaw. Be firm and don't do it. Ever. You will pay 40% to 60% more for your item due to insane commissions and you will be passively encouraging this practice. Do yourself a favour and walk there; or have your ride drop you a block away.

○ Imposter stores are rampant in Varanasi. The places we have recommended are the real deal. Ask for a business card, compare and if the info doesn't match, you have been had.

○ When negotiating with boatsmen, confirm the price **and currency** before setting out. They just love to say '100!' and then at the end claim they meant dollars or euros.

○ Don't book unofficial guides, whether self-found or hostel arranged. If you really want a guide, go through **UP Tourism** (p335) to minimise the hassles listed above. If not, have fun shopping!

---

supplied by Maharaja Ranjit Singh of Lahore 50 years later.

Activities

It's worth getting up early on at least two of your mornings in Varanasi, to take in the action on a river boat trip and, another day, to experience the dawn hubbub on the ghats themselves.

River Trips　　　　Boating
A dawn rowing boat ride along the Ganges is a quintessential Varanasi experience. The early-morning light is particularly inspiring, and all the colour and clamour of pilgrims bathing and performing *puja* unfolds before you. An hour-long trip

south from Dashashwamedh Ghat to Harishchandra Ghat and back is popular, but be prepared to see a burning corpse at Harishchandra.

Tours

Varanasi Walks　　　Walking Tour
(☏ 8795576225; www.varanasiwalks.com; tours ₹1600-2000) ✎ The cultural walks on offer from this foreigner-run agency specialising in themed walks explore beyond the most popular ghats and temples. Walks are usually available on a reservation basis and can be booked online. Five of the eight guides were born and raised in Varanasi. It's a truly fascinating way to explore beyond the Old City.

Sleeping

Many budget hotels, plus some midrange gems, are concentrated in the tangle of narrow streets set back from the ghats along the Ganges River. There's a concentration around Assi Ghat, while many other options are in the crazy, bustling northern stretch of alleys between **Scindhia** and **Meer Ghat**.

At the time of writing, city officials were proposing the demolition of numerous unlicensed ghat-side Old City guesthouses, including some of our favourites. Whether such demolition will be carried out remains uncertain, but do check ahead to find out the current situation.

UP Tourism (p335) lists more than 100 families offering paying-guest accommodation in their homes from ₹150 per bed. Most cost under ₹400.

For five-star luxury away from the river there are some great choices in westerly neighbourhoods such as Bhelpura, Aurangabad Rd and Cantonment.

OLD CITY AREA

Hotel Alka   Guesthouse $
(📞0542-2401681; www.hotelalkavns.com; 3/23 Meer Ghat; r ₹650-1349, with AC ₹1574-5733, s/d without bathroom ₹600/700; ❄@🛜) This excellent ghat-side option could use an attentive eye on its exteriors, but the pretty much spotless rooms, either opening onto, or overlooking, a large, plant-filled courtyard or the Ganges, draw the lion's share of care here. In the far corner, a terrace juts out over Meer Ghat for one of the best views in all of Varanasi, a view shared from the balconies of eight of the pricier rooms.

Teerth Guesthouse   Guesthouse $
(📞0542-2400741; www.teerthguesthouse.com; 8/9 Kalika Gali; r ₹800, without bathroom ₹350, with AC ₹950; ❄🛜) This inner core guesthouse is a pleasant diversion from the undesirable maze of alleyways that leads to it. For the price, it's clean and the 27 rooms, on the smaller side, are quiet and confined from surrounding chaos. The marble-laced lobby hogs a load of sunlight through the open atrium and there's Old City views from the underused rooftop.

Pilgrims bathing, Varanasi

TIM GRAHAM / GETTY IMAGES ©

Homestay
Homestay **$$**

(📞9415449348; www.homestayvaranasi.in; 61/16 Sidhgiri Bagh; s ₹2300-2800, d ₹2500-3000; ❄@🛜) This homestay in a 1936 colonial-era home in a residential neighbourhood 1.5km from the Old City back alleys is a true catch. Good-hearted host Harish, a 30-year veteran of the textile industry (well-regarded, fixed-price shop on premises) has six exquisitely maintained deluxe and enormous super-deluxe rooms that are shielded from light, noise and mosquitoes. You'll truly appreciate the rest.

Kedareswar
Hotel **$$**

(📞0542-2455568; www.kedareswarguesthouse. com; B14/1 Chowki Ghat; incl breakfast ₹1400, with AC ₹2800; ❄@🛜) Housed in a brightly painted, aquamarine green building, this friendly six-room place has cramped but immaculate rooms with sparkling bathrooms. Breakfast is served on the rooftop when it's not too hot or rainy. There's only two cheaper non-air-con rooms, so it might be worth phoning ahead. Chowki Ghat is right beside Kedar Ghat.

Rashmi Guest House
Hotel **$$$**

(📞0542-2402778; www.rashmiguesthouse. com; 16/28A Man Mandir Ghat; r incl breakfast ₹2810-6700; ❄@🛜) Incensed white-tiled corridors and marble staircases lead to a variety of cramped but smart rooms boasting high marks for cleanliness and modernity (many have views of Man Mandir Ghat). **Dolphin**, the hotel's rooftop restaurant, is a fine place for a beer-chased evening meal (emphasis on Kingfisher, not culinary catharsis) and one of the Old City's few non-veg options.

ASSI GHAT AREA

Stops Hostel
Hostel **$**

(📞9506118025; www.stopshostels.com; B20/47A2, Vijaya Nagaram Colony; incl breakfast tent Nov-Feb ₹250, dm from ₹350, d with AC ₹950; ❄@🛜) A true hostel has landed in Varanasi in a four-storey residential mansion 2km or so from Assi Ghat. Dorms in six-, eight- and 12-bed variations are livened up by colourful lockers, and there's ample hang-out spaces on various floors that cultivate the right vibe – a previously scarce atmosphere in much of India.

Lassi (yoghurt drink) with fruit

Sahi River View Guesthouse
Guesthouse $

(📞0542-2366730; www.sahiriverview.co.in; B1/158 Assi Ghat; s/d ₹400/650, r with AC from ₹1250, all incl breakfast; ❄@📶) There's a huge variety of rooms at this friendly place, which is better than it looks from the entrance down a side alley. Most rooms are good quality and clean, and some have interesting private balconies. Each floor has a pleasant communal seating area with river view, creating a great feeling of space throughout.

Hotel Ganges View
Hotel $$$

(📞0542-2313218; www.hotelgangesview.com; Assi Ghat; r with AC ₹4500-6500; ❄@📶) Simply gorgeous, this beautifully restored and maintained colonial-style house overlooking Assi Ghat is crammed with books, artwork and antiques. Rooms are spacious and immaculate and there are some charming communal areas in which to sit and relax, including a lovely 1st-floor garden terrace. Book ahead.

Palace on Ganges
Hotel $$$

(📞0542-2315050; www.palaceonganges.com; B1/158 Assi Ghat; r ₹8993; ❄@📶) Each of the 24 rooms (the four river views are first-come, first-served) in this immaculate heritage accommodation is individually themed on a regional Indian style, using antique furnishings and colourful design themes. The colonial, Rajasthan and Jodhpur rooms are among the best, though the lingering waff of insecticide indicates you might encounter some unwanted roommates.

CANTONMENT AREA

Hotel Surya
Hotel $$

(📞0542-2508465; www.hotelsuryavns.com; S-20/51A-5 The Mall Rd; s/d incl breakfast from ₹2473/3035; ❄@📶🏊) Varanasi's cheapest hotel with a swimming pool, Surya has standard three-star Indian rooms, but a modern makeover in the superior and premium rooms means everything has been tightened up a bit, with stylish new furnishings, upholsteries and the like – yours for ₹1500 or so more above standard rates.

No 1 Lassi in all Varanasi

Your long, thirsty search for the best lassi in India is over. Look no further than **Blue Lassi** (lassis ₹25-85; ⏰9am-10.30pm; 📶), a tiny, hole-in-the-wall yoghurt shop that has been churning out the freshest, creamiest, fruit-filled lassis since 1925. The grandson of the original owner still works here, sitting by his mixing cauldron that fronts a small room with wooden benches for customers. Its walls are plastered with messages from happy drinkers.

Taj Gateway Hotel Ganges
Hotel $$$

(📞0542-6660001; www.thegatewayhotels.com; Raja Bazaar Rd; r from ₹14,062; ❄@📶🏊) Varanasi's best hotel is on nearly 2 hectares of beautiful gardens with fruit trees, a tennis court, a pool, an outdoor yoga centre and the old maharaja's guesthouse. All the rooms were made over between 2010 and 2013.

✕ Eating

Locally grown *sitafal* (custard apples) are autumn treats. Do try *singhara*, a blackish root that tastes like water chestnut.

Many Old City eateries shut during summer months due to unbearable humidity and potential ghat-area flooding.

OLD CITY AREA

Keshari Restaurant
Indian $

(14/8 Godaulia; mains ₹35-170; ⏰9.30am-11pm) Known as much for excellent cuisine as surly service, this atmospheric spot (carved wood panelling dons the walls and ceilings) has been famously at it for nearly a half-century. Indians pack in here for high-quality veg from all over India – a dizzying array of dishes are on offer (over 40 paneer curries alone).

Ayyar's Cafe
South Indian $

(Dashashwamedh Rd; mains ₹20-100; ⏱9.30am-7pm) Excellent, no-nonsense choice off the tourist beaten path for South Indian *masala dosa* (₹40), and its spicier cousin, the Mysore *dosa* (₹90); and one of the few cheapies to serve filtered coffee. It's tucked away at the end of a very short alley signed 'New Keshari Readymade' off Dashashwamedh Rd.

Brown Bread Bakery
Multicuisine $$

(☎9838888823; www.brownbreadbakery.com; 5/127 Tripura Bhairavi; mains ₹110-445; ⏱7am-10pm; 🛜) 🍴 This restaurant and organic shop's fabulous menu includes more than 40 varieties of European-quality cheese and more than 30 types of bread, cookies and cakes. The partly-air-conditioned ambience – with seating on cushions around low tables on the nonsmoking bottom floor, expansive views from the rooftop patio and live classical-music performances in the evenings – is spot on.

Lotus Lounge
Multicuisine $$

(D14/27 Mansarowar Ghat; mains ₹50-260; ⏱8.30am-10pm; 🛜) The food doesn't move mountains, but Lotus is a supremely great place to chill while walking the ghats. The terrace, full of lounge cushions and tatami mats, juts right over Mansarowar Ghat. Free wi-fi.

ASSI GHAT AREA

Open Hand
Cafe $

(www.openhand.in; 1/128-3 Dumraub Bagh; breakfasts ₹105-210; ⏱8am-8pm Mon-Sat; 🛜) 🍴 This shoes-off cafe cum gift shop serves the best espresso and French press coffee we had in India, as well as a range of excellent muffins, pancakes, muesli and juices that will delight you to no end. Take breakfast on the narrow balcony or lounge around the former home all day on the free wi-fi.

Aum Cafe
Cafe $

(www.touchoflight.us; B1/201 Assi Ghat; mains ₹60-180; ⏱7am-3.30pm Tue-Sun; 🛜) 🍴 Run by a hippie dippie American woman who has been coming to India for more than 20 years, this colourful cafe has breakfast all day (good lemon pancakes!), astounding lemon and organic green tea lassis and a handful of light sandwiches and mains that offer a curry respite. There's also massage therapies and body piercing available.

CANTONMENT AREA

Canton Royale
Indian $$

(www.hotelsuryavns.com; S-20/51A-5 The Mall Rd; mains ₹190-380; ⏱11am-11pm) Housed in a nearly 200-year-old heritage building, Hotel Surya's excellent main restaurant has a colonial-era elegance, and on warm evenings you can eat out on the large lawn. Value for money, it's one of the

Sitting Buddha, Sarnath
DENNIS K. JOHNSON / GETTY IMAGES ©

Detour: Sarnath

Less than 20km north of Varanasi, peaceful Sarnath was where Buddha came to preach his 'middle way' having achieved enlightenment at Bodhgaya. In the 3rd century BC emperor Ashoka commemmorated the fact by erecting magnificent stupas and monasteries along with an engraved edict-pillar. When Chinese traveller Xuan Zang dropped by in AD 640, Sarnath boasted a 100m-high stupa and 1500 monks living in large monasteries. However, soon after, Buddhism went into decline. When Muslim invaders sacked the city in the late 12th century, Sarnath disappeared altogether. It was 'rediscovered' by British archaeologists in 1835.

Set in a peaceful park of monastery ruins, the impressive 34m-high **Dhamekh Stupa** (Indian/foreigner ₹5/100, video ₹25; ☉dawn-dusk) marks the spot of the Buddha's first 'sermon'. The floral and geometric carvings are 5th century AD, but some of the brickwork dates back as far as 200 BC. Nearby, the similarly ancient **Ashoka Pillar** once stood 15m tall. All that remains in situ are five fragments of its base, but the pillar's four-lion capital – adopted as India's national emblem – has been well preserved and can be seen in the excellent **Archaeological Museum** (admission ₹5; ☉9am-5pm), whose ticket office is beside the entrance to the Dhamekh Stupa.

Walking distance from here, an incongruous 16th-century tower tops the otherwise 5th-century AD ruins of the large **Chaukhandi Stupa** (☉dawn-dusk) marking the spot where Buddha met his first disciples.

For lunch, a reliable option is the large, modern **Vaishali Restaurant** (mains ₹40-230; ☉8am-9pm) on the 1st floor of a building by Sarnath's main crossroads.

GETTING THERE & AROUND

From Varanasi Junction train station, a prepaid autorickshaw to Sarnath costs ₹120. Inexpensive, unreserved trains for Sarnath leave Varanasi Junction at 7am, 11.30am and 1.20pm, returning fromSarnath at 9am, 7.30pm and 9.50pm. The journey takes around 20 minutes. Everywhere in Sarnath is reachable on foot.

---

best of Varanasi's top-end choices, offering a global hodgepodge that extends from Mexican and Thai to Chinese and Continental.

 Drinking & Nightlife

Note that it is frowned upon to drink alcohol on or near the holy Ganges. Liquor laws regarding proximity of temples ensure that essentially none of the Old City eateries are licensed, but rooftops here can usually discreetly rustle up a beer. For official bars, head to midrange and top-end hotels away from the ghats.

There's nightly live **classical music** at Brown Bread Bakery.

The **International Music Centre Ashram** (☎0542-2452302; keshavaraonayak@hotmail.com; D33/81 Khalishpura) has small **performances** (₹150) on Wednesday and Saturday evenings. A small, easy-to-miss sign on Bengali Tola directs you here.

Prinsep Bar   Bar
(www.tajhotels.com; Gateway Hotel Ganges, Raja Bazaar Rd; ☉noon-11pm Mon-Sat, to midnight Sun) For a quiet drink with a dash of history, try this tiny bar named after James Prinsep who drew wonderful illustrations of Varanasi's ghats and temples, but stick to beer (from ₹325) as the 25mL cocktail pour (from ₹550) is weak.

Mangi Ferra Cafe

(www.hotelsuryavns.com; S-20/51A-5 The Mall
Rd; ⏰11am-11pm) This colourful, laid-back
lounge in the garden at Hotel Surya
(p331) is a relaxing place where you can
sip on espresso (₹50), a cold one or a
cocktail (₹150 to ₹480) in the garden or
on waves of couches and armchairs.

 Shopping

Varanasi is justifiably famous for silk
brocades and beautiful Benares saris,
but don't believe much of what the silk
salesmen tell you about the relative
quality of products, even in government
emporiums. Instead, shop around and
judge for yourself. For musicians, Varanasi
can prove a good place to buy sitars
(₹6000 to ₹60,000) and tablas (₹5000
to ₹15,000), with cost depending primarily on the type of wood used.

Baba Blacksheep Silk

(www.babablacksheep.co;
B12/120A9, Bhelpura; ⏰9am-8pm) If the
deluge of traveller enthusiasm is anything
to go by, this is the most trustworthy,
non-pushy shop in India. Indeed it is one
of the best places you'll find for silks
(scarves/saris from ₹400/3500) and
pashminas (shawls from ₹1500).

ℹ️ Information

Wi-fi is widespread and internet cafes (per
hour ₹20 to ₹30) are everywhere. Try Point
(B1/156 Assi Ghat Rd; per hr ₹30; ⏰7am-10pm).
Several State Bank of India ATMs are to be found
including those in the lobby as you exit the train
station and another near Godaulia Crossing (cnr
Dashashwamedh & Sonarpura Rds).

Heritage Hospital (☎0562-2369996; www.
heritagehospitals.in; Lanka) English-speaking
staff and doctors; 24-hour pharmacy.

Tourist Police (UP Tourism office, Varanasi
Junction train station; ⏰5am-9pm) Tourist
police wear sky-blue uniforms.

UP Tourism (☎0543-2506670; www.up-tourism.com; Varanasi Junction train station; ⏱9am-7pm) The patient Mr Umashankar at the office inside the train station has been dishing out reasonably impartial information to arriving travellers for years; he's a mine of knowledge, so this is a requisite first stop if you arrive here by train.

🛈 Getting There & Away

Air

Lal Bahadur Shashtri Airport is 24km north of town, ₹225/650 by autorickshaw/taxi. Flight destinations are relatively limited but include:

Agra (Air India, thrice weekly)

Bangkok (Thai Airways, five flights weekly)

Delhi (Air India, Indigo, Jet Airways, SpiceJet)

Kathmandu (Air India, four flights weekly)

Khajuraho (Jet Airways)

Kolkata (Jet Airways)

Mumbai (Air India, Indigo)

Train

Luggage theft has been reported on trains to and from Varanasi so you should take extra care. Reports of drugged food and drink aren't uncommon, so it's probably still best to politely decline any offers from strangers.

The main train station is Varanasi Junction train station (BSB), aka Varanasi Cantt. To buy foreigner tourist quota tickets go to the helpful **Foreign Tourist Centre** (⏱8am-1.50pm & 2-8pm Mon-Sat, 8am-2pm Sun), just past the UP Tourism office, on your right as you exit the station.

Handy overnight trains from Varanasi include:

Agra Marudhar Express departs either 5.20pm or 6.15pm, arriving Agra Fort station at 6.10am.

Khajuraho BSB-Kurj Link train 21108 departs on Monday, Wednesday and Saturday at 5.45am arriving next morning at 5.15am (sleeper/3AC ₹265/715).

Kolkata At least three convenient services daily (13½ to 15 hours) to Howrah.

New Delhi Shiv-Ganga Express 12550 departs 7.30pm, arriving 8.10am (sleeper/3AC/2AC ₹415/1095/1555).

❶ Getting Around

Cycle-Rickshaw

Journeys of up to 2km should cost ₹50. Budget around ₹60 from Godaulia Crossing to Varanasi Junction train station, but be prepared for some hard bargaining.

Taxi & Autorickshaw

There are prepaid booths for autorickshaws and taxis directly outside Varanasi Junction train station. Here you pay an administration charge (₹5/10 for autorickshaws/taxis) and take a ticket which you will eventually give to your driver, along with the fare, once you've reached your destination. Note that between 8am and 9pm, autorickshaws and taxis can't proceed beyond Godaulia Crossing and you'll have to walk the remaining 400m/700m to reach the entrance to the Old City/Dashashwamedh Ghat.

During banned hours, autorickshaws line up near Godaulia Crossing at a stand on Luxa Rd.

Auto/taxi destinations and fares include the airport (₹225/650), Assi Ghat (₹90/300) and Godaulia Crossing (₹95/250).

A four-/eight-hour taxi tour costs ₹500/900.

MADHYA PRADESH

Khajuraho

☑ 07686 / POP 23,200

A high point of classical Indian art, Khajuraho's World Heritage–listed temples are best known for their superb sculptures, many of which are openly erotic.

Legend has it that Khajuraho was founded by the son of the moon god

Khajuraho

who was captivated by the sight of a beautiful maiden bathing in a stream. Historians tell us that most of the 85 original temples (of which 25 remain visible or part-excavated) were built from AD 950 to 1050 during the Chandela dynasty. Khajuraho's importance waned thereafter, especially from the 13th century. Its isolation probably helped preserve some of its architecture from later desecration, but as the temples became slowly abandoned, the jungle took over. The wider world remained largely ignorant of their existence until 1838 when British officer TS Burt was guided to the ruins, reputedly by his palanquin bearers.

Today many surviving temples have been expertly restored but little

Khajuraho

⊙ Sights
1	Archaeological Museum	D2
2	Brahma Temple	D3
3	Chausath Yogini	A3
4	Chitragupta	C1
5	Devi Jagadamba	C1
6	Hanuman Temple	C3
7	Javari Temple	D2
8	Kandariya-Mahadev	C1
9	Lakshmana Temple	C2
10	Lakshmi	C2
11	Mahadeva	C1
12	Matangesvara	C2
13	Nandi Shrine	D1
14	Parsvanath Temple	D4
15	Pratapeswar	D1
16	Varaha	C2
17	Vishvanath Temple	D1

⊜ Sleeping
18	Hotel Harmony	C3
19	Lalit Temple View	A1

✗ Eating
20	Madras Coffee House	D2
21	Mediterraneo	B3
22	Raja's Café	D1

⊕ Entertainment
23	Sound-&-Light Show	D1

ℹ Information
24	State Bank of India	D2

ℹ Transport
25	Best Bicycles	D2
	Bus Reservation Office	(see 26)
26	Bus Stand	B4
	Train Reservation Office	(see 26)

Khajuraho still feels like it's in the middle of nowhere. Although touts can be tiringly persistent, it's well worth the effort to get here and contemplate such an array of remarkable religio-artistic gems.

⊙ Sights

TEMPLES

The temples are superb examples of Indo-Aryan architecture, but it's their liberally embellished carvings that have made Khajuraho famous. Around the outsides of the temples are bands of exceedingly artistic stonework forming a storyboard of life a millennium ago – gods, goddesses, warriors, musicians, real and mythological animals.

Two elements appear repeatedly – women and sex. Sensuous, posturing *surasundaris* (heavenly nymphs), *apsaras* (dancing *surasundaris*) and *nayikas* (mortal *surasundaris*) have been carved with a half-twist and slight sideways lean that make the playful figures dance and swirl out from the temple. *Mithuna* (combinations of men and women depicted in erotic poses) display not only the skill of the sculptors but also the remarkable dexterity of the Chandelas.

Western Group – Inside the Fenced Enclosure

The most striking and best-preserved temples are those within the fenced-off section of the **Western Group** (Indian/foreigner ₹10/250, video ₹25; ⊙dawn-dusk). This is the only group of Khajuraho temples that you have to pay to visit. Note that your ticket includes entrance to a small but well-presented **Archaeological Museum** (Main Rd; admission free with same-day Western Group ticket; ⊙9am-5pm Sat-Thu), which is eventually slated to move 700m further north.

An Archaeological Survey of India guidebook to Khajuraho (₹60) and a 90-minute audio guide (₹100) are available at the ticket office.

The large **Lakshmana Temple** is arguably the best preserved of all the Khajuraho sights. You'll see carvings of battalions of soldiers here – the Chandelas were generally at war when they weren't inventing new sexual positions. On the south side is a highly gymnastic orgy, including one gentleman proving that a horse can be a man's best friend, while a shocked observer peeks out from behind her hands. More sensuous figures intertwine between the elephants in the frieze ringing the basement, while some superb carvings can be found around the *garbhagriha* (inner sanctum). Dedicated to Vishnu, Lakshmana took 20 years to build and was completed in about AD 954.

Nearby, **Varaha** contains a 1.5m-high AD 900 sandstone representation of Vishnu's form as a boar. It's meticulously carved with a pantheon of gods.

Kandariya-Mahadev, completed by AD 1050, is the group's largest temple. Representing the highpoint of Chandelan architecture, it also has the most representations of female beauty and sexual acrobatics. Most of the 872 statues are nearly 1m high. One frequently photographed sculpture

illustrates the feasibility of the handstand position. The 31m-high *sikhara* (temple spire) here is decorated with 84 subsidiary spires, which make up a mountain-like rooftop scene evoking the Himalayan abode of the gods.

Mahadeva, a small ruined Shiva temple on the same platform as Kandariya-Mahadev, houses one of Khajuraho's finest sculptures of a *sardula* (mythical part-lion beast). Rather less embellished, the **Devi Jagadamba** has carvings including further *sardulas* accompanied by Vishnu, *surasundaris,* and *mithunas* frolicking in the third uppermost band.

Chitragupta (1000–25 AD) is unique in Khajuraho in being dedicated to the sun god Surya who drives his seven-horse chariot in the inner sanctum. The central niche of the south facade sports an 11-headed statue of Vishnu.

Built around 1002, the **Vishvanath Temple** has further superlative Chandelan sculptures including sensuous *surasundari* writing letters, cuddling babies and playing music while languishing provocatively.

Western Group – Outside the Fenced Enclosure

Skirting the southern boundary of the fenced enclosure, the relatively plain **Matangesvara** is the only temple in the Western Group still in everyday use. Inside it sports a polished 2.5m-high lingam (phallic representation of Shiva).

The ruins of **Chausath Yogini**, beyond Shiv Sagar, date to the late 9th century and are probably the oldest at Khajuraho. Constructed entirely of granite, it's the only temple not aligned east to west. The temple's name means 64 – it once had 64 cells for the *yoginis* (female attendants) of

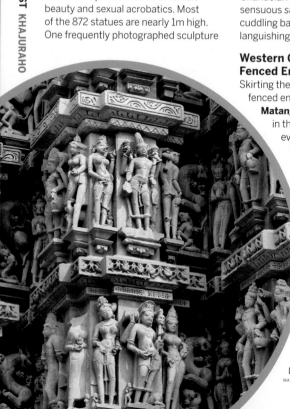

Lakshmana Temple (p337)
MARCO BRIVIO / GETTY IMAGES ©

Kali, while the 65th sheltered the goddess herself. It is reputedly India's oldest *yogini* temple.

A further 600m west is the sandstone-and-granite **Lalguan Mahadev Temple** (AD 900), a small ruined shrine to Shiva. It's down a track and across a couple of fields – ask locals for directions.

Eastern Group – Old Village

Old Khajuraho's dusty narrow lanes of whitewashed and pastel-painted homes are dotted with shrines, old wells and water pumps. Ancient structures scattered around the village include a granite **Brahma Temple** from around AD 900, a small **Hanuman Shrine** (Basti Rd) with pedestal inscription dating to AD 922, and a later **Javari Temple** (1075–1100) with crocodile-covered entrance and slender *sikhara*.

Within a walled enclosure are three **Jain temples** of which the largest and most memorable is **Parsvanath** (AD 950–70). It is notable for the exceptional precision of its construction, and for some of the best preserved of Khajuraho's 'daily life' sculptures including a woman removing a thorn from her foot and another applying eye makeup. Both are on the temple's south side.

Southern Group

A dirt track runs to the isolated **Duladeo Temple**, classical Khajuraho's youngest dating to 1100–1150. Its repetitious sculptures suggest that the temple builders had passed their artistic peak by this point. Further on, ruined **Chaturbhuja Temple** (c 1100) is Khajuraho's only developed temple without erotic sculptures. A signed track leads to the excavated mound known as **Bijamandala Temple**. Unfinished carvings here suggest that it could have been Khajuraho's largest temple, but that it was abandoned before being fully completed as resources flagged.

OTHER SIGHTS

If it has rained recently it might prove worthwhile making the 18km outing to the 30m-high **Raneh Falls**. Or for a full-day 4WD excursion, try to spot one of the estimated two-dozen tigers living in **Panna National Park Reserve** (07732-252135; www.pannatigerreserve.in; vehicle with up to 8 passengers Indian/foreigner ₹1250/2450, 6-person jeep hire ₹2000, guide ₹300; mid-Oct-Jun, closed Wed evenings). In reality you'll have more hope of seeing crocodiles in this peaceful, picturesque place.

 Sleeping

Hotel Harmony   Hotel $

(07686-274135; www.hotelharmonyonline.com; Jain Temples Rd; s/d ₹800/1000, with AC ₹1200/1500;) Cosy, well-equipped rooms off marble corridors are tastefully decorated and come with mostly effective mosquito screens and cable TV. Great food is available at the Zorba the Buddha restaurant and you can eat under the stars on the rooftop. Wi-fi is ₹50 per day.

Hotel Isabel Palace   Hotel $$

(07686-274770; www.hotelisabelpalace.com; Temple Rd; incl breakfast r from ₹1500, with AC ₹2250-2800;) This newish hotel, tucked away off a quiet dirt road in a far more pastoral village than Khajuraho's main drag, is a star. Sparkling-clean rooms are spacious, varying according to view (garden or sunrise), all with sizeable bathrooms and comfortable furnishings (the ₹1500 non-air-con rooms feel like stealing).

Surendra, the manager, is delightful and takes his family's hospitality business very seriously (as he does his great masala chai). You could eat off the floor in the stylish restaurant, which offers sunset views, as does the extraordinary rooftop terrace, the best by far in town and candlelit for romantic dinners for guests at night.

Lalit Temple View
Hotel $$$

(📞07686-272111; www.thelalit.com; Main Rd; r from ₹8570, with temple view ₹14,080; ❄@🛜🏊) Sweeps aside all other five-star pretenders with supreme luxury, impeccable service and high prices. Rooms are immaculate with large-screen TVs, wood-carved furniture and tasteful artwork. If you're not fussed about temple views, it has a block of 'budget' rooms hidden away from the main grounds – all the same amenities for half the price.

Eating

The pleasant main drag is a compact dirt road lined with rooftop restaurants.

Madras Coffee House
South Indian $

(cnr Main & Jain Temples Rds; mains ₹50-200; ⏰8.30am-9.30pm) Three generations of great, honest South Indian fare – dosa, *idli* (spongy round fermented rice cakes), *uttapam* (thick savoury rice pancakes), thali – as well as coffee (Madras style with chicory) and chai. Ideal for breakfast. The house speciality is the tasty egg, cheese and veg dosa (₹200).

Raja's Café
Multicuisine $$

(www.rajacafe.com; Main Rd; mains ₹140-380; ⏰8am-10pm; 🛜) Raja's has been on top of its game for more than 35 years, with espresso coffee, English breakfasts, wood-fired pizzas, superb Indian, Italian and Chinese dishes, and an otherwise eclectic menu full of things you might miss, depending on your passport (rosti, fish and chips, lasagne).

Mediterraneo
Italian $$

(Jain Temples Rd; mains ₹200-440, pizza ₹350-460; ⏰7.30am-10pm; 🛜) Far removed from its Italian roots, Mediterraneo manages acceptable Italian fare served on a lovely terrace overlooking the street. Dishes includes chicken, salads, organic wholewheat pasta and surprisingly good wood-fired pizzas. Beer and wine are also available.

Entertainment

Sound-&-Light Show
Cultural Program

(Indian/foreigner adult ₹200/500, child ₹100/250; ⏰English 6.30pm Oct-Mar, 7.30pm Apr-Sep, Hindi 7.40pm Oct-Mar, 8.40pm Apr-Sep)

Travelling by autorickshaw

BRUCE YUANYUE BI / GETTY IMAGES ©

Technicolour floodlights sweep across the temples of the Western Group as Indian classical music soundtracks a potted history of Khajuraho narrated by the 'master sculptor'. Photography is prohibited.

ⓘ Information

State Bank of India (Main Rd; ⊙10.30am-2.30pm & 3-4.30pm Mon-Sat) Changes cash and travellers cheques.

Tourist Interpretation & Facilitation Centre (⏎07686-274051; khajuraho@mptourism.com; Main Rd; ⊙10am-5pm Mon-Sat, closed 2nd & 3rd Sat of the month) Has leaflets on statewide tourist destinations. Also has a stand at the airport and train station.

ⓘ Getting There & Away

Whether using trains or (especially) flying, travelling from Agra to Khajuraho is likely to be easier than from Khajuraho to Agra. So see the Taj Mahal first!

Air

Set to open in 2016, Khajuraho Airport's new terminal (HJR) feels wildly modern for its rural surroundings. **Jet Airways** (www.jetairways.com) has daily flights to Varanasi (from ₹8178, 40 minutes). Cheaper **Air India** (www.airindia.in) flight 406/405 hops Varanasi-Agra-Khajuraho-Varanasi on Mondays, Wednesdays and Fridays.

Taxi

Yashowaran Taxi Driver Union is under a neem tree, opposite Gole Market. Fares including all taxes and tolls to Agra/Orchha/Varanasi are ₹8000/3500/8000.

Train

Daily train 22447 leaves at 6.20pm to Delhi's Hazrat Nizamuddin (NZM) station (sleeper/3AC/2AC ₹365/935/1365, 11 hours). It stops briefly at Agra Cantt (AGC, ₹280/715/1000, 8½ hours) but arriving at 2.20am isn't ideal. Returning train 12448 departs Delhi/Agra at 8.10pm/11.20pm.

On Tuesdays, Fridays and Sundays train 21107 departs at 11.40pm for Varanasi (sleeper/3AC ₹265/715, 11.40pm, 11 hours).

There's a **train reservation office** (⏎07686-274416; ⊙8am-noon & 1-4pm Mon-Sat, to 2pm Sun) at the bus stand. You must book tickets at least four hours before departure.

ⓘ Getting Around

Autorickshaws to the airport/train station charge ₹80/100. Taxis want ₹300 to either. Cycle rickshaws around town cost ₹20. A great way to get around is by bicycle, rented in varying conditions through **Best Bicycles** (⏎9893240074; Jain Temples Rd; per day ₹50-150; ⊙8am-7pm).

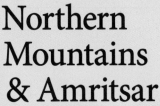

Northern Mountains & Amritsar

Soaring Himalayan peaks and steamy lowland jungles, revered temples and renowned ashrams, peaceful hill stations and busy cities. The Northern Mountains are truly an active traveller's delight, with some of India's best trekking, climbing, rafting, yoga schools, holiday towns and wildlife watching.

In many parts of Himachal Pradesh state, you might think you've accidentally stumbled into Tibet. But the colourful Buddhist monasteries with their red-robed monks and nuns, the troves of Buddhist arts and the home-away-from-home of the Dalai Lama are just another part of the essence of Himachal. And from here you're just a hop, skip and jump away from the realm of the Punjab, with the glorious Golden Temple, Sikhism's holiest shrine, gleaming like a jewel at its heart.

Golden Temple (p378), Amritsar

Monks, Tsuglagkhang complex (p372)

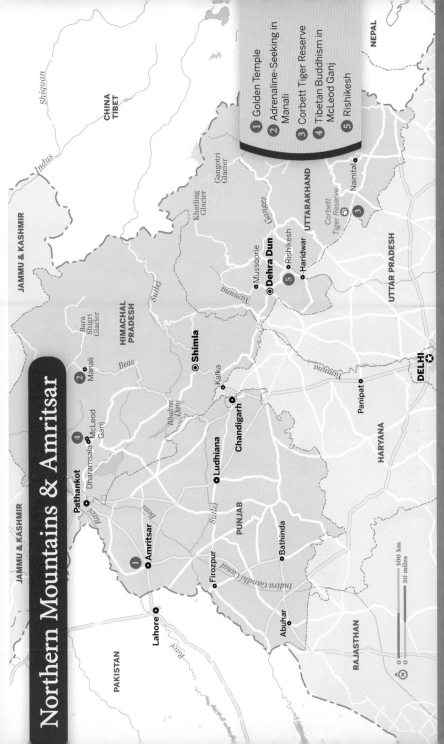

Northern Mountains & Amritsar

1 Golden Temple
2 Adrenaline-Seeking in Manali
3 Corbett Tiger Reserve
4 Tibetan Buddhism in McLeod Ganj
5 Rishikesh

Northern Mountains & Amritsar's Highlights

Golden Temple

Sikhism's holiest shrine (p378), this gold-plated gurdwara (Sikh temple) glitters in the middle of its sacred pool of placid water and draws millions of pilgrims from all over the world. Whatever your faith, Amritsar's gilded temple will undoubtedly be a glowing highlight of your visit to India.

1

2

Adrenaline-Seeking in Manali

Manali (p366) might be one of the mountains' most hippie and laid-back traveller magnets, but there's plenty to get the pulse racing here amid breathtaking mountain scenery. This is one of the best places in India for adventure tourism, with activities such as trekking, paragliding and rafting all at your fingertips.

ANAND PURDHIT / GETTY IMAGES ©

Corbett Tiger Reserve

3

There are around 200 tigers at the Corbett Tiger Reserve (p359) in Uttarakhand, and that's the reason most visitors come here, but even if you don't spot one, the reserve is an end in itself. It's 1288 sq km of grassland, sal forest and river habitats, populated with wild elephants, sloth bears, langur monkeys, peacocks, deer, crocodiles, wild boars, monitor lizards and over 600 species of birds. Black-faced langur

4

Tibetan Buddhism in McLeod Ganj

McLeod Ganj (p371), nicknamed 'Little Lhasa', is situated high in the fresh air of the Himalaya. You may feel as if you've stumbled into Tibet – it is the ideal place to clear your head, see Tibet in exile and understand something about Tibetan Buddhism.

5

Rishikesh

The 'yoga capital of the world' (p354) is a magnet for spiritual seekers, but Rishikesh's laid-back vibe, its outdoor activities and its fabulous mountain setting on the banks of the fast-flowing Ganges, attract all sorts. So if meditation isn't your thing, sign up for a rafting trip, hike your way around the forested hills, or just kick back on a riverside beach and enjoy the view.

Northern Mountains & Amritsar's Best...

Wining & Dining

○ **Imperial Square** Mussoorie's finest, with huge windows overlooking Gandhi Chowk. (p353)

○ **Little Buddha Cafe** An ultra-loungey treehouse restaurant in Rishikesh. (p357)

○ **Indian Coffee House** Uniformed waiters, ageing booths and a blackboard menu: a Shimla institution. (p364)

○ **Lazy Dog Lounge** Riverside restaurant-bar with big plates of fresh, tasty international food. (p370)

○ **Indique** Stylish, romantic McLeod Ganj rooftop restaurant. (p375)

Heritage Accommodation

○ **Kasmanda Palace Hotel** Mussoorie's most romantic hotel; a white Romanesque castle (c 1836). (p353)

○ **Hotel Springfields** Charming Raj-era property in the former summer capital of Shimla. (p364)

○ **Sunshine Guest House** This Manali gem is slightly ramshackle, but still full of colonial-era charm. (p368)

○ **Chonor House** A modern hotel full of the wonderful heritage of hand-made Tibetan artisanry. (p375)

Walks

○ **Rishikesh** Take short walks to nearby waterfalls, or follow pilgrims to Neelkantha Mahadev Temple. (p354)

○ **McLeod Ganj** Take an easy walk through the surrounding pine forests, or test your stamina with the uphill hike to Triund. (p371)

○ **Shimla** Walk along the Mall to the Viceregal Lodge, or head up through the forest to Jakhu Temple. (p361)

○ **Manali** Walk to Jogini waterfall or Lama Dugh mountain meadow, or make a multiday trek across the mountains. (p368)

Need to Know

Adventure Activities

○ **Tiger Safaris** Track tigers in the forests and grasslands of Corbett Tiger Reserve. (p359)

○ **Rafting & Kayaking** Manali or Rishikesh are your best bets for river-based thrills. (p368 & p356)

○ **Paragliding** Popular at Solang Nullah and Gulaba. Sign up with agencies in Manali. (p368)

○ **Mountain Biking** Again, sign up in Manali, although you'll have to take transport out to the best tracks. (p368)

ADVANCE PLANNING

○ **One month before** Book heritage accomm odation or other special hotels, especially in the high season. Book a safari at Corbett Tiger Reserve.

○ **One week before** Book long-distance train journeys or arrange a long-term driver and car through a local agency.

○ **One day before** Call to reconfirm your accommodation; ring ahead if you want to take part in adventure activities.

RESOURCES

○ **Corbett Tiger Reserve** (www.corbettnationalpark. in) Book tiger safaris.

○ **Himachal Tourism** (www.himachaltourism. gov.in) State tourist-board site, with information on destinations, activities and accommodation.

○ **Punjab** (www.punjab tourism.gov.in) The attractions of Amritsar and the Punjab.

○ **US Military Maps** (www.lib.utexas.edu/ maps/ams/india) Useful for trekking.

GETTING AROUND

○ **Air** The region's major airports are at Amritsar and Chandigarh; there are also flights from Delhi to Dehra Dun, Bhuntar (near Manali) and Dharamsala.

○ **Train** The railway will take you as far as Rishikesh, Shimla and Ramnagar (for Corbett Tiger Reserve).

○ **Car & driver** Hiring a taxi for a day or several days is the easiest way to access more remote places.

○ **Bus** Serves smaller towns that the train doesn't reach.

BE FOREWARNED

○ **Best weather** Himachal's best weather seasons are May to mid-July and mid-September to early November.

○ **Amritsar accommodation** Hotels in Amritsar quickly fill during weekends and festivals, so book ahead.

○ **Tiger season** Corbett Tiger Reserve's highlight Dhikala zone is open from 15 November to 15 June, with best sighting prospects from April.

Left: Cyclists near Manali (p366)
Above: Elephants at Corbett Tiger Reserve (p359)

Northern Mountains & Amritsar Itineraries

These itineraries cover tigers, temples, the Himalayan foothills and India's heart of Tibetan Buddhism. Be prepared for some long road journeys...although the scenery should more than make up for the numb bum.

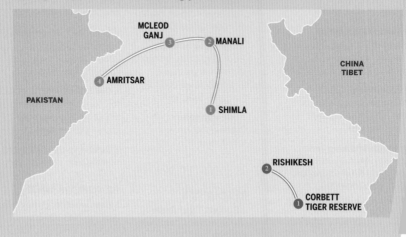

5 DAYS
CORBETT TIGER RESERVE TO RISHIKESH
SAFARIS & YOGA

Easily reached from Delhi by train or bus, ❶ **Corbett Tiger Reserve** (p359) makes a thrilling start to this trip. You'll need to take two or three jeep safaris to give yourself a half-decent chance of spotting a tiger, but even if you don't see one, a couple of days spent exploring the grasslands and forests is a wonderfully peaceful way to begin your Indian adventure.

To experience an even greater level of relaxation, head from here to ❷ **Rishikesh** (p354), either with your own car and driver,

or by bus via Haridwar. Fabulously laid-back Rishikesh is the self-styled yoga capital of the universe, and the serene mountain setting, with forested hills overlooking the banks of the Ganges River, is highly conducive to meditating, contemplating or just chilling out. If you want to stretch your legs, there are riverside beaches to hike to and nearby waterfalls to explore. End your tour with a splash by signing up for a rafting trip.

SHIMLA TO AMRITSAR

10
DAYS

THE MOUNTAINS OF HIMACHAL

Assuming you're starting from Delhi, take the train to Kalka, from where you can pick up the Shimla toy train to the lovely hill station of ❶ **Shimla** (p361). With its colonial-era architecture and grand heritage hotels, Shimla is a beautiful place to relax after India's hectic capital, with walks into the thickly forested green on all sides and sweeping views.

From Shimla, hire a car and driver, or hop on a long-distance bus, to ❷ **Manali** (p366), for its beautiful Himalayan setting, laid-back traveller vibe and adrenaline-pumping adventure activities including mountain biking, rafting, walking and trekking.

Retain your car and driver (or brave another mountain bus journey) to get to ❸ **McLeod Ganj** (p371), home of the Dalai Lama in exile. The mountainous setting is just as gorgeous here, but you'll also get a taste of Tibetan culture and the chance to learn more about Tibetan Buddhism.

Again, either retain your car and driver, or take a long-distance bus from nearby Dharamsala, to travel west to the Punjabi city of ❹ **Amritsar** (p377), home to Sikhism's holiest shrine, the magnificent Golden Temple.

Shimla toy train (p365)
UNIQUELY INDIA / GETTY IMAGES ©

Discover the Northern Mountains & Amritsar

At a Glance

- **Mussoorie** The Queen of the Hills, with colonial-era hotels dotted among the trees.

- **Rishikesh** (p354) India's yoga capital on the surging River Ganges.

- **Corbett Tiger Reserve** (p359) India's first national park, a wild refuge for elephants and tigers.

- **Shimla** (p361) The quintessential hill station with front-row seats facing onto the Himalaya.

- **McLeod Ganj** (p371) A Buddhist mountain escape and home in exile of the Dalai Lama.

- **Amritsar** (p377) Sikhism's most holy town and site of the Golden Temple.

Gun Hill cable car
UNIQUELY INDIA / GETTY IMAGES ©

UTTARAKHAND

Mussoorie

☑ 0135 / POP 29,500 / ELEV 2000M

Perched on a ridge 2km high, the 'Queen of Hill Stations' vies with Nainital as Uttarakhand's favourite holiday destination. When the mist clears, views of the green Doon Valley and the distant white-capped Himalayan peaks are superb.

Established by the British in 1823, Mussoorie became hugely popular with the Raj set. The ghosts of that era linger on in the architecture of the churches, libraries, hotels and summer palaces. The town is swamped with visitors between May and July.

◎ Sights & Activities

Gun Hill   Viewpoint
From midway along the Mall, a **cable car** (return ₹75; ⊘8am-10pm May-Jul & Oct, 10am-7pm Aug-Sep & late Nov-Apr) runs up to Gun Hill (2530m), which, on a clear day, has views of several big peaks. A steep path also winds up to the viewpoint. The most popular time to go up is an hour or so before sunset. There's a mini-carnival atmosphere in high season, with kids' rides, food stalls, magic shops and honeymooners having their photos taken in Garhwali costumes.

WALKS

When the clouds don't get in the way, the walks around Mussoorie offer great views. **Camel's Back Rd** is a popular 3km promenade from Kulri Bazaar to Gandhi Chowk, but there are plenty of other options.

West of Gandhi Chowk, there's a more demanding walk to the **Jwalaji Temple** on Benog Hill via Cloud's End Hotel (about 20km return), passing through thick forest and offering some fine views.

Sleeping

Peak season is summer (May to July) when hotel prices shoot to ridiculous heights. There's a midseason during the honeymoon period around October and November, and over Christmas and New Year. At other times you should be able to get a bargain. The following prices are for midseason.

Hotel Broadway
Hotel $

(☏0135-2632243; Camel's Back Rd, Kulri Bazaar; d ₹650-1500) The best of the budget places by a country mile, this historic 1880s wooden hotel with colourful flowerboxes in the windows oozes character. It's in a quiet location but close to the Mall. Cheaper downstairs rooms could use a refresh, but upstairs rooms are nice; the best has lovely sunlit bay windows.

Kasmanda Palace Hotel
Heritage Hotel $$$

(☏0135-2632424; www.kasmandapalace.com; s/d from ₹5850/7020) Located off the Mall, this is Mussoorie's most romantic hotel. The white Romanesque castle was built in 1836 for a British officer and was bought by the Maharaja of Kasmanda in 1915. The red-carpeted hall has a superb staircase flanked by moth-eaten hunting trophies. All the rooms have charm but the woodpanelled and antique-filled Maharaja Room is the royal best.

Hotel Padmini Nivas
Heritage Hotel $$$

(☏0135-2631093; www.hotel-padmininivas.com; The Mall; d ₹3000-3750, ste ₹4500-5250; @) Built in 1840 by a British colonel, this heritage hotel has real old-fashioned charm. Large rooms with quaint sun rooms are beautifully furnished; those in the main house are significantly nicer than those in the side building. The dining room, with its antique furniture, is an outstanding

feature. The whole place is set on 2 hectares of landscaped gardens.

Eating & Drinking

Lovely Omelette Centre
Fast Food $

(The Mall, Kulri Bazaar; mains ₹40-90; ⊙9am-9.30pm Wed-Mon) Mussoorie's most famous eatery is also its smallest – a cubbyhole along the Mall that serves what many say are the best omelettes in India. The speciality is the cheese omelette, with chillies, onions and spices, served over toast, but the maestro at the frying pan will whip up a chocolate omelette on request. Opening hours can be unpredictable.

Neelam
Punjabi $$

(Kulri Bazaar; mains ₹130-280; ⊙9am-11pm) Around in one form or another since 1949, Neelam specialises in paneer dishes and boasts a long list of chicken and lamb. In high season they break out the *tawa* – a heated metal plate, which slow-cooks meat to perfection. The affable manager, Sam, is exceptionally welcoming.

Imperial Square
Continental $$$

(☏0135-2632632; Gandhi Chowk; mains ₹225-600; ⊙7am-11pm; 🛜) With huge windows overlooking Gandhi Chowk, Imperial Square scores highly on everything – decor, service and food. The menu emphasises Continental dishes, with long lists of platters and sizzlers, plus big toasted sandwiches. For breakfast you can even have waffles. Upstairs features a tea room–cum–hookah lounge, and the attached hotel (rooms from ₹4500) has excellent rooms with valley views.

Information

GMVN Booth (☏0135-2631281; library bus stand; ⊙9am-6pm) Can book local tours, treks and far-flung rest houses.

Om Cybercafe (off The Mall, Kulri Bazaar; per hour ₹60; ⊙10am-9pm) Behind Lovely Omelette Centre.

Trek Himalaya (☏0135-2630491; Upper Mall; ⊙11am-9pm) Exchanges major currencies at a fair rate.

❶ Getting There & Away

Bus

Frequent buses head to Mussoorie (₹56, 1½ hours) from Dehra Dun's Mussoorie bus stand. Some go to the Picture Palace bus stand (📞0135-2632259) while others go to the Library bus stand (📞0135-2632258) at the other end of town – if you know where you're staying, it helps to be on the right bus. There's no direct transport from Mussoorie to Rishikesh or Haridwar – change at Dehra Dun.

Taxi

From both bus stands you can hire taxis to Dehra Dun (₹710) and Rishikesh (₹2200). A shared taxi to Dehra Dun should cost ₹140 per person.

Train

The Northern Railway booking agency (📞0135-2632846; Lower Mall, Kulri Bazaar; ⏱8am-2pm Mon-Sat) books tickets for trains from Dehra Dun and Haridwar.

Rishikesh

📞0135 / POP 102,160 / ELEV 356M

Ever since the Beatles rocked up at the ashram of the Maharishi Mahesh Yogi in the late '60s, Rishikesh has been a magnet for spiritual seekers. Today it styles itself as the 'Yoga Capital of the World', with masses of ashrams and all kinds of yoga and meditation classes. Most of this action is north of the main town, where the exquisite setting on the fast-flowing Ganges, surrounded by forested hills, is conducive to meditation and mind expansion.

But Rishikesh is not all spirituality and contorted limbs; it's now a popular whitewater rafting centre, backpacker hangout, and gateway to treks in the Himalaya.

◉ Sights & Activities

The defining image of Rishikesh is the view across the Lakshman Jhula hanging bridge to the huge, 13-storey wedding-cake **temples** of Swarg Niwas and Shri Trayanbakshwar. Built by the organisation of the guru Kailashanand, they resemble fairyland castles and have dozens of shrines to Hindu deities on each level, interspersed with jewellery and textile shops.

YOGA & MEDITATION

Sri Sant Seva Ashram _Yoga_
(📞0135-2430465; santsewa@hotmail.com; Lakshman Jhula; d ₹200-500, with AC ₹1000; 📶) The yoga classes are mixed styles and open to all. Beginner (₹100) and intermediate and advanced (₹200) sessions run daily. There are also courses in reiki, ayurvedic massage and cooking. Overlooking the Ganges in Lakshman Jhula, the large rooms here are popular, so book ahead. The more expensive rooms have balconies with superb river views.

Parmarth Niketan Ashram _Yoga_
(📞0135-2434301; www.parmarth.com; Swarg Ashram; s/d ₹400/500) Dominating the centre of Swarg Ashram and drawing visitors to its evening _ganga aarti_ (worship ceremony) on the riverbank, Parmarth has a wonderfully ornate and serene garden courtyard. The price includes a room with a private bathroom and basic hatha yoga sessions.

Rishikesh

◉ **Sights**
1 Swarg Niwas & Shri
  Trayanbakshwar Temple.................G1

➋ **Activities, Courses & Tours**
2 De-N-Ascent Expeditions F1
3 Parmarth Niketan Ashram D2
4 Red Chilli Adventure...........................F1
5 Sri Sant Seva Ashram G3

🛏 **Sleeping**
6 Bhandari Swiss Cottage E1
7 Divine Ganga Cottage F1
8 Hotel Surya...G3
9 Vashishth Guest House D3

🍽 **Eating**
10 Devraj Coffee Corner...........................F1
11 Little Buddha Cafe F4
12 Madras Cafe.......................................D2
  Oasis Restaurant ....(see 6)

ℹ **Information**
13 Shivananda Ashram E1

🚌 **Transport**
14 Main Bus Stand...................................B3
  Taxi & Autorickshaw
  Stand .... (see 12)
15 Taxi & Share Jeep Stand....................G3
  Yatra / GMOU Bus Stand .... (see 14)

Rishikesh

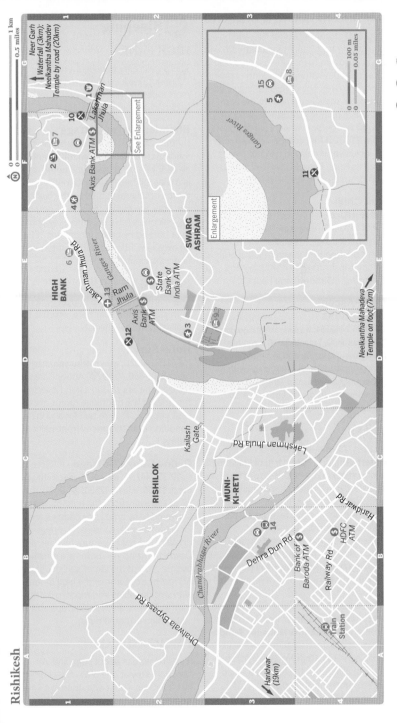

355

RAFTING, KAYAKING & TREKKING

Over 100 storefronts offer full- and half-day rafting trips, launching upstream and paddling down to Rishikesh. Some also offer multiday rafting trips, with camping along the river. The official rafting season runs from mid-September to the end of June. A half-day trip starts at about ₹1000 per person, while a full day costs from ₹1800. Most companies also offer all-inclusive Himalayan treks to places such as Kuari Pass, Har-ki Dun and Gangotri from around ₹3500 per day.

Red Chilli Adventure
Trekking, Rafting

(☎0135-434021; www.redchilliadventure.com; Lakshman Jhula Rd; ◎9am-8pm) Reliable outfit offering Himalayan trekking and rafting trips throughout Uttarakhand and to Himachal Pradesh and Ladakh.

De-N-Ascent Expeditions
Kayaking, Trekking

(☎0135-2442354; www.kayakhimalaya.com; Lakshman Jhula, Tapovan Sarai) Specialist in kayaking lessons and expeditions. Learn to paddle and eskimo roll with an experienced instructor, or go on multiday kayaking or rafting adventures. Also organises trekking trips.

WALKS

An easy, 15-minute walk to two small **waterfalls** starts 3km north of Lakshman Jhula bridge on the south side of the river. The start is marked by drink stalls and a roadside shrine, and the path is easy to find. Four-wheel-drive taxis cost ₹100 from Lakshman Jhula.

On the other side of the river, it's about 2km north to the signposted walk to lovely **Neer Garh Waterfall** (admission ₹30), from where it's a 20-minute uphill walk.

For a longer hike, follow the dedicated pilgrims who take water from the Ganges to offer at **Neelkantha Mahadev Temple**, a 7km, approximately three-hour walk along a forest path from Swarg Ashram. You can also reach the temple by road (20km) from Lakshman Jhula.

Sleeping

HIGH BANK

This small, leafy travellers' enclave is a 20-minute walk up the hill from Lakshman Jhula and has some of the best backpacker accommodation in Rishikesh.

Bhandari Swiss Cottage
Hotel $

(☎0135-2432939; www.bhandariswisscottage rishikesh.com; r from ₹200, with AC from ₹1000; ❄@⎙) The first place you come to, this is a well-run backpacker favourite with rooms in several budgets – the higher up you stay, the higher the price. Rooms with big balconies have expansive views of the river backed by green mountains. It has an excellent little restaurant, internet cafe and yoga classes.

LAKSHMAN JHULA

There are several good budget options on both sides of the river here, which is the liveliest part of Rishikesh.

Hotel Surya
Hotel $

(☎0135-2440211; www.hotelsuryalaxmanjhula. com; r ₹400-950; ❄@⎙) Above Café Coffee Day, the Surya is in a good location by the bridge. The midrange rooms are the best value, as they're quieter and in better condition than the pricey front-balcony rooms.

Divine Ganga Cottage
Hotel $$

(☎0135-2442175; www.divinegangacottage. com; r ₹1500, with AC ₹2500; ❄@⎙) This is tucked away from the hubbub, and surrounded by small rice paddies and local homes with gardens. The huge upstairs terrace has supreme river views. Downstairs non-AC rooms are small and overpriced but the larger stylish upstairs AC rooms are some of the best in town, with writing tables and modern bathrooms. There's an ayurvedic spa and yoga instruction on some days.

SWARG ASHRAM

If you're serious about yoga and introspection, stay at one of Swarg's numerous ashrams. Otherwise, there's a knot of guesthouses a block back from the river towards the southern end of Swarg.

Vashishth
Guest House
Boutique Hotel $

(📞0135-2440029; www.vashishthgroup.com; r from ₹550, with kitchen from ₹1000; ❄🛜) This sweet little boutique hotel has colourfully painted walls, comfortable mattresses and a small lending library. A couple of the rooms boast good-sized kitchens with cooking utensils, table and chairs. For what you get, this is one of the best deals in Rishikesh.

Eating

Virtually every restaurant in Rishikesh, except for some in High Bank, serves only vegetarian food.

LAKSHMAN JHULA

Devraj Coffee Corner
Cafe $

(snacks & mains ₹40-190; ⊙8am-9pm) Perched above the bridge and looking across the river to Shri Trayanbakshwar temple, this German bakery is a sublime spot for a break at any time of the day. The coffee is the best in town and the menu ranges from specialities such as brown bread with yak cheese to soups and sizzlers, along with croissants, apple strudel and more.

Little Buddha
Cafe
Multicuisine $$

(mains ₹100-200; ⊙8am-11pm; 🛜) This funky treehouse-style restaurant has an ultra-loungey top floor, tables overlooking the Ganges River and really good international food. Pizzas are big and the mixed vegetable platter is a serious feast. It's one of the busiest places in Lakshman Jhula, for good reason.

RAM JHULA

Madras Cafe
Indian $

(Ram Jhula; mains ₹100-150; ⊙7.30am-9.30pm; 🛜) This local institution recently underwent a modern facelift but still dishes up tasty South and North Indian vegetarian food, thalis, a mean mushroom curry, wholewheat pancakes and the intriguing Himalayan 'health pilau', as well as super-thick lassis.

Yoga practitioners, Rishikesh

HIGH BANK

Oasis Restaurant   Multicuisine $$
(mains ₹90-170; ⊘8am-10pm) At New
Bhandari Swiss Cottage, this place has
some character, with candlelit tables
in the garden and hanging lanterns
inside. The menu covers oodles of world
cuisines, from Mexican and Thai to Israeli
and Tibetan, and features a number of
chicken dishes. Great desserts include
apple crumble.

ℹ Information

Dangers & Annoyances

Be cautious of befriending sadhus – while some
are on genuine spiritual journeys, the orange
robes have been used as a disguise by fugitives
from the law since medieval times.

The current in some parts of the Ganges is very
strong, and as inviting as a dip from one of the
beaches may seem, people occasionally drown
here. Don't swim out of your depth.

Internet Access

Internet access is available all over town, usually
for ₹20 or ₹30 per hour.

Medical Services

Himalayan Institute Hospital (☎0135-
2471200, emergency 0135-2471225; ⊘24hr)
The nearest large hospital, 17km along the
road to Dehra Dun and 1km beyond Jolly Grant
airport.

Shivananda Ashram (☎0135-2430040;
www.sivanandaonline.org; Lakshman Jhula
Rd) Provides free medical services and has a
pharmacy.

Money

Several travel agents around Lakshman Jhula and
Swarg Ashram will exchange travellers cheques
and cash.

ℹ Getting There & Away

Bus

There are regular buses to Haridwar and Dehra
Dun; for Mussoorie change at Dehra Dun.

Left: Bridge over the Ganges, Rishikesh; **Below:** Shri Trayanbakshwar temple (p354)

(LEFT) KAY MAERITZ / LOOK-FOTO / GETTY IMAGES ©; (BELOW) GOOD LUCK / GETTY IMAGES ©

Private AC and Volvo buses run to Delhi (₹600 to ₹830, seven hours) several times daily. There's also one direct overnight bus to Dharamsala (₹950) at 4pm.

Private night buses from Haridwar to Jaipur (seat/sleeper/AC sleeper ₹500/600/1100, 13 hours) and Pushkar (₹500/600, 16 hours), and from Dehra Dun to Agra (₹840, 12 hours) can be booked at travel agents in Lakshman Jhula, Swarg Ashram and High Bank.

Taxi

Private taxis can be hired from Lakshman Jhula, Ram Jhula, and in between the main and Yatra bus stands. They cost ₹810 to Haridwar (one hour) and ₹1220 to Dehra Dun (1½ hours).

Train

Bookings can be made at the reservation office at the train station, or at travel agents. Only a handful of slow trains run from Rishikesh to Haridwar, so it's usually better to go by bus or taxi.

🛈 Getting Around

Shared *vikrams*)large autorickshaws) run from the downtown Ghat Rd junction up past Ram Jhula (₹10 per person) and the High Bank turn-off to Lakshman Jhula. To hire the entire *vikram* from downtown to Lakshman Jhula should cost ₹80 to 'upside' – the top of the hill on which the Lakshman Jhula area sits – and ₹100 to 'downside' – closer to the bridge. From Ram Jhula to High Bank or Lakshman Jhula is ₹40.

Corbett Tiger Reserve

☑ 05947 / ELEV 400-1210M

This famous **reserve (www.corbettnational-park.in; ☉ mid-Nov–mid-Jun, Jhirna zone open year-round)** was established in 1936 as India's first national park. It's named for legendary tiger hunter Jim Corbett (1875–1955), who put Kumaon on the map with his book *The Man-Eaters of Kumaon*.

Tiger sightings take some luck, as the 200 or so tigers in the reserve are neither baited nor tracked. Your best chance of spotting one is late in the season (April to mid-June). There are also 200 to 300 wild elephants living in the reserve.

Of Corbett's five zones – Bijrani, Dhikala, Domunda, Jhirna and Sonanadi – Dhikala is the highlight of the park. Deep inside the reserve, it's only open from mid-November to mid-June and only to overnight guests, or as part of a one-day tour available only through the park's **reception centre** (☏05947-251489; Ranikhet Rd; ⏱6am-4pm), opposite Ramnagar's bus stand.

Tours

Jeeps can be hired at the reception centre in Ramnagar, or through your accommodation or a tour agency. Jeep owners have formed a union, so in theory rates are fixed (on a per jeep basis, carrying up to six people). Half-day safaris (leaving in morning and afternoon) should cost ₹1500 to Bijrani and ₹1750 to Jhirna or Domunda – not including the entry fees for you and your guide. Full-day safaris cost double. Overnight excursions to Dhikala cost ₹3800. Safaris offered by Karan Singh, who runs Karan's Corbett Motel (p360), are highly recommended.

PERMITS

It's highly recommended to make advance reservations. You can book via the park's website or by signing up for a trip with a safari outfit.

Your total costs will be calculated as follows: Jeep hire (from ₹1500), plus vehicle entrance fee (₹200/500 for Indians/foreigners per day), plus driver's entry fee (₹100), plus visitor entrance fee (₹100/450 per Indian/foreigner per four-hour visit), plus, bizarrely, visitors fees for any spare seats in your six-seater jeep (calculated at the Indian-passenger rate).

Arranging everything yourself is marginally cheaper than taking a safari or hotel tour, but they provide expert guides fluent in English, which can be well worth the few extra rupees.

Sleeping & Eating

For serious wildlife viewing, Dhikala – deep inside the reserve – is the prime place to stay. Book through the park's website at least one month in advance. The town of Ramnagar has budget accommodation, while upmarket resorts are strung out along the road skirting the eastern side of the park between Dhikuli and Dhangarhi Gate.

DHIKALA

Easily the cheapest beds in the park are at **Log Huts** (☏9212777223, 05947-251489; dm Indian/foreigner ₹200/400), resembling 3AC train sleepers, with 24 basic beds (no bedding supplied). **Tourist Hutments** (☏9212777223, 05947-251489; Indian/foreigner ₹1250/2500) offer the best-value accommodation in Dhikala and sleep up to six people. Dhikala has a couple of restaurants serving vegetarian food. No alcohol is allowed in the park.

RAMNAGAR

A busy, unappealing town, Ramnagar has plenty of facilities, including internet cafes (₹30 per hour), ATMs (State Bank of India at the train station, Bank of Baroda on Ranikhet Rd) and transport connections – mostly along Ranikhet Rd.

Karan's Corbett Motel   Hotel **$**
(☏9837468933; www.karanscorbettmotel.com; Manglar Rd; r ₹600-800; ❄) This longtime favourite has changed its name and moved to a new location. It's still surrounded by gardens and mango trees and still has the same terrific owner, Karan Singh – but the rooms and the restaurant are all brand new. Hands-down the best place to stay in Ramnagar. Karan runs highly recommended jeep safaris in Corbett.

NORTH OF RAMNAGAR

Infinity Resorts   Hotel **$$$**
(☏05947-251279; www.infinityresorts.com; Dhikuli; s/d incl breakfast from US$118/135; ❄🛜🏊) The most impressive of the Corbett Park resorts, Infinity has luxurious rooms, a roundhouse with restaurant and bar, and a swimming pool in a lovely

garden backing onto the Kosi River (where you can see hordes of golden mahseer fish). The rooms in the 'old block' are better located and have more character than those in the 'new block'.

ℹ Getting There & Away

Buses run almost hourly from Ramnagar to Delhi (₹178, seven hours) and Dehra Dun (₹171, seven hours) from where you can change for Mussoorie.

Ramnagar train station is 1.5km south of the main reception centre. The nightly Ranikhet Express 15013-Slip (sleeper/3AC/2AC ₹175/485/690) leaves Old Delhi station at 10.30pm, arriving in Ramnagar at 4.55am. The return trip on train 25014 leaves Ramnagar at 9.55pm, arriving at Old Delhi at 3.55am. A daytime run from Old Delhi on train 15035-Slip (2nd class/chair ₹100/370) departs at 4pm, reaching Ramnagar at 8.40pm; the return on train 25036 departs Ramnagar at 9.50am, hitting Delhi at 3.20pm.

HIMACHAL PRADESH

....

Shimla

♫ 0177 / POP 170,000 / ELEV 2205M

Strung out along a 12km ridge, Shimla is one of India's most popular hill resorts, buzzing with a happy flow of Indian vacationers and full of echoes of its past role as the summer capital of British India. The long, winding main street, the Mall, runs east and west just below the spine of the hill, with the bustling bazaar cascading steeply down below it. Traffic is banned from the central part of town, so walking anywhere is pleasant. Porters will carry your luggage uphill (about ₹100 from Cart Rd to the Mall) though many double as hotel touts.

The official centre of town is the junction called Scandal Point. From here, the flat open area known as the Ridge stretches east to Christ Church.

◎ Sights & Activities

Jakhu Temple   Hindu Temple
Shimla's most famous temple, a steep 30-minute hike up from the east end of the Ridge, is dedicated to the monkey god Hanuman, so it's quite appropriate that hundreds of rhesus macaques loiter around, harassing devotees for *prasad* (temple-blessed food offerings). Nearby a 33m-high pink statue of Hanuman looms above the treetops and is visible from most of Shimla.

Viceregal Lodge   Historic Building
(tours Indian/foreigner ₹30/65, grounds only ₹10; ⏱10am-1pm & 2-5pm Tue-Sun, tours about every 45min) The official summer residence of the British viceroys was completed in 1888 and the Indian subcontinent was ruled from here for half of every year from then till WWII. Henry Irwin's grey

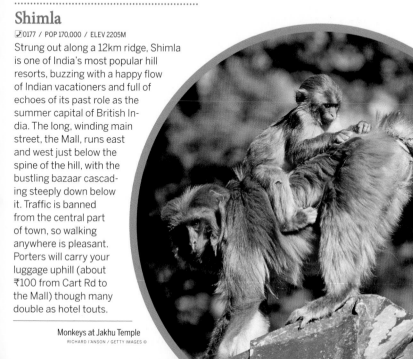

Monkeys at Jakhu Temple
RICHARD I'ANSON / GETTY IMAGES ©

Shimla

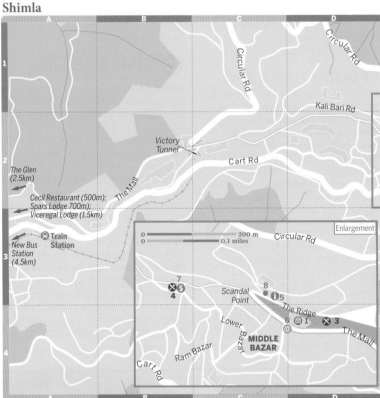

Shimla

⊙ Sights
1 Gaiety Theatre.....................................D4

🛌 Sleeping
2 Hotel Le Royale G2

✕ Eating
3 Ashiana...D4
  Goofa ....(see 3)
4 Indian Coffee House...........................B3

ⓘ Information
5 HPTDC Tourist Office.........................C3
6 Photo Palace C4
7 Punjab National Bank........................B3

ⓘ Transport
  HRTC booth.................................(see 8)
8 Rail Booking Office C3

sandstone creation resembles a cross between Harry Potter's Hogwarts and a Scottish baronial castle. Today it houses the Indian Institute of Advanced Study: you can take a half-hour tour of a few rooms with interesting photo exhibits, but the old ballroom and dining hall are now a library and closed to visitors.

Gaiety Theatre Historic Building
(📞 0177-650173; www.gaiety.in; The Mall; Indian/foreigner ₹10/25, camera ₹15/25; ⊙ tours every 45min 11am-12.30pm & 1.45-6.15pm Tue-Sun) This lovely Victorian theatre, opened in 1877 and now splendidly restored, has long been a focus of Shimla social life. Rudyard Kipling, Shashi Kapoor and various viceroys are among those who have trodden its Burmese teak boards. Today it hosts visiting theatre companies

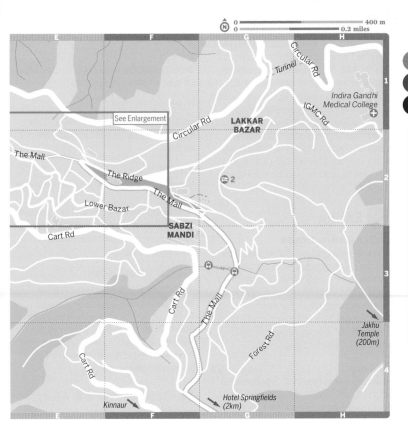

as well as 15 local dramatic societies. Mr R Gautam gives excellent guided tours, explaining its history as you appreciate the view from the viceroy's private box.

Sleeping

Shimla hotels charge steep rates during the peak seasons (April to June, Christmas/New Year and other major holidays), but at all other times, ask about discounts of up to 40%.

Spars Lodge
Guesthouse $$

(☎0177-2657908; www.sparslodge.com; Museum Rd; s/d ₹990/1410, ste ₹2000-2590; 🛜) Though it's 2km west of Scandal Point, on the road up to the State Museum, Spars is worth the trip for its inviting, homey feel, welcoming owners, bright, clean, airy rooms, and lovely sunny dining-cum-sitting area upstairs. The restaurant (mains ₹175 to ₹400) serves great food, including local trout and all-day English breakfasts, and has wi-fi. Room rates are fixed throughout the year.

Hotel Le Royale
Hotel $$

(☎0177-2651002; www.hotel-le-royale-shimla. hotelsgds.com; Jakhu Rd; r ₹2590-4520; 🛜) The front rooms at this hotel on the road to Jakhu Temple, a steep 500m up from the Ridge, are large, bright and comfy and enjoy great views. The cheaper 'deluxe' quarters face to the rear and are smaller but still adequately comfortable. It's friendly, efficiently run and the in-house Green Leaf restaurant is handy.

Hotel Springfields
Heritage Hotel $$$

(📞0177-2621297; www.hotelspringfields.com; opposite Tibetan School, Chotta Shimla; r/ste ₹4670/7640; 📶) The erstwhile summer retreat of the Raja of Sheikhupura, now run by his charming descendants, Springfields features neatly trimmed lawns and bright, spacious rooms with appealing heritage-style furnishings, parquet floors, tea/coffee makers and large, marble-floored bathrooms. Best of all is the huge family suite with balcony, upstairs.

Eating

Indian Coffee House
Cafe $

(The Mall; dishes ₹20-60; 🕐8am-9pm) This Shimla institution is like an old boys' club with its ageing leather seats, uniformed waiters and blackboard menu. Packed with chattering locals for much of the day, it's the most atmospheric place in town for breakfast, cheap dosas and coffee (don't even ask for tea!).

Ashiana
Indian $$

(The Ridge; mains ₹100-250; 🕐9am-11pm) In a fanciful circular building, Ashiana is an almost-elegant restaurant and good people-watching spot with a delightful sunny terrace. As well as tasty Indian dishes there are Chinese and a few Thai favourites. In Ashiana's basement, **Goofa** (dishes Rs80-230; 🕐9am-9.30pm) serves most of the same dishes, from the same kitchen, for about ₹20 less – but without the views.

Cecil Restaurant
Multicuisine $$$

(📞0177-2804848; Oberoi Cecil, The Mall, Chaura Maidan; mains ₹940-1600; 🕐dinner 7.30-10.30pm) For a formal night out, look no further than the colonial-era elegance of the Cecil Restaurant at the Oberoi. The menu is strong on Indian and Thai curries and there are Continental options as well. Book ahead.

 Information

Emergency

Indira Gandhi Medical College (📞0177-2803073; IGMC Rd) Large public hospital with 24-hour outpatient department.

Internet Access

Photo Palace (The Mall; per hr ₹40; 🕐10am-8pm) Decent internet facilities in the town centre.

Money

Numerous ATMs are dotted around Scandal Point and the Mall.

Punjab National Bank (the Mall; 🕐10am-2pm & 3-4pm Mon-Fri, 10am-1pm Sat) Changes cash for major currencies, and American Express travellers cheques.

Tourist Information

HPTDC Tourist Office (Himachal Pradesh Tourist Development Corporation, Himachal Tourism; 📞0177-2652561; www.hptdc.gov.in; Scandal Point; 🕐9am-8pm, to 7pm mid-Jul–mid-Sep & Dec-Mar) Very helpful for local information and advice; also books HPTDC buses, hotels and tours.

Getting There & Away

Shimla's airport had no flights at the time of writing, so apart from the train, the only way to get here is by road. Most hotels and travel agencies can organise car transfers: a cab for up to four people costs around ₹5000 to Manali and ₹6000 to Delhi. Add around ₹500 for air-con.

Bus

The Himachal Road Transport Corporation (HRTC) runs five comfortable Volvo AC buses to Delhi (₹842, 10 hours) each day, as well as 12 cheaper deluxe and ordinary services (₹384 to ₹592). Other HRTC AC buses head to Manali (₹550, nine hours) at 9.30am and Dharamsala (₹926, nine hours) at 5.30pm. All HRTC buses leave from the New Bus Station, a 5km trip west from the town centre: make reservations at the **HRTC booth** (🕐11am-2pm & 3-6.30pm) at Scandal Point.

The HPTDC runs a Volvo AC bus to Delhi (₹900, 10 hours) at 8.30pm, and a non-AC deluxe bus to Manali (₹550, nine hours) at 8.30am, both starting from near the tourist information booth

UNIQUELY INDIA / GETTY IMAGES ©

 Don't Miss
Shimla Toy Train

One of the little joys of Shimla is getting to or from it by the narrow-gauge toy train from Kalka, just north of Chandigarh. Although the steam trains are long gone, it's a scenic five- to six-hour trip, passing through 102 tunnels as it winds up through the hills. Shimla station is 1.5km west of Scandal Point on Cart Rd – a 20-to-30-minute uphill walk to town.

Trains leave Kalka for Shimla at 4am, 5.10am, 5.30am, 6am and 12.10pm, and start the return trip at 10.35am, 2.25pm, 4.25pm, 5.40pm and 6.15pm. The most comfortable option is the Shivalik Express leaving Kalka at 5.30am and starting back from Shimla at 5.40pm, costing ₹415/500 uphill/downhill including food. All other trains have 2nd-class coaches (₹25 unreserved, ₹40 to ₹65 reserved) and fairly spartan 1st-class coaches (₹255 to ₹315).

The convenient Himalayan Queen service runs from/to Delhi Sarai Rohilla, with comfortable connection times at Kalka and fares of ₹435/120 (chair car/2nd class) for the Delhi–Kalka (or vice-versa) leg:

DELHI SARAI ROHILLA	ARRIVE KALKA	DEPART KALKA	SHIMLA	TRAIN NOS
5.35am	11.10am	12.10pm	5.20pm	14095 & 52455
SHIMLA	ARRIVE KALKA	DEPART KALKA	DELHI SARAI ROHILLA	TRAIN NOS
10.35am	4.10pm	4.50pm	10.40pm	52456 & 14096

There's a **rail booking office** (🕙9am-1pm & 2-4pm Mon-Sat) on the Ridge, or you can book at the train station.

on Cart Rd west of Victory Tunnel: get tickets at the HPTDC tourist office (p364).

 Getting Around

The only way to get around central Shimla is on foot. Fortunately a two-part **lift** (per person ₹10; ⊙8am-10pm, to 9pm Dec-Mar & mid-Jul–mid-Sep) connects Cart Rd with the Mall about 600m east of Scandal Point. Taxis from the train station/New Bus Station to the bottom of the lift cost ₹150/250.

Manali

☎01902 / POP 8100 / ELEV 2050M

Surrounded by high peaks in the beautiful green valley of the Beas River, and with mountain adventures beckoning from all directions, Manali is a year-round magnet for tourists. Backpackers come to hang out in the hippy villages around the main town; adventure tourists come for trekking, paragliding, rafting and skiing; and Indian honeymoon couples or families come for the cool mountain air and a taste of snow on a day trip to Rohtang La.

Most backpackers stay in the villages of Vashisht or Old Manali, which have a laid-back vibe and plenty of services, but semi-close for winter from about November to April.

◉ Sights

Hadimba Temple Hindu Temple

This much-revered wood-and-stone mandir, constructed in 1553, stands in a clearing in the cedar forest about 2km west of central Manali. Pilgrims come from across India to honour Hadimba, the demon wife of the Pandava Bhima from the Mahabharata. The temple's wooden doorway, under a three-tier pagoda-style roof, is richly carved with figures of gods, animals and dancers; antlers and ibex horns adorn the outside walls.

Old Manali Area

About 2km northwest of the Mall on the far side of the Manalsu Nala stream, Old Manali still has some of the feel of an Indian mountain village once you get past the core backpacker zone. There are some remarkable old houses of wood and stone, and the towered **Manu Maharishi Temple** is built on the site where, legend says, the ark of the Noah-like Manu, the creator of civilisation, landed after the great flood.

Tours

In high season, the HPTDC offers bus day tours to the Rohtang La (₹310) and other places, if there are enough takers. Private travel agencies offer similar tours.

The **Him-aanchal Taxi Operators Union** (☎01902-252120; The Mall) has fixed-price tours, including to Rohtang

Hadimba Temple
ANAND PUROHIT / GETTY IMAGES ©

Central Manali

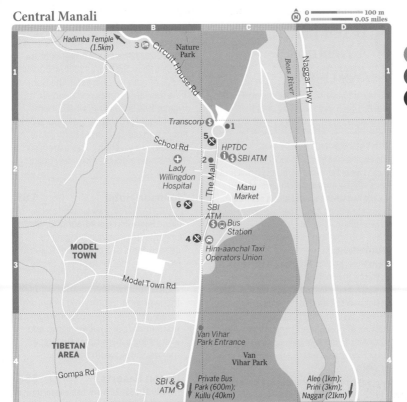

Central Manali

⊕ Activities, Courses & Tours

1 Him-aanchal Taxi Operators
Union C2
2 Himalayan Adventurers C2

⊜ Sleeping

3 Johnson Hotel B1

⊗ Eating

4 Chopsticks..B3
Johnson's Cafe..............................(see 3)
5 Khyber C2
6 Mayur B2

La (₹1800), Solang Nullah (₹900) and
Naggar (₹1100).

Himalayan Adventurers
Outdoor Adventure

(☏01902-252750; www.himalayanadventurers.
com; 44 the Mall) Trekking specialist; also

good for mountain biking, jeep safaris and
motorcycle tours.

Himalayan Extreme Centre
Outdoor Adventure

(☏9816174164; www.himalayan-extreme-centre.
com) This long-running, professional outfit
can arrange almost any activity you fancy.
In Old Manali; it also has a branch in
Vashisht.

Sleeping

Peak season (May to July and Christmas)
rates are listed here but discounts of
up to 50% are standard at other times,
especially at top-end places. Heating is
rare in budget places so be prepared to
dive under a blanket to stay warm.

If You Like…
Adventure Activities

Manali is the adventure sports capital of Himachal Pradesh, and all sorts of activities can be organised through tour operators.

1 MOUNTAIN BIKING
Agencies offer bike hire for ₹350 to ₹850 per day (and can give current info on routes) or will take you on tours ranging from the 51km descent from Rohtang La to two-week trips to Ladakh or Kinnaur and Spiti costing around ₹3000 per person per day with vehicle support.

2 PARAGLIDING
Paragliding is popular at Solang Nullah and at Gulaba (below the Rohtang Pass) from April to October (except during the monsoon). Tandem flights at Solang Nullah cost ₹1000 (a two-minute flight) or ₹3000 (10 minutes). Adventure-tour operators can organise 20- or 30-minute tandem flights for ₹3500 to ₹4000, and also solo-flight training courses.

3 RAFTING
There is 14km of Grade II and III white water between Pirdi, on the Beas River 3km south of Kullu, and the take-out point at Jhiri; trips with agencies from Manali cost around ₹1000 per person, plus transport. May, June, late September and October are the best times.

4 WALKING & TREKKING
Manali is a popular starting point for organised mountain treks. Most agencies offer multiday treks for ₹2000 to ₹3000 per person per day, all-inclusive. June, September and October are the best months. Popular three- or four-day options include 4250m-high Bhrigu Lake, Hamta Pass to Lahaul and Chandrakani Pass from Naggar to Malana.

Shorter walks are possible from Manali. One good hike is up to Lama Dugh meadow west of town (about four hours up, three hours down). A good short walk goes from Vashisht to Jogini waterfall and back. Usual rules on safe trekking apply: tell someone where you are going and never walk alone. Guides for day hikes typically cost ₹1500.

MANALI

Sunshine Guest House
Heritage Guesthouse **$$**
(☎01902-252320; www.sunshineguesthouse.co.in; Club House Rd; d/tr/q ₹3000/4500/5500; ☎) Full of colonial character, the Sunshine has large triples and quads in its original 1920s building, where rooms have beautiful polished walnut and pine floors and old-fashioned bathrooms (pending renovation). There are also four modern doubles in a new building next door.

Johnson Hotel
Hotel **$$$**
(☎01902-253764; www.johnsonhotel.in; Circuit House Rd; r/apt ₹3760/8220; ❄☎) One of a few places belonging to descendants of a prominent Raj-era landowner, the Johnson is a classy wood-and-stone hotel with 12 snug rooms, four two-bedroom apartments in the original century-old lodge, and lovely gardens, as well as an excellent restaurant (p369). It's well run and everything's in immaculate shape, making it well worth the price.

Banon Resorts
Hotel **$$$**
(☎01902-253026; www.banonresortmanali.com; Club House Rd; incl breakfast r ₹7050, ste ₹8220-10,570, cottage ₹21,140; ❄☎) This quiet, luxury hotel is a little slicker than its competition. Centrally heated rooms in the main building are spacious and uncluttered, with huge bathrooms, while the two-bedroom cottages are the last word in luxurious peace and privacy. The balconies and restaurant terrace overlooking the large, lovely garden provide the charm.

OLD MANALI

Tourist Nest Guest House
Guesthouse **$**
(☎01902-252383; touristnest@gmail.com; r ₹900-1100; ☎) In the heart of Old Manali, Tourist Nest has bright, clean, tiled, well-kept rooms with private balconies. Negotiable rates can lead to some of the best value around.

Mountain Dew Guesthouse
Guesthouse **$**

(📞9816446366; d ₹500-800; 📶) This yellow three-storey place offers good-sized, decently maintained rooms with nice east-facing shared terraces. It's one of the best-value places in Old Manali.

Dragon Guest House
Hotel **$$**

(📞01902-252290; www.dragontreks.com; r ₹600-1500, ste ₹4000; 📶) Dragon has good, comfortable rooms opening on to long verandahs on four floors – the higher the better, and the best are in the Swiss-chalet-style top floors. There's a little orchard out front, plus a restaurant and a reliable travel agency for treks and tours.

VASHISHT

Hotel Valley of Gods
Hotel **$$**

(📞01902251111; www.hotelvalleyofgods.com; r ₹2940-4110; @📶) This impressive stone-and-wood building, owned and run by a local family, has bright, spacious, pine-floored rooms with good, big bathrooms and fine balconies overlooking the valley. The rooftop restaurant, internet cafe, in-room wi-fi and on-site trekking-and-travel agency provide a pretty good package of services. Off-season discounts can slash rates by more than half.

Eating

Manali has some fine Indian and international restaurants, and there are lots of cheap travellers' cafes in Old Manali and Vashisht.

MANALI

Mayur
Multicuisine **$$**

(Mission Rd; mains ₹100-300; 🕘9am-10pm) Locals and visitors alike rate Mayur highly for its well-prepared North and South Indian specialities. The decor downstairs is solidly old-school and classy, with uniformed waiters, while the upstairs is bright and more contemporary. The Indian dishes are excellent and there are some refreshingly unusual Continental options including ratatouille, fish in coconut milk, and lamb goulash.

Johnson's Cafe
Continental **$$$**

(Circuit House Rd; mains ₹300-530; 🕘8am-10.30pm; 📶) The restaurant at Johnson Hotel is tops for European food, with specialities such as lamb and mint gravy,

Paragliding at Solang Nullah

ANAND PUROHIT / GETTY IMAGES ©

wood-oven-baked trout with almond sauce, and apple crumble with custard. The restaurant-bar is cosy but the garden terrace is the place to be, especially during happy hours.

OLD MANALI

Numerous places serve all the backpacker standards – momos, omelettes, banana pancakes, apple pie and the three I's (Italian, Israeli and Indian dishes). Nearly all these places close by November.

Dylan's Toasted & Roasted   Cafe **$**
(www.dylanscoffee.com; coffees & breakfasts ₹50-150; ⊙9am-11pm Mon-Sat; 🛜) This ever popular hole-in-the-wall cafe serves the best coffee in town, plus cinnamon tea, hearty breakfasts and wicked desserts including 'Hello to the Queen' – ice cream, melted chocolate and fried banana chunks on a bed of broken biscuits.

La Plage   French **$$$**
(📱9805340977; www.facebook.com/la.plage.manali; mains ₹300-500; ⊙noon-11pm mid-May–Aug, closed Mon Jul–Aug) Dinner at this outpost of one of Goa's chic-est eateries is like being invited to the hip Paris apartment of your much, much cooler friend. Classic French standards such as liver pâté are joined by specialities like overnight-cooked lamb, smoked trout, pumpkin ravioli and a chocolate thali dessert.

Lazy Dog Lounge   Multicuisine **$$$**
(mains ₹220-670; ⊙11am-10.30pm; 🛜) This slick restaurant-bar features big plates of fresh, flavourful international food – from pumpkin-and-coconut soup to oven-baked trout and Thai rice bowls – that's steps above typical backpacker fare. Sit on chairs, benches or cushions in a space that's classy yet earthy, or relax in the riverside garden.

🍷 Drinking & Nightlife

In Manali town, the best places for a beer or local fruit wine are **Khyber** (The Mall; ⊙8am-11pm) and **Chopsticks** (The Mall; ⊙9.30am-10pm; 🛜).

In Old Manali, **The Hangout** (⊙noon-midnight, from 5pm Fri) is popular for its outdoor firepits and frequent live music, and also serves decent food.

Prayer flags at the Tsuglagkhang complex (p372)

Information

Banks in Manali don't offer foreign exchange but there are private moneychangers, and the State Bank of India has three central ATMs.

Lady Willingdon Hospital (☎01902-252379; www.manalihospital.com; School Rd) Church-run hospital with 24-hour emergency service.

Transcorp (The Mall; ☻9.30am-6.30pm Mon-Sat) Changes cash and travellers cheques.

Getting There & Away

Air

Manali's closest airport is 50km south at Bhuntar.

Bus

Government-run HRTC buses go from the bus station. HPTDC buses also go from the bus station but tickets are sold at their office (☎01902-252116; The Mall; ☻8am-8pm, 9am-7pm approx Nov-Mar). Private buses start from a large bus park 1.2km south of the bus station; tickets are sold at travel agencies along the Mall.

Delhi The most comfortable options are the HPTDC's AC Volvo coaches at 5.30pm and 6.30pm (₹1300, 15 hours). Private travel agencies run similar overnight services for ₹800 to ₹1600 depending on season. HRTC also has AC Volvos (₹1285/798 to Delhi/Chandigarh) at 4pm, 5pm and 6.30pm, plus an AC deluxe (₹1005/640) at 5.50pm and 12 ordinary services daily (₹655/442).

Other Destinations HPTDC runs a daily bus to Shimla (₹550, nine hours) at 8am and there are also six HRTC buses (ordinary/AC ₹390/550). For Dharamsala HRTC buses (₹355, 10 hours) go at 8am and 6.30pm, and there's usually a private bus (₹550) at 7.30pm.

Taxi

A taxi to Bhuntar Airport, though the Him-aanchal Taxi Operators Union (☎01902-252120; The Mall), costs ₹1500. To Dharamsala/McLeod Ganj expect to pay around ₹5000.

Getting Around

Autorickshaws from the top of the Mall run to Old Manali bridge for ₹50 and Vashisht for ₹70 (more after dark, if you can get one at all).

McLeod Ganj

☎01892 / ELEV 1770M

When travellers talk of heading up to Dharamsala (to see the Dalai Lama...), this is where they mean. Around 4km north of Dharamsala town – or 10km via the looping bus route – McLeod Ganj is the residence of His Holiness the 14th Dalai Lama and the site of the Tibetan exile community's main temple. The Tibetan government-in-exile is based just downhill at Gangchen Kyishong. Along with Manali, it's the big traveller hang-out in Himachal Pradesh, with many budget hotels, trekking companies, internet cafes, restaurants and shops selling Tibetan souvenirs crammed in just a couple of blocks, like a mini-Kathmandu. Naturally, there's a large Tibetan population here, many of whom are refugees, so you'll see plenty of

Meeting the Dalai Lama

Meeting face to face with the Dalai Lama is a lifelong dream for many travellers and certainly for Buddhists, but private audiences are rarely granted. Tibetan refugees are automatically guaranteed an audience, but travellers must make do with the occasional public teachings held at the Tsuglagkhang (p372), normally in September or October and after Losar (Tibetan New Year) in February or March, and on other occasions depending on his schedule. For annual schedules and just about everything you need to know about His Holiness, check out www.dalailama.com. To attend a teaching you have to register (three or four days ahead is advised) with your passport and two passport photographs at the **Branch Security Office** (☎01892-221560; Bhagsu Rd, McLeod Ganj; ☻9am-1pm & 2-5pm Mon-Fri & 1st Sat each month).

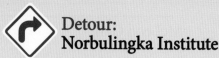

Detour: Norbulingka Institute

About 6km from Dharamsala, the wonderful **Norbulingka Institute** (📞 9418436410; www.norbulingka.org; local & Tibetan ₹20, tourist ₹50; ⏰ 9am-5.30pm) was established in 1988 to teach and preserve traditional Tibetan art forms, including woodcarving, statue-making, *thangka* (cloth) painting and embroidery. The centre produces expensive but exquisite souvenirs, including embroidered clothes, cushions and wall hangings, and sales benefit refugee artists. Also here are delightful Japanese-influenced gardens and a central Buddhist temple with a 4m-high gilded statue of Sakyamuni.

Peaceful and stylish **Norling House** (📞 9816646423; www.norbulingkahotels.com; r/ste ₹3640/5360; ❄ 🛜) offers comfortable rooms decked with Buddhist murals and Norbulingka handicrafts, arranged around a sunny atrium. Vegetarian meals and snacks are available at the **Hummingbird Cafe** (mains ₹150-200; ⏰ 7am-9pm; 🛜).

maroon robes about, especially when the Dalai Lama is in residence.

Sights

Tsuglagkhang Complex
Buddhist Temple

(Temple Rd; ⏰ 5am-8pm Apr-Oct, 6am-6pm Nov-Mar) FREE The main focus of visiting pilgrims, monks and many tourists, the Tsuglagkhang complex includes the Tsuglagkhang itself (the main Tibetan temple), the Namgyal Gompa and the excellent Tibet Museum.

Tsuglagkhang
The revered Tsuglagkhang is the exiles' concrete equivalent of the Jokhang temple in Lhasa and was built in 1969. The central image is a gilded statue of the Sakyamuni Buddha (the name refers to the Buddha's birthplace Sakya). To its left are statues of Avalokitesvara (Chenrezig in Tibetan); the bodhisattva of compassion and Tibet's patron deity, and Padmasambhava, the Indian sage believed to have spread Buddhism in Tibet in the 8th century.

Kalachakra Temple
Before visiting the Tsuglagkhang itself, pilgrims first visit the Kalachakra Temple on its west side, which contains mesmerising murals of the Kalachakra (Wheel of Time) mandala, specifically linked to Avalokitesvara, of whom the Dalai Lama is a manifestation. Coloured sand mandalas are created here annually on the 15th day of the third Tibetan month.

Tibet Museum
(www.tibetmuseum.org; ⏰ 9am-1pm & 2-6pm Sun & Tue-Fri & 1st Sat of month, to 5pm Oct-Mar) The museum tells the story of Tibetan history, the Chinese occupation and the subsequent Tibetan resistance and exodus, through photographs, video and clear English-language display panels. A visit here is a must. Documentaries (₹10) are shown at 11am and 3pm.

Activities

ALTERNATIVE THERAPIES, YOGA & MASSAGE

McLeod Ganj and the neighbouring villages Dharamkot and Bhagsu havedozens of practitioners of holistic and alternative therapies. The **Men-Tsee-Khang Therapy Center** (📞 01892-221484; www.men-tsee-khang.org; TIPA Rd; ⏰ 9am-1pm & 2-5pm Mon-Sat, closed 2nd & 4th Sat each month) is good for Tibetan massages.

Universal Yoga Centre Yoga
(9882222323; www.vijaypoweryoga.com;
Youngling School, Jogiwara Rd; 1½hr class
₹200-300; Apr-Nov) Gets good reports
for daily drop-in classes in a variety of
techniques; also does teacher-training
courses.

TREKKING

Apart from the demanding Indrahar La
trek to the Chamba Valley, the most popular option is the easy four- to six-day loop
to Kareri Lake. All-inclusive treks cost
between ₹1500 and ₹ 2500 per person
per day.

High Point Adventure Trekking
(9816120145; http://trek.123himachal.com;
Kareri Lodge, Hotel Bhagsu Rd) An experienced, knowledgable team offering some
of the best prices in town. There's also an
office (9am-6pm) on Temple Rd.

McLeod Ganj

Sights
1 Kalachakra Temple	A7
2 Tibet Museum	B7
3 Tsuglagkhang	A7
4 Tsuglagkhang Complex	B7

Activities, Courses & Tours
5 High Point Adventure	A4
6 High Point Adventure	A5

Sleeping
7 Chonor House	B6
8 Green Hotel	B2
9 Hotel Tibet	A2
10 Om Hotel	A3

Eating
11 Indique	A3
12 Moonpeak	A4
Namgyal Cafe	(see 10)
13 Nick's Italian Kitchen	B2
14 Peace Cafe	B3

Information
15 Branch Security Office	B2
16 HPTDC Tourist Information Centre	A4
17 Men-Tsee-Khang Therapy Centre	A2

Transport
18 HRTC Ticket Office	A2

McLeod Ganj

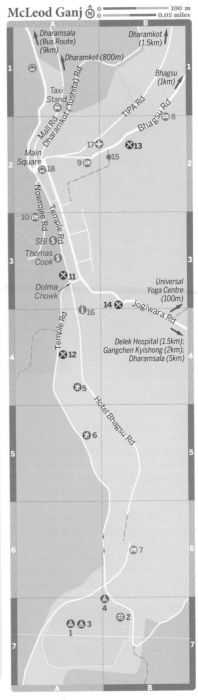

NORTHERN MOUNTAINS & AMRITSAR   MCLEOD GANJ

WALKS

Short walks around McLeod include the 1.5km strolls east to Bhagsu village or west to St John in the Wilderness church, and the uphill walk to Dharamkot village (2km by TIPA Rd, 1km by the steeper Dharamkot Rd). All these follow roads but pass through lovely pine and cedar forests.

To reach the little Gallu Devi Temple, you can walk straight up the path from the top of Dharamkot, or take the track along the left side of the water tank opposite Dharamkot's Himalayan Tea Shop, then turn up a path to the right after 50m. This winds 1km up through the forest to emerge on a jeep track. Head 500m to the right to Gallu Devi, with panoramas both north and south. It's a further 6km, in a strenuous three hours or so, up to the panoramic mountain meadow of Triund (2900m).

🛏 Sleeping

Advance bookings are advised year-round, especially from April to June and October.

Om Hotel   Hotel $
(📞9816329985; Nowrojee Rd; r ₹500-550, without bathroom ₹300-350; 📶) Friendly, family-run Om, just down a lane from the main square, has simple but pleasing rooms with good views. The popular **Namgyal Cafe** (mains ₹80-300; 🕐7.30am-9pm) 🍴 serves well-laden but chewy pizzas, plus decently prepared tofu and potato dishes, soups and more, and its terrace catches the sunset over the valley.

Hotel Tibet   Hotel $
(📞01892-221587; www.hoteltibetdhasa.com; Bhagsu Rd; r ₹880-1770) Bang in the centre of town, this place has a faintly upmarket feel, but very reasonable prices. Rooms have parquet floors and there's a cosy

NORTHERN MOUNTAINS & AMRITSAR MCLEOD GANJ

multicuisine restaurant. Profits go to Tibetan settlements in India.

Green Hotel
Hotel $$

(☎01892-221200; www.greenhotel.in; Bhagsu Rd; r ₹800-2800; ❄ ☎) A favourite with midrange travellers and small groups, the Green has a diverse range of sunny, super-clean rooms in three buildings, most with balconies and valley and mountain views. It's well run and has an excellent cafe.

Chonor House
Boutique Hotel $$$

(☎01892-221006; www.norbulingkahotels.com; r ₹5290-7750; ❄ @ ☎) Up a lane near the Tsuglagkhang, Chonor House is a real gem. It's run by the Norbulingka Institute, and is decked out with wonderful handmade Norbulingka furnishings and fabrics. Each of the 13 bright and sunny rooms has a Tibetan theme that runs from the carpets to the bedspreads to the murals. Even the cheapest rooms are spacious.

Eating

Peace Cafe
Tibetan $

(Jogiwara Rd; mains ₹70-100; ⊗7am-8pm) This cosy little cafe is popular with Tibetans, including monks and nuns, as well as travellers, for dining on tasty *momos* (dumplings), *thukpa* and *thenthuk* (noodle soups with veggies/cheese/egg/tofu).

Nick's Italian Kitchen
Italian $$

(Bhagsu Rd; mains ₹75-175; ⊗7.30am-9pm; ☎) Unpretentious, well-run Nick's has been serving up tasty vegetarian pizzas, lasagne and gnocchi for years. Follow up a ground coffee with a heavenly slice of lemon cheesecake – apparently Richard Gere's favourite when he stayed here. Eat inside or out on the large terrace.

Indique
Multicuisine $$

(Temple Rd; mains ₹190-290; ⊗8am-11pm) With a romantic open rooftop and plenty more tables and a loungey bar indoors,

Indique is McLeod's most stylish eating venue and has live music some nights. Breakfasts and tortilla wraps are good, but the Indian lunch and dinner dishes are probably the best in town, with the chicken mint tikka a standout.

Moonpeak Multicuisine $$
(www.moonpeak.org; Temple Rd; mains ₹120-250; ⊙7.30am-8.30pm; 🛜) A little chunk of Seattle, transported to India. Come for excellent coffee, cakes, imaginative brown-bread open sandwiches (like poached chicken with mango, lime and coriander sauce), plus plenty of well-prepared main dishes – and the Himachali thali (₹200), a sampler of regional dishes.

ℹ️ Information

Numerous travel agencies can book bus tickets, and can also arrange tours and treks.

Medical Services

Delek Hospital (☎01892-222053; www.delekhospital.org; Gangchen Kyishong; consultations before/after noon ₹10/50; ⊙outpatient clinic 9am-1pm & 2-5pm Mon-Fri, 9am-1pm Sat) A small, Tibetan-run hospital practising allopathic medicine.

Money

SBI (Temple Rd; ⊙10am-4pm Mon-Fri, to 1pm Sat) Has a busy ATM.

Thomas Cook (Temple Rd; ⊙9.30am-6pm Mon-Sat) Changes cash/travellers cheques for ₹25/50 commission plus 0.12% tax (minimum ₹30), and gives advances on credit cards for a 5% charge.

ℹ️ Getting There & Away

Air

Dharamsala airport, at Gaggal, 13km southwest of Dharamsala, has daily flights to/from Delhi, though they're sometimes cancelled for bad weather.

Bus

Buses start from and arrive at the New Bus Stand, 150m north of the main square. Buses and minibuses to Dharamsala (both ₹14, 35 minutes) run about every half-hour from 8am to 8pm.

Some long-distance buses start from McLeod but there are more frequent departures from Dharamsala bus station. You can book government (HRTC) buses from both places at McLeod's **HRTC ticket office** (Main Square; ⊙9am-4pm). In addition, the **HPTDC** (☎01892-221091; Hotel Bhagsu Rd; ⊙10am-5pm) runs a non-AC deluxe bus to Delhi (₹700, 13 hours) at 6pm every one or two days, and travel agencies sell seats on deluxe private buses to Delhi (₹1100, 12 hours, 6pm Volvo AC), Manali (₹400, 11 hours, 6am) and elsewhere.

Eternal flame, Jallianwala Bagh
HUW JONES / GETTY IMAGES ©

Buses from McLeod Ganj

DESTINATION	FARE (₹)	DURATION (HR)	FREQUENCY
Dehra Dun	530	12	8pm
Delhi	510-1150	12-13	4am, 6pm & 7.30pm (ordinary); 5pm (semi-deluxe); 6.30pm & 7.45pm (deluxe); 5.30pm & 7pm (Volvo AC)
Manali	330	11	4.30pm

Taxi

McLeod's **taxi stand** (☏01892-221034) is on Mall Rd, north of the Main Chowk. A taxi for the day, travelling less than 80km, should cost ₹1600.

One-way fares for short hops include Dharamsala bus station (₹200), Norbulingka Institute (₹400) and the airport at Gaggal (₹700).

PUNJAB

Amritsar

0183 / POP 1.13 MILLION

Founded in 1577 by the fourth Sikh guru, Ram Das, Amritsar is home to Sikhism's holiest shrine, the spectacular Golden Temple, one of India's most serene and humbling sights. Alas, the same can't be said for the hyperactive streets surrounding the temple – few places can compete with Amritsar when it comes to congestion, air-pollution and traffic noise.

Sights

Jallianwala Bagh　　　Historic Site
(Golden Temple Rd; ☉6am-9pm summer, 7am-8pm winter) Reached through a gatehouse on the road to the Golden Temple, this poignant park commemorates the 1500 Indians killed or wounded when a British officer ordered his soldiers to shoot on unarmed protesters in 1919. Some of the bullet holes are still visible in the walls, as is the well into which hundreds desperately leapt to avoid the bullets. There's an eternal (24-hour) flame of remembrance, an exhibition telling the stories of victims, and a Matryrs' Gallery, with portraits of Independence heroes.

👉 Tours

The Grand Hotel runs good-value day tours of the main sights (₹350 per hour) and night tours to the Attari–Wagah border-closing ceremony, Mata Temple and Golden Temple for ₹650 per person.

The **tourist office** (☏0183-2402452; www.punjabtourism.gov.in; Train Station exit, Queen's Rd; ☉9am-5pm Tue-Sun) runs two-hour Heritage Walks (Indian/foreigner ₹25/75) through the Old City bazaars, starting from the Town Hall at 8am and 5pm daily (9am and 4pm December to February).

Golden Temple Etiquette

Before entering the compound, remove your shoes and socks – there are *chappal* (sandal) stands at the entrances – wash your feet in the shallow footbaths and cover your head; scarves can be borrowed (no charge) or hawkers sell souvenir scarves for ₹10. Tobacco and alcohol are strictly prohibited. If you want to sit beside the tank, sit cross-legged and do not dangle your feet in the water. Photography is only permitted from the walkway surrounding the pool.

Don't Miss
Golden Temple

📞 information office 0183-2553954

🕒 24hr, information office 8am-7pm

Sikhism's holiest shrine, this gold-plated gurdwara glitters in the middle of its holy pool like a fantastical gold bullion bar; a sight some travellers rate as up there with seeing the Taj Mahal. And true to Sikhism's inclusive nature, all are welcome here, making the atmosphere incredibly friendly as well as genuinely spiritual.

Amrit Sarovar

The Golden Temple is actually just a small part of this huge gurdwara complex, known to Sikhs as Harmandir Sahib (or Darbar Sahib).

Spiritually, the focus of attention is the tank – the Amrit Sarovar (Pool of Nectar), from which Amritsar takes its name, excavated by the fourth guru Ram Das in 1577. Ringed by a marble walkway, the tank is said to have healing powers, and pilgrims come from across the world to bathe in the sacred waters.

Golden Temple

Floating at the end of a long causeway, the Golden Temple itself is a mesmerising blend of Hindu and Islamic architectural styles, with an elegant marble lower level adorned with flower and animal motifs in pietra dura work (as seen on the Taj Mahal). Above this rises a shimmering second level, encased in intricately engraved gold panels, and topped by a dome gilded with 750kg of gold. In the gleaming inner sanctum (photos prohibited), priests and musicians keep up a continuous chant from the Guru Granth Sahib, the Sikh holy book, adding to the already intense atmosphere.

The Guru Granth Sahib is installed in the temple every morning and returned at night to the **Akal Takhat** (Timeless Throne), the temporal seat of the Khalsa brotherhood. The building was heavily damaged when it was stormed by the Indian army during Operation Blue Star in 1984; it was repaired by the government but Sikhs refused to use the tainted building and rebuilt the tower from scratch.

More shrines and monuments are dotted around the edge of the compound. Inside the main entrance clock tower, the **Sikh Museum** (7am-7pm summer, 8am-6pm winter) FREE shows the persecution suffered by the Sikhs at the hands of Mughals, the British and Indira Gandhi.

Local Knowledge

Golden Temple Don't Miss List

SHIREEN KUMAR IS A TEACHER, LOCAL CULTURE ENTHUSIAST, AND UNOFFICIAL GUIDE TO THE TEMPLE

1 THE MAIN SHRINE

A confection of white marble. gilded frescoes and ornate domes, the main shrine has three storeys. Under a canopy studded with jewels on the ground floor is the Guru Granth Sahib, the holy book of the Sikhs. Beginning early in the morning and lasting until long past sunset, hymns are chanted to the accompaniment of flutes, drums and stringed instruments.

2 PALKI SAHIB

The Palki Sahib ceremony takes place twice a day where the Guru Granth Sahib is brought to the temple in a decorative palanquin at around 5am (4am in summer), and is taken back to the Akal Takhat at about 9.40pm (10.30pm in summer) amid rousing devotion.

3 PILGRIMS' LUNCH

Langar (meal) preparation takes place in the community kitchen, where all persons, irrespective of race, religion or gender, perform a voluntary selfless service *(sewa)*, serving food to the 60,000 pilgrims who visit the temple each day. The kitchen contains elaborate machines that make up to 6000 chapatis per hour. This is the busiest section of the temple and remains open 24/7. It symbolises the Sikh principle of inclusiveness and oneness of humankind.

4 AKAL TAKHAT

Akal Takhat is the highest Sikh religious authority, located in the Harmandir Sahib. It is decorated with inlaid marble, gold-leafed domes and wall paintings. The Guru Granth Sahib is kept in the Akal Takhat at night. From around 6.30pm to 7.30pm every day, historic weapons are also on display here.

5 THE SIKH MUSEUM

The Sikh Museum is on the 2nd floor of the temple's main entrance, and has fascinating galleries displaying artefacts, coins, weapons, images and remembrances of Sikh gurus, warriors and saints. Details are also given in English.

📖 Sleeping

Tourist Guesthouse　　Guesthouse $
(☏0183-2553830; bubblesgoolry@yahoo.com; 1355 GT Rd; dm/s/d ₹180/250/450; @🛜)
This good-value backpacker stalwart offers pocket-friendly prices and humble rooms with high ceilings and fans. There's a garden restaurant, rooftop seating and traveller-oriented vibe. On the downside, this is one of the few places in town that charges for wi-fi (per day ₹100) and the location, between a flyover and the railway line, is hardly the quietest.

Grand Hotel　　Hotel $$
(☏0183-2562424; www.hotelgrand.in; Queen's Rd; r from ₹1430; ❄@🛜) Across the road from the train station, but far from grungy, the Grand is an oasis of calm amid an otherwise chaotic location. Rooms are spacious – if not exactly grand – and surround a wonderfully charming courtyard garden. The restaurant, with seating overlooking the garden, is also recommended.

Mrs Bhandari's Guesthouse　　Guesthouse $$
(☏0183-2228509; www.facebook.com/bhandari guesthouse; 10 Cantonment; camping per person ₹200, s/d from ₹1840/2300; ❄@🛜🏊) Founded by the much-missed Mrs Bhandari (1906–2007), this friendly guesthouse is set in spacious grounds in the Amritsar cantonment, about 2km from the centre. The large rooms have a hint of colonial-era bungalow about them, and the welcome is warm. The well-kept gardens are vast, and include swings, plenty of seating and a small swimming pool, making this an excellent choice for families, while budget travellers can camp here if they bring their own camping equipment.

Hotel Indus　　Hotel $$
(☏0183-2535900; www.hotelindus.com; 211-13 Sri Hamandir Sahib Marg; r from ₹2140, with temple view ₹2880; ❄@🛜) The dramatic million-dollar view of the Golden Temple from the rooftop is reason enough to stay at this modern-style hotel. Rooms are compact but comfy. Book well ahead to secure one of the two rooms with temple vistas.

Sikh Museum (p379)

SAIKO3P / GETTY IMAGES ©

Eating

Amritsar is famous for its *dhabas* (snack bars) serving such Punjabi treats as *kulcha* (Punjabi-style *parathas* with herbs, potato and pomegranate seeds) and 'Amritsari' fish (deep-fried fish with lemon, chilli, garlic and ginger). Hotels and restaurants in the Golden Temple area don't serve alcohol.

Kesar Da Dhaba Punjabi $
(Chowk Passian; mains ₹70-200; ⏲11am-6pm & 7-11pm) Hard to find (ask for directions in the Old City), this takeway and no-nonsense *dhaba* serves delicious *paratha* thalis (₹200 to ₹250) and silver-leaf-topped *firni* (ground rice pudding; ₹20) served in small clay bowls, as well as arguably the best lassi in town (₹50).

Brothers' Dhaba Punjabi $$
(Bade Bhai Ka; Town Hall Chowk; mains ₹100-200; ⏲7.30am-12.30pm) This fast and friendly upmarket *dhaba* serves some of Amritsar's tastiest *kulcha*.

Crystal Restaurant Mughlai $$$
(☎0183-2225555; Crystal Chowk; mains ₹300-600; ⏲11am-11.30pm) Worth the splurge, this classy, ground-floor restaurant has a fin de siècle air, with mirror-lined walls and ornate stucco trim. The multicuisine menu is dominated by Mughlai favourites – the house speciality is delicious *mugh tawa frontier* (morsels of chicken in a dense onion gravy). It also has a decent wine list.

ℹ Information

Internet Access

Guru Arjun Dev Niwas Net Cafe (Guru Arjun Dev Niwas; per hour ₹25; ⏲6am-1am) Handy internet cafe in the Golden Temple complex.

Medical Services

Fortis Escorts Hospital (☎0183-3012222, 9915133330; www.fortishealthcare.com; Majitha Verka Bypass) International-standard hospital in the city suburbs, 7km northeast of the Old City.

Money

Amritsar has plenty of ATMs, including at the train station and airport. **HDFC** (ground fl, RS Towers, Hall Bazaar; ⏲9.30am-3.30pm Mon-Fri, to 12.30pm Sat) and **ICICI** (ground fl, RS Towers, Hall Bazaar; ⏲9am-6pm Mon-Fri, to 2pm Sat) have Old City branches, both with foreign exchange facilities and 24-hour ATMs. **Manat Travels** (☎0183-5006006, 9815641310; www.mannattravels.com; 5 Dharam Singh Market, Furwara Chowk; ⏲Mon-Sat) is a trustworthy moneychanger in the Old City.

ℹ Getting There & Away

Air

Amritsar's Sri Guru Ram Dass Jee International Airport is about 11km northwest of the centre. Direct flights to Delhi/Mumbai cost around ₹3200/7000.

Bus

Private bus companies operate from near Gandhi Gate, and from Cooper Rd near the train station. Evening air-con buses run to Delhi (₹800, 10 hours) and Jaipur (seat/sleeper ₹700/900, 16 hours).

The main **Inter State Bus Terminal** (ISBT; GT Rd) is about 2km north of the Golden Temple near Mahan Singh Gate. There is at least one daily bus to Dharamsala (₹225, seven hours) and Manali (₹550, 12 hours), plus frequent buses to Delhi (non-AC/AC ₹420/850, 10 hours).

Train

Apart from the train station, there's a less busy **train reservation office** (⏲8am-8pm, to 2pm Sun) at the Golden Temple.

The fastest train to Delhi is the twice-daily Shatabdi Express (AC chair/1AC ₹865/1690, six hours), leaving Amritsar at 5am and 4.50pm and departing New Delhi railway station at 7.20am and 4.30pm.

The daily 6.45pm Amritsar–Howrah Mail links Amritsar with Varanasi (sleeper/3AC/2AC ₹500/1340/1950, 22 hours) and Kolkata (₹695/1850/2720, 37 hours).

ℹ Getting Around

Free yellow minibuses run between the train station and the Golden Temple from 4am to 9pm. Otherwise, from the station to the Golden Temple, a rickshaw/autorickshaw will cost around ₹50/70 but you'll have to haggle like fury for a fair price. Taxis loiter around at the station, and there's a **prepaid booth** (☎9888561615) at the southeast entrance to the Golden Temple. To the airport, an autorickshaw costs ₹250 and a taxi about double.

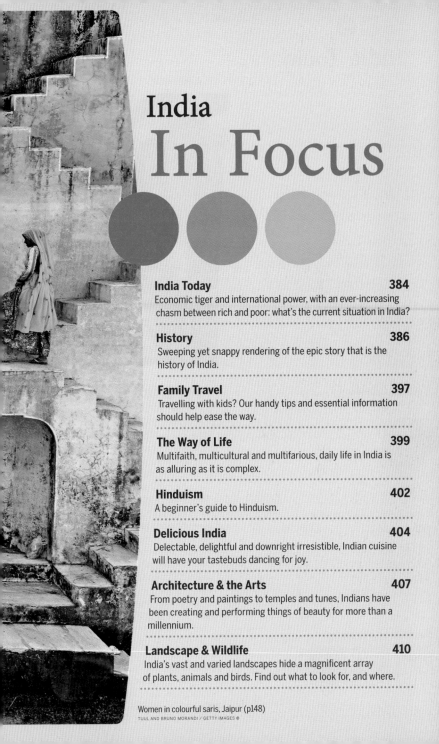

India

In Focus

India Today 384
Economic tiger and international power, with an ever-increasing chasm between rich and poor: what's the current situation in India?

History 386
Sweeping yet snappy rendering of the epic story that is the history of India.

Family Travel 397
Travelling with kids? Our handy tips and essential information should help ease the way.

The Way of Life 399
Multifaith, multicultural and multifarious, daily life in India is as alluring as it is complex.

Hinduism 402
A beginner's guide to Hinduism.

Delicious India 404
Delectable, delightful and downright irresistible, Indian cuisine will have your tastebuds dancing for joy.

Architecture & the Arts 407
From poetry and paintings to temples and tunes, Indians have been creating and performing things of beauty for more than a millennium.

Landscape & Wildlife 410
India's vast and varied landscapes hide a magnificent array of plants, animals and birds. Find out what to look for, and where.

Women in colourful saris, Jaipur (p148)
TUUL AND BRUNO MORANDI / GETTY IMAGES ©

India Today

Cafe-goers, Mumbai

> *Modi has set about to...address social issues such as sanitation, gender equality, poverty and health*

belief systems
(% of population)

80	14	2	2	1	1
Hindu	Muslim	Christian	Sikh	Buddhist	Other

if India were 100 people

55 would speak one of 21 other official languages

41 would speak Hindi

4 would speak one of 400 other languages

population per sq km

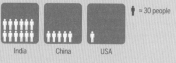

≈ 30 people

India   China   USA

The Political Landscape

In 2014 the Congress-led United Progressive Alliance (UPA) suffered a huge defeat with the BJP-led National Democratic Alliance (NDA) winning by a landslide under the charismatic leadership of Narendra Modi.

With the Bharatiya Janata Party (BJP) securing 282 seats (in the 543-seat Parliament) on its very own, this was the first time since the 1984 election that a party held enough seats to govern outright. Reasons for Modi's success at the federal elections include his former economic reputation as chief minister of the state of Gujarat, his appeal to 'ordinary' Indians due to his working class origins, and his masterful political campaigning which involved savvy use of digital technology, including social media.

Since coming to power, Modi has set about to not only resurrect India's ailing economy but to also address social issues such as sanitation, gender equality, poverty and health. Apart from vowing to build millions of toilets, largely in rural areas, he launched the Swachh Bharat Abhiyan (Clean India Mission) in 2014, a national

RICHARD I'ANSON / GETTY IMAGES ©

When India's BJP won the federal elections in 2014, Pakistan's prime minister, Nawaz Sharif, was invited to attend Narendra Modi's prime ministerial oath-taking ceremony. But it wasn't long before relations between the two nations soured, after Islamabad faltered on certain diplomatic matters and violated cross-border ceasefires. At the time of writing, there had been no formal resumption of dialogue.

Violence Against Women

In December 2012, a 23-year-old student and her male friend boarded a bus on their way home from the movies in Delhi only to find that it was a fake city bus, with blackened windows, where six men awaited them. The men beat the two friends, and raped the woman so brutally that she died 12 days later. Within weeks, India passed a package of new but controversial laws to deter violence against women: rape now carries a seven-year minimum sentence, with the death penalty in cases where the victim dies.

Many in India are also now reflecting on other abuses of women (tens of thousands die over dowry disputes alone each year), widespread police and justice-system mishandling of cases, and the greater issue of gender inequality.

Since becoming prime minister, Narendra Modi has been actively trying to change the national psyche regarding gender equality. In 2015, Modi launched the Beti Bachao Beti Padhao (Save the Daughter, Teach the Daughter) campaign which aims to work towards gender equality by discouraging female infanticide and encouraging education, among other things. With programs, such as this one, it's hoped the way in which society views gender issues will improve.

cleanliness awareness drive that has seen politicians (including the PM himself) along with revered celebrities – from Bollywood stars to cricket icons – publicly sweeping streets and clearing rubbish in a bid to encourage all citizens to do so.

The Kashmir Impasse

Decades of border skirmishes between India and Pakistan, over the disputed territory of Kashmir, have resulted in many casualties and diplomatic stalemates. The predominantly Muslim Kashmir Valley is claimed by both countries (as well as a section of less powerful Kashmiris).

Three India-Pakistan wars – in 1947, 1965 and 1971 – resolved little, and by 1989 Kashmir had its own Pakistan-backed armed insurgency. Talks that might have created an autonomous region were derailed in 2008, when terrorists killed at least 163 people at 10 sites around Mumbai (Bombay) during three days of coordinated bombings and shootings.

Image of elephant god Ganesh

EDDIE GERALD / GETTY IMAGE

Through thousands of years of great civilisations, invasions, the birth of religions and countless cataclysms, the irresistible story of India's long history has proved itself to be one of the world's great epics. From Brahmanical empires and Hindu-Buddhist dynasties through to Islamic sultanates, the British Raj and beyond, India's history has always been a work in progress; a constant process of reinvention and accumulation that is helping to shape one of the most vibrant, diverse and dynamic nations on earth.

Indus Valley Civilisation

The Indus Valley, straddling the modern India–Pakistan border, is the cradle of civilisation on the Indian subcontinent. The first inhabitants of this region were nomadic tribes who cultivated land and kept domestic animals. Over thousands of years, an urban culture began to emerge from these tribes, particularly from 3500 BC. By 2500 BC large cities were well established, the focal points of

10,000 BC

Stone Age paintings first made in the Bhimbetka rock shelters, in what is now Madhya Pradesh.

what became known as the Harappan culture, which would flourish for more than 1000 years.

Early Invasions & the Rise of Religions

The Harappan civilisation fell into decline from the beginning of the 2nd millennium BC. Some historians attribute the end of the empire to floods or decreased rainfall, which threatened the Harappans' agricultural base. The more enduring, if contentious, theory is that an Aryan invasion put paid to the Harappans, despite little archaeological proof or written reports in the ancient Indian texts to that effect. As a result, some nationalist historians argue that the Aryans (from a Sanskrit word meaning 'noble') were in fact the original inhabitants of India and that the invasion theory was actually invented by self-serving foreign conquerors. Others say that the arrival of Aryans was more of a gentle migration that gradually subsumed Harappan culture.

Those who defend the invasion theory believe that from around 1500 BC Aryan tribes from Afghanistan and Central Asia began to filter into northwest India. Many of the original inhabitants of northern India, the Dravidians, were pushed south.

The Hindu sacred scriptures, the Vedas, were written during this period of transition (1500–1200 BC), and the caste system became formalised.

As the Aryan tribes spread across the Ganges plain in the late 7th century BC, many were absorbed into 16 major kingdoms, which were, in turn, amalgamated into four large states.

The Mauryan Empire & its Aftermath

If the Harappan culture was the cradle of Indian civilisation, Chandragupta Maurya was the founder of the first great Indian empire. He came to power in 321 BC and soon expanded the empire to include the Indus Valley.

From its capital at Pataliputra (modern-day Patna), the Mauryan empire encompassed much of North and South India. The empire reached its peak under the emperor Ashoka. Such was Ashoka's power to lead and unite that after his death in 232 BC the empire rapidly disintegrated, collapsing altogether in 184 BC.

None of the empires that immediately followed could match the stability or enduring historical legacy of the Mauryans. Despite the multiplicity of ruling powers,

The Best...
Ancient Cities

1 Qutb Minar (p68)

2 Fatehpur Sikri (p104)

3 Old Delhi (p60)

IN FOCUS HISTORY

2600–1700 BC
The heyday of the Indus Valley civilisation, spanning parts of Rajasthan, Gujarat and the Sindh province in present-day Pakistan.

1000 BC
Indraprastha, Delhi's first incarnation, is founded. Archaeological excavations at the Purana Qila continue even today.

321–185 BC
The pan-Indian Maurya empire briefly adopts Buddhism during the reign of Emperor Ashoka.

this was a period of intense development. Trade with the Roman Empire (overland, and by sea through the southern ports) became substantial during the 1st century AD; there was also overland trade with China.

The Golden Age of the Guptas

Throughout the subcontinent, small tribes and kingdoms effectively controlled territory and dominated local affairs. In AD 319 Chandragupta I, the third king of one of these tribes, the little-known Guptas, came to prominence. Poetry, literature and the arts flourished, with some of the finest work done at Ajanta, Ellora and Sarnath. Towards the end of the Gupta period, Hinduism became the dominant religious force, and its revival eclipsed Jainism and Buddhism; the latter in particular went into decline in India and would never again be India's dominant religion. The invasions of the Huns at the beginning of the 6th century signalled the end of this era.

The Hindu South

Southern India has always laid claim to its own unique history. Insulated by distance from the political developments in the north, a separate set of powerful kingdoms emerged, among them the Satavahanas, who ruled over central India for about 400 years. But it was from the tribal territories on the fertile coastal plains that the greatest southern empires – the Cholas, Pandyas, Chalukyas, Cheras and Pallavas – came into their own.

The south's prosperity was based on long-established trading links with other civilisations, among them the Egyptians and Romans. In 850 the Cholas rose to power and superseded the Pallavas, who had ruled since the 4th century. They soon set about turning the south's far-reaching trade influence into territorial conquest.

The Muslim North

While South India guarded its resolutely Hindu character, North India was convulsed by Muslim armies invading from the northwest.

At the vanguard of Islamic expansion was Mahmud of Ghazni. Today, Ghazni is a nondescript little town between Kabul and Kandahar in Afghanistan. But in the early years of the 11th century, Mahmud turned it into one of the world's most glorious capital cities, which he largely funded by plundering his neighbours' territories. From 1001 to 1025, Mahmud conducted 17 raids into India, effectively shifting the balance of power in North India.

Following Mahmud's death in 1033, Ghazni was seized by the Seljuqs and then fell to the Ghurs of western Afghanistan, who similarly had their eyes on the great Indian prize. The Ghur style of warfare was brutal: the Ghur general Ala-ud-din was known as 'Burner of the World'.

AD 52
St Thomas the Apostle thought to have arrived in Kerala to bring Christianity to India through his preaching. LYNN JOHNSON/GETTY IMAGES ©

319–510
The golden era of the Gupta dynasty, marked by a creative surge in literature and the arts.

In 1191 Mohammed of Ghur advanced into India. Although defeated in a major battle against a confederacy of Hindu rulers, he returned the following year and routed his enemies. One of his generals, Qutb ud-din Aibak, captured Delhi and was appointed governor; it was during his reign that the great Delhi landmark, the Qutb Minar complex, was built. A separate Islamic empire was established in Bengal and within a short time almost the whole of North India was under Muslim control.

The Best...
Mughal Sites

1 Taj Mahal (p98)

2 Fatehpur Sikri (p104)

3 Agra Fort (p97)

4 Red Fort (p60)

5 Humayun's tomb (p67)

North Meets South

Mohammed Tughlaq ascended the throne in 1324. In 1328 Tughlaq took the southern strongholds of the Hoysala empire. India was Tughlaq's for the taking. However, while the empire of the pre-Mughal Muslims would achieve its greatest extent under Tughlaq's rule, his overreaching ambition also sowed the seeds of its disintegration.

The last of the great sultans of Delhi, Firoz Shah, died in 1388, and the fate of the sultanate was sealed when Timur (Tamerlane) made a devastating raid from Samarkand (in Central Asia) into India in 1398.

After Tughlaq's withdrawal from the south, several splinter kingdoms arose. The two most significant were the Islamic Bahmani sultanate, and the Hindu Vijayanagar empire, founded in 1336 with its capital at Hampi. The battles between the two were among the bloodiest communal violence in Indian history and ultimately resolved nothing in the two centuries before the Mughals rose to power.

The Mughals

Even as Vijayanagar was experiencing its last days, the next great Indian empire was being founded. The Mughal empire was massive, at its height covering almost the entire subcontinent. Its significance, however, lay not only in its size. Mughal emperors presided over a golden age of arts and literature and had a passion for building that resulted in some of the finest architecture in India.

The founder of the Mughal line, Babur, marched into Punjab in 1525 from his capital at Kabul. With technological superiority brought by firearms, and consummate skill in simultaneously employing artillery and cavalry, Babur defeated the numerically superior armies of the sultan of Delhi at the Battle of Panipat in 1526.

4th to 9th centuries
The Pallavas, known for their temple architecture, enter the shifting landscape of southern power centres.

7th century
The new religion of Islam spreads to India through Arab merchants and traders visiting the Keralan coast.

1192
Prithviraj Chauhan loses Delhi to Mohammed of Ghur. The defeat effectively ends Hindu supremacy in the region.

Jehangir (r 1605–27) ascended to the throne following Emperor Akbar's death. Despite several challenges to the authority of Jehangir himself, the now-mammoth empire remained more or less intact. He was succeeded by his son, Shah Jahan (r 1627–58), who secured his position as emperor by executing all male relatives who stood in his way. During his reign, some of the most vivid and permanent reminders of the Mughals' glory were constructed, including the Taj Mahal and Delhi's Red Fort.

The last of the great Mughals, Aurangzeb (r 1658–1707), imprisoned his father (Shah Jahan) and succeeded to the throne after a two-year struggle against his brothers. Aurangzeb devoted his resources to extending the empire's boundaries, and thus fell into much the same trap as that of Mohammed Tughlaq some 300 years earlier. He, too, tried moving his capital south (to Aurangabad) and imposed heavy taxes to fund his military. A combination of decaying court life and dissatisfaction among the Hindu population at inflated taxes and religious intolerance weakened the Mughal grip.

The empire was also facing serious challenges from the Marathas in central India and, more significantly, the British in Bengal. With Aurangzeb's death in 1707, the empire's fortunes rapidly declined.

Taj Mahal (p98)

PETER ZELEI IMAGES/GETTY IMAGES ©

1325
Mohammed bin Tughlaq becomes sultan of Delhi, moves the capital to Daulatabad and creates forgery-prone currency.

1336
Foundation of the mighty Vijayanagar empire, named after its capital city, the ruins of which can be seen today close to Hampi.

1398
Timur (Tamerlane) invades Delhi with extreme violence, on the pretext that the Delhi sultans are too tolerant with their Hindu subjects.

The Rajputs & the Marathas

Throughout the Mughal period, there remained strong Hindu powers, most notably the Rajputs. Centred in Rajasthan, the Rajputs were a proud warrior caste with a passionate belief in the dictates of chivalry, both in battle and in state affairs. The Rajputs opposed every foreign incursion into their territory, but were never united or adequately organised to deal with stronger forces on a long-term basis. This eventually led to their territories becoming vassal states of the Mughal empire. Their prowess in battle, however, was acknowledged, and some of the best military men in the Mughal armies were Rajputs.

The Marathas were less swashbuckling but ultimately more effective. They gradually took over more of the weakening Mughal empire's powers, first by supplying troops and then actually taking control of Mughal land, but this expansion came to an abrupt halt in 1761 at Panipat, when they were defeated by Ahmad Shah Durani from Afghanistan.

The Rise of European Power

The British weren't the first European power to arrive in India, nor were they the last to leave – both of those 'honours' go to the Portuguese. In 1498 Vasco da Gama arrived on the coast of modern-day Kerala, having sailed around the Cape of Good Hope. Pioneering this route gave the Portuguese a century-long monopoly over Indian and far-eastern trade with Europe. In 1510 they captured Goa, which they controlled until 1961.

In 1600 Queen Elizabeth I granted a charter to a London trading company that gave it a monopoly on British trade with India. In 1613 representatives of the East India Company established their first trading post in northwest India.

By 1672 the French had established themselves at Pondicherry (now Puducherry), an enclave they held even after the British departed and where architectural traces of French elegance remain. But serious French aspirations effectively ended in 1750 when the directors of the French East India Company decided that their representatives were playing too much politics and doing too little trading. Key representatives were sacked, and a settlement designed to end all ongoing political disputes was made with the British. The decision effectively removed France as a serious influence on the subcontinent.

Britain's Surge to Power

The transformation of the British from traders to governors began almost by accident. Having been granted a licence to trade in Bengal by the Mughals, and following the establishment of a new trading post at Calcutta (now Kolkata) in 1690, business began to expand rapidly. Under the apprehensive gaze of the nawab (local ruler), British trading activities became extensive and the 'factories' took on an increasingly permanent (and fortified) appearance.

1498
Vasco da Gama, a Portuguese voyager, discovers the sea route from Europe to India.

1510
Portuguese forces capture Goa under the command of Alfonso de Albuquerque.

1526
Babur becomes the first Mughal emperor after conquering Delhi. He stuns Rajasthan by routing its confederate force.

Eventually the nawab decided that British power had grown large enough. In June 1756 he attacked Calcutta and, having taken the city, locked his British prisoners in a tiny cell. The space was so cramped and airless that many were dead by the following morning. The cell infamously became known as the 'Black Hole of Calcutta'.

Six months later, Robert Clive, an employee in the military service of the East India Company, led an expedition to retake Calcutta and entered into an agreement with one of the nawab's generals to overthrow the nawab himself. He did this in June 1757 at the Battle of Plassey (now called Palashi), and the general who had assisted him was placed on the throne.

The Best... Colonial-era Architecture

1 New Delhi (p67)

2 Kolkata (p302)

3 Old Goa (p207)

4 Mumbai (p118)

5 Puducherry (p282)

British India

By the early 19th century, India was effectively under British control, although there remained a patchwork of states who administered their own territories. However, a system of central government was developed. British bureaucratic models were replicated in the Indian government and civil service – a legacy that still exists.

Trade and profit continued to be the main focus of British rule in India, with far-reaching effects. Iron and coal mining were developed, and tea, coffee and cotton became key crops. A start was made on the vast rail network that's still in use today, irrigation projects were undertaken, and the zamindar (landowner) system was encouraged. These absentee landlords eased the burden of administration and tax collection for the British but contributed to the development of an impoverished and landless peasantry.

The Road to Independence

The desire among many Indians to be free from foreign rule remained. Opposition to the British increased at the turn of the 20th century, spearheaded by the Indian National Congress, the country's oldest political party.

It met for the first time in 1885 and soon began to push for participation in the government of India. A highly unpopular attempt by the British to partition Bengal in 1905 resulted in mass demonstrations and brought to light Hindu opposition to the division; the Muslim community formed its own league and campaigned for protected rights in any future political settlement.

1540
The Sur dynasty briefly captures Delhi from the Mughals, after Sher Shah Suri's Battle of Kanauj victory over Humayun.

1556
Hemu, a Hindu general in Adil Shah Suri's army, seizes Delhi after Humayun's death.

AMAR GROVER/GETTY IMAGES ©

With the outbreak of WWI, the political situation eased. India contributed hugely to the war (more than one million Indian volunteers were enlisted and sent overseas, suffering more than 100,000 casualties). The contribution was sanctioned by Congress leaders, largely with the expectation that it would be rewarded after the war. No such rewards transpired. Disturbances were particularly persistent in Punjab, and in April 1919, following riots in Amritsar, a British army contingent was sent to quell the unrest. Under direct orders of the officer in charge, they ruthlessly fired into a crowd of unarmed protesters. News of the massacre spread rapidly throughout India, turning huge numbers of otherwise apolitical Indians into Congress supporters.

At this time, the Congress movement found a new leader in Mohandas Gandhi. As political power-sharing began to look more likely, and the mass movement led by Gandhi gained momentum, the Muslim community's reaction was to consider its own immediate future. The large Muslim minority realised that an independent India would be dominated by Hindus and that, while Gandhi's approach was fair-minded, others in the Congress Party might not be so willing to share power. By the 1930s Muslims were raising the possibility of a separate Islamic state.

Humayun's tomb (p67)

1674
Shivaji establishes the Maratha kingdom, spanning western India and parts of the Deccan and North India.

1707
Death of Aurangzeb, the last of the Mughal greats. His demise triggers the gradual collapse of the Mughal empire.

1747
Afghan ruler Ahmad Shah Durani sweeps across northern India, capturing Lahore and Kashmir and sacking Delhi.

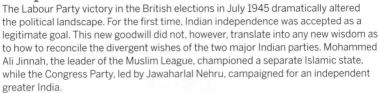

Independence & the Partition of India

The Labour Party victory in the British elections in July 1945 dramatically altered the political landscape. For the first time, Indian independence was accepted as a legitimate goal. This new goodwill did not, however, translate into any new wisdom as to how to reconcile the divergent wishes of the two major Indian parties. Mohammed Ali Jinnah, the leader of the Muslim League, championed a separate Islamic state, while the Congress Party, led by Jawaharlal Nehru, campaigned for an independent greater India.

In early 1946 a British mission failed to bring the two sides together, and the country slid closer towards civil war. In February 1947 the nervous British government made the momentous decision that independence would be effected by June 1948. In the meantime, the viceroy, Lord Wavell, was replaced by Lord Louis Mountbatten.

The new viceroy encouraged the rival factions to agree upon a united India, but to no avail. A decision was made to divide the country, with Gandhi the only staunch opponent. Faced with increasing civil violence, Mountbatten made the precipitous decision to bring forward Independence to 15 August 1947.

Dividing the country into separate Hindu and Muslim territories was immensely difficult; the dividing line proved almost impossible to draw. Some areas were clearly Hindu or Muslim, but others had evenly mixed populations, and there were 'islands' of communities in areas predominantly settled by other religions. Moreover, the two overwhelmingly Muslim regions were on opposite sides of the country and, therefore, Pakistan would inevitably have an eastern and western half, divided by India. The instability of this arrangement was self-evident, but it was 25 years before the split finally came and East Pakistan became Bangladesh.

The problem was worse in Punjab, where intercommunity antagonisms were already running at fever pitch. Punjab, one of the most fertile and affluent regions of the country, had large Muslim, Hindu and Sikh communities. The Sikhs had already campaigned unsuccessfully for their own state and now saw their homeland divided down the middle. The new border ran straight between Punjab's two major cities, Lahore and Amritsar.

Punjab contained all the ingredients for an epic disaster, but the resulting bloodshed was far worse than anticipated. Huge population exchanges took place. Trains full of Muslims, fleeing westward, were held up and slaughtered by Hindu and Sikh mobs. Hindus and Sikhs fleeing to the east suffered the same fate at Muslim hands. The army that was sent to maintain order proved inadequate and, at times, all too ready to join the sectarian carnage. By the time the Punjab chaos had run its course, more than 10 million people had changed sides and at least 500,000 had been killed.

India and Pakistan became sovereign nations under the British Commonwealth in August 1947 as planned, but the violence, migrations and the integration of a few states, especially Kashmir, continued. The Constitution of India was at last adopted

1757
The East India Company registers its first military victory on Indian soil in the Battle of Plassey.

1857
First War of Independence against the British; freedom fighters coerce the Mughal king to proclaim himself emperor of India.

1858
The British government assumes control over India, beginning the period known as the British Raj.

The Kashmir Conflict

Kashmir is the most enduring symbol of the turbulent partition of India. In the lead-up to Independence, local rulers were asked which country they wished to belong to. Kashmir was a predominantly Muslim state with a Hindu maharaja, Hari Singh, who tried to delay his decision. A ragtag Pashtun (Pakistani) army crossed the border, intent on annexing Kashmir for Pakistan, whereupon the maharaja panicked and requested armed assistance from India. The Indian army arrived only just in time to prevent the fall of Srinagar, and the maharaja signed the Instrument of Accession, tying Kashmir to India, in October 1947. The legality of the document was immediately contested by Pakistan, and the two nations went to war, just two months after Independence.

In 1948 the fledgling UN Security Council called for a referendum to decide the status of Kashmir. A UN-brokered ceasefire in 1949 kept the countries on either side of a demarcation line, called the Cease-Fire Line (later to become the Line of Control, or LOC), with little else resolved. Two-thirds of Kashmir fell on the Indian side of the LOC, which remains the frontier, but neither side accepts this as the official border.

in November 1949 and came into effect on 26 January 1950. After untold struggles, independent India had officially become a republic.

After Independence

Jawaharlal Nehru tried to steer India towards a policy of nonalignment, balancing cordial relations with Britain and Commonwealth membership with moves towards the former USSR. The latter was due partly to conflicts with China, and US support for its arch-enemy Pakistan.

The 1960s and 1970s were tumultuous times for India. A border war with China in what was then known as the North-East Frontier Area (NEFA; now the Northeast States) and Ladakh, resulted in the loss of Aksai Chin (Ladakh) and smaller NEFA areas. Wars with Pakistan in 1965 (over Kashmir) and 1971 (over Bangladesh) also contributed to a sense among many Indians of having enemies on all sides.

In the midst of it all, the hugely popular Nehru died in 1964 and his daughter Indira Gandhi (no relation to Mahatma Gandhi) was elected as prime minister in 1966. Indira Gandhi, like Nehru before her, loomed large over the country she governed. Unlike

1869
Suez Canal opens; journey from England reduced from three months to three weeks. Bombay's economic importance skyrockets.

1919
On 13 April, unarmed Indian protesters are massacred at Jallianwala Bagh in Amritsar (Punjab).

1947
India gains independence on 15 August. Pakistan is formed a day earlier. Partition is followed by mass cross-border exodus.

Nehru, however, she was always a profoundly controversial figure whose historical legacy remains hotly disputed.

In 1975, facing serious opposition and unrest, she declared a state of emergency (which later became known as the Emergency). Freed of parliamentary constraints, Gandhi was able to boost the economy, control inflation remarkably well and decisively increase efficiency. On the negative side, political opponents often found themselves in prison, India's judicial system was turned into a puppet theatre and the press was fettered.

Gandhi's government was bundled out of office in the 1977 elections, but the 1980 election brought Indira Gandhi back to power with a larger majority than ever before, firmly laying the foundation for the Nehru-Gandhi family dynasty that would continue to dominate Indian politics to the present day.

1948
Mahatma Gandhi is assassinated in New Delhi by Nathuram Godse on 30 January.

DARREN ROBB/GETTY IMAGES ©

26 January 1950
India becomes a republic. Date commemorates Declaration of Independence proposed by Congress in 1930.

Family Travel

Toys for sale at a village fair

SHIBU BHATTACHARJEE /GETTY IMAGES ©

Travel with children in India can be a delight, and warm welcomes are frequent. Locals will thrill at taking a photograph or two beside your bouncing baby and while this may prove disconcerting for some, remember that the attention your children will inevitably receive is almost always good natured. Kids are the centre of life in many Indian households, and your own will be treated just the same.

Food

India's fabulous food offerings are usually fresh, fragrant, colourful and healthy. The most common problem for families is trying to avoid overly spicy dishes. Safe bets for steering clear of chillies are steamed rice, plain *papad* (crispy chickpea-flour wafer), flat breads (such as naan, chapati or roti), Tibetan *momos* (dumplings) and south Indian specialities like dosa (paper-thin lentil-flour pancake), *idly* (spongy, round, fermented rice cake) and *vada* (doughnut-shaped deep-fried lentil savoury). Fresh fruit is widely available, as is plain yogurt (or curd) - great for cooling spicy mouths. Lassis (yogurt drinks) also go down very well with kids. Traveller-friendly restaurants and cafes usually do Western dishes too, meaning you're rarely too far from pasta and pizza.

Accommodation

India offers such an array of accommodation, from beach huts to five-star fantasies, that you're bound to find something that will appeal. Most places don't mind cramming several children into a regular-sized double room along with their parents. If your budget can stretch a bit, a good way to maintain familial energy levels is to mix in a few top-end stays.

Health

The availability of a decent standard of health care varies widely in India. Talk to your doctor about where you will be travelling to get advice on vaccinations and what to include in your first-aid kit. Access to health care is certainly better in traveller-frequented parts of the country where it's almost always easy to track down a doctor at short notice (most hotels will be able to recommend a reliable one). Prescriptions are quickly and cheaply filled over the counter at numerous pharmacies, often congregating near hospitals. Diarrhoea can be very serious in young children; rehydration is essential and seek medical help if it's persistent or accompanied by fever. Heat rash, skin complaints such as impetigo, insect bites or stings can be treated with the help of a well-equipped first aid kit.

The Best...
Adventures for Kids

1 Tiger Spotting

2 Trekking & Rafting

3 Camel Safaris

4 Elephant Rides

5 Beaches

Need to Know

Changing facilities Not usually available – take a portable changing mat and plenty of wipes.

Cots Bring the lightest fold-up baby bed you can find.

Health Bring a first-aid kit, plus insect repellent, sun lotion and – for those with younger children – nappy-rash (diaper-rash) cream. Calendula cream works well against heat rash, too.

Highchairs Available in some upmarket restaurants.

Kids' menus Found at occasional big-city restaurants, but otherwise there's plenty of cuisine to please all palates.

Nappies (diapers) Available in India, but relatively expensive and may not be your preferred brand.

Pushchairs (strollers) Forget them. Pavements, if they exist, are usually rough, making them a bane rather than a boon. Baby-carrier rucksacks are the way forward.

Transport Book seats in advance if possible, and pack diversions – books, music and movie-loaded iPads.

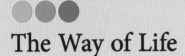

The Way of Life

Wedding ceremony

CHIRAG DAGLI / EYEEM / GETTY IMAGES ©

Spirituality is the common thread in the richly diverse tapestry that is India. And for travellers, one of the most enduring impressions of India is the way everyday life is intimately intertwined with the sacred.

Along with religion, family lies at the heart of society – for most Indians, the idea of being unmarried by their mid-30s is somewhat unpalatable. Despite the rising number of nuclear families – primarily in the larger, more cosmopolitan cities – the extended family remains a cornerstone in both urban and rural India, with males (usually the breadwinners) generally considered the head of the household.

Marriage, Birth & Death

Marriage is an exceptionally auspicious event for Indians and although 'love marriages' have spiralled upwards in recent times (mainly in urban hubs), most Hindu and many Muslim marriages are arranged.

Dowry, although illegal, is still a key issue in many arranged marriages, with some families plunging into debt to raise the required cash and gifts. Health workers claim that India's high rate of abortion of female foetuses (though sex-identification tests are banned in India, they still clandestinely occur in some clinics) is predominantly due to the financial burden of providing a daughter's dowry.

Divorce and remarriage is becoming more common (primarily in India's bigger cities), but divorce is still not granted by courts as a matter of routine and is generally not looked upon favourably by society.

The birth of a child, in Hindu-majority India, is another momentous occasion, with its own set of ceremonies taking place at various auspicious times – the child's first horoscope, name-giving, feeding the first solid food and the first hair-cutting.

Hindus and Sikhs cremate their dead, and funeral ceremonies are designed to purify and console both the living and the deceased. Muslims bury their dead.

The Best...
Places for Spiritual Fervour

1 Varanasi (p325)

2 Pushkar (p159)

3 Hazrat Nizam-ud-din Dargah, Delhi (p71)

4 McLeod Ganj (p371)

The Caste System

Although the Indian constitution does not recognise the caste system, it still wields considerable influence, especially in rural India, where your family's caste largely determines your social standing in the community, and can influence one's vocational and marriage prospects. Traditionally, caste is the basic social structure of Hindu society. Living a righteous life and fulfilling your dharma (moral duty) raises your chances of being re-born into a higher caste and thus into better circumstances. Hindus are born into one of four varnas (castes): Brahmin (priests and scholars), Kshatriya (soldiers), Vaishya (merchants) and Shudra (labourers).

Beneath the four main castes are the Dalits (once known as Untouchables), who hold menial jobs such as latrine cleaners. To improve the Dalits' position, the government reserves around 25% of government jobs and university places for them, though the situation varies regionally.

Women in India

Women in India are entitled to vote and own property. While the percentage of women in politics has risen over the past decade, they're still notably under-represented in the national parliament, accounting for around 10% of parliamentary members.

Professions are still male-dominated, but women are steadily making inroads, especially in urban centres.

For the urban middle-class woman, life is materially much more comfortable, but pressures still exist. Broadly speaking, she is far more likely to receive a tertiary education, but once married is still usually expected to 'fit in' with her in-laws and be a homemaker above all else. Like her village counterpart, if she fails to live up to expectations – even just not being able to produce a grandson – the consequences can sometimes be dire, as demonstrated by the extreme practice of 'bride burning', wherein a wife is doused with flammable liquid and set alight. Reliable statistics are unavailable, but some women's groups claim that for every reported case, roughly 300 go unreported, and that less than 10% of the reported cases are pursued through the legal system.

Following the highly publicised brutal gang rape (and subsequent death) of a 23-year-old Indian physiotherapy student in Delhi in December 2012, tens of thousands of people protested in the capital, and beyond, demanding swift government action to address the country's escalating gender-based violence. The government introduced harsher, but somewhat controversial punishments (including possible death penalty) for sex offenders. Despite such reforms, shocking cases occur with horrifying regularity. It's doubtless that violence against women is a pervasive problem in India.

Sport

Cutting across all echelons of society, cricket is more than just a national sporting obsession – it's a matter of enormous patriotism (especially evident when India plays Pakistan!). And travellers who show even the slightest interest in the game can expect to strike up passionate conversations with people of all types.

The most celebrated contemporary Indian cricketer is Sachin Tendulkar – fondly dubbed the 'Little Master' – who, in 2012, became the world's only player to score one hundred international centuries. He retired in 2014.

India's first recorded cricket match was in 1721, and it won its first Test series in 1952 in Chennai (Madras) against England. Today, cricket – especially the Twenty20 format (the jewel in its crown is the Indian Premier League, or IPL; www.iplt20.com) – is big business in India, attracting lucrative sponsorship deals and celebrity status for its players. The sport has not been without its murky side though, with IPL teams and Indian cricketers among those embroiled in match-fixing scandals over past years.

Internationals and IPL matches are played at various venues throughout the country – see Indian newspapers and/or cricket websites (www.espncricinfo.com is the best) for details about matches that coincide with your visit.

The launch of the Indian Super League (www.indiansuperleague.com) in 2013 has achieved its aim of promoting football (soccer) as a big name, big money sport. With games attracting huge crowds and international players, such as the legendary Juventus player Alessandro Del Piero (who was signed for the Delhi Dynamos in 2014), and Marco Materazzi (of World Cup headbutt fame) as trainer of Chennai, the ISL has become an international talking point.

Field hockey no longer enjoys the same fervent following it once did, though currently India's national men's/women's hockey world rankings are 9/13 respectively. Tap into India's hockey scene at Indian Hockey (www.indianhockey.com) and Indian Field Hockey (www.bharatiyahockey.org).

Hinduism

Statue of Vishnu, Rishikesh

Hinduism has no founder or central authority and it isn't a proselytising religion. Essentially, Hindus believe in Brahman, who is eternal, uncreated and infinite. Everything that exists emanates from Brahman and will ultimately return to it. The multitude of gods and goddesses – the Hindu pantheon is said to have a staggering 330 million deities – are merely manifestations; knowable aspects of this formless phenomenon. Brahman has three main representations, the Trimurti: Brahma, Vishnu and Shiva.

Brahman

The One; the ultimate reality. Brahman is formless, eternal and the source of all existence. Brahman is *nirguna* (without attributes), as opposed to all the other gods and goddesses, which are manifestations of Brahman and therefore *saguna* (with attributes).

Brahma

Only during the creation of the universe does Brahma play an active role. At other times he is in meditation. His consort is Saraswati, the goddess of learning, and his vehicle is a swan. He is sometimes shown sitting on a lotus that rises from Vishnu's navel, symbolising the interdependence of the gods. Brahma is generally depicted with four (crowned and bearded) heads, each turned towards a point of the compass.

Vishnu

The preserver or sustainer, Vishnu is associated with 'right action'. He protects and sustains all that is good in the world. He is usually depicted with four arms, holding a lotus, a conch shell (it can be blown like a trumpet so symbolises the cosmic vibration from which existence emanates), a discus and a mace. His consort is Lakshmi, the goddess of wealth, and his vehicle is Garuda, the man-bird creature. The Ganges is said to flow from his feet.

Shiva

Shiva is the destroyer – to deliver salvation – without whom creation couldn't occur. Shiva's creative role is phallically symbolised by his representation as the frequently worshipped lingam. With 1008 names, Shiva takes many forms, including Nataraja, lord of the *tandava* (cosmic victory dance), who paces out the creation and destruction of the cosmos.

Sometimes Shiva has snakes draped around his neck and is shown holding a trident (representative of the Trimurti) as a weapon while riding Nandi, his bull. Nandi symbolises power and potency, justice and moral order. Shiva's consort, Parvati, is capable of taking many forms.

The Best...
Hindu Temples

1 Meenakshi Amman Temple, Madurai (p288)

2 Kandariya-Mahadev Temple, Khajuraho (p338)

3 Kailasa Temple, Ellora (p135)

4 Vittala Temple, Hampi (p224)

5 Shore Temple, Mamallapurum (p278)

IN FOCUS HINDUISM

Other Prominent Hindu Deities

Elephant-headed **Ganesh** is the god of good fortune, remover of obstacles, and patron of scribes (the broken tusk he holds was used to write sections of the Mahabharata).

Krishna is an incarnation of Vishnu sent to earth to fight for good and combat evil. Depicted with blue-hued skin, Krishna is often seen playing the flute.

Hanuman is the hero of the Ramayana and loyal ally of Rama. He embodies the concept of bhakti (devotion). He's the king of the monkeys, but is capable of taking on other forms.

Among the Shaivite (followers of the Shiva movement), **Shakti**, the goddess as mother and creator, is worshipped as a force in her own right. The concept of *shakti* is embodied in the ancient goddess **Devi** (divine mother), who is also manifested as **Durga** and, in a fiercer evil-destroying incarnation, **Kali**.

Delicious India

Spices for sale, Goa

GREG ELMS / GETTY IMAGES ©

India's phenomenal culinary terrain – with its especially glorious patchwork of vegetarian cuisine – is not only intensely delectable, it's also richly steeped in history. From the flavoursome meaty preparations of the Mughals and Punjabis to the deep-sea delights of former southern colonies, Indian kitchens continue to whip up traditional favourites as part of a national cuisine that combines fresh local produce with an extraordinary amalgam of regional and global influences.

Land of Spices

Christopher Columbus was looking for the black pepper of Kerala's Malabar Coast when he stumbled upon America. The region still grows the world's finest pepper, and it's integral to most savoury Indian dishes. Turmeric and coriander seeds are other essentials, while most Indian 'wet' dishes begin with the crackle of cumin seeds in hot oil. The green cardamom of Kerala's Western Ghats scents and flavours savouries, desserts and chai (tea).

Rice Paradise

Rice is a staple, especially in South India. Long-grain white rice varieties are the most popular, served with just about any 'wet' cooked dish. Rice is often cooked up in a pilau (or pilaf; spiced rice dish) or biryani.

Flippin' Fantastic Bread

While rice is paramount in the south, wheat is the mainstay in the north. Roti, the generic term for Indian-style bread, is a name used interchangeably with chapati to describe the most common variety, the unleavened round bread made with whole-wheat flour.

Puri is deep-fried dough puffed up like a crispy balloon. Flaky, unleavened *paratha* can be eaten as is or jazzed up with fillings such as *paneer* (soft, unfermented cheese). The thick, teardrop-shaped *naan* is cooked in a tandoor.

Dhal-icious!

While the staple of preference divides north and south, the whole of India is melodiously united in its love for *dhal* (curried lentils or pulses). You may encounter up to 60 different pulses. Common varieties include: *channa,* a sweeter version of the yellow split pea; tiny yellow or green ovals called *moong* (mung beans); salmon-coloured *masoor* (red lentils); and the ochre-coloured southern favourite, *tuvar* (yellow lentils; also known as *arhar*).

Meaty Matters

Chicken, lamb and mutton (sometimes goat) are the mainstays; religious taboos make beef forbidden to devout Hindus and pork to Muslims.

In northern India you'll come across meat-dominated Mughlai cuisine, which includes rich curries, kebabs, koftas and biryanis.

Tandoori meat dishes are another North Indian favourite. The name is derived from the clay oven, or tandoor, in which the marinated meat is cooked.

The Best...
Dishes to Try

1 Masala dosa (curried-vegetables pancake), Chennai

2 Bhelpuri (fried dough with lentils and spices), Mumbai

3 Rasgulla (cream-cheese balls flavoured with rose-water), Kolkata

4 Paratha (stuffed bread), Delhi

5 Bebinca (coconut cake), Panaji, Goa

Street Food

Tucking into street food is one of the joys of travelling in India – here are some tips to help avoid tummy troubles:

o If the locals are avoiding a vendor, you should too.

o Unless a place is reputable (and busy), avoid eating meat from the street.

o Be wary of juice stalls. Fresh fruit juices are often mixed with tap water (not good for fragile foreign bellies).

o Likewise, don't be tempted by glistening pre-sliced fruit, which keeps its luscious veneer with the regular dousing of water.

Deep-Sea Delights

With around 7500km of coastline, it's no surprise that seafood is an important staple, especially from Mumbai (Bombay) down to Kerala. Kerala is the biggest fishing state, while Goa boasts particularly succulent prawns and fiery fish curries.

Fruit & Veg

Sabzi (vegetables) is a word recognised in every Indian vernacular. They're generally cooked *sukhi* (dry) or *tari* (in a sauce).

Potatoes are ubiquitous, often cooked with various masalas and other vegetables, or mashed and fried for *aloo tikki* (potato patties), or cooked with cauliflower to make *aloo gobi* (potato-and-cauliflower curry). Fresh green peas are stir-fried with other vegetables in pilaus and biryanis and in the magnificent *mattar paneer* (unfermented cheese and pea curry). *Baigan* (eggplant/aubergine) can be curried or sliced and deep-fried. Also popular is *saag* (a generic term for leafy greens), which can include mustard, spinach and fenugreek.

India's fruit basket is a bountiful one. Along the southern coast are super-luscious tropical fruits such as pineapples and papayas. Citrus fruits are widely grown, and mangoes abound during the summer months (especially April and May).

Feasting Indian-Style

Most people in India eat with their right hand – the left hand is reserved for unsanitary actions such as removing shoes. Before and after a meal, it's good manners to wash your hands.

Vegetarians & Vegans

India is king when it comes to vegetarian fare. However, there's little understanding of veganism (the term 'pure vegetarian' means without eggs), and animal products such as milk, butter, ghee and curd are included in most Indian dishes.

Dear Dairy

Dahi (curd/yogurt) is commonly served with meals and is great for subduing heat; *paneer* is a godsend for vegetarians; *lassi* is one in a host of sweet and savoury beverages; *ghee* is the traditional cooking medium; and some of the finest *mithai* (Indian sweets) are made with milk.

Sweet at Heart

India has an incredible kaleidoscope of *mithai* (sweets), usually sinfully sugary. The main categories are *barfi* (a fudgelike milk-based sweet), soft *halwa* (made with vegetables, cereals, lentils, nuts or fruit), *ladoos* (sweet balls made of gram flour and semolina), and those made from *chhana* (unpressed paneer) such as *rasgullas* (cream-cheese balls flavoured with rose water).

Architecture & the Arts

Ceiling painting, Meenakshi Amman Temple (p288)

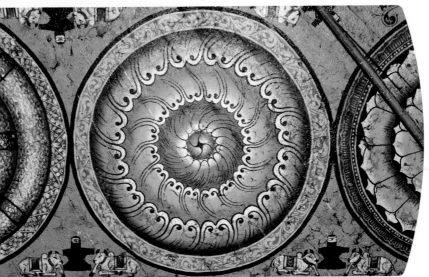

RELIGIOUS IMAGES / UIG / GETTY IMAGES ©

Over the centuries India's many ethnic and religious groups have spawned a vivid artistic heritage that is both inventive and spiritually significant. Today, artistic beauty lies around almost every corner, manifesting itself in everything from poetry and paintings to temples and tombs.

Music

Indian classical music traces its roots back to Vedic times, when religious poems chanted by priests were first collated in an anthology called the Rig-Veda. Over the millennia classical music has been shaped by many influences. The legacy today is Carnatic (characteristic of South India) and Hindustani (the classical style of North India) music.

Both styles use the raga (the melodic shape of the music) and *tala* (the rhythmic meter characterised by the number of beats); tintal, for example, has a *tala* of 16 beats. The audience follows the *tala* by clapping at the appropriate beat, which in tintal is at beats one, five and 13. There's no clap at the beat of nine; that's the *khali* (empty section), which is indicated by a wave of the hand. Both the raga and the *tala* are used as a basis for composition and improvisation.

Both Carnatic and Hindustani music are performed by small ensembles, generally comprising three to six musicians, and both have many instruments in common. The most striking difference, to the uninitiated, is Carnatic's greater use of voice.

Literature

Bengalis are credited with producing some of India's most celebrated literature, a movement often referred to as the Indian or Bengal Renaissance, which flourished from the 19th century with works by Bankim Chandra Chatterjee. But the man mostly credited with first propelling India's cultural richness onto the world stage is the Nobel Prize-winning poet Rabindranath Tagore.

India has an ever-growing list of internationally acclaimed contemporary authors. Particularly prominent writers include Vikram Seth, best known for his epic novel *A Suitable Boy*, and Amitav Ghosh, whose *Sea of Poppies* was shortlisted for the 2008 Man Booker Prize.

Indian-born Booker Prize winners include Salman Rushdie (*Midnight's Children*, 1981), Arundhati Roy (*The God of Small Things*, 1997), Kiran Desai (*The Inheritance of Loss*, 2006) and Aravind Adiga (*The White Tiger*, 2008).

Traditional Musical Instruments

One of the best-known Indian instruments is the **sitar** (large stringed instrument), with which the soloist plays the *raga*. Other stringed instruments include the **sarod** (which is plucked) and the **sarangi** (which is played with a bow).

Also popular is the **tabla** (twin drums), which provides the *tala*. The drone, which runs on two basic notes, is provided by the oboe-like **shehnai** or the stringed **tampura** (also spelt tamboura). The hand-pumped keyboard harmonium is used as a secondary melody instrument for vocal music.

Painting

Primitive cave paintings, thought to be around 12,000 years old, still survive in Bhimbetka, just outside the city of Bhopal. Fast forward to around 1500 years ago and artists were covering the walls and ceilings of the Ajanta caves in Maharashtra, not far from Mumbai, with scenes from the Buddha's past lives. The figures are endowed with an unusual freedom and grace, and contrast with other styles that later emerged from this part of India.

The 1526 victory by Babur at the Battle of Panipat ushered in the era of the Mughals in India. Although Babur and his son Humayun were both patrons of the arts, it's Humayun's son Akbar who is generally credited with developing the characteristic Mughal style. This painting style, often in colourful miniature form, largely depicts court life, architecture, battle and hunting scenes, as well as detailed portraits.

Various schools of miniature painting emerged in Rajasthan from around the 17th century. The subject matter ranged from royal processions to shikhar (hunting expeditions), with many artists influenced by Mughal styles.

By the 19th century, painting in North India was notably influenced by Western styles (especially English watercolours), giving rise to what has been dubbed the Company School, which had its centre in Delhi.

Religious Architecture

Complex rules govern the location, design and building of each Hindu temple, based on numerology, astrology, astronomy, religious principles and the concept of the square as a perfect shape. Essentially, a temple represents a map of the universe. At the centre is an unadorned space, the *garbhagriha* (inner sanctum), which is symbolic of the 'womb-cave' from which the universe is said to have emerged. This provides a residence for the deity to whom the temple is dedicated. Above the shrine rises a superstructure known as a *vimana* in South India, and a *sikhara* in North India.

From the outside, Jain temples can resemble Hindu ones, but inside they're often a riot of sculptural ornamentation, the very opposite of ascetic austerity. Meanwhile, gurdwaras (Sikh temples) can usually be identified by a *nishan sahib* (flagpole flying a triangular flag with the Sikh insignia). Amritsar's sublime Golden Temple is Sikhism's holiest shrine.

Stupas, which characterise Buddhist places of worship, essentially evolved from burial mounds. They served as repositories for relics of the Buddha and, later, other venerated souls.

India's Muslim rulers contributed their own architectural conventions, including arched cloisters and domes. The Mughals uniquely melded Persian, Indian and provincial styles. Examples include the tomb of Humayun in Delhi and Agra Fort. Emperor Shah Jahan was responsible for some of India's most spectacular architectural creations, most notably the milky-white Taj Mahal.

The Best...
Revered Buildings

1 Taj Mahal (p98)

2 Golden Temple, Amritsar (p378)

3 Meenakshi Amman Temple (p288)

4 Temples at Khajuraho (p336)

5 Kailasa Temple, Ellora (p135)

Landscape & Wildlife

Elephants, Corbett Tiger Reserve (p359)

HIRA PUNJABI / GETTY IMAGES

Vast and incredibly diverse, India's landscape encompasses everything from steamy jungles and tropical rainforest to arid deserts and immense Himalayan peaks. Such variety supports an extraordinary array of wildlife, including elephants, tigers, lions, monkeys, leopards, antelope, rhinos, crocodiles, many different species of reptiles and a kaleidoscopic quantity of birdlife.

The Land

At 3,287,263 sq km, India is the world's seventh-largest country. It forms the vast bulk of the South Asian subcontinent – an ancient block of earth crust that carried a wealth of unique plants and animals like a lifeboat across a prehistoric ocean before slamming into Asia about 40 million years ago.

Plants

Once upon a time India was almost entirely covered in forest; now the total forest cover is estimated to be around 22%. Despite widespread clearing of native habitats, the country still boasts 49,219 plant species, of which some 5200 are endemic. Species on the southern peninsula show Malaysian ancestry, while desert plants in Rajasthan are more clearly allied with the Middle East, and conifer forests of the Himalaya derive from European and Siberian origins.

Environmental Issues

With over a billion people, ever-expanding industrial and urban centres, and an expansive growth in chemical-intensive farming, India's environment is under tremendous threat. An estimated 65% of India's land is degraded in some way, and nearly all of that land is seriously degraded, with the government consistently falling short on most of its environmental protection goals due to lack of enforcement or will power.

Animals

Big sprawling India harbours some of the richest biodiversity in the world, with 397 species of mammals, 1250 bird species, 460 reptile species, 240 species of amphibians and 2546 kinds of fish – among the highest counts for any country in the world. Understandably, wildlife-watching has become one of the country's prime tourist activities and there are dozens of national parks and wildlife sanctuaries offering opportunities to spot rare and unusual creatures.

The Big Ones

Elephants (now classified as endangered despite being revered for centuries in Hindu custom) and rhinos (classified as vulnerable, and found mostly in the

The Best...
Wildlife & Birdwatching Experiences

1 Ranthambhore National Park (p163)

2 Kerala Backwaters (p248)

3 Periyar Wildlife Sanctuary (p250)

4 Sunderbans Tiger Reserve (p314)

5 Jaisalmer Camel Safaris (p186)

Project Tiger

When naturalist Jim Corbett first raised the alarm in the 1930s nobody believed that tigers would ever be threatened. At the time it was believed there were 40,000 tigers in India, although nobody had ever conducted a census. Then came Independence, which put guns into the hands of villagers who pushed into formerly off-limits hunting reserves to hunt for highly profitable tiger skins. By the time an official census was conducted in 1972, there were only 1800 tigers left and an international outcry prompted Indira Gandhi to make the tiger the national symbol of India and set up **Project Tiger** (http://projecttiger.nic.in). The project has since established 39 tiger reserves that aim to protect this top predator as well as all other animals that live in the same habitats. After an initial round of successes, tiger numbers in India plummeted from 3600 in 2002 to a low of 1400 in 2008 due to relentless poaching, although numbers are thought to have risen again to around 1700.

Tiger conservationist Valmik Thapar has analysed the perceived failure of Project Tiger, drawing attention to what he calls mismanagement by a forest bureaucracy that is largely not scientifically trained. He criticises the Ministry of Environment and Forests' unwillingness to curb poaching through armed patrols and its refusal to open forests to scholarly scientific enquiry.

northeastern state of Assam) are the two heavyweights of India's big game. Undoubtedly, though, the star of the show here is the tiger.

Also classified as endangered, wild tigers number around 3500 worldwide. Around half of these are found in India, with the population spread across three dozen tiger reserves spanning nine different states. Your chances of seeing a tiger are decent in some reserves; slim in others. In October 2012 a temporary ban on tiger tourism was lifted on the proviso that no more than 20% of each tiger reserve could be open to tourists.

Hoofed & Handed

By far the most abundant forms of wildlife you'll see in India are deer (nine species), antelope (six species), goats and sheep (10 species) and primates (15 species). In the open grasslands of many parks, look for the stocky nilgai, India's largest antelope, or elegantly horned blackbucks. If you're heading for the mountains, keep your eyes open in the Himalaya for blue sheep with their partially curled horns or the rare argali with its fully curled horns that can be found in Ladakh. The deserts of Rajasthan are home to desert-adapted species such as chinkaras (Indian gazelles).

India's primates range from the extremely rare hoolock gibbon and golden langur of the northeast, to species that are so common as to be a pest – most notably the stocky and aggressive rhesus macaque and the elegant grey langur.

Birds

With well over one thousand species of birds, India is a birdwatcher's dream. Winter can be a particularly good time because northern migrants arrive to kick back in the lush subtropical warmth of the Indian peninsula. In the breeding season look for colourful barbets, sunbirds, parakeets and magpies everywhere you travel.

Survival Guide

DIRECTORY   **414**

Accommodation   414

Customs Regulations   416

Climate   417

Electricity   416

Gay & Lesbian Travellers   416

Health   417

Insurance   420

Internet Access   421

Legal Matters   421

Money   422

Public Holidays   424

Safe Travel   425

Telephone   425

Time   427

Tourist Information   427

Travellers with Disabilities   427

Visas   428

TRANSPORT   **429**

Getting There & Away   429

Getting Around   429

LANGUAGE   **435**

Youth in New Delhi (p67)
CHANDAN KHANNA / AFP / GETTY IMAGES ©

A-Z

Directory

Book Your Stay Online

For more accommodation reviews by Lonely Planet authors, check out http://hotels.lonelyplanet.com. You'll find independent reviews, as well as recommendations on the best places to stay. Best of all, you can book online.

● ● ●
Accommodation

Accommodation in India ranges from backpacker dives with bucket showers to opulent palaces with plunge pools. We've listed reviews first by price range and then by author preference.

Categories

Budget (₹) covers everything from hostels, hotels and guesthouses in urban areas to traditional homestays in villages. Midrange hotels (₹₹) tend to offer extras such as cable/satellite TV and air-conditioning. Top-end places (₹₹₹) stretch from luxury five-star chains to gorgeous heritage palaces. Lonely Planet price indicators refer to the cost of a double room, including private bathroom, unless otherwise noted.

Costs

Given that the cost of budget, midrange and top-end hotels varies so much across India, it would be misleading for us to provide a 'national' price strategy. Most establishments raise tariffs annually, so prices may have risen by the time you read this. Prices are highest in large cities (eg Delhi, Mumbai), lowest in rural areas (eg Bihar, Andhra Pradesh). Costs are also seasonal – hotel prices can drop by 20% to 50% outside peak season.

Seasons

Rates given are full price in high season. High season usually coincides with the best weather for the area's sights and activities – normally spring and autumn in the mountains (March to May and September to November), and the cooler months in the plains (around November to mid-February).

In areas popular with foreign tourists, there's an additional peak period over Christmas and New Year; make reservations well in advance.

At other times you may find significant discounts; if the hotel seems quiet, ask for one.

Some hotels in places like Goa close during the monsoon period, or in hill stations such as Manali during winter.

Many temple towns have additional peak seasons around major festivals and pilgrimages.

Taxes & Service Charges

State governments slap a variety of taxes on hotel accommodation (except at the cheaper hotels), and these are added to the cost of your room.

Taxes vary from state to state. Even within a state prices can vary, with more expensive hotels levying higher taxes.

Many upmarket hotels also add an additional 'service charge' (usually around 10%).

Rates quoted in this book include taxes.

Some upscale restaurants may add a service charge (between 10% and 13%) on meals.

Sample Accommodation Costs

CATEGORY	MUMBAI	RAJASTHAN	SIKKIM
₹	<₹2500	<₹1000	<₹1500
₹₹	₹2500-6000	₹1000-5000	₹1500-4000
₹₹₹	>₹6000	>₹5000	>₹4000

Budget & Midrange Hotels

Sometimes you'll luck out and find these in atmospheric old houses or heritage buildings, but the majority of budget and midrange hotels are modern-style concrete blocks with varying degrees of comfort. Some are charming, clean and good value; others less so. Room quality can vary considerably within a hotel so try to inspect a few rooms first.

Shared bathrooms (often with squat toilets) are usually only found at the cheapest lodgings. Most rooms have ceiling fans and better rooms have electric mosquito killers and/or window nets, though cheaper rooms may lack windows altogether.

If you're mostly staying in budget places, bring your own sheet or sleeping-bag liner, towel and soap. Sheets and bedclothes at cheap hotels can be stained, worn and in need of a wash, and towels and toiletries are often not supplied.

An insect repellent and a torch (flashlight) are essential accessories in many budget hotels. Sound pollution can be irksome (especially in urban hubs); pack earplugs and request a room that doesn't face a busy road.

It's wise to keep your door locked at all times, as some staff (particularly in budget hotels) may knock and walk in without awaiting your permission. Blackouts are common (especially during summer and the monsoon) so double-check that the hotel has a back-up generator if you're paying for electric 'extras' such as air-conditioners, TVs and wi-fi.

A room with a TV generally guarantees a working power socket for charging your phone, ipad, etc.

Note that some hotels lock their doors at night. Members of staff might sleep in the lobby but waking them up can be a challenge. Let the hotel know in advance if you'll be arriving late at night or leaving early in the morning.

Away from tourist areas, cheaper hotels may not take foreigners because they don't have the necessary foreigner-registration forms.

Homestays & B&Bs

These family-run guesthouses will appeal to those seeking a small-scale, more homey setting with home-cooked meals.

Standards range from mud-and-stone village huts with hole-in-the-floor toilets to comfortable middle-class homes in cities.

In places like Ladakh, homestays are increasingly the way to go but standards are fairly simple.

Be aware that some hotels market themselves as 'homestays' but are actually run like hotels with little (or no) interaction with the family.

Contact the local tourist office for a full list of participating families.

Top-End & Heritage Hotels

India has plenty of top-end properties, from modern five-star chain hotels to glorious palaces, and luxury eco- and forest resorts.

Practicalities

○ **Newspapers & Magazines** English-language dailies include the *Hindustan Times*, *Times of India*, *Indian Express*, *Hindu*, *Statesman*, *Telegraph*, *Daily News & Analysis* (DNA) and *Economic Times*. Regional English-language and local-vernacular publications are found nationwide. Incisive current-affairs magazines include *Frontline*, *India Today*, *Week*, *Open*, *Tehelka*, *Outlook* and *Motherland*.

○ **Radio** Government-controlled All India Radio (AIR), India's national broadcaster, has over 220 stations broadcasting local and international news. Private FM channels broadcast music, current affairs, talkback and more.

○ **TV** The national (government) TV broadcaster is Doordarshan. More people watch satellite and cable TV; English-language channels include BBC, CNN, Star World, HBO, National Geographic and Discovery.

○ **Weights & Measures** Officially India is metric. Terms you're likely to hear are lakhs (one lakh = 100,000) and crores (one crore = 10 million).

You can browse members of the Indian Heritage Hotels Association on the tourist board website **Incredible India** (www.incredibleindia.org).

Customs Regulations

Technically you're supposed to declare any amount of cash over US$5000, or total amount of currency over US$10,000 on arrival.

Indian rupees shouldn't be taken out of India; however, this is rarely policed.

Officials very occasionally ask tourists to enter expensive items such as video cameras and laptop computers on a 'Tourist Baggage Re-export' form to ensure they're taken out of India at the time of departure.

Electricity

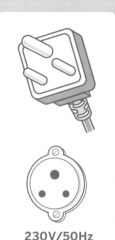

230V/50Hz

230V/50Hz

Gay & Lesbian Travellers

Homosexuality was made illegal in India in 2013, after having only been decriminalised since 2009. Gay and lesbian visitors should be discreet in this conservative country. Public displays of affection are frowned upon for both homosexual and and heterosexual couples.

Despite the ban, there are gay scenes (and Gay Pride marches) in a number of cities including Mumbai (Bombay), Delhi, Kolkata (Calcutta), Chennai (Madras) and Bengaluru (Bangalore), as well as a holiday gay scene in Goa.

Websites & Publications

Gaysi Zine (www.gaysifamily.com/) This is a thoughtful monthly magazine and website featuring gay writing and issues.

Gay Bombay (www.gaybombay.org) Lists gay events as well as offering support and advice.

Gay Delhi (www.gaydelhi.org) LGBT support group, also organises social events in Delhi.

Indian Dost (www.indiandost.com/gay.php) News and information including contact groups in India.

India Pink (www.indiapink.co.in) India's first 'gay travel boutique' founded by a well-known Indian fashion designer.

Queer Azaadi Mumbai (www.queerazaadi.wordpress.com) Mumbai's queer pride blog, with news.

Queer Ink (www.queer-ink.com) Online bookstore specialising in gay- and lesbian-interest books from the subcontinent.

Support Groups

Chennai Dost (www.chennai-dost.blogspot.com) Community space for stories and information; organises events, including parties, exhibitions, campaigns, film festivals and Chennai Rainbow Pride (June).

Humsafar Trust (☎ 022-26673800; www.humsafar.org; Old BMC Bldg, 1st fl, Nehru Rd, Vakola, Santa Cruz East) Gay and transgender support groups and advocacy. The drop-in centre hosts workshops and has a library – pick up a copy of LGBT magazine *Bombay Dost*.

Queer Campus Hyderabad (www.facebook.com/qcampushyd) Student-focused group holds weekly meetings and monthly events including carnival days and film festivals.

Wajood Society (www.wajoodsociety.com) Hyderabad queer-support group, involved in organising events such as Queer Pride (February).

Health

There is huge geographical variation in India, so environmental issues like heat, cold and altitude can cause health problems. Hygiene is generally poor in most regions so food and water-borne illnesses are fairly common. A number of insect-borne diseases are present, particularly in tropical areas. Medical care is basic in various areas (especially beyond the larger cities) so it's essential to be well prepared.

Pre-existing medical conditions and accidental injury (especially traffic accidents) account for most life-threatening problems. Becoming ill in some way, however, is common. Fortunately, most travellers'

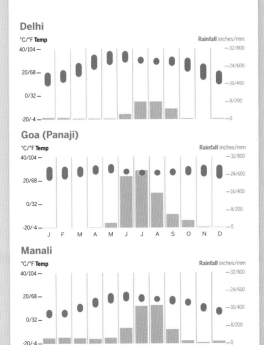

Climate

Delhi

Goa (Panaji)

Manali

illnesses can be prevented with some common-sense behaviour or treated with a well-stocked travellers' medical kit – however, never hesitate to consult a doctor while on the road, as self-diagnosis can be hazardous.

The following information is a general guide only and certainly does not replace the advice of a doctor trained in travel medicine.

Insurance

Don't travel without health insurance. Emergency evacuation is expensive. Consider the following when buying insurance:

○ You may require extra cover for adventure activities such as rock climbing and scuba diving.

○ In India, doctors usually require immediate payment in cash. Your insurance plan may make payments directly to providers or it will reimburse you later for overseas health expenditures. If you do have to

Eating Price Ranges

Prices in this book reflect the cost of a standard main meal (unless otherwise indicated). Reviews are listed by author preference within the following price categories.

₹ less than ₹100

₹₹ ₹100-300

₹₹₹ more than ₹300

417

Drinking Water

○ Never drink tap water.

○ Bottled water is generally safe – check the seal is intact at purchase.

○ Avoid ice unless you know it has been made hygienically.

○ Be careful of fresh juices served at street stalls in particular – they may have been watered down or may be served in unhygienic jugs or glasses.

○ Boiling water is usually the most efficient method of purifying it.

○ The best chemical purifier is iodine. It should not be used by pregnant women or those with thyroid problems.

○ Water filters should also filter out most viruses. Ensure your filter has a chemical barrier such as iodine and a small pore size (less than four microns).

claim later, make sure you keep all relevant documentation.

○ Some policies ask that you telephone back (reverse charges) to a centre in your home country where an immediate assessment of your problem will be made.

Medical Care

Medical care is hugely variable in India. Some cities now have clinics catering specifically to travellers and expatriates; these clinics are usually more expensive than local medical facilities, and offer a higher standard of care. Additionally, they know the local system, including reputable local hospitals and specialists. They may also liaise with insurance companies should you require evacuation. It is usually difficult to find reliable medical care in rural areas.

Self-treatment may be appropriate if your problem is minor (eg traveller's diarrhoea), you are carrying the relevant medication, and you cannot attend a recommended clinic. If you suspect a serious disease, especially malaria, travel to the nearest quality facility.

Before buying medication over the counter, check the use-by date and ensure the packet is sealed and properly stored (eg not exposed to the sunshine).

Infectious Diseases

Malaria

This is a serious and potentially deadly disease. Before you travel, seek expert advice according to your itinerary (rural areas are especially risky) and on medication and side effects.

Malaria is caused by a parasite transmitted by the bite of an infected mosquito.

The most important symptom of malaria is fever, but general symptoms, such as headache, diarrhoea, cough or chills, may also occur. Diagnosis can only be properly made by taking a blood sample.

Two strategies should be combined to prevent malaria: mosquito avoidance and antimalarial medications. Most people who catch malaria are taking inadequate or no antimalarial medication.

Travellers are advised to prevent mosquito bites by taking these steps:

○ Use a DEET-based insect repellent on exposed skin. Wash this off at night – as long as you are sleeping under a mosquito net. Natural repellents such as citronella can be effective, but must be applied more frequently than products containing DEET.

○ Sleep under a mosquito net impregnated with pyrethrin.

○ Choose accommodation with proper screens and fans (if not air-conditioned).

○ Impregnate clothing with pyrethrin in high-risk areas.

○ Wear long sleeves and trousers in light colours.

○ Use mosquito coils.

○ Spray your room with insect repellent before going out for your evening meal.

Other Diseases

Avian Flu 'Bird flu' or Influenza A (H5N1) is a subtype of the type A influenza virus. Contact with dead or sick birds is the principal source of infection and bird-to-human transmission does not easily occur. Symptoms include high fever and flu-like symptoms with rapid deterioration, leading to respiratory failure and death in many cases. Immediate medical care should be sought if bird flu is suspected. Check www.who.int/en/or www. avianinfluenza.com.au.

Dengue Fever This mosquito-borne disease is becoming increasingly problematic, especially in the cities. As there is no vaccine available it can only be prevented by avoiding mosquito bites at all times. Symptoms include high fever, severe headache and body ache and sometimes a rash and diarrhoea. Treatment is rest and paracetamol – do not take aspirin or ibuprofen as it increases the likelihood of haemorrhaging. Make sure you see a doctor to be diagnosed and monitored.

Hepatitis A This food- and water-borne virus infects the liver, causing jaundice (yellow skin and eyes), nausea and lethargy. There is no specific treatment for hepatitis A, you just need to allow time for the liver to heal. All travellers to India should be vaccinated against hepatitis A.

Hepatitis B This sexually transmitted disease is spread by body fluids and can be prevented by vaccination. The long-term consequences can include liver cancer and cirrhosis.

Hepatitis E Transmitted through contaminated food and water, hepatitis E has similar symptoms to hepatitis A, but is far less common. It is a severe problem in pregnant women and can result in the death of both mother and baby. There is no commercially available vaccine, and prevention is by following safe eating and drinking guidelines.

Other Hazards

Traveller's Diarrhoea This is by far the most common problem affecting travellers in India. Treatment consists of staying well hydrated; rehydration solutions like Gastrolyte are the best for this. Antibiotics such as

Vaccinations

The only vaccine required by international regulations is yellow fever. Proof of vaccination will only be required if you have visited a country in the yellow-fever zone within the six days prior to entering India.

The World Health Organization (WHO) recommends the following vaccinations for travellers going to India (as well as being up to date with measles, mumps and rubella vaccinations):

Adult diphtheria & tetanus Single booster recommended if none in the previous 10 years. Side effects include sore arm and fever.

Hepatitis A Provides almost 100% protection for up to a year; a booster after 12 months provides at least another 20 years' protection. Mild side effects such as headache and sore arm occur in 5% to 10% of people.

Hepatitis B Now considered routine for most travellers. Given as three shots over six months. A rapid schedule is also available, as is a combined vaccination with Hepatitis A. Side effects are mild and uncommon, usually headache and sore arm. In 95% of people lifetime protection results.

Polio Only one booster is required as an adult for lifetime protection. Inactivated polio vaccine is safe during pregnancy.

Typhoid Recommended for all travellers to India, even those only visiting urban areas. The vaccine offers around 70% protection, lasts for two to three years and comes as a single shot. Tablets are also available, but the injection is usually recommended as it has fewer side effects. Sore arm and fever may occur.

Varicella If you haven't had chickenpox, discuss this vaccination with your doctor.

ciprofloxacin or azithromycin should kill the bacteria quickly. Seek medical attention quickly if you do not respond to an appropriate antibiotic. Loperamide is just a 'stopper' and doesn't get to the cause of the problem. It can be helpful, though (eg if you have to go on a long bus ride). Don't take loperamide if you have a fever or blood in your stools.

Giardiasis Giardia is a parasite that is relatively common in travellers. Symptoms include nausea, bloating, excess gas, fatigue and intermittent diarrhoea. The parasite will eventually go away if left untreated but this can take months; the best advice is to seek medical treatment. The treatment of choice is tinidazole, with metronidazole being a second-line option.

Food Dining out brings with it the possibility of contracting diarrhoea. Ways to help avoid food-related illness:

o eat only freshly cooked food

o avoid shellfish and buffets

o peel fruit

o cook vegetables

o soak salads in iodine water for at least 20 minutes

o eat in busy restaurants with a high turnover of customers

Heat Many parts of India, especially down south, are hot and humid throughout the year. For most visitors it takes around two weeks to comfortably adapt to the hot climate. Swelling of the feet and ankles is common, as are muscle cramps caused by excessive sweating. Prevent these by avoiding dehydration and excessive activity in the heat. Don't eat salt tablets (they aggravate the gut); drinking rehydration solution or eating salty food helps. Treat cramps by resting, rehydrating with double-strength rehydration solution and gently stretching.

Dehydration This is the main contributor to heat exhaustion. Recovery is usually rapid and it is common to feel weak for some days afterwards. Symptoms include:

o feeling weak

o headache

o irritability

o nausea or vomiting

o sweaty skin

o a fast, weak pulse

o normal or slightly elevated body temperature.

Treatment:

o get out of the heat

o fan the sufferer

o apply cool, wet cloths to the skin

o lay the sufferer flat with their legs raised

o rehydrate with water containing one-quarter teaspoon of salt per litre.

Heat stroke This is a serious medical emergency. Symptoms include:

o weakness

o nausea

o a hot dry body

o temperature of over 41°C

o dizziness

o confusion

o loss of coordination

o seizures

o eventual collapse.

Treatment:

o get out of the heat

o fan the sufferer

o apply cool, wet cloths to the skin or ice to the body, especially to the groin and armpits.

Prickly heat is a common skin rash in the tropics, caused by sweat trapped under the skin. Treat it by moving out of the heat for a few hours and by having cool showers. Creams and ointments clog the skin so they should be avoided. Locally bought prickly-heat powder can be helpful.

Insurance

o Comprehensive travel insurance to cover theft, loss and medical problems (as well as air evacuation) is strongly recommended.

o Some policies exclude potentially dangerous activities such as scuba diving, skiing, motorcycling, paragliding and even trekking: read the fine print.

o Some trekking agents may only accept customers who have cover for emergency helicopter evacuation.

o If you plan to hire a motorcycle in India, make sure the rental policy includes at least third-party insurance.

o Check in advance whether your insurance policy will pay doctors and hospitals directly or reimburse you later (keep all documentation for your claim).

◦ It's crucial to get a police report in India if you've had anything stolen; insurance companies may refuse to reimburse you without one.

◦ Worldwide travel insurance is available at www.lonelyplanet.com/bookings. You can buy, extend and claim online anytime – even if you're already on the road.

●●● Internet Access

Internet cafes are widespread and connections are usually reasonably fast, except in more remote areas. Wi-fi access is widely available; it's usually free but some places charge.

Practicalities

◦ Internet charges vary regionally; charges range from ₹15 to ₹100 per hour; often with a 15- to 30-minute minimum.

◦ Bandwidth load tends to be lowest in the early morning and early afternoon.

◦ Some internet cafes may ask to see your passport.

Security

Using online banking on any nonsecure system is unwise. If you have no choice but to do this, it's wise to change all passwords (email, netbanking, credit card 3-D Secure code etc) when you get back home.

Laptops

The simplest way to connect to the internet, when away from a wi-fi connection, is to use your smartphone as a personal wi-fi hotspot (use a local SIM to avoid roaming charges). However, if this isn't an option, companies that offer prepaid wireless 2G/3G modem sticks (called dongles) include Reliance, Airtel, Tata Docomo and Vodafone. To organise a connection you have to submit your identity proof and address in India, and activation can take up to 24 hours. A nonrefundable activation fee (around ₹2000) has to be paid, which includes the price of the dongle and around 10GB of data. A 20GB recharge costs around ₹1000.

◦ Make sure the areas you will be travelling to are covered by your service provider.

◦ Consider purchasing a fuse-protected universal AC adaptor to protect your circuit board from power surges.

◦ Plug adaptors are widely available throughout India, but bring spare plug fuses from home.

●●● Legal Matters

If you're in a sticky legal situation, contact your embassy immediately. However, be aware that all your embassy may be able to do is monitor your treatment in custody and arrange a lawyer. In the Indian justice system, the

Prohibited Exports

To protect India's cultural heritage, the export of certain antiques is prohibited, especially those which are verifiably more than 100 years old. Reputable antique dealers know the laws and can make arrangements for an export-clearance certificate for old items that are OK to export. Detailed information on prohibited items can be found on the government webpage www.asi.nic.in/pdf_data/8.pdf. The rules may seem stringent but the loss of ancient artworks in places such as Ladakh, Himachal Pradesh, Gujarat and Rajasthan, due to the international trade in antiques, has been alarming. Look for quality reproductions instead.

The Indian Wildlife Protection Act bans any form of wildlife trade. Don't buy any product that endangers threatened species and habitats – doing so can result in heavy fines and even imprisonment. This includes ivory, shahtoosh shawls (made from the down of chirus or rare Tibetan antelopes) and anything made from the fur, skin, horns or shell of any endangered species. Products made from certain rare plants are also banned.

burden of proof can often be on the accused and stints in prison before trial are not unheard of.

Antisocial Behaviour

o Smoking in public places is illegal but this is rarely enforced; if caught you'll be fined ₹200, which could rise to ₹20,000 if proposed changes go ahead.

o People can smoke inside their homes and in most open spaces such as streets (heed any signs stating otherwise).

o Some Indian cities have banned spitting and littering, but this is also enforced irregularly.

Drugs

o Indian law does not distinguish between 'hard' and 'soft' drugs; possession of any illegal drug is regarded as a criminal offence, which will result in a custodial sentence. This may be up to a year for possession of a small amount for personal use, to a minimum of 10 years if it's deemed the purpose was for sale or distribution. There's also usually a hefty fine on top of any sentence.

o Cases can take months, even years, to appear before a court while the accused may have to wait in prison.

o Be aware that travellers have been targeted in sting operations in Manali, Goa and other backpacker enclaves.

o Marijuana grows wild in various parts of India, but consuming it is still an offence, except in towns where bhang is legally sold for religious rituals.

o Police are getting particularly tough on foreigners who use drugs, so you should take this risk very seriously.

o Pharmacutical drugs that are restricted in other countries may be available over the counter or via prescription. Be aware that to take these without professional guidance can be dangerous.

Police

You should always carry your passport; police are entitled to ask you for identification at any time.

If you're arrested for an alleged offence and asked for a bribe, be aware that it is illegal to pay a bribe in India. Many people deal with an on-the-spot fine by just paying it to avoid trumped-up charges. Corruption is rife so the less you have to do with local police the better; try to avoid all potentially risky situations.

●●● Money

The Indian rupee (₹) is divided into 100 paise, but only 50 paise coins are legal tender and these are rarely seen. Coins come in denominations of ₹1, ₹2, ₹5 and ₹10 (the 1s and 2s look almost identical); notes come in ₹5, ₹10, ₹20, ₹50, ₹100, ₹500 and ₹1000 (the last is handy for paying large bills but can pose problems when getting change for small services). The Indian rupee is linked to a basket of currencies and has been subject to fluctuations in recent years.

ATMs

o ATMs are found in most urban centres.

o Visa, MasterCard, Cirrus, Maestro and Plus are the most commonly accepted cards.

o ATMs at Axis Bank, Citibank, HDFC, HSBC, ICICI and State Bank of India recognise foreign cards. Other banks may accept major cards (Visa, MasterCard etc).

o Citibank ATMs generally allow you to withdraw up to ₹40,000 in one transaction (most others have a limit of ₹10,000 to ₹15,000), which reduces transaction charges.

o Before your trip, check whether your card can access banking networks in India and ask for details of charges.

o Notify your bank that you'll be using your card in India to avoid having it blocked; take along your bank's phone number in case.

o Always keep the emergency lost-and-stolen numbers for your credit cards in a safe place, separate from your cards, and report any loss or theft immediately.

o Away from major towns, always carry cash (including a stock of rupees).

Black Market

Black-market moneychangers exist but legal moneychangers are so common that there's no reason to use illegal services, except perhaps to change small amounts of cash at land border crossings. If someone approaches you on the street and offers to change money, you're probably being set up for a scam.

Cash

o Major currencies such as US dollars, pounds sterling and euros are easy to change throughout India, although some bank branches insist on travellers cheques only.

o Some banks also accept other currencies such as Australian and Canadian dollars, and Swiss francs.

o Private moneychangers deal with a wider range of currencies, but Pakistani, Nepali and Bangladeshi currency can be harder to change away from the border.

o When travelling off the beaten track, always carry an adequate stock of rupees.

o Whenever changing money, check every note. Don't accept any filthy, ripped or disintegrating notes, as these may be difficult to use.

o It can be tough getting change in India so keep a stock of smaller currency; ₹10, ₹20 and ₹50 notes are helpful.

o Officially you cannot take rupees out of India, but this is laxly enforced. You can change any leftover rupees back into foreign currency most easily at the airport (some banks have a ₹1000 minimum). You may have to present encashment certificates or credit-card/ATM receipts, and show your passport and airline ticket.

Credit Cards

o Credit cards are accepted at a growing number of shops, upmarket restaurants, and midrange and top-end hotels, and they can usually be used to pay for flights and train tickets.

o Cash advances on major credit cards are also possible at some banks.

o MasterCard and Visa are the most widely accepted cards.

Encashment Certificates

o Indian law states that all foreign currency must be changed at official moneychangers or banks.

o For every (official) foreign-exchange transaction, you'll receive an encashment certificate (receipt), which will allow you to change rupees back into foreign currency when departing India.

o Encashment certificates should cover the amount of rupees you intend to change back to foreign currency.

o Printed receipts from ATMs are also accepted as evidence of an international transaction at most banks.

International Transfers

If you run out of money, some-one back home can wire you cash via moneychangers affili-ated with **Moneygram** (www.moneygram.com) or **Western Union** (www.westernunion.com). A fee is added to the transaction.

To collect the cash, bring your passport and the name and reference number of the person who sent the funds.

Moneychangers

Private moneychangers are usually open for longer hours than banks and are found almost everywhere (many also double as internet cafes and travel agents).

Upmarket hotels may also change money, but their rates are usually not as competitive.

Tipping, Baksheesh & Bargaining

o In tourist restaurants or hotels, a service fee is usually added to your bill and tipping is optional. Elsewhere, a tip is appreciated.

o Hotel bellboys and train/airport porters appreciate anything around ₹50; hotel staff should be given similar gratuities for services above and beyond the call of duty.

o It's not mandatory to tip taxi or rickshaw drivers, but it's good to tip drivers who are honest about the fare.

o If you hire a car with driver for more than a couple of days, a tip is recommended for good service.

o Baksheesh can loosely be defined as a 'tip'; it covers everything from alms for beggars to bribes.

o Many Indians implore tourists not to hand out sweets, pens or money to children, as it encourages them to beg. To make a lasting difference, donate to a reputable school or charitable organisation.

o Except in fixed-price shops (such as government emporiums and fair-trade cooperatives), bargaining is the norm.

Travellers Cheques

o Travellers cheques are becoming harder and harder to change, as credit cards become more widely accepted. They are often more hassle than they are worth.

o All major brands are accepted, but some banks may only accept cheques from American Express (Amex) and Thomas Cook.

o Euros, pounds sterling and US dollars are the safest currencies, especially in smaller towns.

o Keep a record of the cheques' serial numbers separate from your cheques, along with the proof-of-purchase slips, encashment certificates and photocopied passport details. If you lose your cheques, contact the Amex or Thomas Cook office in Delhi.

o To replace lost travellers cheques, you need the proof-of-purchase slip and the numbers of the missing cheques (some places require a photocopy of the police report and a passport photo). If you don't have the numbers of your missing cheques, the issuing company (eg Amex) will contact the place where you bought them.

Public Holidays

There are three official national public holidays – Republic and Independence Days and Gandhi's birthday (Gandhi Jayanti) – plus a lot of other holidays celebrated nationally or locally, many of them marking important days in various religions and falling on variable dates. The most important are the 18 'gazetted holidays' (listed) which are observed by central-government offices through-out India. On these days most businesses (offices, shops etc), banks and tourist sites close, but transport is usually unaffected. It's wise to make transport and hotel reservations well in advance if you intend visiting during major festivals.

Republic Day 26 January

Holi March

Ram Navami March/April

Mahavir Jayanti March/April

Good Friday March/April

Dr BL Ambedkar's Birthday 14 April

Buddha Jayanti May

Eid al-Fitr June/July

Independence Day 15 August

Janmastami August/September

Eid al-Adha September

Dussehra September/October

Gandhi Jayanti 2 October

Muharram October

Diwali October/November

Guru Nanak Jayanti November

Eid-Milad-un-Nabi December

Christmas Day 25 December

Opening Hours

We've only listed business hours where they differ from the following standards. Minor post offices tend to open shorter hours than major ones Monday to Saturday, and not at all on Sunday.

BUSINESS	OPENING HOURS
Airline offices	9.30am-5.30pm Mon-Sat
Nationalised banks	10am-2pm or 4pm Mon-Fri, to noon or 1pm Sat
Government offices	9.30am-1pm & 2-5.30pm Mon-Fri
Post offices	9am-8pm Mon-Sat, 10am-4pm Sun
Museums	10am-5pm Tue-Sun
Restaurants	lunch noon-3pm, dinner 7-10pm or 11pm
Sights	10am-5pm or dawn-dusk
Shops	10am-7pm or 8pm, some closed Sun

Safe Travel

Travellers to India's major cities may fall prey to petty and opportunistic crime, but most problems can be avoided with a bit of common sense and an appropriate amount of caution. Also have a look at the India branch of Lonely Planet's Thorn Tree forum (www.lonelyplanet.com/thorntree), where travellers often post timely warnings about problems they've encountered on the road. Always check your government's travel advisory warnings.

Female Solo Travellers

The following tips will help women avoid uncomfortable or dangerous situations during their journey:

○ Always be aware of your surroundings. If it feels wrong, trust your instincts. Tread with care. Don't be scared, but don't be reckless either.

○ Try always to have a plan of where you're going and what's next. If you haven't, look as if you do.

○ If travelling after 9pm, use a recommended, registered taxi service.

○ Don't organise your travel in such a way that means you're hanging out at bus/train stations or arriving late at night. Arrive in towns before dark.

○ After a time of being in the country, you may start to feel safer and relax your guard. Don't stress, but maintain your vigilance.

Warning: Bhang Lassi

Although it's rarely printed in menus, some restaurants in popular tourist centres will clandestinely whip up bhang lassi, a yoghurt and iced-water beverage laced with cannabis (and occasionally other narcotics). Commonly dubbed 'special lassi', this often potent concoction can cause varying degrees of ecstasy, drawn-out delirium, hallucination, nausea and paranoia. Some travellers have been ill for several days, robbed or hurt in accidents after drinking this fickle brew. A few towns have legal (controlled) bhang outlets such as the Bhang Shop in Jaisalmer.

○ Keep conversations with unknown men short – getting involved in an inane conversation with someone you barely know can be misinterpreted as a sign of sexual interest.

○ Some women wear a pseudo wedding ring, or announce early on in the conversation that they're married or engaged (regardless of the reality).

○ If you feel that a guy is encroaching on your space, he probably is. A firm request to keep away usually does the trick, especially if your tone is loud and curt enough to draw the attention of passers-by.

○ Follow local women's cues and instead of shaking hands say namaste – the traditional, respectful Hindu greeting.

○ Check the reputation of any teacher or therapist before going to a solo session (get recommendations from travellers). Some women have reported being molested by masseurs and other therapists. If you feel uneasy at any time, leave.

○ At hotels keep your door locked, as staff (particularly at budget and midrange places) can knock and walk in without waiting for your permission.

○ Avoid wandering alone in isolated areas even during daylight. Steer clear of *galis* (narrow lanes) and deserted roads.

○ When taking rickshaws alone, call/text someone, or pretend to, to indicate someone knows where you are.

○ Act confidently in public; to avoid looking lost (and thus more vulnerable) consult maps at your hotel (or at a restaurant) rather than on the street.

Telephone

○ There are few payphones in India (apart from in airports), but private STD/ISD/PCO call booths do the same job, offering inexpensive local, interstate and international calls at lower prices than calls made from hotel rooms.

- These booths are found around the country. A digital meter displays how much the call is costing and usually provides a printed receipt when the call is finished.

- Costs vary depending on the operator and destination but can be from ₹1 per minute for local calls and between ₹5 and ₹10 for international calls.

- Some booths also offer a 'call-back' service – you ring home, provide the phone number of the booth and wait for people at home to call you back, for a fee of around ₹20 on top of the cost of the preliminary call.

- Getting a line can be difficult in remote country and mountain areas – an engaged signal may just mean that the exchange is overloaded or broken, so keep trying.

- Useful online resources include the **Yellow Pages** (www.yellowpages.co.in) and **Justdial** (www.justdial.com).

Mobile Phones

- Indian mobile-phone numbers usually have 10 digits, mostly beginning with 9 (but sometimes also with 7 or 8).

- There's roaming coverage for international GSM phones in most cities and large towns.

- To avoid expensive roaming costs (often highest for incoming calls), get hooked up to the local mobile-phone network by applying for a local prepaid SIM card.

- Mobiles bought in some countries may be locked to a particular network; you'll have to get the phone unlocked or buy a local phone (available from ₹2000) to use an Indian SIM card.

Getting Connected

- Getting connected is inexpensive and fairly straightforward in many areas. It's easiest to obtain a local SIM card when you arrive if you're flying into a large city.

- Foreigners must supply between one and five passport photos, and photocopies of their passport identity and visa pages. Often mobile shops can arrange all this for you, or you can ask your hotel to help you. It's best to try to do this in tourist centres and cities, as in many regions – for example, Tamil Nadu, Andhra Pradesh and most of Himachal Pradesh – it's a great deal more difficult.

- You must also supply a residential address, which can be the address of your hotel. Usually the phone company will call your hotel (warn the hotel a call will come through) any time up to 24 hours after your application to verify that you are staying there. It's a good idea to obtain the SIM card somewhere where you're staying for a day or two so that you can return to the vendor if there's any problem. Only obtain your SIM card from a reputable branded phone store to avoid scams.

- Another option is to get a friendly local to obtain a connection in their name.

- Prepaid mobile phone kits (SIM card and phone number, plus an allocation of calls) are available in most towns for about ₹200 from a phone shop, local STD/ISD/PCO booth or grocery store.

- SIMs are sold as regular size, but most places have

Government Travel Advice

The following government websites offer travel advice and information on current hotspots:

Australian Department of Foreign Affairs (www.smarttraveller.gov.au)

British Foreign Office (www.gov.uk/fco)

Canadian Department of Foreign Affairs (www.voyage.gc.ca)

German Foreign Office (www.auswaertiges-amt.de)

Japan Ministry of Foreign Affairs (www.mofa.go.jp)

Netherlands Ministry of Foreign Affairs (www.government.nl)

Swiss Department of Foreign Affairs (www.eda.admin.ch)

US State Department (www.travel.state.gov)

Important Numbers

Country code	91
International access code	🕿00
Ambulance	🕿102
Fire	🕿101
Police	🕿100

machines to cut them down to the required size if necessary.

○ You must then purchase more credit, sold as direct credit. You pay the vendor and the credit is deposited straight into your account, minus some taxes and a service charge.

Charges

○ Calls made within the state or city where you bought the SIM card are less than ₹1 a minute. You can call internationally for less than ₹10 a minute.

○ SMS messaging is even cheaper. International outgoing messages cost ₹5. Incoming calls and messages are free.

○ Unreliable signals and problems with international texting (messages or replies not coming through or being delayed) are not uncommon.

○ The leading service providers are Airtel, Vodafone, Reliance, Idea and BSNL. Coverage varies from region to region – Airtel has wide coverage, for example, but BSNL is the only network that works in remote Himachal areas.

Phone Codes

○ Calling India from abroad: dial your country's international access code, then 🕿91 (India's country code), then the area code (without the initial zero), then the local number. For mobile phones, the area code and initial zero are not required.

○ Calling internationally from India: dial 🕿00 (the international access code), then the country code of the country you're calling, then the area code (without the initial zero) and the local number.

○ Landline numbers have an area code followed by up to eight digits.

○ Toll-free numbers begin with 🕿1800.

○ To make interstate calls to a mobile phone, add 0 before the 10-digit number.

○ To call a land phone from a mobile phone, you always have to add the area code (with the initial zero).

○ Some call-centre numbers might require the initial zero (eg calling an airline ticketing service based in Delhi from Karnataka).

○ A Home Country Direct service, which gives you access to the international operator in your home country, exists for the US (🕿000 117) and the UK (🕿000 4417).

○ To access an international operator elsewhere, dial 🕿000 127. The operator can place an international call and allow you to make collect calls.

Time

India uses the 12-hour clock and the local standard time is known as Indian Standard Time (IST). IST is 5½ hours ahead of GMT/UTC. The half-hour was added to maximise daylight hours over such a vast country.

Tourist Information

In addition to Government of India tourist offices (also known as 'India Tourism'), each state maintains its own network of tourist offices. These vary in their efficiency and usefulness – some are run by enthusiastic souls who go out of their way to help, others are little more than a means of drumming up business for State Tourism Development Corporation tours.

The first stop for information should be the tourism website of the Government of India, **Incredible India** (www.incredibleindia.org); for details of its regional offices around India, click on the 'Help Desk' tab at the top of the homepage.

Travellers with Disabilities

India's crowded public transport, crush of humanity and variable infrastructure can test even the hardiest able-bodied traveller. If you have a physical disability or are vision impaired, these can pose even more of a challenge. If your mobility is considerably restricted, you may like to ease the stress by travelling with an able-bodied companion.

Accommodation Wheelchair-friendly hotels are almost exclusively top-end. Make enquiries before travelling and book ground-floor rooms at hotels that lack adequate facilities.

Accessibility Some restaurants and offices have ramps but most tend to have at least one step. Staircases are often steep; lifts frequently stop at mezzanines between floors.

Footpaths Where pavements exist, they can be riddled with holes, littered with debris and packed with pedestrians. If using crutches, bring along spare rubber caps.

Transport Hiring a car with driver will make moving around a lot easier; if you use a wheelchair, make sure the car-hire company can provide an appropriate vehicle.

For further advice pertaining to your specific requirements, consult your doctor before heading to India.

The following organisations may proffer further information:

Accessible Journeys (www.disabilitytravel.com)

Access-Able Travel Source (www.access-able.com)

Global Access News (www.globalaccessnews.com)

Mobility International USA (www.miusa.org)

Visas

Visa on Arrival

Citizens of Australia, Brazil, Cambodia, Cook Islands, Djibouti, Fiji, Finland, Germany, Guyana, Indonesia, Israel, Japan, Jordan, Kenya, Kiribati, Laos, Luxembourg, Marshall Islands, Mauritius, Mexico, Micronesia, Myanmar, Nauru, New Zealand, Niue Island, Norway, Oman, Palau, Palestine, Papua New Guinea, Philippines, Republic of Korea, Russia, Samoa, Singapore, Solomon Islands,Thailand, Tonga, Tuvalu, UAE, Ukraine, USA, Vanuatu and Vietnam are currently granted a 30-day single-entry visa on arrival (VOA) at Bengaluru (Bangalore), Chennai (Madras), Kochi, Delhi, Goa, Hyderabad, Kolkata (Calcutta), Mumbai (Bombay) and Thiruvananthapuram (Trivandrum) airports.

However, to participate in the scheme, you need to apply online at www.indianvisaonline.gov.in for an Electronic Travel Authority (ETA), a minimum of four and a maximum of 30 days before you are due to travel. The fee is US$60, and you have to upload a photograph as well as a copy of your passport. Travellers have reported being asked for documentation showing their hotel confirmation at the airport, though this is not specified on the VOA website. The VOA is valid from the date of arrival.

It's intended that the scheme will be rolled out to 180 nations, including the UK and China, so check online for any updates.

Other Visas

If you want to stay longer than 30 days, or are not covered by the VOA scheme, you must get a visa before arriving in India (apart from Nepali or Bhutanese citizens). Visas are available at Indian missions worldwide, though in many countries, applications are processed by a separate private company. In some countries, including the UK, you must apply in person at the designated office as well as filing an application online.

Note that your passport needs to be valid for at least six months beyond your intended stay in India, with at least two blank pages. Most people are issued with a standard six-month tourist visa, which for most nationalities permits multiple entry.

Transport

contact your country's representative. Keep photocopies of your airline ticket and the identity and visa pages of your passport in case of emergency. Better yet, scan and email copies to yourself. Check with the Indian embassy in your home country for any special conditions that may exist for your nationality.

Airports

India has six main gateways for international flights; Bengaluru (Bangalore), Chennai (Madras), Delhi, Hyderabad, Kolkota (Calcutta) and Mumbai (Bombay). A number of other cities such as Goa, Kochi (Cochin), Lucknow and Thiruvananthapuram (Trivandrum) also service international carriers. For detailed information, see www.aai.aero.

Getting There & Away

Plenty of international airlines service India, and overland routes to and from Nepal, Bangladesh, Bhutan and Pakistan are all currently open. Flights, tours and other tickets can be booked online at www.lonelyplanet.com/bookings.

Entering India

Entering India by air or land is relatively straightforward, with standard immigration and customs procedures.

Passport

To enter India you need a valid passport and an onward/return ticket. You'll also need a visa, which some nationalities can now obtain on arrival. Other nationalities or those wishing to stay more than 30 days need to get their visa beforehand. See the Visa section for details. Your passport should be valid for at least six months beyond your intended stay in India. If your passport is lost or stolen, immediately

Getting Around

 Air

Airlines in India

Transporting vast numbers of passengers annually, India has a very competitive domestic airline industry. Major carriers are Air India, IndiGo, Spice Jet and Jet Airways.

At the time of writing, the following airlines were operating across various destinations in India. Keep in mind that fares fluctuate dramatically, affected by holidays, festivals and seasons.

Climate Change & Travel

Every form of transport that relies on carbon-based fuel generates CO_2, the main cause of human-induced climate change. Modern travel is dependent on aeroplanes, which might use less fuel per kilometre per person than most cars but travel much greater distances. The altitude at which aircraft emit gases (including CO_2) and particles also contributes to their climate change impact. Many websites offer 'carbon calculators' that allow people to estimate the carbon emissions generated by their journey and, for those who wish to do so, to offset the impact of the greenhouse gases emitted with contributions to portfolios of climate-friendly initiatives throughout the world. Lonely Planet offsets the carbon footprint of all staff and author travel.

The recommended check-in time for domestic flights is two hours before departure (allow for peak-hour congestions when travelling to the airport) – the deadline is 45 minutes. The usual baggage allowance is 20kg (10kg for smaller aircraft) in economy class.

Air India (☎ 1800-1801407; www.airindia.com) India's national carrier operates many domestic and international flights.

GoAir (☎ 020-2566-2111; www.goair.in) Reliable low-cost carrier servicing Goa, Kochi,

Jaipur, Delhi and Bagdogra, among other destinations.

IndiGo (☎ 099-10383838; www.goindigo.in) Reliable and popular, with myriad flights across India and to select overseas destinations.

Jet Airways (☎ 1800-225522; www.jetairways.com) Operates flights across India and to select overseas destinations.

Spice Jet (☎ 098-71803333; www.spicejet.com) Domestic and some regional flights.

 Bus

Buses go almost everywhere in India and are the only way to get around many mountainous areas. They tend to be the cheapest way to travel. Services are fast and frequent.

Roads in mountainous or curvy terrain can be perilous; buses are often driven with wilful abandon, and accidents are always a risk.

Avoid night buses unless there's no alternative: driving conditions are more hazardous and drivers may be inebriated or overtired.

All buses make snack and toilet stops (some more frequently than others), providing a break but possibly adding hours to journey times.

Classes

State-owned and private bus companies both offer several types of buses, graded loosely as 'ordinary', 'semi-deluxe', 'deluxe' or 'super deluxe'. These are usually open to interpretation, and the exact grade of luxury offered in a particular class varies.

In general, ordinary buses tend to be ageing rattletraps while the deluxe grades range from less decrepit versions of ordinary buses to flashy Volvo buses with air-con and reclining (locally called 'push-back') two-by-two seating.

Buses run by the state government are usually more reliable (if there's a breakdown, another bus will be sent to pick up passengers), and seats can usually be booked up to a month in advance. Many state governments now operate super-deluxe buses.

Private buses are either more expensive (but more comfortable), or cheaper but with kamikaze drivers and intense overcrowding.

Travel agencies in many tourist towns offer relatively expensive private two-by-two buses, which tend to leave and terminate at conveniently central stops.

Costs

The cheapest buses are 'ordinary' government buses, but prices vary from state to state.

Add around 50% to the ordinary fare for deluxe services, double the fare for air-conditioning, and triple or quadruple the fare for a two-by-two super-deluxe service.

Rajasthan Roadways offer discounts for female travellers.

Luggage

Luggage is stored in compartments underneath the bus (sometimes for a small fee) or carried on the roof.

Arrive at least an hour before departure time – some buses cover roof-stored bags with a canvas sheet, making last-minute additions inconvenient/impossible.

If your bags go on the roof, make sure they're securely locked, and tied to the metal baggage rack – unsecured bags can fall off on rough roads.

Theft is a (minor) risk: watch your bags at snack and toilet stops. Never leave day-packs or valuables unattended inside the bus.

Reservations

Most deluxe buses can be booked in advance – government buses up to a month ahead – at the bus station or local travel agencies.

Online bookings are now possible in many states including the Punjab, Karnataka and Rajasthan, or at the excellent portals **Cleartrip** (www.cleartrip.com), **Makemytrip** (www.makemytrip.com), and **Redbus** (www.redbus.in).

Reservations are rarely possible on 'ordinary' buses; travellers can be left behind in the mad rush for a seat.

 Car

Few people bother with self-drive car hire – not only because of the hair-raising driving conditions, but also because hiring a car with driver is potentially affordable in India, particularly if several people share the cost. **Hertz** (www.hertz.com) is one of the few international companies with representatives in India.

Hiring a Car & Driver

Most towns have taxi stands or car-hire companies where you can arrange short or long tours.

Not all hire cars are licensed to travel beyond their home state. Those that are will pay extra state taxes, which are added to the hire charge.

Ask for a driver who speaks some English and knows the region you intend visiting. Try to see the car and meet the driver before paying anything.

A wide range of cars now ply as taxis. From a proletarian Tata Indica hatchback to a comfy Toyota Innova SUV, there's a model to suit every pocket.

Hire charges for multiday trips cover the driver's meals and accommodation, and drivers should make their own sleeping and eating arrangements.

It's essential to set the ground rules from day one: politely but firmly let the driver know that you're boss to avoid difficulties later.

Costs

Car hire costs depend on the distance and the terrain (driving on mountain roads uses more petrol, hence the higher cost).

One-way trips usually cost the same as return ones (to cover the petrol and driver charges for getting back).

Hire charges vary from state to state. Some taxi unions set a maximum time limit or a maximum kilometre distance for day trips – if you go over, you'll have to pay extra. Prices also vary according to the make and model of the taxi.

To avoid misunderstandings, get *in writing* what you've been promised (quotes should include petrol, sightseeing stops, all your chosen destinations, and meals and accommodation for the driver). If a driver asks you for money for petrol en route because he is short of cash, get receipts for reimbursement later. If you're travelling by the kilometre, check the odometer reading before you set out so as to avoid confusions later.

For sightseeing day trips around a single city, expect to pay upwards of ₹1000/1200 for a non-aircon/air-con car with an eight-hour, 80km limit per day (extra charges apply for longer trips). For multiday trips, operators usually peg a 250km minimum running distance per day and charge around ₹8/10 per km for a non-air-con/air-con car, for anything over this.

A tip is customary at the end of your journey; at least ₹150 to ₹200 per day is fair.

Local Transport

Buses, cycle-rickshaws, autorickshaws, taxis, boats and urban trains provide transport around India's cities. Costs for public transport vary from town to town.

For any transport without a fixed fare, agree on the price *before* you start your journey and make sure that it covers your luggage and every passenger.

Even where meters exist, drivers may refuse to use them, demanding an elevated 'fixed' fare. Insist on the meter; if that fails, find another vehicle. Or just bargain hard.

Fares usually increase at night (by up to 100%) and some drivers charge a few rupees extra for luggage.

Carry plenty of small bills for taxi and rickshaw fares as drivers rarely have change.

In some places, taxi/autorickshaw drivers are involved in the commission racket.

Autorickshaw, Tempo & Vikram

Similar to the tuk-tuks of Southeast Asia, the Indian autorickshaw is a three-wheeled motorised contraption with a tin or canvas roof and sides, with room for two passengers (although you'll often see many more squeezed in) and limited luggage.

They are also referred to as autos, scooters and riks.

Manning the Meter

Getting a metered ride is only half the battle. Meters are almost always outdated, so fares are calculated using a combination of the meter reading and a complicated 'fare adjustment card'. Predictably, this system is open to abuse. To get a rough estimate of fares in advance, try the portal www.taxiautofare.com.

Autorickshaws are mostly cheaper than taxis and usually have a meter, although getting it turned on can be a challenge.

Travelling by auto is great fun but, thanks to the open windows, can be noisy and hot (or severely cold!).

Tempos and *vikrams* (large tempos) are outsized autorickshaws with room for more passengers, shuttling on fixed routes for a fixed fare.

In country areas, you may also see the fearsome-looking 'three-wheeler' – a crude tractor-like tempo with a front wheel on an articulated arm – or the Magic, a cute minivan that can take in up to a dozen passengers.

Cycle-Rickshaw

A cycle-rickshaw is a pedal cycle with two rear wheels, supporting a bench seat for passengers. Most have a canopy that can be raised in wet weather or lowered to provide extra space for luggage.

Fares must be agreed upon in advance – speak to locals to get an idea of what is a fair price for the distance you intend to travel.

Kolkata is the last bastion of the hand-pulled rickshaw, known as the *tana* rickshaw. This is a hand-cart on two wheels pulled directly by the rickshaw-wallah.

Taxi

Most towns have taxis, and these are usually metered, however, getting drivers to use the meter can be a hassle. To avoid fare-setting shenanigans, use prepaid taxis where possible. Radio cars are the most efficient option in the larger cities.

Prepaid Taxis & Radio Cabs

Most major Indian airports and train stations now incorporate prepaid-taxi and radio-cab booths. Here, you can book a taxi for a fixed price (which will include baggage) and thus avoid commission scams. Hold onto your receipt until you reach your destination, as proof of payment.

Radio cabs cost marginally more than prepaid taxis, but are air-conditioned and manned by the company's chauffeurs. Cabs have electronic, receipt-generating fare meters and are fitted with GPS units, so the company can monitor the vehicle's movement around town. These minimise chances of errant driving or unreasonable demands for extra cash by the driver afterward.

Smaller airports and stations may have prepaid autorickshaw booths instead.

Tours

Tours are available all over India, run by tourist offices, local transport companies and travel agencies. Organised tours can be an inexpensive way to see several places on one trip, although you rarely get much time at each place. If you arrange a tailor-made tour, you'll have more freedom about where you go and how long you stay.

Drivers may double as guides, or you can hire a qualified local guide for a fee. In tourist towns, be wary of touts claiming to be professional guides.

International Tour Agencies

Many international companies offer tours to India, from straightforward sightseeing trips to adventure tours and activity-based holidays. To find current tours that match your interests, quiz travel agents and surf the web. Some good places to start your tour hunt:

Dragoman (www.dragoman.com) One of several reputable overland tour companies offering trips on customised vehicles.

Exodus (www.exodus.co.uk) A wide array of specialist trips, including tours with a holistic, wildlife and adventure focus.

India Wildlife Tours (www.india-wildlife-tours.com) All sorts of wildlife tours, plus jeep/horse/camel safaris and birdwatching.

Indian Encounter (www.indianencounters.com) Special-interest tours that include wildlife spotting, river-rafting and ayurvedic treatments.

Intrepid Travel (www.intrepidtravel.com) Endless possibilities from wildlife tours to sacred rambles.

Peregrine Adventures (www.peregrineadventures.com) Popular cultural and trekking tours.

Sacred India Tours (www.sacredindiatours.com) Includes tours with a holistic focus such as yoga and ayurveda, as well as architectural and cultural tours.

Shanti Travel (www.shanti travel.com/en) A range of tours including family and adventure tours, run by a Franco-Indian team.

World Expeditions (www. worldexpeditions.com) An array of options that includes trekking and cycling tours.

Train

Travelling by train is a quintessential Indian experience. Trains offer a smoother ride than buses and are especially recommended for long journeys that include overnight travel. India's rail network is one of the largest and busiest in the world and Indian Railways is the largest utility employer on earth, with roughly 1.5 million workers. There are around 6900 train stations scattered across the country.

We've listed useful trains but there are hundreds more. The best way of sourcing updated railway information is to use relevant internet sites such as **Indian Railways** (www.indianrail.gov.in) and the excellent **India Rail Info** (www.indiarailinfo.com), with added offline browsing support, as well as the user-friendly **Erail** (www.erail.in). There's also *Trains at a Glance* (₹45), available at many train station bookstands and better bookshops/newsstands. It's published annually so it's not as up to date as websites, but it offers comprehensive timetables covering all the main lines.

Booking Tickets in India

You can either book tickets through a travel agency or hotel (for a commission), or in person at the train station. You can also book online through **IRCTC** (www.irctc. co.in), the e-ticketing division of Indian Railways, or portals such as **Cleartrip** (www. cleartrip.com), **Make My Trip** (www.makemytrip.com) and **Yatra** (www.yatra.com). Remember, however, that online booking of train tickets has its share of glitches: travellers have reported problems with registering themselves on some portals and using certain overseas credit cards. Big stations often have English-speaking staff who can help with reservations. At smaller stations, the stationmaster and his deputy usually speak English. It's also worth approaching tourist-office staff if you need advice.

At the Station

Get a reservation slip from the information window, fill in the name of the departure station, destination station, the class you want to travel and the name and number of the train. Join the long queue for the ticket window where your ticket will be printed. Women should take advantage of the separate women's queue – if there isn't one, go to the front of the regular queue.

Tourist Reservation Bureau

Larger cities and major tourist centres have an International Tourist Bureau, which allows you to book tickets in relative peace – check www.indianrail. gov.in for a list of these stations.

Fare Finder

Go to www. indiarailinfo.com or www.erail.in and type in the name of the two destinations. You'll promptly get a list of every train (with the name, number, arrival/ departure times and journey details) plying the route, as well as fares for each available class.

Reservations

Bookings open up to 60 days before departure and you must make a reservation for chair-car, sleeper, 1AC, 2AC and 3AC carriages. No reservations are required for general (2nd class) compartments; you have to grab seats here the moment the train pulls in.

Trains are always busy so it's wise to book as far in advance as possible, especially for overnight journeys. There may be additional services to certain destinations during major festivals but it's still worth booking well in advance.

Reserved tickets show your seat/berth and carriage number. Carriage numbers are written on the side of the train (station staff and porters can point you in the right direction). A list of names and berths is posted on the side of each reserved carriage.

Refunds are available on any ticket, even after departure, with a penalty – rules are complicated, check when you book.

Trains can be delayed at any stage of the journey; to avoid stress, factor some leeway into your plans.

Be mindful of potential drugging and theft; a padlock and chain are useful for securing your baggage to luggage racks for longer journeys.

If the train you want to travel on is sold out, enquire about other options.

Tourist Quota

A special (albeit small) tourist quota is set aside for foreign tourists travelling between popular stations. These seats can only be booked at dedicated reservation offices in major cities, and you need to show your passport and visa as ID. Tickets can be paid for in rupees (some offices may ask to see foreign exchange certificates – ATM receipts will suffice).

Tatkal Tickets

Indian Railways holds back a small number of tickets on key trains and releases them at 10am one day before the train is due to depart. A charge of ₹10 to ₹400 is added to each ticket price. First AC tickets are excluded from the scheme.

Reservation Against Cancellation (RAC)

Even when a train is fully booked, Indian Railways sells a handful of seats in each class as 'Reservation Against Cancellation' (RAC). This means that if you have an RAC ticket and someone cancels before the departure date, you will get his or her seat (or berth). You'll have to check the reservation list at the station on the day of travel to see if you've been allocated a confirmed seat/berth. Even if no one cancels, you can still board the train as an RAC ticket holder and travel without a seat.

Waitlist (WL)

If the RAC quota is maxed out as well, you will be handed a waitlisted ticket (marked WL). This means that if there are enough cancellations, you may eventually move up the order to land a confirmed berth, or at least an RAC seat. Check your booking status at www.indianrail.gov.in/pnr_Enq.html by entering your ticket's PNR number. You can't board the train on a waitlisted ticket, but a refund is available – ask the ticket office about your chances.

Costs

Fares are calculated by distance and class of travel; Rajdhani and Shatabdi trains are slightly more expensive, but the price includes meals. Most air-conditioned carriages have a catering service (meals are brought to your seat). In unreserved classes it's a good idea to carry portable snacks. Male/female seniors (those over 60/58) get 40/50% off all fares in all classes on all types of train. Children below the age of six travel free, those aged between six and 12 are charged half price, up to 300km.

Language

HINDI

Hindi has about 180 million speakers in India, and it has official status along with English and 21 other languages.

If you read our pronunciation guides as if they were English, you'll be understood. The length of vowels is important (eg 'a' and 'aa'), and 'ng' after a vowel indicates nasalisation (ie the vowel is pronounced 'through the nose'). The stressed syllables are marked with italics. The abbreviations 'm' and 'f' indicate the options for male and female speakers respectively.

Basics

Hello./Goodbye.
नमस्ते ।   na·ma·*ste*
Yes.
जी हाँ ।   jee haang
No.
जी नहीश्व ।   jee na·*heeng*
Excuse me.
सुनिये ।   su·ni·*ye*
Sorry.
माफ़ कीजिये ।   maaf *kee*·ji·ye
Please ...
कृपया ...   kri·pa·*yaa* ...
Thank you.
थैश्वक्यू ।   *thayn*·kyoo
How are you?
आप कैसे/कैसी   aap *kay*·se/*kay*·see
हैश्व?   hayng (m/f)
Fine. And you?
मैश्व ठीक हूँ ।   mayng teek hoong
आप सुनाइये ।   aap su·*naa*·i·ye
Do you speak English?
क्या आपको अश्वग्रेज़ी   kyaa aap ko an·*gre*·zee
आती है?   *aa*·tee hay
How much is this?
कितने का है?   *kit*·ne kaa hay

I don't understand.
मैश्व नहीश्व समझा/   mayng na·*heeng* sam·jaa/
समझी ।   *sam*·jee (m/f)

Accommodation

Do you have a single/double room?
क्या सिश्वगल/डबल   kyaa *sin*·gal/da·*bal*
कमरा है?   *kam*·raa hay
How much is it (per night/per person)?
(एक रात/हर व्यक्ति)   (ek raat/har *vyak*·ti)
के लिय कितने   ke li·*ye kit*·ne
पैसे लगते हैश्व?   *pay*·se *lag*·te hayng

Eating & Drinking

I'd like ..., please.
मुझे ... दीजिये ।   mu·*je* ... *dee*·ji·ye
That was delicious.
बहुत मज़ेदार हुआ ।   ba·*hut* ma·ze·*daar* hu·*aa*
Please bring the menu/bill.
मेन्यू/बिल लाइये ।   men·yoo/bil *laa*·i·ye

I don't eat ...
मैश्व ... नहीश्व   mayng ... na·*heeng*
खाता/खाती ।   *kaa*·taa/*kaa*·tee (m/f)
  fish   मछली   *mach*·lee
  meat   गोश्त   gosht
  poultry   मुर्गी   *mur*·gee

Emergencies

I'm ill.
मैश्व बीमार हूँ ।   mayng *bee*·maar hoong
Help!
मदद कीजिये!   ma·*dad kee*·ji·ye
Call the doctor/police!
डॉक्टर/पुलिस   *daak*·tar/pu·*lis*
को बुलाओ!   ko bu·*laa*·o

Directions

Where's a/the ...?
... कहाँ है?   ... ka·*haang* hay
  bank
  बैश्वक   baynk
  market
  बाज़ार   *baa*·zaar
  post office
  डाक ख़ाना   daak *kaa*·naa
  restaurant
  रेस्टोरेश्वट   *res*·to·rent
  toilet
  टॉइलेट   *taa*·i·let
  tourist office
  पर्यटन ऑफ़िस   *par*·ya·tan *aa*·fis

TAMIL

Tamil is the official language in the state of Tamil Nadu and one of the major languages of South India, with about 62 million speakers.

Note that in our pronunciation guides, the symbol 'aw' is pronounced as in 'law' while 'ow' is pronounced as in 'how'.

Basics

Hello.
வணக்கம். va·*nak*·kam

Goodbye.
போய் வருகிறேன். *po*·i va·*ru*·ki·reyn

Yes./No.
ஆமாம்./இல்லை. *aa*·maam/*il*·lai

Excuse me.
தயவு செய்து. ta·ya·*vu* sei·*du*

Sorry.
மன்னிக்கவும. *man*·nik·ka·vum

Please ...
தயவு செய்து ... ta·ya·*vu* chey·*tu* ...

Thank you.
நன்றி. *nan*·dri

How are you?
நீங்கள் நலமா? *neeng*·kal na·*la*·maa

Fine, thanks. And you?
நலம், நன்றி. na·*lam nan*·dri
நீங்கள்? *neeng*·kal

Do you speak English?
நீங்கள் ஆங்கிலம் *neeng*·kal *aang*·ki·lam
பேசுவீர்களா? *pey*·chu·*veer*·ka·la

How much is this?
இது என்ன வீலை? i·*tu en*·na vi·*lai*

I don't understand.
எனக்கு e·*nak*·ku
விளங்கவில்லை. vi·*lang*·ka·vil·*lai*

Accommodation

Do you have a single/double room?
உங்களிடம் ஓர் *ung*·ka·li·tam awr
தன/இரட்டை ta·*ni*/i·*rat*·tai
அறை உள்ளதா? a·*rai* ul·la·taa

How much is it per night/person?
ஓர் இரவுக்கு/ awr i·ra·*vuk*·ku/
ஒருவருக்கு o·ru·va·*ruk*·ku
என்னவிலை? *en*·na·vi·lai

Eating & Drinking

I'd like the ..., please.
எனக்கு தயவு e·*nak*·ku ta·ya·vu
செய்து ... chey·*tu* ...
கொடுங்கள். ko·*tung*·kal

bill வீலைச்சீட்டு vi·*laich*·cheet·tu
menu உணவுப்– u·na·*vup*·
பட்டியல் pat·ti·yal

I'm allergic to ...
எனக்கு ... உணவு e·*nak*·ku ... u·na·vu
சேராது. chey·raa·tu

dairy பால் paal
products சார்ந்த *chaarn*·ta
meat இறைச்சி i·*raich*·chi
stock வகை va·*kai*
nuts பருப்பு வகை pa·*rup*·pu va·*kai*
seafood கடல் ka·tal
சார்ந்த *chaarn*·ta

Emergencies

Help!
உதவு! u·ta·*vi*

Call a doctor!
ஐ அழைக்கவும் i a·*zai*·ka·vum
ஒரு மருத்துவர்! o·*ru* ma·*rut*·tu·var

Call the police!
ஐ அழைக்கவும் i a·*zai*·ka·vum
போலீஸ்! pow·*lees*

Directions

Where's a/the ...?
... எங்கே ... *eng*·key
இருக்கிறது? i·*ruk*·ki·ra·tu

bank
வங்கி *vang*·ki

market
சந்தை *chan*·tai

post office
தபால் நிலையம் ta·*paal* ni·*lai*·yam

restaurant
உணவகம u·na·va·*kam*

toilet
கழிவறை ka·*zi*·va·rai

tourist office
சுற்றுப்பயண chut·*rup*·pa·ya·na
அலுவலகம் a·lu·va·la·*kam*

To enhance your trip with a phrasebook, visit **lonelyplanet.com**. Lonely Planet iPhone phrasebooks are available through the Apple App store.

Behind the Scenes

This Book

This 3rd edition of Lonely Planet's Discover India guidebook was compiled and written by Abigail Blasi, Paul Clammer, Mark Elliott, Paul Harding, John Noble and Iain Stewart, based on their research and that of Michael Benanav, Trent Holden, Anirban Mahapatra, Daniel McCrohan, Isabella Noble, Kevin Raub and Sarina Singh. This guidebook was produced by the following:

Destination Editor Joe Bindloss
Product Editors Kate James, Kate Mathews
Book Designer Cam Ashley
Assisting Editors Kate Evans, Gabrielle Stefanos
Cover Researcher Naomi Parker
Thanks to Lonely Planet Cartography, Kate Chapman, Catherine Naghten, Martine Power, Luna Soo, Angela Tinson, Juan Winata

Our Readers

Many thanks to the travellers who used the last edition and wrote to us with helpful hints, useful advice and interesting anecdotes:
Don Jones, Ella McDermott, George Wines

Author Thanks

Abigail Blasi

Thank you Joe Bindloss and Sarina Singh, CE and CA supreme, and to my expert co-authors. Thanks in Delhi to Sarah Fotheringham, to Nicolas Thompson and Danish Abbas, to Dilliwala Mayank Austen Soofi, to Rajinder and Surinder Budhraja, to Nirinjan and Jyoti Desai, my Delhi family, and to Luca for holding the fort.

Acknowledgments

Climate map data adapted from Peel MC, Finlayson BL & McMahon TA (2007) 'Updated World Map of the Köppen-Geiger Climate Classification', Hydrology and Earth System Sciences, 11, 1633-44.

Illustrations pp100-1 by Javier Zarracina, pp106-7 by Michael Weldon.

Cover photographs: Front: Taj Mahal, Agra, Peter Adams/Getty; Back: Textiles drying, Rajasthan, Bruno Morandi/4 Corners.

SEND US YOUR FEEDBACK

Index

A

accommodation 49, 414-16, see also individual locations
language 435, 436
activities 29, 42-5, see also individual activities
Agonda 219
Agra 97-104
Agra Fort 97
air travel 429-30
Ajanta 19, 113, 136-7
Alappuzha (Alleppey) 245-50
Amber Fort 149
Amritsar 377-81
animals 410-12
Anjuna 195, 209-12
antiques 421
Arambol 195, 212-14
archaeological sites
Fatehpur Sikri 104-7
Hampi 20
Mehrauli Archaeological Park 70
architecture
Mumbai 20, 112, 116-17
Puducherry 286
religious 409
area codes 427
Arjuna's Penance 279
art galleries, see museums & art galleries
arts 407-9, see also individual arts

000 Map pages

ashrams

Matha Amrithanandamayi Mission 249
Parmarth Niketan Ashram 354
Sri Aurobindo Ashram 283
Sri Sant Seva Ashram 354
Asvem 212
ATMs 48, 422
Aurangabad 133-5
autorickshaws 431
ayurveda 242

B

backwaters, Kerala 13, 230, 248-9
Baga 208-9
baksheesh 423
bargaining 423
bazaars, see markets
beaches 14
Agonda 219
Anjuna 210
Arambol 212-14
Baga 208-9
Benaulim 216-19
Cherai 260
Chowpatty 113, 121
Cola 219
Colva 216-19
Goa 15, 194, 201
Kovalam 240-3
Marina Beach 270
Mobor 219
Palolem 219-23
Patnem 220
Varca 219
Varkala 243-5
Benaulim 216-19
bhang lassi 425
birds 412
birdwatching 411, 412
boat trips
Kerala backwaters 13, 230, 248-9

Kochi 258
Periyar Wildlife Sanctuary 251
Varanasi 296
Bollywood 47
Bombay, see Mumbai
books 47, 408
Brahma 402
British India 392
Buddhism 21
Buddhist temples
Ajanta 19, 113, 137
Bhutia Busty Gompa 321
Dhamekh Stupa 333
Ellora 19, 113, 136
Global Pagoda 121
Tsuglagkhang Complex 372
Yiga Choling Gompa 321
budget 49, see also money
bus travel 430
business hours 424

C

Calangute 208-9
Calcutta, see Kolkata
camel rides
Jaisalmer 28, 186
Pushkar 161
car travel 48, 430-1
Carnival 42
caste system 400
cathedrals, see churches & cathedrals
Cavelossim 219
caves
Ajanta 19, 113, 136-7
Elephanta Island 113, 123
Ellora cave temples 19, 113, 135-6
cell phones 48, 426-7
Chandor 216
Chennai (Madras) 269-78, **272-3**
accommodation 271, 274-5
food 275-6

medical services 276
sights 270-1
tourist information 276
tours 271
transport 276-8
Cherai Beach 260
children, travel with 124, 397-8
Chinnar Wildlife Sanctuary 253
Chowpatty Beach 113, 121
churches & cathedrals
  Basilica of Bom Jesus 206
  Church of Our Lady of the Immaculate Conception 200-1
  Church of St Francis of Assisi 207
  Notre Dame des Anges 286
  Our Lady of the Immaculate Conception Cathedral 286
  Sacred Heart Basilica 286
  Sé Cathedral 207
  St Paul's Cathedral 303
  St Philomena's Cathedral 265-6
  St Thomas' Cathedral 122
cinema 47
climate 48, 417, see also individual locations
Cochin, see Kochi
Cola Beach 219
Colva 216-19
cooking courses 168
  Delhi 72
  Munnar 254
  Periyar Wildlife Sanctuary 251
  Udaipur 168
Corbett, Jim 359, 411
Corbett Tiger Reserve 347, 359-61
costs 49, 414, 417, see also money
Cotigao Wildlife Sanctuary 221
courses, see cooking courses, yoga courses
credit cards 48, 423

cricket 401
culture 384-5, 399-401
currency 48, 422-3
customs regulations 416
cycle-rickshaws 432

D

Dalai Lama 371
dangers, see safety, scams
Darjeeling 15, 293-301, 317-25, **318**
  accommodation 321-2
  food & drink 322-4
  sights 317-21
  tourist information 324
  tours 321
  transport 324-5
Darjeeling Himalayan Railway 27, 320
deities 402-3
Delhi 30, 51-97, **52-3**, **74-5**
  accommodation 56, 75-83
  activities 72
  Connaught Place 66-7, 77, 85-7, **78-9**
  courses 72
  drinking 89-90
  entertainment 90
  food 56, 83-9
  highlights 54
  itineraries 58-9, **58**
  markets 91
  medical services 92
  New Delhi 67-72, 77-8, 87-8, **80-1**
  Old Delhi 58-9, 60-6, 76, 83-4, **62-3**
  planning 57
  shopping 56, 90-2
  sights 60-72
  tourist information 92-3
  tours 73-5
  travel to/from 93-5
  travel within 95-7
  walking tour 58-9, **58**
dengue fever 419

dhal 405
Dharamsala 371-7
diarrhoea 419-20
disabilities, travellers with 427-8
Diwali (Festival of Lights) 45
drinking & nightlife, see individual locations
  language 435-6
drinking water 418
driving 48, 430-1
drugs 422, 425
Dudhsagar Falls 215

E

economy 384-5
electricity 416
elephant rides
  Amber Fort 149
  Kochi 258
  Periyar Wildlife Sanctuary 251
Elephanta Island 113, 123
elephants 411-12
Ellora 19, 113, 135-6
emergencies
  language 435-6
  telephone numbers 427
environment 410-12
environmental issues 244, 411
etiquette 377, 406
events 42-5
exchange rates 49

F

family travel 124, 397-8
Fatehpur Sikri 104-7
festivals 42-5
films 47
food 18, 404-6, see also individual locations
  costs 417
  health 420
  language 435-6
football 401

Fort Cochin 256-7, 259-62, **258**
forts 17
  Agra Fort 97
  Amber Fort 149
  Fort St George 270-1
  Jaisalmer Fort 17, 142, 182-3
  Kumbhalgarh 165
  Mehrangarh 25, 176
  Purana Qila 66
  Red Fort 54, 60

G

galleries, *see* museums & galleries
Gandhi, Indira 395-6
Gandhi, Mohandas 44, 72, 287, 393
gardens, *see* parks & gardens
gay travellers 416-17
Ghum 321
Girgaum Chowpatty 113, 121
Goa 191-225, **193**, **208**
  accommodation 196
  beaches 15, 194, 201
  food 196
  highlights 194-5
  itineraries 198-9, **198**
  planning 197
Golden Temple 29, 346, 377, 378-9
golf 306
gurdwaras, *see* Sikh temples

H

Hampi 20, 223-5
Harmal, *see* Arambol
havelis 187
Hazrat Nizam-ud-din Dargah 71
health 417-20
hepatitis 419
hiking, *see* trekking

hill stations
  Darjeeling 15, 293-301, 317-25, **318**
  Manali 346, 366-71, **367**
  McLeod Ganj 347, 371-7, **373**
  Munnar 231, 253-6
  Mussoorie 352-4
  Rishikesh 16, 347, 354-9, **355**
  Shimla 361-6, **362**
Himachal Pradesh 361-77
  itineraries 351
Hindi 435-6
Hindu temples 403
  Akshardham Temple 87
  Ellora 19, 113, 135-6
  Five Rathas 278-9
  Hadimba Temple 366
  Iskcon Temple 121
  Jagdish Temple 167
  Jakhu Temple 361
  Kailasa Temple 135-6
  Kalighat Temple 306
  Khajuraho 16, 297, 338-9
  Meenakshi Amman Temple 23, 230, 288-9
  Shiva Temples 161
  Shore Temple 278
  Shri Padmanabhaswamy Temple 237
  Shri Trayanbakshwar 354
  Sri Manakula Vinayagar Temple 283
  Swarg Niwas 354
  Virupaksha Temple 224
  Vishwanath Temple 327-8
  Vittala Temple 224
Hinduism 402-3
history 386-96
  British rule 391-2
  European powers 391
  Gupta period 388
  Harappan culture 387
  Independence 394-5
  Indus Valley Civilisation 386-7

  Mauryan empire 387-8
  Mughal empire 389-90
hockey 401
Holi festival 43
holidays 424
hot-air ballooning 153
hotels 415-16, *see also individual locations*
houseboats 13, 248-9
Humayun's tomb 55, 67

I

immigration 428
Independence 394-5
insurance 417, 420
internet access 48, 421
itineraries 32-41, *see also individual locations*

J

Jain temples
  Digambara Jain Temple 65-6
  Ellora 19, 113, 136
  Jaisalmer 183
  Khajuraho 16, 297, 336-41
  Ranakpur 165
Jaipur 148-59, **150-1**
  accommodation 152-4
  drinking & entertainment 156-7
  food 155-6
  medical services 158
  shopping 157-8
  sights 148-51
  tourist information 158
  tours 151
  transport 158-9
Jaisalmer 182-9, **184-5**
  accommodation 184-7
  food 187-8
  shopping 188-9
  sights 182-3
  tourist information 189
  tours 183
  transport 189

Jaisalmer Fort 17, 142, 182-3
Jallianwala Bagh 377
Jama Masjid (Delhi) 61
Jama Masjid (Fatehpur Sikri) 105, 106
Jantar Mantar (Delhi) 66-7
Jantar Mantar (Jaipur) 150-1
Jodhpur 25, 143, 175-81, **176-7**
  accommodation 177-9
  activities 176-7
  drinking 180
  food 179-80
  shopping 180-1
  sights 176-7
  tourist information 181
  transport 181

K

Karnataka 223-5, 265-9
Kashmir 385, 395
kayaking
  Alappuzha 245
  Goa 220
  Rishikesh 356
Kerala 227-65, **229**
  accommodation 232
  backwaters 13, 230, 248-9
  food 232
  highlights 230-1
  itineraries 234-5, **234**
  planning 233
Khajuraho 16, 297, 336-41, **336**
Kochi (Cochin) 24, 231, 256-65, **258**
  accommodation 259-60
  entertainment 262
  food & drink 260-2
  medical services 263
  sights 256-8
  tourist information 263
  tours 258-9
  transport 263-5
Kolkata (Calcutta) 297, 302-17, **303**, **304**, **308-9**, **312-13**
  accommodation 307-10
  activities 306

drinking & nightlife 313-15
food 310-13
medical services 315
shopping 315
sights 302-3, 305-6
tourist information 315
tours 306-7
transport 315-17
Kovalam 240-3
Kumbhalgarh 165

L

language 48, 435-6
legal matters 421-2
lesbian travellers 416-17
literature 47, 408

M

Madgaon, see Margao
Madhya Pradesh 336-41
Madurai 287-91, **290**
magazines 415
Mahabalipuram, see Mamallapuram
Maharashtra 118-37
malaria 418
Mamallapuram 278-82, **280**
Manali 346, 366-71, **367**
  accommodation 367-9
  activities 366-7, 368
  drinking & nightlife 370
  food 369-70
  medical services 371
  sights 366-7
  tours 366
  transport 371
Mandrem 212
Margao 214-16
Marina Beach 270
markets
  Anjuna 195, 211
  Delhi 18, 55, 58-9, 61, 91
  Mumbai 130
  Mysuru 265

mausoleums, see tombs, shrines & mausoleums
McLeod Ganj 347, 371-7, **373**
  accommodation 374-5
  activities 372-4
  food 375-6
  medical services 376
  sights 372
  travel to/from 376-7
measures 415
media 415
medical services 418, see also individual locations
Meenakshi Amman Temple 23, 230, 288-9
Mehrangarh 25, 176
Mehrauli Archaeological Park 70
mobile phones 48, 426-7
Mobor 219
Modi, Narendra 384-5
monasteries
  Ajanta 137
  Bhutia Busty Gompa 321
  Ellora 136
  Ghum 321
  Sarnath 333
money 48-9, 414, 422-4
moneychangers 423
mosques
  Fatehpur Mosque 59
  Jama Masjid (Delhi) 61
  Jama Masjid (Fatehpur Sikri) 105, 106
  Jamali Khamali 70
  Moti Masjid 65
  Quwwat-ul-Islam Masjid 69
Mother Teresa 303-5
mountain biking 368
movies 47
Mumbai 20, 109-33, **120**, **126-7**
  accommodation 123-4
  activities 121-2
  drinking & nightlife 128-30
  entertainment 130
  food 112, 114, 125-8

Mumbai *continued*
  highlights 112-13
  itineraries 116-17, **116**
  medical services 131
  planning 115
  shopping 114, 130
  sights 118-21
  tourist information 131
  tours 122
  transport 131-3
  walking tour 116-17, **116**
Munnar 231, 253-6
museums & galleries
  Archaeological Museum 337
  Chhatrapati Shivaji Maharaj
    Vastu Sangrahalaya 119
  City Palace Museum 167
  Crafts Museum 72
  Desert Cultural Centre &
    Museum 183
  Dr Bhau Daji Lad Mumbai
    City Museum 121
  Gandhi Memorial
    Museum 287
  Gandhi Smriti 72
  Goa Chitra 217
  Goa State Museum 201
  Government Museum 270
  Indian Museum 303
  Indian War Memorial
    Museum 61
  Indo-Portuguese Museum
    256-7
  Marble Palace 305-6
  Mattancherry Palace 257-8
  Mountaineering
    Museum 319
  Museum of Christian Art 207
  Museum of History &
    Heritage 237
  Museum on India's Struggle
    for Freedom 61
  National Gallery of
    Modern Art 72
  National Museum 71-2
  National Rail Museum 72

RKK Memorial Museum 245
  Sulabh International
    Museum of Toilets 72
  Taj Museum 97
music 47, 407-8
Mussoorie 352-4
Mysore Palace 31, 231, 265
Mysuru (Mysore) 265-9, **266**

N

national parks, reserves &
  wildlife sanctuaries 30
  Chinnar Wildlife
    Sanctuary 253
  Corbett Tiger Reserve 347,
    359-61
  Cotigao Wildlife
    Sanctuary 221
  Periyar Wildlife Sanctuary
    250-3
  Ranthambhore National
    Park 19, 143, 163-5
  Sunderbans Tiger Reserve
    297, 314
Navratri festival 44
Nehru, Jawaharlal 394-5
newspapers 415

O

observatories
  Jantar Mantar (Delhi) 66-7
  Jantar Mantar (Jaipur) 150-1
Old Goa 195, 207-8, **208**
opening hours 424

P

painting 408
palaces
  Amber Fort 149
  City Palace (Jaipur) 149-50
  City Palace (Udaipur) 166
  Fatehpur Sikri 105
  Fort Palace 182-3

Hawa Mahal 151
  Jaganmohan Palace 265
  Marble Palace 305-6
  Mattancherry Palace 257-8
  Mysore Palace 31, 231, 265
Palolem 219-23
Panaji (Panjim) 194, 200-7,
  202
paragliding
  Arambol 212
  Manali 386
Pardesi Synagogue 257
parks & gardens
  Lodi Gardens 66
  Mehrauli Archaeological
    Park 70
  Rao Jodha Desert Rock Park
    176-7
Partition 394
passports 429
payphones 425
Periyar Wildlife Sanctuary
  250-3
Pink City 148-51
planning
  budgeting 48-9, 414
  calendar of events 42-5
  children, travel with 124,
    397-8
  India basics 48-9
  itineraries 32-41
  resources 47
  travel seasons 48
politics 384-5
population 384
public holidays 424
Puducherry (Pondicherry) 24,
  282-7
Punjab 377-81
Pushkar 143, 159-63
Pushkar Camel Fair 160

Q

Qutb Minar 55, 68-9

R

radio 415
rafting
  Manali 368
  Periyar Wildlife
    Sanctuary 251
  Rishikesh 356
Rajasthan 139-89, **140**
  accommodation 144
  food 144
  highlights 142, 144-5
  itineraries 146-7
  planning 145
Rajputs 391
Ranakpur 165
Ranthambhore National Park
  19, 143, 163-5
Red Fort 54, 60
religion 384, 402-3, 409
reserves, see national parks,
  reserves & wildlife
  sanctuaries
rice 404
rickshaws 423, 431-2
Rishikesh 16, 347, 354-9,
  355

S

safety 425
Sarnath 333
scams 49
  Delhi 92
  Varanasi 328
Shimla 361-6, **362**
  accommodation 363-4
  activities 361-3
  food 364
  sights 361-3
  tourist information 364
  transport 364-6
Shimla Toy Train 365
Shiva 403
shopping, see markets,
  individual locations

shrines, see tombs, shrines &
  mausoleums
Sikh temples
  Golden Temple 29, 346,
    378-9
  Sisganj Gurdwara 58
sport 401
Sunderbans Tiger Reserve
  297, 314
synagogues
  Keneseth Eliyahoo
    Synagogue 120
  Pardesi Synagogue 257

T

Taj Mahal 11, 54, 97, 98-9
Tamil 436
Tamil Nadu 234, 269-91
taxes 414
taxis 431, 432
tea plantations 26
  Darjeeling 317, 323
  Munnar 253, 254
telephone services 48, 425-7
temples 22, 409, see also
  Buddhist temples, Hindu
  temples, Jain temples, Sikh
  temples
  Bahai House of Worship 66
  Elephanta Island 113, 123
tempos 432
Thiruvananthapuram 236-40,
  238
Tibetan Buddhism 21
tigers 19, 297, 411, 412
  Corbett Tiger Reserve 347,
    359-61
  Ranthambhore National
    Park 19, 143, 163-5
  Sunderbans Tiger Reserve
    297, 314
time 427
tipping 48, 423
tombs, shrines &
  mausoleums
  Bibi-qa-Maqbara 134

  Hazrat Nizam-ud-din
    Dargah 71
  Humayun's tomb 55, 67
  Taj Mahal 11, 54, 97, 98-9
tourist information 427, see
  also individual locations
tours 432-3, see also boat
  trips, walking tours
  Agra 97-102
  Amritsar 377
  Aurangabad 134
  Chennai (Madras) 271
  Corbett Tiger Reserve 360
  Darjeeling 321
  Delhi 73-5
  Jaipur 151
  Jaisalmer 183
  Kerala backwaters 248-9
  Kochi (258-9
  Kolkata 306-7
  Mamallapuram 279
  Manali 366
  Mumbai 122
  Munnar 254
  Mysore 266
  Panaji 201
  Sunderbans Tiger
    Reserve 314
  Thiruvananthapuram 237
  Varanasi 328
toy trains
  Darjeeling Himalayan
    Railway 27, 320
  Shimla Toy Train 365
train travel 433-4
travel to/from India 429
travel within India 49, 429-34
travellers cheques 424
trekking 26, 43
  Chinnar Wildlife
    Sanctuary 253
  Darjeeling 321
  Goa 220
  Manali 368
  McLeod Ganj 373
  Munnar 253, 254
  Mussoorie 352-3
  Rishikesh 356

Trivandrum, *see*
Thiruvananthapuram
TV 415

U

Udaipur 28, 142, 165-75, **166**
accommodation 168-71
activities 167-8
entertainment 173
food 171-2
medical services 174
shopping 173-4
sights 166-7
transport 174-5
Unesco World Heritage sites,
see World Heritage sites
Uttar Pradesh 97-107
Uttarakhand 352-61

V

vacations 424
vaccinations 419
Varanasi 12, 293-301, 325-36,
326
accommodation 329-31
activities 328
drinking & nightlife 333-4
food 331-3
planning 299

shopping 334
sights 327-8
tours 328
transport 335-6
Varca 219
Varkala 243-5
vegetarian travellers 406
vikrams 432
visas 48, 428
Vishnu 403
Vittala Temple 224
volunteering 65
Vypeen Island 260

W

walking, *see* trekking
walking tours
Delhi 58-9, **58**
Mumbai 116-17, **116**
water 418
weather 48, 417, *see also*
individual locations
websites 47, 426
weights 415
wi-fi 48, 421
wildlife 410-12
wildlife sanctuaries, *see*
national parks, reserves &
wildlife sanctuaries
women in India 385, 400-1

women travellers 425
World Heritage sites 21
Ajanta 19, 113, 136-7
Chhatrapati Shivaji
Terminus 119
Darjeeling Himalayan
Railway 27, 320
Elephanta Island 113, 123
Ellora 19, 113, 135-6
Fatehpur Sikri 104-7
Hampi 20, 223-5
Jantar Mantar (Jaipur) 150-1
Khajuraho 16, 297, 336-41,
336
Mamallapuram 278-82, **280**
Mysore Palace 31, 231, 265
Sunderbans Tiger
Reserve 297, 314
Taj Mahal 11, 54, 97, 98-9

Y

yoga courses
Anjuna 210
Arambol 213
Delhi 72
Goa 195
McLeod Ganj 373
Palolem 220
Rishikesh 16, 354
Varkala 243

How to Use This Book

These symbols give you the vital information for each listing:

☑	Telephone Numbers	☎	Wi-Fi Access	☒	Bus
☉	Opening Hours	☰	Swimming Pool	☒	Ferry
Ⓟ	Parking	☑	Vegetarian Selection	Ⓜ	Metro
☺	Nonsmoking	⓪	English-Language Menu	Ⓢ	Subway
❀	Air-Conditioning	☷	Family-Friendly	⊖	London Tube
@	Internet Access	☺	Pet-Friendly	☒	Tram

Look out for these icons:

FREE — No payment required

🌿 — A green or sustainable option

Our authors have nominated these places as demonstrating a strong commitment to sustainability – for example by supporting local communities and producers, operating in an environmentally friendly way, or supporting conservation projects.

All reviews are ordered in our authors' preference, starting with their most preferred option. Additionally:

Sights are arranged in the geographic order that we suggest you visit them, and within this order, by author preference.

Eating and Sleeping reviews are ordered by price range (budget, mid-range, top end) and within these ranges, by author preference.

Map Legend

Sights
- ⓦ Beach
- ⓐ Buddhist
- ⓒ Castle
- ⓒ Christian
- ⓗ Hindu
- ⓒ Islamic
- ⓙ Jewish
- ⓞ Monument
- ⓜ Museum/Gallery
- ⓡ Ruin
- ⓦ Winery/Vineyard
- ⓩ Zoo
- ⓞ Other Sight

Activities, Courses & Tours
- ⓢ Diving/Snorkelling
- ⓒ Canoeing/Kayaking
- ⓢ Skiing
- ⓢ Surfing
- ⓢ Swimming/Pool
- ⓦ Walking
- ⓦ Windsurfing
- ⓞ Other Activity/ Course/Tour

Sleeping
- ⓢ Sleeping
- ⓒ Camping

Eating
- ⓢ Eating

Drinking
- ⓓ Drinking
- ⓒ Cafe

Entertainment
- ⓔ Entertainment

Shopping
- ⓢ Shopping

Information
- ⓟ Post Office
- ⓘ Tourist Information

Transport
- ⓐ Airport
- ⓧ Border Crossing
- ⓑ Bus
- ⓒ Cable Car/ Funicular
- ⓒ Cycling
- ⓢ Ferry
- ⓜ Monorail
- Ⓟ Parking
- Ⓢ S-Bahn
- ⓣ Taxi
- ⓣ Train/Railway
- ⓣ Tram
- ⓣ Tube Station
- Ⓤ U-Bahn
- Ⓜ Underground Train Station
- • Other Transport

Routes
- Tollway
- Freeway
- Primary
- Secondary
- Tertiary
- Lane
- Unsealed Road
- Plaza/Mall
- Steps
-)= = Tunnel
- Pedestrian Overpass
- Walking Tour
- Walking Tour Detour
- Path

Boundaries
- International
- State/Province
- Disputed
- Regional/Suburb
- Marine Park
- Cliff
- Wall

Population
- ✪ Capital (National)
- ◉ Capital (State/Province)
- ● City/Large Town
- ● Town/Village

Geographic
- ⓗ Hut/Shelter
- ⓛ Lighthouse
- ⓛ Lookout
- ▲ Mountain/Volcano
- ⓞ Oasis
- ⓟ Park
-)(Pass
- ⓟ Picnic Area
- ⓦ Waterfall

Hydrography
- River/Creek
- Intermittent River
- Swamp/Mangrove
- Reef
- Canal
- Water
- Dry/Salt/ Intermittent Lake
- Glacier

Areas
- Beach/Desert
- Cemetery (Christian)
- Cemetery (Other)
- Park/Forest
- Sportsground
- Sight (Building)
- Top Sight (Building)

ISABELLA NOBLE

Kerala & South India Isabella's first experience of South India was a masala dosa at Shimla's Indian Coffee House. She has been travelling to India for over five years, but loves the ever-so-slightly more laid-back pace of the friendly south. This time she got lost in tea plantations, checked out Chennai's countless bars, then got stuck in the hills thanks to a landslide. Between trips, Isabella lives in London with a wardrobe of Indian shawls. She tweets @isabellamnoble. Isabella wrote the Tamil Nadu section of the Kerala & South India chapter.

Read more about Isabella at:
http://auth.lonelyplanet.com/profiles/isabellanoble

KEVIN RAUB

Delhi & the Taj Mahal; Darjeeling, Varanasi & the Northeast Kevin grew up in Atlanta and started his career as a music journalist in New York, working for *Men's Journal* and *Rolling Stone* magazines. He ditched the rock 'n' roll lifestyle for travel writing and moved to Brazil. On his eighth epic Indian journey, Kevin was only out-spiced by an Indian chef once and was never outsmarted by a rickshaw driver. Follow him on Twitter (@RaubOnTheRoad). Kevin wrote the Uttar Pradesh & the Taj Mahal section of the Delhi & the Taj Mahal chapter, and the Madhya Pradesh section of the Darjeeling, Varanasi & the Northeast chapter.

SARINA SINGH

Plan Your Trip; In Focus After finishing a business degree in Melbourne, Sarina travelled to India where she pursued a hotel corporate traineeship before becoming a journalist. After five years she returned to Australia and completed postgraduate journalism qualifications before authoring Lonely Planet's first edition of *Rajasthan*. Apart from numerous Lonely Planet books she has written for a raft of newspapers and magazines, and has been a scriptwriter and travel columnist. Sarina is also the author of two prestigious publications – *Polo in India* and *India: Essential Encounters*. Her award-nominated documentary film premiered at the Melbourne International Film Festival before being screened internationally.

JOHN NOBLE

Northern Mountains & Amritsar John, from England, has written about 20-odd countries for Lonely Planet, including covering six very different Indian states. He loves returning to the subcontinent because, in a nutshell, there's never a dull moment there! Biggest thrill of this trip: getting back into the Himalaya (the world's most wonderful landscapes). He tweets @john_a_noble and Instagrams as johnnoble11. John wrote the Himachal Pradesh section of the Northern Mountains & Amritsar chapter.

Read more about John at:
http://auth.lonelyplanet.com/profiles/ewoodrover

IAIN STEWART

Mumbai (Bombay) & Around Iain grew up in Leicester, a very Indian town transplanted to the Midlands, UK (complete with its own curry mile). He first visited India in 1991 and explored the sights at totally the wrong time of year, with temperatures approaching 50°C in parts. For this trip he wised up and travelled post-monsoon: bar-hopping in Mumbai, meandering down the Konkan coast and having several near-misses with tigers in Tadoba.

MICHAEL BENANAV

Northern Mountains & Amritsar A writer and photojournalist who covers issues affecting traditional cultures, Michael has migrated with nomadic water buffalo herders in the Himalaya and joined religious worshippers on mountainous pilgrimage trails. The abundance of fascinating stories in India – and the friendships he's formed there – keep drawing him back. You can see his work at www.michaelbenanav.com. Michael wrote the Uttarakhand section of the Northern Mountains & Amritsar chapter.

TRENT HOLDEN

Goa & Around, Kerala & South India This was the third Lonely Planet trip to India for Trent, a regular visitor to the subcontinent since the 1990s. A freelance travel writer based in London, Trent also covers destinations such as Nepal, Zimbabwe and Japan. In between travels he writes about food and music. You can catch him on Twitter @hombreholden. Trent wrote the Karnataka section of the Goa & Around chapter and the Southern Karnataka section of the Kerala & South India chapter.

ANIRBAN MAHAPATRA

Darjeeling, Varanasi & the Northeast Anirban started his career as a newspaper reporter in 2004, but transitioned into travel journalism some years later after realising that all the good things in life awaited him on the open road. A Lonely Planet author since 2007, he specialises in India and the subcontinent, and loves to trundle routinely through the hinterlands of East and Northeast India, sampling the awesome culture and cuisine of the region. A closet Buddhist (and probably a reborn lama), he takes special interest in Himalayan traditions. Apart from writing, Anirban currently also works on photographic and video projects. He lives in Kolkata. Anirban wrote the Darjeeling section of the Darjeeling, Varanasi & the Northeast chapter.

DANIEL MCCROHAN

Northern Mountains & Amritsar Daniel has been writing for Lonely Planet about India and China for almost a decade now. Originally from the UK, he's based in Beijing these days, but has been travelling to India, on and off, since the early 1990s. Daniel is also the creator of the smartphone app Beijing on a Budget, a host on the travel show Best in China and a 'travel ninja' for planmy.travel. You can contact him through his website, danielmccrohan.com. Daniel wrote the Amritsar section of the Northern Mountains & Amritsar chapter.

Read more about Daniel at:
http://auth.lonelyplanet.com/profiles/danielmccrohan

Our Story

A beat-up old car, a few dollars in the pocket and a sense of adventure. In 1972 that's all Tony and Maureen Wheeler needed for the trip of a lifetime – across Europe and Asia overland to Australia. It took several months, and at the end – broke but inspired – they sat at their kitchen table writing and stapling together their first travel guide, *Across Asia on the Cheap*. Within a week they'd sold 1500 copies. Lonely Planet was born.

Today, Lonely Planet has offices in Franklin, London, Melbourne, Oakland, Beijing and Delhi, with more than 600 staff and writers. We share Tony's belief that 'a great guidebook should do three things: inform, educate and amuse'.

Our Writers

ABIGAIL BLASI

Delhi & the Taj Mahal; Plan Your Trip; In Focus; Survival Guide Abigail has worked on India many times for Lonely Planet, and she was delighted to return to explore Delhi again, learning to love Paharganj, exploring the city's enclaves, and cycling through the mayhem of Old Delhi. She fell in love with the country on her first visit in 1994, and since then she's explored and written on India from north to south and back again. She's covered plenty of other places for Lonely Planet too, from Mauritania and Mali to Rome and Lisbon. Abigail wrote the Delhi section of the Delhi & the Taj Mahal chapter.

PAUL CLAMMER

Rajasthan Paul has contributed to more than 25 Lonely Planet guidebooks, and worked as a tour guide in countries from Turkey to Morocco. In a previous life he may even have been a molecular biologist. He first covered India for LP back in 2004, up in the Himalayas, so he jumped at the chance to explore Rajasthan in more depth this time around, staying on to write the chapter in a converted temple in Pushkar, where it was necessary to lock the doors to stop monkeys stealing his notes. Follow @paulclammer on Twitter.

MARK ELLIOTT

Darjeeling, Varanasi & the Northeast Mark has been making forays to the subcontinent since a 1984 ultra-budget adventure that lined his stomach for all eventualities. He first explored this part of India in 1995 when an Indian Airlines flight to Khajuraho changed route mid-flight and decided to drop him off in Varanasi instead. Over the years his explorations of the remote Northeast have taken him from Tezpur to Tripura to Tibetan Tawang. Mark is passionately enamoured of the region's landscapes and intricate patchwork of cultures, while considering Kolkata India's most inspiring mega-city. Mark wrote the Kolkata (Calcutta) section of the Darjeeling, Varanasi & the Northeast chapter.

PAUL HARDING

Goa & Around, Kerala & South India Paul first landed in India in the mid-'90s and has returned regularly over the years, usually writing about it. He still has a soft spot for the south, where the pace of life is slower, the food tastier and the beer (usually) colder. On his most recent trip he was fortunate enough to return to Goa and Kerala where he researched beaches and backwaters, homestays and bamboo huts, seafood curries and chicken xacutis. This was Paul's ninth assignment on India and the second with his intrepid young daughter. Paul wrote the Goa section of the Goa & Around chapter and the Kerala section of the Kerala & South India chapter.

More Writers

Published by Lonely Planet Publications Pty Ltd
ABN 36 005 607 983
3rd edition – Dec 2015
ISBN 978 1 74321 682 8
© Lonely Planet 2015   Photographs © as indicated 2015
10 9 8 7 6 5 4 3 2 1
Printed in Singapore